D1620999

THE
ENGLISH
ROCK-GARDEN

THE
ENGLISH
ROCK-GARDEN

REGINALD FARRER

Volume II

THOMAS NELSON AND SONS LTD

LONDON EDINBURGH PARIS MELBOURNE
TORONTO AND NEW YORK

THOMAS NELSON AND SONS LTD
Parkside Works Edinburgh 9
36 Park Street London W1
312 Flinders Street Melbourne C1
218 Grand Parade Centre   Cape Town

THOMAS NELSON AND SONS (CANADA) LTD
91–93 Wellington Street West   Toronto 1

THOMAS NELSON AND SONS
19 East 47th Street New York 17

SOCIÉTÉ FRANÇAISE D'EDITIONS NELSON
25 rue Henri Barbusse Paris Ve

First published June 1919
Reprinted 1922, 1925, 1928, 1930, 1938,
1948, 1955

LIST OF PLATES

THE
ENGLISH ROCK-GARDEN

N

Nama Rockrothii, from California, has hairy foliage and white or purplish funnels of flowers in terminal heads on stems of 7 or 8 inches. It should be quite easy in open cool soil.

Nananthea perpusilla, a very minutely dwarf and rather worthless little microscopic-flowered Composite from Colorado.

Narcissus.—The large daffodils are unfitted for the rock-garden, less on account of their stature, indeed, than because they die so untidily, in flopping masses of yellow decay. For its higher reaches, however, if it be large enough in scale, they look superb, and their decadence is not noticed (still less if enshrouded by degrees in the developing leafage of such a thing as *Potentilla nepalensis Willmottiae*). But the smaller daffodils have their place everywhere in the foreground, and the most delicate of them rejoice in the conditions of the water-bed (and, indeed, they all like a generous supply of moisture at the root while growing). The most exquisite of all, the silver-pale *N. Bulbocodium monophyllus*, should have, of course, the daintiest corner, in soil almost wholly sandy, and very damp in spring, under the lee of a hot rock ; and over the whole garden may be peppered the minute charm of *N. minimus*, a real miniature golden-trumpet daffodil of 2 inches or less, that is never in the way ; and, for the rest, are there not elaborate catalogues consecrated entirely to their worship, their needs, their beauties, and their preposterous prices ?

Nardosmia fragrans is no more than *Tussilago fragrans* of former days ; and *N. frigida* is, accordingly, hardly less close itself to the giant Coltsfoots, so valuable for their sweet and dowdy blooms in winter.

Narthecium.—The Bog-Asphodel may be established in the peaty bog and there let alone, to gratify summer with its little fluffy

1

golden spikes as it does in the marshy places of the moors. Other species widely differ botanically, but not in the gardener's eye.

Nassawia serpens is a most curious oddity, wandering far through the coarsest shingle-slopes of the Falklands, with long trunks clad densely in overlapping toothed little leaves, and emerging at last to thicken into a close club-shaped head of blossoms at the end of each.

Nepeta.—Though *N. Mussini* is to some rock-gardeners the first and last word in decoration (being the admiration of all beholders everywhere in summer, with its countless long loose spraying spikes of smoke-blue blossom above the fine silver-grey herbage of the tufts) ; yet neither this nor any other of the race is really of nature sufficiently refined for the small garden, though in the large one a noble effect may be got by filling a broad stretch of worthless sunny soil with *Nepeta*, among drifts of Welsh Poppy and Iceland Poppy. There are many other large species, all easily to be done without, though none, again, are devoid of some value in high and remote corners which it is desired handsomely to fill ; of smaller sorts, however, more fit for our purpose, there are *N. supina*, like a little repent Mint, from the upmost hills of Caucasus, and *N. chionophila*, which is grey, and loves the snows beside the high screes of the Persian Alps. If complete collections of the larger sorts be wanted, here is a selection of names : *NN. caesarea, cataria* (worthless except for the benefit of cats, who pursue the catnip as man pursues alcohol, and with very much the same effects), *nepetella, nuda, Wilsoni, cyanea, grandiflora*, and *macrantha* (two ways of making the same large-flowered promise. *N. macrantha* also = *Dracocephalum sibiricum*).

Nertĕra depressa is a minute half-hardy New Zealand mat of creeping bright-green foliage in spreading cushions, all over which, after the unnoticeable flowers, develop quantities of glowing terra-cotta and scarlet balls of fruit like round comfits. It will be happy out of doors in a sheltered shady corner of the rock-work, in damp sandy loam ; and will even bear our winters, though pieces should always be dug off and potted up in autumn for safety's sake.

Nierembergia rivularis comes from the River Plate, where it sheets the damp muddy banks with its packed masses of small heart-shaped dark-green leaves, which emit an unimaginable profusion of very large and lovely pearl-pale cups or wide bells, like those of some exquisite Convolvulus dropped from heaven. In cultivation the plant is perfectly hardy, but rather uncertain, some people succeeding without effort in having carpets of it, covered with its delicate noble chalices all through the late summer and autumn ; while others with much care never seem to make it happy at all. What is indicated, however (generally speaking), is a gentle sunny slope of very rich, but light and open loam, well-watered from beneath ; in gardens where the sun's heat is southern, it might be better that the slope should turn away from it, but probably *Nierembergia* has no objection to sun in itself, and merely dislikes being parched ; so that abundant water would give it all its needs in open ground or shade. It can most readily be divided, as it rapidly forms wide dense carpets ; but it is too often pulled pitilessly to pieces for the market, which is the reason of many failures with specimens so sickened of division that their only remaining thought in life is to fold their leaves in slumber and pass into the peace of death, where the trowel will no more trouble, nor the spade divide. There are others of this lovely race, but none to be trusted in our climate ; though in warm places success is met with in dealing with the no less beautiful but wholly different *N. frutescens*, which suggests a fine spraying Flax-bush with bigger, blue-white flowers, darkened at the eye, and delightfully abundant through summer.

Noaea spinosissima expresses in the first syllable of its name, what the wise gardener will say when offered it. Nor need he even trouble to add " Thank you."

Noccaea alpina is *Hutchinsia alpina*, and *N. stylosa* is *Thlaspi stylosum*.

Nothoscordon fragrans. See under **Allium.**

Notothlaspi rosulatum.—The Penwiper plant of New Zealand is a most beautiful shingle Crucifer of the high Southern Alps, where it forms a penwiper of thick fat leaves, and then emits a dense and solid pyramid about 9 inches high, of crowded large white flowers deliciously fragrant. *N. australe* is no less snowy and sweet, but not so impressive. They gloriously replace *Thlaspi* in the Antarctic screes.

Nuphar, Nymphaea, and **Nelumbium.**—There is no need at this time of day to expatiate on the glories of these, alike in foliage and blossom. All Water-lilies are of the easiest culture, requiring only to be planted at the bottom of a 3-foot pond, on mounds of grossly rich soil, and there let alone to grow wide every year and glorify the pool far on into autumn with their flowers in every gorgeous shade of colour except, as yet, blue. So much for the larger Water-lilies ; the smaller like a depth of 2 feet, and in the case of such babies as *N. Helvola*, a depth of 6 inches will be ample. And the Nuphars, too, dull Brandy-bottles in flower, but superb in the leaf, may thrive in shallow as in deeper waters (the upstanding foliage of the American species so showing better). But *Nelumbium* should have a depth of nearly a foot, and then, in winter, its department of the pool should be filled with bracken and topped with fir-boughs. *Nelumbium*, indeed, has no right to such affectations as this supposed dread of frost, as anyone will know who has seen it ramping by the railway ditches far up into the frozen North of Japan, while in Tokio itself, of course, the plant is solid ice for half the winter. I should be more disposed to think that our trouble with *Nelumbium* arises always from our experimenting with over-divided rhizomes, that have no more going, nor even staying, power; and that if we could get substantial, solid pieces (of *N. speciosum* at least, and that from the North of Japan or the Tokio Plain), and brought them a little gently on in spring, before putting them out into rich muddy soil and some 9 inches or a foot of water in the sunniest place, we should have no further trouble about enjoying that glorious foliage which sways the Jewel of the World at its heart, when the huge leaves rock the dew-drop that they nurse—a shimmering globule of quicksilver in their glaucous cup; even if we are never to see the holy flower, the type of the human soul, from black mud aspiring high to daylight, and there unfolding a sweet and radiant rosy purity undefiled by all the darkness it has traversed. Yet even of this I cannot think we must despair, if once our Lotus is established and gets all the sunshine there is. Of Lotuses there are many; but let us first succeed with one. Of the Water-lilies there are legion, species and hybrids, all of gloriousness untellable, and ever-increasing from year to year, as more and more colossal pink and crimson beauties appear at more and more colossal prices. But the tale of these things will be found at length in catalogues addicted to such matters; and the rock-garden has no business with them, but to look serenely down on a pond bedecked like the dream of some Indian princess of long ago, and see its own reflection there broken by great blossoms floating on the water, in rose and crimson and pink and pearl and copper and sulphur and saffron and snow, looking incredibly tropical to be, as they are, as hardy and even more vigorous than the poor little common white Water-lily that now seems so very remote and obscure a cousin of such regal gorgeousnesses. The obscurity of these, indeed, lies only in the causes that provoke their unfolding. Full sun is the usual notion of the key that unlocks them; and certainly so it often is; yet no less often have I gone by in the twilight of a sad grey day, or on a tranquil dull evening after rain, and found all the huge blossoms agape and glowing, with the rain still standing in globular diamonds over the marbled and mottled darkness of their leathern leaves.

4

OENOTHERA.

O

Odontospermum maritimum is a silky-woolled neat Composite with golden flowers packed among shoots of greyish foliage, which, with its kin, may be seen tucked into the Maritime rocks of the Levant; but they are hardly hardy with us, nor very well worth the trouble of trying, were it not that failure would bring so little disappointment.

Oenothēra.—American botanists have been having such games with the Evening Primroses that now there is really no knowing what is what, unless we ignore all these superfluous fal-lals, and stick simply to the good old name, without troubling our heads with *Lavauxia, Pachylophus, Galpisia, Chylisma, Meriolyx, Onagra, Anogra*, and all the other tiresome anagrams into which our thicker-blooded-than-water-friends across the Atlantic have lately been mangling the Evening Primroses. At the same time, the words are worth remembering, lest they creep into catalogues, and some day we repent in bankruptcy for having given 3*s.* 6*d.* for a flaming novelty called *Pachylophus caespitosus*, only to find that it was merely *Oenothera caespitosa* after all, of which it luckily chanced that our garden was already full. In any case the American Evening Primroses, ravishing though be the beauty of many (and usually easy to achieve), are not always soundly permanent in our climates, and should frequently be raised from seed or root cuttings, as well as accommodated with choice sunny places in especially light and sandy soil, where it will then be possible for them to despise several of our wet winters without too poignantly regretting the prairies from which they come. All the species are late-summer bloomers, and prodigal bloomers too, so that their merits are thereby enhanced, even if their very beauty have something a little lush and ephemeral and cheap about its look, that makes them seem unworthier still beside the brave brilliancy of a true-bred alpine. Here follow, then, the dwarfer sorts, leaving out the taller ones after the persuasion of our own yellow *Oe. biennis*, which are all adequately dealt with by Herbaceous catalogues.

Oe. acaulis has yellow flowers, lonely on stems of 6 inches or so.

Oe. Arendsii, on the contrary, is the one really first-class plant in the family for the rock-garden—first-rate not only in the beauty of its flowers, that is, but also in the vigour and endurance of its nature. The plant is a hybrid from *Oe. speciosa*, and planted prudently in good open soil on a warm slope, it will take permanent possession of its place, spreading endlessly, and susceptible of endless division, suffering

5

nothing to interfere with the lavish and unceasing display, all summer through, of its large and lovely flowers of melting delicate rich rose-and-white on stems of 5 or 6 inches or so.

Oe. caespitosa is also beautiful, forming tufts and mats about 4 inches high with blossoms of rosy pink.

Oe. eximia or *marginata* is another lovely thing, but specially delicate, running and creeping about in specially hot sandy soil, and producing abundant ample blossoms of white on quite dwarf stalks.

Oe. Fraseri, fruticosa, glabra, are all taller in growth, with handsome yellow flowers; of which *Oe. fruticosa* has given two valuable garden varieties in *Oe. F. Eldorado* and *Youngii,* particularly free and brilliant in the blossom, as well suited to the border as to the rock-garden, if not better.

Oe. Howardii is now the shining light of *Lavauxia* in America, and in our gardens it often masquerades also as *Oe. brachycarpa.* It is a neat ramifying tuft of tall, very narrow leaves, greyish-hoary at first ; among which sit vast lonely Evening Primroses of deep, rich yellow, on stems of 3 or 4 inches. It is a pretty thing, and might be associated perhaps with *Campanula alpestris,* did it not usually come too late into the field to make a contrast.

Oe. macrocarpa or *missouriensis* is an especially fine species for the rock-garden, for, though the stems are tall, they do not stand up, but stagger and lie down over the faces of rocks, in such a way as to give the fullest value to the plant's especially enormous cups of pure clear citron-yellow all through the later summer. It is also a good hearty perennial, asking only for ordinary rich loam in the sun.

Oe. mexicana has a name for pinkness, but is rather to be distrusted.

Oe. ovata is greatly advertised. It makes neat and rather leafy rosettes on the ground, and then, among their leaves produces all through the summer a quantity of little yellow Evening Primroses not quite large enough to redeem the weedish look of the rosette, though in themselves both bright and abundant, it is true, on any sunny slope.

Oe. pumila has the same stature and the same flowers of yellow.

Oe. riparia is advertised. There are far too many obscure plants that go to make up the large and misty personality that is meant by almost all the foregoing names.

Oe. serrulata grows 6 inches high, still with little yellow Evening Primroses.

Oe. speciosa is taller at times than even the rose-pink *Oe. pallida* its relative; this species is notably beautiful, but much the finest form is that called *Oe. sp. rosea,* with flowers of more brilliant rose, and a more modest habit. This, if suited, in a hot garden and sandy hot soil, runs about insatiably and fills the whole place; in cooler gardens and ground it often proves impossible to keep. There is also a *hybrida* of great merit, if indeed it be not synonymous with *Oe. Arendsii, q.v.*

And there are other species frequently advertised and offered, with regard to all of which the collector would be well advised not only to remember the psammophilous proclivities of this sun-worshipping and southerly race, but also that the family, its relationships and differences, are all still wrapped in impenetrable mystery, so that true, definite, finally-established species are not by any means easy to come by in a group of plants as polymorphic as a range of clouds at sundown.

Omphalōdes.—A race of Borrages, as a rule, almost excessively beautiful, from common little Blue-eyed Mary to the rarest new-comer from the East. Their nearest relations are *Paracaryum, Myosotis, Cynoglossum,* and *Lithospermum.* All can be well raised from seed, and most of them divided.

O. cappadocica (sometimes called *O. Witmanniana,* and *O. cornifolia,* Lehm.) makes a neat tuft of oval pointed leaves, dark above and greyish-pale beneath, from which in early summer and autumn, spring many very graceful loose sprays of 6 inches or so, unfurling a string of lovely large Forget-me-nots, beautifully deep-blue, scattered and airy in effect. This thrives quite easily in any rich well-drained loam, in rather shady exposures such as would suit *O. verna;* it is native to similar shady places and copses in Lazic Pontus, Cappadocia, &c.

O. florariensis is said to be a hybrid between *O. Luciliae* and *O. nitida,* from which its beauty, if not its culture, may be imagined.

O. Ikumae is a dainty little lovely Japanese plant, fine and frail, suggesting a compromise between *O. Luciliae* and *O. verna.*

O. japonica is even finer, having more flowers, and greater vigour of port, but otherwise suggesting the same relationship as the last.

O. Luciliae throws down the gauntlet to gardeners. Where happy it runs about and sows itself and turns a weed; in other places, not happy, it yet more promptly turns a corpse. The aim of this fairy's typical need (though occasionally in some gardens it may be otherwise suited), is a light yet rich loam, half filled with mortar rubble and lime-chips, so arranged upon the rock-work as to have the most perfect drainage and the fullest sun, yet without being parched or parboiled. It is so that the plant, a true crevice-lover, forms enormous bushy masses of its lovely glaucous foliage, long and waxy-blue and smooth-oval-pointed, in the sheer walls of Parnassus (above Mana Rachova), Sipylus, Cadmus, and other god-haunted mountains of Asia Minor, delighting those inhospitable rocks with abundant loose sprays of its round blank-looking flat flowers in the most delicate pearly tones of very pale porcelain-blue or sun-kissed snowy rose, seeming there to develop like natural emanations from the blueness of the foliage. In the garden, however, where *O. Luciliae*, if well-drained, will come readily from seed, the glaucousness of the seedlings is not to be trusted ; and, without that, lovely as are the blossoms themselves, thrown out all through the summer, they lose half their value if they do not spring from that cool blue tuft beneath, whose colour they so delicately should complete. And, on the other hand, unless you be specially favoured by fortune, you will not want to hack and harry an established tuft of *O. Luciliae*. So that prescriptions for propagation are apt on many counts to prove unprofitable. In the moraine, too, it grows readily, but slugs will even pursue it across the harsh surface that they hate ; and its safest and most characteristic place will always be in some ancient sunny wall, introduced into a crevice as a young cutting, and there left to grow large if it will, through many successive seasons. In specially hot climates, though, the sun-heat should be counteracted by abundance of water, administered subterraneously if possible (drive a drain-pipe or pot down into the coping of the wall above the plant, and keep it periodically filled), during the growing season, if not indeed from April straight away till the end of August.

O. nitida (*O. lusitanica*) is a pretty species, but perhaps the least worthy perennial of its family. In a damp warm corner it makes large clumps like those of some magnified *O. verna*, that is content to sit at home in a tuft ; from this, all the late summer through, it sprays about a lavish number of fine stems, about a foot high, waving this way and that, with a profusion of blue stars that, brilliant as they are, suffer a little in effect by being rather meanly proportioned for the size of the plant—not so large or stimulating, for instance, as in *O. verna* or *O. cappadocica*. None the less, it is both useful and hearty and beautiful, and should have care, for it is not always perfectly hardy in raw climates, luxuriating as it does most especially in quite damp places such as are often therefore heavy and cloying as cold suet in winter. It is native to cool shady hollows throughout North-Western Spain in the lower mountain region.

O. rupestris must be looked for with eager longing in the cliffs between Vladikafkas and Tiflis, on Bolta at about 2500 feet. For it bids fair to be the loveliest of all—a compact and dense little tuffet, all shining with a pure close coat of silver, and not 2 inches high. The stems hardly emerge from the shining mat of leafage, but throw out very delicate threadlike foot-stalks in all directions, each carrying a single glorious blue flower as large as in *O. cappadocica*, and most lovely to behold, hovering so exquisitely on the gleaming silver cushion, almost as if flowers of Eritrichium were beginning to take flight from one of his cushions, feeling that earth is no more worthy of their heavenly beauty.

O. Thomsoni makes a good sound perennial root-stock, up in the desolations of Western Tibet at 13,000 feet; and from this sends up a rich multitude of fine slender branching stems, roughish to the touch, and showering forth the family stars of azure, lax and airy.

O. verna, they say (whoever They may be), was the favourite flower of Queen Marie-Antoinette; was it part of her hapless naturalness that she brought with her, into the scented court of Versailles, a child's remembered love of Blue-eyed Mary, rambling in the woods of Schœnbrunn far away back in the days of sunlight, across the darkening unnoticed shadow of her world's end? For Blue-eyed Mary is a subject of the Hapsburgs, and in many a mountain copse and stony place of the Eastern ranges may be seen its trailing shoots of heart-shaped bright-green foliage, from which spray forth deep azure Forget-me-nots in a scattered drift of blue sparks from February till May. And even so, no matter under what ill-treatment, will Blue-eyed Mary, the scullion of her cosseted race, behave in copses and woody corners of England, no matter how weedy and worthless and forgotten. There is also a white form, most delicate and beautiful, but hardly to compare with the typical Omphalodean splendour of clear turquoise. As for the multiplication of Blue-eyes, she herself will look to that; and, in any case, can endlessly be divided, and pulled to pieces, and struck.

Onobrўchis.—Not a choice race of Pea-flowers, nor of value in the rock-garden, though in the Alps their pea-flowered spikes of dazzling rose have much attraction, and often so fill the high poor levels as to colour the distances. *O. sativa* is the common Sainfoin, and *O. montana* its more vivid alpine development; it is dwarfer than the lowland plant, and so is *O. lasiostachya*, with spikes of flaming pink. *O. arenaria* and *O. petraea* are about a foot high, the former pink, and the latter purplish. But all are of a lax and straggling habit, and, though melliferous in a high degree, not urgently needed in the rock-garden.

Onōnis.—A family of half shrubby or quite shrubby Pea-flowers, of which the common Rest-harrow is a type (and, in its best forms, by no means without its merits as a carpet for some hot and perfectly worthless place). Much dwarfer yet, however, and fine and frail and quite peculiarly choice and charming, is prostrate small *O. cenisia*, about whose character uncertainty hangs. For the species is one I have never succeeded in finding on the very limited habitat in its name-

ONOSMA.

place, but which I know to be abundant at far lower levels in the burnt barrens about Lanslebourg (as in the pine-zone on all formations here and there in the Alps of Italy, Southern France, and Spain). So that doubt, inspired by doleful experience, leads me to fear that the plant may not be of any sufficing hardiness and endurance. It should be grown from seed, and tried in hot dry places and moraines and so forth, well in the foreground, as fits its small proportions and the surpassing charm of its rosy flowers, which are very fine and large for the plant—little pink-and-white pea-blossoms dancing merrily on fine stems each by itself above the trailing mat of minute and hairless silver-greyish trefoils with toothed edges. *O. fruticosa* is a good shrub of a yard high with blossoms of bright pink, which, like all Ononids, children of the parched and blazing South, should have, in the garden, a parched and blazing place in very deep light soil ; another of the same kidney is *O. Natrix*, being a robustious, sticky herbaceous plant, about 2 feet tall, rank and overwhelming, with heads of large and brilliant yellow flowers. It is uncommon in the Swiss Alps, but becomes quite frequent further South, in dry banks and roadsides and railway cuttings of the warmer ranges. Some accuse it of a special fad for lime ; but in the Alps it has always seemed to me to ask only heat and a worthless rough place, as for a rare instance, in Switzerland, among the rough herbage on the sun-trodden slopes going up to Evolena. Among the best, however, for the rock-garden is really *O. rotundifolia*, which makes a pleasant little bush about a foot high, with large soft scalloped leaves in leaflets of three, among which, all the summer through, appear large and lovely Pea-flowers of rich pink with a paler keel, standing out on stems of their own in groups of two or three. This may abundantly be seen in the grand woods above Lanslebourg, and, like all Ononids, should either be raised from seed, or collected only in yearling seedlings, the roots of these being quite long enough, but those of older plants are interminable, woody, and wholly impracticable in their single-trunked distaste for disturbance. And yet another bushy species is of special value for a sunny place, and breaks fresh ground in colour. This is *O. aragonensis*, which stands boldly up and furnishes the garden with rather crowded yellow blossoms. Even finer than this, however, is *O. speciosa*, the best of all, being a very sticky, twiggy bush about 3 or 4 feet high, with all the upper akils emitting clusters of a few flowers till each shoot seems a loose spire of golden bloom. This is the Rascavieja of Spain, where it abounds in hot rocks and stony places of the South up to about 2500 feet in Granada.

Onosma, a most prime race for the rock-garden, of which we have

PLATE 1

NARCISSUS TRIANDRUS.
(Photo. R. A. Malby.)

PLATE 2.

OMPHALODES LUCILIAE
(Photo. R. A. Malby.)

only yet touched the fringe, and as to which catalogues are still **but** scantily informed and greatly confused. The chief of the family is Southern and Levantine, and insists absolutely on hot exposures and specially well-drained loam, quite light and usually limy. All can be raised freely from foreign seed, and, in England, multiplied by cuttings. The blooming-time is in summer from June forwards, and no race is more noble for hot and open ledges. And, in the first place, to have our ground clear of vain cumberers, the following species are of little value, either on account of their provenance, or their ugliness, or their biennial habit : *MM. microspermum, gracile, molle, kiloujense, Olivieri, chlorotrichum, Kotschyi, rhodopeum, Emodi, Wallichii, giganteum, taygeteum, Sprungeri*, and *hebebulbum.*

O. albo-roseum has the habit of *O. fruticosum.* It is a sub-shrub, very dense indeed with starry down, making masses of oblong blunt leaves, and sending up croziers that uncurl with sumptuous hoary-velvet bugles that range from white to blood-colour and blue, with notably broad lobes to the calyx. This beautiful species haunts the limestone cliffs of Amasia and Eastern Cappadocia, and though often well grown in gardens, is thankful for a little special warmth and protection from winter wet. It is a twin in many ways to our well-known *O. tauricum.*

O. arenarium, from the nearer Alps, has much the habit of *O. tauricum* also, but with flowers of yellow.

O. armenum is like a dwarf pale *O. tauricum*, but the sprays of bloom are in short heads instead of unfurling sprays.

O. bicolor is a foot or more in height, with purple flowers.

O. Bodeanum rises to 6 or 9 inches, with a great number of erect stems, springing from tufts of pale green leaves about an inch and a half long, set with hairs that rise from smooth wartlets. The stems are leafy and graceful, each carrying a few-flowered head of large violet bells. (From Bachtiar in Persia.)

O. Bourgaei grows in the alpine regions of Turkish Armenia, and its stalks are about a foot high, carrying curled-up dense sprays of white blossoms emerging from a fluffy calyx, each depending on a short petiole. The leaves are narrow and as long as their stems, and the whole plant is softly hairy with close-pressed down.

O. bracteatum is an Indian high-alpine, more of an Echium, with stems of 15 inches or so, and dense little sprigs of yellow flower all up the stout bristlish stems in dense array.

O. caespitosum may be seen in the impregnable cliffs of Buffavento in Crete above the ruins of the Queen's Castle ; where it forms tight masses of fat finely-downy foliage lying in rosettes with closely leafy small stems of 2 or 3 inches, displaying ultimately flowers of tawny yellow.

O. cassium has a more stately stature, attaining 18 inches, with unbranched erect or ascendent stalks clothed in smooth, blunt, half stem-embracing foliage, about an inch and a half long, and set with smooth tubercles or wartlets. The flowers are yellow. (From Northern Syria, Amanus, &c.)

O. coeruleum is all rough with short grey hairs, and the stems rise to some 5 or 10 inches, unfolding showers of blue and white in the cliffs of Antilibanus.

O. dasytrichum has few-flowered close heads of violet blossom, on silky-haired erect shoots from a woody stock. (Alps of Southern Persia.)

O. decipiens, Schott and Ky. = *O. nanum*, *q.v.*

O. echioeides ranges from Europe to the Levant, and may always be known from all forms of *O. tauricum* by the *very specially short footstalks* of the flowers that *do not*, as in the others, after flowering exactly equal the calyx in length. It is the *O. stellulatum genuinum* of Boissier. In other words, it is not at all far from *O. tauricum* in garden needs and value. It also has varieties *O. e. brachycalyx* and *O. e. brachyphyllum.*

O. erectum is a small-growing sub-species of *O. stellulatum*, from the sea-rocks of Crete, up to 5000 feet on Cretan Ida. It is most neat and attractive, with bugles of a more golden-orange than in *O. tauricum*, which, it must be remembered, ranked originally as a mere narrow-leaved variety of the very polymorphic *O. stellulatum ;* so that *O. stellulatum* still serves as the standard of comparison for *O. tauricum* and all its kindred.

O. flavum has the full serene beauty of *O. sericeum*, silver coat and all, but sometimes the plant is clothed in russet down instead, and always the seed-nuts are smooth.

O. frutescens is *O. echioeides* of the *Flora Graeca*. It is specially branching, half shrubby at the base, and rough and downy with close-pressed hairs. The leaves are oblong-paddle-shaped, and the bending stems spring up in abundance, and on their 6-inch branches bear the most beautiful big heads of big flowers that range from yellow to pink and violet. This glorious species occupies the rocks of Attica and all Greece, and so down to Palestine, on Hermon and Carmel.

O. fruticosum is found some 2000 feet up in Crete. It has long woody branches and blossoms that vary from white to yellow, some dozen or more to the mound of blossom.

O. halophilum may justly be said to love salt. For it inhabits certain cold salty plains of Lycaonia, beneath Kara Dagh, which in winter are under water. This extreme eccentricity of taste (and doubly extreme in an Onosma) does not deter it from forming tawny-green rosettes of broadish, oblong leaves, round which, from below, spring up stems of 6 or 10 inches, unfurling heads of white velvet blooms. It is not shrubby at the base.

O. helveticum stands quite close in habit to *O. arenarium*. It has green bristlish foliage and flowers of pale yellow, after the style of *O. tauricum*, with which, however (vain words notwithstanding), it has no specific affinity whatever. (German Alps of the South, and away to Crete through the high mountain rocks of Epirus, &c.)

O. Hookeri is a hairy Esau from some 14,000 feet in Sikkim, with stems that vary between 3 and 6 inches or more, carrying fluffy heads of large violet flowers as ample in size as those of *O. echioeides*. This plant it is that yields the red dye of the Lepchas, and has lent itself thus to the long feud between the yellow- and the Onosma-capped monks of Tibet.

O. isauricum comes so close to *O. sericeum* as only to be distinguished by the stellate tubercles on the leaves.

O. lanceolatum comes from the grassy places of Kurdistan, and is all ashy-grey, the lower leaves being three-nerved on the under-side, while the flower-stems are half a foot or a foot high.

O. latifolium haunts the same quarters, but precisely follows the fashion of *O. dasytrichum*, except that it is herbaceous and not half-shrubby, and the whole mass is vested in a thick grey coat ; while the flowers are not violet, but yellow.

O. liparoeides, from the mountains of Cappadocia, is a pleasant little thing, as smoothly and platedly silver as *O. sericeum* itself, but quite neat and dwarf, with stems not more than 4 inches high or a little more. The white flower hardly emerges from the calyx, however, which is cut into strips so thoroughly as even to become feathery.

O. mite makes masses of soft wool, as its name declares, and the masses are but 2 inches high, while the erect-lobed yellow blossoms are borne in heads on stems of seven or nine. This will require cherishing, as its home is in the hot pine-stretches of Lycia and Cyprus.

O. montanum, if this be more than a superfluous form, is only 4 inches high, so it is said, with flowers of clear yellow.

O. mutabile is also about 6 inches high and nobly beautiful, having the general habit and stature of *O. albo-roseum*, all the clump being clothed in grey hairs, and the plant half-shrubby and branching. But the large bell-drops pass from yellow to pink and blue, and the dainty small stature distinguishes it. (From between 6000 to 9000 feet on Berydagh.)

O. nanum is *O. decipiens*, Schott and Ky. It is a beautiful stranger from the high Alps of Cappadocia, on Gisyl Tepe, &c., at about 6000 feet, tawny all over with an abundance of bristlish hair, and closely tufted with a great number of stiff little stems of 2 or 4 inches, rising from the many-headed mass, which is furnished with narrow-oblong blunt leaves, longish and rather rolled over at the edges, and with a conspicuous midrib on the under-side. The stems unfold at last into showers of large velvety white bells, few to a spray.

O. oreodoxum is a Hill-glory on the appropriately named Mount Climax in Pisidia, being very like *O. cassium*, with stems of 18 inches or 2 feet, but the calyces are longer, densely white with downy hairs, and exuding whitish bells with sharper lobes.

O. ovalifolium stands close to *O. Bourgaei*, but has only quite small and scattered tubercles on the leaves.

O. pachypodum, from the schistose rocks of Elburs, has its nearest relation in *O. flavum*, from which it chiefly differs in having pale-green leafage sparingly set with hairs. The stems are about a foot high, but the yellowish corolla is rather longer, being about an inch.

O. polyphyllum makes a sub-shrubby mass in the rocks of Southern Taurus. The leaves are about 2 inches long, and remarkably narrow, pointed and rolled over at the edge, very closely huddled in the cushion, and clad in a double coat of tightly ironed-down short hairs, which, further up, get looser and longer and rather tawny. The stems are some 4 or 5 inches high in nature, and the flowers are large and white.

O. procērum stands near *O. oreodoxum*, but is an obscure species with a hairy nectary for sole distinction at present—and this is only a sort of O.B.E. in the race.

O. pyramidale is a Himalayan, to be quoted with doubt. It is described as being rather tender (perhaps monocarpic), about 2 feet high, with yellow flowers.

O. Rascheyanum is a most longed-for species from Antilibanus, near akin to *O. stellulatum*, but only 6 inches high, yet with a much more shrubby rootstock. And the flowers are in smooth, hoar-frosted heads, of polychromatic variety, while the whole growth is clothed in rough and spreading vesture of hairs and bristles.

O. rostellatum has a much softer character, although its stem be neither taller nor shorter. It is mild in soft down, and its dwarfish shoots are many and frail and branching, emerging from tufts of oblong leaves and unfurling into lax sprays of blue and blue-and-white blossoms about half as long as the calyx, with the blue stamens sticking far out. It hangs from the undercut precipices of Mesopotamia, &c.

O. Roussaei may be found in the rocks by the Cedars of Lebanon, and in the chalky hills of Aleppo. It is a neat dwarf mass and very like *O. armenum,* but that the leaves are much longer, and the yellow flower stands much further out of the calyx, in heads of blossom about 6 inches tall.

O. rupestre, from the Iberian Caucasus, Tiflis, &c., and the rocks of Cappadocia, is a tidy ash-grey mass of foliage with short narrowly paddle-shaped leaves an inch or less in length, and stems of 4 or 6 inches, unbranching, or almost wholly unbranching, and hanging out cylindric citron-coloured bugles.

O. sericeum is one of the most lovely among the most lovely. It makes regular rosettes of rather broad-oval leaves sheeted in quite smooth pure silver of the best quality, untarnishable but by autumnal rains ; from which in due course ascend stems of blossom that divide near the top into two sprays each hanging out a carillon of long creamy-yellow bells. This gem requires the warmest and the best-drained place of all, as we may learn not only by sad experience, but also from the enlightening information that in nature it especially affects the dry sub-alpine stony places in Anatolia, Caucasus, Transcaucasia, &c.

O. simplicissimum.—Simple Simon shows his character by going voluntarily to live in Russia and Siberia, where he makes big tuffets of yellowish-green foliage, sparsely hairy, very narrow, and more or less pointed and rolled at the edges. The plant is almost shrubby at the base, and from the mass ascend a crowd of stems some 6 inches or a foot tall, carrying heads of whitish-velvet flowers.

O. stamineum is also a semi-Russian. It is fairly roughish, in a cluster of many crowns with many uprising unbranched stems of half a foot or more, beset with small sessile narrow leaves, and evolving into almost cylindrical short spikes of blue flowers, with their lobes curling back, and their anthers sticking out. *O. rostellatum* has suggested this, but here the blossoms are twice and a half again as long as the calyx.

O. stellulatum.—This is the species that has given botanists as much trouble as its beauty is worth to gardeners. We may take our common *O. tauricum* as its complete picture, seeing that at first *O. tauricum* was ranked as a mere variety, though now differentiated as a species on small botanical grounds presently to be recounted. The type, anyhow, ranges through Greece into Asia Minor, and takes a large number of varieties, many of which have now been promoted into species. Of such are *O. erectum*, *q.v.*, and *O. tauricum*, Pallas, *q.v.* (formerly *O. stellulatum*); *angustifolium* of Boissier (*O. scorpioeides*, Huet.), a narrower-leaved form, more ashen-grey in its leaf-colouring. Then there were *O. s. pallidum* with whitish flowers, and *O. s. brevifolium*, a neat little mountain form from the higher Alps of Lycia, Caria, &c., passing into *O. erectum;* while even *O. echioeides* was once Boissier's typical *O. stellulatum genuinum*, so that there is but little left of the original *O. stellulatum* to-day ; though you may still know it as a species apart by the fact that its *flower-stems are as long as the calyces after blooming*, unlike the very short pedicels of *O. echioeides*, while from *O. tauricum* (which is the same in this respect) it differs also in broader foliage and much less dense investiture of greyness. But, Lord, what nice quillets are these, in the case of a species so variable and widely spread !

O. strigosissimum is rough as the ways of the world all over. But otherwise a pleasant small plant, having the habit of *O. frutescens*, though not half-shrubby at the base, but wholly herbaceous, with short stems of 6 inches or so, and the same lovely large variable flowers of yellow and pink and violet. (Sea-rocks of the Aegean.)

O. tauricum.—Our well-beloved favourite old Onosma, the one and only Golden Drop of the garden, has already been amply differentiated from its close cousins. Its flower-pedicels do *not equal the calyces after flowering* as in *O. stellulatum*, while the *leaves are narrower*, and the plant greyer altogether with ashen hairs. That being said, we can all rejoice in its wide enormous masses of narrow grey flopping foliage, out of which summer calls such gracious croziers of hanging ample flowers of a waxy and lemony lusciousness peculiar to themselves, and exactly asking for the name of Golden Drop in their melting confectionery clarity of colour and texture. The hot bank that suits all has had this for its inmate many years ; it will strike from cuttings, and always behaves itself in the garden with heartiness and decorum ; one of the best and most characteristic of easy-going beautiful Borragineous rock-plants.

O. Thompsoni is really *Echium* rather than *Onosma*. It is perennial in warm, well-drained soil, forming a deep root with several crowns, and sending up in late summer a number of very stiff and stout stems of 18 inches more or less, set all the way with tight clusters of small ruby-coloured Echium-flowers packed in a spike up the stalks. The whole growth is rough and hispid, and, though noble enough and brilliant in its unyielding way, hardly deserves to enter so brilliant a company as Onosma. (It comes from some 6000 feet up in Sikkim.)

OPUNTIA.

O. Tröodi, from the crevices of Tröodos in Crete, is a twin to *O. nanum* in minute habit, but has even smaller leafage (not rough, but clad in tighter-ironed downy hairiness), and very much smaller yellowish flowers huddled in a head.

O. velutinum only differs from *O. nanum,* the beautiful, in a soft and velvety, not bristlish, vesture, in denser clumps of rather smaller blossom, and in leaves that lack the midrib beneath and the rolled edge. (Alpine region of the Bithynian Olympus.)

Onosmodium molle (and *O. occidentale,* of which it is a variety) are Borragineous plants of no noticeable merit.

Ophelia, a family of Gentianaceous plants, closely allied to Swertia, and sometimes merged in Swertia. Their treatment is the same, and their attractions on a par.

Opuntia, with **Cereus** and **Echinocereus.**—As most of the members of all these races make no pretence at being either hardy or useful generally out of doors, it is only necessary to note some of the more indestructible, that those who like this kind of thing may find these the kind of things they like : for, if you can pardon the arid and unfriendly look of these plants, dusty in colour, and horrible with spines, Rackhamish in weird contortions and Anglo-Saxon attitudes of their indecent stalagmites and ribbed articulations and stars of thorns and mop-heads of frowzy wool or fat great tennis-rackets of dim-green flesh—if you can forgive or enjoy all this, I say, you may easily devote a hot bank of the rockwork to such treasures, any very light soil being sufficient in a warm well-drained situation. Glass should be put over them to keep off wet in winter ; and then in due time, out of their stony grievousness of appearance your confidence (as the Beauty's in the Beast) will be rewarded by the unfolding of their most pure and delicate flowers like heavenly roses, seeming unnatural and misplaced as they protrude in July and August from the dark inhospitable leaf or column, looking as if they had been freakishly pinned there by a thorn, rather than developed in any legitimate course of nature. Among the hardiest and best of Opuntias are : *O. arborescens,* with a branching stem, which, however, relies too greatly upon the charm of its bare branches, for it has never been known to flower in England ; *O. arenaria* is more dwarf, with oval stem branches and yellow flowers ; quite close to this are *O. fragilis* and *O. brachyantha. O. cammanchica* takes high rank in all respects ; it is a specially sturdy grower and free-flowerer, with large flattened joints, and yellow blossoms that vary to red in the form *rubra,* and have also a *major* development. *O. cantabrigiensis* has the largest joints of all the hardy Cacti, and the usual yellow

17

flower; *O. Rafinesquii* is the most indestructibly hardy of the lot, producing light yellow blooms, but varying almost indefinitely, with many good forms to be found quoted in catalogues of such matters, *e.g. arkansana, macrorrhiza, cymochila,* &c. And *O. vulgaris* is not content to be hardy, but has established itself as a wild plant in Europe, though native, like all these others, to the New World; and has not only established itself in Europe, but chosen the Alps for the scene of its prosperity, where, at low elevations in the southerly valleys, it may be seen luxuriating, as on the rocks of Sion, profuse in the beauty of its yellow-silk roses. And there are other beauties, too, in *O. militaris, O. missouriensis, O. rhodantha* (very spiny and very beautiful with noble satiny-pink peonies emerging from flattened little columns of hate). All these to be collected from catalogues. Of *Cereus,* especially seek out only *C. viridiflorus,* which has small odd green blooms in June and July; and *C. paucispinus,* which must have a specially hot dry place, with its back up against the fireplace of a nice hot stove, where it will accordingly burgeon forth freely into flowers of scarlet with a green stigma; and *C. Eyresii,* with dwarf green stems and large white blossoms in July and August; while *Echinocactus tubiflorus* has about a dozen ribs to the trunks, and white trumpets in summer.

Orchis and **Orchids.**—Properly transplanted and re-planted there is no difficulty in the acclimatisation of *Orchis,* and all the English species should have their best forms marked down in bloom, and, either on the spot, or later, be translated to the garden into good deep loam. Superstition vainly imposes all kinds of silly and unnecessary taboos; in point of fact, if an ample sod be taken, and the tubers removed without touch or scar upon themselves, and promptly wrapped in moss to avoid shrivelling on the way home, it is much better and more convenient, and not in the least dangerous, to remove the plant when you find it in flower. Only it must be remembered to take a solid square chunk out of the earth, with no ungenerous slicing that may imperil the tubers; then, having got out the sod, the tuber may be worried clear, and stripped of all its soil, and clad in moss or damp paper, without the slightest peril, while the hole you have made in the world can be put back. Of such, the best of our own are *O. militaris, O. mascula, O. masculata, O. Morio, O. latifolia,* and the two prime rarities, *O. hircina* (*Himantoglossum hircinum*), and *O. laxiflora*— neither of these, of course, on any account to be collected in England, even if you should have the astounding luck to happen on them. The Continent yields a score of lovely species beside, in a tale too long to be recounted here, though on the Alps the pale-lemon spires of stout *O. sambucina* clamour for collection, and on the Riviera and in the

Levant are dozens more, with the moony citron of *O. pallens ;* while Madeira has almost grown tired of giving us her gorgeous *O. foliosa*, which is like a darker, gigantic *O. maculata*, and adapted for the same sort of damp place in a warm and sheltered corner. But pompously-named *O. spectabilis* from America—and the only species there found—is sadly unworthy of its name, having only a few large and scattered hoody flowers of pink and white on the stumpy stems that nestle into foliage excessively ample. Of *Ophrys*, despite their uncanny beauty of plagiarism from bee and bug and bird, no such smooth things can be said as of *Orchis ;* they are matter for the specialist, though in nature no Orchis looks more hearty or happy. In cultivation, though all are worthy (and high above the rest, strange rare *O. Speculum*, with its broad azure patch of looking-glass on the velvet lip, which here and there may very rarely be strayed across in the coasts of the Riviera), all are of brief portion here, and the happiest suggestion will probably be a rather moist and almost wholly sandy mixture, with a scant allowance of leaf-mould and a much more generous one of lime-rubble (though this, considering the provenance of many, can hardly be always essential). And our despair of Ophrys rests hardly so much perhaps on the plants themselves as on the impossibility of getting fresh unshrivelled tubers that have neither been hacked, parched, nor rotted. The delicate lovely little marsh-Orchids of North America had better be left alone in their marshes by all except the most patient, passionate, and prodigal of gardeners ; while marsh-plants as a rule adapt themselves almost with excessive greed to artificial marsh-conditions, the bog-Orchids make a startling and odious exception to the custom—a race of most dainty small fairies, whose tubers sit in the Sphagnum wads, and require constant and especial treatment to keep their temper tame, and their surroundings just exactly and pre-cisely as they please, the slightest dereliction in the matter being fol-lowed by death. Who, in England, has had prolonged success with any of these little lovelinesses, exquisite as the ancient names they bear, of the nymphs whose place they take by fountain-side or pool— *Arethusa, Calypso*, or *Limodoron, Calopogon*, or *Pogonia ?* Less often tried, however, and perhaps more open to hope, is the gorgeous race of American swamp-Habenarias, tropical-looking splendours, with the ample lower lip often slashed and fringed into a fur as fine as that on the labellum of *Dendrobium fimbriatum*. Of such (all most especially to be ensued, and to be acquired by fresh moss-wrapped tubers sent quickly over from America) are : *H. fragrans*, small and white, but deliciously sweet ; *H. ciliaris*, very magnificent, with ample fringy flowers of orange ; *H. blephariglottis*, close akin, but white ;

19

H. grandiflora, stalwart, portly, and splendid, the finest of all, with big spires of fringed great fragrant lilac blossoms ; *H. psychodes*, smaller, in the same way, of pinker colouring and exquisite poise of butterfly bloom ; *H. Andrewsii*, white to purple, and fringed ; *H. fimbriata*, like a larger *H. psychodes ; H. peramoena*, very handsome, violet-purple, but unfringed. All these, when procured, should be planted in deep, rich, and perfectly-drained damp soil by the water-side ; not in grim solitude, but among small ferns and light grasses and so forth, that they may not only look at home but feel so. Imagine their pleasure and consolation of company in a far land, if they found they were hanging their harps beside the waters of Babylon on the same willow-tree as their old neighbour *Cypripedium Reginae*, the Queen of Slippers. Nor, in leaving the water's edge, must we forget how readily and even invasively it may be adorned by our own *Epipactis palustris*, running freely about, and in late summer sending up its loose, few-blossomed showers of large wax-white flowers freaked with rose and gold. Not so very far away, too, we may delight in our own native Habenarias *bifolia* and *chlorantha*, with their fluttering butterflies of greeny-white ; and even more in the long and hyacinth-sweet rosy-mauve spires of *Gymnadenia (Habenaria) conopsea*, flowering in early July, and of especial beauty. But this, alas ! is beaten out of the field by the alpine *G. odoratissima*, taller, ampler, longer-spired, and of the same uplifting fragrance. This may everywhere (like the other) be seen in the alpine coppice and open places of the mountain brushwood ; and while the hill-districts have often yielded me white *conopseas*, once only have I been privileged to see the virgin-snowy spike of the albino *G. odoratissima ;* this was in the debouchure of that gloomy gorge the Val Lorina, by the foot of the Cima Tombea. The *Nigritellas* are found higher up in the fine turf of *Myosotis rupicola* and Flannel-flower ; and here their small pyramids of mahogany or glowing ruby-red fill the air with a vanilla-sweetness that wars with the pervading wine-scent of *Trifolium alpinum*. But so far I have not coped successfully myself with *Nigritella*, and imagine they want warm light turfy loam, rather hard and elastic, in company with a crowd of neighbours such as they have in their home. The *Cephalantheras* are plants of the lower woodland, and offer no difficulties of culture. *C. pallens* is the biggest we possess in England, and would be improved if its white Helleborine flowers would ever open properly. The true Helleborines are of dingy colouring, all except the amethyst and ruby-velvet form called *Epipactis rubra* in old days, a not uncommon form of Yorkshire limestone screes and the same conditions in the Alps ; its name once used to breed confusion with a far auguster thing, the true *Cephalanthera rubra*, the "rarissime" pride of certain Gloucestershire woods, and often to be seen in warm places of the Southern Alps, as in the fringes of the chestnut woods of San Dalmazzo de Tenda, with tall light stems, carrying each three or four large flowers of glowing ruby-amethyst, very brilliant and, from a distance, suggesting *Gladiolus paluster*, but, on nearer approach, a smaller reproduction of *Bletia hyacinthina*, that beautiful and quite hardy Japanese Orchid, with pink and albino forms, which may be trusted no less happily in the same rich-soiled, sheltered, well-drained garden-conditions as Cephalanthera, though it will be long before it there attains the full development of beauty that may be seen crowning the river-bluffs below the Fuji-kawa Rapids in jungles of gleaming swordlike foliage and delicate flights of crimson sparks. The race will be found treated by M. Correvon and Graf Silva Tarouca at ampler length than is fairly possible here—Orchidaceae, in its hardy branches at least, not being a saxatile or essential rock-garden race.

Origanum.—The Marjorams offer us a race of small upshooting herbaceous plants of savoury odour from the Levant, with woolly ample foliage as a rule, and little feeble flowers usually redeemed by the magnificent ruby colouring of the bracts that enclose them. All may be raised from seed, cuttings, or division, and all should have a hot dry place on some sunny ledge of the rock-garden, not too close in the foreground, and high enough up to show the grace of the habit and nodding heads. *O. Dictamnus* is in all the shady rocks of Crete, and is one of the best, with big oval leaves (that are evergreen) flocculent in white wool, and hop-like hanging heads in branching showers; *O. pulchellum* of the Paris Garden has smaller leaves, not so round, and many-bunched panicles of nodding blossom; *O. Tourneforti* is like an almost hairless *O. Dictamnus*, with longer flower-tubes, and the stems leafy all the way up; *O. pulchrum* is especially pretty, quite hairless, with leafy little stems of some 6 or 9 inches, and any number of nodding flower-clusters, enclosed and hidden in bracts of bright purple; and there are many other species, all of merit in the same line and for the same treatment, among their points of importance being the fact that they bloom in later summer and far on into autumn; here are some more names: *O. libanoticum, O. sipyleum, O. rotundifolium, O. Haussknechtii*, &c.

Ornithogálum.—The stars of Bethlehem are adequately coped with in such catalogues as offer them, nor is the race ardently desired in the rock-garden, many of the species, such as *O. nutans* and *O. umbellatum* (both hard to beat among the best), making haste to turn into weeds, and, no more than nature, to be expelled by any amount of forks.

Orŏbus, a beautiful family, leaking into *Lathyrus*, but almost all of the highest value in the rock-garden, *Lathyrus* now tending to possess the ramping trailers, while the neater-habited stay-at-home plants sit quiet under the shadow of *Orobus*. All can be raised as easily from seed as all peas, and the clumps divided in spring or autumn— all the species blooming in spring and early summer.

O. albus. See *O. pannonicus*, Jacq.

O. alpestris has one-sided flower-spikes, and may be seen on Rilo.

O. armenus stands about a foot high, and has purple flowers.

O. aurantiacus has much the same habit, but the flowers are of orange-yellow, a little tawny in their tone. It is hardly, if at all, to be separated from *O. luteus*, unless in the deeper tone of its blossoms.

O. aureus (*O. luteus*, Sibth.) differs from *O. luteus* of the Eastern Alps in having broader leaflets, which are *not glaucous underneath*, while the stems and pedicels are hairy. Otherwise it is the same stately plant that you see as you mount from Cortina to the Falzarego, in the meadow and coppice, amply suited for some such spacious corner at home, which it will occupy with its two-foot growth, with generous loose spikes of large pale-golden Pea-flowers in summer.

O. canescens (*O. filiformis*, Lam.) is a common sight in Southern Europe, belying its name by being glabrous, and standing 18 inches tall, with beautiful blue-and-white blossoms, four or nine to a head. There is also a leafier form, *O. variabilis*, from Eastern Cilicia, with still larger flowers of rich blue-violet. Both plants are of extreme beauty, and run freely in any light soil in a sunny place.

O. cyaneus (*Lathyrus*) comes from Siberia and the stony places of Alpine Anatolia, Caucasus, &c., and is a dwarf treasure of the best, emerging quite early in the year with crumpled leaflets of bright glossy green, from which soon appear handsome sprays or heads of large blooms in the richest and clearest sapphire-turquoise blue. This needs no more trouble than the ugliest weed, but, like many an Orobus, is designed by nature for rather cooler places on the fringe of brushwood. In all catalogues this is *Lathyrus cyaneus*.

O. Fischeri has unbranching stems of about a foot, sparingly furnished, with very narrow and pointed leaflets, only one pair going to a leaf. The flowers are purple, and crowded into one-sided racemes in early summer. (Siberia.)

O. grandiflorus is the finest of all the yellow-flowered species. It grows some 2 feet high in the pinewoods of Lebanon and Amanus, with noble golden flowers an inch across, twice as long as in *O. luteus*, and three times as long as in *O. aureus*, and eagerly to be desired.

O. hirsutus is softly hairy all over, weak-stemmed, with violet flowers in one-sided sprays.

O. Jordani comes prettily into early summer, with stems of nearly a foot, set with leaves made of oval-pointed leaflets in three or four pairs, and carrying rich-blue peas in loose and scanty clusters. (Lucania.)

O. lathyroeides is also called *Vicia unijuga* by those that love variety. It likes shade, and its stems are nearly 2 feet long, and the deep-blue flowers, though not specially large, are specially numerous on the stems that are thrown out in June and July. See also *Vicia*, loc. cit. It is remarkably splendid in effect.

O. luteus may be separated from *O. aurantiacus* by the paler tone of its yellow blossoms; leaning rather more closely—as does the whole plant—to *O. aureus*.

O. niger has the attraction of being a renowned rarity in one or two Scotch alpine glens. It is otherwise not especially distinct in charm from the quite common and most beautiful *O. vernus* (*Lath. macrorrhizus*) that is everywhere to be seen in spring, and by no means to be despised for cool corners of the garden—particularly in its pink form and its very rare white form, in its yet lovelier rose-and-white form, and the double blushing pearly one.

O. pannonicus is also *O. albus*. It forms a thick tuft, sending up in spring a number of elegant 15-inch stems displaying a profusion of white or cream-white flowers, large and well shown on the mass. If possible, its variety *O. p. varius*, with the standards flesh-pink and the wings and keel in tones of soft creamy yellow, is even more beautiful; and both are of the easiest culture and the highest value to leave alone in any open place, where they will form a clump and stay quiet, living and letting live successfully without intrusions.

O. rotundifolius is a fine climbing pea, in reality *Lathyrus rotundifolius, q.v.* (*Lathyrus* has tendrils and climbs.)

O. sericeus is close to *O. hirsutus*, but the leaves are longer and narrower, and the hairs are ironed close instead of standing up in fluff.

O. sessilifolius is a beautiful graceful thing from the mountain copses of Servia, Attica, and the Argolid, with the leaves almost sessile, and the sprays of large violet blossom standing far above them.

O. Smithii is a puzzle without a name, that has nothing to do with the *O. pannonicus* of which it is often sent out as a variety. This strange plant, of most un-Orobian and un-lathyroid habit, makes stiff stems of 2 feet or so, that tend to go flop, straight along the ground; the ample foliole, clothed in white hairs, has a handsome folded effect, and the long-stemmed axillary clusters of large pale-yellow flowers appear in July and August. It will thrive in any fair conditions, and in catalogues is always called *Lathyrus pannonicus Smithii.*

O. tuberosus is *Lathyrus tuberosus,* a very rare English native, very abundant in the one station which it fills with its twining stems and heads of pink peas.

O. variegatus is rather taller than *O. vernus,* with graceful erect wiry stems in spreading clumps from knotty but not running rootstocks. It is most abundant in flower, having ten or a dozen blooms to a stem, daintily borne and making a lovely show a little later in the summer than does *O. vernus,* of blossom rather smaller perhaps, but much more profuse, alike in number of flowers and in number of sprays, and carried too on a plant of smaller leafage, so as to make even more of an effect. The delicate colour varies in pinks and light purples with various garden forms, of which one (very beautiful) is Salmon-and-White in the flower, and in the Catalogue-name also. This will thrive in the common conditions that suit the race, and is indeed native to the mountain copses of South and Mid-Europe, to the Levant. (The species is confused with *O. p. varius* in lists.)

O. varius. See under *O. pannonicus.*

Orontium aquaticum is a shallow-water Aroid that makes tufts of dark-green oval-pointed foliage, among which all round appear in late summer countless 6-inch rat-tails of yellow spathes, bending stiffly this way and that, but not succeeding thereby in eliciting any more attention or enthusiasm.

Orphanidesia gaultherioeides is a most attractive creeping undershrub suggesting *Epigaea repens,* and found beneath the Rhododendrons in the alpine regions of Lazic Pontus.

Ostrowskia magnifica.—Get large trunks of this as thick as your arm, ram down the surface of a sloping and very deep limy loambed in full sun until it is as hard as a threshing-floor. Then, with a crowbar, work a deep enough hole in this to take the trunk, put it in, fill up the hole, stamp it firm, and you need never again have a thought for *O. magnifica,* which for the rest of your lifetime will continue untended to throw up its stout boles and open its colossal Platycodonflowers in June; after which the succulent glaucous stems and foliage die down with a depressing promptitude, and leave their hideous wreckage hanging dolefully all the rest of the season. *Ostrowskia* may be raised from seed if you have profitably studied the virtues of Job;

but it must never be touched, once established, unless you go the length of hacking up the whole vast trunk, to slice it in three or four, and so start the fragments all again as separate plants.

Ourisia, a Scrophulariaceous family of handsome foliage and wandering rhizomes, forming a close carpet of foliage, above which come shooting bare stems with flower-spikes often brilliant in colour. The race is antarctic, and the greater number of the species for which we hope call our eyes to New Zealand. Their needs are a sheltered corner and room to grow in rich deep soil, rather moist in summer but perfectly drained, and in winter kept dry. All could be raised from their minute seeds, but division of the rhizome offers the quickest way of increasing the stock of any species once acquired.

O. brevifolia, a charming little plant like *Linaria hepaticaefolia,* running about in the crevices of the Aucklands, with large single white flowers on the mass.

O. caespitosa is quite a neat close tuffet, close-set with almost sessile leaves, and sending up stalks of a couple of inches or so, with three or four white blossoms at the top.

O. coccinea is a Chilian species, and will always perhaps remain our favourite in the race, at such a rate does it run about when suited, and with such profusion send up stems of such very gorgeous long scarlet flowers in tiers of outstanding trumpets. It succeeds or fails under the most diverse conditions; but if a sound clump, not over-divided, can be got, it will never be amiss to plant it in rich and rather moist well-drained ground, whether in sun or shade, when it will promptly set about sending its fleshy rhizomes creeping far and wide over rock and soil, forming a hearty carpet of crumpled-looking, scalloped, bright-green leaves, above which come starting those 8-inch stems in early summer.

O. Cockayniana is a matted creeper, with the same bright-green leaves, quite smooth, in pairs. The stems are about 6 inches high, purplish in colour, with white flowers of an inch long.

O. Colensoi is a reduced alpine state of *O. macrocarpa, q.v.*

O. glandulosa makes big patches of rather coarse leathery leafage, and has stout branching stems, with flowers half the length of those in *O. Cockayniana.*

O. macrocarpa is the finest of all, with generous whorls of large white blossoms. We may picture the plant from the next species, which we possess, and which is about *half the size in all its parts.*

O. macrophylla has ample dark foliage, rather downy-haired (unlike the last, which is smooth), and stout stems, carrying whorls of white blossom almost suggestive in habit of a Pentstemon. This blooms in the later summer, and the stems are a foot high or so.

O. magellanica has fat leaves of a couple of inches, and large white flowers on stems that begin branching and blooming almost from their base.

O. prorepens is a creeping slender species, with delicate sprayed stalks and large white trumpets.

O. sessilifolia makes a pale-green mat of small scalloped leaves, pressed to the ground ; from this rise stems of some 2 to 6 inches, carrying big white blossoms with a base of purple.

Oxălis.—Our own native Wood-sorrel gives a lovely variety with flowers of bright rosy pink ; but the race has also many exotic treasures to offer, being predominantly a family of the warmth, and of South America, straying over into Europe and reaching the North no less than the cold Antarctic Islands, where *O. magellanica* is like an exquisite small version of the Wood-sorrel. Very lovely too, in the same line and for the same situation, is *O. violacea*, from the Northern States of America, which is a Wood-sorrel with purple blossoms. Unfortunately many of the most beautiful South American or Cape species, such as *O. monophylla, O. rosea, O. lobata* (specially beauteous), *O. floribunda*, &c., though often safe and successful in favoured places in light soil, cannot always be recommended for permanent general cultivation in England, though even in a climate such as Yorkshire's, *O. rosea* on the rockwork was the glory of three unprotected seasons, filling the later summer days with the cheer of its rosy cups ; while even lovelier should be the 2-inch *O. monophylla*, with blossoms of pale pink, and by no means to be denied oneself as an experiment. There is a point at which caution becomes cowardice ; and another at which vain confidence turns into courage ; one is apt, amid the winter wets of Yorkshire, to imagine the glare of the Cape, and sicken sympathetically at the mere thought of subjecting an Oxalis to such a change ; on the other hand, in summer heat the spirit mounts until no Wood-sorrel seems hopeless or foolhardy to attempt. Of two at least a solid tale of satisfaction can everywhere be told ; these are *O. enneaphylla* and *O. adenophylla*. The first occupies the Falklands, there forming masses and long trunks of queer rhizomes that add each year at the end a little scaly bulb like that of some miniature *Lilium auratum*, until at last there is a whole long rope of knubbly beads, sending up, in nature, its leaf-tuft from the youngest. In the garden, in rich soil in a cool and shady (but often in an open and sunny) crevice of the rock-work, *O. enneaphylla* thrives and increases prodigiously from year to year, filling its corner with a mass of sumptuous and finely-

PLATE 3

OXALIS ENNEAPHYLLA.
(Photo. R.B.G., Edinburgh.)

folded foliage, glaucous-blue in tone, among which all the summer through, each lonely on a stem of 2 inches or so, appear the ravishing large pearly cups of clear melting white with a faint flush of life at their heart. At times this flush warms into a positive blush, and then, as often happens when a lovely complexion deepens, the result is unbecoming, and there are many eyes that find *O. enneaphylla rosea* very much too flatteringly named, being of a dim magenta pallor, not in itself of special loveliness, but unpardonable as claiming cousinship with a beauty so unparalleled as the pure and candid type. If we need colour let us leave *O. enneaphylla* unimproved and go on to *O. adenophylla*. This is an even more beautiful thing perhaps than the last, certainly much rarer and more expensive. It does not spread about, but forms a solid bulb like the corm of a Cyclamen, from which springs a profusion of leaves almost the same as in the last, but here rising in a close tuft instead of a running colony. Early summer calls up the flower-stems out of this nest, and here each stalk carries several blossoms, but on pedicels so long and so much in line that the fact does not leap to view. And when summer has called them up, it needs the sun to waken the blossoms from sleep ; at the touch of his rays they unfold and reveal the same wide goblets as in the last, but here of a most gentle and exquisite soft lilac-pink with a streaked eye of crimson at the base. *O. adenophylla* is a rare glory of Valdivian Andes, and should be planted in light good well-drained soil in full sun and a nice sheltered nook to itself, where it will continue for ever, getting sturdier and wider in the tuft, more and more reckless in the profusion of its fairy flowers.

Oxygraphis, a small race differing from Ranunculus in that the sepals continue to hang on. We have two species to hope for in *O. glacialis* and *O. polypetala*, both high-alpines of the Himalaya, the first with little blunt fleshy leaves and yellow flowers, the second with rounded scalloped leaves, and golden ones, on stems of 2 or 3 inches in a neat tuft. Both may be pictured almost precisely by gilding the lilies of *Ranunculus alpester*, which they repeat in gold. They will have the same needs. (Hooker, *Fl. of British India:* some authorities now quote yellow *O. glacialis* as *Ranunculus glacialis*, the snowy-pure !)

Oxyria.—The Mountain-sorrels have no value.

Oxytrŏpis.—Like all clans among the Pea-flowers, this race contains a great many dingy plants, spoiled for the garden by the family touch of inefficiency and dimness in their colours ; on the other hand, it contains a large number of highly successful efforts in blue and violet, large and brilliant heads of blossom, on short stalks from tufts of extremely handsome foliage like that of a dulled *Asplenium trichomanes*. All these species have very long roots and sometimes rather short lives; they are hard to collect, and should, if possible, be raised from seed, and then put out into the moraine, or light sunny deep soil, well filled with chips; and there left alone to cover the floor with flowers in summer and late summer. In the following list I mean to ignore the fat-headed yellow ones, which, though sometimes clear and prettyish on the alpine shingles, are not of charm sufficient to entitle them to the garden, unless of a goodness quite special.

O. Blankinshipii, or *Besseyi*, comes from Wyoming, where they are having fun nowadays with Oxytropis, calling the whole race *Aragallus*, just as Italian botany now tends to merge the whole family into *Astragalus*. In the meantime let us stick stolidly by Oxytropis, of which *O. Blankinshipii* (despite its infelicitous name) is a beautiful species, being a tuft of silver-silk from which rise stems of some 4 to 8 inches, bearing about a dozen big purple flowers nearly an inch long in a dense spike.

O. campestris, however, shall win its way into the list, if only for the favour it has done these islands in alighting on one or two lone rocks of Clova and Lochnagar. That they could have done without it is " dreadful true," for, " facts being stubborn and not easy drove," this Oxytropid has a fat and dowdyish long head of large dim-yellow blossoms. There are, however, more worthy varieties, with white Pea-flowers or blue or of clearer citron ; and one, *O. c. johannensis*, from America, which is of a beautiful pink and very fine.

O. chionophila loves the snows of Alatau. It is near *O. uralensis*, brightly silvery-silky in the tuffet, with the blue flowers emerging from calyces white with soft long down.

O. chrysocarpa is far neater and more precious, not to be found except beside the snow in the high limestone Alps of Persia, where it forms neat scabs of silver, from which rise stems of 2 inches or so with purple blossoms. And on the desolate rocks of remote Khorassan there is a dust-grey variety of this called *O. c. hypsophila*, whose love of mountains is such that it hugs the highest cliffs at 9000 feet, where it cannot grow more than an inch at the most.

O. cyanea has bigger flowers than any other Levantine species, and is neat and lovely, with closely hoary leaves about 3 inches long, made up of many leaflets ; and eight or fifteen big violet-blue Pea-flowers in a head on a 5-inch stem.

O. dasypoda, from Eastern Caucasus and Daghestan, is quite near to *O. cyanea*, of which it has all the beauty but that of blueness ; for the flowers are of much paler tone, verging on white.

OXYTROPIS.

O. dissitiflora is like a more elegant and charming version of *O. grandiflora*, with looser heads and rather paler blooms. (East Siberia.)

O. frigida is probably a mere variety of *O. uralensis*.

O. grandiflora is a hairy thing from the Jenisei, with blossoms of intense pink.

O. Halleri is a part of De Candolle's *O. uralensis*, and the part that is found in the Alps of Scotland. It is a beautiful dwarf shaggy tuffet of leaves, with long purple-blue blossoms in fluffy calyces, gathered in four or five, loosely, on stems of an inch or so, often barely above the condensed mass of the shining leaflets, and standing erect in their cluster. It is nowhere really common (though of general distribution), and is especially rare in the Swiss alps.

O. Lagopus is quite dwarf and dense, silken and silvered, with flowers of bright violet, gathered in half-dozens on stems that surmount the foliage. (From the mountains of Wyoming.)

O. Lamberti stands not far away from *O. campestris*, but is a splendid beauty, adding to the habit of *O. campestris* larger blossoms of violet-purple.

O. lapponica is said to be unworthy, having a more straggly ascendent habit than these last, with rather thick and long stalks, carrying heads of rather small bluish-lilac flowers, well above the long *bright-green*, grey-haired leaves.

O. lazica stands quite close to *O. uralensis*, as also do two closely allied plants, species or forms, *O. Szovitsii* and the smaller *O. Aucheri*. It may be best known from *O. Halleri* by its seed-pod folded in *on one side only*, but on that side so deeply as almost to be divided in two.

O. montana is perhaps the most generally known and loved in the mountains, where, in the upper, though not the upmost, stone patches and bare spaces at some 7000 feet, or lower, on the limestone Alps, you are sure to find its dark fine bluish leaves (made up of many leaflets) lying out in broad tuffets, while from the crowns spring stems of 3 or 4 inches or so, carrying well-furnished heads of splendid flowers, rich red-purple at first, but soon passing to a soft violet-blue, and declining upon the ground in the end, in the form of aldermanic swollen seed-pods of bright and shining scarlet. It is always a delight to meet with, if not to collect, and may at once be known from *O. lapponica*, among its many other points of difference, by the shorter segments of the calyx.

O. multiceps is a silky hoary mat from the granites of the Central Rockies, with weak little stems carrying each one or two purple sweet-peas.

O. neglecta may well deserve its fate, differing only as it does from *O. lapponica* by having its foliage hairy to the point of being velvety. At the same time, so beautiful is *O. montana* that it is as well (short of a proved personal dislike) for every one to reserve his own judgment upon species so nearly allied to it as *O. neglecta* and *O. lapponica*.

O. persica lives beside the snow-lakes, 10,000 feet up in the Persian mountains, where it forms very dense and densely-silvered silken cushions that emit stems of a couple of inches or so, each carrying some half a dozen violet flowers in a round head.

O. podocarpa is quite dwarf and depressed, but turning almost smooth from its first inclination to hairiness. It carries its purple blossoms in pairs on stems among the leaves, and ranges from California into the farthest North.

O. pyrenaica stands close to *O. neglecta*, and gives us another warning against continuing to despise Cinderella. For this is again a most beautiful thing, with *O. montana* the only one to be often seen in cultivation. It is all covered in silvery-silk velvet, sending up here and there frail tufts of foliage with fine long leaves made up of pointed leaflets ; among the leaves come up the stems, some 3 or 4 inches high, ending in a loose bunch of big lavender-blue flowers, at first nodding and then all bending the same way—this whole group, it will be noticed, having a weaker and more rambling habit than the concise and tuffet-forming *O. montana*. And, in any case, it will be worth while to grow even *O. neglecta* on the strength of its acknowledged resemblance to this beauty.

O. Richardsonii is the species sometimes sent out as *O. splendens*. It comes from the mountain valleys of the Central Rockies, and grows a foot high or more, all silvery-silky, erect and spreading, with a great number of spike-like heads of large and refulgent bright-blue flowers, erect and spreading in their cluster.

O. splendens is *O. Richardsonii*.

O. sungarica is an obscure name. The plant should be a silky mat with large pink flowers.

O. triflora (sometimes reckoned only a form of *O. Gaudinii*) is among the choicest jewels—a neat wee wandering mat, after the habit of *O. neglecta* and *O. lapponica*, but quite minute and condensed and fine, with most dainty stems, of 2 inches or so, springing airily up among the delicate foliage, and each carrying just two or three very large and brilliant violet butterflies, standing apart from each other, and of colour much richer than in its parallels. (Eastern Alps, at the usual alpine elevations, in bare and rocky places on the primary formations.)

O. tyrolensis is a neat small thing, about 4 inches high, with purple flowers.

It will be understood that, as with Astragalus, only the likeliest surfaces of this large race have been skimmed, and that there may well be other species discovered to be valuable when the family is further described, and its tangles professionally unravelled.

P

Pachylophus. See **Oenothera.**

Pachysandra terminalis and *P. procumbens* are two not very interesting or hardy Dowds, of mere foliage-interest, useful to cover the ground in shady sheltered places, but of little charm. The former has the merit of coming from Japan, and the vice of variegation.

Pachystigma Canbyi and *P. Myrsinites* are two minute evergreen shrubs, from Northern America, which are valued for their rarity only. They are small evergreen things, of insignificant flower, and in habit suggesting the dwarfest of Euonymus, to which indeed they are related.

Paederota. Now see under **Veronica.**

Paeonia.—This glorious race is so far from being ill-fitted to the rock-garden that the Paeonies are in reality Queens of the stony mountain places, as anyone will know who has seen *P. officinalis* coyly lingering in the rocks of Steep Holmes Island, or *P. peregrina* unfolding its huge Dog-roses of soft pink under the wooded rock-walls and bluffs of Baldo, or *P. japonica* battling with the national Cypripedium for the copsy slopes above Shoji. Let all those, then, that are too wild and small to cope with the bloated beauties of the border, have their acknowledged place in the rock-garden, in some fitting corner of deep hollow or high cool ledge, where they should be planted once and for all, and left for ever to grow larger and finer in deep and very rich soil. They can all be raised from seed, but the method is long, and limbs can easily be lopped in winter and spring from the dormant masses. And see Appendix.

P. albiflora is the mother of many a noble garden plant, yet with white flowers and conspicuous loveliness of its own.

P. anomala is *P. lobata, q.v.*

P. arietina comes out of the East and has flowers of deep red, with the bright purple leaves hairy on the under-side.

P. banatica is much taller and pink, from Eastern Europe. But

PAEONIA.

it must be remembered that in many cases the name alone will be the enthusiast's reward, for a vast number of "species" resolve themselves into *P. officinalis*, *P. peregrina*, or other sorts, and are not clearly distinct in the garden except to the eye of minute love.

P. Beresowskyi is about 2 feet high—a rose-pink Chinaman.

P. Broteri is a crimson Spaniard, bending and smooth, with leaves brilliantly glittering green, and glaucous underneath. It has a variety *P. obovatifolia* which is *P. lobata* (Boiss., not Desf.).

P. Browni delights California with the fragrance of its red blossoms, and the leaves also are tipped with the same rich tone of scarlet.

P. Cambessedesii is a rare species, endemic, like so many startling plants, to Corsica and the Balearic Islands. It stands about 15 inches high, and has pink flowers and erect shining purplish leaves with thin leaflets. I have sometimes found its seedlings tender.

P. corallina is our own Paeony of the Steep Holmes, but probably a member of a vast aggregate, only to be hair-splittingly differentiated from *P. officinalis*.

P. coriacea approaches *P. Cambessedesii*, but has much thicker, more leathery foliage, glaucous-grey below, much resembling in general effect a downless *P. corallina*. This is *P. Russii of* Arno (not of Bivona). From beside the high snows in fat muddy open places in Granada, on the Sierra de Tejeda, &c.

P. corsica, whatever it may be, should stand 2 feet high, and have blossoms of vivid rose-crimson.

P. dahurica, from Siberia, is pink.

P. decora has smaller segments than *P. peregrina*, and blossoms inclining to more of a magenta tint. (Eastern Europe and Levant.)

P. Emodi is a very rare and most beautiful tall wild Paeony from Kumaon and Hazara, with magnificent great white flowers. The leaves are glaucous-grey beneath, and blooms are borne on long pedicels from the upper axils. There is a variety *P. E. glabra* which is quite near to *P. albiflora*, but differs in having but one carpel, and that smooth.

P. humilis is less in stature, only about 18 inches high, with flowers of vivid magenta-red. (South Europe.)

P. japonica, a gracious Paeony with small cups of pearly-white or pink, followed in autumn by gaping tricorned seed-vessels revealing glossy rows of jewels in scarlet and ebony above the splayed ample leafage of pale-green. It used to be called *P. obovata*, and is lovely in the mountain-copses of Japan, among the Cypripediums.

P. lobata is a handsome species, of 2 feet high and more, from South Europe and Asia, with solid goblets of rose. In cultivation it has,

32

however, yielded colour-forms of greater richness than any other. And the form called "Sunbeam" has blossoms of a perfectly pure crimson-scarlet which in the sunshine seem positively incandescent, luminous as globular lighted lamps of blood with a golden heart. (This belongs, in reality, to *P. peregrina, q.v.*)

P. lutea has but newly come to us out of the East. It has most beautiful glaucous foliage like that of *P. Moutan*, amid which droop its unduly small flowers of rich golden-yellow (like those of a Nuphar tied on to a frail shoot of tree-Paeony). It is, none the less, a rarity deserving of the highest consideration, no less on account of its beauty and the interest of the rank it holds in the race, as on that of the monumental nature of the prices asked for it, which are so big that they would make even Dog's Mercury desirable by all who adopt this convenient standard of value. The superior form of *P. lutea* was at one time called *P. Delavayi*, a name belonging by rights to a closely-allied species, with the same beauty of foliage and something approaching to the same excessive modesty of habit, but with flowers of a rich and muffled dark red, verging upon a clarety obscurity.

P. macrophylla is a very rare Paeony, and has the most magnificent leaves of all, and big blossoms of soft yellow, upstanding, splendid, open, and unashamed. (Levant.)

P. microcarpa is said to be pink and to come from Spain.

P. Mlokosievitschii.—This pleasant little assortment of syllables should be practised daily, but only before dinner (unless teetotal principles of the strictest are adopted), by all who wish to talk familiarly of a sovereign among Paeonies—a rare plant, and rendered almost impregnable by its unpronounceable name. It has an ample habit and lovely dark foliage, amid and above which are borne huge flowers like strayed water-lilies of delicate saffron or citron yellow. It is in the wilds of the Caucasus that this temptation has its lair.

P. mollis comes from Siberia and has blossoms of a sad crimson, tragic at being unable to rival its predecessor in the alphabet.

P. Moutan is perhaps the most august of all, for centuries uncounted the centre and heart of far-Eastern Art, and only within the last very few years discovered as a wild plant in the remote mountains appropriately involved in the vast profound heart of China. It is *the* rock-plant of rock-plants ; and, on every plate of every great period, shows us reproachfully how much better the East has understood the wedding of flowers and rocks from the first beginning of history, long before we had even ceased to think of blue Woad as the latest thing in the fashions, to say nothing of blue Lobelias. Let then the wild Moutan be tucked into some high corner of the big rock-garden,

PAEONIA.

and the riotous grace of his branches be so artistically constrained that, thus imprisoned, he learns to give the idea of untrammelled age, and so rejoices the day with his imperious golden-tasselled blossoms of snow, or of sheeny claret-coloured silk that in the sunlight seem to be inspired with a sombre and divine flame. The cultivated forms are of a beauty and variety that no tongue can adequately tell of (at least those that come from the East ; not the coloured cabbages of the Continent that carry the names of queens)—but are too sophisticated for the rock-garden, to say nothing of the fact that in our climate they ask for more consultation of their whims than is implied by a place there. And see Appendix.

P. obovata = *P. japonica, q.v.*

P. officinalis, the type, mother, and fount of wild Paeonies, is a common sight in all the Southern Alps, a downy plant with rosy flowers, and innumerable developments, hailed as species.

P. Pallasii comes from Siberia and is brightly pink.

P. paradoxa is a Southerner with flowers of crimsonish colouring, being quite close to the next, but dwarfer, with smaller more finely-divided leaves, more bluish in tone ; and with blossoms of purplish note and medium size.

P. peregrina is very elegant and splendid and luxuriant, with foliage of bluish-green, still more glaucous or downy beneath, with single flowers of vivid pink. It stands near *P. officinalis*, which with all its many kindred names may be so many local forms or sub-species of this, which is the ultimate mother of the large crimson garden-Paeonies, as *P. albiflora* of the Chinese varieties, and *P. Moutan* of the Trees. It is the scarlet origin of the yet brighter "Sunbeam."

P. pubens is downy and bright pink. (From South Europe.)

P. romanica is no more than *P. decora, q.v.*

P. Russii is a form of *P. corallina* with the leaves puberulous underneath. It hails from Corsica, &c.

P. tenuifolia has leafage cut into a fine fog of green, and smallish cupped flowers of intense crimson. There are various garden forms ; the most notable are a single white and a single rose-pink, both very beautiful indeed, especially with the plant's neat little dwarf habit of not exceeding a foot or 18 inches at the most.

P. triternata has the same stature, or less, with fat-looking dark foliage, however, and blossoms that vary from white to pink and deeper tones.

P. Veitchii is a new rarity with quite fine delicate leafage of pale glaucous-green, forming a wide drooping mass, most graceful in effect, in which proceed stems that carry a goodly number of nodding flowers.

But these unfortunately are of so sad and acid a deep magenta as to make one wish the plant would confine its efforts to the production of leaves.

P. Wittmanniana is a big upstanding Paeony from Caucasus and the cold shady glens of Northern Persia. It is a robustious large spreading thing, with large and little-divided upstanding glossy leafage, and big cup-shaped ample blooms to match, in a delicate tone of pale and gentle yellow, of white and creamy-citron shades. Like all the rest it is of the easiest culture, but just as *P. Emodi* sometimes so snatches time by the forelock as itself to be snatched by a late frost, so does *P. Wittmanniana*, if harried and divided, show a certain amount of resentment, and after years of ever-widening prosperity may suddenly mimp entirely away in a winter, and be little more seen except in leaves of increasing feebleness. It is indeed a fine species, not very refined, but broad and handsome in its effect ; and the parent (with *P. sinensis*) of a most beautiful race of garden Paeonies with single solid flowers of looser design in every possible lovely shade of flesh and cream and sunlit apricot and half-remembered salmon under a bed of melted butter. But this is not the place to tell of such, nor the rock-garden fit territory to display the artificial lovelinesses of *P. Avant-garde* and its kin.

Papāver.—This vast family swarms with annuals and garden plants of no account for us. At the same time many of the larger wild perennial species have value, not only on account of their own beauty, but also as blooming in late summer ; while there are some monocarpics of high worth, no less in the leaf than in the flower ; and one alpine group of the front rank, though not always easy to decipher— any more, indeed, than are many of the others, their most private and vital characteristics turning out sooner or later to be founded on sand. All Poppies, as is well known, will come profusely from seed, and none but the alpine group ask for any special treatment. And now, what *is* the alpine Poppy ? There are in it two species of prime merit, and a meek third.

P. alpinum, L., has the little leaves of the tuft all slit and slit and slit again into thin strips, until the effect is *very* fine and fernlike, or *fennel-like*, and the leaves are almost *hairless* and of a grey tone. It divides into two main types : *P. Burseri* (Crantz), Fedde, with *white* flowers, yellow at the base, ample and beautiful ; this belongs to two ranges, the one in Savoy and the Southern Valais, the other in the limestone Alps of North-Eastern Austria. The second type of the plant is *P. Kerneri* (Hayek), Fedde, being identical in all respects with the last, but that the flowers are bright *yellow* and rather larger. This

PAPAVER.

belongs to the Eastern chains, in the high limestones of the Karawanken and Julian Alps, &c., where in the austere shingles its orbs of *gold* console one for the lost moonlit *citrons* of *P. rhaeticum* left behind in the Dolomites.

P. pyrenaicum is the second branch of the alpine race, inhabiting the same stony places, but usually rather higher up and not descending so low. It is not always quite so woody in its masses, but very dense in their tufts. And it is easily known by its foliage, which *is soft to the touch*, and *all covered with upstanding hair ;* while the grey leaves themselves are *only lobed and cut about once*, with perhaps a tooth here and there on the lobes, so that they have a wholly different and quite simple effect of great richness, not at all fernlike, but suggesting a small neat grey Iceland Poppy. The amplitude of noble blossom is the same, however, but as the first type of *P. alpinum* is white, so that of *P. pyrenaicum* (*P. rhaeticum*) is yellow (the two species thus exactly reversing each other's order : the main form of *P. alpinum* having *white* flowers, with a secondary yellow development, while *yellow* is the main type of *P. pyrenaicum*, which has a corresponding divagation into white. *The leaves are the diagnostic*) ; the white shingles of the Dolomites are filled with the lovely blue-grey masses and big lemon-pale orbs of *P. rhaeticum*, the first type-species of *P. pyrenaicum*—a lovely citron-coloured unvarying development (though once in ten thousand specimens you may see one of a more orange tone). Its range is from the Pyrenees to the Terglou, &c.; rare in Central Switzerland, but not uncommon in the Engadine. There is a specially hairy-stemmed orange-flowered form called *P. p. aurantiacum* on Mount Ventoux ; while *P. Sendtneri* is the second main type of the species, differing in nothing from *P. rhaeticum* but that the hairs are more rusty and the flowers *pure white*. This is *P. Burseri* (Rchb.), and occurs on the Northern limestones here and there, from Pilatus to the Dachstein. In cultivation all these gleaming jewels of the highest screes and shingles ask especially for the moraine, in which they are much safer and happier and long-lived than in the damper conditions of full soil ; as well as looking so much more characteristic. At the same time they will thrive heartily and sow themselves freely in almost any reasonable place, and in the course of doing so have developed countless varieties of colour, at least in the case of *P. alpinum* (for *P. pyrenaicum*—the finer thing—is much more seldom seen in cultivation). There is no need to specify these forms, which will all be found in catalogues; but the most particularly beautiful probably owes its origin in reality to the next species, as it has blossoms of pure soft pink with a heart of pale gold. For *P. suaveolens*,

36

an alpine Poppyling confined entirely to the Pyrenees, differs for the worse from all these last in having smaller flowers (fragrant though they be), and very variable in colour from *orange to pink*, with narrower petals forming a Maltese cross when expanded, instead of a rounded cup. The hairy leaves (there is a hairier variety *Endressi*) are more divided than in *P. pyrenaicum*, but not nearly so much so, nor so finely, as in *P. alpinum*, and they *are green, not glaucous*—thus leading us on to the next allied species, the big brother of all these, the Iceland Poppy. But *P. nudicaule*, in its typical forms, is really too common and large and rampageous and pervasive ; so that its admission to the rock-garden (unless its extent be specially huge) is almost as bad a confession of weakness as the admission of *Meconopsis cambrica*. At the same time it is lovely in itself, and has dozens and scores of variations, alike in habit, size, and colour—*P. radicatum*, Rottboll, being an important sub-species of this, occupying Arctic America to the exclusion of all rivals. And Alpine Asia abounds in more.

A strong generic likeness marks the perennial Poppies of the Pilosum group, all being valuable for decorating out-of-the way corners, though in their habits a little lush and floppy for the choicer places. *P. spicatum* is a most curious species, with its brick-red flowers sitting alternately up the stem, close upon it in the axil of a bract, with the effect of a waved spike ; the whole plant is shaggy in felted white down. It differs from *P. pilosum*, not only in this and in its habits of flower, but in its stem-leaves that do not embrace their stem (except in the variety *P. s. luschanicum* (*P. Heldreichii*, Stapf.), where they do begin to think about doing so). The plant comes from the Mediterranean region, and interbreeds with *P. pilosum*, the results being *P. Balansaeanum* and *P. Boissierianum*, this last being clad in dense tawny fur. *P. pilosum* (*P. olympicum*, Sibth. and Sm.) is terribly variable ; it is in type tall and lax and hairy and bright-green, with large brickred or fierce orange flowers borne singly *on long foot-stalks* from a freely branching stem of 2 feet or so, in a loose shower, and making a very handsome effect. The long oval leaves are soft and velvety, and irregularly, deeply scalloped all round their edges, while on the stem they are smaller and almost embrace it. This is a species of the Mediterranean Basin in its Eastern half, and offers many shades passing into its other relations. The next indeed, *P. apokrinomenon*, has but a shadowy existence, its very name implying that it hardly has a right to one, being a mere transition from the last to the next species (and this, too, often merged into *P. pilosum*). This is *P. Heldreichii*, which replaces *P. pilosum* in northern Asia Minor, and differs from it in smaller habit, smaller flowers, narrower capsule, and less irregular scalloping to the leaves. It has a number of varieties, however, of which two are *P. h. sparsipilosum* and *P. h. pumilum*—this last being a dwarf alpine form from Anemas in Lycaonia, which might have special charm. Both *P. pilosum* and *P. Heldreichii* complicate matters still further by the way they hybridise, alike in nature and in the garden. *P.* × *Cayeuxii* is a fine-flowered child of *P. pilosum* and *P. bracteatum ; P.* × *Pichleri* of *P. pilosum* and *P. Heldreichii* ; *P.* × *pinardianum* and *P.* × *Bourgeauanum* of *P. strictum* and *P. pilosum ; P.* × *sieheanum* of *P. strictum* and another form of *P. pilosum.* But few of these are likely to attain eminence in the garden.

    P. strictum differs from all the last in having *less ample leaves* that make *no effort to embrace the stem ;* its inflorescence aims at copying *P. spicatum,* but carries the flowers on evident foot-stalks, so that the effect is of a much looser and more graceful spire, which is almost wholly smooth, though the rest of the growth is invested in the usual hairiness, clothing its stiffly upstanding stems of some 2 feet and more. *P. pseudostrictum* differs from this chiefly in the broader and more pointed leaves, and their rougher and more irregular scalloping. *P. lateritium* may be known by *very long and narrow leaves,* deeply lobed all along into irregular pointed featherings ; the crown sends up many stems of 2 feet or so, scantily branching about the middle, and carrying one or two brick-red flowers, each on a long stalk of its own. This habit of wearing its flowers *singly* (instead of forming a long raceme of them more or less close) distinguishes it from all the foregoing, no less than does the much narrower foliage ; but its three successors come very close under its shadow, and may be mere local developments. *P. ramosissimum* is merely of specially branching habit, much more diffuse, and with much shorter flower-stems ; *P. oreophilum* is smaller than *P. lateritium,* and forms dense perennial mats at the base of the stems ; *P. monanthum* has the distinction of not making a proper stem at all, but of sending up its large flowers each lonely on a naked stalk of a foot or 18 inches ; these are followed by capsules much rounder than in the rest (that have them of a squeezed and narrow outline). *P. rupifragum* also has the drawn-out narrowness of leaf, but here the feathered lobes are deeper and more ample than in the last, with more of a space between them, and set with rare hairs. The stems are 18 inches high, with a few leaves near the base, but bare all the way up, and but seldom breaking into two equal branches, one solitary brick-pale flower being the more usual rule. This has yielded a useful sterile garden hybrid with *P. orientale* in *P.* × *Ruporient,* with profusion of handsome graceful scarlet blossoms through late summer. *P. atlanticum* is the last of this tangled group, and may

at once be known, if by nothing else, by the *long narrow pointed leaves,*
which are not lobed or feathered at all, but merely cut into irregular
forward-pointing teeth, and vested thickly in silken hairs. The
stem-habits are much as in the last, but the buds are covered in hair,
instead of being perfectly bald and glaucous. (From Atlas, not his
Ocean.)

P. bracteatum is even finer than *P. orientale*, with richer colour and
usually with a large black blot at the base of the satiny-crimson petal.
These are both, however, for the wilder garden ; and the art-nouveau
varieties of *P. orientale*, with sad shrimp-sauce- or vulcanite- or motor-
tyre- or mud-coloured flowers (that look like paper horrors sold at a
bazaar, to hold pins or adorn a lodging-house mantelpiece), are not for
any garden at all that rightly values itself. Other dimmer species in
this important group are *P. lasiothrix* and *P. paucifoliatum*.

In the group of the monocarpic or biennial Poppies there are some
quite valuable wearers of notably lovely leafage, whose predilection for
death can be counteracted easily by always raising the seed they leave
behind them, so as incessantly to have a stock coming on. They have,
for the most part, specially handsome rosettes of long narrow leaves,
deeply feathered and fringed ; from which aspires a spouting shower
or pyramid of blossom 18 inches high or so, pretty much after the effect
of the statelier Meconopsids. Of such are *P. tauricolum*, Boiss. (the
form seems ungrammatical, but authority has iron rules), with a
fountain of ample bricky-scarlet or stale blood-coloured flowers ;
P. persicum, stricter in the pyramid, with a green spot at the base of
the similarly coloured petals (there is a hybrid between these two,
P.×Flahaultii) ; *P. caucasicum*, glaucous-green and set with flavid
bristlishnesses, sending up a fountain of pale vermilion Poppies, rapidly
fleeting ; *P. hyoscyamifolium*, with a very dense stiff fox-brush of
blossom ; *P. floribundum*, the finest of all, with beautiful fine-cut
glaucous rosette-leaves, and a noble two-foot pyramid of gorgeous
scarlet flowers, more tenacious of life than most ; *P. fugax, P. achro-
chaetum*, and *P. Urbanianum* all have the same habit and handsome
rosettes and pyramids, but the petals more quickly drop and are in
paler tones. Sadly fugacious, too, are the light-red petals of *P. armeni-
acum*, a rather dwarfer grower ; while *P. libanoticum* has scarcely any
stem at all, but has to send up the foot-stalks of its pale-purple flowers
naked by themselves from the rosette ; and *P. polychaetum* is even
more definitely stemless still. The most beautiful we have, however
(in foliage at least), is *P. triniaefolium*, which comes, like all these
others, from the hills of Asia Minor. Here the silver-glaucous leaves are
cut and cut again into the finest silver fringe-work, so that the effect of

the splayed-out rosette has an unearthly and almost artificial loveliness which does not suffer when the filigree has caught a number of rain-drops in its mesh, and the whole netting of leaf and water-globules becomes a glistering set of diamond-work almost Etruscan in its fineness. The resulting pyramid of blossom, however, seems hardly a worthy conclusion to so much beauty, for the flowers are small, pale-purple, and so ashamed of their bathos that they make the utmost haste to shed their petals. All these Poppies like any open light soil, but it is on the grey surface of the moraine that the silver of *P. triniaefolium* looks its clearest. The only other perennial to be spoken of (for all the remaining scores of Poppies are annuals) is *P. anomalum*, which comes quite close to some Chinese forms of *P. nudicaule*, but earns definite specific rank by its astonishing possession of a seed-capsule that is very nearly round and wholly bald, instead of being long (as in all Iceland Poppies) and densely clad in coarse black fur.

Paracaryum, a beautiful Borragineous family standing near *Cynoglossum* and *Omphalodes*, taller and stronger than the latter, but not over-weening like the former. They bloom in June and July, may easily be raised from seed, and in due course divided.

P. anchusoeides attains 2 feet or so, and has big Forget-me-not flowers of the most glorious azure-blue.

P. angustifolium (*P. azureum*, Boiss. and Held.) is smaller in habit, making tufts of huddled very narrow radical leaves, clothed in long white silky hairs, and on long stems. The scantily-branching stems are about 6 inches high, loosely set with most lovely wide sky-coloured blossoms. From alpine and sub-alpine regions of Cappadocia, Armenia, Lycaonia, Cilician Taurus, &c., and worthy of the choicest place in the foreground, in light well-drained soil and full sun.

P. erysimifolium has narrow foliage, but has not yet arrived at manifesting further characters ; though it hardly seems likely to be worth great trouble, as it is biennial. The same may be said also of *P. glochidiatum*, which is a yard high, large and lax, and set with minute hooked hairs ; and perhaps of *P. himalaiense*, of which it seems suggested that the flowers are too small.

P. incanum is about 18 inches high, very hoary, with flowers of blue.

P. lamprocarpum is yet another name in a group of biennials hardly to be bothered about, among which are *PP. leptophyllum, ponticum, cappadocicum, stenolophum, modestum, ancyritense, calycinum, longifolium, asperum, corymbiflorum*, &c.

P. microcarpum is a diffuse beautiful plant, dwarf and hairy, from sub-alpine heights of Kashmir, with large brilliant flowers.

P. myosotoeides lives in the cliffs of Crete, and on Lebanon above the Cedars; it makes a matted mass of tufts, with the leaves all ashy in long pressed-down white hairs; the stems are 4 inches or half a foot high, unfolding lovely stars of azure and violet-blue.

P. Reuteri is another great beauty and greatly to be desired. Its home is on the rocks of Berytagh, from 6000 to 10,000 feet, where it makes little masses of soft hoary-grey-velvet oblong foliage, and sends up a lavish number of 6-inch flower-stems, which are either simple or else fork into two branches, carrying large blooms of rich blue-violet.

P. tibeticum is more diffuse than *P. himalaiense*, and has bright blue blossoms a trifle smaller than those of *P. microcarpum*.

Paradisea Liliastrum is the great Saint Bruno's Lily of the alpine meadows that used to be *Anthericum Liliastrum* until it was felt that such beauty ought to stand apart. St. Bruno's Lily must be seen in the mountains to be believed; but, even there, lovely as it is, standing rare and pure (like an understudy for *Lilium candidum*), here and there in the hay-fields, or in open slopes at the edge of the mountain-woods, it has to be seen at its best before its full value is realised: as when in July it floats in a solid shroud of white over the northern slopes of the Mont Cenis, to lay the splendours of spring to rest in fitting purity and state. In the garden it is grown too much in isolated specimens, whereas in any rich loam it should be planted by stretches of dozens and hundreds where there is room, and given its old neighbours *Campanula rhomboidalis* and *Lilium Martagon*, and the field Geraniums, and Astrantia, and *Lilium croceum*. Then the slugs will not be able to eat *all* the spikes, and among the characteristic herbage you will see its tall stems appear in July, hanging out their three or four pure candid trumpets of white, against which (as against the whole plant indeed) the only thing that can be said is that they have an almost too blameless and pietistic look, like something on a text. However, set among the wild herbage the Paradisea looks more appropriate and less preachy, like a clean deed in a rough wild world. It can be easily raised from seed, and clumps divided; there is a superior form in gardens called *P. L. major*, which successfully accomplishes its difficult task of improving on the typical St. Bruno's Lily. And meanwhile the odious Saint Bernard has, very properly, to put up with quite an inferior article in *Anthericum Liliago*, though even such a thing as that, so pretty and innocent, is far too good for the preacher of Crusades.

Parnassia.—The common Grass of Parnassus is the type of the

41

whole race, white-flowered or yellow ; but it is by no means the easiest to grow or keep, succeeding best, as a rule, among coarsish herbage in the bog. The rest are rarer, and many of them really lovely, all asking for abundant water flowing underground.

P. alpestris or *alpina* is a form or sub-species of *P. palustris* which may be found in the Alps, and stands pre-eminent above the type, not only in its taller stature and larger more copious blossom, but also in its much greater readiness to show them in the garden, and form widening healthy tufts from year to year. Like all the rest it can be raised from seed, though the method is chancy, and collected tufts or divided clumps are the best methods of multiplying your stock ; but, unlike the rest, it tends to bloom a little earlier in the season, towards the end of June or middle of July—its blooming-time being prolonged till the rest are well in flower.

P. fimbriata is one of the best—a stalwart hearty grower from the damp alpine places of the Rockies, of ready good-temper in cultivation, and very fine large white flowers, most beautifully fringed at the base of the petals. And other American species of merit are : *P. asarifolia*, *P. caroliniana*, *P. grandiflora*. *P. rivularis* is *P. fimbriata ;* and *P. Kotzebui* is a tiny 3-inch Arctic plant, to match the tiny *pusilla* variety of *P. ovata*, on the high Alps of Sikkim and Kashmir.

P. mysorensis and *P. parviflora*, the one Indian and the other American, are of but little worth, the flowers in either case being small.

P. nubicola, however, is a notable species from the heights of Sikkim and Kashmir, growing from 4 inches to 18, with flowers an inch across, hardly clawed at all, with ovate-oblong leaves, heart-lobed at the base. It is like a larger stouter version of the same-flowered *P. ovata*, which is only some 3 to 8 inches high, and altogether smaller.

P. Wightiana, which ranges from the Nilghirries into Yunnan, is a foot or more in height, with flowers of pale yellow.

Parochaetus communis runs about all over the place like a rather lush green clover, but from the tangled long-armed mass there emerges all through the late summer an indefatigable flight of big Pea-flowers, each borne lonely on its separate stem of 2 or 3 inches, and of a most brilliant azure-blue, tinged with something of that same faint touch of yellow which gives its ferocity of tone to *Gentiana verna*, but clearer and lighter and softer, and fading into a dozen subtleties of emerald, opal, sapphire, and mild sad pink. Though this wonder of the garden comes from the East Indies and the mountains of Central Africa (so it is said), it may none the less be looked upon as perfectly hardy in England in sheltered places, kindly climates, and well-drained soil. It likes to grow in the sun, and shows especial

PLATE 4.

PAPAVER TRINIAEFOLIUM.
(Photo. R. A. Malby.)

PLATE 5.

PARONYCHIA ARGENTEA.

(Photo. R.B.G., Kew.)

happiness in *warm and swampy* ground, though its growth is by far too vigorous for choice company, and it must be put where it can be unquestioned king of many square feet and almost yards, where it forms a tangled jungle 3 inches high or so, perpetually twinkling with multitudes of its light azure butterflies. And in any case, should you suspect the caprices of your climate, you have no more to do than to take off as many sprigs of *Parochaetus* as you please in autumn and pot them up indoors. If not already rooted they will lose no time in becoming so.

Paronychia, a curious little race of creeping matted cousins of the Pinks, that run about in the poorest dry and hot soil, with shoots of small smooth leaves and bunches of minute flowers without any petals at all. However, this lack is compensated by the bracts that enclose them, which are fine and large, and bright silver-white, giving not only the full effect of petals, but of exceedingly full and snowy petals into the bargain. *P. polygonifolia* may be seen in the Alps; but by far the most beautiful are silver-headed *P. Kapela* from Istria, and *P. capitata* from Spain, with very striking crowded heads of broad white bracts looking most lovely on the minute little humble plant. There is also a sub-species of this, *P. serpyllifolia*, of the same brilliance, but more perfectly prostrate, and with more rounded tiny leafage, though the beauty of the pure glistening bracts remains the same. This may be found in hot places in the South, as, for instance, on Monte Toraggio in the Ligurian Alps; it flowers like the rest in June, should be raised from seed, and then propagated by cuttings, and treated only to the hottest, driest foregrounds of the garden in worthless soil and near the level of the eye, a position which the charm of this whole group will well repay, even apart from their secondary use of making a carpet for rare little bulbs, Crocus and Daffodil, to peer up through, in a moment when the Paronychias have not yet begun to think of flowering.

Parrya.—These are very near relations of Cheiranthus and Erysimum, both attractive and useful in their way, the best known of which is *P. Menziesii* from the Rockies, which makes tufted rosettes of narrow grey leaves on rather woody shoots of 2 or 3 inches or more, and then in spring and early summer sends up spikes of flowers like those of a lax purple Aubrietia. Cuttings should be taken of this, and seed sown. It is of easy culture in any light open soil and in full sun. More remote from our hands are the high Himalayan Parryas, dangerously densely woolly things, of which one at least, *P. macrocarpa*, has stiff blossom-spikes of 6 inches or a foot, while others are *P. exscapa*, *P. lanuginosa*, and *P. platycarpa*. But perhaps the most to be longed for is *P. pinnatifida* from Afghanistan, which offers precisely the look and habit of *Morisia monanthos*, but that here the single flowers are *red* upon the fine ground-hugging rosette.

Pascalea glauca is a free-flowering Chilian Composite for a light and sunny place, with broad slightly toothed bluish foliage and tall two-foot branching stems of golden blossom in later summer.

Passerina dioica and *P. nivalis* are a brace of microscopic and dowdy Daphnes from South Europe. Their heads of flower are quite negligible, and their only value is as minute evergreens that ramp quite flat and tight across the face of a sunny rock, and clothe it with small neat tufts of little Daphnoid foliage, suggesting fraudulent imitations of *D. petraea*.

Patrinia.—These may briefly be described as yellow Valerians, by which their worth and the value of the fuss that has attended at least one of them into cultivation may be gauged. This one is *P. rupestris*, a pretty enough thing for a corner of a rock, with stems of 6 inches or a foot carrying relaxed Valerian heads of golden-yellow flowers in late summer—their season of bloom enhancing their value, which is quite sufficient to win it admission for the plant, though by no means enough to justify the price at which it rates that admission, seeing that it may rapidly be multiplied by division at your pleasure. Others of dwarfish habit are *P. sibirica* and *P. villosa ;* and taller species, almost always with yellowish or bright-yellow flowers, are *P. intermedia, P. palmata, P. scabiosaefolia,* and *P. gibbosa,* all being too precisely Valerian-like in tall stem and loose habit to be fitted in the garden for any place more choice than the wilder parts where Paradisea is growing among the Astrantias and *Campanula rhomboidalis*. This they will greatly help with their golden show in the duller days of August, when they would admirably suit with the bending sapphire swathes of *Gentiana asclepiadea*.

Pedicularis.—Although the Louse-worts make a special show of beauty on the alpine pastures, with their brilliant coloured parrot's-beak flowers, and their ferny fine tufts of foliage, yet there is a look about them of softness and unwholesomeness that prepares one for the news that they are almost all parasites, and impossible to grow unless by seed sown in tussocks taken from the mountains, on the chance of their pet host being present. Also their ephemeral air of effectiveness makes them seem rather like vicious fungoid emanations that will soon collapse into rottenness and disappear in half an hour ; so that one is doubly consoled for their impossibility. There is, however, one honourable exception at least. For *P. Barrelieri* has the courage to grow almost wholly on its own root (more solid than that of most others), and accordingly, if reverently transplanted, will thrive heartily on a moist well-drained sunny slope of the garden, sending up tufts of lush asplenioid green foliage, and 9-inch spikes of handsome clear yellow blossoms. It is not a common species, but may abundantly be seen on the Mont Cenis; it is possible also that *P. tuberosa* may have the same powers, as it is closely related, and has a similar self-sufficient-looking root. But this is not so desirable, as the spike is shorter and stumpier.

Peganum Harmala has interest if no great show. It is a little low wide bush of very finely-divided fine foliage, from the hot places of the South, with stars of greenish white from May to July. It should have a specially sunny corner on the rock-work, and be multiplied at need by division. It was a sudorific in old days; but the effect was probably due to the rocks it inhabited rather than to any beauty of the plant itself; at least, nowadays, so far from causing the cultivator to perspire, it leaves him wholly cold.

Pelargonium Endlicherianum is hostile to tapeworms. But it is not so hostile to our climate, and is, in fact, the sole member of its vast and noble race that is faithfully hardy anywhere in Great Britain, if planted securely in a sunny sheltered nook of the rock-garden, in light and perfectly-drained calcareous soil. At least in nature it is lime that it likes; filling the crevices of the high limestone Alps in the Cilician Taurus, making ample bushes of a foot high or more, thick with stalked Geranium leaves, soft and scalloped and aromatic with the best, and emitting in the later summer large clear rosy-carmine flowers in loose clusters of four or five.

Peltandra virginica, an Aroid of North America, growing about 2 feet high or more, with handsome foliage, and green spathes of blossom about 8 inches long in May and June.

Peltaria alliacea in happier days used to be *Sisymbrium Alliaria*, and under that title will be recognised as a tall white-flowered Cruciferous weed from every hedgerow, with ample rounded toothed leaves embracing the stem, and a vile stink of garlic proceeding from every part of the plant with equal virulence.

Pentachondra pumila is a pleasant small Ericaceous shrub of a few inches from the mountains of the North Island of New Zealand, up to 5000 feet, with flowers sitting lonely at the tips of the shoots and followed by red berries.

Penthorum sedoeides, a worthless Crassulaceous weed from North America, producing wide heads of greenish-yellow bloom on the top of erect smooth stems of some 18 inches or so, set with narrow toothed foliage. For culture in dampish places.

Pentstēmon.—Catalogues contain long strings of names of these, often wrong, and almost always without adequate descriptions; so that there is no knowing where one is, a dangerous deficiency in all plant-races, but especially in such a case as this, where, among many species of the greatest charm, there are also an enormous number of dim or gawky weeds, to say nothing of those that hail from countries and States and conditions too tropical to offer hope that their inhabitants will here stay happy. And, among the lovely species, too, the names are mixed and cloudy. So that now we must fare across the Atlantic for profounder study of this family, which seems to have one Old-World outlier, and one only, in the Russian *P. frutescens.* When suited with their various treatments (and all Pentstemons in England clamour for light and very perfectly-drained soil, as well as for the most lavish allowance of sun), the different species can all be raised from seed and propagated from late summer cuttings. Late summer, too, and autumn, see the climacteric of their blossom, which is brilliant in proportion as the life of the individual plant is inclined to be brief, Pentstemons usually having but a lush constitution, preferring a crowded hour of glory rather than a longer existence of mere usefulness.

P. acuminatus, from sandy rocky places in Missouri, Texas, &c., stands about a foot high, with small narrow-ovate glaucous leaves, fat and thick and firm, with a graceful spire of long narrow funnels of lilac-lavender, or blue, or purple, or all three, that open suddenly into a wide mouth.

P. albidus is a dullness of no merit.

P. alpinus has at times been reduced to a variety of *P. glaber,* and has also had specific rank of its own as *P. riparius, P. oreophilus, P. Bakeri.* It is one of the most beautiful in the whole race, but impermanent, as is often the case with beautiful things (yet this one not only leaves a memory behind, but also seed). *P. alpinus* may be 5 inches high, or five times as much, but the stems are weakly and unable to bear their burden of big sprayed flowers in the most heavenly shade of violent clear-blue with a white throat. Its ample leaves are also glaucous-blue, but deficient at the base, oblong-spoon-shaped and narrower as they mount the stem; the stock is woody, and the plant belongs to the high mountain gravels of the Central Rockies. In the garden, to be truly permanent, it wants the same treatment—in a soil nutritious, indeed, but quite full of stones and lightness and drainage.

P. ambiguus is a diffuse species of the central prairies, making a

46

branching mass of some 8 to 20 inches, beset with thread-like foliage, and breaking into loose showers of narrow curved flowers about half an inch in length, and varying from white to rosy flesh-colour.

P. angustifolius is also *P. coeruleus*, and another queen in the race— a leafy thing of 8 inches or so, forming an almost bushy mass of lovely blue-grey shoots from which later summer elicits spikes of ample blossom such as only the high gods, pillowed on the Empyrean, could have imagined—beginning gently in dreaming tones of lavender and rose, from which the sunlight of maturity stiffens the dawn-softness into clear coerulean tones that herald day, yet never arrive at its hard and shadowless certainties. Not even in Omphalodes is there any matching the tender yet assured magnificence of the pale azures deployed in time by *P. angustifolius*, which should have the same site and soil as *P. alpinus*, if long life is desired for its loveliness.

P. antirrhinoeides need have little note. It is yellow, foot-high, and tender.

P. arenicola is some 8 inches or a foot tall, with unbranching stems, hairless, and glaucous-blue with oblong leaves. The flowers in their time are no less blue also—tubes of half an inch or so, in short spike-like spires, leafy below. (From sandy deserts in the region of the Central Rockies.)

P. aridus is a beautiful glandular-downy one-flowered sub-species of *P. laricifolius*, *q.v.*, with blue blossoms. (From Montana.)

P. arizonicus is tall and reddish-purple, with smallish flowers, being no more than the variety *stenosepalus* of *P. glaucus*, *q.v.*

P. azureus is a doubtful name. Plants bought under it ought at least to be of good colour.

P. baccharifolius should be a scarlet-flowered species from Texas, about a foot in stature.

P. Bakeri. See *P. alpinus*.

P. barbatus is *Chelone barbata*, a wand-like delicate stem of a yard high or so, set delicately with long thin scarlet tubes. There are many varieties in gardens of this : and all are most daintily effective in drifts and billowing masses of fine colour in late summer.

P. Brandegeei is a variety or sub-species of beautiful *P. cyananthus*, with thick leathery, fringed leaves, and flowers of pure pale azure suddenly gaping wide, and borne in loose clusters in an almost dense spire.

P. brevifolius (not *P. breviflorus*) sends out subterraneous shoots, and is woody and branching, with slender weakly-rising stems spreading about the ground and in length some 4 to 12 inches, set with almost round smooth-edged leaves at the base of the stems and on the barren

47

shoots, thin in texture, and with very slender foot-stalks as long as themselves. The flowers are blue, nearly an inch in length.

P. Bridgesii is also woody at the base, and the sprays are about a foot or more in height, set with narrowly paddle-shaped small foliage, and ending in a twiggy one-sided spike of narrow scarlet trumpets in clusters on short foot-stalks, with their lips about a third of the length of their tube. (Nevada, California, and South-West Colorado.)

P. caespitosus makes depressed wide mats all finely downy till they are ashy-grey in effect. The leaves are narrow, about half an inch long with their stalk, and the stems are not more than 2 or 3 inches high, with upturned tubular-funnel-shaped flowers arranged in a one-sided spray on their foot-stalks.

P. canescens has no worth for us ; nor has its form *P. pallidus*.

P. centranthifolius is a tall and leafy scarlet-flowered Californian.

P. Cobaea has no more. It is a leafy tall coarse plant of no marked hardiness, with enormous bloated bells of dim and washed-out lilac.

P. coeruleus. See under *P. angustifolius*.

P. collinus is a matted mass of smooth elliptic-oblong little leaves on foot-stalks as long as themselves, from which arise a great number of downy stems from 4 to 16 inches in height, set with slender-tubed flowers of deep blue, about half an inch long, gathered in knots of half a dozen or so in a broken spire. (Gravel hills of Montana and Wyoming, &c.)

P. commarrhenus, from West Colorado, Utah, &c., is 8 inches high (but can attain to more than a foot), and is glaucous-smooth or else minutely hoar-frosted above. The blossoms are of rich purple-blue, large and handsome, about an inch long, carried in lax and feathery spikes, each with long and narrow tube.

P. confertus marks a descent. It is a neat massed and matted plant, with many wiry stems of about a foot high, crowded with disappointing and common-looking little sulphur-pale flowers in a series of packed heads. The species is very variable, and there is a variety, *P. c. purpureo-coeruleus*, which has a rather more compact habit, and flowers of purplish-blue ; but *P. confertus*, altogether, does not rank as high as its tidy preliminary habit would lead us to hope.

P. cordifolius is a half climber, coarse, with scarlet blossoms.

P. corymbosus is half shrubby, and its stems are about a foot high or a little more. The leaves are hairless and oblong, and pointed at both ends, while the more downy flower-shoots are ended by plumes of br.ght scarlet blooms each about an inch long. (From dry rocky ledges all along the coast ranges to Shasta, at high elevations.)

P. Crandallii has a woody base and notably branchy stems of not

PENTSTEMON.

more than 8 inches, beset with notably narrow foliage, and carrying wide-open flowers—the whole growth forming a neat mass or cushion.

P. crassifolius = *P. fruticosus, q.v.*

P. cyananthus stands quite close to lovely *P. glaber*, but is taller and more slender, with the leaves all broad, and dense spires of bright blue blossoms, suddenly swelling as they emerge from the calyx.

P. Davidsoni, a vexed name for a very dwarf and prostrate small Pentstemon with fleshy little oval toothed leaves of bright green, clothing the stems of a fat and minute branching shrublet of an inch or two in height, that end in baggy bugles of a ferocious aniline red-mauve most terrible and breath-taking to look upon in the sun. It thrives perennially in light open places, in perfectly-drained warm soil or granitic moraine, and is essentially a rock-plant for a sunny deep crevice : and can be multiplied from cuttings like a Pelargonium. It has appeared every season under a new name, *P. Menziesii, Douglasii*, &c. The frail human mind is not willing so to continue burdening itself, on behalf of a gem so little pleasing to the subtler senses, though in itself of a brazen brilliancy quite inimitable.

P. deustus is little worth indeed.

P. diffusus is even less worth, being a very coarse and leafy weed about 18 inches high or less, lush and rampageous-looking, with dismal and undistinguished purple bells half lost among the rankly-toothed foliage.

P digitalis is a variety of *P. laevigatus*, and of no use or value.

P. Douglasii, a name to discard and ignore.

P. Eatoni is tall and leafy, about 2 feet high, with the leaves clasping the stems, and a strict spike of fiery crimson flowers widening at the mouth.

P. erianthera has stems of nearly a foot, beset with almost un-toothed foliage, and ending in dense spikes of red-violet blossoms, each about an inch long, and set each in a bract of leafage, sticky above and with fluff on the lower lip (*P. cristatus*).

P. exilifolius, from the dry and stony places of Wyoming and West Colorado, has a neatly tufted habit, and its stems of not more than 6 inches are set with a remarkable abundance of channelled little leaves, pointed and finely narrow. The flowers are white, carried in a crowded shower, each on a slender foot-stalk ; and the shoots are so delicate in their leafage as to suggest the sprigs of a larch.

P. Fremontii lives in the Red Deserts of Wyoming. It is a neat thing, with stems of half a foot, more or less, and the whole plant dense with a hoar-frosted down ; the flowers are purple-blue funnels

49

suddenly yawning, borne in a close spray like a spike, and each about three-quarters of an inch in length.

P. frutescens, unless it greatly lies, is the one species to cross the sea by way of Unalaska into Asiatic Russia, where it makes sub-shrubby masses with oblong leaves, smooth-edged, or toothed here and there, sitting tight to the branches and fringed at their edge, but otherwise nearly bald, while the fluffy-piled flowers are borne in terminal showers.

P. fruticosus is the beautiful and attractive little plant that delights one in the high and stony places of the Canadian Rockies. It makes straggling mats through the shingle—a woody and branching dwarf, with sprays of some 8 to 20 inches, set with thick oblong narrow leaves, dark and toothed, some 2 inches long (or more or much less), the twigs ending in a flight of single stemlings, each carrying one enormous swollen upright Snapdragon nearly 2 inches long and usually of a luscious red-violet, but varying into bluer and hotter shades. It is no less a joy to meet meandering in the grey shales beyond Lake Louise, than to see wandering in one's own—a really alpine species in a race where such are the exception.

P. gentianoeides deserves respect as being the parent of the gorgeous garden Fatties—though how it dares call itself like a Gentian we must leave admirers of *Gentiana purpurea* to decide.

P. glaber, with lovely *P. Brandegeei* for an offshoot, occupies moist sandy places from Dakota and Nebraska far into the West. It is leafy and more or less glaucous-blue, with firm and toothless foliage, the lower leaves (no less than those at the base of the tuft), having footstalks : and the spikes stand or flop some 12 or 24 inches, narrow and protracted in outline, filled with flowers of the loveliest pure clear blue, expanding abruptly as soon as they leave the calyx. *P. speciosus* is simply a variety of this, standing more erect, taller, more slender, and with a looser spire of blossom.

P. glandulosus is tall and leafy, and goes easily out of these pages, with its large but dimmish lilac flowers.

P. glaucus belongs to the Northern Rockies, and is worth the seeking there. It has thick fat oblong foliage, entire or a little toothed, and stems that flop or rise to some 4 to 16 inches, ending each in a short compact spike of baggy great violet flowers, about an inch long, in simple or branching clusters. The whole growth is hairless till you get to the spikes, which are sticky : and forms a matted mass with many slender stems of blossom. Its variety, *P. g. stenosepalus*, sometimes called *P. arizonicus*, is taller and commoner, more lax and showery in effect, with dull pale trumpets.

P. Gordoni is a form or synonym of *P. glaber*.

P. gracilentus is only half the height of the last, and has foot-high stems of clear blue blossom.

P. gracilis is a slender smooth plant of a foot high or more (or much less), with narrow paddle-shaped leaves, either toothed or smooth at the edge, and loose open spires of lilac bugles each about an inch long. It loves moist places and meadows from Colorado to Minnesota.

P. grandiflorus is a large tall leafy species, with big lavender flowers, from the Prairies.

P. Hallii lives high up in the Alps of Colorado. Its stems rise about 8 inches or less, and the leaves are rather thick, and narrowly paddle-shaped. The flower-spike is short and dense, carrying some five to fifteen flowers, dimly sticky, of lilac-purple, bagging out from their tube, which is shorter than the calyx.

P. Harbourii is yet another covetable high-alpine, from the Colorado Rockies, where it forms low dense masses and mats of smooth thick green little leaves, obovate-oval, with some three pairs of them on the 2- or 4-inch flower-stems that carry two or three blossoms crowded in a cluster.

P. Hartwegii, a wild original of plants so civilised that now they have forgotten their parent, like the gorgeous daughters of Père Goriot.

P. Haydeni is more or less glaucous and rather floppety, with stems of 1 or 2 feet, set in linear-narrow leaves that half embrace them, and are pointed at their tips. The flowers are blue, swelling as soon as they get out of the calyx, and are borne in narrow dense thyrses, embraced by large leafy bracts.

P. heterophyllus, Wats. (*P. sepalulus*), is one of the loveliest of all. It is slender and erect and wiry in growth, with narrow leaves and loose spikes of the most exquisite narrow-tubed wide-mouthed flowers of a serene dawn-blue, pale-throated, lined, and shadowed sooner or later with a sheen of very soft external amethyst that doubles the effect of the already entrancing clear tender blues of the mouth. These dainty trumpets of opalescent loveliness sound their music in August and September, and the plant is a hearty erect grower of a foot or more, easily to be raised from seed, even if it show too much of that fashionable American weakness for impermanence.

P. humilis.—The leaves of this are dark-green, or occasionally bluish, oblong-lanceolate, and with those on the stems marked with teeth. The shoots are not more than a foot high, but usually much less, with smoothness all over, unless it be for a sticky inflorescence. The flower-spike is strict and straight, about 3 inches long, with clusters of about half a dozen flowers, or less, on short pedicels. These blossoms are narrowly funnel-shaped, and about half an inch in length, dark-blue, or white in part—especially in the variety *P. h. pseudohumilis* (it surely should take an American, so to bastardise two immortal languages in a name so grotesque), which, like the type, is a high-alpine from the rocks and cañons of the central ranges.

P. Jamesii, Benth., is a very lovely little jewel, forming a bush like some lax Rosemary, rather flopping and not more than 6 inches high, so narrow are the many small leaves, all vested in a fine dense hoar of down ; the flowers are ample and baggy, of the loveliest blue and white, with a lined throat, borne in dense sprays protected by narrow bracts usually at least as long as the flower-stems. In any likely open place this dainty thing, with its seductive little bright blooms in later summer, forms ever-spreading masses, and, apparently, is a startling example of goodness emerging from unlikely quarters, seeing that its home is in the Bad Lands of Wyoming and South Dakota. One only wishes Wyoming would exchange some of its Bad Lands for some of ours.

P. Jamesii (Gray) = *P. similis*, *q.v.*

P. Kingii makes a woody base, from which it sends up a great number of stems about 6 inches high, more or less. The foliage is narrowish-oval, almost untoothed and unstalked, and the whole clump is rimy with down beneath. The one-sided flower-sprays are short and leafy to their base, with one to four flowers gathered together on foot-stalks. They are purple, and not far from an inch in length, widening upwards.

P. laevigatus is the type from which springs *P. digitalis*. They are both large, coarse, and leafy things of a yard high, with stolid swollen bells in dowdy shades of lilac.

P. laricifolius is smooth and tufted, from a woody stock which keeps level with the ground. The leaves are very narrow, crowded at the base, and set more loosely in the many shoots of 4 to 8 inches, ending in few-flowered loose clusters of purple blossoms, each on a delicate foot-stalk, the whole effect being of delicate habit and branch to match, like a spray of larch stuck into the ground. (See *P. aridus*.)

P. Lemmoni has little claim on us. It is a bush of 2 or 4 feet, bright green, with flowers of purple and dull yellow.

P. linaroeides stands near to *P. caespitosus*, and has the same woody stock, but is looser in habit, with quite narrow pointed leaves and one-sided sprays, the lower clusters having some four flowers, and these being tubular funnels of blue, nearly an inch in length. (*A. coloradensis*, Nels.) And there is also a dwarfer form, *P. l. Sileri*, with only one blossom at a time up the spray, instead of clusters, and this rather smaller, while the leaves are longer.

P. Menziesii appears not to be in cultivation. It is a variable species, which has given us at least one noble thing in *P. M. Scouleri, q.v.*

P. Moffattii sends up several stems of from 4 to 20 inches, glandular, with hairs above, and crowded at the base with smooth-edged egg-shaped, paddle-shaped little leaves of which the upper ones sit close to the stem and half embrace it with their heart-lobed base. The flowers are many and purplish-blue, borne in separate clusters up the stem. (From dry plateaux in the Central Rockies.)

P. montanus is herbaceous from the perennial woody root-stock, and sends up a number of stems of 4 to 8 inches, clothed up to the spikes in grey-downy foliage, oblong-narrow, and very conspicuously toothed. The fine ample flowers are pink in the tube, and purple in the face, borne in several pairs, and about an inch long. (This is a high-alpine from the mountains of Idaho, Wyoming, and Montana.)

P. Murrayanus need not enter into these pages, being too large to fit, and too tender to suit.

P. Newberryi sounds like the charming Newbury Gems in name alone. The species sends up foot-high stems from a perennially woody base, and they are set with leathery little round or roundish leaves, and end in sprays of bright scarlet flowers sitting tight and lonely to the stem. It lives in the upper mountain rocks of the coast ranges, and is sometimes called *P. sonomensis.*

P. oreophilus=*P. alpinus, q.v.*

P. ovatus blooms from August to October. It is about a yard high, light green in the thin-textured leaf, and carrying heads of little dark blue or purple flowers, by no means attractive on so gawky a stem.

P. Oweni is a much better plant in the relationship of *P. procerus,* much dwarfer, only about 6 inches high, downyish, and with larger bugles of blue violet. (From the high mountains of Wyoming.)

P. pallidus. See under *P. canescens.*

P. Palmeri is 18 inches tall, with flowers of dim lilac on slender foot-stalks, in a lax and twiggily branching naked spire.

P. procērus likes moist parks and meadows. It has lanceolate stalked leaves of which the longest are to be met with *midway* up the many slender stems of 4 inches or nearly a foot and a half. The blue-violet flowers are rather small, borne in dense whorls, about half an inch long. Though often praised, this is not among the most dainty and attractive. There is also a variety, *P. p. pseudoprocerus,* with longer blossoms, wider in the gaping mouth and (with great imprudence, therefore) less fully protected by a beard at the throat.

P. procumbens = *P. suffrutescens*, *q.v.*

P. pseudohumilis. See under *P. humilis.*

P. pubescens stands nearly 2 feet high at its strongest, with hairy leaves, and flowers that vary from white to deep purple. The garden plant, "Southgate Gem," makes us say glad farewell to its parent, if we care for such things.

P. puniceus may be left out of reasonable count, being a yard-high Mexican with vermilion-scarlet blossoms.

P. pygmaeus has the catalogue-description of being quite wee, not more than 6 inches high, with "opal" flowers, whatever this, unannotated, may mean. It possibly comes in the group of *P. alpinus.*

P. radicosus forms tufted mats, so dense as to be unbreakable by craft of man or spade, in the moist places of the Coloradan deserts and those of Utah and Wyoming. The leaves are very tiny, packed at the base of the slender erect fine stems of 8 inches or even twice that height. But there are many leaves also on these stems, that end, each, in a compact thyrse of dark-blue tubular flowers about three-quarters of an inch long, with purple anthers.

P. Richardsonii has a height of 18 inches, with spreading branches and violet blossoms.

P. riparius = *P. alpinus*, *q.v.*

P. rotundifolius is tall and brilliantly red-flowered, from Mexico.

P. rubricaulis is yet taller, and merely called " red."

P. Rydbergii is a strong perennial with horizontal root-stocks that emit vertical branches, from whose crowns come slender stems on specially short leafy shoots ; the stems are smooth, a foot or a foot and a half in length, bearing whorls of pale-blue or purple flowers. The basal leaves are oblong, and rather less, as a rule, than the length of their foot-stalks. (Moist coppices of Colorado and Wyoming.)

P. Scouleri, though the name is now lost, may here stand as a reminder of the most magnificent of all shrubby Pentstemons, making a loose bush in any sunny place, of perhaps 2 feet high and as much across, composed of wandering fleshyish branches, set with toothed fat foliage, and with the shoots ending in the most glorious and enormous of lilac-rose or lavender Snapdragons, ample and baggy and splendid and incredible, in the early summer and continuing on for many weeks. (It is a form of *P. Menziesii.*)

P. secundiflorus is glaucous-blue, erect, and strict, with stems of not more than 2 feet at the most, with many firm smooth-edged leaves, of which those at the base have stems, and all are obovate-narrow. The flowers are blue, gradually dilating from the tube, and often, but not always, borne in the long and one-sided spire that the plant's name implies. It lives in the sandy plains of Wyoming and New Mexico, and there is a pleasant variety, *P. s. caudatus*, in which none of the leaves have any stems at all, and all are more fleshy, while the flowers vary from pale violet to a pinky tone.

P. sepalulus (Nels.) = *P. heterophyllus*.

P. Sileri. See under *P. linaroeides*.

P. similis (*P. Jamesii*, Gray), has either few or many frail delicate stems about 8 inches or a foot long, the plant being usually glabrous, or else with a sparse rimy down ; and the stem-leaves are scantily toothed, oblong in form, and very narrow. The thyrse of blossom, too, is narrow, and inclined to be one-sided ; bearing blue-and-white flowers like those of *P. Jamesii*, Benth. (of which the entire tuft is the precise picture, altered only in the points specified), but rather longer, about an inch, and abruptly expanding from their tube into a wide cup-form. A lovely small species from South Colorado and New Mexico.

P. speciosus. See under *P. glaber.*

P. spectabilis is a perfectly hairless leafy 2-foot gawk with flowers flattered as being " lilac and blue " in a long foliaceous spire.

P. strictus stands about 18 inches high, an erect smooth blue-grey plant with a long narrow, drawn-out spike, and rather one-sided sprays of short-tubed ample foxgloves of blue-violet, bell-shaped and baggy, about an inch long ; the lower leaves are oblong paddle-shaped and stalked.

P. suffrutescens is lower, and slender, in its habit. The older branches most properly lie down in meekness, while the young, with no less propriety, stand up. But none of them are much more than 9 inches long, or a foot at most. The leaves are very small indeed, green and almost smooth, narrow-spoon-shaped, and bearing in their uppermost axils some one or three large violet-rose flowers, the branches all being clad in downward-pointing fine down. It makes quite a wee shrub, low and slender and divergent, and comes from the arid places of Colorado, having also had the name of *P. procumbens.*

P. Torreyi stands very close to *P. barbatus*, and may even be no more than a variety, more slender in the habit and more graceful in the long, loose spire of especially brilliant scarlet flowers.

P. trichander is pretty much the same as this last, but is dwarfer in habit, with a shorter tube to the blossoms.

P. triphyllus is about 18 inches high, leafy and branched, with inferior purplish flowers.

PERICOME CAUDATA.

P. tubiflorus is another species not for admittance here.

P. unilateralis is almost (if not quite) a synonym of *P. secundiflorus*, except that here the tube of the blossoms expands suddenly, instead of gradually. But, for the rest, see *P. secundiflorus*.

P. utahensis is tall and strict and erect, attaining 40 inches or so, with long-petioled, oblong-narrow leaves crowded at the base, and a protracted spire of ample, specially baggy-belled, violet-blue flowers nearly 2 inches in length.

P. venustus has a stature of 2 feet, and a loose spire or pyramid of large purple bells in June.

P. virgatus is more modest, and only aims at about one and a half, with blossoms in a proportionately diluted tone of lilac-lavender.

P. Watsoni attains a foot or 15 inches, with weakly-ascending stems that are smooth and blue-grey below, but sometimes rather downy in the inflorescence. The stem-leaves are oblong-narrow and pointed, leading up to a longish and contracted thyrse of flowers, violet and white. The spray-stems are fine and slender, yet each carries several blooms. No part of the plant is ever sticky, as in *P. humilis,* nor are the stem leaves (or any of the leaves) diversified with teeth. (Mountains of Colorado and Nevada.)

P. Wrightii, it is suggested, blooms in June, with stems of 18 inches and flowers of lilac-rose ; from which euphemism of kindliness the worst may probably be augured.

Pericŏme caudata.—A little herbaceous bush a foot or two high, from the Cordilleras of New Mexico, to be grown in a warm, sunny corner, and multiplied by cuttings or by any seeds which it may produce from the hay-scented, golden, Composite flowers that it produces in August and September in thick and clustered heads, which do not last long in the very hot exposures that are required to assure the plant's complete hardiness.

Pernettya, a race of Ericaceous neat bushes, quite hardy in England, with evergreen foliage and abundance of large berries in lovely shades of white, blue, violet, grey, pink and crimsons, which make a fine effect, as the plants are tidy and small in growth. The race occupies the Antarctic Islands, &c., where the wind blows them, as it blows the little beeches and other temerarious growths of those inhospitable regions, into tight, flat masses on which one can walk as on a roof. They are not by any means lime-lovers, yet are not so calcifuge as Rhododendrons, thriving comfortably in any clean loam. Cuttings.

Petalostēmon.—A family of graceful Pea-flowers from the prairies, asking for light soil in a sunny position, where they will send up many stems about a foot high, set with finely-divided foliage, and ending each in a tight cone of small purple peas. Such is *P. violaceus;* but *P. candidus* has white heads, and *P. tenuifolius,* pink.

Petasites.—The great Coltsfoots are only fitted for the remotest parts of the wildest bog or wilderness, where *P. japonica* is nearly as ample and tropical as a Gunnera in effect.

Petrocallis pyrenaica is the Rock Beauty of the highest stone shingles and ridges, where it sits tight in neat rounded cushions often a foot across, and still more often hidden from view beneath a mass of delicate lilac-pale crosses, filling the nose with the sweetness of vanilla, as the neat, profuse beauty, so gentle and persuasive, fills the eye with satisfaction. *Petrocallis* is a locally abundant delight, especially but not exclusively on the calcareous mountains, here and there along the main chains from the Pyrenees to the Carpathians : on the gaunt ridges immediately above the Mont Cenis it may be seen especially prodigal and ample, and on the limestones of lower Austria, less wadded and wide in the mass. Under cultivation the Rock Beauty makes its proper tight cushions of finely cloven, wedge-shaped, minute green leaves, serried into the densest congregation of shoots ; but, like many high alpines, is by no means so apt as at home to conceal them beneath a carpet of flower. It can best be induced to do this by growing it in full sun, and in a poor part of the moraine. Its seeds can, of course, be raised, but the plant is best multiplied by pulling away a lateral column or two from the clump, and striking them as cuttings in sand about the end of the summer, say in the beginning of September.

P. fenestrata is quite near the last, with patches of smooth bluish-green leaves cut into three sharp teeth and very tiny. The stems, however, are rather longer, some 2 or 3 inches high, and the flowers are white, in longer sprays, and with the fruticulose little branches of the mass not downy but bald. It asks for the same treatment, to remind it of its home in the stony places above the Val Loura on Elburs ; flowering, like *P. pyrenaica,* in early summer, and like the last to be propagated by cuttings.

Petrocoptis. See under **Lychnis.**

Phaca.—None of these Alpine Astragalids have any value for the garden, being dim in colour and undistinguished in habit.

Phacelia sericea and **idahoensis** may be tried in specially warm and sandy places. They are dwarf or foot-high plants, hairy, with leaves cut into narrow jags, and then a naked crowded spire of smallish blue or lilac cups in May and June. Seed. They are perennial, if not rotted off by rain in winter.

Philesia buxifolia or **magellanica** is a noble Liliaceous

57

shrublet, with arching sprays about a foot high or more (at the best), clothed in long, evergreen foliage dark and oblong, rolled at the edges of the leaves, and glistering in a sombre healthiness of green ; from these sprays depend solid waxy flowers in late summer like those of a rather smaller Lapageria (of which this plant is indeed a small cousin, so close in relationship that the two have interbred and produced a hybrid, *Philageria*). This species comes from Chili, and is quite hardy, but likes a very cool and shady place distinctly on the damp side in summer, and rather high upon the rock-work, that its pendent bells may best strike the eye amid the arches of the shoots ; its soil should be a heavy, rich and clammy mixture of sand, leaf-mould, and peat, with lumps of sandstone dug in for the roots to grip. Thus planted, in a shaded ledge, *Philesia* will send out fat goose-quill runners pink as pigs, and soon possess the whole space, filling it with banks of lovely overhanging sprays of deep glossy green all the year, and kindling its darkness with noble roseate waxy trumpets through the later summer. Once established, *Philesia* may be propagated by pieces pulled off and restarted, but is otherwise best left alone. It also appears, in limestone cracks, sometimes to die vehemently and thoroughly at a week's notice, and it will therefore do no harm to act on the hypothesis of *post hoc, propter hoc*, and conclude it a lime-hater, departing out of life as soon as its runners have impinged on rock containing the accursed thing.

Phlomis.—The Jerusalem Sages are, for the most part, too large for admission to the rock-garden, to say nothing of the fact that they have a goodly share of that coarseness which is the lot of all the larger Labiates ; and nothing, even, of the further fact that they are all rank Southerners, with leaves of wool, and very often hearts of wool to match. They make, however, stately subjects for high, hot ledges of the great rock-garden, in light and limy soil (or indeed any soil that is safe from stagnation in winter), and many can be found in catalogues. The choicest, however, for lower places, are *P. rigida*, which is only a foot or a foot and a half high, with heads of pink flowers up the stem. This, like all the rest, blooms in late summer, and comes from the dry mountain valleys of Armenia. Yet choicer and rarer is *P. crinita* from fat and stony ground high in the alps of Atlas, Valencia, and Granada. This makes great woody masses, and the obese, egg-shaped leaves are snowy-white with reverend wool in their young days, and reverse the process of nature, by growing less ash-white as they advance into the season ; the stems too are snowy with wool, and the dim tawny flowers, borne in whorls of nine or ten in dense clusters up the stalk, emerge from calyces and bracts that are

PLATE 6.

PETROCALLIS PYRENAICA.

(Photo. R. A. Malby.)

PLATE 7.

PENTSTEMON NEWBERRYI.
(Photo. R.B.G., Edinburgh.)

PENTSTEMON COERULEUS.
(Photo. R.B.G., Kew.)

PLATE 8.

PHLOX SUBULATA (var. "NIVALIS").
(Photo. R.B.G., Kew.)

PHYTEUMA COMOSUM.
(Photo. R. A. Malby.)

venerable in the same candid fluff. And yet another more attractive Phlomis is *P. fruticosa*, forming a bush about 2 or 3 feet high, with dense rings of clear-golden flowers up its flower-spikes.

Phlox.—That we should sit contented with even *Vivid* and *G. F. Wilson* among the Phloxes makes one ashamed, as one goes through the long list of exquisite and longed-for alpines that are still vainly offering themselves to us on the desert mountains of America. Therefore we will go straight through the list, that we may know our possibilities and recognise them in the future, as one by one they come to hand. Nor will we despise to mention the taller species, though more briefly, if only that we may know what Flames we do not want. So now for the *complete perennial roll-call* of this race, incomparably the most important that America has yet evolved for the benefit of the rock-garden, and one of which it has an almost undisputed monopoly.

Ph. alyssifolia makes more or less prostrate mats, with thick, flat, oblong-narrow foliage, each smooth leaf having a hard white edge, and a white vein below. The flowers are scattered and large, varying from pale purple to white.

Ph. amabilis is a small woolly-stemmed mass or bushlet of 3 inches high, with narrow, but not intensely narrow, leaves, hairy on both faces, and running to a short, sharp point. The big flowers are white or pink, produced in clusters from the end of every stem. This species, then, is the first of the type that we already worship under the many-headed name of *Ph. subulata*. Therefore, we may here mention that light and open loam in the sun causes all these cushion-Flames to blossom like the rose and burn as fiery as the day. Their one prime need is perfect drainage, and as much light as was loved by Little Nell. They must never be overshadowed, never be clogged in winter. But, this being said, there is no more advice to give, or caution to suggest. And all these species can be layered with sand worked down among the mats, or struck more simply in the form of cuttings.

Ph. amoena, Sims, is *Ph. procumbens*, A. Gray (probably because it is starkly erect). It has simple, downy, upstanding stems of about a foot high in a neat bush, and throwing *no offsets;* these are set with quite narrow downy leaves, and end in many leafy clustered heads of pinky-lilac blossoms, smooth in the throat, but otherwise, like the whole plant, very much suggesting *Ph. pilosa*. (Atlantic North America.) This group requires, to make it happy and permanent, a rather more specially light soil than the last, and a rather more especial place in the sun ; for they are inclined to be frail and straggly in growth as in character, not having the glorious amplitude of the

PHLOX.

Divaricatas, nor the neat and massed profusion of the Subulatas, nor the creeping stoloniferous habit of *P. stolonifera.*

Ph. andicola. See under *Ph. Douglasii.*

Ph. aristata (Lodd.), is a form of *Ph. subulata,* or perhaps a hybrid of *Ph. divaricata* × *Ph. subulata.*

Ph. assurgens is a graceful, creeping, ascending plant from the pine-woods of Pacific North America, with smooth, longish leaves in opposite pairs, and clusters of white flowers at the ends of the shoots.

Ph. austromontana must immediately be quested, from the Peach Springs of North Arizona, Santa Rosa, San Bernardino, and the other saints that keep guard over the loveliest, perhaps, among the Phloxes. It is a downy thing, but not glandular, making low masses of shoots, set with very narrow pointed foliage, which is thickly powdered, like a Christmas card or a micaceous rock, with countless glistening sparks of pure silver in the sunlight, till the whole tuft glisters and twinkles again. The large flowers almost sit close over this loveliness, and are themselves of a glorious lavender-blue or paler, or white. And there is also a perfectly flat creeping form called *Ph. a. prostrata.*

Ph. bifida is a diffuse species of a foot high, or more or less, finely downy all over, and with clusters of starry pale violet blossoms, with each lobe deeply cleft into two or three minor lobes.

Ph. bryoeides is the first member we come to of a section that calls the water to the mouth—a group of tiny massed domes from the upmost rocky ridges, where they take the place and scorn the poor beauties, of the high-alpine Androsaces of the Old World (a scorn which the high-alpine Androsaces requite or provoke, by utterly refusing to set root in America at all). *Ph. bryoeides,* then, is a rare plant in this group ; it makes dense masses of very densely woolly foliage of packed little narrow leaves arranged up the shoots in four rows, but all blurred by the wool they wear ; all over the cushion are set the ample, round-faced, white flowers, like blossoms of an uncloven-lobed Primula, poked into a ball of fluffy moss. It need hardly be added after that alarming word " wool," that when we possess the high-alpine Flames, they must have all the care and nicety of culture that go to make success with the Aretian Androsaces ; though they will not, indeed, insist on growing in rock, but will ask for a choice corner in the under-ground-watered Gentian-bed or moraine ; and will certainly wish to be protected severely against excessive rains in winter.

Ph. caespitosa is another, but less tight and perilous, of the same group, making close mats of longish shoots in effect exactly like that of *Douglasia Vitaliana* in the abundance of the little green leaves, narrow and spiny on their sprays, flat, more or less edged with membrane,

PHLOX.

and more or less fringed with minute bristlinesses. This is a most variable type, though ; *Ph. c. rigida* has the leaves curving outwards and spiny-pointed ; *Ph. c. muscoeides* is a quite minute high-alpine, like a hoary small scab of moss, in effect suggesting the domes of *Ph. bryoeides*, but that the leaves are not arranged in four rows, and are not woolly ; *Ph. c. Colvilei* is another tiny form with white flowers ; *Ph. c. condensata* has also been ranked by Gray as a variety of *Ph. Hoodii*, and is specially dense and hoary-green, with overlapping, packed, stiff leaves and white blossoms ; *Ph. c. Hendersoni* has also the same colour ; whereas in the type the more favoured tone for the ample flowers is a pale blue.

Ph. canescens is another dense mass, densely woolly-hoary, with the little fine leaves prickly and recurving. The flowers are white with a yellowish tube. There is a yet thornier variety, *Ph. c. spinosa.*

Ph. carnea is *Ph. Carolina*, Sweet. It is a giant attaining two and a half feet, minutely roughish all over, and suggesting that it is a hybrid between *Ph. maculata* and *Ph. glaberrima.* The stars in their clusters are pinkish mauve.

Ph. Carolina, Sweet. See above.

Ph. Carolina, of gardens, is *Ph. ovata, q.v.*

Ph. cernua is only some 2 inches or perhaps half a foot high. The lower part of the stem is purple, and the growth is more or less smooth all over, except between the pairs of leaves, which are very narrow indeed, and outspreading. The flowers are a trifle inclined to nod upon their slender footstalks, and are white with a tinge of purple.

Ph. Criterion has come and passed, like the memory of a beautiful dream. It was a treasure of garden origin, which was nothing more nor less than *P. Drummondii ;* but it was perennial.

Ph. dasyphylla makes a woody mass of densely leafy branches some 3 inches or half a foot long, prostrate or ascending, with pink flowers gathered in groups of three or four, at the ends of the hairy-leaved shoots, in the shape of expanding trumpets or funnels.

Ph. densa again calls out our warmest longings. For it may possibly be a variety of *Ph. austromontana*, but with pink blossoms very much more numerous, and sheeted over a very much closer tight tuffet of a couple of inches or so, in an even greater profusion. But it also has a longer style. From Frisco of Colorado, Walnut Cañon, Slate Mountain, &c., at nearly 8000 feet, with a flat smooth form, *Ph. d. depressa*, from the wet plains.

Ph. detonsa. See under *Ph. pilosa.*

Ph. divaricata makes its own bush, and there is no need to advertise its stately June-borne profusion of royal lavender-blue flowers

61

that smell like those of *Lilium auratum*. This only wants room in a light rich loam, to form wide carpets and drifts of pure colour, through which in the spring could have come Daffodils, and in the later season, Lilies. There are various forms of this, including an albino ; *Ph. Laphami* is no more than a rather neater variation of the type *divaricata*, with slightly larger stars of a slightly richer colour, which lose some of the type's charm of clarity when they deepen into the form called "Violet Queen." And G. Arends has lately raised a whole hybrid race between these and the Paniculatas, in order to obtain the immense flower-trusses, rather loosened, much earlier in the season, and of laxer dwarfer habit. These are generically called *Ph. × Arendsii*, but their garden-names can all be studied in catalogues, they being florist-flowers as much as the varieties of *Ph. paniculata*.

Ph. dolichantha has a singular beauty of its own. It is a loosely erect species of 10 inches or a foot, set with pairs of smoothish eye-lashed leaves, long and sword-like, with distinct nerves, about a couple of inches in length. Then, from the upper axils of these, at the top of the shoots, emerges from each a minute footstalk, on which unfolds a noble flower, rose-pink or purple, large and comely, but with a tube of quite ridiculous length, 2 or 3 inches, so that the blossoms with which the loose clump is bespattered have the look of rich tropical oddities dropped there by accident, and making an effect of exotic magnificence. From the San Bernardino Mountains in California, where also lives *Ph. austromontana*, so that the two lovely birds could be bagged with one trowel.

Ph. Douglasii is the most abused and crowded name in the race. The type is a dense tuft, either downy or nearly glabrous, with stems of 6 inches or less, fairly thickly-set with narrow little leaves, not quite so stiff as in the varieties of *Ph. caespitosa*. The blooms either sit tight in the shoots, or have short footstalks ; in colour they are of lovely lilac as a rule, and *their lobes are perfectly rounded, not cloven or notched at all*. It has, however, countless varieties in the course of its range through the Eastern and Western Rockies from Montana and Utah. One, *Ph. D. scleranthifolia*, has white stars, and the leaves stiffly upsticking ; and *Ph. diffusa* and *Ph. longifolia* are developments that explain themselves. In gardens the genuine plant is not common, and seems to be confused in catalogues with *Ph. pilosa*, a species utterly distinct, of looser, taller, straggly, spindly growth, and flowers in clusters here and there, instead of being like *Ph. Douglasii*, in every form, a neat mossy tuffet, besprent with beautiful blossoms of pink all over.

Ph. floridana stands quite close to *Ph. glaberrima ;* not a thing

PHLOX.

of value, tall and erect, with bunches of bloom too small for the long narrow pairs of leaves that enclose them, and continue in longer and longer pairs down the stem.

Ph. glaberrima stands tall and erect, with long and very narrow leaves, and rose-pinky flowers in clusters at the top of the stems, with specially sharp long lobes to their calyces, but otherwise lacking in notable attraction ; and the habit of its growth shares the faults of the last species. There is a variety, *Ph. g. suffruticosa*, of this.

Ph. glabrata is another minute, lovely, high-alpine tuffet, neat and tight, with the leaves closely overlapping, and packed down on the shoots, at the end of each of which peers forth a rounded white flower, sitting close to the mass, and rather longer in the tube (which is usually more or less shorter than the length of the calyx) than in *Ph. Hoodii*.

Ph. gladiiformis from the Alps by Cedar City in Utah, is also a small cushion, but woolly, with the leaves very tightly tiled and serried on the tiny shoots. The flowers are white, protruding from the mass, each by itself, and hairy on the outside of the tube.

Ph. glandulosa stands quite near to *Ph. paniculata*, but the blossoms are smooth and bald in the throat.

Ph. hirsuta is a hybrid from Siskiyou, between *Ph. Stansburyi* and *Ph. speciosa*.

Ph. Hoodii should much resent the way its name is now being taken in vain by nice little ordinary *Gilia pungens*, a pretty light spiculous bush in its way, but by no means worthy to usurp the name and the prices that rightly belong to one of the neatest, smallest, densest, and most charming of the cushion Flames, a plant of woody base, intricately branched and very compact, and massed with white stars. From the high plains and foothills of the Central Rockies.

Ph. Kelseyi is a beautiful, cosily spreading mat of 16 inches wide or less, made up of thickly-leafy shoots, spreading and cushiony. The narrow neat foliage is smooth and green and spiny, white-margined, and rolled over at the edge. The flowers are of a lovely bright lilac-blue, and broad in the lobe ; almost sessile in their multitudes over the mat. There are local varieties of this, too—*Ph. K. costata, Ph. K. collina*, and the charmingly suggestive *Ph. K. diapensioeides*.

Ph. lanata comes from the Steins Mountains of Oregon, &c., and is a specially charming, white-woolled tight tuft of 2 or 3 inches, set all over with big stars of the most brilliant purple.

Ph. longifolia lives in the sandy places of the Pacific Coast Alps, &c. It grows about 9 inches or a foot high, sending up, from the half-woody base, a great number of erect stems, set here and there with pairs of long, pointed, one-nerved leaves (some 2 inches in length), and

63

concluding in clusters of some half a dozen pink blooms. It has a narrow-leaved form, *Ph. l. linearifolia*, and yet another, *Ph. l. humilis*, whose charm is amply foreshadowed in the name, even had it not so struck other observers as to make them give the neat, rosy-flowered mass specific rank as *Ph. speciosa*.

Ph. maculata stands very close to *Ph. paniculata*, but has dark spots on the stem, yet the same typical magenta-pink little blossoms in long clusters, and with a strong scent.

Ph. multiflora is in the neighbourhood of *Ph. alyssifolia*, a depressed tuft of flattened leaves, with a large number of flowers on short footstalks, starry in outline.

Ph. nana.—A most variable species from North Mexico, but never by any chance a dwarf, attaining as a rule about a foot of height, with stems either glabrous or fluffed with glands, beset with pairs of long, very narrow pointed leaves with a conspicuous nerve. Each stem concludes in one, or usually two, large and handsome flowers, in outline suggesting a well-built Linum's, and in colour of almost every tone in the race ; with the varieties, *Ph. n. albo-rosea*, *Ph. n. lutea*, *Ph. n. purpurea*, *Ph. n. ensifolia*, *Ph. n. glabella*, *Ph. n. triovulata* (tall and graceful), and, finally, the one exception which may be held to prove the preposterous name—*Ph. n. depressa*, a beautiful downy-white dwarf-form, from some 6000 feet up on Chihuahua.

Ph. Nelsoni, Brand (*Ph. triovulata*, Nelson, in part), is an erect grower of a foot or so, with the lower leaves in pairs, smooth, and gradually drawing to a point at either end, while the upper ones are alternate, and inclined to be a little downy. The flowers are carried in few-blossomed loose sprays at the tops of the stems (which only branch sparingly, if at all), on footstalks that are woolly and without any glands. Their lobes are half again as long as their tube, and the style much shorter than the calyx. (Rucher Valley in South-East Arizona.)

Ph. Nelsoni of gardens is an unjustified name, covering a white form of *Ph. subulata*, *q.v.*

Ph. nitida is nothing but a name.

Ph. nivalis has no right to be even this—being the same thing as the white form of *Ph. subulata*, which is also so often called *Ph. Nelsoni*, and well worthy, in its sheeted, snowy beauty, of the most laudatory name that could be invented, so long as it is invented by someone who has Latin enough to know that "nivalis" is not descriptive but territorial, and means a plant that lives in the snow regions, not a plant whose whiteness calls theirs to mind ; the descriptive epithet to suggest a comparison with snow is *niveus*, and *niveus* alone.

Ph. ovata is *Ph. Carolina* of gardens, no less than *Ph. triflora* and

PHLOX.

Ph. latifolia. It comes from the open woods of Alabama and Pennsylvania, making no bones about being happy in our gardens, where it develops its character freely—a low, creeping, prostrate species, with its shoots set with *oval or oblong green leaves*, of which the lowest have footstalks of their own. The blossoms are borne in terminal clusters at the top of the slender foot-high stems, and are of a magenta-rose, rather crowded, and poorly proportioned, one of the forms (once called *Ph. Carolina*), approaching almost to *Ph. glaberrima.* It is not among the most attractive of its race.

Ph. paniculata has no place in the rock-garden, for the wild forms are too ugly in their colours, and the garden ones too artificial in their gorgeousness for admission even to the bog.

Ph. pilosa belongs to the dry woods and coppices of the Atlantic regions. It is a stragglingly erect grower of a foot or 18 inches, all sparsely hairy (except in its glabrate variety, *Ph. p. detonsa*), and its stems are set here and there with pairs of long-pointed leaves. The flowers are of purplish-rose, in loose clusters, profusely produced at the ends of the stems and of all their branches, and with long articulate hairs, but no glands, on the calyces and pedicels of the blossoms. It is a strong contrast to *P. divaricata*, much less pleasant in the colour, and taking deeper shades of carmine and purple, often to be seen in catalogues as "Purple Queen," "Brilliant," "Splendens," and so forth; all the improvements, as well as the type, liking best a particularly sunny exposure, with particularly good, light and sandy soil.

Ph. pinifolia is a dwarfish tuffet, made up of very many, very leafy shoots, thick with pairs of opposite little prickly leaves. The blooms emerge from the tips of these shoots, and are gradually-expanding funnels of about an inch, some one to three in a cluster, set in calyces whose lobes wear a beard of wool. (Oregon.)

Ph. procumbens, Lehm., Sweet, Loddiges and gardens, is a hybrid between *Ph. pilosa* × *Ph. subulata.* It is a weakly thing, hairy in all its parts, with flopping or ascending stems of 10 inches or so, and clustered lax stars of rosy-mauve.

Ph. procumbens (A. Gray), is a hybrid of *Ph. amoena* × *Ph. subulata*, but standing so close to *Ph. amoena* that most recent authorities take it as a synonym. See under *Ph. amoena.*

Ph. puberula. See under *Ph. Stansburyi.*

Ph. reptans is *Ph. stolonifera, q.v.*

Ph. Richardsoni dwells in the gaunt lands of the far North, where it may be seen beside the ice-lakes of Arctic America—a tiny close mass of shoots forming a hedgehog of erect, incurving, prickly foliage, woolly-white in all the upper part, in which nestle the goodly blossoms of a lovely lilac-blue.

Ph. Rugelii is another hybrid, from stony wood-borders in Tennessee. It has the leafage of the one parent, *Ph. amoena*, and the ample blue flowers of the other, *Ph. divaricata*.

Ph. " setacea " of gardens is usually *Ph. subulata*.

Ph. " setacea " of gardens is sometimes *Ph. sibirica*.

Ph. sibirica, which sometimes does duty for *Ph. setacea*, is the one member of the family to escape across, by way of the Arctic islands, into the Old World, thus ranging from Alaska to all Northern Asia. It is a villous-downy mat of 6-inch shoots, set with narrow little leaves, more or *less withered at the edges*, and clad in rather long down all over. For the rest, its blooms and beauties are those of the much more glabrous *Ph. subulata*.

Ph. speciosa is sub-shrubby and rather erect, with pairs of leaves, quite hairless, and half an inch to two and a half inches in length, and with one conspicuous nerve. The flowers are white or pink, but most variable, borne in loose showers, one to three or four in a cluster. In all its development *Ph. speciosa* stands not far from *Ph. pilosa*, from which it differs in the obvious characteristics given, among others. It also has varieties beyond number : *Ph. s. elatior*, taller, with thinner foliage ; *Ph. s. latifolia, Ph. s. lanceolata, Ph. s. nitida, Ph. s. Woudhousei* (with the blossoms on short footstalks, and the whole plant so dwarf as to bring it near *Ph. amabilis*, but that the style is short and the lobes of the corolla not cloven to a quarter of their depth as in that species) ; *Ph. s. lignosa, Ph. s. Suksdorffii* (with dense blossom-sprays and long footstalks to the flowers) ; and *Ph. s. Whitedii*, with loose showers of lilac-blue.

Ph. Stansburyi makes a stout little tuffet of 4 inches high, downy below and developing to roughness above. The shoots are set with thick, recurving, spreading, small foliage, very narrow and prickly-pointed. The flowers are pink, and the plant is *Ph. dasyphylla* of Brand. There is a variety of this, similar in habit, with larger flowers of light blue, an inch across. This is *Ph. St. puberula*, which, as its name justly observes, is vested in a certain amount of glandular down It flowers earlier in the year than *Ph. longifolia*.

Ph. Stellaria is familiar to all our gardens—a rather lax mossy Phlox of long, straggly arms and starry flowers of pale French-blue, with deep-cleft lobes in loose clusters here and there over the curtain, on stems of an inch or two in June—a pretty thing enough, but unfortunate in coming into competition with *Ph. subulata*, a rivalry for which nature has not equipped it.

PHLOX.

Ph. stolonifera often appears in catalogues as *Ph. reptans* and *Ph. verna.* It may at once be known by its unique habit of *emitting runners and rooting stolons,* the whole growth being rather clammy-downy, and the prostrate long, weak branches set with pairs of oval leaves, which are quite large about the base of the red flower-stems that rise up here and there, but much smaller on the runners. The stems are some 6 inches high, and set with, here and there, a pair of small oval leaves ; at their top is a loosely branched head of large and lovely rose-carmine blossoms in spring before the others, and very often again in autumn. *Ph. stolonifera* has all-round charm, the stalks uprising at intervals from the carpet of runners, making far less of a crowd and giving far more of an effect to both groundwork and blossom alike than in some of the other species, where only a dense clump or mat is formed. This favourite joy comes from the damper woods in Alleghany, Kentucky, Pennsylvania, and Georgia ; and in the garden is of the easiest culture, sheeting any good space of soil with the insatiate ramification of its runners, thrown out in all directions from the flower-stem's rosette, after the hen-and-chickens fashion affected by *Androsace sarmentosa.* The only note to make is one of caution against the confusion of some catalogues, which, besides often calling it " *reptans* " or " *verna,*" seem to think that it is the same thing as *Ph. procumbens.* It stands apart *from all* in its stoloniferous habit, and the others are sufficiently differentiated, each in his several place.

Ph. subulata.—There is no end to the kindliness and glory of this little Flame, whether we have to thank it in winter for the cheery shimmer of its wide mats of green, or in early summer for the way in which it conceals them from us with a carpet of comfortable full-faced stars in an indistinguishable mass of snow or lavender-blue, or pink, or vehement rose or lilac. The day that saw the introduction, more than a century since, of *Ph. subulata,* ought indeed to be kept as a horticultural festival ; for so hardy and so hearty is the plant, that not even the timorous veneration of a hundred years ago could do it harm, and it continued to survive even in the dank and gloomy hollows of shelter then prescribed for a thing so precious, till at last the clouds rolled by, and now it makes mats of loveliness over every high rock of the garden in June. In America it has a general distribution through the sandy, woody places of the Atlantic border (which is why it came to us so much sooner than its tarrying Pacific sisters), and in its range varies into many forms, of which the archetype is the one called *Ph. subulata ciliata,* while the perfectly smooth-leaved, glossy one is the variety *Ph. subulata setacea,* so that the species has often, therefore, appeared in catalogues as being the same thing as itself.

unless the name were used to cover *Ph. sibirica*, which differs finally from this in having its leaves less stiff, and hairy all over instead of only at the edge, where they also tend to wither in a rim, unlike those of *Ph. subulata*. Yet other forms of this species are *Hentzii*, and the lovely snow-white jewel called *Ph. subulata " nivalis,"* which also in gardens usurps the name of the inferior species, *Ph. Nelsoni*. This is neater than many, and incredibly profuse and pure in flower, blooming a few days earlier than the others, which then come on in a roar of beauty with the opening of June, so brimming the garden over with colour that one wonders how it can ever have room for anything else. Of these precious garden varieties there is no need here to speak, as every catalogue amply states their charms. But the best of all at present are the wild form *Ph. sub. " nivalis,"* the no less free and beautiful electric-blue-flowered *G. F. Wilson* or *lilacina*, and the unsurpassable *Vivid*, which unfortunately has some of the caprices that its beauty allows, and does not show the heartiness or the invariable hearty indestructibility of the species in all its other forms, until one almost suspects some other blood in this much smaller plant, much tighter and more condensed in the smaller and shorter shoots, much slower and more concise in growth, perhaps less hardy, and especially avid of sun and light soil; but, when all is said and done, above the price of rubies in its display of rather small flowers in the most piercing tone of hot flesh-pink—the one member of the race rightfully to wear the name of Flame, unless we are to suppose that the Greeks had foresight of electricity, so that we may think of the race-name as meaning the cold electric fire of *Ph. divaricata* or *Ph. sub. lilacina*.

Ph. suffruticosa is a variety of *Ph. glaberrima, q.v.*; and, though mixed up, with all its hybrids and garden-forms, by every catalogue with *Ph. paniculata*, has nothing whatever to do with that perfectly distinct species.

Ph. superba stands erect, and has a stature between 2 inches and 12, the lower part of the growth being smooth, but the upper vested in white wool. The leaves are quite narrow, and *Ph. superba* magnificently justifies the challenge of its name when the neat mass of shoots breaks forth into as many loose clusters of two or three very large and long-tubed roseate flowers about an inch and a half in length, with rounded lobes and generous outline, so that their face is about two-thirds as wide as their throat is long. It is in far Nevada that the mystic word " Jonopah " gives hope of seeing this lovely thing in the bare gravelly shingles, 6000 feet up in those mountains.

Ph. tenuifolia sends out a rich profusion of stems, twiggy and upstanding, to a height of 2 feet or so, bearing funnel-shaped blossoms of varying colour nearly an inch long, with deepish clefts to the lobes, in loose and few-flowered sprays. (South Arizona.)

Ph. triflora = *Ph. ovata.*

Ph. variabilis is a dwarf mat-forming species from the Colorado Rockies, with the leaves flat and pointed, and fringed with longish hairs, while the rest of the plant is rather bald, and the flowers sit tight over the tuft by ones or twos.

Ph. verna is a false name for *Ph. stolonifera, q.v.*

Phyllodŏkē taxifolia is also **Menziesia coerulea,** and its beauties have been hinted at under that head. There are others of the race, all delicate bushlings of fine yew-like foliage, which eject from the tips of their shoots a varying number of drop-shaped or bubble-shaped flowers in pinks or lilacs, each hovering on a delicate footstalk of its own. *Ph. Pallasiana* has more blossoms and shorter stems to them than *Ph. taxifolia ;* and there is also, among the rest, the most dainty little pink-belled *Ph. nipponica*, and the inferior *Ph. aleutica.* All these, indeed, are dainty things, and for the daintiest treatment, lest they too poignantly remember the cool, arctic air and the conditions of their birth. They should have, then, a specially gritty, stony peat, light and spongy, and perpetually kept moist from below in summer, if they are to continue prosperous and long in the land. There is no question of their propagation ; and their chime of bells rings out in summer and late summer.

Physălis. —After *Phlox* and *Phyllodoke*, who will not be made sick by the mere name of these rank and leafy weeds, with their ostentatious "Japanese Lanterns" of orange and red ? These are, of course, the dismal sere decorations of winter ; and any flower that allows its corpses out for so grim a purpose can only be reckoned as a blackleg in the floral Union, going out to illegitimate employment when all decent plants are enjoying the night when no man can work ; and earning by this treachery a place in the garden to which their rank ugliness of summer would certainly not entitle them.

Physaria. —An American race of small Crucifers close to *Lesquerella* and *Vesicaria*, for cultivation in dry soils and sunny places, where they will bloom in spring, and then may occasionally, but not by any means invariably, die ; and in any case can be abundantly replaced from seed. *Ph. didymocarpa* has a leaf-tuft of quite singular beauty, for the leaves are broad and oval, and clothed in pure shimmering silver. But they are also arranged round the rosette at rare intervals, in flattened, inclined planes like the vanes of a wind-fan, which gives the plant quite sufficient charm in itself, even did not the rosette send up a spire of such handsome, clear-yellow flowers. There is also a form of this where the leaves are not only silver, but fluffy with silver. And there are also *Ph. vitulifera* and *Ph. floribunda*, quite tufted and perennial, and *Ph. Newberryi*, large and silver, but with white flowers. All these from the dry places of Colorado, and to be considered accordingly.

Physochlaina orientalis is a weird Solanaceous species out of the East, with a big fleshy root, and uncurling, branching sprays, some 8 inches high, of coppery-blue flowers most strange and odd, in April and May, before the hairy, dark-green foliage has developed to anything like its subsequent amplitude. This should have a sheltered nook in profound and well-drained woodland soil or garden loam not too much visited by the sun, and may be multiplied by seed or division. There is also *Ph. grandiflora* from Tibet, which is more stiffly hairy, and has much larger flowers of greenish yellow in loose spikes.

Physoptychis gnaphalioeides is almost **Vesicaria**—a small tufted Crucifer from high in the Persian Alps, half shrubby in its small way, with spikes of golden crosses, and rosettes of numerous leaves all hoary grey with stellar hairs. The whole thing is only about 3 inches high, so should have a choice foreground place in full sun in light limy soil or moraine or warm crevice. Seed, or cuttings.

Phyteuma.—What this race has done to be called especially *The Plant* or *the Vegetable Growth*, beyond all other plants and vegetable growths, is not to be known by man. The rock-garden need make no long tarrying over consideration of the taller spike-headed Rampions; but in the wild meadow among the Anemones and the Paradiseas, the sombre pokers of *Ph. Halleri*, *Ph. spicatum*, *Ph. Michelii* (with its paler blue form *Ph. betonicaefolium*) may well have their place, gloomily flowering in full summer, and standing boldly up on bare stems of 18 inches or so. But there are very much more precious and immediately important things in the race, and the Alps are carpeted in many small, neat Rampions, which every one who sees them is always trying to tell apart, and never succeeding. Here then, we will make an effort at each portrait.

Ph. austriacum, *Ph. Carestiae*, *Ph. globulariaefolium* will give no trouble: they are all rare small species of which *Ph. Carestiae* comes from Corsica, and *Ph. globulariaefolium*, the smallest of all, with stems of 2 inches or so, from the Eastern ranges, while *Ph. serratum* is another small Corsican, very nearly stemless and flat on the ground, with broad, pointed, toothed leaves, almost nursing a dishful of little blue bottles in an ample plate of bracts.

Ph. comosum, however, far harder to collect, is far better worth the effort, and far more worthily repays it. *Ph. comosum* is so utterly unlike the rest that it has now been put by Dalla Torre into a race apart : however, for the moment we may stick to the old name. In the hardest and sheerest limestones of the far Southern and Eastern ranges it chooses the most adamantine precipices for its home, and there alights in only the most microscopic crannies of an apparently unbroken cliff-face. Here its rootstock, yellow and fat, flows out and in and far until it has precisely moulded the cranny as if old wax had been poured in and hardened. From this, on fine stems, spring a number of leaves not unlike the evanescent basal leaves of the Harebell, but quite thick and fat, and of a green so dark and metallic in tone that it looks like cast-iron, so that no one who has ever seen *Phyteuma comosum* will ever mistake it again, in flower or out of flower, for anything else—although, curiously enough, as all precious plants seem to have their jackals, so the Phyteuma is roughly mimicked in the colouring and sombre gloss of its foliage by *Veronica Bona-Rota*, which inhabits the same walls and from afar often gives false hopes of the other, alluring one in haste up the stony scree to the base of the cliff, there at once to be disillusioned by the wholly different shoots and leaf-shape of that delusive and snobbish Veronica. So then, in the summer, up from amid the waving tuft of leaves, deriding all trowels from their crevice, arise several stout stems of 3 or 4 inches, set with dark, oval-pointed foliage, deeply and coarsely-toothed, and ending in a head of flowers more eccentric than need of insect ever designed before. Sitting, as it seems, among the scalloped leaves of sombre greenish-black, unfold the clusters of immense diaphanous yet solid flowers like bunched soda-water bottles of pale purple deepening to their tip, from which the curly stigma goes frisking forth in manner weird and wild. It is indeed the strangest of all children of the cliffs, and, I may also say, the hardest to dislodge. This being so, I may safely instance the stark iron walls behind the Hotel Faloria at Cortina, as a place where it may be observed in notable abundance and fine character ; but all over that region it occurs in the high limestone crags, and there only, and only there if the hardness of the rock exactly suits its view. There is an ancient tuft, the great-grandfather of tufts, in an impregnable cliff by the bridge going down to Storo in the Val di Ledro, that yearly greets the pilgrim of *Daphne petraea* with increasing flaunts of its magnificence, until it has grown an old friend, always to be looked for and waved to in passing ; while high, high above this gorge, in the rocks of the Daphne itself, the Phyteuma grimly clings, and finds that even *Daphne petraea* is too loose in its notions, and but few of its precipices quite hard enough for a person of really sound and rock-bound root. In cultivation, however, the plant most paradoxically drops all these principles at once: we should expect the little mat-forming Phyteumata of the alpine turf to be very easy, and in point of fact they are rather difficult : we should expect *Ph. comosum* to be the most paralysingly impossible of its race, and it is in reality one of the easiest of all alpines. There is, indeed, an immense fund of vitality stored in that stout fleshy rootstock ; mutilate it as you may (and neither hammer nor crowbar nor the rod of Moses will secure you perfect roots of more than one Phyteuma out of a hundred), the fragments will push forth life, and burgeon anew, and gradually get re-established. If you have a little patience you will ere long be able to plant it out ; when, to your surprise, this intractable species of the most unmalleable mountains will show itself perfectly happy and robust, sitting in any deep soil of limy rich loam on the rock-work, perfectly drained. Here it will produce a pride of tuft and blossom unknown before, and not to be repressed unless by the nemesis of slugs, who seize upon this new prosperity and pursue it from afar, and seem to have a special nose for it, and for its sake leap walls of zinc, as Romeo scaled the parapets of Verona for his love. Having then got so far as this, you will now, if the slugs permit, be able to adore those amethystine heads of wild pale bottles in July, and afterwards collect the seed and lay foundations for more. But, supposing the counsel were not such a mockery, and the collector compelled to be only too thankful for what Phyteuma he can get, I would urge him to have an eye for forms ; for often the bottles are livid and sombre, or of a cold and bilious pallor that looks as if they were designed for drinks that neither inebriate nor cheer ; while now and then they are of so transparent an amethystine blue, deepening to darker tones of translucent purple at their tip, that they seem like carved jewels from long ago of T'ang or Sung, phials wrought by great artists to hold the wine of ghostly ancestors, or the sacred tears of the Emperor for Tai-Ch'ên the Beautiful. Let such then be sought, and even if when found they prove impregnable, in the mere sight of them the spectator will still be none the poorer for a beauty that he has seen and worshipped, even without being able to drag it down into the garden for the delight of vile creatures that walk upon their bellies, and think of nothing else.

Ph. confusum is not a species likely to trouble either traveller or gardener. It is too rare for the one, and too ugly for the other. It may possibly prove a large and very much coarsened form of *Ph. hemisphaericum,* with much broader leaves abruptly cut short in such a way as to end in three teeth, a bigger and two smaller, almost in a line. The flower-head is large and flat and dull, en-saucered by an ample involucre, and the uninteresting thing is rare in the Alps of Styria and Carinthia.

Ph. humile now asks our notice, the noble species of the cliffs being settled. *Ph. humile* is wholly distinct and never to be mistaken, being a spoiled version of *H. hemisphaericum.* It is larger, leafier, with broader, stiffer, and much longer, duller foliage, *often hairy and faintly toothed at the edge;* the flower-stems are a trifle taller, and though the blossoms are larger, yet the enveloping bracts (which are usually sharply toothed) are so much larger still that the flower-head can never overflow and form into a ball of blue, but must always sit more or less flat in the saucer of the involucre. Altogether it has a coarse tone which is no reproach that can ever be brought against either of its successors, whatever their other faults; and the leaves contribute to that effect, with their narrow length suggesting an Erysimum's. And now come the tourist's twin problems.

Ph. pauciflorum and *Ph. hemisphaericum* are the two most general Alpine species, and the two most generally confused, though in themselves readily distinct. Let it be pictured then, that the foliage of *Ph. hemisphaericum* is *thin and narrow and pointed, just like a glossy little grass,* with well-furnished tufts of leaves, arching and graceful, about an inch or two in length and forming wide mats. Thus runs the neat plant about in the highest fine turf, especially in the non-calcareous ranges, and in later summer sends up a number of stems 2 or 3 inches tall, set with a leaf or two, and ending in a cup of bracts or leaves pointed and finely-hairy, that give issue to a very *great number* of tiny, *clear-blue,* soda-water-bottle flowers arranged in a crowded and almost globular head, with the forked stigma (as in all these) protruding far, and waving about in a most vivacious manner, like the tongues of many imprisoned snakelings, making the orb of clear-blue blossom look quite fluffy and living.

Ph. pauciflorum is wholly different, though this also runs about as freely, and forms the same wide stretches in the highest ridges of the non-calcareous ranges. But here the leaves are *much fewer, much stiffer, darker, fatter, shorter,* not at all *grass-like or wavy or pointed,* but solid and firm and blunt, and so far from being finely narrow, that they are almost of a *squeezed oblong outline.* The bloom-stems, again, are rather shorter and rather stouter, ending in a cup of much more rounded bracts, from which overflows a head of only *quite a few blossoms*—some eight or six perhaps—but these *very much larger and more ample and swollen;* not pale-blue, but of a gorgeous *dark-blue violet,* especially at the tips, most delicately paling downwards to the bellies of the bottles till they look indeed as if they had been blown by fairies in some imperial factory of Myrrhine glass. And, beautiful as are the fluffy sapphirine balls of *Ph. hemisphaericum* upon the mats of its fine foliage, the prize of glory must go, I think, to the more solemn-flowered clusters of *Ph. pauciflorum*, as you may see it, for instance, on the crest of Malamot, threading Eritrichium in and out with the ramifying tissues of its rootage, and combating the round azure patches of the King with the serried battalions and dotted clumps of its own blobbed violet darkness. In cultivation, however, neither of these jewels is of easy temper, nor, indeed, any other of the alpine " Plants "—to give them their invidious name, though the title lacks precision. Abundance of stone, in the peaty, and for preference *most certainly non-calcareous mixture* of their soil, is clearly to be indicated ; the most perfect drainage also, and abundance of water underground in the growing period, with dryness and rest in the winter. There seems no reason why little growths so hearty and invasive at home should not be as easy in cultivation as their kindly hearty cousins from a little lower down. Especially as they bear no trace of wool nor the slightest outward warning of danger, either in look or habit. Yet so it is, the alpine Phyteumata are often hard to satisfy, though amply worth the labour that their satisfying calls for.

   Ph. Scheuchzeri and *Ph. orbiculare* are larger species with big graceful wild balls of blue, on bare foot-high stems in the summer. The latter is a lime-craving native ; but *Ph. Scheuchzeri* is much more generous in the habit and valuable all round, slender and delicate in the abundant stems, but a very free grower and forming lavish masses that are always attractive. *Ph. Charmelii* is a frailer, weaker thing altogether, with the lowest leaves of all quite little and heart-shaped and rounded, on long slender stalks; but the next are quite unlike them, amply swordlike and drawn-cut ; while the heads of flowers are smaller and the whole effect more puny, and the leaves of the saucer are specially narrow and pointed. *Ph. Balbisii* is rarer still, and yet more frail, making a fat root-stock in a hard cliff, and then trailing about its gentle weak stems, with rather large heart-shaped pointed leaves, coarsely toothed, and soft in texture, springing from the base on long foot-stalks, while there are even one or two leaves, still of the same ivy-pattern, on the floundering stalks that end in egg-shaped heads of blue or pale-blue flowers. This species may occasionally be seen, floating from the limestone cliffs about the Col di Tenda ; it is quite impossible to collect, and there seems no reason why it should be any less impossible to grow.

   Ph. Sieberi, on the other hand, may often be seen in the Eastern

PLATE 9

PHYTEUMA SIEBERI.
(Photo. R. A. Malby.)

POLYGONUM VACCINIFOLIUM.
(Photo. R.B.G., Edinburgh.)

ranges, and might give trouble to the unwary. But it is an altogether larger growth than any of the alpine species already recounted, and with whom it shares the high fine turf (though perhaps not as a rule ascending to such elevations). In the first place, it is not of matting habit, but forms a *single tuft of two or three stems;* in the second place, the scanty tuft is of thick and stocky build, with only a very few stalked leaves at the base, and those broadish-oval, pointed, coarsely toothed, and clothed, *like the whole plant, in a hoar of velvety grey hair.* The two or three thick stalks, set with a largish leaf or two like those at the base (but not stalked), are some 3 or 4 inches high, ending in a saucer of ample coarse-toothed leaves, yet not ample enough not to be successfully overflowed by a quite conspicuous fine large head of large blue flowers distinctly bigger than in any of the foregoing, and of notable effect, on a clump so neat and small in habit, and so chary of its stems. Indeed the whole tuft looks like that of some hoar-frosted lowland Phyteuma, being philosophic in a high mountain station to which it has unadvisedly strayed.

Pimelea.—None of these New Zealand Daphnes are officially reckoned hardy, but considering the many surprises that occur, there would be far less about this than about many others, if two or three at least of the species were to prove possible in light peat and a sheltered warm corner. *P. arenaria* might be tried, with its leathery leaves so beautifully silky below, and its heads of white blossom ; and *P. Lyallii;* and the most beautiful of all, *P. Traversii,* which gives us hope by ascending to alpine elevations and in the South Island—a dense branched erect shrub of a foot or two, with the leaves arranged in overlapping fours and often red-edged, and every shoot ending in a bunch of large Daphne-flowers of white or pink.

Pinguicula.—The Butterworts ask absolutely for abundant moisture in their soil, but when this is arranged for, give no further trouble whatever : and in winter their carnivorous fat leafage dies all away, and a fat nodule of greeny scales alone remains, just underground, to promise a renewal next year. All answer to the same treatment in rich cool ground, kept rippling with dampness above and below. Our own *P. vulgaris,* with its violet little Gloxinias, has quaint charm, but its Irish cousin, *P. grandiflora,* has twice or three times the bulk of flower and charm, with a flapping lip of purple and white, like that of some tropical Zygopetalum. Another larger-blossomed species in the way of our own is *P. macroceras* from Unalaska ; while *P. spatulata,* from Transbaikalia, wears a big spoon-shaped lip. Very large in the flower, too, is *P. vallisneriaefolia,* with erect wormy-looking filmy leaves of pale pellucid green ; and great lilac Streptocarpus-flowers of about an inch and a half long. This is a plant of the South, from the warm damps of Granada ; while Greece and the Balkans yield us *P. hirtiflora* with rose-coloured blossoms and a red capsule. Nor must one forget the alpine varieties of *P. vulgaris* itself. For this greatly varies, and whereas in some ranges you get only pinched and screwed little trumpets not as good as our own in form or colour, in others *P. vulgaris* advances into the most beautiful rotund development of lip, clear violet, with either one big oval patch of clear white, or else a trefoil patch, contained by the purple hem of the swelling three-lobed lip. These are specially often to be found in the Dolomites and Southern ranges ; often the difference of a few hundred feet will mean the difference between good and bad forms ; as, for instance, about St. Martin Vésubie, the type is sadly inferior, both in colour and form, while up towards the Madonna della Finestra, the violets grow larger, and the whiteness of the lip more evident, even though they never arrive at the amplitude and clarity of the flowers that you see above the Val di Daone or in the high Monzoni-Thal. Another interesting Butterwort of those southerly parts, however, is *P. longifolia*, which may be seen hanging in curtains and dense unhealthy-looking masses of long sickly pallid flopping leaves of yellow-green on the hot shaded rocks of the Roja Valley below San Dalmazzo de Tenda, a rare species, but there abundant, and from stations so warm that it hardly seems possible for it to be as hardy as the rest—a grief which may be mitigated if it prove to be as parsimonious with us of its blue and lilac flowers as it there seems to be on its native cliffs and shining slime-slides. More beautiful and profitable than this is *P. Reuteri*, from the Jura, which has blossoms little larger than those of *P. vulgaris* indeed, but of a soft lilac-pink. The white-blooming species, *P. alpina* and *P. lusitanica*, are both found in England and Scotland, and another, more yellowish in tone, *P. flavescens*, in the Eastern Alps ; but *P. alpina*, the best of these, is usually but a poor little wizen thing as you see it in the mountains. But here, too, localities produce the most astonishing variations, and the woods of Misurina are filled with a white-and-gold Pinguicula which can only be *P. alpina*, but in a form so magnificent as to be like an albino *P. grandiflora*, though much firmer and more refined in flower, lighting up the long mossy stretches of the larch-wood with thousands of flowers like snow-pure Gloxinias, with a throat of golden velvet.

Pisum.—One of this useful family has escaped the thraldom of respectable utilitarianism, and taken refuge high up in the shifting screes and moraines of Lycia, Lebanon, Eastern Caucasus, and the Cilician Taurus, where *P. formosum* rambles happily among the stones, a wandering Odysseus of an inch or two high, roaming far and wide with fine thready fibres, and perking up every here and there from the greyness in tufts and shoots of hairless paired leaflets, above which hover the big pink Sweet Peas, each lonely on its fine stem, rejoicing in the thought of not having to provide anybody but itself with green peas. By a green pea, however, must it be ultimately introduced to our notice, and in the moraine made happy enough to secure its succession with more.

Platycōdōn.—The Wide-Bells stand between Campanula and Ostrowskia. They develop on a diminished scale the fat huge stock of the latter, the fleshy glaucous foliage and stem ; and the big fat-faced flowers of rich powder-blue have something of the same effect, except that in the grandest of the race, *P. grandiflorum*, they are bulged and ballooned in shape, borne in long sprays, opulent and splendid, and the more precious that, like those of all the rest of the family, they appear in latest summer when the garden is beginning to go into mourning for the approaching departure of the Maiden. Other species are *P. glaucum*, and *P. autumnale ;* their culture is of the simplest, the only thing they dread being stagnant damp in winter that corrodes the stout stock. But let them be planted in very deep and well-drained light loam, and they will be perennially happy ; as the tall-stemmed species are fleshy and stiff in the stalk, and often nearly 2 feet high, they suffer the weight of their great flowers, and should be established either on lofty ledges where they can flop and fall with good effect, or in the neighbourhood (not under the shadow of) light little bushes on which they can decline and rest their weariness. (For in the rock-garden the stake should no more be seen than now, for the present, it is in the Church.) The most valuable, however, of all the species is, therefore, the one that needs no precautions ; this is *P. Mariesii*, which makes a sturdy mass of 8- or 10-inch shoots, so stocky and short that they need never flag, but bravely uphold their noble open fleshy-looking bells throughout the autumn. There are lighter, and darker, and white-flowered forms of all these ; they are beauties of high worship in Japan, where the bulk of them are native ; and may easily be raised from seed, and also multiplied by most careful division, which, however, in fleshy-stocked plants is always best avoided, as no one wants to break up a fine happy clump.

Pleurophyllum speciosum is indeed a splendid plant, though very far away at present from our hopes. For it dwells in the wet places of the Auckland and Campbell Islands, ascending even into their mountains in a dwarf and stunted form, but in the damps making a superb growth of 2 or 3 feet high, its base wrapped in vast corrugated oval leaves like those of *Gentiana lutea*, or like some colossal Plantain, ribbed and vested in silk, with prominent nerves ; then from this goes mounting a stiff spire all set with enormous violet daisies or Senecios, close on the stem in a mace of magnificence, each with a central eye of purple darkness. There is also there a second *Pleurophyllum*, but this one wipes out every other, and is most ardently to be longed for.

Plumbago Larpentae. See **Ceratostigma plumbaginoeides**—by way of a pleasant change of name.

Podanthum.—There are a large number of these plants, and some occasionally stray into the pages of catalogues, where they should, however, as a rule, be allowed to remain undisturbed. For the race is not one of garden value—a sub-group of Campanula, approaching Phyteuma, with clustered small heads of pinched flowers on stems that are often leggy, produced from clumps that are most often biennial. *P. cordatum* is sometimes offered as *Campanula michauxioeides*, and *P. virgatum* as *C. virgata ;* not even under the auguster name are they anything but feeble and spindly biennials. There is no need to go through a string of names unworthy of note ; rather more graceful in their fine stalks and spider-heads of blue are *P. limoniifolium*, *P. anthericoeides*, and *P. leianthum ;* interesting, though monocarpous, is *P. giganteum*, 4 or 5 feet high, carrying its small flowers in a rather dense spike of enormous length—some 2 or 3 feet long, so that the effect is that of a dark-blue snake turned into a plant. *P. lanceolatum* and *P. tenuifolium, P. Otites, P. scoparium* all have the comparative merit of not being more than a foot high : even smaller, and therefore even more hopeful, are *P. lobelioeides* and *P. linifolium*—this last a rare species from the rocks of Taurus and Lycia ; while *P. trichostegium*, from the high-alpine cliffs of Argaeus, in Cappadocia, soars to such a point of ambition as to produce a quite creditable imitation of *Phyteuma hemisphaericum*, alike in flower and stature. All these bloom in early summer and onwards ; all may be raised from seed, and cultivated in any open limy loam in a sunny place.

Podophyllum.—The May-Apples are plants of lush opulent beauty, all for easy culture in deep rich soil in a rather cool place. *P. Emodi* is a stately species of 2 feet high or so, unfurling in the spring large glossy umbrella-shaped leaves on tall stems, marbled and blotched with mahogany and green and pallors, most beautifully ; then, among these, little pearly cups like narrower-petalled blooms of *Paeonia japonica*, each of which is followed in autumn by a huge pendent fruit like an oblong Persimmon, of brilliant scarlet and orange, beloved by birds, but of rich effect if these can be induced to permit.

POLEMONIUM.

On old clumps you may see a dozen at a time, glowing and swaying from the stalks that look so slight to hold them. Even taller is *P. Emodi majus*, and there is now news of yet a third giant provisionally called *P. Leichtlini*. Smaller than these is *P. peltatum*, from America, with leaves more deeply lobed, and flowers more filled with stamens, and fruit of yellowish tone ; but stout and stately are *P. pleianthum*, and *P. versipelle*, both from China, with leaf-lobes very deep, and hanging clusters of rather smaller flowers of dark and dusky red. All these can freely be raised from the seeds that lie buried in the large fleshy pods ; and in time can easily be divided at the end of summer.

Polemonium.—As this alphabet advances towards the appalling shadows of *Primula* and *Saxifraga* now darkening grimly across its path, it is met once more and impeded by many races asking for especial attention. And here is one ; the Jacob's Ladders are so beautiful, so useful, so pleasant and deserving of their general popularity, that they must needs be dwelt with awhile, and have their creases of confusion rolled out and their names set straight. Fortunately culture offers little trouble ; the greater number seed like cresses, and can be grown perpetually in any light open and rather rich loam, not parched or water-logged, where they make a practice of profusely blooming in high summer, and on into its later months, and can at need be taken up in autumn and have their clumps divided and put back again. The race is predominantly American, wholly alpine and sub-alpine, with at least one species not only native to the Old World but extraordinarily pervasive and variable there, in all its mountain chains. The following list contains every species known up to date ; no others are genuine.

P. antarcticum has a stimulating name, but no other merit of any sort.

P. Brandegeei (*Gilia Brandegeei*) comes from Colorado, and there forms a neat tuft of wholly sticky foliage, from which rise unbranched stems of a foot at the most, but usually less, carrying a leafy spire of narrow-tubed golden flowers, with an inch-long, very narrow tube, and a delicious fragrance.

P. carneum is a rather rank grower, but attractive for a remoter corner, where its ferny masses of foliage may have full sway, and its carillons of abundant long flesh-coloured and creamy and rosy bells may hang and sway in full luxuriance without suffering the hurtful challenge of some neat austere alpine. Indeed, so lush is the plant that seed should surely be annually collected.

P. coeruleum ranges over the mountains of the Old World, North, South, East, and West, greatly varying as it goes, in stature, colour, and size of blossom. Our own Jacob's Ladder holds up its head with the best ; a species of sub-alpine copses in the North of England, and eminently able to take care of itself in the garden, and see to its own propagation. The Albino is beautiful too, and the plant called *P. sibiricum* is only a cultivated form of *P. coeruleum*. See Appendix.

P. confertum brings us to a choicer group, where care is asked. It has a vigorously-shooting little stock, creeping across the face of the ground, and emitting tufts of small glandular sticky leaves, composed of countless leaflets tucked and packed together in whorls as it were, till the whole leaf has the effect of a broad fat shoot of Galium. On fine stalks of their own do these wave, but on fine stems of about double their height do the flower-stalks aspire, with a little leaf or so to clothe them, to the height of 6 or 8 inches, and then unfold a very dense head of the most beautiful wide-eyed ample saucer-bells of clear rich blue. It is a treasure from the highest Alps of the Rockies and the Californian Sierra Nevada ; in the garden it wants light and specially well-drained ground, with sufficiency of subterraneous water in early summer as a counsel of perfection ; though it will be quite happy and perennial in a mixture of chips and rich soil, stony almost to the point of being moraine. Unless it can be kept from thirst it will not usually enjoy being sun-burnt excessively, though by no means averse from the light of day. It is one of the loveliest of the whole race, either sticky or smooth, and far preferable to its variety, *P. c. mellitum*, which is so much commoner in gardens and catalogues. This has flowers of a soft bluish-white ; the whole plant is taller and the spike laxer, and the look of brilliancy and distinction diminished,— though by no means destroyed, for the clustered pale tubes of *P. c. mellitum*, in their close ample sprays, have much elegance and charm, though they miss the concision and the clear rich colour of the type— of which, for the rest, it has the needs and habit, though forming more of a clump than the mat into which *P. confertum* will tend to expand if happy. It also smells so violently of beer that, when exhibited, it makes its cultivator an object of deep suspicion in abstaining circles.

P. Ehrenbergii is a spreading species of about 8 inches high from the mountain woods of Mexico, where its branches spread about, carrying two or three very large and bell-shaped yellow flowers at their top.

P. eximium is a taller plant of a foot high from Rio Grande, all clad in glandular down, with leaflets in whorls on the leaves, and un-branching stems that end in a pyramid of golden blossoms, which, however, in the variety *P. e. Lambornii*, are of a livid red.

POLEMONIUM.

P. filicinum is a tall-growing sort after the style of *P. coeruleum*, with no particular distinction of its own.

P. flavum comes from New Mexico, and may be pictured as being a version of *P. coeruleum* with flowers of clear yellow, tinted with mahogany-red outside.

P. foliosissimum is a tall and leafy thing, of the group that is crowded out of the garden by *P. coeruleum*.

P. Gayanum would have no value in any case.

P. grandiflorum is a most stately stalwart branching species from the high Alps of Orizaba in Mexico, between 9000 and 12,000 feet, carrying specially large bells of blossom, lilac or yellow, each almost alone on its foot-stalk.

P. Halleri, from California, stands close in many ways to *P. occidentale*, but is as far as possible removed, not only from this but from all the rest of the race, in that the anthers have hardly any stamens to stand on, but are almost sessile to the base of the flower.

P. Haydeni has no specific rank, and had better be reduced to *P. pulcherrimum*. It has a woody branching stock, and many stems varying from 4 inches to a foot. The leaves are crowded and the leaflets especially numerous, while the tubular blue bells of blossom are no less numerous, too, each half-drooping on its slender foot-stalk.

P. humile.—"There ain't no sich a person." See under *P. lanatum* and *P. pulcherrimum*.

P. lanatum.—This is the rock-garden Queen of the family—a little running spreading mat, with tiny leaves packed with leaflets till they suggest those of some crowded and slender Astragalus ; here and there come up several short stems of 2 or 3 inches or less, unfolding a most lovely bunch of great wide flowers of rich blue, hairy and almost *woolly (like all the rest of the plant)*, gathered in a close cluster. This will want moraine of the best, or, better still, the Gentian-bed. For it is a species of the Arctic region, ranging across the top of America and over far Northern Asia too, developing many different forms, of which *P. l. humile* was figured in the *Bot. Mag.*, T. 2800, as *P. Richardsonii*, as if its own varietal name were not sufficiently likely to create confusions ; as, indeed, do the other ones, *P. l. pulchellum, speciosum, moschatum, boreale*, and *villosum*, all beauties of the most beautiful, tiny alpine growers with heads of enormous round-faced blue blossom, among which, perhaps, for almost stemless dwarfness and undiminished size and brilliancy of blossom, *P. l. humile* may bear away the palm. None, alas, are as yet in cultivation, though.

P. Lemmonei, however, is a high-alpine, hardly less choice and lovely, hailing from 12,000 feet up in the San Francisco mountains

POLEMONIUM.

of Northern Arizona. It makes an erect-growing tuft, *densely glandular-hairy*, and with the leaves as long as the flower-stem or longer. The tubular blue blossoms are packed in huddled heads on a stem of 2 inches or so, and the uprising leaves are built of very very tiny leaflets arranged round their stalk in whorls of four.

P. mellitum. See under *P. confertum.*

P. micranthum has only the credit of honestly proclaiming its worthlessness of little blossom in its name.

P. occidentale can hardly be separated from *P. coeruleum.* The flowers are a trifle smaller as a rule, and vary from white to cream, and then on into violet and deep purple; while the plant forms a short creeping rhizome, sending up unbranching stems.

P. pauciflorum stands about 18 inches high, and has tubular flowers of yellow, with the leaflets not tight-packed upon the leaves.

P. pectinatum is a species of quite special rarity, from the Eastern part of Washington State. It has ferny foliage and yellowish flowers.

P. pterospermum, from Colorado and New Mexico, is weakly in habit, and sends out a number of stems of 4 inches or 8 inches, that lie about spread over the ground, specially leafy and glandular in the upper part, but smooth below. The flowers are purple saucers, half an inch wide, and half an inch deep, carried in dense sprays.

P. " pulchellum " does not exist. See *P. pulcherrimum.*

P. pulcherrimum is the lovely thing that has confused catalogues so sadly. Every garden plant called *P. humile* and *P. pulchellum*, or *P. humile pulchellum*, is nothing but a diminished form of the species *P. pulcherrimum.* The type is a slender, sparingly-branched grower, *minutely sticky*, with stems that vary between 4 inches and a foot, very graceful in their habit, and very numerous, spraying out into clusters of slender-stemmed blue blossoms, *saucer-faced*, and white in the throat, and deeply cleft in the lobe. It is a high-alpine with many varieties, in which *P. p. humile* and *P. p. pulchellum* are included, and differ from it only for the worse, in having markedly smaller flowers. But there is another variety called *P. p. parvifolium*, with the lobes almost uncloven, fine and full, much longer and larger than the tube. *P. pulcherrimum* indeed deserves its name, and in cultivation is as good as it is beautiful; so that, within reason, no decent culture comes amiss to it. *P. p. humile* is the gardener's *P. " Richardsonii."*

P. reptans has *no stickiness at all ;* the leafage is after the pattern of *P. coeruleum,* and the plant forms a widening clump, having a creeping rhizome, but very rarely throwing runners. Its stems are about a foot high, carrying pendent *bell-shaped flowers* of lovely light-blue tone and most dainty design, in loose and delicate showers. It is of perfectly easy culture, especially in rather cooler soils and exposures, and is a darling of slugs. There is an albino, and a form called in gardens *P. himalaicum*, being more rightly to be styled *P. r. himalayanum* (a name which, if not mendacious, means a strange straying of the species from its distribution far away in New York State, Missouri, Minnesota, and Alabama), which is finer even than the type, having larger blooms, though by their deepened colour they lose that lucid flaming note of cool blue that is so lovely alike in *bell-shaped P. reptans* and in the *saucer-faced*, white-throated *P. pulcherrimum*.

P. Richardsonii is a name to be specially guarded against. We have seen that *P. Richardsonii* is a false name for *P. lanatum humile* (which is so good-tempered that it never loses its wool in any of its forms). But *P. humile* is also a varietal name under the shadow of the much larger and woolless *P. pulcherrimum*. What has happened then, is that the two Humiles have got mixed, and catalogues have then continued the mixture by raking in the name Richardsonii and making it a synonym of *P. pulcherrimum's* variety Humile, whereas it was really a *Bot. Mag.* error for *P. lanatum's*; with the result accordingly, that for the name *P. Richardsonii* in all catalogues (and even in authorities so much greater as Count Silva-Tarouca), you will get merely the minor forms of *P. pulcherrimum*. And thankful enough you may well be for them anyhow, for *P. pulcherrimum* in all variations is a hearty, lovely treasure, and the Humile variety earns especial commendation by blooming first of all in April and May, and then again in July and August. So remember: there *is no P. Richardsonii*.

P. rotatum must be invoked from Arctic North America, where it forms a matted tuft, sending up a number of little stems 4 to 6 inches high, striped, and sticky with glands, that break into loose showers of round, open, blue blossoms, very beautiful, and better worth going to Klondyke for than much fine gold.

P. sibiricum. See under *P. coeruleum*.

P. speciosum is a lovely tube-flowered alpine, from Mount Garfield in Colorado, &c., at about 12,000 feet; it is probably a hybrid between *P. pulcherrimum* and *P. confertum*.

P. van Bruntiae lives in the mountain swamps, and is a hairless, glandless stalwart, from 2 to 3 feet tall, with blue flowers.

P. viscosum is a rare and precious high-alpine of the Pacific coast ranges, between 9000 and 12,000 feet; it is a neat, woody-stocked rarity with tiny, tiny leaves made up of tiny, tiny packed leaflets, and erect stems of 3 or 4 inches, all sticky like the leaves, and bearing dense heads of large blue blossoms in the shape of noble expanding trumpets. There is a variety of this, *P. v. Grayanum*, with longer hairs on the calyx among the glands.

Polygala.—The brilliant Milkworts of the Alps have never come to their own in culture, and probably have something ephemeral or ghostly about their rootage. The race is a most crowded, difficult, and complicated one, however, and the eyes of the gardener need not stray far beyond the common English Milkwort that in the mountains develops into a thing of tropical and orchideous gorgeousness, with long spikes of large flowers in the most flaring tones of violet. And there is also a very handsome *P. nicaeensis*, with violet blooms, that ascends to some 2000 feet in the Maritime Alps, and is worth the trowel; as is another Southerner for a wall or sunny, hot place, *P. alpestris*, though the name is so much in dispute, and so indiscreetly shared among different members of the race, that perhaps the gardener had best make his choice with his own eye in the mountains, without troubling the pages of bewildering print. The value of the family, however, finds its high water-mark in *P. Chamaebuxus* and *P. Vayredae*. *P. Chamaebuxus* is universal in all the lighter alpine woodland, with its sheeted carpet of dark little evergreen leaves sparkled over almost all the year by great butterflies of white and yellow, with wings of rose and crimson especially deep after fertilisation, so that in the same flight may be seen a dozen different tones. The type is variable, however, and the Southern and Eastern ranges produce the glorious form, *P. Ch. rhodoptera* or *atropurpurea*, in which the wings are always of the brightest carmine, and the blossoms of size and brilliancy to match. And other forms are sometimes offered by catalogues, *P. Chamaebuxus* having an almost universal distribution throughout the main alpine chains, and being of inordinate abundance, not at the greater elevations, but in the woods and open places lower down. It is extremely unpleasant to collect, wandering far and wide with yards of naked fibre that strike no root; once established, however, it thrives ardently in the garden in sandy peat or loam, whether in sun or shade, to such a pitch indeed as sometimes to be degraded into serving for a border. It should instead be planted in broad drifts for fine bulbs to come up through, and Pyrolas and such old neighbours of the woodland to make common cause with. In course of no long time, too, a garden specimen can be divided, for in cultivation it no longer roams so readily far afield, but forms into neat clumps and close stretches full of rootage that can easily be pulled to pieces. And, in the garden also, the plant does not lose its perpetual wakefulness; even in middest winter some of the golden-winged white butterflies, pink-tipped, are sure to be seen hovering doubtfully

84

over the dark carpet, wondering whether any bee or fly will share their courage, and come by to turn them to a rosy blush with its embraces. As for *P. Vayredae*, this is a neater species yet, from the Sierras of Spain—the most brilliant of all, a prostrate bushlet of an inch or two, with very dark-green narrow leaves, and butterflies of flaming crimson, with a body of gold; it answers to the culture that suits the other; but, being rarer and smaller, should have a more select and prominent place in the sun, with rarer bulbs to come through it, lest it feel their presence an indignity.

Polygonatum.—The Solomon's Seals do not need description, and the times and seasons of their opulent arching sprays and small hanging clusters of greeny-white bells are no less well known than the perfectly ordinary treatment in any ordinary soil that will cause them to flourish and spread. Of larger sorts are *P. biflorum, P. giganteum, P. multiflorum, P. japonicum* (white and pink in the bell), *P. oppositifolium* (pinkish), *P. vulgare*, and tall handsome strange *P. verticillatum* with the narrow leaves in whorls round the stem, a plant of acute rarity in England and Scotland, but not by any means uncommon in the Alpine woods (on the Mont Cenis it abounds in the gypsum-ghylls). Of smaller and choicer species none could be prettier than our own *P. officinale*, that fills the copses under the limestone cliffs in the Yorkshire highlands, and shares the deep cracks of the level scar-limestone pavement higher up with Actaea and Lily of the valley; it is a neat thing, about 8 inches high, and especially stiff-necked. Its solid, pale-green leaflets, folded back in pairs, like the wings of so many butterflies, seem to be settling on a stem strained backwards almost to the point of breaking its spine, the better to hang out from each pair the couple of large, whitish-green bells in which the plant rejoices so openly. Of different habit is little *P. roseum* from the Altai, with sword-pointed leaves of verticillate persuasion, and clusters of smaller rosy-lilac flowers; with another in the same line, *P. graminifolium* from the Himalaya, of the same span-high stature, but with even narrower, more crowded foliage, and purplish bells. These two, being rare, should have a choice place in deep woodland soil in the fringe of woodland, among the Cypripediums, but no such consideration is necessary for the rest.

Polygŏnum.—The rock-garden is no place for the large knot-weeds, gigantic tropical plants for the wilderness only; by the water-side, however, the 3-foot bushes of *P. alpinum* or *P. polystachyon* (falsely called *P. oxyphyllum* or *P. amplexicaule*), beset with clouds or spires of white or pink in high summer, produce a fine effect and ransom the leafiness of the plants' many upstanding shoots; while our own *P. Bistorta* and the American *P. bistortoeides* may wander in wild, wet places, with their poker-spikes of pink on tall, bare stems (and *P. peregrinum* and *P. amplexicaule* are leafier in the same line). And there are others to be found in catalogues. But the rock-garden has its eye on smaller things only, and from this point it may be taken that all species included in its glance are of neater habit, all of the easiest culture anywhere, anyhow, readily to be divided or struck, and usually flowering late in the season.

P. affine (*P. Brunonis*), forms a quite dense wide carpet of almost evergreen narrow leaves, from which, from August to October, rises an interminable succession of neat little clear pink spikes on naked stems of some 6 inches. It is an admirable coverer of the ground, and always gives pleasure, in flower or out of it. (From Kashmir and Kumaon, a high-alpine, up to 13,000 feet.)

P. capitatum flops about with vulgar freedom, and has countless little round pink heads of flower and spotted foliage. Somehow the whole plant, though dwarf enough, has a coarse and ill-bred look, a disproportion of the dimmy orbs to the rank and weedy dull foliage; so that one is consoled for learning that it is half-hardy, and closes one's ears to the murmur that every fragment will strike if potted up.

P. Emodi has the habit and the charm of *P. affine*, but that the leaves are longer and narrower, making much more spindly stars, therefore, as the plant runs over the ground, and throws up its red spikes above a scantier carpet. It should always, in specially inclement places, have a few sprays taken off and potted up in autumn, for it is not so high an alpine as the other, coming from Bhotan and Daghestan, where it is not found above 11,000 feet.

P. equisetiforme (*P. scoparium*) is a most beautiful Corsican species, to be planted on the top of a high sunny cliff. From this it will fall and foam and wave in a great wild surf of innumerable long wiry branches, set with myriads of tiny white flowers, producing an effect of the most bewildering dainty grace in late summer and autumn, suggesting some of the finest tender white-flowered Brooms, but especially airy and delicate in its springy spray, and with the added advantage of being hardy.

P. hayachinense is a Japanese species, of more refined habit than *P. Bistorta*, and, though with the same pink spike on a bare stem, taking a median position between this and the habit of *P. viviparum*.

P. perpusillum is a minute species, in the way of *P. sphaerostachyon*, but a hundred times more attractive. It forms a wee clump of matted wee leaves, very thin and narrow, recurving and smooth at the edge, and almost stemless; then from these are sent up bold little erect stalks that vary between half an inch and an inch and a half, and end in spikes of white or pink flowers, drooping on the stem in their dense mass. It is a high-alpine, from some 14,000 or 15,000 feet in the Himalaya.

P. sphaerostachyon is a species for which high prices are asked, and to which high praise is given. I can understand neither the one nor the other. In my eye the plant is coarse and quite unworthy of pains, and not particularly worthy of cultivation at all. It forms a tuft of leaves like those of *P. Bistorta*, stalked, long, and narrow, and from among these sends up the characteristic spike of its section, on bare stems. The flowers, it is fair to say, are of brilliant pink and borne in autumn, but the stems are 10 inches or a foot high, and there is an utter lack of elegance or breeding about its look. And it is even a liar in its name, for the blossoms are not worn in a ball, but in the usual stodgy oval tail-tip, the whole plant having the weedy lushness with which the charm of so many Knotweeds, such as it is, is tainted. Its one value (I am tempted to believe) is its rarity, which is only owing to the fact that it furnishes no seed and makes no runners, sitting tight in a clump which the pious have too much feeling to divide. It is a Himalayan species from elevations between 11,000 and 13,000 feet.

P. vaccinifolium, however, not only escapes the charge of coarseness to which this race is open, but escapes it so handsomely as to be one of the loveliest and most refined treasures in which the garden rejoices. All the year it is lovely, in any sunny place in good soil, making close carpets and cataracts over the edge of the rocks, with its long, woody trailers, set with narrow, glossy, evergreen little leaves of the heartiest and most immortal appearance ; and then, in autumn, there breaks up, on stems of 2 or 3 inches, so unbelievable a profusion of little rose-pink spikes that the ground and the green below are almost hidden from view ; and when in their midst tower up also the violet wide goblets of *Crocus pulchellus* or *C. speciosus Aitchisoni* among the crowded pink spires, the sight is one to make even the most sedate give tongue. This beauty requires careful propagation by cuttings, and should not be put in too exposed a position in the garden's battlefield, as, though perfectly hardy, it repays a sheltered slope or ledge, and insists on fullest sunshine if it is to repay you with its fullest generosity of flower.

P. viviparum is a meek thing, wholly different from all the rest, not always of very long life, but often appearing in clumps of other things collected abroad, which it benefits rather than harms with the companionship of its neat tuft of long, dark, little leaves rolled over at the edges, from which arises, in May or June, one single stem of 3 inches or so, almost bare, and ending in a long spike of tiny, white, starry flowers, which are replaced, half-way down the stalk, by glossy mahogany bulbils or bulbillules, from which it can at pleasure be propagated. It is an abundant species of the upper alpine meadows, and no less common in the alpine meadows of England, where it occurs, as, for instance, in the fields round the High Force, which so lavishly back up their imitation of alpine pastures by making *Viola lutea*, in colour and abundance, if not in size, take up the rôle of *Viola calcarata* in painting the distances with purple-and-golden veils, amid which stand finely up the little white lances of the *Polygonum*.

Polyschēmōnē nivalis=**Lychnis nivalis,** *q.v.*

Pontederia cordata is a handsome water-plant from North America, for a warm corner in a pool of some 12 or 18 inches deep (that it be fully protected from frost). It throws up swathes of long, glaucous leaves, narrow-oval, at the ends of tall stems ; and then, in very late summer and autumn, 3-foot stalks, with spires of fine blue blossom. If the water be shallow, or the climate cold, bracken should be piled about the roots in winter to keep them safe.

Potentilla.—This race may be said, in a way, to own the privilege of having given birth to this book. Into so swirling and wild a sea does the name plunge us, and with no faintest hint of a lifeline, that my many years of suffering over unannotated lists of Potentillas in catalogues had long made me yearn for some handbook that should cope concisely with these and similar obscurities. Few races are larger, and certainly few more largely quoted. Catalogues are filled with strings of Potentilla-names, stretching out into infinity like the Pharaohs, and each with no more individuality to the uninstructed. In this family, then, where jewels are concealed in such a frippery of worthless brass, how is the gardener to know the one from the other by nature's bare and insufficient guidance ? I turn up M. Correvon's new work, and I read this :—"VI. ; 20 c : jaune vif ; Eur ; I ; 3 "— a most searching problem in algebra, evidently, or Rule of Three, or some other high mystery of mathematics ; but how, out of this unenlightening Abracadabra, is the unenlightened to learn that the species thus compendiously pictured is *P. anserina*, one of the commonest of weeds, and one of the most fatal to admit to the garden ? Yet no race is harder to deal with, for the average is good, and there are many kinds only to be disregarded because they are inferior to the best that they so closely resemble. Yet this generic resemblance is at once the weakness of the race, and the trouble of the describer, who feels that he is called on to diagnose every name, lest he should by chance be missing a good one. Not so we; out of much disappointment and much laborious study, I will first compile a list of such Potentillas as seem secondary or tertiary in their claims for admittance to the garden; and then we will proceed to sift the rest. It may well be that the list will contain some plants upon whom such a condemnation unjustly rests; but it will, probably, also be found on experiment that they are not, even if as good, any better than some species such as *P. alpestris* which have the first claim, and which the discarded cousins so closely resemble that the garden which finds room for the one would be overcrowded if it began to include all the species that take after it. For if few families are so large, also few are so unoriginal and repetitive; every country has a range of Potentillas representing a similar range across the border, separated indeed by sufficient botanical differences, yet all in a ruck of demerit for the garden; yet all no less paraded in full catalogues of the species, to the undoing of the wretched gardener who has no inner light of knowledge to tell him by instinct what to choose, yet at present no help from outside to save him from putting his last half-crown on what has looked like a dark horse indeed in a list, but soon turns out to have been an absolute wrong 'un. Here, then, is a provisional list of such Potentillas as it may possibly prove useful and even helpful to avoid : *PP. bifurca, coriandrifolia, sericea, desertorum, kashmirica, pteropoda, monanthes, Clarkei, Mooniana, Griffithii, leuconota, peduncularis, glomerata, viridescens, diversifolia, decurrens, glaucophylla, Nuttallii, gracilis, glutinosa, fissa, glandulosa, pseudorupestris, arguta, Convallaria, flabelliformis, pinnatisecta, Meyeri, mollissima, de Tommasii, collina, lazica, heptaphylla, opaca, adenophylla, Bungei* (many of these last being nice things, but inferior to *P. verna*), *pannosa, radiata, argyroloma, nuda, geranioeides* (secondary to *P. alpestris*), *pimpinelloeides, poteriifolia, elvendensis, sericea, argaea, hirta, recta, inclinata, pennsylvanica.* So is the ground encumbered for the gardener's feet; not all of these are weeds absolute, but certainly weeds comparative by the side of the best; and the best, the best alone, is what the wise gardener alone has room for, when it comes to coping, in ground not conterminous with wide earth, with a race so enormous yet so monotonous as this of the Potentillas. And now, here follows a brief annotated list of the more possible species —very many more are to be found in some very catholic lists, but whether more possible or not who shall say? For the lists don't. See Appendix.

P. adjarica, 8 inches, with yellow flower. No special use.

P. agrimonioeides, of half the height and half the use.

POTENTILLA.

P. alba, a valuable species with large grey spreading tufts, like those of a glorified silvery-smooth *P. Fragariastrum:* and pleasant showers of white small blossoms all the summer, more or less hovering among the leaves. A pretty and useful rambling plant developing into a wide mass, but never a weed.

P. alchemilloeides is like an *Alchemilla alpina*, as its name justly tells us, but glorified beyond all recognition, with finely-fingered and long-stalked foliage, silky all over, and sheening white below, from which come spraying far above the foliage gracious stems of 6 inches or a foot, with diverging clusters of large and in a long succession through the summer lovely pure-white flowers about an inch and a half across. It belongs solely to limestone cliffs and screes of the central and Western Pyrenees, on both sides of the range, and is a species of special beauty and value : and easy of culture in the sunny rock-garden.

P. alpestris brings us into a confused land. This is a most handsome thing, too, and common in the alpine pastures—more or less low-lying, with showers of very large golden-yellow flowers, usually with an orange blotching at the base. Its false names are *P. salisburgensis*, Haenkel ; and *P. maculata*, Pourr ; or *P. aurea*, Sm. (not Linnaeus, *q.v.*). But it *may* be no more than a luxuriant and splendid mountain form of our own *P. verna*. (It is also found in Teesdale.) But from all forms of *P. verna* it may be known by its greater size and brilliancy, alike of growth and of blossom ; while from *P. aurea*, L., it can easily be distinguished by having a number of *five-fingered stalked leaves in a basal rosette or tuft*, while *P. aurea* has but a pair (or none at all at flower-time), and those *glossy*, while the leaves of *P. alpestris are always quite dull on their surfaces*. It is of the easiest culture in light open soil in full sun, where it produces a prostrate profusion of its wide golden blooms in loose showers from midsummer far on into the season.

P. ambigua is a truly precious Indian species that runs freely about, and yet never makes itself a nuisance, with its tufts of greyish-green leaves and big golden suns on stems of an inch or two all through the season, produced in profusion in any open and reasonable place, where the neat little rambling runner may have ungrudged room to wander.

P. anserina.—No, no, no. Though many a new Chinese weed at seven-and-six has flowers far less beautiful than those of the common Goose-weed, to say nothing of its plumed silvery leaves and its extra-nutritious tubers, as delicate as new potatoes, when washed and boiled.

P. apennina is a very choice rock-tuffet, with sprays of golden blossom in early summer. Its chief charm, however, lies in its stalked leaves, which are solid, wedge-shaped trefoils, cut into teeth almost straight across the end of each, and all clothed in the closest plating of fine silver, that shimmers and shines again in the sun. As in all this group, *P. apennina* is of the easiest culture in decent soil and in open, sunlit positions. In fact it may be taken that, except where cultural notes are given for Potentilla, none are needed.

P. arbuscula is a 6-inch bushling in exile from Siberia, with yellow flowers in later summer.

P. argentea.—A tall, common, and valueless English weed with small yellow blossoms, which tries to impose itself on the unwary with its seductive title.

P. arguta is another tall species from America, with yellow stars. And it may be taken as axiomatic, as far as the rock-garden is concerned (apart from the border and so forth), that the taller-growing Potentillas, with the rarest exceptions, have little value, their growth being so heartrendingly lush and untidy, that even if the flowers here and there be fine, they cannot outweigh the length of stem and leafy straggliness of habit.

P. argyrophylla is yet another of these, without place in the rock-garden, though here again the description of the beautiful silver leaves does not belie them. This includes yet another plant of even larger and leafier habit, *P. atrosanguinea*, which differs chiefly in having blood-red blossoms—produced, however, in such a way as to give this original variant no more value than the rest, though it is a good border-plant for those who do not object to large straggling growth and partial displays: it has freely hybridised with others of the big species, including *P. nepalensis*. And there is also a variety, *P. a. Gibsoni*, which has stars of light scarlet, instead of the deep blood-colour of the type, which, for the rest, like all these larger sorts, blooms on from summer into the later months.

P. aurea must be remembered and guarded against in the Alps, as being a diminished *P. alpestris*, always to be known by the fewer leaves and the smaller habit and flower, the leaves being five-lobed as in the other and very nervy, *but velvety at the edge*, hairy underneath, and on the upper surface *bright shining grass-green*. It has every claim, however, to a good place in the rock-garden or moraine, for it is very beautiful and gay in its decumbent showers of golden blossoms, orange at the base; and only differs from the other, to the gardener's eye, by their lesser size. The two species, moreover, are found to be rather shadowy in the field, and, either by hybrids, or by intergrading forms, seem often to melt into each other.

POTENTILLA.

P. baldensis is a little white-flowered thing that makes no claim.

P. calabra is a variety of *P. argentea*, with decumbent stems and the leaflets canescent only above, but hoary below, divided, fan-shape, into narrow strips. It follows, a dullness of little value.

P. canadensis.—Say no.

P. carniolica.—A 3-inch grower of the Eastern Alps, with flowers declared to be of pinkish-white in April. To be seen before purchase.

P. caulescens is not an uninteresting or unworthy species, although not among the most showy. In the limestone rocks of all the Eastern ranges it forms wide mats of five-fingered, stalked leaves, grey and silky and silverish, and from the thick crown summer elicits a great number of stems some 5 or 6 inches high, that contrive on the ashy plant to make a pretty effect, spraying this way and that, though the petals of the many white flowers are narrow and starry, showing the sepals in between, and thus giving a greenish tone to the inflorescence, which deprives it of any brilliancy it might have had. It is of the easiest culture anywhere on lime (or anywhere else, probably).

P. chrysantha is yellow, and 2 feet high.

P. chrysocraspeda stands quite close to *P. aurea*, but the leaves are always *in three leaflets* and *clad in silk*, which distinguishes it from its larger relations *P. aurea*, *P. alpestris*, and *P. gelida*. The stems are short and fine and hairy and depressed, with big bright-yellow flowers, and golden silk to the edge of the leaves and on their ribs beneath. (From the Alps of the Levant, Macedonia, &c.)

P. cinerea should not be trusted. It is minute in flower as in growth.

P. Clusiana takes high rank among the noblest of beautiful alpine plants, forming a pendant to the glorious *P. nitida*. It is in the far Eastern limestone cliffs that this rare species at last appears, hanging from the rock like *P. nitida* in huge wide mats of foliage that are only just a trifle less silvery. The flower-clusters, however, are leafier and longer, and carry more flowers above a looser-looking mass, and the *leaves themselves are five-fingered* instead of three-fingered as in *P. nitida*. The blossoms themselves are large and full in the segment as Nitida's, and of a pure milk-white; shining from afar in their clusters over the clump, rather than sheeting it in a dense constellation as in *P. nitida*. As it has much the same habit, however, so it has the same temper: the chosen mat upon the mountains should be broken from its woody great root at the neck, and laid in sand; by the next spring it will have made new fibres, and may be planted out in any good crevice in any sunny situation in any good open soil, though lime is especially indicated for almost all the saxatile Potentillas.

P. concinna (*humifusa*) is another species poured out upon the ground, with the leaves in fives, and white on the under side.

P. corsica is *P. rupestris pygmaea, q.v.*

P. crassinervia makes a very pretty rock-plant, clad in sticky down, with five-lobed, scalloped leaves, and stems of 6 inches, more or less, with sprays of golden blossom, which are much finer than in *P. nivalis*, which otherwise in some ways *P. crassinervia* recalls, though it has *five-lobed leaves* and a definite aversion for the limestone, to which *P. nivalis* is more or less partial, while *P. crassinervia* haunts the high granites of Corsica, and there develops a quite squat peak-form called *P. c. viscosa*, which makes scabs of stickiness in the topmost cliffs and ridges.

P. crinita is a golden-flowered American of a foot high or more.

P. dahurica is a small Siberian bush of a foot and a half or so, in the way of *P. fruticosa*, but finer and straggly in growth, with twisted sprays and yellowish bloom.

P. delphinensis is a tall yellow-flowered species of 18 inches or more from the Western Alps.

P. deorum, from the rocks of the Thessalian Olympus, imitates the lovely silvered style of *P. apennina*, but improves upon it by having showier white blossoms, of ampler and longer petal, gathered in heads of three or five, on graceful almost bare stems of a few inches that emerge from the silver-sheening tufts of foliage.

P. effusa is large and yellow and American.

P. elatior is merely a larger Strawberry in general effect.

P. eriocarpa lives on the high frontiers of Tibet, at some 14,000 feet. It has a very few trefoiled leaves, bright-green, and cut again and again; and then a number of notably graceful stems that vary from 2 inches to 18, floppeting finely about, and each spray carrying a single splendid golden flower about an inch and a half across.

P. Fenzlii is quite microscopic, and with little yellow stars of no value.

P. formosa. See *P. nepalensis.*

P. fragiformis calls up the Strawberry again to mind, and is an American species, with 8-inch stems, and sprays of white blossom all through the summer and autumn.

P. Friedrichseni is a hybrid between *P. fruticosa* and *P. dahurica*. The result is the loveliest of neat wee crabbed bushes, with stiff depressed arms, and fine foliage that leads to very little else, for the plant is so pleased with its habit as to think there is no need for it to do anything else. Accordingly not a flower does it usually put forth.

However, it is justified of its opinion, and suits especially well with the moraine, stiffly weeping in a dome, and looking like some ancient pride of Japan some 8 or 10 inches high at the most, and never seeming to grow any more.

P. frigida is minute and valueless and yellow ; and universal in the high Alps.

P. fruticosa may be seen in rich glory filling the sandy banks of Tees with deep boskets and coppices of its neat shrubs, bespattered all the summer through with royal golden flowers. Plants of this are best bought and put in their places and there left alone to grow into masses 3 or 4 feet high and as much across, glittering with stars of gold, and now and then cut back into shape in winter should the bush grow bare and leggy with age. *P. fruticosa* is the type of a very large number of similar beautiful bushes, and has itself an enormous range over Europe, Asia, and America, while of late days many fresh developments in the way of it have come to us out of the mountains of Central China. Such are *P. Veitchii,* which seems a small and low-growing neat bush of straight branches, with profusion of large lovely white blossoms and silvered foliage ; silvered, too, and white in the blossom, but erect in its growth is *P. Vilmoriniana;* and there are white-starred forms officially allowed to *P. fruticosa* itself, as well as a thing called *P. floribunda*, which is much the same, but more procumbent in habit, with special abundance of rather paler yellow flowers. And every season, without doubt, will now bring us more names and more, out of prize-packets from China. Every form in the group is of the easiest culture in any good open loam. And see Appendix.

P. fulgens is a high Indian alpine, tall in the stem and lush in the leaf, with blossoms of golden yellow.

P. gelida stands near *P. alpestris*, and can only be separated by minute differences from *P. grandiflora*, but that its stems are shorter and slenderer, carrying a loose shower of large bright-golden flowers from a central tuft of rather long-stalked basal leaves, trefoiled and hairyish and soft and green, with the lobes deeply and coarsely toothed. It is almost universal across the Northern hemisphere.

P. geoeides has the basal leaves, which are softly sticky-hairy, made up of some four to eight pairs of leaflets, in the way of *P. anserina ;* the stems are hardly longer than they, about 6 inches in length, and the blossoms are yellow with persisting petals in erect, branching, forking sprays.

P. geranioeides from the East is very small and early and yellow.

P. glandulosa from the Mediterranean region is very large and lush and yellow.

POTENTILLA.

P. gracilis, though fine in the 6-inch stem and golden in the star, establishes no special claim upon our place or purse.

P. grammopetala is an Italian, of nearly a foot high, with white-petalled but not very effective blossoms.

P. grandiflora may often be seen in the hot alpine turf of the high pastures. It may always be told at a glance from all forms of *P. aurea* and *P. alpestris,* in that all the leaves are *lobed in threes* not in fives, the three lobes being broad and oval and coarsely sharp-toothed, soft and hairy and lax, until they are like those of some small bright-green Strawberry, instead of having the stiffer alchemilloid look of the others. The stems are bare and hairy and erect, about 6 inches or a foot high, branching into sprays of large flowers of brilliant golden yellow.

P. Haynaldiana comes quite close to *P. valderia,* but has its leaves narrower and smooth on the upper surface, though forming into the same heavy foliose masses, from which rise the same tall, leafy, branching, erect stems of 2 feet or so, which carry heads of blossom even inferior to those of *P. valderia,* with the sepals and petals alike a great deal more starved into strips. (Rocky places in the Balkans.)

P. Hippiana, from America, has pinnate silvery leaves, and yellow flowers on 6-inch stems; not a species of outstanding merit.

P. hirta is tall and rather coarse and worthless, with yellow flowers, on stalks of nearly 2 feet high, from June till August.

P. intermedia stands close to *P. pyrenaica,* but the leaves have *seven* lobes and are on specially long foot-stalks.

P. lanuginosa makes a curling, quirling, tangled bush like *P. dahurica,* very slow indeed in growth, but attaining with years to some 2 feet or so. It shines with lovely leafage of silky-woolly silver, and has large golden blossoms late in the summer.

P. Leschenaultiana is hardly worth the lockjaw provoked by its name, for it is a large robust and coarse weed from India.

P. libanotica forms trunky masses in the limestone cliffs of Lebanon; a glandular-hairy thing, with the whitish flowers serried in a corymb, and their petals longer than the calyx.

P. microphylla is a variable Himalayan species, of which the high-alpine forms have distinct charm, for they are so massed and minute that the little feather-lobed leaves are indecipherable, and on the hard lichenous mass the solitary golden stars sit almost close.

P. minima has no merit at all. Its microscopic flowers are yellow.

P. montenegrina grows a foot high, but also has yellow flowers.

P. Mooniana has the notoriety of little worth; sprays of profuse tiny yellow stars all through the later summer.

POTENTILLA.

P. multifida may easily be recognised in the high non-calcareous pastures of the Southern Alps by its little cottony-white leaves, which are feathered and cut again and again into a number of small straight toothless oblong strips. The branching cottony stems are about 5 or 6 inches high, or less, but the yellow flowers have no special interest or brilliancy or size.

P. nepalensis (*P. formosa*) makes a large lax tangle with lush soft silky leafage and straggling flower-stems of 2 feet or so in later summer. All this, however, has to be forgiven for the sake of the blossoms, which are big (though not outweighing the mass of the growth), and of brilliant rose-crimson. It is, however, banished finally from the rock-garden by its variety *P. n. Willmottiae*, which is really a most glorious form, having flowers of the same amplitude, but of a more resplendent and lucent vivid tender rose, on stems of 8 inches or half a foot, straggling indeed this way and that, but so exactly balancing the silky foliage that the mass has a neatness of port which makes it no less precious in the upper ledges than do its lovely bright-faced flowers that stare down in so serene a blush, making a specially beautiful combination with the paler flesh-toned cups of *Geranium lancastriense*, and the lavish china-blue bells of *Campanula haylodgensis*, all filling their ledge or bed with a simultaneous chorus of beauty from July far on into November, the Potentilla being the last stayer in the race. It comes true from seed (or might even vary excitingly), and can be otherwise multiplied by cuttings or division in spring.

P. nevadensis in the great altitudes of the Sierra Nevada grows in compact grey-green tufts an inch or two high, and in May emits a quantity of fine prostrate shoots 3 or 4 inches long, and liberally beset with three or four lovely orbed flowers of brilliant yellow. It is a delightful species in the garden, too, where it does the same thing handsomely, like all the others, in light loam and a sunny place. There is also a most beautiful higher alpine form yet, called *P. n. condensata*, which has the same display, but on much tighter tufts, shining with a coat of pure and gleaming silver.

P. nitida, however, is the glory of the race. All over the Eastern limestone at high altitudes, it forms huge mats and masses and carpets of small trefoiled foliage, purely silver and grey ; or hangs out in huge ancient curtains from its woody trunk in the stark limestone cliffs of the Grigna, Baldo, or the Boé. (I have only once seen it on non-calcareous rock—one small and pallid-flowered mangy tuft, sad and in exile, on the granites of the Cima Torsoleto above the Val Camonica.) And then, as if that refulgent moonlit carpet were not enough, it covers all the mass with a close constellation of vivid rose-pink dog-roses, peppered singly over the sheet in such profusion as only to give a hint of the silver shimmering here and there beneath, till all the dunes of the Forcella Lungieres in August and September are filmed with pink wherever a grey cloak of Potentilla has been laid over the rippled silt of the ridge. It varies readily, however, and there are pallid forms of less worth by comparison with the refulgent rich roses of the best. Nor is the pure-white form at all uncommon ; but, though a lovely thing, it is no improvement on the blood-heats of the type, and seems to trench a little on the domain of *P. Clusiana*, which that pearly beauty is perfectly well qualified to occupy for itself without interference. (It differs in having *cinq-foil* leaves and taller stems, with a *loose* allowance of blossom.) *P. nitida* is often desperately hard to collect, owing to the sheer trunked woodiness of its one and only root, more concentrated in the sole tap than are the more liberally-fibred though still tap-rooted masses of *P. Clusiana*. Nor will *P. nitida* root quite so readily from the broken cushion. It should, however, be quested from the high level ridges where it makes carpets in the gravel ; for there the mat forms more and more woody trunks to each cluster as it spreads, and these trunks are stimulated by the clammy silt into sending out a few subsidiary threads. Wads, then, should be thus taken, and sent home, and laid in sand. By the spring they will have formed so pleasant a number of hungry new threads that they will be glad to move out of the sand-bed into some sunny crevice of good light loam, where they will at once set to work, growing and spreading to such good effect that by the summer's end they will have formed a curtain over the rock, or filled your crevice with a hearty reminiscence of the Drei Zinnen Ridge. And, if ever these cushions are slack in flower, it will be because the fatness of the soil has sent the plant into so sybaritic a sleep that, like many of the soddenly rich, it has lost care for the continuation of the race. It should then be put into poorer stuff, and have its root tight-squashed between the stones of adversity, which will cause it once more to blossom like the rose it resembles. Catalogues offer various forms, including the white one, and another which they call *atrorubens*. The two finest of all blushers, however, that have met my eyes, are a pair of tussocks that passionately flamed against their cold white wall, at the laden end of a cold and cheerless day of winds as cutting as the words of the wicked. These have not lost their radiance in more kindly conditions, and stand (for I do not love the multiplication of Latin varietal names), as *Autumn Sunset* and *Rose of Dawn*—beauties no less hearty in habit than the type, but larger in the flower, and of that especial brilliancy of flaming pure pink which claimed my reluctant labours on that bitter day.

cultivation *P. nitida* blooms perpetually from **June to August** if well suited, though not always in the same high pressure of blossom that it shows here in early summer (whereas on the Alps it is never at its best until August is in, and even over).

P. nivalis is rather a liar, not having quite such an addiction to snow as its name would import. It is at high levels, but not the highest, that the plant will be found in the rocky places of the French ranges. It is a woody, woolly and herbaceous species in the way of *P. valderia*, with tufts of long-stemmed leaves from the base, made up of five or seven lobes very broadly oval, toothed at the tips, and green and velvety on both faces. The shaggy stems are set with narrower trefoils, and are some 4 to 12 inches high, carrying (in summer, like all this section : the Verna-group belongs to June) a head of rather baggy and bell-shaped flowers of creamy-white, with the sepals longer than the petals, and projecting from between each of them in pointed green rays.

P. nivea, however, is a far worse species, and a far worse liar, having neither any resemblance to snow, nor any inclination to live near it. It is a common-looking little underbred plant, with trefoiled leaves, often not lobed to the base, greyish-green above, and greyish-white below. The stems, almost bare, are some 5 or 6 inches high, carrying a few little yellow stars of no size or brilliance. It has nothing to do with the group of the last, but is an inferior and widespread infester of all the great Northern ranges, in the kinship of *P. grandiflora*, but *quantum mutata ab illâ*.

P. nudicaulis comes from the high Alps of Cappadocia, where it makes a dense stock and sends out numbers of fine naked stems, with showers of beautiful blossoms as large as in *P. aurea*, but of pure white.

P. pedemontana is an early-summer bloomer, with golden-yellow flowers and stems of about a foot. It makes no especial claim.

P. peduncularis should have the treatment of a pestilence.

P. pennsylvanica should share it.

P. petiolulata belongs to the limestone crevices of the Eastern Alps, and stands quite close to *P. caulescens*, from which, however, it differs in being clad in hairy stickiness, instead of downy silk ; the lobes of the cinq-foil leaves are broader, and the three middle ones are hardly notched at the tip, or only slightly.

P. pulvinaris is a beautiful little close high-alpine tuffet, from the Cilician Taurus, forming dense rosetted masses of silky-downy small cinq-foils, toothed in the lobes ; and emitting from these a number of thread-fine stems, each bearing perhaps a couple of large bright-golden flowers.

P. pygmaea. See under *P. rupestris*.

POTENTILLA.

P. pyrenaica is an intimate relation of *P. aurea* and *P. delphinensis.* From *P. aurea* and *P. alpestris* it differs in that the stems are thrown out from the *lateral axils* of the stock, instead of from the centre of the crown ; and the rosette-leaves are living at the time, instead of being dead as they often are in the others when the flower-stalks emerge. The whole growth is weaker than *P. delphinensis,* floppier and smaller ; the stems only rise up after creeping, instead of standing straight from their birth ; the lower leaves are five-lobed, but the lobes are narrower and often do not run to the base, oval-pointed in outline, and scalloped along their edges ; instead of being very ample, obovate, and deeply toothed all round. *P. pyrenaica,* finally, is truer to its name than many rivals that bear it, and is found only in the Pyrenees. The flowers are large and golden as in all this group, one or two to the stems, that may be 4 inches long or 18.

P. recta.—No. It is a coarse thing, yellowish-flowered and poor.

P. reptans, a lovely but devastating English weed, with a double form as rampageous as the type.

P. Reuteri is a Spanish high-alpine, of very much the same beauty and charms as *P. nevadensis,* to which it is extremely closely allied.

P. rubricaulis is a red-stemmed, white-flowered species of 2 or 3 inches from the high Alps of North America, where it also takes a yet smaller impoverished form in *P. r. depauperata.* The leaves are feathered, not fingered, in a tuft, and white-felted underneath, while the blossoms are produced on few-flowered sprays in opposite pairs.

P. rupestris makes a complete change for our eyes. For this, from its hard crown makes a spraying mass of long leaves, each made up of toothed oval leaflets in pairs at rare intervals, and a longer, larger, oval-pointed lobe at the end ; these sprout gracefully from the stock, and in the middle rises a tall and gracefully-branching erect stem of 12 inches, more or less, breaking in summer into a loose fountain of fine white flowers. It may be seen here and there in the Alps, but never at alpine elevations, and almost always on warm limestone rocks or in their crevices. And there are one or two most secret spots in Great Britain where its delicate sprays may be seen waving. In the garden it is as hearty as the worst weed among its kindred, and beautiful no less in the grace of its port and the clear whiteness of its large blooms in late summer, than in the reddish-bronzed tone often assumed by the stems and foot-stalks. In Corsica, moreover, *P. rupestris* has taken a strange and precious development. For it is here in the high Alps, either of lime or granite, that it varies into the minutely-dwarf form which is sent out by catalogues as *P. pygmaea,* being in reality *P. rupestris var. pygmaea,* a neat and most exquisite thing of an inch

99

or two in height, with the grace of foliage and habit of its parent, unaltered except in actual size, and with the beauty of the blossom unimpaired, so that it is fit for choicer places than the grandeur of *P. rupestris* will suit, and flowers also through late summer into autumn.

P. Salessowii is a woody bush, with fine large foliage, glossy and finely leafleted. But the flowers are not always common, and when they come are not particularly desirable ; being very big indeed, but with the white petals so narrow that all the sepals are shown and predominate, and make the whole wide star of dullish-green effect. (Starve it : it hails from river-shingles of North Tibet.)

P. salisburgensis = P. alpestris, q.v.

P. sanguisorbaefolia is an 8-inch species with yellow flowers and no especial value, from South Europe.

P. Saxifraga is a rare and beautiful little treasure very seldom seen in cultivation, but very abundant in its district, where, from all the limestone cliffs of the Roja Valley or the Vésubie, it hangs from the rock in masses like clumps of dead bats or abandoned swallows' nests. It forms, as may be pictured, hard tight cushions of small cinq-foil leaves, leathery and dark and shining above, silver-white beneath ; and from this cushion spray out thread-fine stems of an inch or two, in endless number, each carrying a few delicate white stars of blossom, not very large, but specially dainty and pretty in their multitudinous effect when they all break into bloom in early summer. It should have the treatment, though it cannot claim quite the glory, of *P. nitida* and *P. Clusiana*.

P. saximontana comes from the Alps of Colorado, where this also forms tight tufts, but the small leaves are feathered and not fingered, though they have the same silky reverse ; the stems are hardly 2 inches long, bearing two or three fine flowers of ample petals.

P. Seidlitziana is beautiful, a plant closely akin to *P. chrysocraspeda*, from the Alps of Russian Armenia, which, from its close-trefoiled tuft, emits stems of 2 or 3 inches, bearing blossoms as large and full and golden as in *P. aurea*, but with the outer segments of the calyx cut into three quite blunt little lobes.

P. speciosa has its chief beauty in its foliage. For the leaves are of a rare loveliness : stalked trefoils of goodly shape, notably thick and firm and fleshy, toothed round their generous ovals, and all gleaming and shimmering under the sun in a pure smooth coat of silver. The flowers are not always freely produced from among the waving stout-stocked tuffets of foliage, and their lack is not greatly felt, for they are of a creamy-white not especially distinguished, though of reasonably good size. They are borne in a rather dense long head, and their petals, though more or less exceeding the sepals, are narrow and grooved, and contract to a claw at the base, while at the top of their narrow length they expand suddenly into a definite rounded lobe, so that each petal has rather the outline of an infinitesimal salt-spoon. It is a plant of calcareous hot crevices all through South-eastern Europe from Dalmatia to the Levant.

P. splendens is not so good as all that. It is a whitish-flowered species with flowers two to a spray, on stems of 4 or 5 inches, and in themselves about half an inch across, produced in April. The leaves, however, have the beauty of silver plate. It is in the kinship of *P. nivalis*, and therefore well worth the growing. But its name is an unfair handicap, and provokes a disappointment from which the plant unjustly suffers.

P. stolonifera comes from Kamchatka and has the habit of *P. fragarioeides*, but with white flowers of twice the size.

P. subacaulis makes a neat golden-flowered tuffet of ash-grey leaves, which are ample wide-spread small trefoils, toothed all round their lobes, while their stem emerges from the oddest two-horned wing-flaps that contract below the horns and then widen out again, so that the effect is rather as if the leaf-stem lay under the fore-quarters of an earwig with unclenched pincers.

P. subpalmata hugs the cliffs of Ararat, forming tufts of tiny leaves, in two little pairs of leaflets. The stems hardly get clear of the cushion, and the flowers are large for the minute scale of the mass.

P. Thurberi is a large American species, lax and lush and in the way of *P. nepalensis* alike in habit and in blood-coloured flowers.

P. Tonguei is a treasure of the garden, whatever be its history. It makes a dark cinqfoiled mass of tufts, near *P. reptans* in the leaves, though they are larger and more solid ; wide clumps are formed, and ramifying masses, from which, all through the later summer, spring numbers of large flowers on stems of 3 or 4 inches, in a delicious shade of apricot colour, deepening to a crimson suffusion at the base of each petal. It runs about happily in the sun in any light rich soil that is not arid or torrid, and is a thing of the greatest charm and value.

P. tridentata makes a neat small bush after the style of *P. fruticosa*, but about a foot high, beset with white blossoms, and often to be measured rather by the inches of one hand.

P. uniflora recalls *P. nivea*, but is altogether a marked improvement on that dowdy weed, having flowers of twice the size, sitting lonely over a close dense mat of trefoils. It is a rare species from great elevations in the Rockies, and away North to the Arctic regions.

POTENTILLA.

P. valderia is yet another whited sepulchre. In the hot rocky places below the Baths of Valdieri it may be seen earning its name, and making masses of the most lovely silver foliage, large and regal, of stalked leaves waving in jungles from the silky crowns of the tuft, and made up of some five or seven wedge-shaped oval toothed lobes, velvety on both sides, and of an inimitable sheen. July calls up the flower spikes, which lead one to expect a loveliness to match that foliage. But alas, Potentilla is often niggardly of its beauties, and is rarely guilty of so double a generosity as in *P. nitida* and *P. Clusiana*. The stem of *P. valderia* comes up tall and stout and leafy, 18 inches high, as a rule, and bearing crowded branching heads of blossom. And when those flowers open, the white petals prove so narrow that the ample long green sepals stand out and show on every side, so that the general effect of the inflorescence is of dull greying green that by no means redeems the leafiness and lush amplitude of the flower-stems, and goes far to discount the superlative merit of the foliage. The species is a most rare one ; abounding in the Valdieri valleys in the hot stony tumbles of granite and porphyry, and then not seen again till you get to the Balkan provinces. It must have full sun, and light stony soil of ample depth ; and the garden will not go into mourning if the flower-stems be nipped off betimes, so as to allow full play to the noble glistering clumps of silver foliage.

P. verna cannot well be distinguished from *P. alpestris*, which is its magnified mountain form. Therefore divide the description of *P. alpestris* by a third, and the result will give a picture of *P. verna*, but that the beautiful abundant blossoms on their many fine branching flopping sprays are not only smaller, but also of an undiluted, clearer, lighter golden yellow in early summer, *without* orange spotting at their base. It is a most variable type, however, and has a very wide range, occurring here and there all over England in isolated specimens, and particularly refulgent as you sometimes see it in the Yorkshire highlands from afar, lighting up the cold grey wall of a limestone cliff in June with a blotch of gleaming yellow light.

P. villosa is a foot-high plant from America, whose stature is con-doned (like that of many, no doubt, in the preliminary list of super-fluities) by specially brilliant heads of clean golden flowers springing from June to August above neat tufts of foliage clothed in a vesture of long tawny silk.

P. viscosa. See under *P. crassinervia*.

P. Visiani is said to have a stem of 8 inches, and bright yellow stars in June.

P. Woodfordii has an unknown history, but is an old rare garden-plant, making exquisitely neat small cushions of bright-green trilobed foliage about 2 inches high ; and then in May (and on spasmodically through the year), profusely generous with half-inch flowers of clear golden yellow, delightful in themselves as in the freedom with which they are ejected in showers on their fine stems in a quite dwarf cloud like that of some concise and alpine form of *P. verna*. It thrives anywhere in the sun, like most of the rest, and is readily divided at pleasure in the spring or autumn, deserving a choice foreground place, alike for its small matted habit and its beautiful generosity of blossom.

Poterium. See under **Sanguisorba.**

Pratia, a small Campanulaceous family, from New Zealand and the Himalaya, to be distinguished from Lobelia by producing a berry and not a capsule. They should all have a sheltered place in soil rather moist in summer, and very sandy and well drained. Here they will run about and form close dense carpets of green studded with flowers all the season through, and followed by large coloured fruits in autumn. They should not always be looked on as so invariably hardy as to lure the gardener into leaving all his Pratias in the one basket of the garden through the winter ; but pieces of each should be cut off and potted up securely, no less to increase the stock than to guarantee it. *P. arenaria* is the ugliest, with coarse and thin-textured toothed little pale-green leaves, and flowers of a starved spideriness insufficient to make any good effect. Another comparatively unworthy one is *P. begoniaefolia*, from the Himalaya, with roundish hairy foliage, and flowers less pretty than usual, followed by purple berries. And yet another worthlessness is *P. montana*. But when we turn to the rest there is no room for anything but praise of their neat carpets starred with flights of delicate lilac-and-white Lobelias. *P. perpusilla* is especially minute, forming dense patches, a few inches wide, of microscopic foliage, close upon which appear the blossoms from the axils of the shoots. *P. angulata* forms a mat of fleshy oval little leaves, waved and coarsely-toothed, from which springs a great number of long starry white flowers. *P. ilicifolia* has larger and more roughly-toothed leaves, and Lobelias larger also and more solid, though no less white. And *P. macrodon* breaks the record of the family, forming, in the Alps of the South Island, matted patches nearly a foot across, of roundish wedge-shaped fleshy foliage, roughly and coarsely toothed, which is a setting for a profusion of flowers springing almost stemless from the axils, and covering the carpet with conspicuously long-tubed yellow stars of broad spreading rays and delicate fragrance, most curiously swollen at the base of the tube.

Prenanthes is a strange group of Composites, hardly to be recognised as such, but seeming, in the typical instance of *P. purpurea*, from the alpine woods, as if an oat had gone mad and swung out in purple ears. This is the style of the family, which is not showy, but easily to be cultivated in any worthless out-of-the-way place on the cool side of the rock-garden, or under its worst bushes ; where all will look delicate and quaint, when their tall stems of a yard or so have pierced the boscage in July and August, and above the leaves float out their loose sprays of fine purple ears. There are many other species too, especially from the Indian Alps ; as, for instance, *P. khasiana*, *P. Brunoniana*, *P. violaefolia* (small and neat and slender), *P. Hookeri*, *P. sikkimensis*, and *P. scandens*—all worth a trial if they could be got, though not grievously to be missed if they can't.

**Primula.*—A cold awe sweeps across the gardener as he comes at last into the shadow of this grim and glorious name, which, there is no question, strikes terror no less than rapture into the mind of the boldest. For this royal race has acquired a bad reputation in the garden, not on its own demerits but on the obstinate misconception of gardeners, which no preachments or experience of advisers seem to prevail against. For the most alpine plants of this family are usually treated by cultivators, with careful worship, to the selectest, dampest, shadiest, and dankest depressions of the rock-work, in the clogged humid soil that it is considered they particularly affect. With the result that, though they do not die indeed (for it takes more than hard words to kill an Arthritic or an Erythrodose Primula), they linger sadly and miserably, because they do hate it all so, and would be so glad to die and go hence if only they could. But no, there from season to season they sit leaden in flowerless gloom, and their leathern dark leaves cry out incessantly for the sun, and the springy well-drained turf of the Cima Tombea or the Frate di Breguzzo ; and if only the cultivator who has never seen them growing, but has merely taken his cultural notions from the timid books of thirty years ago (in the old drainless condition of the garden, all alpines of any preciousness were regarded with the awe of Verlot's time, when the only two that were considered, pavidly, as even *possibly* hardy were *Arabis albida* and *Gentiana Gentianella*), if only the cultivator, I say, would shake off these foolish chilly nightmares, and emerge with his Primulas into the bold and blessed day, he would have them flowering round his feet in

* Since this attempt at a compendium was compiled in 1913, and revised at Lanchow in the winter of 1914, so vast a quantity of new species and fresh information has been acquired that it would be hopeless now to incorporate it in the text. Accordingly a special Addendum will be found at the end of the book (exclusive of my own field-notes on Chinese species), in which all unknown names may be looked up, with a hope of there finding them if they are valid.

regal tussocks from year to year in perpetually increasing splendour; and the race would at last be cleared of an ill-fame that it has done nothing of itself to earn. Not, for a moment, that one denies the existence of capricious Primulas, both miffs and mimps, especially among the Asiatics, now come into a too-kindly and cosseting exile. But the bulk of our own mountain-species have the heartiest tempers, the most indestructible vitality, and the greatest willingness to flower. But they are *children of the broad sunlight* on the high rolling turf of the mountain tops, and the rocks of crest and summit; they are *not* woodland plants, and detest to be immured in low dank hollows, when their every fibre is clamouring for light and air. Therefore let each cultivator release nine of his Primulas out of ten from their gloomy death-beds, and plant them in loose and sandy turfy mould, full of lime-chips, with very well-rotted old manure, in full sun and with abundance of water (perfectly drained away), perpetually percolating beneath their feet in summer. Then there will be no more word of difficulty or shy-flower or sad habit (and oh, the tragic Arthritics and Minimas one has seen and yearned over, being killed year by year in some stagnant hollow of specially well-meant horror!), not even in the hottest, driest counties; while in the cooler North they will be seen, as seen they may be here, growing and waxing like cabbages, planted in rows in kitchen-garden soil, where they flower each spring in a blaze of splendour, and usually again in autumn.

Let a few general rules, then, be suggested. The enormous majority of our own alpine Primulas are of easy culture. And what they want is not dead darkness, but abundance of well-drained water and full sun. For the four Arthritic Primulas, a rich peaty loam filled with limestone chips is the ideal mixture, though they will thrive magnificently, as I say, in old kitchen-garden fatness; but they *must* have full exposure to light and air, so long as neither light nor air are rendered pernicious by being either sodden or parched. If only they can have water underground they will be happy in the hottest places. The saxatile species, such as *P. Allionii*, are certainly more difficult; and their highest hopes are set in a perfectly firm and downward-draining crevice of hard limestone rock, where, in rich loam, they will dread neither winter nor summer. The Rhopsidion and Erythrodosum sections often have in nature antipathies to lime, but in the garden offer no difficulty, and will even put up more cheerfully than the others, very often with a shady exposure; yet are still at their happiest on a well-drained slope or in a comfortable rock-niche, with ample rooting-room (for all Primulas have roots as long as a Scotch sermon), in succulent but properly-drained loam, with peat and leaf-mould and chips and grit. The Auriculas are all comfortable with the culture of the cabbage, and the man has not yet been born who can kill *P. marginata* or *P. carniolica*. The *Farinosa*-group will be found catered for under its type-species ; and the choice Gentian-bed is the best place at present for unproven Asiatics (see Appendix) at ten and sixpence each. Every special species whose needs are known will find them dealt with in the following list, which makes an attempt to cover every species and hybrid and synonym so far known.

Primula acaulis.—Neither description nor cultural notes are needed for this, one of our best-beloved of native plants. The Primrose occupies woods and sheltered shady places throughout the length and breadth of Europe, far away into Asia Minor, Armenia, and Turkestan. Native to Great Britain and abundant, *Primula acaulis* has been in our gardens for centuries, and in the lapse of time has developed into many varieties of more or less beauty, whether single or double. These will be found in any florist's catalogue, under descriptive or personal names. Some of the most specially favoured are double forms of rich colour, such as Pompadour (deep crimson), Derncleugh (splashed crimson and white), Miss Massie, a single glowing Pompadour, and many other names to the pleasure of their raisers, fresh developments perpetually appearing. From the days of Parkinson, freaks, reduplications and virescent forms have been frequent, and particularly valued among gardeners, in the various species of the vernal Primroses. Nowadays, however, the passion for Hose-in-hose, Jacks-in-the-green and Galligaskins, has passed away, or survives here and there as a curiosity, such deformities being of more precarious life than even the fashion that cherished them. The coloured forms of *P. acaulis* need no more attention than the type, when single ; when double, however, they are often apt to prove of less easy and perennial cultivation in the well-prepared gardens of the rich and mighty than in the im-memorial cottage-borders of the humble and meek. A very stiff, rich and greasy soil (with no stint of liquid manure, for which their thirst is insatiable), seems to be their desire ; and many a village, especially in the Midland counties, can show borders of the precious old Double White or Double Lilac that are richer and finer and older than any of hall or manor. Though occasionally colour-forms of *P. acaulis* are found in English copses, the original white is a variety, *P. a. balearica*, endemic to the Balearic Islands. Yet more important, however, is the beautiful early-blooming or perpetually-blooming single carmine variety, that has for so long been productive of so much confusion in catalogues. Robinson wrongly published it as *P. amoena*, and now Dr. MacWatt in the *R. H. S. Journal* has perpetuated another

PLATE 10.

POTENTILLA ALPESTRIS.
(Photo. R. A. Malby.)

PRIMULA CONCINNA.
(Photo. R.B.G., Edinburgh.)

PLATE 11.

PRIMULA CITRINA.
(Photo. W. Purdom.)

PRIMULA BEESIANA.
(Photo. R.B.G., Edinburgh.)

error by calling it *P. a. Sibthorpii*. It is, in point of fact, *P. a. rubra* of Sibthorp and Smith (1813), whereas the name *Sibthorpii* was not applied till 1824 and 1842 (*P. amoena var. Sibthorpii*, Koch.; and *P. Sibthorpii*, Hoffmansegg,—as a species). *P. a. rubra* is a most interesting and valuable plant, by no means so rare as one might fear, lying " perdue " in many old gardens under one or another of its false names. It is the Byzantine and Levantine form of *P. acaulis*, occurring, to the exclusion of the type, from Constantinople down through Asia Minor. It is of delightful beauty, as easy of cultivation as the species; and is the parent, over the several centuries that it has been in cultivation, of all the coloured primroses that figure in catalogues as *P. lilacina*, *P. rosea*, *P. purpurea*, and *P. atropurpurea*. The most illustrious of its breed, for those who love such things, is the rather farouche old Double Lilac, which those who want to cannot keep, and those who do, ignore. *P. acaulis genuina*, however, the wild type, has yielded us from an English copse one superb and glorified edition of itself in *Evelyn Arkwright*, a magnificent primrose, undistinguishable in flower from her common sisters except in the fact that she is at least double their size. Evelyn hails from the woods of Cornwall, I believe, Nature's belated tribute to the megalomania of that over-favoured land, and may always be known, even when not in flower, by the especial dark greenness and the exaggerated crinkliness of her large sombre foliage. (Look up any doubtful name in lists under *P. officinalis*.)

P. Aitchisoni is an Afghan species in the section of *P. nivalis*. It is not yet in cultivation, and the very colour of its flower was not known to Pax. The scape is nearly as long as the leaves, which are stalked, entire, rather fleshy, and perfectly glabrous and without powder when adult : in bloom it clearly has the lilac-purple of the Nivalids,

P. albiflos leads us far from the humble haunts of Primroses. It is a plant almost legendary in its beauty, not yet attained, nor for many years to be attainable by the small garden. It carries two noble white flowers at the top of its scape, and glorifies the high Atuntzu Range by the Mekong-Salwen Divide, the special paradise of new beauties in the race. Kingdon Ward discovered it and named it ; on Kingdon Ward depend our hopes for its introduction. No peril at the hands of fierce Tibetan monks should be too high a price to pay for it. Like the last it belongs to the Nivalis group.

P. algida, as I have known it, is not a species of particular merit, resembling a rather dowdy and enlarged *P. farinosa*, demanding the same treatment, and responding to it. *P. algida* is nearly related to

P. farinosa, and its many varieties have even been published as varieties of *P. farinosa*. The species is of extended range, stretching from Siberia down through the Caucasus to Armenia and Turkestan, a lover, like its cousin, of mountain meadows and marshy places. In the course of its travels it develops many forms, of which *P. a. sibirica, armena*, and *Brotheri* may be remarked.

 P. Allionii is the jewel of jewels among our European saxatile species. It is a most rare treasure, existing only in some dozen stations or more, within a radius of as many miles or less, on the low, hot limestones of the Maritime Alps from Mentone to San Dalmazzo de Tenda. Here it inhabits small shallow grottoes, or outlines the minute crevices of the hard rock with its irresistible little tight cushions of ovate leaves, grey-green with the sticky exudation of its glands. Upon these cushions appear for months together, on scapes so short as to be imperceptible, glorious great rose-pale flowers, in number from one to six on each rosette. In the shady caves, where neither sun nor rain can ever penetrate, *P. Allionii* forms enormous cushions a yard and more across, the leaves never dropping, but drying into withered tags along the perpetually elongating trunks, that push out at the end the rosette of the current year, while further down their length still linger the capsules of summers long bygone and forgotten. In such situations the growth is more luxuriant, and the masses larger; but on the open rock, exposed to some hours of the grilling sunshine of Provence, the serried tight tufts of the Primula are no less thriving and prosperous, though far harder to acquire than in the grottoes, where each trunk plucked from some pendent hassock that may have watched Napoleon pass, will come away with promising white points of new rootage at the base. This precious Primula has an undeservedly bad reputation for difficulty in cultivation. In reality it gives no trouble, when once its first necessity of perfect drainage has been granted. I find the plant of perfectly easy culture on the Cliff at Ingleborough, whether in sheltered hollows or on the face of rock, exposed to the merciless winds and rains of my climate. At the same time, excessive moisture is the one trial that all specimens dread, and I have known good tufts decay away within a day or two, if afflicted with a too unbearable series of downpours. A place secure from such should then be chosen for *P. Allionii*, which objects neither to sun nor to shade, prefers hard limestone rock to grow in, and must, indeed, always be treated as a species essentially saxatile in its requirements. As a rule, even if a suitable chink, firm, minute, and immovable, be secured, the difficulty of introducing into it the foot-long white fibres of an established clump will be found insuperable. In this case, rosettes should be taken off and struck as cuttings in sand about the end of July. They will immediately proceed to root, and at the end of August, with two or three young tentacles just beginning to push, can be easily inserted into the crevices that they are to occupy for ever. Thus it was that my original fragments on the Cliff were established there without difficulty some four years since, and now, in the darkest hours of spring till far on into April, their wonderful royal flowers come forth, lying flat upon the tiny tufts, and glorify the grey walls of rock against which they shine like living jewels. In fact, in any circumstance, I prefer August for the planting of all the more tricky Primulas ; as being the moment when the old roots are stationary, and just before the new ones issue forth to anchor the plant in its new situation. In size and shape of blossom *P. Allionii*, like all its race, is extremely variable, some flowers being of aniline colouring and thin shape, whereas the best are of the most beautiful amplitude and rotundity, and of the blandest softest rose-pink, very often diversified with a clear white eye. *P. Allionii* can easily be raised from seed, but the quicker and surer method of multiplying it is by offshoots and cuttings taken off in July or August. It is not, I think, patient of pot culture for many seasons together (unless kept on the move), though an exquisite object in pans in a cool greenhouse ; in ordinary circumstances the trouble is to keep the soil in the pot from growing stale and stagnant. In the open, however, with sufficiency (but no excess) of moisture, and in some firm, deep, perfectly-drained and downward-draining limestone crack or crevice, as small and tight as possible, *P. Allionii*, whether in sun or shade, is well capable of forming the annually increasing glory of the rock-garden, now that the pernicious days of pockets and fussments have passed, giving place to sound initial ideas of hygiene in the original compilation of the rock-work and its drainage.

P. alpina (Lois.) is a false name for *P. viscosa*.

P. alpina (Salisb.) is a false name for *P. auricula*.

P. alpina (Schleich.) is a false name for *P. × pubescens*.

P. altaica of gardens is an altogether false name. It is usually meant to apply to *P. acaulis rubra ;* whereas, in fact, it belonged once in part, and unlawfully, to the type-form of the true *P. amoena*, which is not in cultivation ; *P. altaica* has also been a name for *P. Pallasii*, Lehm. (a form of Oxlip), while its only true proprietor is a variety of *P. farinosa*, *P. altaica*, Lehmann.

P. ambita is a form of *P. obconica*, and therefore quite unsuitable to outdoor cultivation in Great Britain.

PRIMULA.

P. americana is merely a sub-name for the universal type of *P. farinosa genuina.*

P. amethystina is a Chinese species for which as yet we must vainly long. It bears beautiful violet bell-flowers on drooping pedicels—a dainty little loveliness with firm foliage resembling a daisy's, from damp mountain-meadows, 12,000 feet up on Tsang-chan in Szechuan.

P. amoena, whose name has too long served in gardens as a disguise for *P. acaulis rubra,* is, in point of fact, a perfectly distinct and lovely species which has passed into undeserved oblivion. It may be roughly described as a mauve or purple Polyanthus. It ranges through Caucasus and Lazistan, developing local forms, differentiated as *P. a. intermedia, P. a. Meyeri, P. a. grandiflora,* and *P. a. hypoleuca.* The type-form *genuina* has long, indeed, been introduced into cultivation, but so universal is the false name of *P. amoena* for the red Primrose that I cannot now tell where the genuine *P. amoena* may still be to be found.

P. androsacea is a pretty little Yunnanese annual akin to *P. Forbesii,* and of no use for outdoor culture, with a neat basal rosette of leaves, and delicate bare stems carrying whorls of pink flowers on half-drooping pedicels. It is the prettiest of its group.

P. angustidens is rightly *P. Wilsoni,* and has come to us from Yunnan. It is a handsome, damp-ground species belonging to the easily recognised section of *P. japonica* and *P. Poissoni.* It resembles this latter in its smooth, dentate, glossy foliage, stout and succulent as a cabbage. The tall, slender spires are set at intervals with close whorls of rounded blossoms that have the vindictive magenta-purple tone so painfully prevalent in this section. No difficulty attends the culture of *P. angustidens* in any cool rich ground, and it seeds profusely. The name " angustidens " covers a mixture of species.

P. angustifolia is one of the few American species, and is not in cultivation, a minute, delicate, powderless little plant, with entire stalked leaves of remarkable narrowness, and one or two rosy-purple flowers on hardly any scape at all, nestling among the foliage. It inhabits the Rockies from Colorado to New Mexico.

P. × anisiaca is a name that sometimes figures in catalogues. It covers one among the many forms of hybrid between *P. acaulis* and *P. elatior*—the Primrose and the true Oxlip. However, when this disappointment is surmounted *P. anisiaca* is found a really delightful tufty plant, amazingly profuse of its loose heads of short-scaped pale Oxlip flowers from the blackest days of January onward, until all the forms of *P. acaulis* are in full chorus. Other developments of this hybrid, to be guarded against in lists, are *P. digenea*, *P. Falkneriana*, *P. caulescens*, and *P. purpurascens* (this last a garden-form, of a dull red).

P. apennina is the obscurest species in the red-haired group of our alpine Primulas. It has the densely-hairy rosettes of *P. hirsuta* and *P. villosa*, but, altogether, is closest in habit to *P. pedemontana*, from which it differs in its furrier and paler vesture, and its smaller capsules. It was only recorded in 1891, and belongs to the Northern Apennines ; not a species of any remarkable distinctness or charm, when weighed against beauties so refulgent as *P. pedemontana* and *P. hirsuta*, though no less easy of culture in similar conditions of good drainage, and a light peaty mixture of soil, for preference among firm rocks in full sun.

P. Arctotis often appears in lists, and is yet another false name for the painfully confused and painfully vast group of intermingling undecipherable hybrids that originate between *P. auricula* and *P. villosa*, *P. viscosa*, and *P. hirsuta*, and are all to be covered by the huge and unsatisfactory general name of *P.* × *pubescens*, *q.v.* All the forms are well worth growing, remarkably brilliant, beautiful and easy rock plants for light rich loam in sun or partial shade, but none has any claim to be differentiated from *P.* × *pubescens*.

P. × *Arendsii*, if ever met with in a list, should be disregarded, as a hybrid, useless for ordinary gardens, between *P. megaseaefolia* and *P. obconica*.

P. argutidens belongs to that glorious impregnable group of Bell-flowered Primulas, which droop their fringy great blooms from frail stems on the heights of the Himalayan and Chinese mountains. All are difficult, some are possibly monocarpous, all are very rare and hard to procure. *P. argutidens* figures as a name of *P. amethystina* in Pax and Knuth ; and, though a distinct species, figures not at all in any garden, nor is likely to do so for years to come. The inflated bells are of purple-violet, and fine spongy soil with subterranean water turned on throughout the summer, with perfect drought in winter, will undoubtedly prove our best answer to the riddle of these delicate mountain-fairies, if ever we possess them.

P. atrodentata. See under *P. capitata.*

P. Aucheri is a rare member of the whorled, stout-leaved, succulent-looking, yellow-flowered section that inhabits damp rocks in warm climates from India to Abyssinia, and is nowhere hardy in the North.

P. auricula heads another yellow group, but one of quite different nature from the last. Of all alpines most precious and universal and easy and hardy is *P. auricula*, with its huge mealy leaves, lying out upon the grey rock like fat hoary star-fishes; and its stalwart heads of blossom, mealy-mouthed, of the imperial Chinese yellow. This glorious plant, one of our oldest friends in the garden, belongs to the main alpine chain, and ranges eastward *only*. On all the central Alps it will be seen universal and abundant at the upper levels, growing often in masses in the moorland turf, but much more stolid and splendid on sunny cliffs of limestone, and occasionally seeding down on to the moraines, where it grows with the amplitude of a cabbage. In its wide distribution and diversity of situation *P. auricula* divides into many marked variations. Splendid as is the type, so abundant for instance in the Bernese Oberland, much more noble still is the yet greater *P. a. Bauhini*, which appears in lists under the secondary name of *P. a. albocincta*. *P. a. Bauhini* is the prevalent form of the Southern limestones of Monte Baldo and the Judicaria. Though found through almost the whole range of the type, it is here, I think, most notable, and may be known by its magnificent development, and by the heavy silver powdering that covers the leaves, and gathers into a clear and brilliant white line round their rims. The flowers are borne in vast generous trusses, and are very large and wide-eyed, with a circular ring of white meal at their throat. Then there is *P. a. monacensis*, a curious relic of the glacial period, on high moors by Munich, with smaller development, a neat rosette, leaves much greener and many times longer than their breadth. *P. a. serratifolia* hails from the Banat, and has serrate leaves; *P. a. Widmerae*, from the Black Forest, and has powderless hairy leaves of thin texture. *P. a. Obristii* is the *P. similis* of catalogues; it has more or less glandular powderless foliage, edged with soft hairs. This form belongs chiefly to the North-eastern Alps and Western Carpathians. And next comes *P. a. ciliata*, which, if catalogues had any conscience, should appear under this name alone. As it is, they often offer Primulas called *Balbisii, bellunensis*, or *Dolomitis*, which are all in reality nothing but *P. a. ciliata*. This is a magnificent small form, with broad foliage, powderless, glandular, densely hemmed with hairs. The flowers of this type should be sweet-scented, and, in at least one development, from the Forcella Lungieres, the leathery bright-green leaves are regularly and deeply dentate, the noble wide open flowers on 4-inch scapes being of an exceptionally deep and gorgeous golden-yellow. But, indeed, the variations of *P. auricula* are endless; and though the variety *ciliata* centres in the Southern limestones, it may be found overlapping and grading into the rest elsewhere. I have to add two other specially well-marked forms; one a glabrous, small-growing plant, from rock-faces on the Fedaja Pass, with large wide flowers, very sweet, of a beautiful pale butter-yellow; the other, from one spot on the Cima Tombea, most distinct, to be known as *P. a. moschata*, with large soft leaves, notably lax and limp, powderless, hairy, and densely glandular, with glands emitting a violent odour of musk. The flowers are small and screwed-up as in the worst forms of *P. auricula*, of tubular outline and deep golden colour. All the forms of *P. auricula* are of the easiest culture anywhere in the rock-garden, to such a degree, indeed, that its children and grandchildren have become ordinary border plants. For *P. auricula* freely breeds with the other species that share its alps—never, indeed, with the Arthritic section, but quite freely with the Redhairs. All the offspring have to be lumped under the one name of *P.* × *pubescens*, and to *P. pubescens* belongs the whole vast race of garden Auriculas, being descendants, interbred and interbred through ages, of the original crosses, *P. auricula* with *P. viscosa*, *P. hirsuta*, and *P. villosa*. These hybrids are fertile too, and breed again in and out with each other endlessly and then back again to their parents; so that there is no real differentiating them, or distinguishing them by any but fancy names such as The General, or Mrs. J. H. Wilson. These hybrids, with their children, have been in cultivation at least since the sixteenth century, when Clusius saw them in the garden of his friend Dr. Aicholtz of Vienna about 1560, and vainly sought them accordingly in the Austrian and Styrian ranges, but understood them to abound in the Œnipontine Alps. So far now have the garden Auriculas departed from the tradition of their golden parent that they wear—even, indeed, from their first generation—every colour in the red scale, but never the pure imperial yellow of *auricula* itself—until, at least, they have bred so far back towards their origin as to be almost pure *auricula* once more. One named form, however, deserves to be remarked; it appears in catalogues as *P. decora* (a false name for *P. hirsuta*), and is a clear and most handsome *P* × *pubescens*, of neat free growth, attractive rosette of dentate leaves, and generously-borne heads of large round mealy-eyed flowers of a rich and beautiful blue-purple. This, being a cross-breed, does not come true from seed, producing every shape and shade of garden Auricula. Seed of the species, however, germinates freely; or the stock may be cut into lengths, or offshoots detached from the main trunk about July. In all its forms *P. auricula* is of the most permanent and trustworthy nature. Although by choice a glory of the limestone ranges, it suffers from no fads in the garden; and tolerates sun or moderate shade with equal equanimity, so long as its soil be deep and wholesome, and as rich as can reasonably be made. One of the greatest splendours on the Cliff at Ingleborough is a mass of *P. a. Bauhini*, raked off its rock five years since, at four in the morning, in the Val di Ledro, and now yearly increasing in robustness and magnificence and number of rosettes and flower-trusses.

P. auriculata, as I have seen it, is not a specially attractive species of the Farinosa section. It is, in fact, close akin, alike in habits and appearance, to *P. algida*, which is Siberian in its distribution, whereas *P. auriculata* is clearly limited to the hills of Bithynia, Cappadocia and Paphlagonia. It is a variable type, and its best form, *P. a. Bornmuelleri*, is occasionally to be seen listed as a species.

P. Balbisii. See under *P. auricula*.

P. Balfouriana, Watt, is *P. Tanneri*, King. *P. Balfouriana* of catalogues is a very fine garden form under *P. × pubescens*. See *P. hirsuta*.

P. Barbeyana is a form of the tender *P. Forbesii*.

P. barbicalyx is a form of the tender *P. obconica*.

P. batangensis is like a glorified Celsia. It is a yellow-flowered cousin to *P. malvacea*.

P. Beesiana is a recent introduction by the firm whose name it somewhat unworthily bears. For despite the glowing cries of catalogues, it is rather coarse in growth, and has blossoms suggesting a virulently-magenta form of *P. japonica*, alike in shape and spike. No difficulty unfortunately attends the cultivation of this plant, which has the requirements, as it has the style, of *P. japonica*.

P. bella is a tiny treasure of extreme beauty, first recorded from the summits of Tsang-chan, and introduced into cultivation in 1908. This is a fluctuating name belonging to a small high-alpine group, and one of its forms, *P. b. Bonatii*, may ultimately take rank as a true species. The plants of this family have small, spatulate leaves, so deeply toothed as to have a curly fringed look, and powdered with a lighter or heavier coating of meal. The flowers of *P. bella*, carried singly on a scape about an inch high, strongly recall those of *P. minima* in size and shape, but the throat is blocked with a mass of white hairs —the diagnostic of this group—and the colour is of a soft lilac-purple. Among other variations is a form neat and tight and dense as *Sax. oppositifolia*. For this, as for the type, the general public will probably have to pine for many years in vain ; *P. bella* has only looked in upon us, and may not stay long enough to be distributed. If ever such a golden day should dawn, *P. bella* will be most likely to answer to cool alpine treatment in a spongy soil, rich and rough and very stony, with underground water turned on through the bed in summer.

P. bellidifolia, from the Sikkim-Himalaya, is a flaccid-leaved, powderless species of the Muscarioid section, with blue-purple little bells after the style of *P. Giraldiana*, gathered in a dense and sessile head on a stem from 4 to 6 inches high.

P. × Berninae, which also appears in lists as *P. Salisii*, is the natural hybrid between *P. hirsuta* and *P. viscosa*. It is fertile and produces secondary forms. In appearance it is midway between the parents, having the smaller stature of *P. hirsuta*, and the wider, larger flowers; together with the added height of *P. viscosa*, *viscosa's* one-sided umbel, violaceous colouring and odorous glands. At best it is a beautiful production, gathering the virtues and not the faults of either species; it may be found, but not commonly, growing among them, in the ranges where they overlap, throughout the Rhaetian Alps, from the Engadine, as far south as the Val Seriana in the Bergamask range. Like many hybrids, it seems to occur often on high necks and passes, as at the end of the Heu-thal above the Bernina. In cultivation it is as easy as its parents, in similar conditions.

P. × Bilekii. See under *P. × Steinii.*

P. Biondiana is so far a doubtful and obscure Chinese species of the Auriculata section, standing suspiciously near *P. stenocalyx.*

P. blattariformis is probably useless for the garden, a plant of the Yunnanese limestones, forming a close rosette of foliage from which rise spikes of lilac flowers, giving the appearance of a little Verbascum in their close arrangement on the scape.

P. Bonatii. See under *P. bella.* [The name *Bonatiana* covers a form of *P. obconica*, the largest and handsomest in that group; and *P. × Bonatii* is a supposed hybrid of *P. farinosa* with *P. marginata* (!)]

P. borealis is a minute powdery microform of *P. farinosa*, from the extreme North-western corner of Asia. It is said by Pax to be nearer to *P. sibirica* than to *P. farinosa*, although so different in appearance. See also Appendix.

P. Bornmuelleri is a form of *P. auriculata* and a particularly fine one.

P. Boveana is the commonest form in cool-house cultivation of the yellow-flowered group aggregated under *P. verticillata.*

P. bracteata is a yellow-flowered Primula in the group of *P. Forrestii*, from damp and shady rocks in the mountains of Yunnan.

P. × brennia, a false catalogue name for the splendid *hirsuta × minima* hybrid, whose primary title is *P. Steinii, q.v.*

P. brevifolia is a beautiful Chinese cousin of *P. amethystina*, and not yet in general cultivation.

P. breviscapa belongs to the Davidian section, which contains some of the loveliest of the Chinese species. They have large flowers of rich blue-purple, on a short well-proportioned scape, rising from a neat rosette of oval sessile leaves (most membranous in *P. breviscapa*) invested in a cluster of rich brown scale-leaves. *P. breviscapa* haunts damp shady rocks on Tchen-fong-shan in Yunnan, and is not yet introduced.

P. bullata is akin to *P. Forrestii*, forming thick, massive stems, clothed all along their length in the withered dry leaves of bygone seasons, and ending in the wrinkled evergreen rosettes of the current year, which send up a tall-stemmed umbel of large yellow Polyanthus. *P. bullata* is hairless, but clothed in golden meal, and, like the rest of its race, dwells in the sheer limestone cliffs of Yunnan, where nine others of its kindred are found, including *P. Forrestii*. The sub-shrubby, ligneous habit is rare in Primula, and other species that have relation to this strange group in their growth-habits are *P. Lacei*, the American *P. suffrutescens*, and lovely *P. dryadifolia*.

P. Bulleyana.—The introduction of this magnificent Primula by the enthusiast whose name it justly bears, marks an epoch in horticultural history. It may be described, if description is nowadays necessary, as a counterpart, in size, habit, robustness and requirements, of *P. japonica*. But the big round flowers that crowd the rich whorls up its stems are, at their opening, of a fierce red-gold developing into a clear pure yellow. *P. Bulleyana* is of the freest growth and bloom in any cool rich soil such as suits *P. japonica*. It seeds with great profuseness, and so readily hybridises with others of its sections that before long we shall have a vast confusion of named beauties intermediate between *PP. Bulleyana, pulverulenta, Cockburniana,* and *japonica.* Already an exquisite hybrid, *Bulleyana × Beesiana,* has been raised in Edinburgh, with tiers of blossom rich and round, of the most subtle and shaded apricot-salmon. Unfortunately such seedlings vary violently from the pod, and others of this cross have merely perpetuated or intensified the worst faults of *P. Beesiana*.

P. cadinensis, a superseded name of Porta's for *P. oenensis, q.v.*

P. calliantha has so far barely looked into our gardens, and then liked them so little that it did not even stay long enough to flower, and the young plants (from seed sent home by Forrest in 1908), made haste to return to China, or wherever it is that dead and disappointed Primulas disappear to. *P. calliantha* is a species of splendid beauty in the miffy and capricious Nivalis section, all of whose members seem to want underground water and perfect drainage and an even, humid temperature about them during the growing period. It comes from dense shade in the pine-forests of that marvellous chain of Tsang-chan which produces such a store of Primulas from its skirts and folds and crests, including *P. bella* and *P. amethystina*. The

116

leaves are 2 or 3 inches long, arranged in a tuft, oblong, dentate-crenulate, and clothed with golden meal beneath. The scape rises above them, and carries very large flowers, of a brilliant violet-purple.

P. calycina, a varietal name of *P. glaucescens*, which far too often is made to figure in catalogues as a separate and distinct species, or as a substitute for the proper name, *q.v.*

P. Candolleana = *P. integrifolia*, *q.v.*

P. capitata is a garden name embracing a whole number of allied but quite definite species, of which, to increase the confusion, several are now in cultivation. *P. capitata*, true, is one of the miffiest and poorest of the lot ; then comes *P. crispa*, the commonest *P. "capitata"* of gardens and catalogues (*P. erosa* of *Bot. Mag.*, T. 6916*a*); *P. Mooreana* is by far the finest species, though ; long-lived and stout, with stalwart white-powdered stems, contrasting beautifully with the ample round head of Tyrian violet flowers in August and onwards—in short, a first-class treasure for any rich, cool, well-drained position, and the one "capitata" that deserves diligently ensuing : I have had plants four and five years old, more and more lavish of loveliness each season. *P. nano-capitata* has a dwarf habit and very brief life for its portion—it has probably got *P. "capitata"* its bad name as a biennial ; *P. lacteo-capitata* has notably creamy meal, and unlike sulphur-powdered *P. Craibiana* is now in cultivation, as is also *P. atrodentata* with its black-tipped sepals. These are all from Sikkim and Bhutan ; but China offers us *P. sphaerocephala*, and has already given us *P. pseudo-capitata*, a notably vigorous grower in our gardens.

P. capitellata is a little species from Afghanistan, not in cultivation, akin to *P. farinosa*, with pink flowers, in a close umbel. The plant often shown under this name is only a form of *P. auriculata*.

P. carniolica, one of the rarest and remotest of European Primulas, is confined to a few wooded hill-tops in the Idrian Alps just north of Trieste. The whole growth is glabrous to the point of being glossy, the oval, smooth, brilliantly-green leaves having a special charm of their own, only surpassed when up come the 6-inch scapes, carrying from three to eight large round blossoms of a delicate, delicious soft rose, with a solid round eye of white meal at their throat. On its native hills *P. carniolica* grows frail and straggly in the moss and damp rocks beneath the densest shade of firs ; but in the garden it proves everywhere a species of the most perfect adaptability and charm, in any cool rich soil. There has been known a lovely white form ; it is only, at this present hour, a "Has-been." The type has thriven in cultivation for many years, and figures in catalogues so freely, and at so cheap a rate, that I have often wondered whether their plant be indeed the true *P. carniolica*, or whether the august name may not really be cloaking *P. glaucescens*, that vain and vulgar usurper of so many titles, which so rarely appears in the market under its own. *P. carniolica* ramifies and forms spreading trunks along the ground ; and may readily be increased by seed or division. It has produced one hybrid, which will be found under the name of *P. venusta*.

P. x *Carueli*, a rare and not horticulturally valuable natural hybrid of *P. glaucescens longobarda* x *P. spectabilis*, on neither of which is any improvement conceivable.

P. cashmiriana, so profusely catalogued and universally grown, is usually only one of innumerable and undecipherable forms or hybrids of *P. denticulata*.

P. caucasica should be a form of *P. auriculata ;* but under the name also appears in lists an object which, being purchased for large sums, proves to be indistinguishable from a Cowslip.

P. Cavalieri is a form of *P. obconica*.

P. cernua is perhaps the finest of that spicate, cluster-headed lop-sided-belled section, headed in gardens by *P. Littoniana*. It hails from mountain-meadows on the limestones of Hee-gni-chan by Ho-kin, to the north of Tali. It has a large truss, and fragrant flowers of a good clear blue. All the species of this section have hairy leaves, a very definite indication that they will stand no nonsense in the way of winter-wet. This difficulty attends their culture in all damp climates, and they are not prompt at seeding, either owing to natural perversity, or lack of suitable butterflies.

P. chartacea is an unintroduced and barely known species, with large papery leaves, glaucous beneath. It will probably be tender, as it comes from shady bamboo-groves in Szechuan.

P. ciliata (Schrenk), is a discarded subname for *P. hirsuta*. But *P. ciliata* of all gardens and catalogues (with its varieties *coccinea, purpurea, eximia*, and so on), is simply an unjustifiable name applied to some among the innumerable forms of the vast hybrid race of *P.* x *pubescens, q.v.*

P. cinerascens, a central Chinese species, akin to *P. mollis*.

P. Clarkei, a glabrous little thing in the group of *P. Gambeliana*, with all the habit of a Viola,—big cordate leaves, no scape, and a big baggy calyx to the handsome flowers. *P. Clarkei* comes from Kashmir ; or would, if brought.

P. Clusiana carries us leaping back across the world, to where, on high limestones of Austria and Styria, this magnificent Primula forms masses and wide stretches in a carpet composed also of *P. minima*,

PRIMULA.

Viola alpina, Loiseleuria procumbens, Androsace lactea, A. villosa, Dianthus alpinus, Primula auricula, Campanula pulla, and *Campanula alpina.* *P. Clusiana* forms stout clumps of broad, pointed, glossy-green leaves, from which shoot up the 3- or 4-inch scapes, carrying as many as half a dozen enormous round flowers of glowing carmine, with a white eye, and the lobes of the corolla so deeply divided that the blossom has the air of possessing ten petals. No difficulty whatever attaches to the cultivation of this beloved and splendid species, which adds to its virtues that of being even ampler of growth and freer of flower in our gardens than on the windswept uplands of the Hoch-schneeberg and the Raxalpe. It has suffered in gardens, indeed, from the curious superstition that has doomed all the European Primulas to dank and shady places. In many such may *P. Clusiana* and *P. spectabilis* be seen sadly lingering in exile, never flowering ; in point of fact all the four great Arthritic Primulas (and nearly all the other European species, too), want as much light as they can get. They are lords of the sun-trodden high bare lawns in the limestone Alps, and like a good open position, in light, well-drained peaty loam, mixed freely with sand and limestone chips. This being granted, *P. Clusiana* stands high among the easiest and most manageable glories of its race ; varying, like all the European Primulas, in size and amplitude of blossom, but always magnificent and worthy of regard. It has bred at least one hybrid, even more remarkable if possible than itself. See *P.* × *intermedia.*

P. Cockburniana is in all gardens by now, though few years have passed since its whorls of fiery copper-orange flowers first staggered the gardening world. It is a small species of the Candelabra section headed by *P. japonica,* and responds quite readily to cultivation in any light cool soil, not parched or sunburnt. It seeds, too, with exemplary generosity, and it is as well thus to multiply it from year to year ; for, though no more necessarily biennial than a *P.* " *capitata,*" it has true *capitata's* way of dying off sometimes after too profuse a blooming season, or of disappearing from damp, rich, or imperfectly drained soil in the winter, unless it be divided annually, crown from crown. In no case, probably, will *P. Cockburniana* be very long-lived, but its easy habits and ready germination imply a minimum of annual trouble in keeping relays of its flat basal rosettes of wrinkled leaves, from which so freely rise the powder-white stems beset with rings of large blooms of that refulgent scarlet orange.

P. coerulea of the Davidi's, still mocks our longings from afar.

P. cognata was collected by Purdom in 1911, but has since been suspiciously little heard of. At present it is a vague name, covering

119

perhaps several species, all being rock-tufts, with heads of fragrant large blue-pink blossom. See Appendix.

P. Columnae, a name that frequently appears in the lists of foreign collectors, is a handsome, large, pale-yellow Cowslip, one of the prevalent forms in the Southern Alps. See under *P. officinalis*.

P. commutata, a thin-leaved, large and lax sub-form of *P. villosa*, found on porphyry, near Herberstein in Styria. This is wrongly given as a species in some handbooks. See *P. villosa*.

P. concinna is a most exquisite little species for which at present we call in vain. It is, indeed, in cultivation, but not within reach of ordinary hands. *P. concinna* forms dense cushiony masses not an inch high, among the grey grit and damp gravel of the highest moraines in Sikkim ; and the clump is set with minute scapes, carrying two or three lovely round rosy flowers, with a notched yellow eye. It is a Himalayan species, there making good the Himalayan lack of *P. farinosa*, to which it is nearly akin, differing in its tufted habit, minute growth, and powdering of golden meal beneath the leaves. In cultivation such a treasure ought to promise well.

P. confinis (Schott), one of the countless old false names for *P. hirsuta*, which occasionally, thus disguised, makes several appearances in the same catalogue under different epithets.

P. conspersa. See Appendix.

P. cordifolia is another Sikkim species, akin to *P. Gambeliana*. It is not, I believe, in cultivation ; a plant of small growth, with from three to four flowers in an umbel.

P. × coronata is the natural hybrid between *P. minima × P. oenensis*. It takes two forms, the one, *P. × pumila*, closer akin to *P. minima*, quite minute with two lovely round rosy flowers on a scape barely as long as the microscopic leaves ; and *P. × Widmerae*, verging more towards *P. oenensis*, of rather larger habit, and less distinguished in growth. These two developments of *P. coronata*, with intermediate forms, are only to be seen in the Pass of the Frate di Breguzzo, close to the Adamello in Judicaria, being the one point at which *P. minima* meets *P. oenensis*. They are of rare occurrence and great charm ; perfectly easily cultivated under the conditions that suit *P. minima*, and under cultivation growing more strongly and flowering more freely than in nature. *P. coronata*, it will be understood, is the covering name, and now, under Viennese rule, the one justified name for all forms of the hybrid. In old days, any conspicuous form of a mule was given a distinct title, with the result that our catalogues are now crowded and clouded with many such superfluous epithets, all of them cloaking one variable family of intermediates.

PRIMULA.

P. cortusoeides (see notes to *P. saxatilis* and *P. Sieboldii*) is a name universally to be met with in gardens and catalogues, where it is always confused with *P. Sieboldii*. Unfortunately the species it belongs to is practically unknown in cultivation; all the plants thus described being either *P. Sieboldii* in differing forms, or else *P. saxatilis*. The true *P. cortusoeides* is a native of the Asiatic mainland, and not of Japan; it is taller and more graceful than *P. Sieboldii*, with the leaf-stalks often much longer than the blade of the leaf itself. It should be cultivated, when obtained, like *P. Sieboldii*.

P. cottia brings us back once more into the European ranges, where, in a few dark volcanic cliffs in the Cottian Alps, this extremely rare species of the red-haired Erythrodose group may be seen. It is near *P. villosa :* a small group of neat rosettes of furry oblong spoon-shaped leaves, often entire, and sometimes slightly toothed toward their tips. The glandular scape rises well above the rosette, and carries a number of large rose-pink flowers, with calyx-tube much exceeding the calyx. The seed-vessels are amply vase-shaped, standing erect on lengthened pedicels. *P. cottia* has been for some years in cultivation, and answers readily to the same treatment that suits *P. hirsuta*. I found a new station for it near Bobbio one season, however, and on the higher rocks the clumps were all crinkled and dried with heat. When I returned a few summers later it had there died out, and those upper rocks were wholly bare of it, though lower down it still throve. The sun, however, is so very different a proposition in the Southern Alps from what might be guessed from its pallid manifestations even in the hottest parts of England, that I do not fear *P. cottia* will ever prove a sun-hater with us, so long as reasonable water is supplied at its roots.

P. × cridalensis, a false list-name of Gusmus (together with *micrantha, adulterina, valmenona*) for the hybrid between *P. tyrolensis* and *P. Wulfeniana*, whose only right name is *P. × Venzoi, q.v.*

P. crispa, the commonest garden plant called *P. " capitata."*

P. cuneifolia, a species akin to *P. suffrutescens*, from the Arctic Islands of the Behring Seas. It is a variable small thing, dividing into two named forms, *P. Dubyi* the larger, and *P. saxifragifolia* the smaller; the habit is tufted, with leathery leaves and a short graceful scape carrying rosy flowers among them, or not rising far above. It is a quite smooth and hairless copy, in effect, of our Erythrodose Primulas, and of no less value.

P. Cusickiana is a species quite near *P. angustifolia*, if not merely a form of it. It comes from the South-eastern Rockies, and is not in cultivation.

PRIMULA.

P. daonensis, a false name (mistakenly formed from the Val di Daone in Judicaria, above which it is found) for *P. oenensis, q.v.*

P. darialica resembles *P. farinosa* in habit and needs. It is a Caucasian plant, and has powdered and powderless forms. It is in cultivation, and offers no difficulty, but I do not think it competes in charm with *P. farinosa*, though a little larger.

P. Davidi comes from the cold region of Moupin. It has large flowers of very rich violet, carried on a well-proportioned scape above the rosette of sessile, oblong, wrinkled leaves. It has not yet arrived in cultivation, though ardently desired, like all its kin.

P. × Davosiana, a false name for the glorious hybrid *P. × Heerii, q.v.* (*P. hirsuta × P. integrifolia*), which has so impressed its discoverers whenever and wherever they see it, that each time they give it a distinct name, local or personal. Thus the unlucky plant has at various times appeared as *PP. Davosiana, assimilis, Laggeri, Thomasiana, incerta, globulariaefolia, montafoniensis,* and *Trisannae,* the first four being Sündermann's names and the last four Gusmus's, all for the same hybrid.

P. davurica is one among the myriad named forms into which diverges, in the course of its enormous distribution, the universal *P. farinosa.* It occurs in Siberia and again in Saskatchewan.

P. decipiens (Stein), one of the catalogue-names under which lurks *P. hirsuta.*

P. × decora, a garden hybrid of great beauty from *P. auricula, q.v.*

P. deflexa was the first in cultivation, and still perhaps the most generally useful, of that Chinese section which produces small flowers pendent in a spike, with hairy leaves and a general miffiness in respect of excessive moisture in winter or drought in summer. *P. deflexa* is also the most exquisitely fragrant in a group where all the species compete for the palm of sweetness. The little hanging bells on the spire are of a clear periwinkle-blue.

P. Delavayi is yet another of the glorious species which decorate Tsang-chan. It occurs there in damp cool places, and in cultivation appears of slow growth and some reluctance to flower, and exacting in respect of streams of water flowing beneath its roots throughout the growing period. The stalked hairy leaves form a close clump, shooting up from a long bud, and before them are thrown up on taller scapes still the huge solitary Pinguiculoid or even Gloxinioid blooms of fulminating violet.

P. delicata is a form of the untrustworthy *P. Forbesii.*

P. denticulata.—This vast and cabbage-like species is one of universal utility, and spread throughout our gardens, even into our

PLATE 12.

PRIMULA DEALBATA.
(Photo. W. Purdom.)

PRIMULA CONSPERSA.
(Photo. W. Purdom.)

PLATE 13.

PRIMULA × DISCOLOR [form].
(Photo. R.B.G., Kew.)

PRIMULA FRONDOSA.
(Photo. R.B.G., Edinburgh.)

wild damp woods. It flowers before the huge primrose-like leaves, in earliest spring, with huge tight round heads of lilac-purple on stout scapes. The plant enjoys any cool rich soil, and is indispensable for spring effects, though too coarse and massive to be accused of charm. It varies copiously from seed, has blossoms in differing degrees of purple, lilac or mauve, and leaves more or less endowed with powder. One form, rather neater in habit and choicer in colour, with dense golden meal on the reverse of the leaves, is distinguished in catalogues as *P. cashmiriana*. *P. denticulata* colours the hillsides of the North-Western Himalayas in spring, and its young leaves are recommended for salads, while its roots, when powdered, are said to be destructive of leeches. Sometimes in our gardens, the huger, older masses may moulder off in a wet winter, but seed is always abundant, and prompt to germinate, nor need *P. denticulata* be looked on as anything but a sound perennial. Its colour-forms are often named, and are too rarely an improvement on the better blues of the type. *P. d. cashmiriana Ruby*, for example, is an instance of misplaced zeal in nomenclature, having far more resemblance to a dingy amethyst of poor and dirty water. The white form, on the contrary, is beautiful indeed, with rather larger flowers than the type, not quite so densely huddled in a head.

P. deorum has in its time aroused much excitement and subsequent heartburnings. It is a stout species, alone in a group with exquisite *P. glutinosa*, and comes from high meadows and rill-sides near the melting snows in the mountains of Thrace and Bulgaria. It forms a tuft of uprising, narrow entire leaves, leathery and glandular. Well above these stand stout scapes bearing one-sided generously-furnished umbels of nodding flowers, large and round, of a deep magenta-purple. In cultivation it has proved hard to grow, hard to keep, and hard to flower. Nor, when the rare flowers have appeared, have their colour and size been of a nature to rouse enthusiasm. Clearly *P. deorum* requires the same abundant running water throughout the summer that is demanded by *P. glutinosa*; but, despite its pretentious name, it is not really so well worth the trouble as that most delicious of plants and most exacting of jewels.

P. × Deschmannii is the natural hybrid between *P. minima × P. Wulfeniana*. It is intermediate, being variable, taller than *P. minima*, and with small leaves, dentate after the habit of *P. minima*. This has also been divided into two extreme types; the one nearer *P. minima*, with no scape at all, and the other with a short scape, larger size, and fewer teeth to the tip of the leaves, thus showing closer approach to *P. Wulfeniana*. This last is listed sometimes as *P.*

vochinensis, while the former development is quite common in catalogues under the name of *P. serratifolia*, to the utter confusion of the real *P. serratifolia*, Franch, *q.v.* D. *Deschmannii* occurs at the meeting point of its parents, on the high limestone meadows of the Karawanken. Gusmus, who called it *P. Deschmannii*, has also called it *P. Kankeriana* and *mutata*. It is of perfectly easy culture by anyone who grows *P. minima* and *P. Wulfeniana*. And who is there who does not ?

P. diantha.—A quite tiny tufted miniature, with little lilac stars, collected by Prince Henri d'Orleans, and otherwise unknown. But the Petrograd Herbarium under this name shows a beautiful plant, to my eye identical with my own *P. scopulorum*, Balf. fil.

P. Dickieana is a variable and doubtful species of medium height in the group of *P. Gambeliana*, with scentless large flowers ranging from yellow and white to purple. The species includes *P. Pantlingii*.

P. × *digenea* is the English form of the cross between the Primrose and the true Oxlip, a most various many-named invention.

P. × *Dinyana*, which also appears in catalogues as *P. Muretiana* or *Mureti*, is the natural hybrid between *P. integrifolia* and *P. viscosa*. It occurs not uncommonly in districts where its parents abound, such as on the high moors of the Engadine, and may at once be known by the intermediacy of its appearance, being shorter in stature and much laxer in umbel than *P. viscosa*, but taller, freer and more brilliant in colour than *P. integrifolia*, of which, nevertheless, it has the large wide flowers instead of the pinched long trumpets of *P. viscosa*. It will be found further noticed under its invalid later name *P.* × *Muretiana*, which ought to represent it in lists, yet too seldom does.

P. × *discolor* is yet another natural hybrid, between *P. oenensis* and *P. auricula*. In appearance it rather resembles a small, spoiled Auricula, the gold of one parent having diluted the magenta of the other into a dingy, dirty brownish tone, with a blurred yellowish eye. *P. discolor* also occurs on the ridge of the Frate di Breguzzo, where four species meet (*auricula, oenensis, minima,* and *spectabilis*), there producing the four hybrids, *discolor, Facchinii, Dumoulinii, coronata*.

P. diversa is a false name for *P. Steinii*.

P. dolomitis. See under *P. auricula*.

P. Drummondiana.—A plant very close indeed to wonderful *P. Winteri*, from which it differs in having smaller flowers not fringed, and with the segments of the corolla bi-lobed.

P. dryadifolia whets our expectations with hopes of one of the loveliest Primulas in the race, now ripening towards distribution in careful hands. We are to imagine a spreading woody mass of *Dryas octopetala*, set with heads of large round fragrant blossoms of rich rose-pink emerging from a bag of dark purple bracts. *P. dryadifolia* grows beside the great Li-kiang glacier in Yunnan in the wet rocky places close to the melting icefield, and so high up that only *P. bella* is its companion. Here it undergoes unthinkable vicissitudes of climate, very late in emerging from its snow-shroud, and very quickly covered up again. Its robust suffruticose habit, and its lack of perilous down, no less than its radiant happiness in such untoward conditions, give us good hope that it may really be an addition to the garden as permanent in the underground watered moraine-bed as it will assuredly there be glorious.

P. Dubernardiana is another suffruticose Chinese Primula, with flowers among the ample foliage.

P. Duclouxii.—A species in the group of *P. malacoeides*, and therefore unsuited to the open air. It is quite dwarf, as it grows on the mountain, with short scapes nestling among the leaves. The only two undoubted species in this group are *P. Forbesii* and *P. malacoeides* (with a distinct and less robust form, occurring in cultivation, which is the so-called *P. pseudo-malacoeides*). Both these plants were ushered into civilisation with a loud flourish of trumpets, and true to say they are easy, pretty little useful things. But they have a lush, lax ephemeral look which betrays their character, for neither is hardy, nor has the group even a perennial tendency, despite the persistence of *P. Forbesii*. The brightest of the group is *P. androsacea*.

P. Edgeworthii is a beauty which has with difficulty secured itself from being overshadowed by the large name of *P. petiolaris*. It is now reckoned as a distinct species, differing from all forms of *P. petiolaris* in the shape of the leaf, though otherwise similar, except in the broad ovate lobes of the calyx, which recurve after flowering. As *P. Winteri* has emerged from under the shadow of *P. petiolaris*, it will well be understood that all the kindred of this glorious thing are greatly to be longed for in our gardens, where a proud and happy future may be foretold for most.

P. efarinosa is a pretty neat sort from Central China which might prove akin to *P. Knuthiana*. It is said to be in cultivation, but little known.

P. egallicensis is a Greenland form of *P. farinosa*.

P. elatior is the true or Bardfield Oxlip, always to be distinguished from the much wider-flowered false Oxlip, the hybrid between Cowslip and Primrose, frequent where both occur together, whereas *P. elatior* has but a limited distribution in the midlands.

P. elegans. See under the garden labels of *P. rosea, q.v.*

PRIMULA.

P. elliptica stands quite close to *P. rosea*, but its flowers are purple instead of pink, and its leaves are elliptic on long stalks. It will come to us from Kashmir and Turkestan.

P. Ellisiae, proclaimed lately as a novelty, is only *P. Rusbyi*.

P. elongata is a beautiful yellow-flowered new arrival in our gardens, possibly to be grouped near *P. Stuartii*, and of similar needs.

P. Elwesiana is a glory of the Omphalogrammas; but, unlike the five other species of that odd group, comes from the mountains of the Chumbi Valley in the Sikkim-Himalaya, whereas the rest are all Chinese. From a long stock enclosed in dark membranaceous scales, rises up a tall, stout, and densely hairy stem, well before the leaves, which are long, broadly-oval, leathery, acute and glabrous. The flowers, singly produced, are very large, fringed at the edge and richly violet. *P. Elwesiana* can now be found in cultivation, but is of slow development, and requires the same conditions as those insisted on by the rest,—*PP. Engleri, Franchetii, vincaeflora, Delavayi, and Viola-grandis.*

P. Engleri stands nearest to *P. Delavayi*, offering the same beauties, and demanding the same conditions. It is hardly distinguished from *P. Franchetii*, but comes from further North about Tatsien-lu.

P. erosa is hardly known in cultivation. It is like a very frail *P. denticulata*, but produces its numerous delicate incurving flower-stalks at the same time as its leaves. These are either smooth or puberulous, toothed with a nibbled-looking effect round their edges. The blossoms are pretty, of a pleasant lilac, gathered in a head on short fine pedicels. The false *P. erosa* of gardens is a coarser plant, and quite easily thrives under reasonable conditions of cool rich soil. I have from Nepaul a closely similar species, puberulous all over, with corollas irregularly lobed. This, whether a mere form or no, grows vastly in deep moist soil, in the company of *P. japonica*.

P. × Escheri is the natural hybrid of *P. auricula P. × integrifolia.* It is easily recognised as intermediate, being taller than *P. integrifolia*, with more flowers, marginate leaves, a powdered calyx and a sweet scent ; while it differs from *P. auricula* by its lesser stature, fewer flowers, longer calyces and deep dull-red colouring. It is to be found on the high moors of the West-Rhaetian Alps in the Engadine, &c. It is in cultivation, but I have never seen it listed, nor set eyes on it, either in gardens or on the wild hills. I should suspect it of sharing the ugliness of *P. discolor*.

P. Esquirolii is at present a species of uncertain place and needs. It is placed for the moment near *P. Davidi*, and was collected in Kwei-chou.

126

PRIMULA.

P. eximia, from the Kurile and Aleutian Islands, is a magnificent dwarf form of *P. nivalis* (*q.v.*), very closely allied to *P. Macounii*.

P. Faberi, which is found on the summit of Mount Omi in central China, ought to be a precious treasure when at last it arrives. It belongs to that exquisite and dainty bell-flowered group in which great pendent goblets are produced by twos or threes on delicate short scapes. In *P. Faberi* the leaves have a horny margin, and the flowers are yellow. No one is yet sufficiently intimate with it to prescribe precise conditions for its culture.

P. × Facchinii, which must also include *P. Dumoulinii* of lists, should be the inclusive name for all forms of the natural hybrid each way round between *P. minima × P. spectabilis*. Formerly the two names were given, the one to the development approaching nearer to *P. minima*, and the other verging more towards *P. spectabilis*. This, *P. Facchinii*, Pax, is the commoner, though both forms are to be found together on the ridge of the Frate di Breguzzo, where, in earliest June, with *minima* and *spectabilis* gleaming all around, their brilliant blossoms glow like little amethystine fires upon the sere brown herbage of the ridge from which the snow has barely melted yet. The hybrid freely varies, and the more attractive in nature is the scapeless one-flowered form known as *P. Dumoulinii*. This is comparatively uncommon on that slope, a round-flowered beauty like a glorified *P. minima*. In nature, too, all forms were a trifle disappointing in colour and size and shape of flower, taking too much after *minima's* thin, ragged design and pale aniline pink, a fault which makes it the more surprising that in the garden, where they all grow robustly in the conditions that suit *P. spectabilis*, their character should alter so violently for the better: the habit magnifies, the scapes grow tall and stout, the blossoms big and round and splendid almost beyond recognition, and of a cleared soft tone of brilliance with a clean white eye.

P. × fallax is a false name for magnificent *P. × intermedia*.

P. Fargesii has not yet come down upon us from damp rocks above Cheng-kou in Szechuan. It is a Bell-flower of delicate growth, with horny margin to the leaves. (It is also *P. nutantiflora*.)

P. farinosa, besides being the loveliest of all our native alpines, is the largest name, and has the widest distribution, in the whole race. No gardener is a stranger to the wistful beauty of Pretty Bird e'en, with its little rosettes of grey and mealy foliage, and its delicate scapes, all powdery-white, carrying that loose round head of fragrant soft-pink flowers with a twinkling yellow eye. *P. farinosa* ranges right across the Northern world from east to west. In the course of its wanderings

127

PRIMULA.

it varies according to climatic conditions so vastly that almost every country or county has its named form, often attempting specific rank, and as species occasionally appearing in catalogues. In all the alpine chains of the Northern hemisphere the species, or forms very closely allied, are to be found ; though it is but poorly represented in China, and not at all in the Himalaya. In England *P. farinosa* belongs to the Northern counties, and is especially notable in Westmorland and the Craven Highlands. Here, on all the grassy open fells round Ingleborough the Primula sheds a wide glow of pink in early summer ; by no means restricted to the marshes (though in marshes also most generously occurring), but abounding especially on the high scars of rough turf. It also descends into the valleys, and is glorious, for instance, on the railway cuttings between Settle, Ribblehead and Bentham. It is often, even, found in glowing colonies by the road-sides, with heads as ample as some Verbena's, and in these valley stations it is curious to note that it is much later in blossom than on the fells, where it is nearer to primeval conditions, and preserves the tradition of the alpine summer, so short that plants must needs rush out into flower the moment the snow disappears, before, in another moment, the early snow returns again. Therefore, when all the hills are sheeted in a film of lilac, at the end of May, no bud will yet be found open in the valleys a thousand feet below. Rabbits have a taste for picking its flowers, and so have tourists. But, where the Primula can be protected from these enemies in the animal kingdom (as, for instance, round the Lake at Ingleborough, and on the high places of the fells where tourists do not go, and the Primulas by far outnumber even the rabbits), there is no doubt that the precious beauty is yearly increasing in abundance, so that long ranges of turf that used to be dully green in spring are now roseate with veils of Primula-pink as definite as the rosy haze it sheds over the Alps. In cultivation *P. farinosa* has had a gloomy reputation ever since the days of Parkinson, who declares that it " will hardly abide to be noursed up." It is possible that too much care may be the cause of its frequent failure to survive for long in Southern gardens : that, and a slavish imitation of imagined natural conditions. The crown, too, which is essentially gregarious in nature, and is only found densely wadded up in grass and other vegetation (the matting of many roots thus ensuring equableness of humidity and steady drainage), is usually planted in gardens in reverend loneliness as a tribute to its rarity, difficulty, and reputation. There is an instinct in us that prescribes isolation and particular care for all such ill-famed subjects, which in reality only want the struggle for life among their fellows to spur them into a hearty vitality which they can never attain in the dull grandeur of a pocket to themselves with nothing to interest, stimulate, or support their growth. I feel sure that comradeship is the answer to the problem of many uncertain or impish treasures, such as *Gentiana verna;* and is especially to be commended in the case of *Primula farinosa.* This should be planted among kindred spirits in a heavy rich and sticky loam, on a slope, well drained, and with abundance of water from March to June. Sow among it then some fine perennial grass, such as *Festuca ovina tenuifolia,* and take no more care; for the Primula should soon be established, and there abide from year to year. It is not a marsh-plant, and is independent of water after the flowering-period, so long as it has the copious wet of the alpine spring, when the melting snows turn all the ranges into a sop of moisture. But prescriptions for such a rover can only be approximate, and my suggestions need only be understood as offering themselves to gardeners who may hitherto have failed to grow or keep the Bird's-eye Primula. The typical Bird's-eye varies greatly in depth of colour and shape of flower. I have found deep-red forms, and once a beautiful precocious blue one; but, as a rule, though round-flowered stout forms should be secured, there is no point in naming or specially marking out the varieties of a species so elusive and impermanent. There is, however, a stemless, cushiony form, now very rare, but always most desirable (*P.f. acaulis*); and there is the true lovely albino, *P. farinosa alba Saundersae*—the final possessive being applied no less to commemorate its enthusiastic discoverer and guardian as to differentiate this special and superb form from the ordinary albino, an extremely "sometime person," but not so good, which I have only seen myself near the Grindelwald Glacier, and in Sulber Nick under Ingleborough. Mrs. Saunders' albino is a stout and stalwart variety, perfectly pure, large-flowered, and breeding true, whenever it condescends to produce seed at all, instead of the fine soot with which it too often fills its capsules instead.

Of the innumerable geographical forms and sub-species of *P. farinosa* notice will be found in due course under each name that covers them (and occasionally, in catalogues, deludes the unwary with hopes of a striking strange Primula). Such are *P. groenlandica; P. Hornemanniana,* a mealless alpine and Pyrenean form; *P. magellanica* from antarctic South America; *P. borealis,* North America; *P. modesta,* Japan; *P. davurica,* Russia, Siberia, North Mongolia, &c. (this is the one true and original *P. altaica,* Lehm.—a name so clouded with error and confusion that now it has lapsed by general consent); with its little frail Bulgarian variety *P. denudata* (or *exigua*); and finally

PRIMULA.

P. stricta, of sub-arctic Europe, Lapland, and Norway, is best taken as only a sub-species of *P. farinosa*.

P. Faurieae (*P. Fauriei* of Pax) is a dry-ground form of the very useful and charming little gold-powdered Farinosa sub-species *P. modesta* from Japan.

P. Fedschenkoi has glabrous toothed oval-rounded leaves in a neat upstanding tuft; and then on a most gracefully-proportioned scape, a most graceful umbel of big wide purple flowers. But unfortunately it is not yet in cultivation, so further commendations would be vain.

P. Filchnerae comes from the Tsin-ling range in China, and stands in a section all to itself, having affinities with *P. sinensis*, but differing in the leaves divided again and again and again.

P. filipes is an obscure small-flowered plant from rocks in Bhutan, which may be taken as a form of *P. obconica*.

P. flagellaris has only just emerged to recognition as a species; its nearest relation is tiny androsaceous *P. minutissima* from great altitudes in Kumaon, Kashmir, and Western Tibet. These species are spreading and stoloniferous, with small starry flowers usually sitting close upon the tuft. *P. flagellaris* differs from the rest by throwing out long threads, with rooting plant-buds at the end, after the fashion of the Saxifrages *flagellaris* and *Brunoniana*.

P. ×*flatnitzensis* is the natural hybrid of *P. minima*×*P. villosa*. It should closely, considering its parentage, resemble the wonderful *P. Steinii*, from *P. minima*×*P. hirsuta*. *P. flatnitzensis*, however, thanks perhaps to its forbidding name, is unknown in gardens, and yet more certainly in catalogues, although, besides being beautiful, it clearly should be as robust and easy as the other hybrids of similar parentage. It has been, as usual, divided into two named forms, for the two extremes, leaning to *P. minima* on one hand and to *P. villosa* on the other. Of these the one produces only two flowers, and those almost sessile on the little rosettes of roundly wedge-shaped leaves, glandular, dark and toothed at their point. This is the Minima-end of the scale, and has been called *P. truncata*, and also *P. Jiraseckiana*. The other has scapes very slightly taller, and bears as many as five blossoms on them. The name under which this form has occasionally appeared in lists is *P. Sturii*. The hybrid occurs with its parents on the high moors of Styria, never on the limestone, but no doubt indifferent in cultivation. *P.* ×*variiformis* is a false name.

P. flava I believe to be a xeromorph of *P. citrina* (see Appendix) from the bleak arid mountain region of the upper Hwang Hor.

PRIMULA.

P. × *Floerkeana* often appears in lists. This is the natural hybrid of *P. minima* × *P. glutinosa* either way round. It is a most important and beautiful thing, but unfortunately the range of variation is here so immense that no fewer than four distinct names have been applied to different developments. All these forms interbreed and grade into each other, until there is now no choice but to sweep the whole range into the one wide net of *P. Floerkeana*. This, or rather that special form to which the name was originally applied, is a most marked and magnificent thing at its best, having the habit of *P. glutinosa*, but forming wide dense masses, from which shoot up 3-inch scapes, each carrying three or four flowers as large as *P. minima's*, but of a fulminating vinous rose, which glows like fire from afar among the soft violet films with which *P. glutinosa* veils the high granitic moors. It is a very robust grower, too, in any light wellmixed peaty soil, and a garden-plant of great value. It is, on the whole, the commonest and most typical form of the cross. Then comes another called *P. Huteri*, tending more towards Minima, but with violet flowers ; yet a third is offered often as *P. salisburgensis*, a plant much closer to Glutinosa, but with two or three violet-red flowers to the scape ; and last of all the rare *P. biflora*, which is almost pure *P. minima*, but with two magnified blossoms to the scape.

P. floribunda is, of course, useless out of doors.

P. Forbesii was annual when first described, but has now developed, from other seed, into a useful greenhouse perennial, without value for the outdoor garden. The species varies indefatigably, and among its named varieties or microforms are *PP. androsacea, multicaulis, Willmottiae, Duclouxii, delicata, pellucida* (*speluncicola* and *debilis*), and *Barbeyana*. None of these have separate value except pretty neat *P. androsacea*, and this is no more hardy than the rest.

P. Forrestii was received into cultivation with a roar of acclamation. Those shouts have now died down into silence after many sad and expensive attempts to keep *P. Forrestii* in the land of the living. Never did a species look so robust and indestructible ; everyone felt that the Polyanthus now had a rival. In point of fact *P. Forrestii* is a sturdy suffruticose species, which forms enormous aged trunked masses in the hot limestone cliff-faces of Yunnan ; and in cultivation it proves to dread and detest superfluous wet in winter. In future it must be grown purely as a saxatile subject, in high and dry crevices, perfectly drained, of warm dry limestone rock, open to all the sun there is. In appearance, indeed, the clump is misleading, owing to its general resemblance to a gorgeous but orange-coloured Polyanthus ; of which it has the solid crinkled, stalked leaves (but here oblong heart-

131

shaped), the upstanding scapes, and the stout well-furnished graceful heads of blossom, which in *P. Forrestii* are smaller, more numerous, of a fiery golden-yellow, and entrancingly delicious perfume. It will come to its right place in our estimation when we have forgotten the exaggerated clamours of its introduction, and forgiven the disappointments into which it led us with its apparently hearty habit and its secret valetudinarianism.

P. × Forsteri. See under *P. × Steinii.*

P. Fortunei is a prettyish little Chinese species, recalling *P. farinosa* in appearance. It has often been in cultivation but is not hardy.

P. Franchetii is the rarest and least known of the six species at present under the leadership of *P. Elwesiana.* It has distinct Gloxinias, large and long and wide and lonely, of violet-purple; and *P. Engleri* comes close beneath it, if not actually the same thing.

P. frondosa is very welcome by now in all our gardens, though for long it has lain under the reproach of being wrongly named. Now, however, it has been cleared by the discovery that the original types in the Herbarium *are* mealy, like the garden plant, whereas Pax had declared true *P. frondosa*, Janka, to be destitute of powder. In effect *P. frondosa* is incomparably the most valuable garden species we have in the kindred of *P. farinosa.* Of this it lacks not only the daintiness and charm, but also the miffiness of temper; it is a robust cabbagy little thing, like a large coarse Farinosa, with a dense coating of white meal on the under-side of the crinkled grey leaves, and countless scapes carrying blossoms no bigger than in *P. farinosa*, but more numerous, in looser heads, and of a rather harsher pink. *P. frondosa* comes from Northern Thrace, where it lives in cool corners of the mountains, wet with the melting snow. In spite of this, however, it grows freely in any light soil in any open place of any garden, seeds itself freely all over the place, and only seems to dread excess of moisture in winter.

P. × Fumana.—Yet another false name of Gusmus for *P. × Facchinii, q.v.*

P. Gaignepainii = *P. heucherifolia, q.v.*

P. gaisbergensis.—Though I have never yet seen this name in a list, there is no knowing what iniquity may not some day occur. So it may as well be recorded that this is a cowslip-hybrid from Lower Austria.

P. Gambeliana must indeed be a most lovely little gem, closely akin to *P. rotundifolia*, but differing in its larger flowers and glabrous inflorescences. It is of tiny stature, with rounded, serrate, stalked

PRIMULA.

leaves looking like those of *Ranunculus bilobus*, and short scapes carrying three or four very large round flowers of brilliant purple-pink with a golden throat. *P. Gambeliana* occurs only in Sikkim, at higher altitudes than *P. rotundifolia*, and affects banks of damp moss in the dense forest, growing almost epiphytically. It is by now in cultivation, and we may well long for the day when we all can attempt its conquest.

P. Gammieana represents *P. Roylei* in East Sikkim, and both have been largely confused with *P. obtusifolia*.

P. gemmifera is described as a handsome annual from rocks overhanging the Czan-ho river in Kansu. Its habit is that of a Saxifrage: it produces reproductive bulbils in the axils of its leaves, and the large flowers are said to be violet.*

P. geraniifolia is a charming little plant, simulating the habit of a Cortusa, with graceful loose trusses of large round rosy flowers rising well above the stalked, crinkled leaves so like those of Geranium or Cortusa. This is a native of the Chumbi Valley, and is in cultivation. It comes readily from seed, but I have little experience of it in its later stages. It will probably enjoy the same treatment as its close relative, *P. cortusoides*, but, being smaller and frailer, may well exact a little more care in some more special place.

P. Giraldiana is the proper name of the pleasant but rather miffy little species introduced by the Bees, Ltd., as *P. muscarioeides*. It is small in growth, with quite small purple flowers packed into close drooping heads at the top of a stem rising some 8 or 12 inches above the neat rosette of long-oval upstanding hairy leaves, neatly scallop-lobuled at the edge, and of thin membranous texture. Like the rest of this group it should have a choice place in the underground-watered bed; but no Insurance Office will accept it as a really sound life.

P. glabra is a small hairless Indian alpine, with a rosette of outspread leaves, distinctly and delicately toothed, and then a stem of 3 or 4 inches carrying six or more flowers like those of an exaggerated *P. farinosa*. It should have the same treatment, but its heads are not so well proportioned to the ample rosette.

P. glacialis.—It is beside the Li-kiang Glacier that *P. glacialis* earns its name, and opens its wide saucers of violet blossom, many in a head, on a stem of an inch or a good deal more, surmounting the

* I leave this note, from the Paxian diagnosis, but the classical specimens of *P. gemmifera* in the Petrograd Herbarium are merely (α) a poor Sibirica-form found also by myself in the Da-Tung Alps, and (β) my own *P. "acclamata,"* Balf. fil., a very beautiful and valuable species, which is not an annual, throws no bulbils, and is not in the least degree like a Saxifrage. In fact, it contradicts the above diagnosis in every point, having large round flowers of rosy lilac, and standing very near to *P. conspersa* in the obvious group of *P. farinosa* and *P. stenocalyx.*

leaves, which are stalked and papery in texture, coarsely freely toothed at the edge, and white with powder underneath. The wide lovely flowers have the lobes entire and rounded, so that their face has a full and cheerful look ; and in the Petrograd Herbarium *P. glacialis* shows as a notably sturdy and splendid species in its splendid group.

P. glaucescens refreshes us by leading up our feet once more on to the copsy levels of the upper Lombard limestones, where it makes wide great cushions in and out of the bushes, thus doing such sad disservice to the race of which it is the least distinguished ornament. For it is the only one of the four Arthritic species that is not found in the high and open sunny turf of the mountain ridges so much as among the opener places of the brushwood below the summits. And as *P. glaucescens* is the commonest of the group, and one of the commonest of all Primulas in gardens, under many names, it follows that *P. glaucescens* has set a rule in gardeners' minds of shade and coolness for all its kindred, which shade and coolness, on the contrary, all its kinsmen most profoundly resent. *P. glaucescens* is confined to the alps of Bergamo, just advancing upon the Judicarian territories of *P. spectabilis*, and there, on Monte Cadi, near Brescia, has resulted the hybrid *P. × Carueli*, which, being between two parents so closely related, has no special value for the garden. *P. glaucescens* has the smooth firm leathern leaves of this group, forming into wide mats, and brightly gleaming. They are much stiffer than those of *P. Clusiana*, larger than those of *P. Wulfeniana*, wholly lacking the gland-pits and dulled-leather tone of *P. spectabilis;* and from all of these might easily, besides, be known by the extra-visible broad band of membrane they wear round their edge, no less than by the chalky glaucescence that they sometimes wear beneath. The purplish flower-stems are some 3 or 4 inches high, carrying a head of large lilac-purple flowers in varying tones, with deeply cloven lobes and a rather thin texture ; so that, for all their beauty, they do not compete successfully with those of their wearer's nearest relations. There are two main forms of it : the one called *P. g. calycina*, Duby and Pax (and catalogues), is the more robust and large in all its parts, and the commoner in the Lombard Alps ; the second, *P. g. longobarda*, is altogether smaller, and adventures higher on to the open turf of the Judicarian hills, meeting the other type on Bondol and on Resegone, while the Grigna seems exclusively occupied by *P. calycina*. There was also a thing once sent out as *P. intermedia* (Hegetschw. and Heer.) ; this is no more than *P. glaucescens*, as sent out by foreign nurseries ; whereas the true plant, if true such a pretender can be called, should belong to *P. Clusiana*. In cultivation *P. glaucescens* is quite easy and popular, growing freely

in any rich soil; here on the Cliff it has formed a handsome clump
in a crevice (though in nature by no means addicted to such), and
there most gloriously hides itself with loose heads of flower in March,
while the rows of garden clumps are not often without blossom even
in the depths of winter.

P. × *globulariaefolia* is one of Gusmus' many superfluous names for
P. × *Heerii* (Brügger), *q.v.*

P. glomerata is a rather obscure and difficult species in the neighbourhood of *P. denticulata*, from which it differs in unfurling its foliage
simultaneously with its flowers, while, though its leaves are almost
those of *P. erosa* (a plant very like this, and possibly a hybrid, has been
wrongly figured in the *Bot. Mag.* under the name of *P. erosa*), the
flowers are carried in a dense round head, on a stout scape, and each
on the very shortest pedicel consistent with being a pedicel at all.

P. glutinosa is the despair and the delight of the enthusiast—the
delight, when he sees the alpine acreage of the Monzoni-Thal, or
Kraxenträger, or the Pasterze, veiled with a film of clear violet from
afar, beneath the countless clumps of its delicious blueness dotting
the sere brown turf of the upmost levels; his despair when he hopes
to make so hearty-seeming a thing do the same at home, and sees,
instead, the squinny little stars on a dumpy stem that now and then
appear at shows, to be clucked over with gasps of awe by those who
know. *P. glutinosa* is violently calcifuge, and will only be seen at high
elevations in the ranges to East and South of Switzerland, just im-
pinging on that frontier in the Bernina range, but wandering far into
the South and East, abundant wherever it is found as the sands of
the sea, in the upper moorlands of the Hohe Tauern as on all the
volcanic outcrops of the Southern Dolomites. Here it covers the
earth in a profusion of neat massed clumps, not forming into mats,
but remaining concise clusters of narrow little strap-shaped toothed
leaves, densely sticky, from amid which shoot up several 2- or 3-inch
sticky dark stems, from the baggy bracts of which escapes a head of
most lovely flowers of pure blue-violet, with the lobes so deeply cloven
that it looks as if each corolla had ten segments. And not only are
they grateful to the eye almost beyond any other of their kind, but
they are no less pleasant to the nose, exhaling a delicious clean warm
sweetness that always suggests a translation, into terms of odour, of
the clean sweet white powder that decks the leaves of many species,
though not of *P. glutinosa;* which is also so distinct in the family, as
being the one *blue-violet* species of the Alps, that it seems wonderful how
people can still be in a maze about it, and mix it up with the quite
inferior and wholly different *P. integrifolia*, which occupies the same

situations indeed, but has much larger flowers, and fewer of them, and those of a washed and ugly magenta-lilac ; to say nothing of the many other points of difference. In cultivation *P. glutinosa* has always proved a problem, until the invention of the underground-watered bed, in which conditions it finds the soaking summer circumstances that it enjoys, and is evidently prepared to grow away as heartily as on the Alps, though it yet remains to be seen how heartily it will bloom. But even on the hills, although by dint of sheer abundance it clothes their expanses in blue, it is not a free-flowerer ; and where in a hundred yards you will have a thousand half-nodding heads of delicious violet springing from their clumps, yet, if you look, you will see that the number of flower-stems is but one in ten to that of all the masses that might be sending them up. So that there need yet be no reproach against the plant on this score in cultivation. On the hills it varies but little, though very fertile of hybrids with *P. minima*, which are found treated in their place. Once I met two specimens of a pure albino in the Monzoni-Thal, but these had more the look of a little white Allium than of anything else, and, but for their rarity, could not compare with the loveliness of the violet-blue type, which, to be loved as it deserves, must not be read of in cold pages but seen for oneself, veiling the hills, high and far, with a colour rich as the robes of Theodora on the walls of Ravenna, but less evanescent than the imperial purples of Rome, never fading to the present mud-colour of the great Augusta's vestment, but preserving always its invariable splendour, inspired with a fragrance that seems the essence and everlasting spirit of the hills, when Spring has once more trailed her coat of many colours for man to tread that carpet of constellated lovelinesses. There is a little ledge, man-high, under Colbricon, which is filled with *P. glutinosa* (descending from its higher places just above on the moor), where it nods its shaggy heads of soft colour in one's face, and fills the air with a sweet thought of the year's recurrent dawn, until one feels that no garden, save that of forgotten Eden, is worthy to contain a thing so beautiful and so good. However, the gardener need labour under no artificial humility on this point—the Primula is quite capable of agreeing with him on its own account, and will very soon judge of his worthiness by infallible methods of its own : and behave accordingly. It is a challenging fairy, to be conquered and tamed with wise love : not impossible, but difficult like all good things, and amply worth the wear of winning.

P. glycosma hovers on the fringe of cultivation. It belongs to the great easy group of *P. japonica*, glories of the bog, and its especial eminence lies in the fact that every part of the growth exhales a sweetness as delicious as the lives of saints.

P. × Goeblii (Kerner)=*P. pubescens*, Jacq., *q.v.*

P. gracilenta is a dim and minute-flowered species of the Muscarioid group. It is now in cultivation, but not worthy of much attention.

P. grandis stands by itself. The foliage is heart-shaped, and of an almost tropical splendour, like that of some Petasites, and well worth planting for its own sake in some rich corner of the bog, where it will have room to develop. The tall scapes shoot up high above these in the summer, and then break, like a rocket, into a thick crowd of trailing little sparks—long tubular small flowers in great numbers, hanging and shooting from graceful long pedicels, the whole effect being delicate, but the blossoms in themselves preposterously mean for a stalwart of such size and pomposity of promise. It is a Caucasian species, and can easily be raised from seed ; or else the clumps divided—a method most popular among Primulas, a race whose seed is slow and uncertain of germination, even under conditions of the most experienced care, and even when it is fresh ; but where the established mat or clump seems positively to enjoy being divided in the later summer, a fact which lends extra happiness to the long summer hours spent upon the Grigna in holidays from *Campanula Raineri*, or on the Tombea in the few off-moments allowed by *Daphne petraea*.

P. graveolens. See under *P. viscosa*.

P. Griffithii is a species in the troublesome but most beautiful group of *P. Roylei*, which is a plant in the same kinship as *P. petiolaris*. The real *P. Griffithii* remains quite unknown in cultivation, and has suffered long, like its cousins, *P. Gammieana* and *P. Roylei*, from confusion with the equally unknown but quite remote *P. obtusifolia* of the Nivalis section. True *P. Griffithii* is a glory of the Rhododendron-zone, standing close to *P. Tanneri* and with much the same large and lovely flowers of lavender-blue, though with the stalked oblong leaves and the general habit of *P. Roylei*.

P. groenlandica is a sub-species of *P. farinosa*.

P. hakusanensis is a Japanese microform of *P. cuneifolia*.

P. Harrissii comes from Chitral, and there stands between *P. elliptica* and *P. rosea* in habit and character, having the brilliant and violently-pink flowers of the latter.

P. hazarica stands near *P. Jaffreyana*, from which, among other points, it differs in having its adult leaves powdered underneath. Its beauty is more that of *P. elliptica*, however, with scapes of 2 or 3 inches, bearing many-flowered heads of big purple-rosy blossoms hardly rising out of the leaves as they appear. It is a common beauty high up in the Western Himalaya, having, like *P. elliptica*, the same looks and ways as *P. rosea*, but with violet flowers.

P.×Heerii is the natural hybrid between *P. hirsuta* and *P. integrifolia*, which has had such a quantity of unnecessary synonyms, some four of them contributed by one collector and three by another, both of whom ought to have known better. It is a strikingly beautiful little cross, always to be looked for (but very seldom found) where the two parents are growing together (as, for instance, throughout the high moors of the Engadine). It forms ramifying masses, and has flowers of far greater size and brilliancy than either of its parents—though it is variable, and should be bought and collected only in its best forms, where the blossoms, on stems of 2 inches or less, are of an amplitude and splendour altogether exceptional: brilliant pink with cloven lobes and waved loose wide outlines, and a white fuzz of glands in the blurred white throat. It may, apart from its own personality, be always known from *P. integrifolia* by its broader, softer, bright-green leaves, *never entire*, but always more or less toothed ; and from *P. hirsuta* by its much scantier down, much *larger fewer flowers on longer foot-stalks*, and the head swathed in longer, broader, baggier bracts. It seems, in the garden, to retain its native prejudice against lime, which comes to it strongly through both its parents, and may therefore be an inexpugnable heritage.

P. helodoxa is a superb acquisition in the Japonica-group, of the same hardiness and stature and use and beauty—a stately splendour with tall stems and whorls of large flowers of soft rich yellow, well indeed to be called the Glory of the Bog. (China.)

P. × helvetica (Don.)=*P. × pubescens*, Jacq.

P. helvetica (Ktze.)=*Androsace helvetica*.

P. Hemsleyi is a Chinese species allied to *P. cuneifolia*, from the bogs of Tatsienlu. It has a neat charm, forming a basal rosette of stalked toothed leaves elliptic in outline, and sending up a Farinosa-stem, with a similar head of mauve flowers with a deep-cut bell-shaped calyx, and an oval seed-head afterwards sticking far out.

P. Henrici lives in the rocks between Lhasa and Batang. It is a cushion-forming plant, possibly of the Suffruticose section, making long trunks in the way of *P. Allionii*, thickly clad in long narrow wavy-edged leaves (and their dead further down), glandular-downy above, and white-powdered beneath, blushing to a dark bronzy note as they

PLATE 14.

PRIMULA GEMMIFERA.
(Photo. W. Purdom.)

PRIMULA FARRERIANA.
(Photo. W. Purdom.)

PLATE 15.

PRIMULA HIRSUTA (var. MRS. WILSON).

PRIMULA GLAUCESCENS.

grow old. Among these, lonely on each shoot, sits a single solitary lilac-rosy star of blossom with deeply-cloven lobes.

P. Henryi remains wrapped in obscurity in the mountain-woods of Yunnan. We only know that it is a strange oddity. The leathery oval leaves are of immense length, standing boldly upright, to the height of 18 inches or more, on foot-stalks usually longer than themselves, and set with spiny teeth all round. The graceful stem overtops them and opens into an almost umbellate shower of small flowers at present imperfectly known, but the general effect is hardly that of a Primula at all.

P. heterochroma lives in Persia, and has its little leaves downy-white on the under-side. It is merely a small gem-like form of the Primrose, with the same yellow blooms though much diminished.

P. heterodonta, a Japanese high-alpine, is a microform of *P. cuneifolia*, to be distinguished by the leaves, larger and thinner, with coarse irregular toothing, and more luxuriant. (Pax's note misleads.) This group stands near our own species of the Erythrodose section—neat rock-plants, with quite short stems and heads of large and brilliant flowers. But they are wholly smooth and glandless; *P. heterodonta* is quite the brightest and best—like our own alpine friends in dense rosette and stout flower-head.

P. heucherifolia is the thing cultivated usually as *P. Gaignepainii*. It has a general resemblance to a neat and charming *Cortusa Matthioli*, with fuller pendent bell-flowers of rich and sombre purple, on graceful little stems of 6 inches or so, standing high above the tuft of soft and crinkled deep-lobed leaves. It should have the treatment of the Cortusa it mimics, and be shielded from wet in winter.

P. Heydei is much more original. It forms wide and wandering masses of small rosettes, emitting long runners that terminate in more, made up of congregated narrow tiny leaves, so deeply and sharply toothed as to have a spinulous look, yet not rigid either to eye or touch. Here and there, from these rosettes, rise up stems of an inch and a half or less, giant for the minute size of the plant—carrying a wide head of some six or eight pale-lilac flowers like those of *P. farinosa*, standing in a laxer flatter cluster. A high-alpine from Western Tibet. It should go into the choicest moraine; it is noted that species of the Denticulata-group that are covered with snow in winter are usually annual or biennial, so that the rule might apply here, but that *P. Heydei's* running habit immortalises it. For one may take it for granted that snow occasionally lies on the Roof-beam of the World in winter. At lower elevations the section is addicted to open glades on the hillsides, among the buttercups and Anemones, such species being then robustly perennial as in the group of *P. denticulata* itself.

P. hirsuta, All., has no doubt at all about its name. It is quite definitely and finally described by Allioni as *P. hirsuta* in 1785, so that Villars's subsequent name of *P. viscosa,* 1787, was obviously invalid from the beginning (see note on *P. viscosa,* All.). However, though the arch-breeder of confusion in catalogues, this most generally known and grown of the Erythrodose section is one of the most precious of its race in the garden. It is a variable species, and not only have varieties been accorded specific rank, but synonyms have been multiplied and advertised with reckless prodigality. The following names must henceforward be discarded absolutely from all serious lists and catalogues : *P. ciliata* (Schrank), *P. pubescens* (Loiseleur), *P. decora* (Sims), *P. confinis* (Schott), *P. decipiens* (Stein). All these appear too often in catalogues, and all are to be reduced to the single name of *P. hirsuta.* The type is easily recognisable by its very broadly-ovate or rhomboidal leaves, always obtuse, always more or less dentate, always narrowing sharply to a longer or shorter petiole, and clothed in yellow, tawny or golden fur, which only rarely deepens to red. The plant is viscid, and the flower-scape rarely rises at all, and never rises much, above the leaves. The height of the whole growth is from 2 to 4 inches at the most. The umbels are many-flowered, the corolla-tube long, the blossoms bright pink or mauve, occasionally white, very large and brilliant and beautiful at their best.

This species has been for centuries in cultivation, is the most robust of the section, and the widest in distribution. It occasionally occurs on limestone (as, quite starveling, in crevices of the Grigna), but prefers granitic formations, and ranges through all the central alpine chain, on rocks and moorland ridges of the primary formations, from the Pyrenees, through the Graian, Bernese, Valaisan, Rhaetian, South Tyrolese, Austrian, and Dolomite Alps. Its varieties are not to be clearly distinguished ; *P. hirsuta angustata* hails from the Maloja, and has narrower leaves ; *exscapa* is stemless ; *nivea* is an albino, and is the correct name of " *P. nivalis.*" I do not know if the genuine *P. hirsuta nivea* is now obtainable ; and the many things sold under the name of *P.* " *viscosa* " are very often clearly of mixed parentage. *P.* " *viscosa* " *Mrs. J. H. Wilson,* a beautiful, vigorous, and most free-blooming treasure with rich purple-lilac flowers, seems to be certainly a *P.* × *pubescens,* and the same must be said of the lurid-scarlet and dark-violet forms, *P. hirsuta* (*ciliata*) *coccinea* and *purpurea,* as well, I think, as of *P. hirsuta purpurea* and *eximia,* &c., and many another named colour-variety. But *P. hirsuta* is so free a seed-bearer, in fact, and so prolific a parent, that a large percentage of its children in nature, as in the garden, show a greater or a less degree of alien blood.

P.×Hoelscheri is an interesting, rare, and beautiful hybrid between *P. rosea* and *P. luteola*. It has more the habit of the latter, but the flowers are pink as in *P. rosea*, though with a yellow eye, and carried in heads on taller stems above foliage that unfolds contemporaneously and is more closely toothed. It should have the culture of *P. luteola*, and be divided every other year to keep it in permanent condition. And it has *P. luteola's* value of flowering in full summer.

P. Hookeri is a dainty small high-alpine from Sikkim, in the huge and polymorphic group of *P. petiolaris*. It is, however, quite minute, hardly an inch and a half tall, flower and tuft and all, while the toothed little oval leaves are frail and smooth and powderless. And whereas the less mountaineering species in this group make large masses in rocks, or in the shadow and spray of waterfalls, these higher developments are seen to prefer the shadow of pine and bamboo far up on the mountain, like *P. viscosa* on the Col de la Croix. The flowers of *P. Hookeri* are round and white, nestling among the leaves, and making in their time the massed solid splendour of bloom so noted in this group, where all the colony marches into blossom together with the unanimity of a regiment, and marches out again, so that the whole neighbourhood is either naked of everything but green, or else at a day's notice imperialised in colour, and then in a week or two dethroned into mere verdure again.

P. Hornemanniana is a form of *P. farinosa*.

P.×Hugueninii, Brügger, was detected on the Parpaner Rothhorn among its parents, *P. glutinosa* and *P. integrifolia*. The specimen was, however, indiscreetly removed to a new home that it did not like, so departed promptly to a better and final one. So that the record needs confirming, and the hybrid describing.

P.×Huteri is a name for one of the large sliding-scales of hybrids between *P. minima* and *P. glutinosa*. This name applies to a form standing near to *P. minima*, but with sticky blunt-toothed leaves and broadly-ovate overlapping bracts, longer than the calyces. The flowers are two or so to a short scape, not very full, and purple-red in colour, with their face hardly as wide as the tube is long. This form is a rare one, difficult to come across in culture, or anywhere else.

P. imperialis is a stalwart giant of the Japonica-group that has the romance of breaking far away from the neighbourhood of all its race. It is the only Primula to trespass on the Equator, where at some 9000 feet on Pangerango in Java it grows great and stately, and yet is by no means indisposed to do so in England, even out of

141

doors. For in the Javan land of Cornwall it is grown in beds, and even in Yorkshire it will blossom in the open, though here the amplitude, indeed, of its Japonica-like foliage is fine (though no finer than Japonica's), but the tiered tall spikes of rich golden-yellow flowers cannot be expected to reach their full magnificence unprotected. It should be grown in the very rich and humid conditions beloved by *P. japonica*, and, in cold climates, potted roomily in fat soil to show its splendour more happily indoors.

P. Inayatii flutters at present, like a malicious butterfly, just out of reach of man's hand, here and there to be seen flourishing in botanical collections, but there guarded as if it were the " di'mond jewelleries of Pharaoh's Ma " that it is really hardly worth. The leaves in their tuft are about 10 inches or a foot in length, narrowly-oblong, membranous, irregularly scallop-toothed at the edge, and yellow-powdered below, with a reddish stem to each, along which, in flaps, the leaf continues, till the outline of the foot-stalk is blurred. The scape stands boldly up, but above the excessive length of foliage and on the tall stem the flowers are not such in size as to justify this boldness, or qualify it as anything but " bragian." For they are rather small and funnel-shaped in themselves; and, for so lavish a growth, little more than a derision, even if not lacking in beauty of their own. It lives in moist rocks high in Hazara.

P. × *incerta* is one of Gusmus' four false names for *P. Heerii, q.v.*

P. incisa belongs to the noble, dainty, and glorious section of the great-belled Soldanella group. It has a tuft of hairy stalked leaves, about 2 inches long in all to start with, but then developing the leaf-stalk to another inch or so. The leaves themselves are deeply toothed and gashed as in the Bella-section, and from the tuft rises a scape of 3 or 4 inches, swinging a little chime of royally blown-out bells of pink or violet, with deeply-cloven lobes. It lives in the upper wood-region of Omei, Moupin, Tatsienlu, and should have the reverent observation that attends all this miffy gathering of loveliness, the most delicate of the race, craving for porous moist soil in summer and perfect dryness in winter.

P. infundibulum, in the Petrograd Herbarium, reveals a very lovely small species of the Szechwanese Alps, close on whose close tuffets protrude single enormous funnels of roseate flower.

P. integrifolia, L., is a species abundantly to be seen on the high moors of the Engadine, and away to the Voraarlberg in the East and the Pyrenees in the West, usually on the granites, but occasionally on the limestones too. In the high turf it forms running clumping masses and lawns of broad-leaved rosettes, brightish green and close and almost shining, until one might mistake it for an Arthritic Primula. But the leaves are *softer* and more strap-shaped, they have *no edge of membrane*, and they are always set all over with *fine glandular hairiness*, besides being smaller and forming looser, not dense-clumped cushions. The stems, too, are glandular, about an inch or two in height, with large reddish bracts and a reddish tinge to the baggy calyx too. The flowers are borne in heads of two or three; they are very large and densely glandular-furry in the blurred white throat, but of a washy magenta-lilac that makes *P. integrifolia* the least pleasing of our European alpine species, though quite ready of culture in full sun in open porous peat. Its most beautiful aspect is offered, I believe, on the Joch Pass in the Oberland above Engelberg, where it colours the alps with its millions of lilac-purple blossoms, relieved by millions of *Ranunculus alpester* standing up in snowy moons among the magenta-red masses of the Primula. (There is also a sub-species or form of *P. farinosa* that bears the same name, to say nothing of the fact that it has been used by many other authors to cover many other pretenders.)

P. × intermedia, Port., if it likes, can be by far the grandest of all our mountain Primulas, species or hybrids. It is the cross of *P. Clusiana* and *P. minima*, occurring, very rarely indeed, in wide colonies among its parents, on the high limestones of Styria, threading the open fine turf with laxly-carpeting rosettes, distinct at once in size and habit from either parent, running more freely and widely than *P. minima*, and larger in the tuft of shining, oval-pointed leaves; and less stay-at-home in a clump than *P. Clusiana*, with leaves, indeed of the same shape and glittering scheme, but half the size, and *always cut at the edge into a varying number of quite spiny-looking fine teeth*. There are several leaf- and flower-forms: one, the smaller, is clearly nearer to *P. minima*, and is probably the reverse cross, having little scapes of an inch or so, carrying two Minima-flowers of richer colouring, which are followed by fertile capsules of seed, while the plant itself has the carpet-habit of *P. minima*, expanded into great laxity, but still recognisable, though the rosetted leaves are pointed and up-standing in small glossy clusters. The other cross clearly has *P. Clusiana* for its mother, and is the noblest of its kind I know. Here the rosettes are larger, the toothing of the foliage more evident even to the casual eye, the colour of more glaucous pale-green, and the habit a series of small clumps of two or three crowns together, scattered here and there over perhaps half a dozen square yards of moor, and then nowhere again to be beheld. The flower-stems, too, are taller, some 3 or 4 inches high, and furnished more fully with flowers whose

PRIMULA.

dimensions it is hard to understand. For at their best they leave *P. Clusiana* gasping on the shelf, and *P. Clusiana* type comes near to being the grandest species in the grandest group we have. Yet, out of *minima* and *Clusiana* a child has been born which has not combined the two blossoms so much as added them together and produced blossoms of almost unseemly enormousness and magnificence, glowing pink with wide white eyes, as large as a five-shilling piece and larger, ample in outline, firm in texture, and of such dominating beauty that both its parents sit and sulk when it blossoms, and refuse to enter into competition. For to its own natural merits *P. × intermedia* adds that of being perhaps the freest and easiest of all the European Primulas to grow, multiplying its crowns as quickly as a Primrose in any rich loam or sterile moraine, with equal speed, but luxuriating most fatly in the fattest soil, and rejoicing to be divided in late summer ; while from every crown Spring never fails to call up a stem of those superlatively splendid flowers in early April. The plant is sterile and sets no seed, unlike the inferior reverse cross ; and in nature it is interesting to note that both follow that curious law which seems to indicate that hybrids are best born on high and wind-swept ridges. It is on such, and only there, that *P. × Juribella* will be seen, *P. × Facchinii*, *P. Dumoulinii*, *P. coronata*, and the rest ; while on the Schneeberg you will tramp miles of moorland made of nothing but *P. minima* and *P. Clusiana* (intertwined with *Dianthus alpinus*, *Viola alpina*, *Campanula alpina*) without ever seeing any hybrid until you reach a certain high ridge, and there, and there alone, and there only, within a range of a few hundred yards, will the intermediates at last be found dotted about in all their wonder and splendour. (They should be seen in flower before purchase.)

P. intricata, Godr. and Gren., is nothing but a form of *P. elatior* from the Southerly Alps. But nevertheless most valuable and charming, for it forms neat tufts in any good soil, and there flowers with an unimaginable profusion of large creamy-lemon oxlips on scapes of 3 or 4 inches, without any intermission through the whole year, but most especially brilliant in spring and autumn.

P. intrusa (Rchb.) is merely a microform, but has the look of a quite tiny *P. farinosa*, with enormous flowers and a large involvement of bracts.

P. involucrata, Wall., 1828 (*P. Munroi*, Lindley, 1833), is a most lovely and easy-going bog-plant, so free and anxious to grow that our cries for the rest of the group grow louder. It loves a wet clogging spot in rich soil, and there forms hearty spreading clumps of small dark oblong leaves on stalks, lush and glossy and smooth ; high above which in May shoot brave 6-inch stems, unfolding a head of very large flowers, very round and opulent in outline, very deliciously sweet-scented, and of a white so profound and cold that it sometimes chills off into an icy blue. *P. involucrata* needs no other prescription than wetness and richness, seeds freely, can be divided at any time (but best in late summer), and often sows itself about in the most improbable places, or comes up in the bed of a stream half a mile or so beyond the rock-garden and its bog.

P. Jacquini. See under *P. villosa.*

P. Jaffrayana is another of the remote lovely group of the Lovely-flower section. It forms a tuft of little smooth and ultimately powderless leaves, toothed and blunt, about an inch and a half in length, from which ascends a scape of two or three, only just surpassing the foliage, and carrying some half a dozen noble pale-purple blooms almost in the shape of widening funnels, opening suddenly into a flat cheerful face about an inch across. (From 12,000 feet up in the Chumbi valley.)

P. japonica still stands at the head of its group, and will not readily be displaced. Every garden where there is water or rich soil rejoices in some favourite form of this stalwart and established species, which has a much longer record of friendship with England than the country whose name it bears, and where alone it may be found. There are good golden-eyed white forms, and there are inferior white forms with blurred weeping eyes, sore-edged and conjunctivitic ; there are bad magenta forms, and pale pinks of indecisive merit, and superb forms of hot clear scarlet-rose like sunlit blood, or salmon suffused with tomato sauce : but nothing will easily oust the best old types, superb tiered giants of deep and velvety crimson. *P. japonica* should be used to fill wide acres in the open bottoms of woodland, in such multitudes that not all the rabbits of Australia could eat them down ; and, once established in rich soil of garden, lake-side or stream, the clumps will look after themselves and go on for ever, and so robustly occupy the ground with the children that even in the most unlikely corners they will persist in coming up for many years, and defy the most indefatigable efforts at eradication.

P. jesoana is a woodland Primula of the soft-leaved Geranoid group, rather smaller than the Chinese species of which it continues the race in Japan and the tradition across the sea ; but it has no special charm to make us long for it.

P. Jelenkae is *P. × venusta, q.v.*

P. × Jiraseckiana (Tratt), the hybrid *P. minima × P. villosa*, whose correct prior name is *P. × truncata.* See under *P. flatnitzensis.*

PRIMULA.

P. Jonarduni need not trouble us yet awhile with its affinities. It is a tiny tufted species from Bhutan, with densely neat rosettes of overlapping little leathern leaves, powdered underneath. The crown is perennial, but of its flowers no tale is yet told.

P. Juliae has taken the plunge into civilisation amid cries of general applause, and now swims so eagerly on the tumbled sea of horticulture that its value in money must rapidly go down, as its value in the garden no less rapidly goes up. It has only been in cultivation some three or four years, but was only discovered in 1901, and then in the Caucasus, which gives great hope of further treasures yet lurking in byeways, even close at hand, of our overtrodden earth. In the Caucasus it is to be seen in wet dripping rocks and under the spray of waterfalls. In the garden it has no such fads, but continues to appreciate all the moisture it can get, though growing quite happily in any rich soil, where it makes huge masses of very attractive smooth and sombre little crinkly heart-shaped leaves on stalks, from which, alone on their stems, comes a profuse procession of starry Primroses in spring, autumn, and winter, varying in tones of soft or virulent lilac that would sometimes be called magenta if the plant were still not priced at five shillings. But they are always somehow beautiful, and are harmonised perhaps by the blurred or pencilled crimson at the base of the blossoms, which so have the happiest effect, nestling in such radiant abundance among their dark leaves through the darker hours of the year. And then, when tired of blooming, Julia's Primrose takes her walks abroad, on runners that strike fresh root and widen the lovely patch. And is no less easily multiplied by the seed that she no less freely produces.

P. × Juribella has so far only one recorded station. It is the natural hybrid between *P. minima* and *P. tyrolensis*, and is found in the grass with *P. minima* its mother, on the limestone ridges by the Rolle Pass beneath the frowning and tremendous peak of the Cimon della Pala. Even the most casual eye could distinguish it among the others, for the tiny leaves of the rosettes do not close in a straight toothed cut across their end as in *P. minima, but are oval* and toothed finely and irregularly *round their outline;* they are also not glossy like Minima's, but of a more opaque green, because they inherit a certain legacy of sticky glands from *P. tyrolensis.* From this, on the other hand, it may be known by never being found with its father in the rocks; while it has something of Minima's gloss, all Minima's mat-forming habit, and nothing of the dense columnar formations of *P. tyrolensis* (which has the rosettes standing each on a dense aged trunk of dead ones from many bygone years). In fact the plant is very much closer to *P. minima*, and has Minima's flowers, carried

146

PLATE 16.

PRIMULA GIRALDIANA.
(Photo. R.B.G., Edinburgh.)

PRIMULA JULIAE.
(Photo. R. A. Malby.)

PLATE 17.

PRIMULA LICHIANGENSIS.
(Photo. R. A. Malby.)

PRIMULA LISTERI (left) ; P. FORRESTII (right).
(Photo. R.B.G., Edinburgh.)

one or two to a most minute scape, and rather ragged in outline, though inheriting an added intensity of magenta from the rather aniline Tyrolensis. In culture it is quite easy in a place suited to this group, and thrives with *P. Facchinii* and *P. Dumoulinii*, but is not a thing of especial loveliness, though interesting on account of the remoteness of the cross and its extreme rarity.

P. × Kankeriana, a false name for the hybrid of *P. minima P. Wulfeniana*. See under *P. Deschmannii*.

P. Kaufmanniana stands quite close to the true *P. cortusoeides*, having the same very short pedicels to the flowers, but can be distinguished by the leaves, which are more rounded and deeply incised. (Turkestan.)

P. × Kellereri. See under *P. × Steinii*.

P. × Kerneri (Stein) is a synonym of *P. × pubescens*, Jacq., *q.v.*

P. kialensis belongs to the dainty little section of *P. yunnanensis*, to which it is closely allied. It is a rock-plant of the central mountain ranges of China, and makes a neat tiny single rosette of oval toothed leaves diminishing quickly to a stem as long as themselves, thin in texture, and thick with golden powder underneath. The stalk is perhaps 2 inches high, hardly taller than the leaves are long, and carries a graceful head of some half a dozen very large lilac flowers, bowl-shaped and with a long pale tube, deeply cloven lobes, and a green calyx with hardly a trace of powder on it.

P. kichanensis is sometimes offered or spoken of (for it rarely gets so far as an offer) as *P. Clementinae*. It is a most dainty delight, standing near the last, and quite easy to cultivate and keep. Here also we have a neat tuft of outspreading little oval toothed foliage, diminishing gradually to the base. The stem is 2 inches high or so, carrying a radiant head of long large blossoms that have to droop because they are so big and so beautiful with their comely faces of pale lavender-blue. The leaves are greyish, and the whole growth is more or less powdery, with the whiteness especially conspicuous on the umbrella of spreading calyces when the flowers are gone.

P. Kingii flowers at 14,000 feet on the mountains of Sikkim and Tibet, and, with its rich claret-purple bells, so sombre as almost to be of satiny black, mocks at collectors who see them with awe but have never yet been able to return into those inhospitable regions in time for the seed. It makes a neat tuft of small leathery dark leaves, fat and thick and oval, from which rises the stem of a few inches to hang out those tragic and splendid blossoms. Its beauty is allied to that of *P. amethystina*.

P. kisoana is a close cousin to *P. Sieboldii*, and is endemic to

147

P. Veitchii, but has foliage less hairy, and *not white beneath,* while its flowers are larger, and with a larger yellow eye, and anthers *not yellow but purple.* It is possible that these both belong to *P. polyneura.* In any case they all appreciate the treatment of Cortusa in the light woodland, and are of easy culture. And see Appendix.

P. Listeri will take the place of evil-minded *P. obconica,* with which it is connected by a long series of intergrading forms. But it will only do so indoors, standing the winters outside, indeed, but not with strength to develop flower next year. Therefore, outside the green-house we need take no more note either of *P. Listeri,* King, from the Himalaya, with its strong scent of Herb-Robert, nor of its Chinese substitute, *P. sinolisteri,* Balf., fil., originally sent out as the same species, but distinct in many ways, and especially in absolutely lacking the scent, though both alike form masses of handsome lobed leaves like dark-green dulled ivy, broken by countless trusses, over a very long season, of lovely large lilac or white blossoms, much finer and more gracefully borne than in the doomed *P. obconica.*

P. Littoniana is the most striking species, if not the most beautiful, in the Spike-flowered group—not a hard thing to grow and flower well in light rich soil, but it so upsets insects with its unheard-of spikes that the most faithful Primula-lover refuses to recognise it and passes it by on the other side, so that it does not bear seed and, like all the Hairy-leaves, is painfully apt to miff off if the winter is wet and the situation undrained. It makes a tuft of upstanding oval foliage, ribbed and downy and soft; and then up shoots a tall powdered stem, terminated by a spike often 6 inches in length, of brilliant scarlet bracts, from which, as the stem grows taller, unfold the innumerable pendent little packed flowers of lavender-lilac or deep violet, till in mid-bloom the spikes seem tapering ghost-flames of blue aspiring to their long tips of crimsoned fire, making an unparalleled effect as they hold up their millions of tall steady candle-lights in the lush grasses of the Yunnanese alps, among the sulphured spraying bells of *P. sikkimensis,* and the rich claret-rose and bloomy flesh of *P. secundiflora.* *P. Littoniana* is not a synonym of *P. Viali,* as sometimes said; *P. Viali* is a much smaller plant, after the same image, but shorter in the spike and altogether inferior, except in the fact that it lacks the hairiness of *P. Littoniana.* It is possible, of course, that *P. Viali* may prove merely a minor form of the grander species. (*P. Viali* of Pax is a portmanteau-name, containing, besides itself, *P. deflexa, P. Watsoni,* and *P. gracilenta.*)

P. Loczii is said to be a microform of *P. borealis,* Duby (*P. mistassinica* of some catalogues); but it hails from Kansu, and it is a far jump from Kansu to Alaska, where *P. borealis* has its nearest home. *P. Loczii* is rather a mystery, still, having affinities both with *P. farinosa* and with *P. sibirica*, nearer in nature to the latter, and in appearance to the former. But see Appendix for further news.

P. longiflora sets our feet once more on the high-alpine meadows of Europe. Even in the wilds it is a notable and delicate species, making small tufts of leaves larger, yet more condensed, than those of *P. farinosa*, so that in the end the rosette itself is often of less diameter ; seeming almost inadequate to the stalwart stems that it now sends up to carry half a dozen golden-eyed rosy-lilac flowers like those of a very large *P. farinosa*, but of fuller outline and deeper tone, and set on very long conspicuous tubes of dark purplish-pink that make the plant recognisable immediately. Its range is from the Central Alps, far away through Bosnia to the Caucasus. In Switzerland it is rare, and occurs here and there in single specimens, but in the Eastern ranges on the high limestone meadows, especially in the Dolomites, it becomes extremely abundant and beautiful, dotting all the grassy lawns of the Forcella Lungieres, the Schlern, Castellazzo, &c., with its long bugled stars of dim rose, above the shimmering pink carpets of *P. minima*, and leaving *P. farinosa* far down below in the damp places of humility. In cultivation the growth takes a new character ; it becomes colossal as a cabbage in any rich moist soil, and is so incomparably easier to grow and keep than *P. farinosa*, that one wonders how it is that while everybody wrestles bitterly with the one, the other is hardly if ever seen in the garden. The only point at which it needs safeguarding is in the matter of winter wet ; for if the tuft have made excessive growth, and its situation be not adequately drained, it may possibly prove too soft to stand the damp. Otherwise it offers no trouble at all, seeds as profusely as it grows, and adds to all its benefits that of sending up its magnified heads of blossom in July and August, and indeed at intervals throughout the season, till winter positively says " Cease." Something about the blossoms, however, displeases the taste of slugs ; they have a way of eating off all the pink-and-golden star of the flower's face quite neatly, and leaving nothing but the long bugle of the tube behind. It has no hybrids, none of the records of such satisfying either investigation or the demands of possibility.

P. longifolia, Bieb.=*P. algida, var. sibirica, q.v.*

P. longifolia, Curtis=*P. auriculata, q.v.*

P. longobarda, Porta=*P. glaucescens* (type 2), *q.v.*

P. luteola dislikes being water-logged in winter, but is otherwise so perfectly easy to grow in any rich deep cool soil, and so splendid see them. Therefore, in asking him for guidance the gardener will not only be gaining profit, but giving pleasure also—a holy and a pleasing thought. In yet other districts of those Alps the most lovely varieties of *P. marginata* may also be seen, that make even the lovely common type seem like silver in the time of Solomon. Some or many of these will often be offered under pompous names at high prices ; the gardener may hereby learn that if he chooses to take his summer holiday in that direction in May, he will be able to fill his garden with a hundred forms as good and better, for the mere trouble of taking his feet to the level of its rocks—where it is not necessary, indeed, to collect it by the root, since a few trunks pulled off here and there from the undisturbed mass will immediately strike fibre for themselves if sent home and reasonably treated. Culture already knows a white variety which is rather squinny and pink and impure ; but the personal eye will always offer the best satisfaction to the personal taste, which in this case runs less risk than usual, seeing that there is no form of *P. marginata* that is not of delightful charm and as easy of culture as couch-grass. Of hybrids the plant has yielded several beauties of the first rank. *Linda Pope* bears the name of the species, but has clearly other blood in her, though this has not spoiled her free and spreading habit, and the leathery toothed beauty of the grey powdered leaves ; while she also has blossoms of a quite especial size and amplitude, especially rich in soft clear blueness, and with a quite special round white eye of powder—a rare treasure at present, but one of the highest value. Then there is *P.* × *marven*, a hybrid between this species and *P.* × *venusta*, itself a hybrid of *P. auricula* and *P. carniolica*. From parentage so splendid a noble and a thrifty beauty is born—a thing of the easiest temper anywhere on the rock-work, with the grey leathern leafage of *P. marginata*, but taller stems carrying slightly smaller flowers, more round and numerous, of a sumptuous pure violet-purple with an eye of white, in loose heads on the stout stalks. This not only comes copiously from cuttings, but also seems fertile in seed. In nature hybrids were long looked for in vain, until at last 1913 yielded in the Cottian ranges a most regal intermediate which is to bear the name of *P.* × *Crucis*, Bowles. For on certain passes *P. marginata* dwells among the stones and cliffs and mossy places, while about among the roots of the pine-trees luxuriates also a notably full-faced and beautiful form of *P. viscosa*. And here accordingly, after years of doubt, it has been discovered that the two species in the same sub-section of their family will interbreed. *P.* × *Crucis* yet awaits its full description ; of *P. marginata*, however, it has the habit (though more tufted and less procumbent), no less than

PLATE 18

PRIMULA LITTONIANA.
(Photo. R. A. Malby.)

PRIMULA INVOLUCRATA.
(Photo. R.B.G., Edinburgh.)

PLATE 19.

PRIMULA LUTEOLA.
(Photo. R.B.G., Edinburgh.)

PRIMULA MALACOEIDES.
(Photo. R.B.G., Kew.)

the toothed and more or less powdered foliage, which, however, is less leathern and stiff than in the species its mother. And the flowers are intermediate, having the beauty of both parents and an added intensity of colour, though leaning more towards the loveliness of *P. marginata*, which clearly is the dominant original of the cross. The hybrid has many splendid colour-forms, and seems to breed back again into secondary crosses with either or other of its parents—but always a glory not to be mistaken or misunderstood among the species by the most uninstructed and unobservant of passers-by. There was one form among them of a beauty so overwhelming that it can only be realised when I say that it was three times offered by its finder to the eponymous discoverer, and no less than three times refused, thus postulating a heart-breaking degree of virtue on the part of the refuser, no less than on that of the offerer, such as could be called out by no less momentous occasion than a matter of horticultural life and death. Let it be known that *P. ⨯ Crucis, Blue Bowl*, to all the vigour of one parent, and the stalwart volume of the other, unites flowers of a clear and lucid sapphire-blue like the finest Chinese glass of Kien-lung, that simply laughs at everything in Europe, and joins hands across the world with *P. sapphirina* and *P. Viola-grandis*. In time, however, virtue, it is hoped, may be rewarded all round ; for *P. ⨯ Crucis, Blue Bowl*, continues to thrive as heartily as it should, and promises to be no less a friend to cultivation than its beautiful mother.

P. Maximowiczii, Regel, is a fat and thriving fraud in a superb race. The whole tuft is lush, green, hairless and downless, rich and rank and large, in a great clump of oval-pointed leaves, very finely toothed, luxuriantly emerald, from which stand up tall stems of 18 inches or more, stout and smooth, bearing tiers of blossom that can be compared to nothing but a whorled spike of some mahogany or dirt-coloured hyacinth. In fact I believe that there is no valid distinction between *P. Maximowiczii* and *P. tangutica :* both occupy the Tibetan Alps of North-West China, and from one large bed of blatant *Maximowiczii* you will get no two flower-spikes of the same colour, dull-browns being the general tone, reds and scarlets (such as have been delusively exhibited) very rare, and the ugliest flowers (where all are so ugly) merging indistinguishably into the full frightfulness of *P. tangutica*. In cultivation *P. Maximowiczii* is as rank and easy as its habit imports. But under careless conditions it may acquire the name of a miff. In winter a large pane of glass should cover all, to keep off wet and supplement the drainage. The tuft should also be kept, like a rival empire, in a wholesome state of and brilliant, of rich violet-blue, with a yellow or white throat about half an inch long.

P. mirabilis, in case the name should ever clamour for the undoing of purse-strings, is merely *Androsace mirabilis*, and an object, at that, wonderful only in the egregious measure of its ugliness.

P. mistassinica is a form of *P. farinosa*, confined to North America.

P. Miyabeana, from Formosa, is a new species in the habit and alliance of *P. japonica*, tall and stalwart, with purple flowers in ample tiers.

P. modesta is a most pleasant sub-species of *P. farinosa*, widespread in Japan, and abundant in the high places of Nyo-ho-zan and Nantai-san the Holy. It has precisely the look, the vigour, and heartiness of *P. frondosa*, but the meal with which the rosette is invested is not silver but golden ; also the scapes are shorter, but the pedicels of the individual blossoms much longer, so that the heads have a far more graceful radiating look. It should soon be a staying guest in every garden. *P. Faurieae* is a condensed, dry-ground development of this.

P. mollis has no place out of doors—a downy, soft species with small lilac-pink stars in tiers, on stems of 10 inches or so above the much too ample leafage.

P. Monbeigii, like *P. Dubernardiana*, belongs to the sub-shrubby group, and is enviably distinguished in it by also having much larger pink flowers than are there the fashion, even with *P. Forrestii*.

P. × montafoniensis is a false name of *P. × Heerii*, *q.v.*

P. Moorcroftiana is a dwarfer form of *P. nivalis*, *q.v.*

P. Mooreana is the very best of the various Primulas grown in gardens under the name of *P. capitata*.

P. mupinensis sits along the lips of the mountain streams on the eastern slopes of the Tibetan Alps. It is a most lovely small gem, in the group of *P. petiolaris*, making neat tufts of perfectly smooth little green thick leaves about 2 inches long, coarsely and irregularly toothed. The scape rises up 3 or 4 inches, carrying a simple umbel of very large soft-pink flowers, with a funnel-shaped tube, opening out into a wide round face nearly an inch across.

P. × Muretiana (Moritzi, 1829) and *P. × Mureti* (Charp., 1846) are both discarded names of *P. × Dinyana*, Lagger, 1839. This is the natural hybrid between *P. integrifolia* and *P. viscosa*, which may not uncommonly be found in the Engadine, affecting, very often, moss-cushions by waterfalls and other damp places, by no means to the taste of either parent. From *P. viscosa* it differs in being much dwarfer, with fewer, much larger blooms, larger calyces, and smaller

P. oculata stands close to *P. heu[ ]*

P. odontocalyx comes near *P. pe[ ]*
still. Its flowers are said to be on [ ]
some 2 inches tall, above the powd[ ]
home is in the rocks above the Yan[ ]

P. oenensis carries many names, [ ]
any of them, though catalogues ofte[ ]
P. cadinensis, *P. stelviana*, *P. Pooli[ ]*
throdose, and close akin to *P. hirs[ ]*
obviously in having much narrowe[ ]
blossoms, too, seem longer and thin[ ]
arrangement. It is a rarity to be lo[ ]
district of the Western Rhaetian Al[ ]
where, on the high granites, its sin[ ]
glanded rosettes may be seen dotte[ ]
beset closely with glowing loose [ ]
The most obvious place to see it i[ ]
top of the Stelvio, covering the [ ]
the Dreisprachenspitz; but it als[ ]
thereabouts; as, for instance, the t[ ]
ridge opposite the Adamello. In [ ]
species, but quite outclassed by *P.* [ ]
nothing of other members of the g[ ]

P. officinalis.—The Cowslip is [ ]
need not linger on it too lovingly o[ ]
however, sometimes offered with [ ]
varieties of the Cowslip, and thei[ ]
and by no means matter for disa[ ]
has not led the innocent into hop[ ]
out of China : *PP. oo. ampliata, ho[ ]*
calycina), macrocalyx, with sub[ ]
canescens (pannonica, inflata, m[ ]
cinerascens, hardeggensis, and *com[ ]*
pyrenaica, cordifolia, discolor), wh[ ]
hands with each other indeed—in [ ]
forms. And here, too, it may be [ ]
all the Bastard Oxlips, the hybr[ ]
always to be distinguished from [ ]
however, has no idea of not addi[ ]
ducing hybrids alike with Cows[ ]
there is no need here to unravel th[ ]
be given, and the rough notion of t[ ]

capsules; from *P. integrifolia* in having toothed leaves, more flowers to an umbel (inclining to be one-sided), on longer foot-stalks, of a beautiful rich blue-purple or violet, rather smaller, and with no white glandular fur in the throat, though there is a scanty peppering of powder. It is a beautiful plant, taking the best from each parent and leaving the worst; its neat habit and large head of large bright-purple blossoms will always distinguish it, in the districts where they all occur; it varies in form, of course, like every hybrid. The long bracts and *baggy calyx* inherited from *P. integrifolia* would always be diagnostics to separate it from any other hybrid of *P. viscosa*. Unfortunately, in gardens, the names of *P. Muretiana* and *P. Mureti* are applied with indiscriminate wrong-headedness to a small and specially vigorous mat-forming Primula with clumped rosettes of shining smooth foliage, faintly toothed, sending up empurpled stems of an inch or two, with large dark lilac-magenta flowers with darker touches yet at the base of the five lobes, and in calyces purple as the stems. There can be no doubt that this is some form of *P. × Venzoi*, the natural hybrid between *P. minima* and *P. tyrolensis*, unless occasionally it be a development of *P. × Deschmannii, q.v.*

P. muscoeides is the smallest of the race, a microscopic jewel on the highest passes of Sikkim, where it forms dense, moss-like masses in and out among the roots and rhizomes of other high-alpines, and has very much the look of *P. minutissima*, but that it is smaller still, and with the lobes of the flowers deeply cloven into narrow lobes, so that they have a starrier face.

P. × mutata.—A superfluous name for *P. × Deschmannii, q.v.*

P. nanocapitata, a very poor, small miff, under the name of *P. capitata*.

P. nessensis is really *P. polyphylla*, with bunches of pink blooms on tall stems, like a young *P. denticulata* that is trying to be *P. farinosa*.

P. neurocalyx stands near *P. malvacea*, and has no place out of doors in the garden, nor, indeed, a high place anywhere; for it is a small-flowered species in its large-leaved group (*P. Rosthornii*, Diels).

P. nipponica is abundant in alpine pastures of Japan—a dainty white *P. farinosa* with neat rosettes of fleshy tiny leaves.

P. "nivalis," of gardens=*P. nivea*, Sims (1809), being the only possible correct name for this beautiful and favoured albino form of *P. × pubescens*, upon which so false and ludicrous a label as "*nivalis*" has been long fixed by the ignorance of catalogues. It is an ample-headed, smoother, and creamy-white version of *P. villosa*, remarkably vigorous, but too crowded in the head to equal another cross in the same name, which is usually called *P. "helvetica" alba*, and has

P. nivalis sinopu...
repetitions of the f...
native land. *P. n. s...*
wrappings of bright g...
Its imperial violet flo...

P. nivea, Sims, ...
P. × pubescens.

P. norica. See u...

P. nutans belong...
spiked congeners, m...
which are sweet-scent...
kin. It must be soug...

P. nutantiflora = ...

P. obconica is an...
purposes. To save t...
intemperance (like ...
extravagance), we m...
mere forms, and mic...
begoniaeformis, Bona...
sinolisteri, and *Vilm...*

P. obliqua, so fa...
are rumours of a won...
flowers, and a slanti...
of Sikkim in July ; a...
obliqua ready for it t...

P. obovata belong...
is less unlike a Prin...
Yunnan, and there, o...
in outline and stem...
which 1913 armed t...
affording such a lux...
one. In a thin sta...
thin stem ending an...
each on an aspiring f...

P. Obristii, a for...

P. obtusifolia, th...
tion. The name h...
Roylei, P. Gammiea...
kinship of *P. petiola...*
folia is a Nivalid, ...
and in the Confere...
merely plain *P. Roy...*

cousin, *P. imperialis ;* and, considering its beauty, there is something suspicious about its infrequency in cultivation.

P. pseudo-bracteata is a mealless twin to *P. Forrestii.*

P. pseudo-capitata is smaller and darker in the ball of blossom.

P. pseudo-denticulata is a valueless species of its group, flowering even earlier than *P. denticulata.*

P. pseudo-elatior is a microform of *P. elatior.*

P. pseudo-Forsteri is a false name of Gusmus for the hybrid between *P. hirsuta* and *P. minima*—to which, with his usual generosity, he has given no fewer than four distinct names : *P. pseudo-Forsteri, P. brennia, P. diversa,* and *P. venalensis.* All forms of this glorious hybrid will be found under *P. × Steinii,* the central type.

P. pseudo-malacoeides is the worse form, weaker, uglier, and miffier, of *P. malacoeides* as grown in gardens.

P. pseudo-sikkimensis really deserves better than to be included in this gallery of liars. For though it is not *P. sikkimensis,* it has a beauty in the same line, delicate and slender (though not so noble as the shorter and broader-leaved *P. microdonta*), with larger flowers than even in *P. sikkimensis.* These all are easy and lovely in the same conditions.

P. × pubescens, Jacq., is the name that has to cover, like a cloth cast over a heap of unsortable untidiness, the whole vast family of primary, secondary, tertiary hybrids (always fertile), not only of *P. auricula × P. hirsuta,* but also of *P. auricula* with *P. viscosa* and *P. villosa.* These two last crosses, of course, ought each to have had a distinct name of their own, leaving *P. pubescens* quite enough to do in successfully embracing all the children, grandchildren, and remoter tangled descendants of *P. auricula* and *P. hirsuta.* However, the complications are by now too vast and old for any unravelling ; but, to make the matter worse, the countless collected and developed forms in this chaos have often proved so distinct that, as each enthusiast found—as each enthusiast still may, wherever the parents, any of them, abound—especially brilliant and beautiful developments in the group, he was pardonably tempted to follow Sairey's example, and "give it a name, I beg," of its own. And all these, at one time or another, have slipped into catalogues, so that not only have we three definite lines of descent to look for under the name of *P. × pubescens,* but also a whole host of synonyms and pseudonyms and unauthorised names that must properly be discarded. Among these are : *P. rhaetica* (Gaud), *P. helvetica* (Donn), *P. alpina* (Schleicher), *P. intermedia* (Van Houtte), *P. Göblii* (Kerner), *P. Arctotis* (Kerner), *P. Kerneri* (Göbl.), and *P. Peyritschii* (Stein).

PLATE 20.

PRIMULA MARGINATA.
(Photo. R. A. Malby.)

PRIMULA MODESTA.
(Photo. R.B.G., Edinburgh.)

PLATE 21.

PRIMULA PULVERULENTA.

PRIMULA MALVACEA.

PRIMULA.

When it is remembered how wide a gulf separates *P. hirsuta* from *P. viscosa*, it will easily be seen that a name which is intended to cover all hybrids of both these species with *P. auricula* can only be described as a cry of despair. It results that *P. pubescens* is a name even more vague and wild than *Saxifraga aeizoon ;* there is no analysing this series of hybrids. " More or less " has to be appended to every descriptive detail. Wherever *P. auricula* occurs with *P. viscosa*, *P. villosa*, or *P. hirsuta*, there their bewildering polymorphic children are sure to be found. In culture, *P. pubescens* is the oldest of all hybrid Primulas. Clusius saw it in the rich garden of Dr. J. Aicholtz, at Vienna, about 1580, and understood it to abound in the Oenipontine Alps. And *P. pubescens* is still, perhaps, the most important of hybrid garden Primulas, for the name covers every florist's " *Auricula*," Green-edged, Alpine, or Border, and such a multiplicity of other forms, too, that the brain reels in contemplation. There are, in particular, the two albinoes, called by catalogues *P.* " *nivalis* " and *P.* " *helvetica* " *alba*. They are both of them, of course, according to present classification, *P. pubescens alba*. " Ut mihi videtur, absurde," since the one is much nearer to *P. hirsuta*, and the other to *P. villosa* (in shape of flowers). There is also an absolutely different albino *P. pubescens*, which is typical *P. auricula* × *P. viscosa alba*. This plant, an ancient inhabitant of some north-country gardens, has the habit of *P. viscosa*, almost pure, with dense one-sided bunches of narrow white trumpets, carried on tallish stems, the whole clump tending to grow stalkily out of the ground. Finally, as a small straw to cling to in the maelstrom of confusion—*P. pubescens*—it may be remembered that that hybrid is, by preference, of almost every colour in the rainbow except Auricula's golden-yellow ; while it differs always from *P. hirsuta*, *P. villosa*, *P. viscosa* in being *less hairy*, and also, usually, to a certain extent, *farinose in some of its parts*. But the name of *P. pubescens* is hopelessly strained and artificial, especially as the primary hybrids are fertile, and fertile again, to the third and fourth generation. There is, for instance, the beautiful violet-flowered *P. decora* (of gardens) ; it is a distinct enough form of *P. pubescens*, but its seedlings yield only border Auriculas in every imaginable colour. See *P. auricula*.

P. pulchella is almost patronised by its name. It is so far from being a Little-pretty as to be among the very loveliest of the race ; however, its dainty neatness may accept the name without dishonour, so pleasant are its tufts of small and solid upstanding oval-pointed leaves, gold-powdered beneath, greyish in shade, and at their curling edge most delicately scalloped and goffered. But from this come up fine stiff stems of 6 inches or even a foot, carrying a head of lovely-faced great golden-eyed blossoms of soft pure lavender-blue, delicate to the nose as to the eye. It is a glory of the Nivalis group, but often impermanent, and sharing that sensitiveness of theirs about excessive damp, which, like that of the leather trade, might almost be described as morbid. High on the limestone mountains of Yunnan it lives, but no less heartily in the garden, in light rich soil full of stones, and well-watered from beneath (though such a precaution is not so much a necessity here, as rather the extra luxury that extra loveliness is felt to deserve).

P. pulchelloeides.—Here the name is a flattery. For this is but a spoiled version of the last, although the resemblance is undeniable. But *P. pulchelloeides*, of the same habits, ease and needs, is narrower, longer, floppier in the leaf; the stems seem taller, because they carry fewer flowers, ragged and starry and thin, on stiffer pedicels, and so in less gracious and almost gawky heads. Yet it is fair to say that this species might take high rank if it were not for the model with which it deals so ill and so brazenly claims to resemble.

P. pulcherrima (of gardens) is a really Disraelitish piece of flattery for various forms of *P. denticulata.*

P. pulchra is a lovely thing, in the group of *P. Gambeliana.* The whole plant is quite small, quite smooth, quite green, and quite powderless. The little leaves are roundish, lobed on their stalks, and in all about 3 inches long at the most, pointed and wavy at the edge. Hardly emerging from the tuft arises a 2-inch scape, carrying a big sheath, and then a loose head of large purple blossoms, ample in the lobe. It is a species from considerable altitudes in Sikkim.

P. pulverulenta is well known by now, almost damaging the supremacy of *P. japonica* by the contrast between its whitewashed stems and its larger flowers of a rather richer crimson. It has, moreover, yielded a form or hybrid standing far up in the race; *Mrs. R. V. Berkeley* is not to be distinguished in ease and vigour from the type, but has blossoms of a most lovely shell-pink pallor, suffused with a tinge of apricot, overflowing from the golden eye. With *P. Cockburniana,* again, the plant has produced, and goes on producing, a race of bloodscarlet, salmon, and vermilion Primulas, all to be found under their several names in catalogues, but those names multiplied with unbearable generosity, seeing that the generic resemblance is so strong between them all, and their parentage the same.

P. pulvinata is a cushion-plant in the group of *P. Forrestii.*

P. × pumila, Kerner, is the second branch of the hybrid *P. × coronata* (Porta), *q.v.*

P. pumila, Led., is a microform of *P. nivalis, q.v.*

PRIMULA.

P. pumilio is a tiny high-alpine from Kansu, making clumps of leaves, barely half an inch long, stem and all, powderless and smooth-edged ; and on these mats sit close the heads of soft pink flowers, each of them about a quarter of an inch across, and making a lovely effect when they are crowded upon the generous cushion. (Specimens in the Petrograd Herbarium show no sign of the " wide carpets " that figure in its description.)

P. Purdomii arrived in 1913, a brand-new species (as species it is), and among the most royal in the royal kinship of *P. nivalis*. It forms tufts of rather long, thin, and very pointed foliage, thick with grey glandular powderiness till the whole tuft looks as if it had lived all its years beside a popular motoring road, instead of in the fine sandy cool peat of a grassy mountain-slope high in Tibet ; the stems are grey no less, rising up a foot or so, bare and elegant, breaking out at the top into a rocket-spray of specially large stars, perfectly flat across their faces, with five ample blunt and oval lobes, so that they look, on those stalks and above that leafage, like the head of some most weird and cupless Narcissus that has watched the motors go by until not only has it grown powdered as the footmen of the great, but has changed the tone of its blossoms into the most sad and subtle tone of pale lavender, that seems just the exquisite complement and development of these ash-grey stems and leaves. Far away from all rivalry, far away from all comparison, is this gracious lilac Tazetta-Narcissus that has so strangely strayed into a race so remote. In culture it has uttered no warning as yet ; but seems a good and vigorous hearty perennial ; though calling, of course, for the special care that its price and perfection combine to demand ; and sometimes, like so many of the Nivalis group (to which it is in suspiciously close alliance, barely separated by its larger stigma), inclined to give up the ghost after the strain of producing those lovely blossoms. In nature it gives the cultivator a significant hint ; it lives among the long grass, in rich loam, high up on the well-drained alpine slopes of Tibet. In autumn the deep hay dies down over the dead crowns of the Primula, and covers them all in a dense thatch of perfect dryness, beneath the dry warm coverlet of snow that overlies the mattress of the grass. (Purdom, 1911 ; and see Appendix.)

P. purpurea has but just emerged from a confusion with *P. nivalis macrophylla*. Await enlightenment.

P. pusilla looks a miffy little plant. Botanically it stands near to *P. bella*, but differs in being hairy, though with the same fluffy beard blocking its throat. It has no relation to *P. glabra*, for while *P. glabra* has the short scape and rather large flowers, too small in comparison with the ample rosettes of toothed oval leaves, so *P. pusilla* has a very tiny tuft of foliage, very deeply feathered into teeth at the edges, and making so neat a little star, outspread upon the ground, that the frail stem of four inches or so, beneath its load of one, two, or three glutinosa-like blossoms, deep-violet and deeply-cloven in the lobes, seems altogether too heavily laden. It will want care and specially dainty treatment in the special bed or moraine, yet proves an easier, better doer than *P. bella* under similar conditions.

P. pycnolŏba takes us back to the woods of Szechuan, there to find one of the oddest freaks in the race—yet another species that shares the longing of *P. Purdomii* to be a Narcissus, though it has chosen a different model. Close to the ground, on quite short and densely fluffy fat stems, appear the typical fat and crinkly glossy-green lobed heart-shaped leaves of the Woodland section ; then in their midst a shaggy stem rises well above them, to some 4 or 5 inches. And now, having been a characteristic forest-Primula so far, the plant suddenly declares that it is a Daffodil. The loose heads of flower unfold. The shaggy calyx is their dominant feature. This is of immense size, dowdily green (said to be creamy white, however, by some), and cut into five very long, sharp, and ragged lobes, like a perianth, in the middle of which appear the long narrow white trumpets of the flower, ending in its five-lobed mouth of dark red —so that the loose clusters on the stems seem exactly like a collection of most eccentric shaggy little five-segmented Daffodils, with a dim red rim to the minute five-flanged trumpet. This ambitious oddity is quite easy to cultivate in the woodland soil and conditions that suit Cortusa, and rapidly spreads in the ground by little root-buds, that can easily be taken off and grown on elsewhere. Its only fad is a craving for being allowed to rest in peace in the winter without getting water-logged or rained on excessively. As I have seen this it is like a very poor Galligaskins.

P. racemosa is only a poor *P. batangensis.*

P. redolens is a pink-flowered cousin to *P. Forrestii.*

P. reflexa stands doubtfully in the Sikkimensis group, but has rather different foliage. The tall stems bear a drooping head of flowers that have not quite made up their minds to be of clean pink or clean purple, so compromise on an unalluring chalky tone. It is of easy culture in any conditions of rich soil and reasonable moisture.

P. Reidii, however, is not only one of the loveliest jewels in the race, but in the world. It comes from damp rocks high up in Kumaon, near the glaciers ; and its leaves are like those of a Primrose, if a **Primrose-leaf** can be imagined densely shaggy with long hairs of blown-glass from Murano. Then ascend the stems of 4 or 5 inches, powdered pure white, and hang out an even bunch of four or five stout bells of soft cream-colour and thick waxen bloom, with their calyx-lobes and bracts above the pendent chime all white with meal, and making a sort of inadequate snowy penthouse or umbrella for the blossoms. *P. Reidii*, however, like most supreme things, is very difficult of achievement, and until established (as now so marvellously on the rock-work at Wisley), hard to keep as love (even in nature it is always as rare as perfection). It should have a light spongy mixture of peat and sand and leaf-mould, with abundance of chips ; and water should be kept as steadily running beneath its roots all the summer as it should be diligently held off all the winter, and this treasure kept as dry as if it were indeed the pearls and diamonds that it is so like, and so well worth.

P. Reinii has taken a long time to arrive, but now there is no fear of its departure, for this delicate and dainty little Japanese woodland species from Hak'san in Kanga turns out to be quite hardy and easy and ready to thrive and spread in light rich soil under almost any con- ditions, so as to be neither parboiled nor water-logged. The small stalked leaves are hearts or kidneys (according to taste) of softly velvety texture ; and among them and above them the short stems throw out a loose spray of cheery-looking flowers, enormous for the plant, of delicate pink, with a radiant star of darker colour from the centre, the segments being straight-sided, heart-shaped and deeply lobed, with the lobes standing apart, so that the whole bloom does not make a circle or a face of fatness, but a dainty expanded star, of ten full rays, not plump enough for rotundity, nor lean so as to look scraggy and ill-furnished. So then, when these are over by mid-May, and the seed matured by later summer, the entire clump dies down to a tidy collection of brown budlings, waiting the call of spring to rise up again next year and play the whole game again with redoubled vigour. So free is it of increase that either in spring or in summer can it happily be divided. Of all the woodlanders it is easily supreme in charm, small in stature, gigantic in blossom, clean and sweet in colour, graceful in all its outlines, and graceful no less in demeanour and temperament.

P. reptans is much tinier than *P. minutissima*, and creeps over the ground on the highest passes of Kumaon, rooting as it goes in a hearty manner, and forming little wandering mats of infinitesimal outspread- ing foliage, so deeply toothed that the wee stalked ovals look like those of some gin-fed *Chrysanthemum alpinum;* and on the mass stand stemless the wide-eyed, long-tubed stars of soft pale purple, staring straight up to the day. This should have the choicest of morainy-mixtures when caught, and be kept constantly damp below while growing.

P. reticulata gives the family trumpet a holiday. It is only a feeble *P. sikkimensis*.

P. x *rhaetica*, Gaud, is a belated synonym of *P.* x *pubescens*, Jacq., *q.v.*

P. rosea is so labelled in all gardens by now, calling for its relations *P. elliptica*, *P. Bornmuelleri*, *P. Harrissii*, and *P. hazarica*. In point of fact, so common is *P. "rosea"* with us that it seems impossible to ascertain how many of the countless Roseas we cultivate are really *P. rosea* at all, and how many belong instead to the rather larger *P. elegans* (*Bot. Mag.*, T. 6437, as *P. rosea*)—*P. rosea* itself being, like *P. nivalis*, a large aggregate, involving also such forms or species as *P. rhodantha*, *P. rosiflora*, and *P. radicata*, all tightly dwarf high-alpine developments. But our typical *P. "rosea,"* the cosy gloss of its tufts, and then, before they appear, the incredible rose-carmine of those noble loose heads—these are all engraved so deep in the heart of anyone who has ever handled a trowel as here to ask no picture ; the tufts can be divided too at will, and seed with amazing profusion even on their own account in the open bog, so that almost every garden has its favourite and especial form eminent in size, or fire of pink, or freedom of bloom. Such are often advertised in catalogues. Any damp and even water-logged soil will admirably suit each type ; it will there make enormous masses, with its roots in actual running water, and will even do as much in dank and sunless shady places under walls and so forth, in which, *a priori*, it seemed madness to imprison a race whose home is among the glaciers on the Roof of the World, where, amid the sapphire and emerald splendour of the crevasses and terminal ice-falls, break through, wherever a tongue of grit be exposed, the mounded gold-and-ruby sparkles of these astonishing children of hope.

P. Rosthornii x *P. neurocalyx, q.v.*

P. rotundifolia is, like Cerberus, at least three gentlemen at once. The true species is not yet known at all in cultivation, but a relation from Sikkim has been figured under this name in the Report of the Primula Conference. This looks a most precious species, suggesting a *Ranunculus bilobus*, with two or three very ample round bright-eyed flowers of brilliant purple-pink. In time, however, it grows out of this dainty kitten-stage into a cathood of no less merit, forming clumped tufts of upstanding violet-like leaves on long stalks, over-lapping-lobed at the base, and powdered with gold beneath ; while

176

the flower-stems easily overtop all these, rising to **7** or **8** inches, and carrying one or two tiers of the brilliant fragrant blossoms. (*P. Gambeliana* is much like this, but always small in habit and with much larger flowers.) Its home lies throughout the Himalaya from Kashmir to Sikkim, where it loves dry rich peat in shade—as under the shelving rocks in Rhododendron glades. This must be remembered in attempting the cultivation of *P. rotundifolia*, which, if not suited, is sadly apt to prove perverse and impermanent, and will be best pleased with very perfect drainage in a sheltered dry and warm position, with not only drought but even protection in winter. For it is not a high-alpine, and Primulas that cannot climb higher than a mere 12,000 feet in the Himalaya are by no means to be universally trusted in England, where 900 feet often means far more cold and trying conditions in winter than those which send up their influence so far from the profound and steamy valleys of Sikkim or Yunnan, that there 10,000 feet is as 2000 on the Alps.

P. Roylei, with *P. Tanneri*, *P. Griffithii*, and *P. Gammieana*, form a group of Petiolarid Primulas long confused under the name of the unknown *P. obtusifolia*, itself a Nivalid. *P. Roylei* has crinkled, wrinkled, undulate, small oval leaves on very short stalks that distinguish it from *P. Gammieana*. The dainty flower-stems of 4-6 inches carry an ample head of large round-lobed purple blossoms. In light soil it is free in growth, yet not always so free with its blooms, which, in violet multitudes, arouse sick headaches with their metallic scent, in all who traverse its native Indian Alps.

P. rufa, like *P. bullata*, is a yellow-flowered cousin to *P. Forrestii*. It differs from *P. bullata* in having hairy foliage, though it has the same investiture of golden powder.

P. Ruprechtii is the better development of *P. leucophylla*, q.v.

P. Rusbyi is an outlier of the race, representing it in the Rockies of New Mexico and Arizona. It makes tufts of leathery toothed foliage, rather narrow and without powder. The stems are about 6 inches high, bearing loose clusters of more or less nodding blooms, rather funnel-shaped, with the face expanding into a bowl of livid and obscure red-purple, like an old bloodstain on faded velvet. It should have an open warm place in moist but well-drained peaty loam, where it will flower in later summer and keep up the succession. It is a curiosity, and has a certain sad and sinister attraction, though by no means among the beauties of the family, at least in its poorer forms, for others are of much cheerier colouring and charm. It follows the habits of *P. japonica* by seeking, at home, for rich damp soil at low elevations—so that with us it should probably be treated as a plant for the warmest of places in the choice bog or underground-watered moraine-bed.

P. × *salisburgensis* is another of the names given in the long range of hybrids between *P. glutinosa* and *P. minima*. The form that typically bears this name is suggestive of *P. glutinosa's* motherhood, and stands near the form called *P.* × *Huteri*, from which it differs in having the leaves wedge-shaped instead of oblong, while the 2- or 3-inch scapes are not sticky (but the variations are endless). The flowers are altogether suggestive of *P. glutinosa*, but are of a hot red-violet, fewer in the cluster and longer in the tube. Its habit is intermediate, running in a small compass, and forming loosely matted clumps and patches, which have a curious predilection for places much wetter than those liked by either parent—as, for instance, where water is perpetually trickling over a wide level of rock, or diffusing itself across a shallow hollow of the moor. It seems, like others in this range, to be of quite local distribution ; the high bogs of Kraxenträger and Colbricon seem to contain no other form of the hybrid ; yet there is no sign of it in the Monzoni Thal, where *P.* × *Huteri* and *P.* × *biflora* may both be found, while *P.* × *Floerkeana* blots the blue distances of *P. glutinosa* with flaring patches of hot amethyst blazing from afar. In cultivation no difficulty attends these crosses, though they are not always more generous than *P. glutinosa* in flower. There are many forms and shades of them all ; one especially beautiful and dwarf variety of *P.* × *salisburgensis*, with large flowers of clear pure pale-blue, I can hardly concede to be *P.* × *salisburgensis* at all, as it has neither the points nor the habits, but turns towards the Minima-side of the family. The whole question of names among these hybrids is, however, academic and illiberal ; the two species yield so endlessly variable and fertile a progeny, that there is no use in trying to stereotype any of the forms with rigid certainty, though a few of the more salient states of the more salient may be singled out for the purposes of convenience, that their names may indicate well-marked stages of the interbreeding.

P. × *Salisii*, Brügger=*P.* × *Berninae*, Kerner, *q.v.*

P. × *Sanctae-Coronae*, a form of the hybrid between Primrose and Cowslip. See under *P. officinalis*.

P. sapphirina has not yet shown a smile to civilisation, though it has several times been coaxed into flower. It is a most dainty gem, tiny in leaf and small in bloom, forming dense clumps of minute toothed oval foliage diminishing to the base and virtually without hair, and sending up numbers of little stems of some 2 inches high, each carrying

PLATE 22

PRIMULA POISSONI.
(Photo. R.B.G., Edinburgh.)

PRIMULA PYCNOLOBA.
(Photo. R.B.G., Edinburgh.)

PLATE 23.

PRIMULA REIDII.
(Photo. R.B.G., Edinburgh.)

PRIMULA REINII.
(Photo. R.B.G., Edinburgh.)

PLATE 24.

PRIMULA ROSEA.
(Photo. R.B.G., Edinburgh.)

PRIMULA ROTUNDIFOLIA.
(Photo. R.B.G., Edinburgh.)

PLATE 25.

PRIMULA SERRATIFOLIA.

PRIMULA PURDOMII

from one to four wide-rimmed bells of rich and brilliant blue, upturned or nodding, stemless in their head, and shining with inimitable brilliance on the emerald moss-cushions which it occupies in the face of the high damp rocks and grit-banks, bringing out its jewels in the first moment when the snows begin to melt. It should clearly be welcomed to the choicest place in the Gentian-bed, should be kept sedulously dry in winter, and not in any case be counted upon, even after the most successful summer, to prove perfectly perennial. (Sikkim-Himalaya.)

P. saxatilis, Komarow, is the species almost universally in cultivation as *P. cortusoeides* (not *P. Sieboldii*). It is also *P. oreodoxa* of gardens, but not *P. patens* (Turcz), which is *P. Sieboldii*. Under any name it is a pleasant easy thing of ready spreading habit, with masses of rather limp-stemmed foliage after the fashion of all the Cortusoeides group, and then sending up an endless profusion of tall naked-looking 10-inch stems far above the leaves, which stay flopping and flagging down below. The flowers, in generous heads, are round and cheery in their shades of pinky-mauve. From all forms of *P. cortusoeides* the plant may be told by the fact that each flower here has *a very long foot-stalk of its own* (so that the head is quite loose), while in *P. cortusoeides* they are *very short indeed*, and the head therefore much tighter. It ranges right across the rocky woods of Northern Asia to Alaska, and has been in cultivation for more than a century; the "doyen" of all specimens has lived in the botanical gardens at Berlin ever since 1806. It can be divided as frequently and freely as the rest of the group, and seeds with unparalleled profusion.

P. saxifragifolia is a form of *P. cuneifolia*, and a delicate pretty little thing, from the Aleutians, Alaska, and Unalaska.

P. Schlagintweitiana is a neater thing than its name, suggesting a powderless *P. farinosa* at first glance, the many-flowered head of graceful blossoms being carried high above the tidy incurving rosettes of oval-rounded leaves, on stems of some 3 or 4 inches. Its real relation is to *P. denticulata*, while from *P. glabra* it may, among other points, be distinguished by the longer flower-tube. The calyx, too, folds into a sort of minute pocket at the base between each lobe. (Kashmir and the Western Himalaya.)

P. scotica is a smaller form of the type *P. farinosa*, with fatter foliage, shorter stems, and rather larger golden-eyed flowers of deeper purple tone. It is *P. farinosa Warei* (Stein), for which laments are sometimes heard. *P. scotica* is stocky and pretty; though a miff, it will seed freely, even if the seeds take a year to germinate; it wants neither more nor less than the treatment of the type, and flowers so freely and long as often to exhaust itself.

P. secundiflora.—It is not easy in simple words to convey the beauty of *P. secundiflora.* Plant it in any rich cool loam, and it will at once start growing into a perfect cabbage of long oval-pointed finely-toothed leaves, bravely upstanding, bright-green and glossy, of a noble and healthful appearance, continuing through the summer as the stock goes on adding fresh lateral crowns to the clump (which can then be taken off and grown on as fresh specimens). Early summer calls the flower-stems up. These are like those of the plant's cousin, *P. sikkimensis*, but not nearly so tall, hardly rising to a foot. They hang out a one-sided shower of very wide bell-shaped flowers like those of *P. sikkimensis* in shape, emerging from dark calyces beautifully striped with longitudinal bands of powder. And the colour of the hanging bells is, like Uncle Joseph's stores of knowledge, "a thing that beggars language, Julia." In texture they are thick, and the outside of the bell is of a waxen dulled flesh-colour, filmed with a strange powdery bloom, and suffused with lines and nerves and flushings of claret and deep rose, with blue mysteriously suggested as a veil over the whole, omnipresent as the faintest of tints, like a whiff of onion in a good salad ; the inside of the bell is of deep dim satin, in a muffled tone of crimson-rose, with the lines and nerves intensified and darkened to a glowing flush. Their beauty, against the waxen bloom of the exterior, is ravishing ; their colour is such that they just miss the absolutely frightful, and in the missing achieve with precision the absolutely beautiful. And *P. secundiflora* is as vigorous as *P. japonica*, for a higher and less boggy place indeed, but no less robust ; seeding profusely, and as profusely multiplying its crowns. Confusion is said to rage between this and *P. vittata*. Prof. Balfour describes the right *P. secundiflora* as having horizontal, while *P. vittata* has upstanding leaves ; but his own photograph rather reverses this, and shows under the name of *P. secundiflora* the thing described above with bold and stalwart foliage ; while his plate of *P. vittata* gives an inferior crowded head of smaller flowers, and the floppeting feeble foliage that his text ascribes instead to *P. secundiflora*. In any case the two are nearly related, and in their less characteristic forms are said to be hard of discernment the one from the other.

P. × Sendtneri is said to be a garden hybrid between *P. auricula* and *P. pedemontana*, two species that could not interbreed in nature, as they do not share the same ranges. It has not been described, and little need either be said or thought of it—*P. auricula* having done its best by the Erythrodose group in its breedings with *P. hirsuta*.

PRIMULA.

P. septemloba, with rather longer and more trumpet-shaped flowers, exactly recalls *Cortusa Matthioli*, and has the same habits, ease, and temper. It is taller, and at the same time narrower in the tube, and less generous in the bell than its much more attractive fellow-woodlander, *P. heucherifolia*, which sometimes appears in lists as *P. Gaignepainii*. See Appendix.

P. × seriana is the hybrid between *P. oenensis* and *P. hirsuta.* See *P. oenensis.*

P. Serra (Small) is *P. Rusbyi, q.v.*

P. × serrata (Gusmus), a false name of his for his own *P. × serratifolia*, being the first type of the hybrid *P. × Deschmannii, q.v.*

P. × serratifolia (Gusm.). See *P. Deschmannii.*

P. serratifolia of Pax is a portmanteau packed with *P. Beesiana* and *P. pulverulenta*, as well as the true *P. serratifolia*, Franch.

P. serratifolia, Franch., is attributed to the Candelabra section, but is very much less in the style of *P. japonica* than in that of *P. sikkimensis*, sending up no tiered tower of blossoms above its tuft of sharply-gashed and saw-toothed foliage, but a stem of 8 inches or so, bearing a head of graceful pendent bells precisely after the habits and portraits of *P. sikkimensis* and *P. secundiflora*, except that a second feebler shower may sometimes be unfolded above the first. It is the least and weakest of this gorgeous and cabbage-like group, though of especially gracious delicate port of its own, between the charm of both sections, and catching some from each. The flowers may best be figured by imagining so many bells of a rich orange, which has faded all round the rims and lobes to a soft primrose, leaving only a central radiating suffusion of the original colour, till the blossom-heads absurdly recall those of *Lewisia Howellii* on a smaller scale. The culture should rather be that advised for *P. secundiflora* than the bog-treatment and heavy fatness in which the rest of the Japonica section do their best.

P. sertulum makes a neat tuft of small blunt leaves, sharply toothed and oblong-oval; with stems twice their length, carrying a heavily-furnished head of large saucer-shaped violet or white blossoms, deeply cloven in the lobes, and emerging from bell-shaped powdered calyces on pedicels twice or thrice as long. No more can yet be said of *P. sertulum*, which hails from Tatsienlu.

P. sibirica, when true, is but a poor thin thing, with two or three pink flowers to the umbel. Fortunately it is now represented in gardens by what is called *P. s. chinensis*, more rightly to be now known as *P. Wardii*—a very variable and valuable development of the Alps up the marches of Tibet and over the north of China. It is evident that we have been fortunate in getting, and keeping, an exceptionally fine type, which seeds so copiously too, and from seed so copiously varies, that out of one's own batches one may select half a dozen better developments of fuller flower or dwarfer growth or more brilliant colour or brighter white eye. Our type is a real treasure in fact, in the habit and tuft of *P. involucrata*, but three times the size, with foliage lush and green, that goes flop in summer beneath the sun, even if sustained by any amount of underground drinking. The stems rise up, countless and tall, at the end of May and far on into July, with a second burst in September, carrying large loose heads of large and broadly starry flowers of bright lilac-pink with another star in their centre of white, and the most delicious sweetness adding to their charm. Any cool rich soil of the bog will suit this species, which may easily be divided in spring, and comes prodigiously from seed. See Appendix.

P. Sibthorpii (Hffmsgg., 1842), is rightly *P. acaulis rubra*, Sibth. and Smith, 1813, and is that beautiful single Primrose, red, lilac, purple and crimson, which is the prevalent form, throughout the Levant, of *P. acaulis*, and has been the parent of all our coloured garden primroses. This is *P. "amoena"* of Robinson; it has also unlawfully shared with the true *P. amoena* (Bieb.) (in which, as originally described, *P. Sibthorpii* had a share) in the name *P. "altaica."* But the name *altaica* had also previously been given to the form of *P. elatior*, whose valid title is *P. Pallasii*, while all the time it only belonged to *P. farinosa altaica* (Lehmann), figured in the *Bot. Mag.* of 1809 as *P. intermedia*. After all this confusion we utterly drop *P. "altaica,"* renounce *P. "Sibthorpii,"* reinstate *P. acaulis rubra*, and let the rightful *P. amoena* come at last to its own again.

P. Sieboldii, Morren, is a beloved and immemorial ally from Japan, with its running masses of soft crumply oval leaves, scalloped and stalked; and its tall bare stems opening wide heads of beautiful flowers in almost every colour and conceivable design of fringing segment. These varieties all may be collected from the catalogues that contain them; and in cool soil, rich and light, the jungles of the growth will in time cover the ground far and wide, easily to be divided in spring and raised from seed. *P. Sieboldii* is always confused in lists with *P. cortusoeides*, L., a species with which it has nothing to do. All forms of genuine *P. Sieboldii* may easily be recognised by *the widely spreading lobes of the calyx;* nor is the true *P. cortusoeides* to be found in Japan at all, or anywhere further east than Korea. Unfortunately the Japanese plant (*P. Sieboldii*, Morren) was subsequently called *P. cortusoeides* by Thunberg, Lindley, and Verschaffelt—these latter two making it a variety of the true *P. cortusoeides*. It has also been called *P. patens* (Turcz.) and *P. gracilis* (Stein)—the one valid name being the oldest, *P. Sieboldii*, Morren ; while the only *P. cortusoeides* is the original and distinct species of Linnaeus, a native of Northern Asia (very rare to-day in gardens, where its place is always taken either by *P. Sieboldii* or *P. saxatilis*). *P. Sieboldii* is restricted to Japan and Transbaikalia ; whereas *P. cortusoeides*, ranging all over Russia and Mongolia, does not cross the sea to Japan, and has close tight short-pedicelled heads of blossom.

P. sikkimensis is one of the grandest beauties of the race, with its great tall tufts of long oval saw-edged leaves, and the many much taller powdered stems in June, swinging out a wide loose head of hanging wide bells in the loveliest shade of soft milan-soufflé yellow, waxen in texture without, and bloomy with delicious white meal within, as clean and sweet as the sweet clean fragrance of the flower. This is the ready and hearty glory of any deep rich and boggy soil ; it must not be looked on to attain the Psalmist's term, but is most wisely to be treated as a triennial, with seed annually raised from the pods it so profusely produces, and among whose results occasionally a strain of even especial grandeur and loveliness may be secured and fixed.

P. silaensis is a lovely unknown species of the Amethystine group, with horny margins to the foliage, and pendent bells of blue-violet, on foot-stalks longer than among the Soldanella section, though the flowers are the same in their shape, and in their reduced number on the gracious stems of 4 or 5 inches.

P. simensis is the only African Primula—an extension of *P. verticillata*, from the neighbouring coasts of Asia into the mountains of Abyssinia. It has, of course, no use for us.

P. similis, Stein, is *P. Obristii*, Beck. See under *P. auricula.*

P. Simsii (Sweet). See under *P. villosa.*

P. sinensis has no use for us—though in cool wet places by the waterfalls of the large rock-garden it might be permissible, and would certainly be beautiful, to use the simple stellate wild forms as annuals, as is done on the Riviera.

P. sinensis (nivalis), Pax. See under *P. nivalis,* Pallas.

P. sinolisteri is a microform of *P. obconica.*

P. sinomollis, a greenhouse thing from China, there replacing the Indian *P. mollis*, and having the same immense soft crinkled and lobed foliage to the same tiered and shaggy spire, scantily set with red-pink flowers. It proves hardy with us, if planted out under Rhododendrons.

P. sinoplantaginea. See under *P. nivalis*, Pallas.

P. sinopurpurea. See under *P. nivalis*, Pallas.

PRIMULA.

P. sinuata waits our urgent call in the mountain woods of Szechuan. It is a beautiful small species, with tufts of oblong toothed leaves, horny-hemmed and drawing to a long foot-stalk. The stem is shorter than they, carrying from one to three flowers that emerge from a tubular bright-green calyx with overlapping lobes. The blossoms are noble bells of pink with a very long tube about an inch in length.

P. Smithiana is like a paler, poorer *P. Bulleyana* of similar needs.

P. soldanelloeides, like all members of the marvellous group to which it gives its name, is a species august in its rarity no less than in its beauty. It is a tiny frail jewel of the high passes in Sikkim, with delicate tufts of soft little oblong-obovate foliage, deeply feathered into many lobes, and sending up a fairy-fine stemling of an inch and a half or so, whose bell-shaped calyx is the base of a swelling pendent bell of waxen snow-pure white, preposterously large for the plant, and turning outwards with what seem like ten blunt lobes, suggesting the outline of a Soldanella, though without the full fringiness. For its due rites of worship, see under *P. Reidii*, which is a sort of gross and glorious incarnation of this unearthly elfin beauty.

P. sonchifolia got as far as germination once, but would come no further—a reluctance the more to be deplored when we learn that its charm so kindled the heart of its finder with rapture that he first named it *P. gratissima*, until it took its proper name after the strange sow-thistlish design of its outspread leaves, which are hairless, greyish-green, papery, and rough with raised dots. They are about 6 or 8 inches long, and very deeply and doubly gashed into blunt lobes, toothed sharply all round, and, when the summer is old, almost seeming to point backwards after the barbed style of Sow-thistle and Dandelion. These, however, are not what cause the heart to leap in gladness on the high summits of Tsang-chan in the dawn of the year. For there, in the first moments of the melting snow, among the open brushwood of the mountain glens, no leaves at all are seen, but only rich wide heads of rich wide lavender-blue flowers, delicately fringed all round their lobes, sitting close over the dank earth in ample raying domes of blossom, emerging from the crown before all else, on fat stems so short that it seems as if each bloom sprang directly from the stock on a stem of its own, as in *P. Winteri*—whose beauty of fringed lavender blossom is here recalled, though the five lobes of *P. sonchifolia* are more starry and distinct than the fuller orbs of *P. Winteri*.

P. Souliei, also from Szechuan, is a little species remarkable for the long, definite, and delicate stems of its blunt and rounded leaves, oblong and scalloped and powderless, though roughish with a short down ; it is generous with many dainty scapes of 4 or 5 inches, each carrying one or several long-tubed violet bowls on graceful pedicels, and cloven in the lobe.

P. spathulifolia is the form of *P. minutissima* once called its mere variety *spathulata*, but now raised to specific rank on account of its larger flowers and foliage.

P. spectabilis is the most royal of the four royal Arthritic Primulas— a majesty confined to one small district of the Alps, from the utmost ridges of Judicaria, across Monte Baldo, to Monte Summano and the high sunny hill-tops of Venetia, until it is stopped by the advance, from the East, of *P. Wulfeniana*. It would almost seem as if *P. spectabilis* had its especial cradle on the Cima Tombea, so marvellous there is the abundance and glory of its masses, cushioning all the long grassy ripples of the topmost downs to the summit in cascades of cushions covered in their time with such a profusion of sturdy stems crowded with those full-fed wavy splendours of white-eyed pink, that all the mountain blushes in your face as you cross from the Northern side (where the Primula is rare though lovely in isolated tufts and clumps in the rocks), and come over suddenly into the full sunlight of the rippling emerald arêtes and lawns that range away towards the precipices of the Daphne. Each crown there sends up its stems ; and as the most casual tussock you may kick out by the pathside will consist of some eighty odd crowns, it may be imagined what spectacle is offered to the mountain marmots in the first week of June. For the flowers in themselves are enormous and comfortable ; while no 3-inch stem of the lot would consider its powers properly employed if it were not carrying more than four of them. The plant must be seen at home in glory to be believed : it must also be so seen to be collected. For among the rosy millions lurk hassocks of especial loveliness ; and the eye of devotion, in the course of a day that dulls the hope of heaven, may select the richest harvest of notabilities among the rest—forms ox-eyed as Hera with their clear white centres against the pink undulations of their face, forms of colour especially rich and clear, blossoms especially round and full, wavy at the edge, or folded or fringed most exquisitely : forms white as milk (but starry in outline), forms like apple-blossoms, all of snow within and sun-flushed snow without, forms as blue as *P. marginata* and as red as *P. japonica*—forms so dizzying in their various loveliness that in the end one swoons before the problem as to which are the best of the best among these beautiful myriads. In cultivation *P. spectabilis* bears out its promise of heartiness on the hills : it is impossible to harm it, in any rich deep loam or peaty mixture, or even old kitchen-garden soil, where it grows fat in rosettes like cabbages, making increasing tufts of those broad dim leaves of dulled-green leather, slightly recurving at the tip, so as to give them a rounded effect in the matted clump, and marked with the especial sign by which you may always know *P. spectabilis* among its kin. For they are *pitted all over their surface with minute half-transparent dots* that give the foliage the look and feel of being made of green skin elastic with pores, dimmed in its sheen and offering a faint, but false, suggestion of stickiness. And if only gardeners will realise that this Primula, especially of its especial group, abominates darkness and shade, they will get it out into the full light of day, where it will blossom,—but not as freely as it always grows—a thing so accommodating that it will even continue no less happy, though it sit in pools of water all through the summer.

P. sphaerocephala is the Chinese cousin of the Indian *P. capitata*, for the same use and purposes and treatment.

P. spicata has often come and gone again like the dream of beauty that it is, moving even the hardened heart of experience to declare it the most lovely Primula in the world. Unfortunately it is the only one that seems certainly monocarpous (though some very recent Catalogues are betrayed by pride of possession into a blessed doubt of this); so that, unless the flowers can be taught to set seed, their appearance is but a heart-rending flash of sunlight before the night of their final departure. The leaves are oblong in outline in a brave upstanding small rosette, rather leathery and shortly downy. They are deeply feathered into lobes all up, and these lobes are lobed and sharply toothed again, so that the outline has a sumptuous lacy effect; in the middle rises the powdery stem of 3 or 4 inches, bearing perhaps half a dozen flowers. And the name of the plant is misleading though true; for these are indeed arranged in a spike, and yet they do not look it, the flower-clad portion of the scape just gently elongating with a very short interval between blossom and blossom, so that the effect is rather that of a loose long head of those amazing wide-open bell-shaped saucers, a little jagged in the lobes, and of the serenest pure china-blue, veiled with a faint haze of silver meal. It should have the worshipful treatment of *P. Reidii*, and be sat up with night and day when in flower, that it may be prevailed on, with food and flattery, to set fertile seed.

P. × spinulosa, a false name of Gusmus for *P. × intermedia*, Portenschl., *q.v.*

P. × Steinii is the central point of the hybrid between *P. minima*

PLATE 26.

PRIMULA SAXATILIS.
(Photo. R.B.G., Edinburgh.)

PRIMULA SUFFRUTESCENS.
(Photo. R.B.G., Edinburgh.)

PLATE 27.

and *P. hirsuta,* which contains some of the most gorgeous treasures in the garden. Unfortunately, though they are quite easy to grow, the hybrids are all painfully rare in nature, only to be found here and there after long prying, and the most exhaustive and painful researches in the Brenner Alps, where alone the parents achieve a meeting—and this only with difficulty, because *P. minima* sticks to the open moor, while *P. hirsuta* hugs the rocks and precipitous gullies above the little waterfalls, so that it is there, and just above, on the shelves of their cliffs, that there is best hope of the hybrids. *P.* × *Steinii* stands in the median position between its parents, with toothed, shining, half-sticky little leaves, and trusses of huge blooms on almost no stem at all; it may be seen in the limestone shingle of the Hintere Onne. The cross, however, is fertile and various; there are two principal lines of divergence, one towards *P. minima,* the other towards *P. hirsuta.* The name of the central type is *P.* × *Steinii,* Widmer, and from its many and subsequent shades and intershades, crossings and re-crossings (for these plants are fertile), stand out superbly *P.* × *Bilekii* (as I believe, though I have never collected it), *P.* × *Forsteri,* Widmer (*minima* > *hirsuta*), and *P.* × *Kellereri,* Widmer (*minima* < *hirsuta*). These crosses are of unparalleled splendour, perfectly dwarf, almost as much so as Minima, but with flowers larger, wider, and more solid than those of either parent, and of an almost startling intensity of rich red or pink. This, of course, is true of the best forms only; the names can never be taken as fixed rigidly on any one development, and I have seen types called *P.* × *Kellereri* and *P.* × *Forsteri* that are pale and starry by comparison with the regal orbs of claret-crimson velvet that I have long cherished as those of *P. Kellereri,* and the expansive glowing stars that classically belong to *P. Forsteri.* This last, but for the size of its flowers, and a certain unmistakable different look in the leaf (owing to a minute legacy of glandular dots and oval-shaped end from Hirsuta, is apparently a gigantic Minima with two or three flowers to a minute scape; *P. Kellereri* is larger in leafage, darker in its green, more glandular, and altogether approaches rapidly towards Hirsuta in a smaller scale of growth and larger of flower. *P.* × *Brennia* is a false name.

P. stelviana, Vulp. = *P. oenensis, q.v.*

P. stenocalyx reserves the full psalm of its glory and value for the Appendix. It also embraces *P. leptopoda, P. Biondiana,* and possibly *P. cognata.*

P. Stirtoniana is a lovely little alpine, making rosettes like that of some Drosera, or a very toothy oval-leaved *P. minima,* from which stand up scapeless the single noble blossoms of lavender-blue. While the no less dainty *P. Hookeri* belongs to the group of *P. petiolaris*, *P. Stirtoniana* finds its affinities among those other wee high-alpine treasures, *P. minutissima* and *P. reptans*.

P. stricta (which is also, though in part only, *P. Hornemanniana*, Lehm.) is no more than a smaller and poorer *P. farinosa* from sub-arctic Europe, lacking the meal of the type.

P. Stuartii has bred a great deal of confusion in lists, which can now be finally cleared away by realising that there *is* no purple or "*purpurea*" form of *Stuartii*, which is *a uniformly yellow-flowered* species, a copy of *P. sikkimensis*, growing in running watercourses, and for precisely the same needs and of the same value in England. All purple-flowered pretenders that bear this name belong to *P. nivalis*, and will there be found described.

P. × Sturii is the first branch of the hybrid between *P. minima* and *P. villosa*, for which see *P. × flatnitzensis*.

P. suaveolens is *P. Columnae, q.v.*

P. × Suebtitzii is a garden cross between *P. denticulata* and *P. rosea*. It has interest, but no beauty or value.

P. suffrutescens adds another to the few valuable American species. It is an undershrub of high exposed positions in the Central Rockies, and is hardy and easy in cultivation, as much more so than *P. Rusbyi* as the plant itself is more beautiful—in warm sandy, stony, and well-drained peat, in a sheltered and warm situation, where it will run about, making long prostrate branches thickly set all along with abundance of narrow long leaves, green and glossy, swelling to ampli-tude at their ends, and there more or less sharply toothed or scalloped. From the ends of all these shoots rise up in early summer tall bare stems that seem a little excessive in height and gawky from a mass so humble, carrying loose heads of most brilliant aniline-pink flowers with a golden eye, suggesting a reminiscence of *P. rosea*, but lacking that flaming purity of violent clear rose.

P. szechuanica has the hyacinthine persuasion and lush habits of *P. Maximowiczii*, but is much less valuable, its stems not greatly ex-ceeding the leaves, and carrying smaller flowers from larger calyces. It is little more than a weaklier yellow *P. Maximowiczii* of divergent habit (Purdom, 1910).

P. taliensis belongs to the group of *P. petiolaris*, which it helps to replace in China, though not in cultivation ; and quite inadequately anywhere, not having any sort of endowment for sustaining a rôle so arduous, or competing with *P. Winteri*, though in itself a pretty thing. But the whole group of Chinese Petiolarids yet awaits much fuller

PRIMULA.

information before the popes of Primula will be able properly to pronounce upon it.

P. tangutica I believe to be not specifically distinct from *P. Maximowiczii*, of which typically ugly plant it is typically the ugliest development. In a thousand diversities of dowdiness both the (supposed) species grow together over the huge grass-downs of Northern Tibet, among *P. Woodwardii*, *P. Purdomii*, and a fine yellow Nivalid. At its very best the tall lax tiers of blossom in *P. tangutica* resemble inferior and lunatic hyacinths of green, varnished with mahogany on the outside and rimmed round their rays with pale citron ; at their average they are in varying shades of dull chocolate, and at their worst sink to a dirty blackness.

P. Tanneri is a Himalayan from the high Rhododendron glades, making tufts of toothed, stalked violet-shaped leaves, which are glaucous underneath when young ; and the stems rise up to some 5 or 8 inches, unfolding simple graceful heads of large and lovely lavender-blue flowers with a notched or fringy edge and a golden eye. It stands very near to *P. Griffithii* in the group of *P. petiolaris*.

P. taraxacoeides is another Chinese species, with blue blossoms, after the habit of *P. sonchifolia*, and with the same eccentricities of leafage, which here, however, is held more markedly to recall the Dandelion.

P. tenella produces mealy little stalked leaves, obovate or rhomboid, scallop-toothed to the tip from the middle, with delicate threadlike stems of an inch or two, each carrying one large smooth blossom of bluish-white, deeply notched along the edge of its heart-shaped lobes. (High altitudes between Sikkim and Bhotan.)

P. tenuiloba was originally reckoned only a variety of *P. muscoeides*, *q.v.*, but has now been given rank of its own, because, although the same in its densely matted habit, the foliage is evenly and minutely (instead of quite deeply and coarsely) toothed, while the flowers are two or three times as large, with specially narrow lobes, deeply cloven into two more strips, starting apart, so that the whole wide blue blossom has a rich spidery effect.

P. tenuissima = *P. odontocalyx*.

P. tibetica belongs to the highest highlands of its high land, and is a beautiful thing, akin to *P. pumilio* in some ways, but more suggesting a *P. sibirica* so much dwarfed that there is hardly a trace of the stalk left, but only the pink or blue great flowers with cloven lobes, almost as if each had only its own stem on which to spring from the tuft, which is very small and neat and dense.

P. × Tommasinii is among the Cowslip-inclining hybrids of *P. acaulis* and *P. officinalis*.

PRIMULA.

P. tongolensis stands beside *P. sinuata* in a group of its own. It is a small plant with little fat horny-rimmed leaves, blunt and scalloped and stalked, lobed at their base. The stems just overtop the foliage, these being a little over an inch high, each carrying one flower—an inch-long tubular bell with rather narrow lobes at the mouth, each just nicked into two more.

P. tosaensis belongs to the group of *P. Reinii*, but comes from realms so southerly of the Rising Sun that there is little hope that it will be of any use in our gardens.

P. Traillii, Watt, is a species imperfectly described, and so far unknown in the garden ; though greatly to be desired, according to its author, who found it growing at high altitudes in upper Kulu, in soft powder-dry woodland soil under the shadow of large rocks—despite the fact that it belongs apparently to the Sikkimensis group, though, apart from its habitat, rather resembling *P. japonica*, but that the flowers are rather smaller, and of a lovely pale-blue. Unfortunately, though *P. Traillii* seems to have two blooming-seasons, so that Sir G. Watt was able to get ripe seed, as well as revel in the blossoms of his find, this seed got mixed in its packet, and, when at last it came home to Wisley and germinated with much gladness, the promises thus raised proved to yield nothing else but *P. involucrata*, though confidingly described by Mr. Wilson in the *Gardener's Chronicle* under the name of Traillii, which they ought to have had a better right to bear. The real species accordingly remains a treasure still to seek.

P. × *Trisannae* is a false name of Gusmus for *P.* × *Heerii*, *q.v.*

P. × *truncata*. See under *P. flatnitzensis*.

P. tyrolensis is the only close relation of *P. Allionii*, though separated from it by the width of Northern Italy ; for, while *P. Allionii* belongs only to a very small district of the limestones in the Maritime Alps, so *P. tyrolensis* occupies another, hardly larger, in the limestones of the Southern Dolomites, where it may sometimes be seen in the crevices of the cliff, forming vast ancient loose cushions, the rosette of the year springing at the end of a trunk matted with the dried relics of a century. The plant does not form the dense masses of the other, and its rosettes are much smaller, the tiny leaves being almost round, toothed, stemless, and very sticky, and stinking if squeezed ; while the flowers are of the same size, but of thinner texture, and of a more aniline red-lilac colour, usually with a white eye, and sometimes with a fading blurred star of darker colour radiating from its centre. Better and worse forms of this, as of all the others, may be chosen in June when the blossom is at its full ; but it does not very readily vary, and the thin magenta-rosy stars, large and abundant though they be, are

PRIMULA.

no specially worthy fulfilment of the tiny foliage and the cushioned habit, which has given hope of a charm as potent as *P. Allionii's*. In cultivation it likes moraine, or a sunny deep crevice in calcareous loam, with perhaps a little lightening enrichment of peat and sand ; and it can freely be divided, while shoots taken off in August can easily be struck as cuttings.

P. tzetzouenensis belongs doubtfully to the group of *P. sikkimensis*, though its leaves are so definitely stalked as to suggest that it should go rather with the Heart-leaved group, of which *P. rotundifolia* may be taken as a type. No more can at present be said of it.

P. Umbrella resembles *P. kichanensis* in many respects. It makes a neat rosette of powdery-grey oval-pointed leaves, curling along the roughly toothed edges ; the sturdy mealy little stalk comes up in the middle, and rises 2 or 3 inches high. And round it on their pedicels stand out the large lavender-blue flowers in such a neat radiating ring that an umbrella is not so much suggested as a merry-go-round at a village fair, swinging out all the blossoms at the full length of their attachment-cords, as round and round the stem goes whirling at full pressure of the machinery, till the cars swim out straight at right angles to their axis, like the joy-boats at Earl's Court. It is no robust thriver.

P. uniflora goes modestly in the matter of a name, and is guilty of under-statement. For its flowers are almost invariably two ample pendent bells from ample calyces, hanging from the top of a powdery stem of 4 inches or so—*P. uniflora* being most closely allied to *P. Reidii*, but that it is altogether frailer, with lilac-blue or rosy bells, and oblong little leaves, very shaggy, and very deeply feathered into toothed lobes, standing out on foot-stalks longer than themselves. High-alpine Sikkim, and for the special care devoted to the group.

P. urticifolia inhabits rocks like the coneys, but it is not at all a feeble folk, as you see its delicious colonies outlining the cool, dank moss-crannies of the shadiest limestone ghylls that occur rarely in the granitic wilderness of the Da-Tung Alps. With its tiny tufts of tiny foliage, gashed into ferny strips, and its lovely profusion of big pink flowers, *P. urticifolia* quite absurdly suggests a hybrid of *P. minima* and *P. bella*, with the beauties of both parents reinforced. The diagnosis of this now visually realised treasure in Pax is so frigid as to fill me with fear lest I may also have underrated other charmers likewise known only, at the time of writing, from similar descriptions.

P. vaginata is another, poor-flowered lilac species, of the Geranioid group, with soft rounded leaves, and an obviously half-hardy temper, undeserving of love or longing.

P. × *valbonae* (Gusmus), one of his four superfluous names for the hybrid between *P. minima* and *P. spectabilis,* whose type-name may be *P.* × *fratensis,* but which is better known under its branch-names of *P.* × *Facchinii* and *P.* × *Dumoulinii.* See under *P.* × *Facchinii.*

P. × *valmenona,* a false name of Gusmus for his own *P.* × *Venzoi, q.v.*

P. × *variabilis :* forms of the hybrid between *P. acaulis* and *P. officinalis.*

P. × *varians,* another extra name of Gusmus. See under *P.* × *Facchinii.*

P. × *variiformis,* another extra name of Gusmus. See under *P.* × *flatnitzensis.*

P. Veitchiana, like *P. chartacea,* approaches the Sinensis group in handsome round-bladed leaves, definite in outline and devoid of hair ; but the habit of growth and beauty of blossom seem to lead on towards *P. Davidii.* They are both, at present, unknown and ungrown.

P. Veitchii is a stalwart and gorgeous species of the Woodland group, quite easy to grow and quite hardy. It has the typical lobed ample leaves of the section, crinkled and veined, with many tall stems, carrying whorl over whorl of large golden-eyed flowers of a colour which its admirers call lively and brilliant, and its detractors, the most crude and remorseless magenta in the race. It is usually therefore to be seen grouped at exhibitions in close association with the pure fire-scarlet of *Habranthus pratensis ;* it is rumoured that many a venerable Chelsea pensioner has been blasted into blindness by the spectacle thus offered.

P. × *venalensis* is a superfluous name of Gusmus for *P.* × *Steinii, q.v.*

P. × *ventricosa* is a superfluous name of Gusmus for nobody knows what.

P. × *venusta* is a natural hybrid between *P. auricula* and *P. carniolica* —a fertile parent itself, and most variable in form, differing from *P. carniolica* chiefly in the possession of meal, and from *P. auricula* in the rosy, crimson, purple, or brownish colouring of its flowers. It is invariably offered in catalogues, but the true primary cross is almost, if not always, there represented by secondaries or tertiaries— if indeed by anything that has even so remote a legitimist right to bear the style of *P.* × *venusta* at all, the name by now having become almost as blurred as that of *P.* × *pubescens.* It is quite possible that the very lovely blue-purple Auricula form called *P.* " *decora* " may belong to this group, while there is no doubt about the parentage of the smaller-flowered yet more brilliant *P.* × *marven,* with heads of round sapphire-violet blossoms with a powdered eye, which represents a secondary cross from *P.* × *venusta* on to *P. marginata*. All these are perfectly easy to grow ; they all multiply readily from cuttings, but most of them, from seed, will show every kind of reversion into dulled and damaged colours, returning towards *P. auricula.*

P. × *Venzoi* is probably the impostor that emanates from nurseries under the name of *P. Muretiana.* It is the hybrid of *P. tyrolensis* × *P. Wulfeniana*, a willing mass-forming little clump, most various, but differing typically from *P. tyrolensis* in being larger, stiffer, glossier in the more ample leaf, which has an indefinite horny hem, but occasionally a vague toothing or so at the edge. It is smaller altogether than *P. Wulfeniana*, shorter in the similarly empurpled flower-stem, and smaller in the similarly stiffish and glossyish lessened leaves. The flowers are large, two or three in a cluster, and of a rather impure lilac-rose, often with deeper blots at the base of their lobes. It grows very readily in any reasonable conditions (and in unreasonable ones no less), and may be pulled to pieces unresenting at any moment. Those who wish to see it for themselves must seek the ranges where *P. Wulfeniana* meets *P. minima* in the mountains of Venetia about the ridges of Cimolais and over the Val di Torno.

P. veris is the aboriginal name that held the Primrose and the Cowslip and the Oxlip and all their children in its vast embrace.

P. verticillata is the tropical Arabian Primula with tiered yellow flowers, which, by its kinsman or sub-species *P. floribunda*, has yielded a far better greenhouse plant than either, in *P.* × *kewensis*, a chance-gift of the gods. *P. Boveana* is a microform of the species, and has often been confused with it ; the *Bot. Mag.* plate of *P. verticillata* in 1828 in reality represents *P. Boveana.* And *P. simensis* is another.

P. Viali, Franch., is a hairless small species, of which, on present information, *P. Littoniana* seems only an expanded version.

P. Viali, Pax, contains *P. deflexa*, *P. gracilenta*, and *P. Watsoni* as well.

P. villosa replaces *P. hirsuta* in the Noric Alps, and very often in catalogues. It is another clump-forming alpine, not easy, like many of the Erythrodose section, to tell from its cousins, except by its geographical distribution. For they each occupy a different district, so that it is easy enough in nature to know which kind you have come upon ; but the happy information fails in the garden, in the case of a bought specimen, so that in the personality of *P. villosa* what must be looked for, to distinguish it from *P. hirsuta*, are rather longer, limper leaves, more *densely vested in longer darker coarser fur ;* and taller stems, carrying their flowers on rather shorter pedicels, and thus in rather closer heads, though otherwise their beauty of big ample white-eyed rose-pink blossom is unaltered. In nature *P. villosa*, like others of the section, is wholly calcifuge, but in the garden seems indifferent to the presence of lime. It divides into two main types, of which it is to be regretted that either should continue to figure in modern handbooks as a species. *P. v. commutata* has thinner foliage, still limper, longer, and more often coarsely toothed. The scapes are 5 inches high or so, carrying a head of large bright rosy blossoms; it may be seen on the porphyry rocks about the castle of Herberstein in Styria. The main form is *P. v. Jacquini*, Pax (*P. Simsii*, Sweet.), with broadly obovate or oblong leaves, drawing to a short or minute short leaf-stalk and lightly toothed. The variety *P. v. norica*, is hardly more than an indistinguishable development with narrower leaves and a less dense coat of fur.

P. vincaeflora has at last yielded its face to the photographer, so that all is over except the shouting and the seeding. A characteristic of the blossom is the way in which the two upper lobes turn back, so that the whole flower takes on the look of some exaggerated violet or Pinguicula rather than a Periwinkle. Like all this group it wants rich and perfectly-drained soil, flooded with underground water all through the period of its growth, and then turned off in winter, so that the tight and bulb-like bud into which it dies may rest, like the knop of the dormant Pinguicula that it so faithfully imitates, too, when fully awake, at its other extremity. Then, in spring, come up by fold over fold the small shaggy oval leaves, merging at the base into membranous dusky scales that only gradually begin at last to change their character, until finally the uppermost and largest open out into the rosettes ; and then, if luck and water favour, the single stems arise, each bearing its weird prognathous flower of violet-purple. Having outgrown its youth, *P. vincaeflora* is perfectly vigorous and free—a most happy surprise.

P. Viola-grandis. See Appendix.

P. violodora is an ungrown tender species in the group of *P. mollis*.

P. viscosa is offered in catalogues under almost any other name than its own, which has been misappropriated too long for the use of *P. hirsuta*—an error which has bred much trouble and is yet so gratuitous and the state of the case so simple and beyond dispute that one greatly regrets to find the author of an authoritative modern handbook on Alpine Plants asserting that the nomenclature of *P. hirsuta* (which he actually still calls *P. " viscosa "*) is "rather involved." Nothing could be further from the facts. *P. hirsuta* is the name given by Allioni in 1785 to the only species that has now any right to bear it—the dwarf pink-blossomed Erythrodose Primula

PLATE 28.

PRIMULA VITTATA.
(Photo. R.B.G., Edinburgh.)

PRIMULA URTICIFOLIA.
(Photo. W. Purdom.)

PLATE 29

PRIMULA VIOLA-GRANDIS.
(Photo. W. Purdom.)

PRIMULA VINCAEFLORA.
(Photo. W. Irving, Kew.)

PLATE 30.

PRIMULA VISCOSA.
(Photo. W. Irving, Kew.)

PRIMULA WINTERI.
(Photo. R.B.G., Kew.)

PLATE 31.

that catalogues, however, try to call *P. viscosa* (on Villars' most unfortunate name, which was, however, only bestowed in 1787, and therefore is incapable of standing against Allioni's prior description of two years before). So much for *P. hirsuta :* the question being perfectly simple, as will be seen, and by no means involved. We now turn to the true *P. viscosa*, where again Allioni steps in first, by applying this name to the big stinking-leaved glandular Primula of the Southern granites—lax in texture, running woodily about in wide masses, sending up luxuriant flopping tufts of very long oval-pointed foliage, sometimes toothed, and of a dusky grey-green with glands that smell rancidly of goat ; to be followed by tall stems of 10 inches or more, carrying serried and one-sided bunches of hanging narrow trumpet-shaped flowers usually of a hot and vinous violet, rather squeezed and cylindrical in outline, large indeed in themselves, yet not by comparison with the lush and leafy plant. But then, Allioni having got in first with his name, Villars came leaping in as before, two years later, and once more exactly reversed matters, making his *P. hirsuta* out of Allioni's *P. viscosa*, just as he had turned Allioni's *P. hirsuta* into a new *P. viscosa* of his own (and Allioni's *Campanula alpestris* into a complimentary but untenable *C. Allionii*). However, the priority of date settles the matter finally and quite simply in favour of Allioni's names of 1785, as against those so mischievous transpositions attempted by Villars in 1787. There can be no further room for doubt or error. Nor need we trouble about the catalogue-names of the species, except as mere varieties. *P. graveolens* (Hegetschw.) and *P. latifolia* (Lapeyr.) are invalid synonyms of *P. viscosa*, All., which name has the prior right over all. The type, however, occupies a very large range, from the Pyrenees through all the Southern granites (never on limestone) to the Voraarlberg ; accordingly it takes various local developments, of which three are fairly well marked, though by no means to be insisted upon, since each district will yield many shades of difference, and many a valley may be found with special forms as beautiful as that rarity, for instance, of broad-toothed leaves and round powdered eye to the flowers of pure blue-violet, that is so precious by certain rocks of the Mont Cenis among abundance of an uglier type. However, as some of these try to figure as species sometimes in catalogues, it may be well to point out the three main streams of variation as at present recognised—all forms of the species being equally ready to grow, when once re-established in warm deep and perfectly-drained light peaty and stony soil, *especially among roots or under the edges of granitic rocks,* so that they can send their fibres far in beneath into the dry shelter they often seem to like ; or in among the rootage of light mountain-pines, which seems to have the same effect of securing drainage, and is especially affected by that especially beautiful form which haunts the Cottians, and there with *P. marginata* produces *P.* × *Crucis*—a form of much more slight and tufted habit, much smaller in general development, much larger and fuller and more widely honest-faced in the big round bloom. These, then, are the more marked local or national forms ; to save the unwary, in case they ever appear as species, uncommented, in catalogues, I quote them here in order :

P. viscosa pyrenaica (Pax).—This is evidently the finest type : larger, broader leaves than those of the other types, coarsely toothed ; a multitude of flowers to the umbel. (Eastern Pyrenees.)

P. viscosa cynoglossifolia (Widmer), smaller leaves, oval, entire, or slightly toothed ; many-flowered umbels. This is the prevalent form of the Valais, the Graian, Cottian, and Maritime Alps ; Mont Cenis, Combes de Barant, Valdieri, Boréon (with *P. marginata*). This variety seems, in my experience, usually to insist on possessing rocky places, cliffs, and crevices. It readily acquiesces and luxuriates in a shady aspect, as also does *P. marginata.*

P. viscosa graveolens (Pax)=*P. graveolens* (Hegetschw. and Heer.) ; the form belonging to the Western Rhaetian Alps. Smaller leaves, oblong or lanceolate, narrowing straightly to their base, and more or less toothed from their middle to their point ; many-flowered umbels. This form belongs essentially to the Engadine, though reported from as far south as the Bergamask Alps (Widmer) and as Paznaun in West Tyrol (Engadine : above Samaden ; Piz Languard). As I know it this development prefers to form very wide masses in full open soil and in full sun.

P. vittata.—See the note on *P. secundiflora.* This species, apart from other differences, has more and smaller flowers to the umbels, of which there are often one above another ; and the plant has the same needs and habit as the other, and with the same stripes of meal down the empurpled calyx—although, unless there be a considerable tangle among the species, this seems much inferior to *P. secundiflora* of nurseries as sent out by those who say they have it.

P. × *vochinensis* is the second branch of *P.* × *Deschmanni, q.v.*

P. Walshii, Craib, is a small and lovely high-alpine rarity from Tibet, which stands quite close to *P. pumilio* (*q.v.*) for needs and character, but can easily be distinguished by its abundance of glandular hairs, whereas *P. pumilio* is wholly bald.

P. Wardii. See note on *P. sibirica*, and also Appendix.

P. Warei, sometimes seen in catalogues and lamented in lists, is nothing but either *P. farinosa scotica,* or else the *genuina* form of typical *P. farinosa* itself, so called by Stein in 1888.

P. Watsoni is the most worthless species of the Grape-hyacinth group. It makes rosettes of shaggy oblong foliage, and sends up rather tall bare fat stems that end in a spike of small and wizen flowers ridiculously insignificant at the top of such a powdered maypole.

P. Wattii, on the other hand, is one of the treasured lovelinesses in that terrible group of the Soldanellas, of whom it wants all the usual care and reverence, and perfect drainage, and rich stony soil, and underground moisture, and subsequent rest in winter ; which it will reward, if the mood so take it, with a thick little well-furnished rosette of upstanding primrose leaves, very shaggy all over with long glistering white hairs, and crinkled and feathered on either side from the middle in toothed and scalloped lobes. From their midst shoot up the powdered sturdy smooth stems of some 4 or 5 inches, ending in a well-furnished head of especially fat and solid fringy-edged bells of sapphire-blue, depending, in much larger domes, from the rounded Byzantine cupolas of their comfortable calyces.

P. Whitei is a close cousin to *P. petiolaris* (*q.v.*), and that is all that can yet be said about it except that it comes from Bhutan, and may easily at a glance be mistaken for its rival.

P. ✕ Widmerae. See under *P. ✕ coronata.*

P. Wilsoni is the only correct name of the species described under *P. angustidens, q.v.*

P. Winteri.—It is unfair to say that the name of *P. Winteri* is a base and unpardonable pun, yet true it is that in mid-winter always seem to emerge the crowded new rosettes of powdered, rounded, toothed leaves on their firm foot-stalks, and in their heart an interminable cabbage of these glorious wide lavender-lilac flowers with their fringed lobes and noble outline, succeeding each other for many months, in a rivalry of beauty, against the grey and mealy beauty of the robust leaves, if only the weather will allow. There is no other fault than this—which perhaps is merely due to the plant's inexperience—to be brought against this unparalleled introduction, which is perfectly hardy anywhere, and perfectly perennial too, in any well-drained rich soil, moist in summer (or merely rich), and not water-logged in winter. It will in time very likely begin to throw out runners also, such is its almost cruciferous rampageousness of hearty habit, and such the general fashion in the race of *P. petiolaris,* to which species it stands so near that, though now acknowledged a true species, it was known for years as *P. petiolaris pulverulenta.* And in the meantime it will freely come from seed (which, however, as becomes a jewel, requires some setting), or is so robust that, in the end of the summer, its added crowns of the year may readily be removed from the main stock and grown on for the next season. Care, however, should always be taken with this, as with all Primulas, to see the specimen you are buying in flower. Pick it out then and there, order it, and make sure you get it ; for the species, like the race and its hybrids, is as variable as woman, and the best should as carefully be chosen of the one as of the other, and artificially fertilised accordingly.

P. Wulfeniana is the last and smallest of the four royal Arthritic Primulas of the European Alps, where it occupies the Eastern limestones, on the same high and sunny ridges of grass along the necks of the mountains as afford such revelling-ground for *P. spectabilis* on the Cima Tombea. Even so grows *P. Wulfeniana* on the upper lawns of the Karawanken, not growing into huge rounded hassocks, but extending over the herbage in solid flat masses of glossy foliage, hidden in their time from view by the myriads of short purple stalks, sometimes touched with powder, bearing heads of enormous ample and wavy-edged flowers of richest rosy-mauve, with a white eye of fur at their throat. It is the lowest in habit of the group, but in beauty stands high, and forms such matted masses, gleaming emerald in the grass of the mountains (which they occupy like many square yards together of battalioned glossy plantains, threaded in and out by the pale sapphires of *Gentiana Froelichii*), that even the calloused chronicler of the race has to break into cries of joy over its " lordly rosy carpets." Note that the stiff and shining little pointed leaves of the notably clear and lucent green rosettes have a most characteristic tendency to curl *inwards* at their edge, and are bordered with the broad family band of membrane, which here is glandular at the rim. The lobes of the calyx are broad and blunt, not half the whole length of the calyx, and the 2-inch stem does not carry more than three flowers, and lengthens mightily and blushes more shinily after blooming. It is quite as easy as its three sisters, in the same conditions : the peer of the best. And, like the other two, far superior to *P. glaucescens*, the least brilliant and the most common of the four, though no heartier than the rest.

P. yargongensis is a gorgeous and desirable treasure in the group of *P. glacialis*, with ground-hugging rosettes of thick oblong little stalked leaves, and great brilliant blossoms so splendid in their colour that it has to overflow into the calyces as well.

P. yedoensis is *P. jesoana, q.v.*

P. yunnanensis, from limestone crevices by the Li-kiang Glacier, is after the habit of *P. kichanensis* (from which it chiefly differs in having its flowers on long foot-stalks of their own instead of sitting close to the head), but much weaker and more sickly in growth, with its flowers in grudged pairs, on the top of long and spindly stems of 3 or 4 inches. In the garden it is utterly wiped out by *P. kichanensis* and *P. Umbrella, q.v.*, being a puny little thing like a tense and wizen *P. farinosa*, with just a pair of flowers on stilts above a starveling tuft.

P. yuparensis is a most beautiful new Japanese, in habit like *P. farinosa*, but with very much larger long-tubed blossoms in the way of *P. longiflora*, borne erect, by twos or threes on a dainty scape of 3 to 4 inches.

P. zambalensis clamours to the collector from the far Alps of Batang, where it replaces its close kinsman *P. yargongensis*.

Priva laevis, an 18-inch half-hardy Verbena of no merit.

Prosartes Hookeri=**Disporon Hookeri,** *q.v.*

Prunella. See **Brunella.**

Pseudopyxis depressa is an attractive small woodland species of Japan, suggesting that the blooms of Trientalis have strayed on to an Enchanter's Nightshade.

Psilostēmon orientalis has also been called *Nordmannia cordifolia, Trachystemon orientalis*, and *Borrago orientalis*. This last name gives the picture ; it is a thing for the wildest places only, among scrub or on rough outlying slopes where it may freely spread. In the spring come up 18-inch loose spikes of very starry hanging Borrage-flowers in blue and pink, which are followed in later April by the unfolding of taller rank heart-shaped leaves, wrinkled and rough as is the fashion of the race.

Psoralea, a race of almost shrubby Pea-flowers, with blossoms in spikes. Their place is on dry warm slopes in arid soil. They have no special charm, but *P. subacaulis* is quite dwarf, with egg-shaped heads of blue blossom in April ; still dwarfer is *P. acaulis*, which wears purple flowers ; *P. macrostachys* is a yard high, with spikes of violet-blue in late summer ; *P. bituminosa* has the same season, but half the stature, with flowers of dark violet ; and *P. formosa* (now ana-grammed into *Perosela*) is a branching small bush with minute leaves, and few flowered spikes of large and brilliantly purple flowers. Seed.

Pteridophyllum racemosum is a curious and pleasant little Japanese Poppywort, which from its fleshy stock unfolds in spring a tuft of dark-green fleshy leaves just like those of the Hard-fern, except that they are not hard ; then in the midst rises in July a stem of 6 inches or a foot (or more), unfolding a spike, most airy and graceful, of tiny white flowers, which, though Poppies, look much more like the loose spire of some small-flowered white Crucifer. This can easily be grown in sheltered places and woodland soil, but must be shielded from slugs.

Pterocephalus Parnassi is a cushion plant, covered with pinky-lilac Scabious flowers, on stems of 2 or 3 inches all the later summer; it thrives well and grows wide in any open sunny place in light well-drained soil. *Pt. Pinardi* is smaller, with the same silver-grey foliage much more divided; and the feathering becomes finer yet in *Pt. pyrethrifolius* from Kurdistan. Division and seed.

Ptilotrĭchum contains some half-shrubby Crucifers left over from *Iberis*, and some others which, if not white or pink, would be *Alyssum*. They have, then, the same needs and values, will thrive in sunny places of the rock-garden, in light soil, profusely bloom in spring, and set seed for their reproduction, if you do not prefer propagating them from summer cuttings.

Pt. cappadocicum appears also as *Ib. cappadocica* in catalogues. It comes from the alpine pastures of Armenia and Cappadocia, making a neat small mass of stems, beset with huddled elliptic leaves, very tiny and stiff and untoothed, smooth at the edge, and all clad in finest starry down, getting narrower higher up the stems of 3 inches or so, that each end in a firm head of white candytuft. So that the whole thing is a rounded hump of simultaneous bloom.

Pt. cyclocarpum (*Alyssum*) suggests *Alyssum rupestre*, but the leaves are broader, and the pod scaly; it forms a neat tufty mass of branches, thick at the base, with little narrow silver-scaled leaves that tail off into upstanding naked spires of white blossom, 6 inches to a foot high.

Pt. emarginatum has no merit.

Pt. glabrescens makes a neat humped dome about 6 inches tall, almost hairless, with the branches thick with fat narrow foliage, and ending in spikes of white flower. (Masmeneudagh in Cappadocia.) Akin to *Pt. spinosum*, which comes from Spain.

Pt. longicaule is a depressed heap, forming loose silver rosettes, and with flopping boughs of a foot or two in length, with bare and quite frail stems carrying showers of white blossom—the whole effect being that of a white-flowering *Alyssum saxatile* in habit. (From the limestone crevices of Granada, &c.)

Pt. purpureum is one of the loveliest Crucifers anywhere known, and sometimes is called *Alyssum Lagascae*. In the upmost schists of the Sierra Nevada, from 8000 to 11,000 feet, it huddles itself among the rocks almost into hiding, growing a very dense thornless and branching tidy mass of close-congested silver-scaled leaves, oblong-oval, small and neat; and the mass is covered with clusters of the most beautiful bright flowers of purple and pink in spring.

Pt. pyrenaicum makes a loose mass about 10 inches through, springing from a woody trunk about an inch thick. The base of the lax cushion is thick with fat leathern obovate foliage, above which aspire the dense spikes of large white blossoms, arising from the branches of 3 or 4 inches that break from the main shoots and form the silver-scaly, woody, tortuous bushling. It is a fine species, but of the greatest rarity, to be seen here and there in the sheer precipices of Catalonia and the Eastern Pyrenees.

Pt. spinosum.—This is the favourite commonplace called in gardens *Alyssum spinosum.* It forms neat thorny masses that may be nearly a foot high, and many more across, hidden in time by sheets of little white blooms suggesting those of *Koeniga maritima* (which also used to be *Alyssum*); it luxuriates on warm dry soils and exposures, and there is a pretty variety, *Pt. sp. roseum*, in which the flowers have a varying flush of faint lilac or pink, most attractive, even if not quite deserving this high epithet so often charitably extended (by kind catalogues) to cover even the faintest of mauve blushes.

Pulmonaria will not easily find a lovelier representative than the narrow-leaved brilliant Spotted-dog of the Dorsetshire woods, with its 6- or 8-inch stems, and its hanging lovely bugles of rich clear blue in April—so much more modest in the leaf, well-bred in the growth, and brilliant in the flower than the towzled and morbid-looking heaps of leprous leafage made by the common Lungwort of gardens, with leafy stems and indecisive heads of dim pinky-blue flowers that look as if they were going bad. This is sometimes *P. saccharata* of the Southern ranges, a species of even startling foliage-beauty when you come upon the marvellous and awful mottlings and splashed whitenesses of its lush leaves in the woods, for instance above the Boréon, seeming as if some Suffragette had been liberal in those parts with vitriol. But the flowers are grievous. *P. azurea* (Bess.) is simply *P. angustifolia*, of which English woods have one form, perhaps the best, and the upper Alps another; *P. "arvernensis"* of catalogues is one of its developments, and so are the white and the pink ones sold simply as *P. alba* and *P. rubra*—leafy things all, but of clear-coloured beauty in early spring (and even into summer), and perfectly easy of culture anywhere in cooler soils and aspects, positively rejoicing in division. Others of much less clarity of tone and general merit are *P. officinalis*, often the Spotted-dog or Jerusalem Cowslip of gardens, and probably no more than a poor form or sub-species of *P. angusti-folia*, larger, broader and limper in the leaf, as well as much more muddle-headed about the colour of its flowers : *P. mollis*, from Siberia ; *P. styriaca*, dimly purple-blue ; and *P. tuberosa*, of a reddish violet.

Puschkinia.—These are lovely little bulbs of the Levant, with stems of 3 inches or more in spring, and rather large china-blue flowers in loose spikes, lined with a richer shade, and so of the loveliest effect of pale-blue blown glass in the ample bell. *P. scilloeides* is the best known ; *P. libanotica* is larger in the bloom, and *P. hyacinthoeides* (from the highest snows of Kurdistan) is the smallest of all and the palest in blue. All thrive easily in light sunny soil.

Putoria calabrica is worth the pains of cosseting in light soil in an especially warm and sheltered spot between sunny rocks, in order that it may remember the cliffs of Spain and Greece and remain with you as a hardy perennial, forming more and more of a delicate flopping bush of 10 inches or so, with narrow shining leaves, and heads of wax-pink trumpets all the summer through, as large and fine as in *Daphne Cneorum* (but emitting unpleasant instead of celestial odours), and followed by black berries from which the plant may be raised anew, if not, in England, more surely propagated from careful cuttings.

Pycnanthemum lanceolatum will prosper in dry shady places of the copse, where it will throw out 18-inch or yard-high stems beset with whorls of little white or purplish labiate flowers. This is a North-American, finely hairy, aromatic, and also called *Koellia virginica*, but under no name a thing of especial value.

Pyrethrum is almost the same, if not quite, as *Chrysanthemum*. *P. roseum*, however, from the alpine and sub-alpine fields of Pontus and Caucasus, is the parent of all our garden forms ; *P. fruticulosum* is a very branchy, woody, dense bushling from the upper Alps of Asia Minor, with flowers as in *Chrysanthemum alpinum ; P. Kotschyi* shares the cliffs of Berytagh with the last, and is a perfectly compact little mound of small, silky, finger-cut leaves, from which stand out the large white marguerites ; *P. nivale* has many stems of 6 inches or a foot, gracefully rising this way and that, smooth and bluish-grey, and bare only at the top, where they each carry one wide white daisy ; and there are countless others to name, though these are the chief of those that carry one blossom to the stem. The best of them, perhaps, is *P. carneum* (*Chrys. coronopifolium*), with bigger flowers of the same pink as in *P. roseum*, both being of the same value as insecticides ; and *P. densum*, with heaps of dense and soft-grey velvety curled foliage. All are of easy culture in light open soil, and may at pleasure be pulled to pieces or struck as cuttings, or raised from seed, according to their habits.

PYROLA.

Pyrŏla.—When once these are obtained in good sound pieces, rooted and ready, they are all quite content and hearty in light woodland soil at the fringe of bushes, in cool aspects, where they will spread heartily and give more joy from year to year. Unfortunately it is very difficult so to obtain them, owing to their odious habit of running through their native forests in long, fibreless runners like fine macaroni, that never stop to rest, and offer no opportunity to the collector, and are shy about striking out fresh life for themselves. Even in pots they are most deceptive ; for the clump of evergreen foliage is immortal ; you take up the pot which for months has had a goodly glossy tuft of Pyrola sprouting from it, and which is obviously, therefore, ready by now to be put out, having clearly filled its receptacle with new roots. Out it accordingly goes, and lo, there is still nothing more than 2 inches of inert spaghetti (exactly as the nurseryman potted the shoot a year ago), on which the clump has immovably lived, but made no preparations for a fresh start. If, however, sound plants can be got, the best species are : *P. rotundifolia* (perhaps the best of all), a rare native, and most abundant in open stony and bushy places on the Alps, where it is perpetually being picked as a summer-flowering Lily of the Valley. Especially ample are its tufts of long-stemmed, leathery, round leaves, dark and glossy, and its sturdy spire of 10 inches or a foot, well furnished with fine white waxen cups with style and anthers of orange scarlet. Very similar is the American *P. asarifolia*, but that the duller leaves are not only round, but lobed at the base on either side of their stalk. But this has a variety which is the loveliest thing in the race, *P. a. incarnata* (*P. uliginosa*, Torrey), indistinguishable in vigour and stature, but with bells of the most exquisite true and tender waxy pink, clear and strong and clean and rich in colour as raspberry cream. *P. media* and *P. minor* are smaller stages of *P. rotundifolia*, as far as the garden is concerned, though *P. minor* is distinct by a very short, instead of a very long style ; while *P. media*, though much nearer to *P. rotundifolia* and with a style as long, wears it nearly straight instead of violently curved. Inferior in value are *P. arenaria*, *P. elliptica*, *P. chlorantha*, and *P. secunda*, with bells that verge towards a greenish tone, as is also the case with the plant one buys with hoping heart as *P. picta*, which turns out only to be *Chimaphila*, and only " picta " so far as white mottlings on the dark leaves go, instead of having the rose-painted waxen face that one had hoped. *P. umbellata* is also *Chimaphila*, *q.v.*, and the sweetest of all has struck out a line of its own so distinct that it is usually set nowadays in a race to itself as *Moneses grandiflora*. This is *P. uniflora*, which may often be seen in the moss-banks round the stones and the fir-roots in the alpine woods, and very rarely in North England and Scotland, studding the needled ground or the wide emerald sponge with flat rosettes of round-toothed leathern leaves in a pale-yellow shade of green, nursing next year's bud at their heart, or sending up the single 3-inch stems from which hangs a single enormous star of dense and waxen creamy-white, crystalline and pure in texture as blended ivory and snow, haunting the whole wood with a scent of orange-blossom so poignant in its deliciousness as to be almost a pain to remember. This delicate loveliness is terribly hard to collect, and when got, by no means easy to grow. In nine cases out of ten, it will be found running underground with threads as fine as cotton, never arriving at any root at all, and quite useless to collect. It should accordingly be looked for in unusual places ; as, for instance, beside a woodland path near the Mont Cenis, where it is growing in moist grey silt of the gutter, and there, not called on to meander far and wide before it roots, forms compact balls of dense fibre like a mass of clumped Lobelia seedlings. These, then, do really offer hope, and should be given a shaded place in light, rich, gritty sand or soil, with water flowing underneath in summer. Or else they might be inserted in the woods, beneath the pine-trees in the mossy masses, there to make themselves at home.

Pyxidanthera barbulata.—See under **Diapensia.**

R

Raillardella Pringlei makes a good companion to Ptero-cephalus, a creeping American Composite, with linear leaves and stems of a foot or more, each carrying a head of orange-coloured Scabious in summer.

Ramondia Heldreichii=Jankaea Heldreichii, *q.v.*

R. Nataliae is, to some thinking, by far the finest of the Ramondias. It makes much neater rosettes, with flatter and more overlapping leaves than *R. pyrenaica*, of oval foliage more corrugated than crinkled, and not dull and dusty, but of brilliant glossy green with a dense fringe of dark hairs. The flower-stems are more numerous, and the flowers in a much clearer, brighter tone of lavender-blue, with the usual eye of golden orange, but only *four lobes* to the crown. A well-flowered clump of this, staring glossily from some rich-soiled shady crevice or ledge (in which every Ramondia is as happy as linnets on a text), wipes out all the rest of the race ; there is also a tragically pale form, whose blossoms seem as if they were carved from lavender-tinted snow, and a white one of purity and brilliance and solidity unsurpassed, with the golden-scarlet pointil at the centre enhancing its candour. (Servia and Bulgaria.)

R. × *permixta* stands between *R. serbica* and *R. Nataliae* and has no distinguishing claims.

R. pyrenaica represents a most ancient outlier of the family (whose main home is the Balkans, with *R. pyrenaica* breaking out far away in the Pyrenees), with an unbridged gap of many a hundred mile between its nearest relations (though there is at least a rumour now of the plant's being recorded in one valley or so in an alpine chain of Central Europe). It is a noble species, very old in cultivation, and ranked by Parkinson among the Primulas, to some of whose clumps, indeed, the great rosette of hairy dull-green leaves, shaggy and ear-shaped and crinkled, do have a resemblance almost as rough as themselves ; but how different are the lilac-blue potato-flowers, three or four on a stem of 4 inches, springing all round the crown, with five lobes to the corolla, and a pointil and eye of orange and gold. Neither the white form, nor the pink, is quite worthy of the love and the prices bestowed on it, for it is usually inferior to the type, thin and ragged in outline, no less than washy and feeble in colour (all Ramondias seem to vary, like *Primula*, in amplitude of contour, as well as in brilliance of tone, and so should be bought or collected in flower). And as for the Ramondias pompously sent out as *R. querci-folia*, *R. peregrina*, and *R. leucopetala*, these are merely forms of the quite ordinary type or albino, thus insidiously trying to slink into circulation under names and prices grossly beyond their deserts. The clumps of all the race may be divided, or leaf-cuttings may be struck in heat as with Begonia, but the best method of propagation is by seeds ; these, being microscopically minute, and in number as the stars of the Galaxy, should be sown on the surface of a pot, filled with fine peaty mixture, and then stood in a saucer of water with a piece of brown paper (for darkness) held down over its top by a pane of glass (for close humidity) ; they should there be carefully watched from day to day, and will germinate like a cress, and be good little flowering crowns in a couple of seasons.

R. serbica, like its hybrid *R.* × *permixta*, sinks down into obscurity between *R. pyrenaica* and *R. Nataliae ;* it is more saucer-shaped than either in the more cupped flowers, which are smaller (like the whole plant), with a shorter style, *five lobes*, and the general colouring of *R. pyrenaica*, rather than the braver lavender brilliance of *R. Nataliae*.

RANUNCULUS.

Ranunculus.—In catalogues this race is far too fertile of unannotated names. In point of fact the family is no less fertile of indistinguishable or worthless weeds, filling every wayside and pasture up to alpine levels all the world over, with a superabundance of species, many of them annuals, some of them uglies, and a vast army of them not sufficiently distinct to rival the best. These are the lowlanders ; the alpine section of the family contains few that are not supremely beautiful, and solitary in their especial charm. We are yet strangers to many a white high-alpine buttercup from the Rockies, and other ranges of America, that may some day threaten the secure thrones of *R. alpester* and *R. glacialis.* The following list, then, can be guilty only of suggestions, and sifted though the choice has been with a sympathetic eye, it may very well be that among the species omitted there may prove to be several deserving of a warmer fate.

R. abnormis is a most curious species from the Alps of Central Spain, having precisely the foliage of *R. graminifolius*, though still narrower and more grasslike and (like the whole growth except the flowers) on a very much smaller scale, making a neat tuft of grassy foliage in the alpine herbage, with large golden blossoms on short stems of 4 or 5 inches, made up of some eight or ten petals instead of the fashionable five of the family, thus justifying the plant's claim to abnormality. It should have open sunny places in light soil.

R. acetosellaefolius we have long been wanting, and now our desires seem in a fair way to be achieved. The plant is sadly rare, only to be seen in the highest damp fields and slopes of the Sierra Nevada, where it forms clumps of foliage really like *Rumex Acetosella*—long leaves lying out in a larger or smaller rosette upon the ground, in the shape of a long, savage spear-head with one or more pairs of backward-pointing barbs. From the neck in early summer are thrown up a protracted profusion of quite naked stems spraying up all round to the height of 3 inches or so, but lengthening in fruit to 5 or 6 inches. They never branch, and bear one large white flower, till the plant looks as if a number of stems had been picked from snowy *R. pyrenaeus*, and stuck in round the stock of a mountain-sorrel. It should have, like all the alpine field-buttercups, the open, cool, and rather moist rich soil, perfectly drained and in a sunny place, that is indicated for the whole group that has *pyrenaeus* for its type.

R. aconitifolius, with its pyramids of lucent handsome leafage, and its yard-high loose showers of lovely white stars, is the joy of any bog or rich waterside border, as it is of so many an alpine water-meadow or open woodland recently cleared. In the Alps an eye should be kept open for forms of special amplitude and size in their blossom,

206

and in the garden that eye should be kept firmly shut to any suggestion of merit in the fat-packed little double-flowered form called Bachelor's Buttons, which sometimes dares to appear in lists even to the exclusion of that noble fairy, the type, with which it is not worthy to share a catalogue, to say nothing of a garden.

R. adoneus is a very high-alpine from beside the snow-fields of Colorado, quite dwarf in growth, with claw-cleft leaves, and large golden-yellow flowers. For the gritty, underground-watered moraine.

R. alpester, L., is perhaps the most lovable of all the alpine group, and one of the few treasures that are at their best and happiest in Switzerland. It is hardly possible to tread the high, stony places of all the main chains (especially on the limestone) towards the upper shingles beside the water-courses trickling from the snow, without having your recognition clamoured for by clustered clumps of stalwart and shining pure-white buttercups with a golden eye, standing so sturdily up on their stems of 2 or 3 inches from those hearty tuffets of intensely dark-green leaves, three-lobed or five-lobed, and then usually cut deeply again in ample or pointed scallops, and all veinous with yet darker nerves. The type, however, varies greatly, and some forms are as ample as other local developments are poor. In the Oberland (as, for instance, above the Gemmi, and about Rosenlaui) it is specially notable ; in the far Alps of Styria, on the limestones of the Schneeberg as on the granite above Heiligenblut, it is rather less full-fed in outline of lovely snow-saucer, and has much less inclination to swell into big clustered clumps with as many as twenty blossoms all out at once. And its chief dereliction is in the Graians, where it occurs very rarely, and not at all about the Mont Cenis. In the Maritime Alps it is not at all to be seen either, but as soon as you have crossed the Col de Tenda, from the Rocca del Abisso on to limestone Marguareis of the Ligurian Apennines just opposite, the plant is once more in possession of the white stony places. In the garden it loves almost any deep, rich, moist soil, but is especially happy in the moraine close by running water, where it forms widening tufts from year to year, and never wholly ceases to blossom from March to the end of November. Division.

R. amplexicaulis is only known in the alpine pastures of the Pyrenees, Asturias, and Estremadura. It is a most hearty and well-known dweller in rich places of the garden, much larger and less choice than the last, with tall stems of a foot or so, branching, and embraced by ample pointed-oval leaves of glaucous blue-grey that contrast admirably with the very big and full-petalled blooms of pure and pearly whiteness in early summer.

RANUNCULUS.

R. anemonifolius is a high-alpine from Armenia, of half a foot or more, with handsome foliage and large golden blossoms.

R. angustifolius is a Pyrenean species, best to be described as a close cousin of *R. pyrenaeus*, but rather smaller, with foliage more narrow and grassy still, while the white flowers tend not to be so large. It has, however, a really charming sub-species, *R. alismoeides*, a plant confined to the alpine fields of the Sierra Nevada, much dwarfer, with stems of 2 or 3 inches at the most, each carrying only one much ampler white flower. The leaves are all at the base, rather broad and tapering to a long point, in all about an inch in length, and only a few of them, spreading out upon the grass.

R. arizonicus, from the Rockies, is golden, but only about 8 inches high.

R. asiaticus.—Except in warm, dry gardens of the South, in light, warm soil, England is but a cold stepmother to the blazing single scarlet buttercup of the Levant, like a royal Anemone; and the double forms have no place in the rock-garden.

R. bilobus has the habit and the tastes of *R. alpester*, but is confined entirely to a small limestone district in South Tyrol, in the mountains round the head of Garda, and away towards Venetia, where it haunts the cooler, shadier shingle-slopes, and there makes clumps of rich beauty, as in certain places on the Cima Tombea. It may easily be told from *R. alpester* by its leaves, which are perfectly round and uncloven in outline, fatly roundly scalloped along their kidney-shaped contour. In cultivation the plant is no less easy and delightful than its cousin, with the more abundant petals more deeply notched, so that, while *R. alpester* (at its best), holds up solid saucers of whiteness, the flowers of *R. bilobus* are more like the most exquisite of wee and pure-white dog-roses above the tufts of lucent green foliage, dark as night, which are *evergreen* instead of dying down in the winter as in *R. alpester*. It has sometimes been sent out by misguided ones (myself included), as *R. crenatus*, a distinct and separate species of wholly different tastes and distribution, *q.v.*

R. brevifolius (*R. Pythora*, Crantz) is a rather ugly yellow Buttercup from the Abruzzi and Asia Minor, etc., where, in the high limestone screes, it forms a sub-species of *R. Phthora*, with small glaucous-grey leaves on longish thin stems, and very much broader than they are long (as if they had been squashed-to, like a concertina), and with three or five deep lobes along their outer edge. There is one of these leaves on each 3-inch stem, that each supports a single little flower of shrill yellow; but here the lobes are deeper and much more pointed and less ample in outline than in those at the base.

RANUNCULUS.

R. Buchanani is a New Zealander, erect and sturdy, with the handsome foliage kidney-shaped and then cut into three lobes to the base, the middle one often having a short foot-stalk of its own. The blossoms are large and white, most abundantly furnished with petals. It should have the treatment of *R. Lyallii*, and is about a foot in height.

R. bullatus lives in damp, shady, sandy places among the Olives from Spain to Asia Minor, with a rosette of leaves at the base, blistered and coarsely double-scalloped, while from the crown spring many naked stems of 6 inches or so, each carrying one large golden flower.

R. bupleuroeides is a form of *R. pyrenaeus*, confined to the Pyrenees, and differing in the greater length of fine stem that carries the much broader, long-pointed oval of the leaf, which in true *R. pyrenaeus* seems to have no foot-stalks at all as a rule, so do they taper narrowly downwards. Here they diminish quite suddenly from their amplitude, and the whole plant is more delicate and thin in effect.

R. carinthiacus is a sub-species or only a mere form of the variable *R. montanus*, slender in habit and with the foliage much more freely, profoundly, and narrowly claw-cut, the stems more slender, and the bright golden flowers not so large. It has no special claim, any more than have two other golden mountaineers, *R. carpathicus* and *R. caucasicus*, all this section having little look of their high station, but seeming rather stunted field-buttercups out of place.

R. Chamissonis, from Eastern Siberia, is quite close to *R. glacialis*, having only one flower to the stem and a hairy calyx.

R. cortusaefolius is a gigantic 2-foot golden buttercup (flowering in July) with handsome foliage. It comes from the Canaries and is of no long-enduring hardiness, though worth attempting in a hot and specially well-drained corner in light soil.

R. crenatus has much the look and habit of *R. bilobus*, but here the leaves are only rounded to the stem, and not bi-lobed at the base. They are also of limper texture, dull dark green, and with the scallops much deeper and definitely pointed instead of rounded. The stems, too, are a little stouter and stockier, though the great white flowers are quite as beautiful, and even more amply furnished in effect, as the petals are not so deeply notched. It likes the same places as the other white alpine buttercups, but resolutely avoids the limestone, instead of seeking it. It has only one district in Central Europe, in the chain of the Bosenstein in Styria, after which it occupies four or five quite small mountain tracts, widely isolated, and far away from each other as from the last, in Bosnia, Servia, Transylvania and Macedonia.

RANUNCULUS.

In the garden it is as easy and as lovable as all the rest, in the same situations.

R. creticus is a handsome golden buttercup of the field-persuasion, a foot high, with soft foliage and brilliant blossom.

R. cupraeus is a most exquisite treasure, with fern-fine frail foliage like that of some tender alpine poppy, and then dainty and almost naked little thready stems of 2 or 3 inches, each carrying one large flower which continues copying the poppies, at the price of departing from all the family traditions, in being of a hot coppery orange. Want at present, however, must long remain our master in this matter ; *R. cupraeus,* in the whole world, inhabits only the highest rocks of Lassiti in Eastern Crete.

R. demissus, from Greece and Asia Minor (with a variety *R. d. hellenicus*) and again in the Sierra Nevada (*R. hispanicus* is spindlier), has fine foliage on fine stems from the crown, and golden big flowers that sometimes seem specially large when the whole plant is only an inch or two high instead of its usual four or five.

R. Enysii is a large New Zealander of small use or merit.

R. eximius lives in the high places of the central Rockies. It has only one fan-vaned leaf, or very few at the most ; and the dwarf stems carry great golden stars an inch and a half across.

R. flabellatus (*R. chaerophyllos*) is worth a hot, dry place in the sun. It is an extremely rare native that used to occur in Jersey, the rest of it reaching the Levant. It is like a minute and hairy *R. bulbosus,* with the finely feathered and claw-cut leaves all at the base of the stems, that thicken to a sort of bulb at the bottom. The flowers are borne on the usually unbranching stem of 6 or 9 inches, and are very bold, upstanding, and large, of shining glorious gold.

R. geraniifolius is a form of *R. montanus.*

R. glacialis, sometimes calling itself *Oxygraphis glacialis,* has a most curious distribution. It clothes the whole of the European Arctic North, descends all down Western Norway, and so across Iceland to the far coasts of Greenland. But it will not set foot either in Arctic Asia or Arctic America, and, unlike most other Arctic types (which, if they put up with the conditions at all, put up with all of them), never descends at home from its high places on to the level of shore or tundra. And the same trait may be noticed when *R. glacialis* begins again in Southern Europe, where, after having ceased for so long, it suddenly erupts upon the Alps into amazing vigour, and occupies all the gaunt granitic, porphyry and schistose screes, shingles, moraines, and so forth, in the highest alpine zone, especially abundant in the damp upmost hollows where the mountain flanks are brought to bed of the first stumbling trickles that are in time to be the Rhine, the Rhone, the Inn ; or by the shores of the glacial lakes, sheeting the stony levels in a shroud of pink and white. It is especially abundant in the main chains, the highest climber of our phanerogams, ascending to 14,000 feet on the Finsteraarhorn. It wanders eastwards, and abounds throughout the Lombard Alps, Tyrol, Styria, Salzburg and Carinthia, never on the limestone, and never at all descending from the highest places. It then ceases, but for one last outbreak in Transylvania far away, and one isolated mountain of Bavaria where it is extremely rare. To the West it roams more feebly, is a rarity in the Pyrenees, and rarer still in the Sierra Nevada. No one who has ever trodden the high places of the non-calcareous Alps has failed to rejoice over the world-hiding profusion of those fleshy-fat grey-green tufts, with their branching stems crouched under enormous full-faced flowers of dazzling whiteness that after fertilisation pass into a deeper and deeper rose colour till they fade into stale blood. But the species greatly varies ; the levels of the Lac Savine above the Mont Cenis are solidly pink with it over the distances, making an effect like daisies on a vicarage lawn, but as the comparison suggests, the form here is poor, starveling, and one-flowered, as compared to the sturdy jungles of it on the Monzoni Thal, covered with snowy flowers the size of five-shilling pieces, or the less upstanding but no less comely-saucered type of the upmost screes in the Engadine and Oberland. The gardener should choose his forms with care, and with no less care get them up. For the fat roots, bunchy and countless, wander far down and wide ; ice-axes are the fittest implements of collection. And then it should be cultivated in heavy stony loams kept constantly flushed with water below in summer : thus *R. glacialis* may be led to thrive almost as heartily as by the shores of the snow-lakes up towards the stars and the great silences of its home. Clark's elaborate recommendations about making a 6-inch-deep (!) pocket for it, are a pathetic reminder of the dear dead days when you built your rock-garden of any garbage, and then had to spend the rest of your life and money in pecking little unsatisfactory " pockets " in it for anything special you wished to grow ; so that the poor dying alpines there earned a reputation for difficulty that was the last thing they wanted. Now that the garden is well-built from the base, and *in toto*, the Ranunculus offers less of a problem, so long as the underground water-supply be constant and abundant, the soil solid and rich, but perfectly drained, with abundance of large, sharp stones as well as chips, for the plant's stout roots to take hold of and luxuriate beneath. It is, perhaps, of all the granitic group of high-alpines, the most blatant and dominant in its magnificence, though making no pretence to rival the concise azure cushions of His Celestial Majesty the King of the Alps. Forms of it are sometimes needlessly distinguished; one of especial fluffiness and deep colour has been called *R. roseus*, and an enthusiast has reported and photographed a most splendid thing with creamy flowers, which sounds as if *R. glacialis* had been wooed and won by *R. montanus*.

R. Gouani is a taller version of *R. montanus*, about a foot high, with the segments of the deep-cut, ample leaves folded rather than flattened out. The whole tuft is lush and velvety, and belongs only to the cold alpine fields of the Pyrenees, where it is abundant.

R. gracilis and *R. geranifolius* are synonyms of *R. carinthiacus, q.v.*

R. graminifolius is a really handsome species, hardly appreciated at its due worth. Its habit, much larger and looser, together with its narrow, glaucous-blue foliage, suggest a lax, exaggerated *R. pyrenaeus*, but the large and abundant flowers, each on a long foot-stalk, are of glossy, clear, rich citron-yellow. It is a plant of the Seaward ranges, and quite easy, free, and handsome in the garden.

R. Haastii lives in the Alps of New Zealand, and wears all its leaves at the base; these are of glaucous blue-grey, irregularly cut into five or seven deep irregular lobes. The blossoms are ample and golden, on stout stems of 3 to 6 inches, which exude venomous milk when pinched, or otherwise annoyed.

R. heterorrhizus has much the charm of *R. flabellatus*, with the same sized flowers, though on stems of only 3 or 4 inches, with the leaves on long foot-stalks. (High alps of Phrygia.)

R. hybridus (Biria, 1811), is superseded by the older name, *R. Phthora* (Crantz, 1769), *q.v.* It is *R. Thora* × *R. brevifolius*.

R. illyricus stands among the many field Buttercups that, in the ruck of description, might escape notice. It is a beautiful easy native of Bulgaria, for any light, open place, with tri-lobed, silvery leaves, and tall, branching stems of a foot high or more, carrying sprays of large pale-yellow blooms.

R. insignis is a hairy counterpart, with noble golden suns, to smooth, dark, and glossy *R. Lyallii*, from the Alps of New Zealand. It is most variable in the size and splendour of its blooms, and the stalked leaves are large and round or kidney-shaped and scalloped.

R. lanuginosus is a tall and woolly yellow European, only to be cautiously admitted.

R. Lingua, with a *grandiflora* variety, is a splendid rampant water-plant of England, with long foliage and tall stems of 3 feet and more, very abundant in brilliant large blossoms of golden yellow throughout the summer. It is a treasure for shallow waters, where it can have free room to run wild.

R. Lyallii is always ardently talked of. It belongs usually to high glacial places of the New Zealand Alps, where it grows in banks of rich loose silt, or in the black mountain soil, on slopes that are torrid bogs in the summer and frozen snow-fields all the winter. In habit it is stout and stalwart, with big, glossy, scalloped leaves (on sturdy stems), leathern and dark and round ; and an 18-inch stalk that breaks into a wide shower of many-petalled white flowers that, as a rule in England, do not seem quite large enough for the general dimensions of the plant, and suggest a loosely-wired bunch of *R. crenatus*, stuck up above the tropical foliage of *Caltha polypetala*, on the top of a tall stalk. It is not at all easy, either, seeming to require a consistency of temperature such as our artistically erratic climate cannot admit ; however, it will thrive quite as well, either as it deserves, or as its grower, after experience of it, desires, in very deep, rich, chippy, gritty, and well-drained peaty loam on a sunny or sheltered slope, with abundant water flowing beneath throughout the growing season, until the plant dies down into its fat great tuberous rhizome to rest for the winter (when it must lie dry, on pain of rotting). There is also a smaller variety, *R. L. Traversii*, with cream-coloured flowers, and as the species is splendid enough to elicit notice even from the most inexperienced colonist, it is to be charitably hoped that we have either not yet succeeded in importing the finest type, or have not yet succeeded in making it show its fineness.

R. macrophyllus is a big, tall, and noble-flowered yellow species from the Caucasus, with kidney-shaped leafage hewn into three or five lobes, and clad in a close coat of hair, on notably long foot-stalks.

R. magellensis can only be seen in the high places of the Central Apennines, especially on the Majella (with a variety, *R. m. arcuatus*, on Monte Sirente in the Abruzzi). It is a smaller local sub-species of *R. crenatus*, with long-stalked, deeply, amply, and irregularly scalloped little dark leaves, which, with their gloss and their lobes at the base on either side of the stem, approach nearly to *R. bilobus*, and establish a link between this, the calcareous species, and *R. crenatus* of the schists and granites. In cultivation it is quite easy under the rich- and moist-soil conditions that suit the other two, than which it is usually smaller in habit, and most attractive with its white flowers, with petals nearly as dog-rosy as in *R. bilobus*.

R. Marschlinsii is a spindly yellow gawk of no merit, with in- finitesimal stars, closely akin to *R. demissus*, but fortunately peculiar to damp fields in Corsica.

RANUNCULUS.

R. Mathewsii is a splendid New Zealander, very much in the way of *R. Lyallii*, but with golden flowers. It has the same habits and exactions and doubts.

R. millefoliatus is another bright and handsome field Buttercup, after the fashion, and for the same treatment, as *R. flabellatus*, and with much the same range, though larger and more ample, with the leaves even more elaborately feathered and feathered again.

R. monspeliacus grows taller yet, about a foot high, with golden flowers.

R. montanus is almost universal in the Alps, and so variable a species that although its average or poor forms deserve no more note than *R. auricomus, R. bulbosus, R. reptans*, or any other English weed of the race that the garden thinks itself lucky if it can escape in the ordinary course of nature, some of its neater, dwarfed, huge-flowered alpine forms are well worth marking and collecting. There is a splendid one called *R. m. Villarsii* in the Western Alps, stunted in the growth, and exaggerated in the golden sun of blossom ; but the observant eye, among the ordinary types, no more worthy of the garden than any of our field-weed Buttercups (though not so big in the growth or so small in the flower), will be able, every now and then, to mark down varieties for itself ; for instance, an especially notable and royal rich-golden dwarf lives in the roadside gutters of the Dolomitenstrasse, on the first violent coilings of the road on its way up to the heights of the Pordoi from Canazei. This has flowers that make one think of *Geum reptans*, but that they are far brighter in their sheen, and far richer in their gold. And there is a form with flowers pale and creamy, called, of course, *R. m. albus*.

R. nivalis is not alpine, but entirely Arctic, alike in Europe, Asia, and America, where it descends a little down the Rockies. It is a small species, with hardly more than one little five-lobed leaf on a stalk at the base, with an Anemonoid frill of one or two more on the 3-inch stems, that each carry a single yellow flower, large for the stature of the plant. It should go into the moraine, if thought worthy.

R. nivicola cultivates the snows of the South Island of New Zealand, and there makes tufts of stalked kidney-shaped leaves, cut into five or seven lobes. The stems are slender and branching, the blooms large and of golden yellow.

R. nyssanus is a hairy-leaved, handsome thing that very soon runs about and occupies a wide space of ground, whether in light soil and full sun or moist soil and shade, filling it with fine furry-green foliage, and sending up in June abundant foot-high stems of golden flowers, after which they soon die down again, and leave the foliage once more master of the field.

R. Pallasii has a creeping stock, and all its leaves are stalked, oval wedge-shaped, and more or less tri-cleft. The flowers are large, with eight or nine petals and only three sepals. (Arctic Asia and America.)

R. parnassifolius is always a rare and local treasure, occurring in high silty beds of the limestone Alps from the Pyrenees to the Reiting in Styria, but always a find to be thankful for, and nowhere a common-place to expect. It has a most distinct and sombre beauty of its own with its single (as a rule) tuft of stalked, oval-pointed, fat leaves, thick and dark, of glossy solemn green, with deep lines of care engraved upon their face, outlined with woolliness, and with a special fringe at their crimsoned edge ; the fleshy and hairy stems bend lowly to the earth beneath their branching burden of three or four most glorious pearly moons of white blossom, sometimes tinted with pink on the reverse, and built of very broad, overlapping petals, round and notchless. It is to be seen especially in damp places of the finest silt, often rooting into white wet clay as heavy as hate, with the long, fat roots that emerge from its bulb-like frog-bit root that always seems to have rotted away on the under side. In the garden it is the heartiest thriver, I think, of all the hearty alpine section, in any fair and congruous treatment, with free water allowed. It will even go the length of seeding itself in the most improbable dry banks, and there continuing to prosper as successfully as in the chosen and fussful places especially prepared for it. But great care must be taken in buying a specimen. The best forms, as I have said, are glorious, and never vary in their beauty. But the type has a wide range of variation in the hills, and should be collected from stations where its ways are beyond suspicion. On the Piz Padella, for instance, where it abounds on the saddle, it tends more than elsewhere to form up into close, large patches rather leafier and laxer and smaller and duller in the foliage than elsewhere. And here the abundant blooms never have any petals at all, but only a few little twisted chaffy green tabs. This form, introduced to cultivation, and often sent out by innocent nurserymen, has brought much discredit on the grandest of the alpine white Buttercups, as you may see it in the white clay of the Forcella Lungieres, sumptuous and pure. But on the highest rippled ridges of the Monzoni Thal, where it has the isolated habit and the sober gloss of foliage of the last, the flowers are still not successful in avoiding the bad example of Padella. For, though they do their best, they never seem able to achieve even the five perfect petals that are the fashion of the race, but two or three of them are reduced to wizen tags of membrane, thus giving the blossom a sad air of lopsidedness. But, if once the sound form be acquired, it will never cease to be itself, or produce you flowers in any way false to its best beauty. So that it is essential either to buy or collect your *R. parnassifolius* in flower. Nurserymen sometimes give you guidance in the matter; what they call *R. p. major* is, in reality, the right *R. parnassifolius*-type.

R. Phthora has its descent from *R. brevifolius*, but here the leaves are much larger, in the same style, and much more ridiculously broader and shallower than their depth, along which they are more freely and irregularly toothed and lobed and scalloped. The stem-leaves, one or two, have the same alteration as the other, and the glaucous-grey little stalk ends in the same erect little flower of vindictive and venomous yellow. It is abundant in the alpine screes of the Lombard and Tyrolese limestones (and away through Salzburg, Styria, and Carinthia to Lower Austria), where it is often taken for *R. Thora*, which is a lower-level species of twice the size, always to be known by the more or less vast kidney-shaped and scalloped leaf that sits *halfway up the stem*. *R. Phthora* has curiosity, to make up for a lack of charm; and is *R. hybridus*, Biria (*R. Thora* × *R. brevifolius*).

R. pinguis lives in the damp rocks of the Campbell and Auckland Islands—a dwarfish thing, altogether fat, with fat stem and fat leaves and fat great flowers of many yellow petals veined with purple, sitting fatly among the fat leaves on their fat stalk.

R. platanifolius differs chiefly from *R. aconitifolius* in being yet taller in stature, and ampler of port, with its large leafage less divided, and so rather plane-like, while the blossom-showers are launched on rather weaklier stems. Same uses as the other.

R. pygmaeus is a most diminutive yellow high-alpine, of no merit, but with a curious distribution. For it abounds all round the fringe of the Arctic circle of Europe, Asia and America, and then it breaks out again, very rarely, here and there, in the highest damp granites of Salzburg, of South-eastern Tyrol, the Western Carpathians, and the Val Zeznina in Switzerland. There and there alone may its minute yellow flowers be seen clinging close to the gaunt earth between its stunted little pairs of plump, five-fingered leaves.

R. pyrenaeus is abundant in the alpine grass of all the Southern ranges, bursting into blossom after the passing of the snow in such illimitable profusion that the plains and folds of the huge greening hills soon look as if the snow had not gone at all. It makes varieties, too, of which *R. plantagineus* is taller, with longer leaves, swelling to the middle, and finally diminishing rather quickly to their tip.

RANUNCULUS.

But it also, on the gully-sides of the Mont Cenis, develops two double forms of singular loveliness, for which it is as well to ascend the merciless slopes on a day of rain when the many millions of 6-inch stems are nodding their royal white flowers to escape the wet, for then your eyes immediately confront the blank stare of *Rosa bianca*, where all the carpels have turned petaloid as well, so that all you see among the tossed pure foam of the flower are a few tinges of green such as those on the snowdrop ; it is like a perfect little double white Banksian Rose, and has a chill purity hard to express. The more normal double form, *Rosa Bella*, is more after the Baby Rambler style, preserving the cheerful golden eye of stamens, surrounded by double or treble rows of round white petals in a rich reduplicated saucer, more tidily overlapping than in the loose and Moutan-like elegance of *Rosa Bianca*. Both these prove more or less constant in the garden (especially in their first, and terminal flowers), and, like all other forms of *R. pyrenaeus*, are remarkably easy to grow in any cool and enriched soil, such as that of the kitchen garden, where, in alternate rows with the alpine Primulas, they grow quite beyond themselves from year to year in amplitude. Indeed, it is a most significant thing that on its own wild hills where it so abounds, *R. pyrenaeus* is one of the very few alpines that not only does not wither away under the corruptions of manure, but grows fat immediately, and clamours for more. The most splendid specimens I ever saw sprang on an ancient heap of garbage by the outlet of the Mont Cenis Lake, while in the manured high-alpine plain of the Granges Savines, the Buttercup in its time is like a solid tablecloth of moonlight. Indeed, from all I have now so often seen of lovely *R. pyrenaeus*, I should urge that it never be bought or collected out of flower ; for, manure or no manure, it varies copiously in nature, and, while one bank is covered with nothing but solid orbs of purity, its rival, on the other side of the gully, will show you nothing but starveling squinny stars ; and, a month later, you could have no chance of knowing which was which. *P. pyrenaeus*, besides being the most abundant by far of the white alpine Buttercups, has also proved the most fertile parent, though as yet none of its progeny have come into the garden. On Marguareis it meets *R. aconitifolius*, and there is born *R.* × *lacerus ;* in the Western Maritimes it runs across *R. Seguieri* and begets *R.* × *Yvesii*, and by *R. parnassifolius* it becomes the origin of *R.* × *Luizetii* and *R.* × *Flahaultii*.

R. rupestris lives in the grassy damp rocks and warm limestone crevices in the mid-region of the Sierra Nevada, &c. Its leaves are fluffy, roundish kidney-shaped, stalked, and cut in threes ; and its

RANUNCULUS.

stems are about 9 inches or a foot high, carrying from one to four ample golden flowers about 2 inches across.

R. rutaefolius = *Callianthemum coriandrifolium, q.v.*

R. scutatus is a taller and larger variety of ugly *R. Thora*, with larger, though still mean, yellow stars by twos and threes at the top of a 9-inch or foot-high stem, leafless from the base, but with one or two enormous and very broadly-rounded, tooth-edged leaves sitting to the stems about half-way up, lobed deeply into a depression in their upper edge, with a point or so sticking forward in the middle, this depression being its distinction from *R. Thora*, which merely has the outer edge of the leaves comparatively larger and rounder, and roundlier-scalloped (as if it were blunted and nibbled), where the point should be, with only perhaps a shallow flattish tooth or two here and there.

R. Seguieri is the least known of the white high-alpine Buttercups, and yet quite as beautiful and easy as the best. It is the limestone counterpart of *R. glacialis*, occupying the stony screes of the calcareous ranges, though not ascending to elevations quite so austere, and with a most curious distribution, for, while its main area lies from Dauphiné down into the Maritime Alps, it also has an outbreak in the Abruzzi, and yet again, across Lombardy, another, where it is generally common in the higher limestone silts and screes of the Dolomites on the Italian frontier-ranges and on both sides of the Fassa Thal. It is a specially lovely thing, forming, unlike the others, widely ramifying masses from tough roots that spread underground, and send up tufts of very fine and ferny green smooth foliage, delicate and strange in effect, suggesting a much smaller, frailer, paler-green *Anemone baldensis*, with profusion of round-faced, milk-white flowers on stems of 3 inches or so from each clump. It is a perfectly easy and delightful species for the limestone bed or moraine; so intensely calcareous is it, and so intensely anti-calcareous *R. glacialis*, that it is curious to note their rare contacts. For instance, on the Passo delle Selle, at the summit, there is a strip of limestone silt about three yards wide; this is filled with *R. Seguieri*. But the strip of lime is a thin channel between broad continents of red porphyry and syenite on either hand; these are occupied by waving jungles of *R. glacialis*. Yet as " east is east and west is west, and never the twain shall meet," so here the two buttercups never trespass by a hair's-breadth on each other's ground, but keep separate houses like Montague and Capulet, eyeing each other jealously over the wall, though they do not yet seem to have produced a Romeo and Juliet to overleap the borders and reconcile the families and blend their tastes. Nor, on the Forcella Lungieres, where it abounds in the silt-

218

PLATE 32.

RANUNCULUS ACONITIFOLIUS.
(Photo. R.B.G., Edinburgh.)

RANUNCULUS GLACIALIS.
(Photo. R. A. Malby.)

PLATE 33

RANUNCULUS THORA.
(Photo R.B.G., Edinburgh.)

RAOULIA.

pans of *R. parnassifolius* (and yet more copiously in the drier scree beyond) do there seem any traces as yet of any offspring.

R. sericophyllus is an alpine from the South Island of New Zealand. The whole growth is clothed in silky wool, and the leaves are all at the base, broadly oval and then feathered into three cloven leaflets. The naked stems are some 2 to 8 inches high, bearing big golden flowers about 2 inches across.

R. Sommieri is a 4-inch yellow-flowered species of the Caucasus.

R. Thora has been pictured under *R. scutatus*, its amplified form. The type is smaller and slenderer, a mean and venomous worker of iniquity—filled with an intensely poisonous nature, and found often in the lower woody and rocky places of the Southern limestones. It has many varieties, of which *R. dubius* has also been called *R. hybridus* (not our *R. hybridus*, Biria, which should be *R. Thora* × *R. brevifolius*); there is also *R. carpathicus*, which is the same as *R. Tatrae* (Borbas). As for *R. Pythora* (Crantz), this is clearly *R. brevifolius*, Ten.

R. Traunfellneri is a sub-species of *R. alpester*, and in Switzerland (where it is very rare), can only with the greatest difficulty, if at all, be distinguished. Its real range, however, is through the high limestones of the Eastern Alps, and then again in Transylvania. It may be known by its much smaller, slighter habit, and duller leaves, more finely cleft into narrower, divergent, and much less veiny segments. And the 2- to 3-inch *stems never carry more than one blossom*. It may be seen in fine character round the snow-patches high on the Grigna, almost its last westerly extension, and is a dainty miniature of dainty *R. alpester*, of the same needs and the same charm.

R. Traversii is a cream-coloured variety of *R. Lyallii*, *q.v.*

R. uniflorus is a garden form of *R. montanus, q.v.*

R. Villarsii is a wild and high-alpine form of the same, dwarf, and with flowers of notable size and brilliance.

Raoulia.—A little race of creeping small mats from Tasmania and New Zealand, not of any startling effect, even in foliage, but useful for running over the surface of warm soil, sand, or moraine, and acting as a carpet. There are innumerable species ; *RR. glabra, subsericea, Hectori, eximia, tenuicaulis, Haastii, Monroi, Buchanani, rubra, mamillaris* (these three last form specially dense, hard masses). *R. subulata* is a tiny mosslike thing, in patches of a few inches ; and *R. grandiflora* makes fine sheets of shoots clad in overlapping little oval-pointed leaves, stiff and silvery with close-pressed wool, each shoot ending in a head of flowers frilled with white radiating bracts, about two-thirds of an inch across, all the flowers of *Raoulia* being of the same kind as in *Helichrysum*, to which the race stands close.

Rehmannia.—The Rehmannias suggest in their flowers that a Foxglove has married a Salpiglossis. Of this last they have the floppy, limp texture, the veinings and suffusions of colour; and their shape is intermediate between the long bell of the Foxglove, whose spire they flaccidly emulate, and the wide bell of the Salpiglossis. They are a lush, soft-looking race, but may be grown as hardy plants in well-sheltered, warm corners of loose, rich soil, well-drained, where they have their value in summer, when they help to fill the interval with their loose and leafy spires of hanging, wide-mouthed Foxgloves. It may be well to grow 18-inch *R. elata* (wrongly called *R. angulata*) and *R. sinensis* (*glutinosa*), and the dwarfer hybrid, *R. kewensis*, of the yet dwarfer Chinese novelty, *R. Henryi*.

Reineckia carnea is a little Japanese Liliaceous plant, freely stoloniferous and spreading and easy, with tufts of narrow grassy foliage like that of Ophiopogon, with small violet flowers coming up at the sides, on stemless spikes, close to the ground, all the summer through.

Reseda.—The wild Mignonettes have no real value. *R. complicata* is a 2-foot semi-shrub from Spain, for rather shady slopes, while much dwarfer, and for warmer, sunnier slopes may be chosen 10-inch *R. glauca*, with bluish foliage and the usual little insignificant spikes of flower, all through the summer; while *R. sesamoeides* (like both the others, a Spaniard), is quite dwarf, creeping and ramping. Seed and division.

Rhabdothamnus Solandri is a fine, greyish-leaved, straggling shrublet from New Zealand, with little orange-red foxgloves striped inside with scarlet. Its hardiness is rather more than doubtful, and it seems often a sullen and reluctant grower even in good soil.

Rhamnus alpinus is the rock-sheeting shrub, tight-pressed, with bright green foliage and subsequent black berries, that often gives pleasure on the alpine cliffs, and can easily be made to do as much at home. *R. pumilus* is no longer so adherent to the pavement, and there are many other species, not germane to this garden.

Rhaponticum must all be looked for, either as *Serratula* or as *Centaurea*. *Rh. cynaroeides* is a large Artichoke, and *Rh. scariosum* a large *Centaurea*.

Rhazya orientalis and *Rh. stricta* both want the sunniest of places on the warmest of well-drained slopes. They are Dogbanes. The latter is pretty hopeless—a yard-high bush like *Daphne Laureold* with heads of whitish stars; the former is more practicable—a 10-inch plant of unbranched leafy shoots, enveloping a head of little blue stars among the uppermost leaves in late summer. The first is tropical, the second only Levantine.

RHODODENDRON.

Rheum.—The stately splendour of the great Rhubarbs, such as *Rh. palmatum* and *Rh. officinale*, &c., needs no further passport to the waterside, from which they trample out poor Gunnera, superb no less in their vast gashed foliage than in their 10-foot stout spires of spouting creamy or currant-red foam in early summer. *Rh. Alexandrae* is yard-high, with large yellow oval leaves flopping on the spike. *Rh. Emodi* has the same stature and red-flowered spikes; and for huge columnar overlapping-leaved *Rh. nobile*, that stands a stern column of downward-tiled foliage on the cliffs of Nepal, and up through the everlasting snows of Tibet, we long in vain. And there are countless other species, yet never one as yet for which the rock-garden essentially craves. All can be easily raised, divided and grown, in any rich soil.

Rhexia virginica has been unwisely praised. It is at once a worthless and impossible species of the pine-barrens and swamps of the Southern States, growing about 18 inches high, with opposite egg-shaped leaves all up the stems, and pink-magenta flowers about an inch across, in thick spikes through July and August. It is an erect and gawky grower, suggesting a stiff and inferior Loosestrife. In the same condemnation, and no less impracticable as well as ugly, are *Rh. Mariana*, *Rh. ciliosa*, and *Rh. aristosa*.

Rhododendron asks for a book, not a page. Such as are fitted for the rock-garden will be found amply annotated in all catalogues that offer them; and apart from such exquisite jewels as *Rh. elaeagnoeides*, minute and dainty, with flowers like a little yellow *Pyrola uniflora*, on stems of about an inch, China is pouring in more and more species, in the way of prostrate high-alpine delights, at present only to be designated by numbers. In the early year the rock-garden rejoices in *Rh. praecox*, *Rh. dauricum*, *Rh. ciliatum*, &c., neat bushes hidden by big lilac-pink flowers (or noble creamy-rosy trumpets in the case of the last); smaller, neater, and more exquisite are *Rh. anthopōgon*, with yellow clusters, and bronzy leaves in winter that are almost dauntingly aromatic; and *Rh. imbricatum*, with hoary blue little packed shoots headed by clusters of lovely starry blue-violet blooms with golden eyes. *Rh. kamschaticum* is minutely dwarf, with broad hairy deciduous leaves of pale-green, and half-nodding large singly-borne flowers, flat and wide, of deep satiny claret-purple; *Rh. lapponicum* is very dwarf and rare (*Rh. myrtifolium* always being sent out wrongly under its name); *Rh. chrysanthum* is prostrate, with heads of large yellow trumpets, and a sullen mimpish temper; *Rh. racemosum* has lost half the family hate of lime (living as it does in China on a limestone sub-soil), and makes stalwart bushes, fine in the white reverse of the leathery little dark-green oval leaf, with fluffy flowers of lovely pink in wands of colour all the way up, instead of merely in heads at the top ; and there are more and more beyond hope of numbering. But I find no place here for the Alpenrosen, in whose glowing clusters there is mingled a tone of chalk, or something that usually makes their colour seem squalling and mysteriously vulgar ; though the albinoes are good, and the Alps will yield the eye of love a number of exquisite pale flesh-coloured forms a great deal more easily than these will then proceed to yield themselves to the trowel.

Rhodothamnus Chamaecistus, on the contrary, is incomparably more beautiful than any of these, a native only of the Eastern and Southerly Alps, and there only on the limestones, where, in cliff or scree, it makes vast tussocks of shoots, clothed in tiny oval-pointed, fringed leaves of bright green, emitting from the ends of each shoot in summer a pair or so of the most exquisite saucer-wide flowers of pale pure pink, each dancing bravely before the world on a fine and dainty stem of its own. So delicately lovely a fairy can no longer, indeed, be counted among the crude and clownish Alpenrosen to whose family it was formerly assigned. In cultivation Rhodothamnus is easy, once it has recovered the pain of transportation. But this takes time ; the stocks and subterranean trunks are long and woody, the fibres far and few and very fine, drying up in a moment unless the greatest care is taken, and then never seeming able to recover vitality. It is as well never to touch Rhodothamnus unless you find some slab of a ridge that can be levered off to deliver you a perfect clump ; or unless you at last find a little cave or cañon of damp clayey silt where the plant has seeded and grown into compact mats. If such as these are got, and got down to the post without drying, and got home to England without either drying or mouldering, the clumps will offer no further difficulties, but, after a year of recuperation in the sand-bed, may hopefully be put out on the rock-work in some not too fiercely sunny place, with water flowing far underground if possible, in quite perfectly-drained and spongy mixture of peat, leaf-mould, and rough sand, leavened and lightened with innumerable chips of limestone, with larger blocks, as the plant develops, hammered firmly down to act as comfortable conductors to its trunks and wandering fibres. It is the joy and glory of the Dolomites, and all the South-eastern limestones—not coming westward at all of Garda, but lovely indeed along the crests of Baldo, where it makes no such rampageous jungles of display as the coarse flaring Alpenrosen, but offers cushions of unsurpassable charm, danced over by these delicately staring pearl-pink fairies of blossom.

ROMULEA.

Rindera canescens is a Borragineous plant from the Levant, close to Cynoglossum and Mattia, with greyish foliage and reddish flowers. *R. cyclodonta*, from the high granites of Turkestan, is only half a foot high, and hairless, with narrow-oblong leaves.

Rodgersia.—All these are superb, alike for foliage and for bloom, and are the delight of the rich border by the waterside, where they all thrive vastly. In *R. aesculifolia*, from China, the noble glossy crinkled green foliage is like that of a huge horse-chestnut, and the rose-white plumes of blossom stand a yard high, almost suggesting elongated spires of *Saxifraga longifolia;* *R. pinnata* has similar, more bronzed foliage, more finely divided, and the flowers are borne more aloft in a looser feather of pink or white; *R. podophylla* has plumes like those of a richer *Spiraea Aruncus,* in tiers of foamy crests above mahoganised metallic-shining foliage, of which all the lobes are deeply cut with picturesque teeth; *R. sambucifolia* has dark-green leaves like an Elder's, and spires of creamy-white; and *R. tabularis* has the hugest leafage of all, like that of a limp green Lotus or *Saxifraga peltata*—round umbrellas, scalloped irregularly at the edge, while far above them, on tall naked stems, wave small feathers of white blossom. All these bloom in summer and onwards; all are easy to divide and to raise from seed. See Appendix.

Rohdea japonica, a Liliaceous plant of Japan for any half-shady place of which it may be thought worthy, with tufts of ever-green leathery foliage 2 feet high or so, and little white bells among the leaves, succeeded by red berries.

Romanzoffia sitchensis is usually confused with *Saxifraga ranunculifolia,* the one being a Hydrophyllad and the other a Saxifrage. The true species makes tufts of stalked kidney-shaped scalloped leaves, about 3 inches high, dark-green, and brown underneath; the flowers are small white stars in branches unfurling like the tail of a scorpion; whereas in *R. unalaschkensis* the spike is dense and incurling and one-sided. Both can easily be grown in the damper parts of the rock garden on its shady side.

Romulea, a race of small and delicate bulbs that send up in spring their flowers, like Crocus, often of the most gorgeous deep violet. They are not trustworthily hardy except in the warmest soil of the warmest driest places; though they will live elsewhere, if planted far down, they do not flower properly nor make headway. *R. Columnae,* which is wild on the Warren at Dawlish (though never noted by Mr. Robert Ferrars), is unfortunately a dowdy and ugly little thing, like many; the best we have are the best forms of *R. Bulbocodium,* which in some southern gardens is glorious with clumps of imperial dark-violet Crocus-blooms in spring, followed by very long thin rushlike leaves that flop about in grassy tangles; *R. rosea* is from South Africa, pink, with a yellow eye, and purple lines on the three outer segments; and among many others are *R. Requieni, R. candida, R. Linaresii,* and *R. ramiflora.*

Rosa.—There is no room here to say more than that the rock-garden should not lack *R. alpina,* all the prettiest forms of *R. spinosissima, R. altaica, R. dahurica, R. pyrenaica;* golden little dainty *R. berberidifolia Hardyi,* with a purple blotch at the base of its petals, making its golden flowers look like a Cistus on their dainty arching sprays. (It must have a warm place and full sun; *R. berberidifolia* is a miff, and so is *R. sulfurea.*) And there are many others to be admitted, such as neat little *R. Sicula,* or the long glaucous pinky-blue fine-leaved boughs of *R. Willmottiae;* but all these will be found amply commented in catalogues, and are in any case adornments for only the largest rock-gardens, and there, though delightful, by no means essential to salvation, as they all tend to be rather tyrannous shrubs, and may well be set apart in ground apportioned for such: but the prostrate *R. alpina* is a treasure.

Roscoea purpurea had never raised its family into any high favour. It is a tuberous Himalayan species, to be planted deep in rich well-drained soil, from which it will send up foot-high stems, sheathed in ample corrugated oval foliage, and ending in an autumnal spike of dark-purple strange flowers, like a compromise between a Gladiolus and a Cephalanthera. There is also *R. sikkimensis.* But these rather dim additions to the garden have suddenly been illuminated by the moonlight radiance of *R. cautlioeides,* introduced by Messrs. Bees from China. For this is a plant of quite singular loveliness, thriving readily in rich woodland soil, increasing freely, and apparently of perfect hardiness, though it should be planted at least 6 inches deep. In spring the graceful stiff stems arise to the height of a foot, swathed here and there with narrow iridaceous leaves of glossy green, that shoot also in long pointed lances from the base. The flowers may be six or seven in a head, opening in succession; they are extremely large, with a narrow hood and then a huge bilobed expanded fall or lip, wide and open, and seeming as if cut from the finest of crimpled silk as delicate as that of the most delicate poppy. And their colour is of a yellow unparalleled in the garden, uniform, soft and clear, seeming to contain living luminosity in its texture, but a luminosity more mellow and pure and cool than that of our crude and dusty daylight here upon earth. Its nearest match is in the lucent citrons of *Meconopsis integrifolia,* but here the tone is yet blander

and more serene, shining with a solemn and unearthly radiance as
the blossoms, like ghostly butterflies of light, hover pale and vivid
upon the background of dark pine-branches and fern-frond that
makes the best setting for the plant's beauty; their presence affords
the comfort and surroundings that its health most enjoys. And this
sudden leap of Roscoea from dullness into the heights of glory is not
made solely by *R. cautlioeides*, for it has a sister as yet unpublished,
precisely twin in size and habit, but with flowers of a rich and brilliant
vinous purple.

Rubia Aucheri, a 6-inch plant like an Asperula, with creeping
spreading root, and whorled foliage topped by scantily furnished
heads of blossom in summer. It comes from the Levant, and should
have the treatment of the Asperulas, to which it is related.

Rubus.—Upon England has China in these latter days cast
forth from all her hedgerows and highway-sides so appalling a collection of invasive and hideous great brambles that we have given up
all effort to say pleasant things about them (as at first their cultivators
pathetically and piously attempted), and have even developed an
undiscerning general disgust, in consequence, with the whole misguided
country that has burdened us with such horrors. For the rock-
garden, however, there are some pleasant and quite small brambles,
all well suited in a sunny but not parched place in stony peaty loam.
R. arcticus from the far North, that once was thought to have lodg-
ment in Scotland, is an erect little running raspberry of 6 inches or so,
with large cheery pink flowers, followed by fruits no less exhilarating
in their own way. Care should be taken, however, to get the fruit-
bearing form of the plant, which is sold as *R. a. fecundus*. *R. saxatilis*,
a common species of our Northern limestones, is hardly worth a place,
though neat and modest ; and no one seems ever for long or thoroughly
to succeed with the Cloudberry, though on the moors of Ingleborough
and all the North it makes carpets of many a hundred-yard width,
with its one or two broad-lobed leaves on the upstanding stem of
4 or 5 inches, which first bears up a single erect white blossom, and
then replaces it with a succulent fruit, which is of a golden amber when
ripe, like a very big and large-carpelled Raspberry, with the sharp
sweetness of the Pomegranate. This is the staple jam-fruit of the
Scandinavian moors, but the Cloudberry, though so placid a native of
our high places, seems almost more reluctant to descend from its
ridiculous molehills and be happy in the garden, than does the King
of the Alps himself from the great mountains of the world. And,
finally, there are the Bush-lawyers of New Zealand—terrible spiny
affairs with long thin arms beset with millions of minute but efficient

ivory spines and hooks. Such are *R. parvus* (dwarf and prostrate, with a large fruit—an eccentricity in an Australasian Rubus), *cissoeides, schmideloeides,* and *australis*—this last being the only one that has effected a home in English gardens, where its chief merit is that it is not quite hardy, so that in time you may be relieved from the inhospitable massed mess that it forms of spidery-thin and almost leafless branchage, accumulating into an inextricable mound of white wiry whipcord, armed with insatiable little teeth as numerous, vicious, and ivorine as those of sharks, though not so large. There is practically no foliage, and neither flower nor fruit would be worth contemplation even if they ever condescended to appear. This should be planted in a cold dank place (if you want it to die); if, however, the giver of it lives near, and pays you frequent visits, you will have to assign it a warm sheltered and sunny place in the foreground, in light and well-drained soil—under no other pressure of circumstances to be so wasted.

Ruellia ciliosa is an Acanthad from North America, which is hardy, but must have a dry sunny place in light and well-drained soil if it is to be happy. It attains 2 feet, and is hairy, with oval leaves and blue flowers, either solitary or in clusters, from June on into the autumn. *R. strepens* is yard-high and more beautiful, blooming from May to July, no less blue than the last, but preferring a damper and more shady corner. Seed.

Ruscus.—Of the Butcher's-brooms, the garden in its out-of-the-way and shady slopes, otherwise useless, may be glad of *R. hypophyllus* and *R. hypoglossus*, neat little evergreens of a foot high, neater than our own *R. aculeatus*, and with big crimson berries like jewels seeming to adhere to the under-sides of the leaves.

Ruta.—All the Rues have most aromatic foliage, fine and fat and blue-grey, but as a rule rather large in development for the rock-garden, where they require the very hardest and driest place that it affords. The only one that in any way needs admittance is *R. patavina,* which makes neat little shoots about 8 inches long, clad in narrow grey leaves and leaflets, and set with numbers of ample cream-yellow stars of blossom from May to September, making a pleasant effect as it flops over a sunny rock.

S

Sagina.—All these are precious carpeting plants for any open soil and place, valuable for the sheets of minute moss in which they clothe the ground and sheathe the base of any choice bulb that may come shooting from below, but valuable no less in the profusion of white stars with which their carpet is set in summer. They are, in effect, quite dwarf mat-forming Arenarias. Of these, then, *S. Boydi*, *S. Linnaei*, *S. bryoeides*, and *S. procumbens* all have the merits of the family, while the best known is *S. subulata*, which is often seen in catalogues as *Arenaria caespitosa*, when it is not called *Spergula pilifera*, and *Sagina acicularis*. This makes a notably charming fuzz-floor of green (or of yellow in the case of the *aurea* form), sprinkled all the summer through with white stars on dainty fine stems of an inch or so. *S. Linnaei* is dwarfer, with less needly little leaves, but no less brilliant in the green, and rather larger in the blossom ; it is sometimes offered as *S. saxatilis*.

Sagittaria.—The Arrowroots are all delightful for shallow waters, where they bloom on and off throughout the summer. It is sad that one of the finest of the race, *S. montevidiensis*, is not safely hardy here. *S. latifolia* is North American, taller than our own *S. sagittifolia*, but thriving no less readily in 5 or 6 inches of water, in rich mud, with wider leaves and larger flowers ; there is a double form of *S. sagittifolia*, too, a foot or 2 feet high, like its parent, and often quite falsely sold as *S. japonica* or *S. jap. fl. pl.*, when it is not sent out under the name of *S. sinensis*, which ought to be a yard-high plant with specially handsome large white flowers, and leaves that are not *barbed arrow-heads* as in the others, but simply *long lances*.

Salix.—In the rock-garden it is not possible to do without rock-hugging *S. retusa*, with its even smaller-leaved variety *S. serpyllifolia*, that both make dense wide carpets, or hanging tight cataracts down the face of the rocks, with long elastic branches, set with wee shining leaves, close-packed in myriads, and in early summer powdered with the multitudinous fine gold of the microscopic flowers. Both these will grow almost anywhere, and from the merest fragment ; as has been sadly found by many, when the choice bishopric of some dead alpine Gentian has been occupied, and the whole bank soon swept, by some minute fragment of willow that had been lurking in the tuft. Far less important than these, but admissible, are the egg-leaved silky creepers, *S. reticulata* and *S. herbacea*, but these have not the gloss, the minute and crowded leafage that give the first two their inimitable charm and sets them quite outside the race of alpine willows, of which there are very many more, though none that so insist on admittance to the garden.

Salvia.—The rock-garden is hardly a place for these, and the family is so full of leafy weeds that, but for many brilliant exceptions, one might say that no other garden was either. However, though here it is not possible or fitting to deal with the large species, it may be said that even the rock-garden may be glad of dainty vermilion *S. Souliei*, neat in habit, too, though not to be trusted as hardy; no less than in the beautiful grey-leaved bush with feathered leaves (for a sunny dry bank) of *S. ringens*, from which shoot tall stems in late summer, carrying very large whorled flowers of soft lilac-blue, with a delicate contrast in the white lip. A little smaller than this is *S. scabiosaefolia* with helmets of violet. Another plant greatly to be desired, and always most rare, is *S. bicolor* from Spain and North Africa, 2 or 3 feet high, branching. The flowers are in whorls of six, the whorls being many and close together, but with the blossoms standing out on longish foot-stalks; they are nobly large with a big white lip, and a hood of violet-blue, dotted with gold. *S. libanotica* also has fine flowers of blue, spotted with white, while of low-growing species there are several, though *S. acaulis* proved so far a dismal fraud, sending up a gawky stem of a foot or so from the basal rosette, and studding it with whorls of insignificant little flowers at that. By the feet of Allad'agh, 5000 feet up in Cappadocia, lives *S. eriophora*, with very wrinkly narrow leaves and a great number of woolly bluish fine stems of 6 inches or so, carrying close-set whorls of handsome blue blossom in woolly calyces; *S. frigida* (*S. oreades*), from Anatolian Alps, is about the same height, and also has blue flowers; *S. caespitosa*, from the same alpine regions, is densely tufted and sub-shrubby, yet closely dwarf, with stems of only 3 or 4 inches, clad to their top in feathered foliage, with splendid purple helmets in a scanty head, sitting amid the leafage at the top of each shoot, so that the whole wide mass of the plant is a carpet of flower.

Samolus, a race of small Primulas that are not satisfied with their family, and try to look as much like Shepherd's-purse as possible, or *Kernera saxatilis*. One is universal, *S. Valerandi;* and, as we have it wild, we have scant need to burden our gardens with it. The rest are all hopeless of cultivation, even were they worthy, with the exception of *S. repens* (*Sheffieldia repens*), which by no means creeps, but stands more or less erect, with terminal clusters of little pinky stars. It has countless forms, and comes mainly from Australia, and may be coped with, if considered worth the trouble, in moist warm places, where it will flower in summer and may perhaps have cuttings struck, or seed sown, in case it dies in winter.

Sanguinaria canadensis, the Bloodroot of Canada, is a lovely thing for planting about under deciduous trees, and in good out-of-the-way corners among Dog's-tooth Violets and so forth, where Spring, from the solid creeping fat root (so susceptible to sorrow that it weeps tears of blood if hurt, and refuses to be comforted) calls up here and there one lovely blue-grey leaf, daintily lobed and scalloped, silvery-smooth beneath, which emerges modestly folded-up on a stem of an inch or two, and gradually, as it develops, is surpassed by the flower-stalk on which opens a frail wide blossom of transparent opalescent white, like the ghost of a bland Anemone that died of starvation. There is no other *Sanguinaria*, but the species varies widely, and nurseries offer a form they call *S. c. grandiflora*.

Sanguisorba.—The Poor Man's Pepper of our fields asks no admittance to our gardens, but *S. canadensis* is superb for the water-side in rich soil, with elaborate masses of foliage, and the long leaves delicately made up of toothed oval green leaflets, spaced at intervals down each leaf-stalk; and then come tall upstanding spikes of close fluffy flowers in long white tails like those of a Cimicifuga, in the latest hours of summer, standing 2 yards high or little less. *S. tenuifolia* has the pinkish flower-head much shorter, and thereby loses merit, becoming like our own *S. officinalis* on a big scale. And there are various other species, none calling for note except the very rare and rather splendid *S. Vallistellinae*, which is only to be seen in the upper meadows of the Valtelline, as, for instance, about Bormio—a stately plant 2 feet high, with ample glaucous-blue foliage, and long furry tails of sweet-scented creamy-white. All these are quite easy and rampageous in cool rich soil, and can be divided at will. Among dimmer cousins are *S. sitchensis, S. carnea, S. alpina,* &c.

Santolina.—None of these need ever be thought of for their flowers, which are no more than rayless yellow pompons; but they are tiny little composite bushes, with fine and very aromatic neat foliage, and so employable in hot dry and worthless places, to be kept in shape when they grow leggy with an annual cutting-back like Helianthemum. Their various names need no further specification; catalogues may offer any they choose, but the French Lavender remains their best type. But many of the Anthemids are also rayless, and have got mixed, rayless or no, with *Santolina;* this should be remembered, and, especially, that *S. alpina* means merely *Anthemis montana, q.v.*

Saponaria has lately had a distinguished recruit; but, with that one exception, the Soapworts are all easy and pleasant to grow, enjoying light loam in an open place. All of them bloom in early summer, and all are easily to be raised from seed and multiplied by cuttings.

S. bellidifolia is a species of Eastern Europe, Greece, &c.—a rare plant and near akin to *S. lutea*, but taller in the growth, attaining sometimes to a foot or more, with huddled heads of straw-coloured flowers with dark anthers. It should have a warm and perfectly well-drained place, but is not by any means of special loveliness.

S. × *Boissieri* is a hybrid between *S. caespitosa* and *S. ocymoeides*—from which parents have resulted altogether admirable offspring—a neat and dwarf mat-forming thing, with decumbent stems much more profusely set than *S. caespitosa*, with flowers twice as large as in *S. ocymoeides*, and of no less clear a pink than in both.

S. caespitosa is a peculiar glory of the Pyrenees, where, in the high limestone alps, it forms wide and woody-rooted lawns of huddled small leaves, thick and narrow and fleshy and pointed, from which arise graceful reddish stems of 5 or 6 inches, carrying at the top two or three buds of reddish velvet, from which unfold large oval-petalled flowers of bright pink.

S. calabrica is a bedding annual too common to be more than mentioned here.

S. cerastioeides. See *Gypsophila cerastioeides.*

S. cypria is pretty and neat and pink for a warm dry place.

S. depressa comes from Thessaly and Sicily. This also forms mats of smooth and bluish-green foliage, with rather sticky and downy stems from 2 inches to a foot in height, carrying one or two large pink flowers.

S. × *laeta* is another beautiful and brilliant low-growing hybrid, this time secondary, between *S.* × *Boissieri* and *S.* × *Boissieri's* pollen-parent, *S. ocymoeides*, of which, accordingly, it has more the character.

S. lutea is a rarity that suffers from the anticipations aroused by its name, which leads one to expect a golden counterpart of *S. caespitosa*, so that when we only get a huddle-headed crowd of pale straw-yellow stars on a stem of 2 or 3 inches, we are apt to overlook the real and personal charm of the neat little bright-green mat of flattened pale foliage springing from the woody trunk, and to turn blind eyes upon the diaphanous subtlety of the small hyaline flowers themselves, with their woolly calyx and blackened eye of dark anthers. *S. lutea* need not often so afflict us, though ; it is a most precious speciality of the southern slopes of Monte Rosa, and far away from there, on the Mont Cenis, where it is abundant indeed but extremely local, being found for choice in close crevices of the huge grey granite boulders of the Little Mont Cenis and the Val Savine most especially, but also among the hillocks below the Lake. In cultivation *S. lutea*, paradoxically enough, is not so perfectly hardy as scores of plants from far lower and even maritime elevations ; it requires non-calcareous peaty soil or moraine, in full sun, and in an especially well-drained, dry, and warm position.

S. ocymoeides belongs to warm places and open rough banks all South Europe over, but attains its zenith of rosy glory in the Alps, where whole barren mountain-sides in the Engadine are seen to be crimson with it from afar; while it fills the scant woods below the Brenner with sheets of colour, and blots the banks and rocks and railway-cuttings of the Pass with hassocks of pink. In the garden it is a noted treasure for hanging about over rocks in light soil and full sun; it has no alpine look indeed, and suggests the bedding annual, but is in point of fact perennial to the point of being immortal, and flops each year further and further, the prostrate boughs beset with loose heads and showers and sprays of rosy stars. There is a white form, too, and various improvements offered by catalogues, of which the one called *S. o. splendidissima* claims highest rank; but every traveller should take note of the type for himself as he goes, for it varies very widely; in districts where it is straggling and poor there is no turning the trowel that way at all, but in its favoured hills there may quite often be found forms of especial brilliancy and fullness of face. In nature, as in the garden, it seems to have no rigid preference about soils; but certainly, so far as my own experience goes, I have usually seen it far more abundant and generous of growth and flower on the granitic than on the calcareous ranges (as in the instances given—the Engadine and the Brenner).

S. officinalis. — The common Soapwort, tall and ample, and no bad anticipation in early summer of a paniculate Phlox, will go into the wild garden. There are better forms and double forms; and below Botzen here and there from the train the traveller to Verona may espy lovely shades of salmon-rose well worth breaking the journey to collect.

S. pamphylica in the rocks of its native Alps makes mats of foliage, and sends up great numbers of flower-stems half a foot or a foot high.

S. × peregrina is a hybrid between *S. bellidifolia* and *S. ocymoeides.*

S. × pulchella is a most attractive neat and bright hybrid between *S. ocymoeides* and *S. pulvinaris.*

S. pulvinaris (*S. pumilio*, Boiss.) lives in the Alps of Anatolia, on Lebanon, &c., making tight mats of minute narrow leaves, rather blunt and keeled, and densely huddled, in effect like cushions of *Silene acaulis*, from which are sent up short stems that carry one pink flower as a rule, but sometimes as many as five or seven.

[*S. pumila* = *S. pumilio.*]

S. pumilio is *Silene pumilio* of old years, and it is possible that the last species is merely the child of confusion. For the same picture paints *S. pumilio* as it may be seen in the high granitic alps of Colbricon, beneath the frown of the Cimon della Pala in the Southern Dolomites, where, sandwiched between vast slabs of weather-riven granite, its huge tap-root spreads inwards, and over the rock flows flat and hard the brilliant lucent pale-green mat of foliage, in point of fact never to be confused with *Silene acaulis*, on account of the broader, longer, blunter, glossier, paler, ampler foliage of wholly different and much more sumptuous effect. Or sometimes it may be found higher up, growing in open bare peaty earth-pans of the mountain (but never at its happiest in the turf, if at all), there forming great lucent domes as big as footballs sitting about upon the black soil, into which they drive roots like fat fierce whip-thongs of a yard and more. The flowers come forth in summer from baggy reddish sticky calyces, on hardly any stem at all—wide flimsy single Godetias or ragged carnations of soft rosy pink. After which the capsule matures inside the withered undecaying bag of the calyx; and in time the little stem, such as there is of one, fades quietly away, so that in the spring you find the sere bags, with their unscattered seed-pods inside, lying in such neat piles round the parent plants that it looks as if they must have been nipped off and hoarded there in heaps by some squirrel or mountain-marmot. In cultivation *S. pumilio* is not easy; it is not hard to collect, with care; it bears removal well, and re-establishes with beautiful promptitude in sand. But nearly all other conditions seem distasteful to it, when the time comes for its translation into the garden—where it certainly does best in perfectly-drained slopes in the fullest sun, in a rich compost, mixed with stones, of about a third part of mingled leaf-mould, peat and sand, very deep—at least 3 feet—with a very coarse bed of drainage-blocks below (whether water be to flow far down or not), and nowhere, as it seems, the *slightest perceptible trace of lime*, which has the same effect on the Saponaria as the parched pea in the Princess's bed; no matter how deep and pure the plant's soil, if lime to the size of a pea-pod be there discoverable by its haughty sensibility, it will at once make haste towards a better world, accepting no apologies. In cultivation, if happy, it seems to flower profusely, but on the Alps a strange irregularity attends it. I have heard, in the Hohe Tauern, of high moors that blush with its blossom; on Colbricon, where *S. pumilio* is certainly abundant and in fine form, I have collected abundant seed in early spring left from the foregoing season; but another year, being up there in July, my closest scrutiny could nowhere detect the remotest promise of a bud, on cushions no matter how solid and healthy, that ought by that time to have been showing swellings preparatory to flower in August. At home *S. pumilio* flowers in later summer, however, and need nowhere be hoped for on the Alps west of the Brenner, being entirely a species of the Eastern ranges, locally, but only locally abundant, on the upmost granitic and volcanic ridges from the Noric Alps to the Southern Dolomites, and again in the Carpathians. In the garden it flowers in June.

S. × *Suendermannii* bears the name of the raiser who is responsible for all these attractive crosses. The parents of this are *S. bellidifolia* and *S. caespitosa.*

S. × *Wiemanniana* is the only one of the group in general cultivation, and this usually under the name of " *Weinmanniana.*" It gives a fair notion of how little the dull yellows of the flavid species influence the charm of the hybrids in which they have a share. For it is a most neat and pretty matted thing in growth, with decumbent stems, and heads of flowers as numerous (though more freely spaced) as in *S. lutea,* while the other parent contributes their size and their brilliant rose-colour handed down untarnished from *S. caespitosa.*

S. × *Willkommiana* (Sündermann, 1910) is yet another hybrid, making neat mats, and copiously emitting rose-red stars.

Sarracenia.—The weird charm of the Pitcher-plants is well known, and the hardy one of the large family, *S. purpurea,* so heartily enjoys European conditions that alike in Switzerland and in England it has quite successfully established itself in the Sphagnum-patches of the wild bog, and there catches flies in its deep urn-shaped leaves of marbled red and green, and hangs out its indescribable huge yellowish flowers (like some of the great ivory belt-buttons of old Japan) to such good effect on their 10-inch stalks that young seedlings subsequently arise all over the face of the spongy tract.

Satureia, a race of quite charming little wiry bushlings from the South, like erect-growing, dainty Thymes of delicate foliage and larger flower. They are all children of the sun, and enjoy light well-drained soil in full warmth, where they will be happy without attention from year to year, delighting the eye with their axillary clusters of blossom in late summer, while all the year through, on a pinch of the finger, their aromatic tiny leaves will delight the nose, and send the mind on a far journey to the warmth and light and colour of the Mediterranean. There are various species, all of charm, and none more than 8 inches high, standing, in their family, between Thymus and Micromeria (nowadays the race is even made to absorb Micromeria, *q.v.*). *S. pygmaea* is a variety of the more common *S. montana,* and is especially delightful—a very small bush of wiry straight stems, set with dark sweet little leaves, and rather large crowded flowers of soft violet in the upper axils of all the shoots through August and September.

Then there is *S. spinosa*, a thorny mound with white blossoms and spines ; *S. parnassica*, in the same line, but not so hostile ; *S. diffusa*, clear pink ; *S. montana*, *S. intermedia*, *S. illyrica*, in varying shades of mauve ; *S. rupestris*, white ; *S. stenophylla*, pink ; with many another—*S. subdentata*, *S. mutica*, *S. Boissieri*, and a variety *macrantha* of *S. mutica*, about a foot and a half in height, a rare giant in the race. *S. spicigera* has yellow flowers, and *S. longiflora*, hoary and woody, carries especially large long blooms of clear pink. (Seeds or cuttings.)

Saururus may all be unregretfully avoided. They are ramping weeds of 2 or 3 feet, leafy, with flopping tails, atop, of mean little whitish flowers in a spike through later summer. They might take possession of a wild and worthless bog. (America and Japan.)

Saussurea, a curious little race of high-alpine thistlish flowers, quite dwarf in the stem, and often woolly in the dull dark foliage, with huddled heads of blue, reddish or purple florets, intermingled often with white fluffs. They are not of any startling beauty, and several species often seen in the high stony places of the Alps do not elicit shrieks of joy from climbers trampling them unnoticed ; these are *S. depressa*, *S. discolor*, *S. pygmaea*, *S. macrophylla*, and *S. alpina* (a rare native on the highest ridges of our Lake Country). They may all be grown in deep and stony soil, with water flowing far beneath. On the Roof of the World, however, *Saussurea* takes on more interesting forms, finding it necessary so elaborately to wrap itself in wool against the awful cold, that at last the strangest of the race, *S. gossypiphora*, making little grey stalagmites along the bleakest limestone ridges at 17,000 feet, has become nothing but a 9-inch sugar-loaf of fluff, looking like a very ancient sodden wasp's-nest congealed in everlasting frost, with the flowers lurking far down in the cell-like holes of the mass. Hardly less strange is *S. leucoma*, which attains much the same stature in the vast screes about 1000 feet lower ; this has visible and sweet-scented flowers of crimson and blue, huddling at the top of the stem, but from them the specially long thin leaves, feathered into a few fine lobes at the end, weep away earthwards in a dense and widening column, till, as all their long stems are furred with soft white wool, the effect in the end is like the column of some lachrymose-looking ancient Mammillaria, venerable with a drooping fleece of white. *S. sacra* is close akin to *S. gossypiphora*, but here the wasps'-nests of wool are pink ; while *S. tridactyla* almost repeats *S. gossypiphora*, but is more woody and leafy in habit. *S. sorocephala* is much smaller, and makes tiny stemless mounds of wool in the Altai ; and among many others are *S. subulata*, *S. Stolickzai*, *S. Yakla*, and *S. Sughoo*.

Saxífrăga.—This huge race is the backbone of the rock-garden,

PLATE 34

RODGERSIA TABULARIS.
(Photo. R. A. Malby.)

PLATE 35.

RODGERSIA PINNATA.
(Photo. R.B.G., Kew.)

SAXIFRAGA × BOYDII.
(Photo. R. A. Malby.)

SAXIFRAGA.

and no less. Its English name is Saxifrage—a singularly apt, easy, expressive, and beautiful one, in universal use except in Wardour Street, where the appropriate Ruskinian faddists sometimes try to talk of it in print (but never in words) as *Rockfoil*—a dismal and tedious affectation which all reasonable people unanimously ignore. In general average of beauty the race is not so dazzling as those of Primula and Gentiana, but in furnishing value, ease, robustness of temper and stately charm of port and foliage alike, Saxifraga undoubtedly obliterates every other alpine race in the garden. A vast proportion of the species are both spreading and easy ; nearly all can be pulled to pieces and propagated at will, and all will come readily from their fine seeds, which should be sown *on the surface* of a pot filled with soil as fine as themselves, and not earthed over, but with glass and paper atop to keep them close and dark. Their flowering season begins with *S. Burseriana magna*, affronting the rains of February, followed by nearly all the rest of the Kabschia group and their hybrids, until with early summer the Mossies and Euaeizoons break into a blaze of beauty. Summer is poorer except in the golden stars of *Hirculus*, but autumn yields the fluffy white clouds of *S. cortusaefolia* and *S. Fortunei*. The family is of universal range throughout the Northern hemisphere, alike of the Old and New World ; in many situations its members have developed needs and characteristics so diverse that the race, for the sake of convenience, is divided into seventeen very definite sections. It might here be well done to arrange the species according to these classes, yet, for the sake of reference, pitying in advance the seeker after truth who vainly quests his Saxifrage from group to group, it is more convenient to treat the sorts alphabetically, first giving a synopsis of the sections, their needs and characters and claims ; and then, wherever possible, assigning each plant (in its due order as it comes) to the particular class to which it belongs. Thus I hope the labour of memory will prove less than otherwise the work of cross-reference would have proved arduous. There is not yet, of course, any finality in the family, which lies at present in a fearful welter of confusion, largely owing to its popularity in the garden, which has impelled nurserymen to go on perpetually issuing unauthorised and synonymous and false species, as well as multiplying varieties with a zeal only to be paralleled by botanists themselves; to say nothing of the family's own perplexing and insatiable passion for natural interbreeding, no less on the hills than in cultivation. The result accordingly is an interminable string of entanglements, superfluities, repetitions, and confusions, all tending to the bewilderment of the buyer, and the merciless elicitation of his pence ; and matters are now yet further complicated by the enormous new issue of garden seedlings in the Mossy-group, particularly emanating from *S. decipiens*, and for ever being announced in more and more flamboyant tones, as more and more marvellous and brilliant novelties with pompous names—all being, in fact, mere seedlings, no more deserving separate titles outside their own territories than the thousands of Aubrietias that could annually be christened out of a well-born packet. With such horticultural waywardnesses neither commination nor Conference can cope ; in the meantime, as a forerunner, earnest and humble, the following list shall try to clear a few blocks from the path which the Conference will ultimately make smooth and straight for ever— until China begins to contribute its enormous quota to the confusion.

GROUP I. *Bergenia.*—Only doubtfully included now under *Saxifraga*, and here for the purposes of convenience. These are *vast plants of round leathern glossy leafage*, and uncurling spreading rays of very large pink or white flowers on short stout stalks in the early year. Their needs are rich border-soil in half shade, and their type is *S. crassifolia*. (Spring.)

GROUP II. *Boraphila.*—Soft leaves, *all at the base*, forming a rosette ; flowers in a spike or shower, usually rather insignificant and ugly. Their preference is for a dampish cool place ; their type may be our own *S. nivalis*, and their best example our own *S. stellaris*. (Summer.)

GROUP III. *Cymbalaria.*—Frail little annuals with glossy leaves and flowers usually golden. *S. Sibthorpii* (*S. Cymbalaria*, Sibth. and Sm., as of gardens) is their exemplar, and they all love cool damp places, shady walls, &c. (All the summer.)

GROUP IV. *Dactyloeides.*—The mossy Saxifrages may be represented by *S. hypnoeides* or *S. × Wallacei*. Their form is that of *vast loose and mossy cushions* with fine large blossoms on slender stems. They are among the most useful of all, but not among the most choice, although they have a section of small high-alpines that are sometimes lacking in charm, but as difficult and miffy as the rest of the group is easy and hearty, in any good clean soil, in sun or partial shade. (Early summer.)

GROUP V. *Diptĕra.*—These are stoloniferous runners, not of any note in the garden, for the section is not very hardy. The Mother of Thousands, *S. sarmentosa*, hangs in sheets from every greenhouse pan and cottage window, and stands as the type of the section ; it may be made happy if not permanent in sheltered damp places of well-drained shade in any garden not too arctic and raw. (Summer.)

GROUP VI. *Euaeizoonia.*—This there is no need to prescribe or describe. Hats off for *S. aeizoon* and *S. Cotyledon.* Almost all the Silver Saxifrages are the easiest glories of the rock-garden, as they are the greatest, thriving in any light good soils in full sun, and no less lovely when winter embroiders the rock-work with their matted rosettes of pearl-beaded silver-green, than in summer when the ledges are awave with their gracious plumes of pink or white or cream. (Early summer.)

GROUP VII. *Hirculus.*—All these form mats of *undivided* oval leaves, with yellow or orange flowers gathered at the top of stems usually set with foliage. They are plants for the careful bog, or the wet moraine bed ; and their type is our own very rare *S. Hirculus* itself. (Summer to autumn.)

GROUP VIII. *Isomeria.*—Claims little comment. These are wood-land plants of dullish bloom, with large rounded and lobed leaves on stems at the base. They come from America and Japan, and have no popular type ; we may take *S. tellimoeides* from Japan as their representative, but, like the rest of the group, it is better left than taken. (Summer.)

GROUP IX. *Kabschia.*—Under this repulsive and irrelevant name lie the dearest (in every sense) jewels of the family. They need not go further for a representative to be proud of than *S. Burseriana,* which almost flatters their habit of large brilliant blossoms on short stems, over compact mounds of *narrow un-divided leathern or spinous foliage* early in the year. They deserve, and ask, more care than the rest, requiring a light and rich soil, mixed with about half its own weight of lime-chips, in an open place, but with every precaution taken against their being parched or clogged. If possible, water should flow about a foot or 18 inches beneath their roots in summer, or sunk flower-pots must be filled periodically to supply the deficiency. Large stones may also be buried with the chips amid their equal mixture of half loam, quarter leaf-mould, and quarter sand (but each garden will, of course, make its soil to the mind of its master and the needs of its Kabschias), and if water be unobtainable, the shadow of a great rock in a thirsty land may be attempted as a " pis aller," by planting your Kabschias under the lee of a big boulder which may keep off some of the sun's ferocity, though not his geniality. The thing to remember with the general run of these lovely things is that, while they love light and air, they usually detest being parboiled nearly as much as they would detest being water-logged. They are plants of the rocks and screes and shingles, and some of them, even in nature, turn towards the cooler aspects, but however fiercely the sun may kiss the Italian and Levantine Alps, it is never the same fury in that mountain air ; with the melting snow percolating far beneath, and filling all the upper air with a soft veil through which the darts of Apollo can never smite with such lethal ferocity as down on the unprotected sands of Surrey or Kent. (Spring.)

GROUP X. *Engleria.*—This group comes near the last, containing a set of silver-leaved Saxifrages, with taller and ampler spires of small flowers (red or yellow) in large fluffy calyces of kindred colour. The group is distinct and important, and filled with confused names; their type shall be our nearest neighbour, *S. media* of the Spanish middle-alpine region, which probably covers more names than it knows of; and their requirements are those of Kabschia, though some of them seem to like more sun, and one at least is native to less. (Spring.)

GROUP XI. *Miscopetalum.*—Stout clumps for the shade and damp woodland, with rounded fleshy notched leaves on long stalks, and small uneven-petalled white stars in loose showers. These all, large or little, are plants for cool soils and exposures, in woodland or bog or damp ledges; and their representative is the common *S. rotundifolia* of stream-sides in the alpine woods. (Summer.)

GROUP XII. *Nephrophyllum.*—Here the basal foliage is fleshy, kidney-shaped, lobed or many-cleft, while the plants often have *bulbils at the base* and in the *axils of the flower-stem.* They are all medium-sized, slight or frail things for quite cool and sometimes boggy conditions, and the type is our own *S. granulata* of the Teesdale meadows. (Early summer.)

GROUP XIII. *Peltiphyllum* contains only the noble Californian *S. peltata* with its Bergenia-flowers on tall stems, before the tall-stemmed splendid leaves unfold. This for the waterside.

GROUP XIV. *Porphyrion.*—Lawn-forming prostrate alpine and high-alpine mats with rose-purple flowers. They ask for damp moraine or cool open soil, and need no better illustration than our own *S. oppositifolia.* (Spring to early summer.)

GROUP XV. *Robertsonia.*—The look and habits of all these may be drawn from London Pride. (Early summer.)

SAXIFRAGA.

GROUP XVI. *Trachyphyllum.*—This group is characterised by close tumbled masses of narrow, stiff, glossy and often spinulous little leaves, packed upon the wandering shoots, from which stand up the stems of yellow or white blossom. Its best type is *S. aspera*, and any open culture suits the section so long as the plants are not kept too dry and baked. (Summer.)

GROUP XVII. *Tridactylites.*—Little flimsy annuals for the most part, typified by our own *S. tridactylites.* (Spring.)

With so much preface, an indication of its group will supply general directions for each kind's culture, except in all such cases as need special treatment.

S. aconitifolia stands half a yard high and is only *Boykinia*, *q.v.*

S. adenophora, Boiss.=*S. androsacea*, *q.v.*

S. adscendens, L., is little more than a larger *S. tridactylites*, not quite so bronzed and blushing. It can only be grown from seed, which it scatters freely. There is a variety *S. a. Blavii*, with broader leaves on the little stems, and several flowers on each of the branches.

S. Aegilops. See under *S. umbrosa.*

S. aeizoeidoeides (Micq., 1865).—This ridiculous name stands for a very doubtful find, recorded from the top of Mont Perdu, with the usual leaves of *S. aeizoeides*, but toothed petals of white.

S. aeizoeides is quite the finest of the Trachyphyllum group, and almost the best of the race for any cool soil in a rather moist but quite open sunny and well-drained place, where it makes its matted masses of fleshy bright-green foliage as freely as it does by every alpine stream, and as freely sends up, but rather earlier in the summer, its many stems of 4 or 5 inches, carrying many red-spotted stars of clear yellow, with orange anthers and central disk of the ovaries, maturing to a darker shade. It is a common plant, no less, in the alpine marshes of Scotland and Northern England, and has developed also a saxatile form that flowers much later in the summer. This is *S. aei. autumnalis* (the original *S. autumnalis*, L.), whose rather richer and more brilliant blossoms may be seen, for instance, in the stark limestone cliffs on the Western face of Ingleborough in late August. There is also a rich striking form sometimes sent out as *S. atrorubens*, in which the flowers are of a violent brownish blood-colour, deepening to more fiery tones in their later stages ; as well as a most beautiful form with blossoms of very brilliant and strong clear orange. This I have only once seen, and, as a rule, *S. aeizoeides* may be said hardly to vary, except into the Atrorubent form ; for many years will show you many miles of alpine stream and bog and slope all golden with the type, yet never yield you any variety but the lurid wonder of flame and blood.

S. aeizöön gives the gardener that feeling of launching out upon a vast uncharted sea such as must have lowered the heart of Columbus when first he loosed from Cadiz for the Atlantic. Let us hope that the Conference will provide us with a chart by which we may learn at last to reach the firm land. At present, as *S. aeizoon* is by far the most abundant of the Euaeizoon group, hybridises with every species of its own kind that it touches, and varies incessantly on its own account in every range where it occurs, each collector and each gardener goes on affixing names to every variety he finds, until the pages of catalogues are crowded with synonyms and superfluous or unauthorisable names. Not only that, but as *S. aeizoon* crosses so readily with the other species of its section, so the children are again fertile interminably, so that the turmoil is not lessened. It is, as a species, the commonest of all alpine plants, the first to be seen on the hills, and one of the first to be introduced to our gardens. It does not ascend to very great heights, and, on the other hand, may often be seen quite low down, as for instance on the lip of the Lombard Plain at the foot of the passes from Genoa. It is perfectly indifferent to its soil and treatment in cultivation, in almost all its forms, and practically unkillable if granted open air and sun. Yet in nature it is predominantly and undoubtedly a species of the *non-calcareous* ranges— a fact which has long been obscured and denied by the inveterate habit of observers not to observe but to take a confident statement eternally for true. And nothing, *a priori*, could seem more certain than the calcareous proclivities of lime-beaded and indestructible *S. aeizoon.* And yet, though often found and sometimes abundant on the limestone Alps, it is incomparably larger, freer, finer on the granites and sandstones, and obviously at home instead of in exile ; as some seasons of alpine travel will convince anyone who looks for himself ; and has seen its huge healthy towzles of white breaking forth the moment you leave, for instance, the calcareous slopes of Venanson (where it is so measling and cramped and worthless) and cross over on to the granites of the Madonna della Finestra, or the Bernina group, or Puflatsch, or the road of the Rolle Pass, or any other of the myriad places of the Alps where primary rock either reigns or suddenly crops out of limestone or Dolomite—and where, accordingly, *S. aeizoon* either reigns, too, or else immediately crops out in regal abundance the moment that the limestone is left behind. But the plant wanders very far, and makes no vital point of any stone ; it is the only Euaeizoon to cross into America, and in the mountains of the Old World you may flee into the uttermost parts of them and never escape its silver-beaded neat immortal rosettes and its 6- or 10-inch plumes of creamy white in early summer. The type, if doubt ever arose or could arise, may always be told from kinsmen such as *H. Hostii*, *S. incrustata*, &c., by the fact that the *serrations of the leaves point upwards and forward*, instead of being minute triangular saw-teeth standing out-wards. And the chief varieties of the species are these:

S. aei. atropurpurea, a most iniquitous invention of catalogues to sell you *S. aei. rosea* under another name.

S. aei. balcana is smaller, and paler in the green of its leaves, which seem shorter and broader than those of the type, because they curve inwards more strongly. The stems are sturdy and red, about 5 inches high, bearing large stolid flowers very densely covered with large crimson dots. This form is not always as hearty of temper as the others, having a tendency to go brown and miff off in parts. It seems to have a special dislike to any excess of water, and may quite possibly bring into the garden, unlike the rest, the family disinclination for limy soils. It is one of the most beautiful—short and sturdy in the stem, and amply furnished with large, solid, and ample flowers dotted almost to duskiness with crimson on their white ground.

S. aei. baldensis is a very minute and huddled form from the high limestones of Baldo, where its aspect is so minute and massed that on first sight from afar I thought I must be approaching *S. diapensioeides*. In cultivation it keeps almost as small as at home, rapidly covers wide stretches, and has the further charm of being of burnished crimson on the under-sides of its tiny foliage. The flowers are of no account, as is so commonly the case in the limestone Aeizoons, being rather cramped and mean in shape, dingy and creamy in colour.

S. aei. brevifolia is a smaller form than the type also sent out as *A. aei. minor.*

A. aei. Camposii, *carniolica*, *carinthiaca* (with petals unspotted), *cultrata*, *cuneata*, *dubia* are all local or horticultural forms not satis-factorily distinct, and *S. cartilaginea* (Willd.) may count as a species.

S. aei. Correvoniana bears minute flattened rosettes, in the line of *S. aei. venetia* and *S. aei. baldensis*, and it is to be hoped may be worthy of the august ascription it bears, especially in a group so crowded with unnecessary names.

S. aei. elongata is a large-rosetted, very spidery-leaved green form, which has the look of being merely an etiolate woodland development in the shaded places where it may rarely be seen in the Alps (*e.g.* Iseltwald, by Brienz), yet keeps its habit in cultivation, and is strikingly distinct, accordingly, in the rosette; the flowers continue the drawn effect, being loosely borne on rather tall stems of a foot and more, comparatively few in number, large and round in outline, and of a good creamy-white.

S. aei. flavescens.—In many places, notably on the Southern side of the Bernina, the prevailing form of the species (there especially fine and abundant) is surprisingly flavescent, but the name belongs particularly to a form found above Arolla among the creamy type, and of a greener tone of leaf, and an even clearer note of palest citron (rather than thickened cream) in the flower. The plant is a most healthy grower, free in flower, and with elegant and elegantly furnished little spikes of 5 or 6 inches.

S. aei. gracilis is like a smaller *S. aei. Sturmiana,* with the leaves of the amassed rosettes rather more pointed, slenderer stems, and slightly smaller flowers.

S. aei. hirsuta comes from Corsica, and is, indeed, hairy all over in a very minute way. Otherwise it is only a medium-sized *S. aeizoon,* with poor stodgy blossoms.

S. aei. intacta is probably a hybrid between *S. aeizoon* and *S. Hostii.* It is the large coarse long-leaved form so common in gardens, with tall, rare, and rather gawky stems of a foot or so, furnished scantily with branches whose flowers vary in the degree of their spotting, or in the possession of any spots at all. There is another form called *S. aei. farinosa intacta;* and both plants are copious growers, handsome in the foliage, and generally useful.

S. aei. labradorica is a delightful tiny form of the species, with pretty flowers, as well as neat diminutive rosettes, round and charming.

S. aei. laeta is *S. aei. Sturmiana,* though the confusion of course is infinite, and some authorities suppose it, instead, a synonym of *intacta.*

S. aei. lagraveana belongs to the miniature group, and offers a worthy pair to *S. aei. labradorica,* both being larger than *S. aei. baldensis,* and not having quite that expansion of the wee rosette, nor the conspicuous crenelated effect due to the presence of serrations on leaves so small that there is hardly room for them.

S. aei. lutea is yet more definitely yellow than *S. aei. flavescens* (as it ought to be). It is also a much larger plant, though with the same pale-green note about the well-furnished rather narrow-leaved rosettes. The habit, however, is twice the size, and so are the flower-spikes—pale-yellow blossom-spires of a foot or so, admirably adapted for planting in and out of a plantation of *S. aei. rosea,* if the two be set in broad drifts together, with *Aster alpinus* for a further beautification of the slope.

SAXIFRAGA.

S. aei. major, Koch, earns our gratitude. For it helps us out of various confusions by swallowing up the following synonyms: *S. aei. Malyi*, *S. robusta* (of Schott, Nyman, Kotschy, &c.), *S. aei. robusta* (Engler), *S. aei. recta, flabellata, linguifolia*, and *valida*. It is the dominant form of Dalmatia—a fine form and a notable grower; the ample rosettes of broad leaves are markedly incurved, and are always tinged with red (which deepens in autumn), and the teeth on the upper part of the incurving leaves are not conspicuous through the lime-rim. The gawky flower-stems are not generously produced, but stand about 18 inches high, set with glands; and the handsome amply-petalled flowers are well set on the scant branches, and strongly speckled with red all over.

SS. aei. marginata, micrantha, microphylla, and *minima* explain their own merits and distinctions with quite sufficient definiteness. The number of such varieties could be increased without end.

S. aei. minor, again, only sues for a name *in forma pauperis*, being small in the rosette, as poor in lime as an unfinished egg, and with stunted spikes carrying little flowers few and dull.

S. aei. nepalensis had better apply for its description to Mrs. Betsey Prig, who will reply without doubt that its correct name should be *S. Harrisiae*. See *S. Cotyledon* and *S. " nepalensis."*

S. aei. notata is a compact plant after the kind of *S. aei. major*, but much smaller, pleasant and comely and compact in the incurved broad-leaved little rosettes, never enlarging even when the spike shoots up, and with the backs of the foliage always reddened. It is a fine grower and pretty in the growth; but the blossoms are poor, spotless, starry, and of a bad cream-colour, pink in the bud, crowded on their short foot-stalks, on the scanty sprays of stunted little scantily-branched red-glandular stems of about 6 inches or so.

S. aei. orientalis is merely a slender-stemmed and few-flowered form.

S. aei. paradoxa. See *S. paradoxa.*

S. aei. pectinata. See *S. pectinata.*

S. aei. punctata has a large rosette of strap-shaped leaves rather feebly beaded with lime. The flowers are densely spotted, and the spire of blossom especially well-furnished on a stout glandular stem.

S. aei. punctatissima.—I am under the necessity of thus distinguishing a development of my own that is a seedling from a beautiful form found years ago on the Hubel by the Rosenlaui glacier. The parent was of the best small-habited larger-flowered graceful type of rather slender Aeizoons, and attracted my notice only because of the dense pink spotting on the round petals. The child, however, losing nothing of the fine gracious little habit, the small rosette and neat mat, has developed a spotting so dense and fine that the whole bloom appears of a dusky and blushing tone—its whole style of growth being absolutely distinct from *S. aei. balcana*, no less in the much slighter, smaller, slenderer habit, and proportionately larger and fewer flowers, than in the minuteness of the thick red-peppering which gives them a quite different effect, on their dainty stems of only 3 or 4 inches. It is, however, as ready to grow as the best of the wild types, and no less charming in the tumble of small and comfortably-rounded rosettes, vividly beaded, than in the few large blossoms.

S. aei. pusilla is small and frail.

S. aei. recta = *S. aei. major, q.v.*

S. aei. Rex springs from one clump discovered among thousands of the finest sandstone-type on the upper moraine of the Dossenhorn in 1903, and sent home in the same box that was also illustrated by *Campanula Bellardii Miranda*. The plant stands the test of time, and of examination, even in the welter of Aeizoons. It is a supreme and culminating form ; the crowded neat masses of stiff expanding rosettes have not so much of the common triangular look at the tip of the leaf, and are notably handsome with their broad overlapping outlines, richly beaded with silver ; the flower-stems are mahogany-red, very numerous and sturdy, arising to 8 or 10 inches, and set in fine proportion with a number of branches carrying well-rounded flowers of great size and amplitude in a tone of cream-white unusually pure and striking in an Aeizoon. It is a perfectly free grower and flowerer in the garden.

S. aei. robusta, Schott. = *S. aei. major*, Koch, *q.v.*

S. aei. rosea is really pink. It was introduced from the mountains of Bulgaria, and is a variety of outshining value among all, lavish and hearty alike in growth and flower, with handsome medium-sized and well-silvered open rosettes of strap-shaped triangle-ended leaves, forming into dense domes a foot and more across (and then to be divided ; every fragment grows as if it were a hated water-weed instead of a beloved alpine). The flower-spikes are about a foot high, or even more, well and gracefully furnished with many sprays of lovely ample blossoms in a soft clear shade of pink, fading in the sun, and with development, to a paler shade.

S. aei. rosularis is the largest of the incurving-leaved forms, surpassing Notata and even Major. It does not always grow so vigorously as they, but blooms, on the other hand, more generously. All the leaves incurve, and are pointed. The flower-stems are green and nearly glandless, set with green unblushing foliage ; they are taller than in Major, and may attain 2 feet. The flowers are not poor and narrow-petalled as in Notata, but ample and well-rounded as in Major, borne in better trusses and of creamy white, freckled with red about the middle of each petal.

S. aei. Sempervivum is a large form, with incurving rosettes of thick leaves.

S. aei. Stabiana, or *S. aei. Sturmiana,* is a rather small plant, making wide tumbly mats of neat rosettes with blunt small broad leaves ; the stem is only about 4 inches high, freely branching at the tip, and carrying fat stars of creamy-white. It shares the cliffs of Palinurus with Palinurus' Primula. (See *S. aei. laeta.*)

S. aei. triternata of Glasnevin is a small and down-hearted Aeizoon with flowers of pale pink and a rather poor constitution.

S. aei. " venetia," sometimes called *S. " venetia,"* is a very pretty thing, belonging to the group of miniatures, though not yet quite attaining the absurd and lichen-like density of habit that *S. aei. baldensis* never loses even when the rosettes have developed just a little (they never do more) from their first fine baldensian rapture of minuteness.

S. afghanica of gardens is a form of *S. Stracheyi.*

S. afghanica, Aitch. and Hems., is an unacquired Kabschia, like a quarter-sized *S. marginata,* with hardly any stems to speak of, from the scablike huddles of tiny rounded rosettes, bearing clusters of three or four white-petalled blossoms veined with purple. (Shendtoi Pass in Afghanistan.)

S. ajugaefolia is much commoner in catalogues than in gardens— the plant most often sold instead of the rare true species being the form *aprica* of *S. aquatica.* The real thing is a rarity of the high Spanish mountains (top of Maladetta, &c.)—a tiny prostrate Mossy, with very fine shoots about 3 or 4 inches long, set with leaves cut into five or seven lobes as thin and fine and sharp as in *S. hypnoeides.* There are no rosettes or tufts, and the flower-stems rise up from the axils of the lower leaves on the shoots—a thing that happens *in no other* mossy Saxifrage except *S. perdurans* (which has blunt leaf-segments instead of sharp ones). They are 2 or 3 inches high, and the flowers are white. It must have conditions of healthy and constant moisture if it is to do well : and, if it be indeed Parkinson's *S. chamaepityfolia,* is one of the oldest of its race in cultivation, though its later Linnean name of *ajugaefolia,* of course, remains the only valid one.

S. × Alberti is a garden-hybrid of the same blood as *S. × apiculata,* and hardly to be usefully distinguished from that unsurpassable plant. All the same its masses of evergreen spiny foliage and clumped heads of yellow flower in earliest spring on stems of 2 or 3 inches are never to be despised, come they under never so many vainly-multiplied names. This section of the Kabschias, too, thrives and spreads like couch-grass in any good open loam in the sun.

S. Allionii is a quite minute white-flowered Mossy about 2 inches high, from a carpet-like minute moss indeed ; for the choicer damp cool places of the open rock-work or damp gritty moraine-bed.

S. altissima.—This is a most noble Euaeizoon which is hardly ever seen in gardens that abound in plants of not half as much merit. It forms clumps of particularly handsome wide rosettes, the leaves being very long and very narrow and *always recurving outwards*, of leathern blue-grey, margined with silver-beaded teeth that, as in *S. aeizoon*, are always sharp and pointed upwards along the leaf, instead of being rounded and scalloped as in *S. Hostii*. But the reddish and notably glandular stems are half a yard high, branching into pyramids of blossom almost as ample as in *S. Cotyledon ;* while the flowers do no disgrace to the comparison, for while they have rather the creamy note of the Aeizoons than the flagrant whiteness of the Lingulatas and Cotyledons, they are also fuller-faced than in many forms of either, and in all but the best ; and at the base of the petals are freckled with red. It is a splendidly hearty grower, and comes from the lower regions of Upper Styria, where it is widely spread and common.

S. ✕ Andrewsii is a hybrid between, as it seems, *S. aeizoon* and *S. umbrosa.* The narrowly spoon-shaped leaves are set with countless little teeth which give them a distinct effect, and the flowers are little stars of pink, freckled with purple, and borne in loose branching showers of about 6 inches high. A perfectly easy thing to grow.

S. androsacea.—A difficult but rather beautiful species of the highest damp places of the alpine peaty stream-sides and soaked edges of the snowdrifts. It wants the same peat, the same pervading humidity in England, and is easily established in the underground-watered moraine-bed. It makes humbled, flat-squashed matted clumps of narrow-oblong leaves (that perhaps have a tooth or so towards the tip), of a greyish pale-green, and fringed with long hair ; from the rosettes rise densely glandular-hairy stems of a couple of inches or so, carrying from one to three flowers, enclosed in a rather large glandular cap that seems to give a blunted look to the oval-petalled milk-white blooms, that yet have a strange meek charm of modest and circum-scribed purity, dulled and sad, yet serene, against the groundwork of the sere and sodden brown earth from which they spring.

S. aphylla is another high-alpine Mossy, but this time from the limestone ranges. It wants the same conditions as the last, and is hardly worth them, being a minute cushion of *tri-cleft* blunt foliage, from which rise many *bare* stems of an inch, carrying each a single starved yellow star of very narrow-pointed petals, making no effect against the ampler calyx-segments expanding in an alternate star between them. The specially narrow and pointed petals have also earned it the name of *S. stenopetala*, and will always be found its certain diagnostic on the Alps, no less than the *perfectly naked* little stems.

S. ✕ *apiculata* is the oldest of the hybrids in the Kabschia group, and still remains perhaps the best of the early-flowering Saxifrages, in any fair place making wide lawns of evergreen glossy bright-coloured pale-green rosettlings, packed into serried masses, and built of narrow strap-shaped small leafage, flat, not keeled, with not one lime-pit only at the tip (which ends in a tiny spicule), but with two more, one on either side. Then in February and March up rises a profusion of glandular pinkish leafy stems of 3 or 4 inches, carrying a loose head of large primrose-yellow flowers, beautifully enhancing and fulfilling the yellow green of the carpet from which they spring, and each standing on a footstalk of its own, so that the head does not have the more crowded effect that you get in *S.* ✕ *Elizabethae*. The parentage of this plant is *S. sancta* ✕ *S. marginata*, and it labours often under many false names. *S. Malyi*, *S. luteo-viridis*, and *S. scardica* are all names to beware of in catalogues, lest they prove only to cover *S.* ✕ *apiculata*. And akin to this may be taken a new and probably secondary hybrid, now being sent out as *S.* ✕ *Primrose Bee*. This has more trace of *S. marginata*, and is very beautiful, with specially large and full primrose flowers in characteristically loose heads, above the same neat and spreading mat of brilliant green rosettes, on the same short stems, and in the same free and easy early robust habit.

S. aquatica is a handsome large-growing and vigorous Mossy, making loose lawns and masses by the high stream-sides on all formations in the Pyrenees (where this section is as largely represented as poorly in the Alps). It is all hairy and glandular, and the lower leaves are large and fleshy and thick, divided and divided and redivided into pointed strips until they have the look of some dark and fat Field-buttercup's; the stems are from 12 inches to half a yard high, leafy all the way, and freely branching into noble sprays and showers and clusters of big and brilliant white flowers. The form *S. a. aprica*, often sent out for *S. ajugaefolia*, is smaller in all its parts, with shorter inflorescence and diminished blooms. Both form and type ask for the sunny bog or waterside. (Catalogues often call this *S.* " *petraea*.")

S. arachnoidea belongs to the Nephrophyllum group—a typical and terrible little annual, impossible to collect or keep. In the damp silty grottoes under the Daphne's cliff on the Cima Tombea this very rare species (confined to that district) may be seen, making masses so filmy and evanescent that you expect them to be blown away on a breath like the yellow-starred films of cobweb that they seem. It is as frail in root and stem as the hope of a lost cause, then spreads into a lax flopping jungle of weak fine branches set with broadly oval and minute toothed leaves as flimsy and frail as lovers' vows; and the whole mass is interwoven with a long soft twining fluff of shaggy silver that gives it the frosted and dew-dropped iridescence of a dream. The little stars of blossom spring here and there on fine stems at the ends of the branches, and are of a pale diaphanous yellow in keeping with the ghostly unreality of the whole apparition. In cultivation it should have damp sand and mud in shade, among stones; and no drop of water should ever be allowed to fall upon the plant itself.

S. aretioeides is a typical and attractive Kabschia from the Pyrenees and the mountains of Northern Spain, where it lives in the limestone rocks of the sub-alpine and lower-alpine zone. It makes mats of characteristic huddled and hard little greyish-green shoots, all the narrow short leaves, stiff and fat, tending to stand erect. The stems are dense with glands, and barely 2 inches high, carrying three or four bright-yellow blossoms, each on a foot-stalk of its own, and each emerging from a baggy and densely glandular calyx. The central flower does its work first, while the secondaries grow up a little on their lengthening foot-stalks on either side, so that the effect is loose and widely branched. Finally, *S. aretioeides* has an absolutely certain strawberry mark, for the golden oval petals are *notched and waved* at the edge, and below each notch the end of each petal-vein can be seen expanded. There are two forms of the type, of which the rarer and more difficult makes a tighter tuft, and has shorter, stouter stems with flowers of a darker yellow. But the form called *S. a. primulina* belongs in reality to *S. diapensioeides, q.v.* In nature it shares the upper woods and lower rocks with *S. media*, and from this association, accordingly, has sprung a vast and by now unnecessarily confusing set of hybrids, a number of them bearing quite superfluous names. The first to know is the true *S. × luteo-purpurea*, Lap., 1795. (Our gardens swarm with sham Luteo-purpureas, if we let them, nurserymen seeming to use the name as a sort of blessed Mesopotamia for any obscure plant they wish to sell.) This has the habit, stem, and inflorescence of *S. media*; intermediate calyces, and the golden flowers of *S. aretioeides*, with stems, stem-leaves, calyces, and foot-stalks all purpled as in *S. media*. That is to say, *S.* × *luteo-purpurea* is precisely the golden mean between the parents. Then comes *S.* × *ambigua*, DC., 1815. This is a secondary cross of Supra-media tendency—that is, having more in it of *S. media* (which no doubt crossed again on to the primary hybrid *S.* × *luteo-purpurea* to produce it), so that *S.* × *ambigua* has a double dose of its original father. It has the purple petals of *S. media*, but the foliage and habit are those of *S.* × *luteo-purpurea*. Then, on the other side of the family stands the Supra-aretioeid, *S.* × *Lapeyrousei*, Don., 1882, where the influence of *S. aretioeides* predominates in this, the primary hybrid, which has spreading flower-panicles, and not the elongating spike of *S. media;* and the habit and golden flower of *S. aretioeides*, with larger and broader foliage due to *S. media*. Thus we have on the one side a primary hybrid leaning to *S. aretioeides* (*S.* × *Lapeyrousei*), a primary hybrid standing midway between the parents (*S.* × *luteo-purpurea*), and a secondary hybrid of this (*S.* × *ambigua*) leaning away towards *S. media*. All hopes of certainty and safety in the matter are, however, doomed. For these hybrids breed with each other backwards and forwards in and out interminably, and not only has Sündermann of late years sent forth many named forms representing various shades of interbreeding among them, but he has also got the original relationships of the primaries confused and reversed; so that his *S.* × *luteo-purpurea* is not the old primary and intermediate hybrid of Lapeyrouse, but a plant coming close to one of its parents. His other forms—said to have been collected among the species in the Pyrenees, but which may equally well be raised by any one who can induce the two parents or any of their hybrids to seed side by side in the garden (a good action in which they are especially profuse)—are, elaborately labelled (and priced), as follows : *S.* × *flavescens, aurantiaca, erubescens, ambigua*, and *luteo-purpurea*—all these, of his naming, being Supra-aretioeids, that is, with *S. aretioeides* predominating in all the forms, which are pleasant and easy-going tuffets of foliage, with spreading fluffy-calyxed panicles of flowers in many Water-Avens shades of apricot, orange, and terra-cotta. On the other side he emits a second string of names, these all being Supra-medias, with *S. media* dominant in habit and flower— larger tufts, broader leaves, in goodly rosettes, and taller stems with blossoms in loose and showering spikes, with the fading Water-Avens tones here inclining to old rose and mud-colour and sad worn salmon and crushed bad strawberries ; these are they : *S. racemiflora*, " *Lapeyrousei*," *Godroniana*, and *Grenierii*. The whole range, indeed, is most interesting and fascinating ; of the last group the best, I think, are

S. ×*Godroniana* and *S. Grenierii*, with ample bells in subtle and delicate colours. The race is of hearty growth and easy to deal with, so long as it be remembered that while neither *S. media* nor *S. aretioeides* is very fond of hot sunshine (*S. media* especially detesting it), they are both no less intolerant of dankness and excessive moisture. They, and all their children and posterity, should have quite perfectly-drained situations on open slopes and corners of the rock-work or moraine-bed, in a light mixture of peat and loam and leaf-mould and sand, with abundant chips of limestone or mortar rubble, and with abundant water far down beneath their roots in summer, with no possibility of its vexing their fibres or necks either in winter or at any other time. With such supplies of moisture they will of course bear far more sunshine than if left to take their drink from overhead at the capricious help of heaven (a haphazard, heedless, or heavy-handed Hebe to whose services no choice Saxifrage is partial). But if water be lacking, their happiest place will be along the lines of some high rock that may avert the full fury of the midday, without cutting off the milder influences of the sun, or in any way cloistering them off from light and air.

S. × *arguta*, Sündermann, is a prompt and easy grower, and one of the best hybrids among the smaller Mossies. It makes bright-green cushions of rosetted shoots with the leaves almost translucent as in the one parent, *S. tenella*, yet not entire, but trifid and sharp-cusped, as in the other, *S. tricuspidata*. The flowers are snow-white, borne on rather long foot-stalks, in loose and generously branching showers of 5 or 6 inches. (*S. arguta*, Don, is quite different, and a genuine species near *S. punctata*.)

S. aristulata is a pretty and minute Himalayan high-alpine of the Hirculus group, closely akin to *S. saginoeides, q.v.*

S. aspera is both familiar and distinct, everywhere to be seen in the Alps, making dense rambling mats of rough and mossy shoots, like those of some very narrow-leaved and condensed Mossy Phlox, with bristly edges and a bristly end to all the stiff huddled little needle-like leaves of clear glossy green, sometimes taking a dusted look from their bristliness, and bearing gem-buds embedded in their wandering shoots. The fine frail stems ascend weakly some 4 to 6 inches; often they are of a purple or bronzy polish, and set here and there with a rare narrow leaf. The rather large flowers are two or three in a loose spraying head, of pale butter-colour or straw-colour, deepening to their base; either pointed or oval in the petal, with orange frecklings and bright golden anthers. It is of the easiest culture in any open place. Higher up and in drier places (like many of the Mossies), it

PLATE 36.

SAXIFRAGA BURSERIANA (var. GLORIA, Farrer).
(Photo. R. A. Malby.)

SAXIFRAGA CAESIA.
(Photo. R. A. Malby.)

SAXIFRAGA.

takes a condensed aspect, *S. a. bryoeides*, with the foliage less bristly, smaller and shorter, and packed more closely round the gem-buds, so that the briefer condensed shoots look much more like masses of grey-green balls. This form makes tight and tumbled heaps, from which rise shorter, sturdier, fine flower-stems, usually carrying only one blossom which is larger, clearer in colour, more brilliantly freckled with red and gold, and altogether a good deal more attractive, while quite as easy to grow in any open soil and conditions. (The species and its variety are duplicated in America by *S. bronchialis, q.v.*)

S. atlantica belongs to the Western Mediterranean region, and stands in the Nephrophyllum section, closely allied to *S. granulata*, but that it has no naked bulbils. The leaves of the basal rosette are roundish and deeply scalloped or lobed, on short stalks, with bulbils in their axils; but though there are numerous leaves on the ascending 6- to 8-inch stems, these produce none; the flowers are few and large and fragrant, pure-white, with the central one always overtopped undutifully by the laterals. It was introduced by Dammann and Co. from Naples, in 1895; and its smaller variety, *S. a. carpetana*, Boiss. and Reut., is the plant sometimes seen or offered under the name of *S. veronicaefolia*, Duf., and there is a large group of similar Nephrophyllum Saxifrages awaiting cultivation or clearance, on the Alps of Spain and elsewhere, that we may ultimately know the individualities and claims of *SS. glaucescens, arundana, Rouyana, biternata, gemmulosa* (a dwarf of the last), *hispanica, Bourgaeana, Haenseleri*, and *blanca*—some of which will probably prove to owe their existence as species rather to the beautiful and bountiful zeal of botanists than to any specific merit of their own.

S. augustana is a high-alpine Porphyrion of no special distinction, and the usual exacting temper.

S. australis, Moric. See under *S. lingulata*.

S. austrina is an improved and slenderer *S. nivalis* from Colorado.

S. austromontana lives aloft on the Alps of Colorado, and is possibly a dwarfer and yet more brilliant development of *S. bronchialis*, with stems of half a foot or less, and big white stars freckled with gold and purple.

S. Baldaccii of the Maritime Alps is the precise typical form of that elusive and protean species *S. pedemontana, q.v.*

S. × *Bertoloni*, Sündermann, 1907, and *S. Biasolettii*, Sündermann, 1912, are Engleria-hybrids, of which the first is a spine-leaved plant, no improvement on *S. thessalica*, while the second is a noble-foliaged silver-rosetted combination of *S. thessalica* and *S. Grisebachii*, with leaves much ampler than in the one, and much more pointed than those of the other. The red-flowered Englerias form a difficult and tangled group, which has too liberally been described and synonymised. Pending further researches, it may be suggested that the confusion has largely arisen through *S. porophylla*, which in South Italy is a divergent type of *S. media*, and in the Balkans has again been met with and there again described, at least in part, under the name of *S. Federici Augusti*. But this name was originally given by Biasoleto to the narrow spine-leaved plant otherwise known as *S. thessalica* (Schott), so that thus we get a confusion between *S. porophylla* and *S. thessalica*, these being the two opposite and widely divergent extremes covered by the disastrous doubled name of *S. Federici Augusti*. Simplifying this race, then, there would remain two main groups only (with *S. Grisebachii* as a link); *S. media*, containing sub-species or varieties, *S. porophylla*, *S. montenegrina*, *S. Federici Augusti*, and possibly *S. Stribnyri*—all these being of the broad-leaved and loose-racemed habit; and the other, *S. thessalica* (Schott.), to include the spine-leaved plant sometimes offered as *S.* "*porophylla*" (and seeming a mere synonym of what is here called *S. thessalica*)—this type being narrow and spinous in the foliage, with flowers on much shorter pedicels, and borne accordingly in a close spike rather than on more or less open sprays.

S. × *Biasolettü*. See under *S.* × *Bertoloni*, above.

S. biflora is a similar fat-leaved and weakly species of the shingle-slopes and beds of shale among the melting snow-patches. It is, as a rule, curiously unattractive. The trailing branches are about 6 inches long, set with thick pairs of oval fringed leaves that make the twin or triplet flowers of ragged purplish petals, huddled in the ends of the shoots, seem strangely mean and flimsy in effect, even setting aside the unpleasantness of their unclean madder-rose or dullish-purple colouring (which is often dimmed, too, by the glacial mud in which the plant goes floundering). There is, however, a larger-flowered ampler-petalled white form, by some distinguished as a species under the name of *S. macropetala* (Kerner), which is more desirable, though rarer. It may be seen at great elevations above the Mont Cenis. The species has also produced a more brilliant thing in *S.* × *Kochii*, a hybrid with *S. oppositifolia*. The entire group, to be grown successfully, requires rich muddy soil, with abundance of stone-chips, and water running through the whole mass throughout the whole summer. In such conditions it will readily succeed.

S. × *Bilekii* is a microscopic and lovely-looking hybrid-Kabschia, obviously owing most of its blood to *S. tombeanensis*, and worthy, no doubt, of the botanist whose name it bears. At present, however, it is only a May-be, and its beauties and capacities are unproven.

S. Blavii. See *S. adscendens.*

S. blepharophylla is a quite dwarf high-alpine Porphyrion, allied to *S. biflora.* It is, like all these plants of the upmost snow-shingles, neither easy to grow nor worth the wear of growing, the habit being straggling, and the clumped effect of the aniline purplish flowers not handsome on the comparatively rank leafage of the flopping shoots. It may be known by its broad blunt leaves eyelashed nearly to their tips with hairs.

S. × Borisii is a hybrid between *S. Ferdinandi Coburgi* and *S. marginata.* The leaves have the blue-grey tone of the first, but spread into neat rosettes after the fashion of the second, though the leaves are not so sharply pointed. The little 3- to 4-inch stems are glandular and pinkish, beset with glandular red hairs; and the flowers are specially charming, wide-clustered stars of bright pale citron-yellow: an easy Kabschia, but a most choice one of the daintiest charm.

S. Boryi is not easy to separate from the Coriophylla variety of *S. marginata,* except that its shoot-stems are clad in old leaves all their length, instead of being naked, or only shortly-columned with débris. It is distinct, however, in appearance by the specially smooth snug look of its little rounded thick leaves, each neatly edged with white, and arranged in the neatest of massed and mounded rosettes, spreading rapidly into wide cushions and mats. The stems are about 2 inches high, carrying a spray of four or five large white flowers in the early year—an easy-going rare and precious Kabschia from the upper rocks of Taygetos, &c.

S. × Boydii has miffiness for its chief remaining attraction since the introduction of *S. × Faldonside* and *S. × Paulinae.* It was a seedling from *S. Purseriana,* juxtaposed with *S. aretioeides.* The result is a very neat compact cushion of shoots clad in stiff short narrow needle-like leaves, stiff and fat and bluish-grey in tone, emitting crimsoned stems of an inch or two that bear noble blossoms, one or three to a head, of clear citron-yellow, with the widening veins at the edge of the notched petals that clearly show their descent from *S. aretioeides.* It may have suffered from excessive division in the past, but is certainly a plant of evil and uncertain habit, only to be tried in the choicest of well-drained limy mixtures on a sunny but not torrid slope of rockwork or moraine, with a sufficiency but no superabundance of water.

S. × Boydii alba has nothing to do with the hybrid whose name it bears, but is obviously of wholly different parentage, containing none of *S. aretioeides's* unvarying legacies, but suggesting the influence of *S. marginata*. It makes lax and rather tumbled wide tuffets and mats of much broader, looser, longer, bluer leaves, not spiked, and with four or five pairs of lime-pits arranged (as in *S. marginata*) along their edge. The stems are many, reddish, about 2 inches high, carrying a close stemless clump of fine white blooms with oval-petals smooth and notchless at their edge. It is quite an easy Kabschia to grow, but I can never acquire a liking for it, nor escape from a feeling that it has an underbred untidy floppeting look. It also blooms so early that, what with rains and slugs and mice, the snowy displays rarely have a chance of doing the cushion justice.

S. brachypoda is a high-alpine Kabschia from Bhotan and Kumaon, making very dense mats of very densely overlapping little needle-narrow leaves, sometimes spinulous at the edge, but usually smooth ; the stems are one-flowered and minute, seeming to scatter yellow stars over the brilliantly green and shining tufts.

S. brevifolia, a form of *S. aeizoon*, *q.v.*

S. bronchialis adequately replaces *S. aspera* in Northern Asia and America. The habit and the culture are the same, but the foliage is of much darker green, making a sombre carpet ; American botanists now patriotically try to divide off their own national form from the Yellow Peril over in Asia by saying that this always has lanceolate sepals and orange frecklings ; while their own true-born American plant is to be called *S. cognata*, and has oval sepals and the petals freckled with purple as befits an imperial republic, instead of with the beggarly orange of the Asiatic saint. However, the type in all countries varies as widely as do saints and republics too, and alpine forms may be segregated, as *S. bryoeides* from the European *S. aspera*. In particular there is one, often sent out as *S. Stelleriana* (Merck.) and sometimes as *S. cuspidata*. This stands to *S. bronchialis* exactly as does *S. bryoeides* to *S. aspera*, being neater, tighter, dwarfer, denser, shorter in the stem and larger in the single bloom. Its especial value in the garden, however, lies in the fact that it bronzes to a rich metallic tone in autumn, and keeps its new splendour undiminished through the winter.

S. Brunoniana belongs also to the Trachyphyllum group, and grows readily in any open and not too torrid place of sandy peat, but should have ample space to itself, for it forms remarkable spiny rosettes of pale-green leaves, long and stiff and narrow and pointed, with bristles all up their edges and a longer bristle at their tip ; and these rosettes throw out fine thread-like pink runners this way and that, 6 inches long and more, arching gracefully in their search for a comfortable spot on which to develop the bud that lurks by a leaf-scale at their end. When this is found, the runner comes to earth, the bud lodges, and a new rosette unfolds. A slope several feet across, filled with *S. Brunoniana*, has quite the effect of a carpet of fine stiff rosettes, doddered over with innumerable pink threads of Cuscuta, and sending up many dainty leafy stems with large flowers of bright golden-yellow in summer.

S. bryoeides. See under *S. aspera.*

S. Bucklandii. See under *S. cuneifolia.*

S. bulbifera is a cousin of *S. granulata*, producing a tall gaunt stem set with leaves and bulbils, and carrying at the top a closely clustered head of white flowers. It has no particular attraction.

S. × Burnati owes its existence to *S. aeizoon* and *S. cochlearis*, and is a singularly beautiful and successful cross, for the rounded rosettes are thicker in the leaf than those of *S. cochlearis*, while they still have not the overlapping fullness of *S. aeizoon*, but retain that lovely blue-grey colouring and elongate form of *S. cochlearis*, to which they add Aeizoon's delicate beaded margin of silver ; they lie curling outward, as in the Lingulata group, instead of inward as in the Aeizoons. The many spikes are 6 or 9 inches high, and the flowers, in loose and lovely sprays, have almost the solidified contour of an Aeizoon (though more refined), together with the perfectly pure-white colour that distinguishes *S. cochlearis*. It is as ready a grower as either of its parents, and a treasure of special note.

S. Burseriana has long taken rank as one of the stock plants of the choicest garden, and reams of correspondence constantly flow between successful and unsuccessful cultivators. It is the choicest and earliest, and the largest-flowered, and altogether the loveliest of the Kabschias, forming mats a foot across, dense with thick and spiny glaucous-blue leaves, from which arise in February and March red stems of an inch or two, bearing each a single enormous pure-white flower, wide open, solid and splendid. The distribution of the species is almost entirely within the quadrilateral of the Dolomites, where it is to be seen locally in the cañons and silt-beds under the cliffs, affecting rocks and banks which do not get the whole fierce heat of the sun. As a rule it is not alpine, and the most magnificent form of all its developments belongs to quite low levels in the valley of the Adige, as in the Salurn Klamm, or higher, in the Schlern Klamm ; but everywhere and always on the limestone, and especially happy in rippled shady banks of limy silt, clammy and cool and fine as grit, up against the foot of a great precipice from whose inhospitable crannies its aged tufts can seed their children down into happier homes. Its distribution is most strange ; in the Salurn Klamm and the Adige valley, this typical-looking mountaineer is at its most luxuriant at about 200 feet above the sea ; in the Schlern Klamm at some 6000 feet the form remains the same, while far away in the Karawanken, high on the neck of the Hoch Obir (where it makes very wide flat masses under the step-like ledges of grass in the steepest places), the form is the compressed, flattened, and diminished Minor variety. There are, of course, many other named developments of the plant. Particularly beautiful is *S. B. speciosa*, tight, small, and huddled in the rosettes, which pile up into tight mounds, and emit an astonishing profusion of astonishing fine blossoms on stems of especial redness and brevity ; *S. B. major* and *S. B. grandiflora* are both ample in the blossom, but not always so free of showing them as they should ; *S. B. crenata* has the petals deeply nibbled all round their edges instead of merely waved, and looking as if a slug had been at them, reducing them almost to that famous form *S. B. skolēkobrôtos* or *herodioeides*, which sooner or later occurs in all gardens where slugs are not rare and infrequent cultivators (and could so readily be dispensed with when their special taste confines itself to the corona of *Primula longiflora* and the petals of *S. Burseriana*). All forms, however, sink into insignificance beside the common endemic type of the Southern Dolomites. This, because it lives chiefly in the Prince-bishopric of Trent, has received the name of *S. B. tridentina*, which name our nurserymen, unlearned in the Tridentine Decrees, failed to understand, and substituted for it the almost unbelievably silly name of *tridentata*. For no Burseriana Saxifrage by any possible chance could ever be tridentate in any sort of way. The form, however, mocks at mistakes, in its supreme and crushing splendour—the largest in the leaf of all, the largest in the rosette, the largest in the football-like masses, the largest in snow-white flowers, and the most generous of all in their display. Out of this, too, have issued even better plants still, in *S. B. Gloria* and *S. B. magna*. Of these, *S. B. Gloria* may briefly be described as the greatest, finest, freest, and grandest of the Burserianas, with tall stems of 3 inches or so, usually more greenish in tone than in most of the others, and occasionally with more than one blossom to the stem ; it is a wonderful grower, constant, unchanging, and indefatigable. *S. B. magna*, at its best, beats even this, being much neater and dwarfer, red-stemmed, with flowers borne in unimaginable profusion all over the ample tuft, and of even ampler splendour than those of the last, with rounder and more overlapping petals. This, however, requires good treatment if it is always to be at its highest levels ; and, though quite as easy, has not always the serene and unconquerable triumph of *Gloria* in the garden, to say nothing of the fact that it blooms some ten days earlier, the advance-guard of the race—so that its lavish pearly moons are apt to be saddened by the muds and slugs and rains of February. Both *magna* and *Gloria* have come out of *tridentina*; *Gloria* developed here many years ago from a lot of imported plants of whose habitat and history I then knew nothing (the name *tridentina* had not then been invented), but I have since bloomed it from among batches collected by myself in the Schlern Klamm; *S. B. magna* was from the same lot, but no other foreigner has yet paralleled its tidy and copious magnificence, though imported clumps of *S. B. tridentina* yield endless surprises in the way of splendour and brilliancy and size—no two specimens blooming precisely the same, but each one of startling loveliness in its own line, with never a lame duck in the lot. With regard to the halo of difficulty that is made to hover round *S. Burseriana*, is not this in reality a legacy from the bad old days of " pockets "—when we had, too, only the less vigorous North Tyrolese type to deal with, and usually dealt with that in dense shade ? I have so often seen cosseted *Burserianas* miserably dying in dank dark corners of special selectness, or their owner hopping in ecstasy round one sad moribund blossom that the tuft had mustered force to emit after five years, that I believe the plant, especially now that we have healthy hearty *tridentina* for our subject (to buy the old type-*Burseriana* now is like buying *Lilium auratum* instead of *L. a. platyphyllum*), is far more often killed by uninstructed kindness and fuss than by anything else. Let it be remembered that *S. Burseriana* insists *on open air, clean and unfogged by dampness, darkness, or the discouragement* of dismal bushes, but that it equally prefers not to be baked and burned and frizzled by the sun (sun is usually less its enemy than stagnant shade). Then let a place be chosen where there shall be the shelter of a rock against the fiercest heats of the day, but perfect openness to light and air. Let the soil consist of one-half good loam, with half its weight of mortar rubble, and another half of blended peat, leaf-mould, and rough sand. Let its bed be made of this, among an equal bulk, or less, or more, of limestone chips ; so, if water underground be adequately applied in spring, there will be no further trouble with *S. Burseriana* in any of its forms. At the same time these precautions are only offered to those who are sickened and sad with incessant failures. Many are the gardens where the plant riots in despite of rule, in the most improbable places ; I myself have seen big cushions, apparently contented, sitting on knobbles of blazing hot rock, with no more soil or depth than 3 or 4 inches, dabbed down on the stone, of stone-hard caked loam and manure, as if the thing had been a Sempervivum, to be treated after the disastrous principles of **W. A.** Clark; I have heard of *Gloria* grown consistently, and evidently with success, in the fullest sun; I have seen all forms turn green and tired from a sunless summer; and finally, in the alpine climate of West Yorkshire no *Burseriana* gives any trouble anywhere, but remembers the Salurn Klamm with equal stoicism in sun or shade, loam or underground-watered moraine-bed. As for *S. Burseriana elegans*, this stands so remote from the type, in its outbreak into flowers of a very dim pink, that it hardly deserves to bear the family name undifferentiated, and will be found, accordingly, under a heading of its own as *S. elegans*. (It has now, indeed, received separate rank as *S. Irvingii*.)

S. x *bursiculata* is the hybrid between *S. Burseriana* and *S.* x *apiculata*. Its inflorescence is rather that of an enlarged loosened *S. apiculata*, with Burseriana-white flowers, but in a slackened head, carried on stems of 3 or 4 inches, above cushions of glaucous spines, after the style of *S. Burseriana*. It is a fine and easy novelty.

S. caesia, as sent out by some nurseries, is *S. stricta*, *q.v.*—a specially neat and brilliant sub-species or hybrid of *S. incrustata*.

S. caesia, L. (sometimes sent out as *S. recurvifolia*, Lap.), is the commonest of the choice wild Kabschias, alike in cliff and in cultivation; and always one of the most delightful, with its crowded masses of *tiny* packed rosettes, built of broad recurving little leaves, dark and leathery, brightly pitted with lime; and its thread-fine delicate stems of 3 or 4 inches, bearing each a loose spray of charming milk-white round-rayed stars. In cultivation it is quite easy on rock-work or moraine, liking a rather cool place, as a rule, and of course, like all its kindred, clamouring for lime. Where found in the Alps it is usually abundant; the form sent out sometimes as *S. c. major* being a form prevalent at high altitudes in the Dolomites, whereas the ordinary type is abundant in company with *S. squarrosa*, lower down. In the screes above the Antermoja Lake, for instance, and on the Forcella Lungieres, the *Major* form prevails—a splendid thing about twice the size of the type in leaf and flower and all parts, with the rosettes more loosely built and compiled.

S. caespitosa.—The true species is almost unknown in cultivation, though the name is often given in catalogues to its hybrids, or to forms that shade out of it towards *S. decipiens* or *S. hypnoides*, between which the plant stands undecided—a difficult species, and not attractive, requiring to be pulled to pieces or raised from seed anew every year, and in appearance exactly suggesting a small tight mass of *S. hypnoides*, without any barren runners, but formed into cushions of almost hairless tri-cleft little leaves, conspicuously broader and blunter, with quite short (hardly any) purplish stems, carrying from one to three dull-white flowers, always *erect in bud*.

S. calyciflora, Boiss. and Reut., is the far better and more expressive, but unfortunately subsequent and ten years younger, name of *S. media*, Gouan, *q.v.*

S. Camposii has nothing whatever to do with the glorious garden hybrid *S.* × *Wallacei* which sometimes pretends to bear it. The true species is a neat cushioned Mossy, an extremely rare and fine mass, almost wholly hairless and fairly sticky, with the leaves three-lobed, and the two side-lobes again cloven, and each gash ending in a point. The stems are stout, carrying dense clusters of chalk-white flowers; and the plant may always be known by the fact that these scapes are slightly winged—that is, with a *little leafy line or rim running down along them*.

S. canaliculata is a much more beautiful Mossy from the limestone Alps of Calabria, up to the snow level. It forms wide aromatic cushions of deep dark lucent-green foliage, fleshy and sticky. The branches are woody from the base, and the rosettes packed at their ends, with very long and *deeply-grooved* stems to the leaves, which are cut into three lobes, and then the two laterals gashed again, and perhaps again, all the lobes being firm and quite narrow and pointed, *deeply grooved like the petioles*, which characteristic will always distinguish the plant whose name it has earned. These broad and shining hassocks send up abundant erect trusses of large white flowers.

S. Candelabrum is a Chinese monocarpic novelty of rather tender nature, with tender green leaves arranged in a most lovely wide rosette of fine foliage. The flowers are unfortunately tarnished in their brightness by the conspicuous narrow segments of the calyx, standing out between the petals.

S. capitata seems likely to be a hybrid between *S. aquatica* and the much smaller *S. ajugaefolia*, whose name it is sometimes made to bear in gardens. It is by now a fixed species, occasionally seeding, "though rarely in cultivation," but varies greatly, either towards the one parent or the other. Some hold it, though, a mere form of *S. aquatica*, *q.v.*, and in gardens it is identical with *S. aq. aprica*, while it belongs in nature to districts where *S. ajugaefolia* is unknown.

S. carinthiaca. See under *S. aeizoon*, of which it is a local form.

S. carniolica. See under *S. aeizoon*, of which it is a local form.

S. caroliniana. See *S. pennsylvanica*.

S. cartilaginea, Willd., in all probability only a form of *S. aeizoon*, is treated in its place here because it is always made in catalogues a synonym of lovely *S. Kolenatiana*, Regel—though the true species has the saw-teeth of the leaves more acute than in *S. cartilaginea,* where they are usually rather blunt. This variety is a remarkable *Aeizoon* of ready growth and easy culture, which prevails all through the Caucasus and is lavishly variable. The rosettes are larger than in *S. aeizoon rosea,* and of a greener note, broader, more overlapping and expanded, with a clearer triangle at the apex of the straight strap-shaped leaf. The glandular stems are about 6 or 8 inches high, with an oval panicle of flowers usually in a considerably paler tone of spotless pure pink, but varying at home alike in size and in depth of tone, fading to white and deepening to purple. A garden plant sent out as *S. Sendtneri* seems merely a form of *S. cartilaginea* with doubled size and laxer inflorescence. It is also called *S. Kol. major.*

S. catalaunica. See under *S. lingulata,* although it has a fair claim to specific rank as a handsome silver Saxifrage, standing, as it seems, between the Lingulata type and that of *S. aeizoon.*

S. " ceratophylla " of gardens is a useful Mossy, forming vast mats of fine shining foliage, finely divided, and curly like a stag's horn. This is *S. Schraderi,* a species in the vast series between *S. hypnoeides* and *S. sponhemica.* But the name is also applied to many other garden forms and hybrids that have the finely divided stag's-horn foliage. The blossoms are large and white and abundant, on delicate stems of 6 or 8 inches, above the rolling masses of evergreen and lucent leafage.

S. cernua requires the bog or underground-watered moraine-bed. It is always a rare treasure, and has one British station only, near the summit of Ben Lawers, where it exists in quantity but is as shy of flowering as sometimes it is in the garden. The few basal leaves are very fat, of dull fleshy-green, kidney-shaped, and cut into some five shallow and wide triangular lobes. The stems are 3 inches high, bearing a single large and nodding flower of pure white, and with little bright-red bulbils in the axils of its little stem-leaves, which not only make a brilliant effect, but scatter themselves freely about the garden and make new plants.

S. cervicornis. See under *S. pedemontana.*

S. × Cherry Trees is a Burseriana hybrid of perfectly free and easy growth, forming wide cheerful mats of close yellow-green spiny rosettes, from which, at blue-moontide of the Greek Kalends, emerge yellow moons of blossom on short stems. Sun and light poor soil seem to be the only means of eliciting these; but the neat massed carpet has attractions of its own, even though it be never graced by that of flower.

S. chrysantha lives far up on the mountains of Colorado. It is a moist-ground plant, in the kinship of *S. flagellaris* but with much fewer leaves on the almost bare stems of 2 or 3 inches, rising from clumps of leaves at the base, and each carrying one or two large golden stars of blossom.

S. chrysosplenifolia should more properly be called *S. rotundifolia repanda*, and is a Miscopetalum, close akin to typical *S. rotundifolia* in habit as in habits, but of tenderer consistency, and with blunt toothing to the leaves.

S. Churchillii, Huter (*S. elatior*, Stein), is a valuable and beautiful Aeizoon hybrid, having all the appearance of a much larger and freer flowering *S. aeizoon*, but with quite distinct rosettes, large and stiff-leaved and grey, deriving clearly from its other parent, *S. Hostii*, from which it differs in having the broad conspicuous silver-beading rather sharp on the forward- and upward-pointing teeth, instead of bluntly scalloped as in *S. Hostii*, though they are broader than in *S. aeizoon*, and the whole growth on a larger scale.

S. ciliata is a Bergenia, and merely a slimmer form of the hopeless *S. ligulata*, with flowers of flushing pink. It has a further variety *S. Milesii*, and two white ones, *alba* and *afghanica*.

S. circinata does not exist. The name adumbrates *S. incrustata*.

S. circuenta exists still less, and its name adumbrates nothing, unless perhaps a misprinted memory of the last. *S. pectinata* and *S. paradoxa* are the old friends most usually thus disguised.

S. × *Clarkei*, Sündermann, 1908, is another rosy-flowered hybrid of the Englerias, whose various children are now much too copiously and unauthoritatively named in catalogues.

S. Clusii may be taken as a magnified *S. stellaris*, with big coarsely-toothed leaves from the basal rosette, with a large leafy-bracted shower of loose pink-freckled white stars. There is, or was once, a form much beloved in gardens called *S. c. propaginea*, with bulbils in the axils of the basal leaves, and many scapes coming from the rosette, branching into a pyramid of flower that often is no pyramid of flower at all, the blossoms being replaced by bulbils. Both these are for the moist-ground treatment indicated for *S. stellaris*.

S. cochlearis is a variable and most beautiful Euaeizoön, whose place in the race is less certain than that which it holds in our hearts and gardens. It stands between two marked forms of *S. lingulata*, though typically much smaller than either; and was formerly ranked by Engler as a mere variety of *S. lantoscana*. It makes humped and massed domes of stiff rounded rosettes, built of very fat thick little outward-curling leaves, narrow, and with the characteristic Lingulata-swelling at the tip, here so condensed as to make a sort of spoon-shape effect. From each of these rosettes springs an *invariably glandular* reddish spike of 6 or 8 inches, carrying loose and one-sided sprays of fine-stemmed flowers of pure milk-white, usually ample in the star, and always lovely in their show. This beautiful thing is entirely confined to the calcareous districts of the Roja valley, and eastward of the Col de Tenda into the limestones of the Ligurian Apennines, having almost its last station, like so many less happy mortals, high up on the Port-Fino summit. It varies extravagantly; when it seeks the shady stations affected by *S. lantoscana* it approaches more and more closely to the Lantoscana-form itself, growing larger and laxer, alike in leaf and rosette, and of a more ochreous green, instead of the powdered pale-blue and silver-white of its cushions where they are tightened by the sun. The typical shade- or gully-form may be seen on the limestone cliffs overhead as you drive up the bed of the Roja to San Dalmazzo ; and the more normal sun-compressed type on the drier rocky slopes of the Rio Secco behind Briga. In the Val de Caïros, again, it takes the yet minuter shape which is sent out not only as *S. coch. minor,* a perfectly fair, proper, and prevalent name, but also of late years as *S. Probynii,* a name nearly as unjustifiable as the alternative one of *S. " valdensis,"* under which it is so universal in gardens as to make the genuine *S. valdensis* almost unknown. Yet the Probynii-name is the more provoking in its mere irrelevance ; the tiny tight masses of the plant *do* bear a definite resemblance to the tiny tight masses of *S. valdensis,* and, when the latter grows drawn and stouter, the two are not easily separable at a glance, until it is realised the leaves of *S. cochlearis* in all its forms are *flat on the upper surface,* no matter how much their tips be swollen, nor how condensed they be ; while in this form they tend, as usual, to stand distinct, despite their diminished outward curve, instead of lying pressed down tight in the hard impenetrable domes of *S. valdensis* that give your hand the feeling of pressing some warted reptilian hump, instead of the hundred little resilient points that you feel on laying it over a mass of *S. cochlearis minor.* Further differences will be noted under *S. valdensis.* With regard to other forms, the rocks of Briga and San Dalmazzo may yield opportunities for more names ; the species is always graceful in stem, and always pure and beautiful in flower, but there are ampler forms as well as starrier. That called *S. c. major* is the larger-leaved, looser, greener-grey, rosetted plant developed in the gorge of Saorgio, and it is not insignificant that just as *S. Burseriana* develops into special amplitude in close Southern valleys, with forms thence emerging of even added beauty, so does *S. cochlearis* also, in the same conditions, majorify, and emit a superior form, at present distinguished only with three stars, but also by blossoms of quite remarkable size and brilliance, on 5-inch stems, on large and very broad-leaved bluish-white rosettes. The type is extremely local in its own valleys, and I have not yet seen it growing with the Lingulatas—which, however, are so close at hand that this year revealed a clear hybrid of *S. cochlearis* with the great *S. l. Bellardii*—a plant obviously intermediate, with the lovely leafage of the smaller parent rather enlarged, and the loose milky plumes of the other rather diminished. In the garden all the forms of *S. cochlearis* are of the most admirable and indestructible vigour, whether on the sunny or the shady side of the rock-work, and whether endowed with lime in their rocks or no. If the site be *very* torrid, however, and the water-supply inadequate, it might always be preferable, in hot countries, to plant this race (the whole of it, and the Lingulatas too) on the cooler and shadier exposures of the rock-work. On the almost sunless cliff at Ingleborough the entire group is naturalised in perfect comfort and vigour, in crevices of the mountain limestone, making wide fat cushions as at home.

S. cognata. See under *S. bronchialis.*

S. compacta is a Kabschia like a *S. Burseriana*, with rather smaller yellow flowers, above mats of specially dense and spiny glaucous-grey foliage, sending out offsets like a Sempervivum, on stems that are never pink or sticky-glanded, but always quite smooth and more frequently set with leaves. (Cliffs of Lena, East Siberia.)

S. conifera is a small Mossy with small and feeble white stars on short stems, from rosettes of narrow bristle-pointed *and always lobeless and toothless leaves*, very tightly packed and overlapping along the shoots, and emitting oblong gem-buds clothed in densely-webbed and bristly-pointed membranous leaves. It is neither pretty nor easy to grow ; the plant sent out under its name is *S. globulifera* in various forms, but here the leaves are *always more or less lobed*, the *entire* packed foliage along the shoot being the invariable diagnostic of *S. conifera* among all its Mossy kin.

S. cordifolia is a yet larger-leaved form of *S. crassifolia, q.v.*

S. cordigera is a high Himalayan Hirculus, with dense tufts, and golden flowers on stems of 3 or 4 inches, invested in cordate leafage.

S. coriacea comes close into the relationship of *S. stellaris.*

S. coriophylla. See under *S. marginata.*

S. corsica is a pretty little pygmy of *S. granulata*, but the name (or that of " Corsicana ") is often given in catalogues to *S. pedemontana*, especially in its form *S. p. cymosa.*

S. cortusaefolia is a splendid and valuable plant of the Diptera group. It thrives in the same rich soils and sheltered well-drained conditions as suit *S. Fortunei*, from which it may typically be distinguished by flowering about three weeks earlier—towards the end of September—with taller, looser showers of more abundant, smaller, and starrier white flowers, above the same nobly handsome waxy-glossy dark-green foliage, ample and lobed. These are both quite hardy species, but sound drainage ensures the safety of the clumps, and shelter secures their blooms from damage.

S. corymbosa, Boissier, Fl. Orient., lives on the damp rocks of Cadmus at about 6000 feet, and is practically the same thing as *S. luteoviridis* of Transylvania, with narrower, more pointed leaves and sharper calyx-lobes. Its picture is that of small neat rosettes of greyness in the fashion of *S. media*, with loose heads of little yellow flowers in large and very glandular fluffy green calyces, giving the effect of a Cowslip gone mad. It should have a shady place, and there grows with the utmost readiness.

S. corymbosa, Hook., F. and T., is a much smaller *S. diversifolia*, a high-alpine *S. Hirculus* with the flower-pedicels glandular, indeed, but not clothed in brown hairs.

S. Cossoniana has the largest and most magnificent blossoms of all the Spaniards. It is a Nephrophyllum, living in the shady limestone rocks of Valentia at alpine and sub-alpine levels, where it makes close tufts of huddled, little rounded sticky leaves, heart-lobed where they meet the petiole (which, like the lower part of the plant, is cob-webbed with fine fluff). The flowers are borne on long foot-stalks in a branching loose fountain of 8 or 10 inches.

S. Cotylēdon.—It is a complete mistake to describe the grandest of all the big Plume-silvers as monocarpic. What does happen is that the *flowered rosette invariably dies*, but the stock, if happy, has meanwhile thrown out a dozen more, which carry on, undiminished, the magnificent traditions of last season, and prepare their own successors by the spring, against the summer when they shall all themselves have flowered and died. The mass, in fact, is immortal ; it is only the bloom-spires that die. So that this noble species, with nothing more to show than its mats of twenty or thirty rosettes of noble strap-shaped leathern bead-edged leaves in noble rosettes of 6 inches across and more, is in itself the glory of the rock-work, alike by winter and summer, without " proticipating " on the wonder of its waving yard-high plumes of delicate snow-white, sometimes pink-freckled and sometimes pure, but often as many as twenty at a time, mopping and mowing with their inimitable ample grace from some high slope, exactly as they wave over masses more than a yard across, from all the black granites of the Simplon and its southward valleys, even by the highway-sides, in lucent cushions like church-hassocks on every ledge, whitened with the dust of the motors, and in the summer flagging and flopping—even those undamageable impermeable leaves—beneath the awful heats of summer in the lowland South. It is always superb, but should be sought out in flower, that the best varieties be chosen. Some of these bear names already; such is the stocky and red-stemmed *S. c. montafoniensis;* and *S. pyramidalis* of gardens is simply another, perhaps of especially splendid port and wide pyramidal towers of blossom. The finest of all is the superb *S. c. islandica* from the far North, which has enormous rosettes often more than a foot across, of very long narrow strap-shaped foliage in tones of iron and bronze; with the most amazing spike to match, of 4 or 5 feet, bowed with the drifted soft glory of their snow. Unfortunately it does not seem a ready grower everywhere, though on the oolitic limestone of the garden at St. John's at Oxford (whence it first broke forth upon a dazzled world) it thrives or throve with all its might, a thing that would be more strange than it is, in a species so passionately calcifuge as *S. Cotyledon,* were it not that in the garden, so long as it has light and air and sun, it does not seem possible to find a soil or a treatment that will disagree with it. Yet *S. Cotyledon* is, with *S. florulenta,* the one Euaeizoön that in nature is absolutely faithful, in the Alps at all events, to the dark granites towards the Italian slope. But in the garden it revels in any rich and heavy limy loam, between the most melting of calcareous rocks; showing, in fact, the same genial lack of faddishness that distinguishes the no less naturally calcifuge *S. aeizoon,* which, however, foreshadows its willingness of temper by overflowing also in the Alps on to limestone, in a manner not favoured by *S. Cotyledon.* This species has also given us its influence in many a hybrid, named and unnamed; so that there are few gardens long established that have not some special Saxifrages that owe part of their blood and nobleness to *S. Cotyledon* (Miss King's is one of particular freedom and beauty of rosette, and so is *S.×Launcestonensis*); even if their owners have not been buying other forms, not necessarily better, under fancy names. In especial, the thing that bears the ridiculous name of *S. nepalensis* is probably a hybrid of *S. Cotyledon* and *S. Hostii,* while all the innumerable forms called *S. Macnabiana* have more or less of *S. Cotyledon* in their nature, no matter who the other parent may have been—or parents indeed, seeing that the family is indefinitely fertile, so that there is no use in final definitions among the later generations.

S. crassifolia is a big Bergenia, with Elephant's-ear *smooth* foliage, and pink flowers standing *erect* when open, each on a *bald and hairless* foot-stalk. It has innumerable forms and hybrids; among them are: *S. c. rubra, ovata, compacta, nana, alba, cordifolia* (notably large in the leaf), *cord. purpurea, media, aureo-marginata*, &c.

S. × *crispa* owes its origin to *S. Geum* and *S. cuneifolia*. The result is a pleasant little intermediate London Pride, with most graceful showers of white stars. Quite easy anywhere.

S. crustata and *S. cristata*. See under *S. incrustata*.

S. cultrata. See under *S. aeizoon*.

S. cuneata often masquerades in gardens as *S. Willkommiana*. It is not a trustworthy species, having, like many of the thick-leaved Spanish Mossies, a tendency to miff off; but, if established happily in a light and sunny place, it makes a really effective mass of wedge-shaped broad leaves, fleshy-fat and sticky, cloven into three lobes and borne on foot-stalks shorter than themselves (or of the same length). The blossoms are large and white and beautiful, borne in loose branching showers on many valid stems of 8 inches or so.

S. cuneifolia makes one of the most charming of spectacles in shady woodland places, where it forms a carpet of tiny London-Pridish rosettes, dark bright green, tapering at the base and scalloped at the edge. The dainty spikes are 3 inches high or so, delicately bending to unloose a dainty shower of white stars, with a yellow dot at the base of each oval little petal. It is very widely distributed through all the alpine woods, and varies in the course of its distribution. Among the forms especially distinguished are *S. c. Bucklandii*, a rather larger development, with the leaves less scalloped, and two yellow dots at the base of each petal. *S. c. Infundibulum* exists merely by virtue of an inconstant and artificial distinction; the neat cup or funnel of the unfolding foliage is supposed to be deeper and more evident. But the symptom is not certain, and the plant as it develops further is indistinguishable from the type. *S. c. subintegra* is also *S. multicaulis* (Lange) and *S. apennina* (Bert.), as well as being usually sent out by gardeners under the name of *S. capillaris*, by a gardener's misspelling for *S. capillipes* (Rchb.). This is a specially delightful little form, of much paler green all over, and with the flower-stems green instead of red as in the others, even more freely produced and more freely branching from nearer the base, and consequently carrying a greater number of larger and snowier-white flowers, which not only have the basal golden dot but also a freckling of pink spots as well.

S. cuscutaeformis is a Mother of Thousands, to be seen in every greenhouse, but not permanently to be trusted out of doors.

S. cuspidata. See under *S. bronchialis*.

S. Cymbalaria figures more often in catalogues than in gardens.

PLATE 37.

SAXIFRAGA COTYLEDON [hybrids].
(Photo. R. A. Malby.)

SAXIFRAGA CUNEATA.
(Photo. R.B.G., Edinburgh.)

For it is a rare species, not so easily kept as *S. Sibthorpii*, which is the pretender that bears its name in general use. The true *S. Cymbalaria*, L., gives its name to the section of damp shade-loving annual little fleshy-leaved species with golden flowers; in growth, form, and foliage it justifies its name by exactly recalling *Linaria Cymbalaria*, but, though in all its parts it so resembles the common Toad-flax of the wall, the kidney-shaped leaves are not succulent, and have the brown striping characteristic of the section, with a good number of pointed lobes. The blossoms are golden stars, and the calyx-segments curl backward only at fruiting time.

S. cymosa. See under *S. pedemontana.*

S. dalmatica is a catalogue-name for a small yellow-flowered Kabschia, possibly no more than *S. Ferdinandi Coburgi* or *S. Desoulavyi.*

S. debilis is a weakly small alpine of Colorado, with stems of 2 or 3 inches with scalloped little kidney-shaped leaves at the base, and two or three flowers of pinkish white.

S. decipiens.—This huge name covers the largest group of Mossies in the garden, being really only a despairful aggregate-description to embrace a vast series of forms ranging from fat-leaved fleshy *S. caespitosa* at one end, to thin and fine-leaved *S. hypnoeides* at the other. Its chief diagnostics are the *erect flower-buds*, the big flat fat flowers, and the *rather broad and rather blunt lobes* to the foliage. All the forms vary widely in nature, according to situation, and freely interbreed, there as in the garden, so that the bestowal of endless names in cultivation is as profitable as weaving ropes of sand. All that can be said is that all forms are invaluable big Mossies for any reasonable situation, very solid in growth as well as very fine and large and free in bloom. Of late years a race has arisen called *S. d.* "*hybrida.*" These are huge and obese, with broad plate-like coarse blossoms of red or pink or cream, that have exchanged their birthright of grace and charm for heavy ostentation and a blowzy coarseness of appeal. Accordingly they are most dearly cherished by catalogues, which give them fine and finer names each year; among them are *S. bathoniensis, Clibrani*, and many more—not indeed to be unjustly despised, any more than preposterously praised; for, while they have lost the elegance of their race, they have a noble showy value of their own, indestructible rough strong growers and abundant in flower. Some of the smaller varieties, too, approaching *S.* × "*Rhei*," and partaking of the same blood, are not only really brilliant in their crimsons, but pleasant and neat in their smaller habit. Such are Red Admiral and many others. As for *S.* "*Rhei*" of gardens, this originates between *S. decipiens* and *S. sponhemica*, together with many another seedling in the same lot—Guildford Seedling (crimson), Stormonth's Seedling (smaller and earlier), Fergusoni, Craven Gem, &c. ; these have all sprung from the same crosses in various forms, making up so vast a series, both natural and artificial, that the wise gardener, recognising their utter invalidity as species, and the uselessness of multiplying their names, will yet gladly acquire every one of them by catalogue-descriptions, to adorn the lower and outlying parts of the rock with wide mats of their beautiful, neat, and hardy foliage that changes neither by summer nor winter, except when it is half hidden in early summer by the forest of stems that are to carry the glowing or blushing little platters of stout blossom. Any fragment of these will grow, if stuck into the earth at any moment ; but seed should always be collected and sown broadcast, where the strains in culti- vation are brilliant, on the chance of a development more brilliant still, that shall outshine the reddest seedling of them all, and make the most fiery Admiral go pale. Of the more justly-named forms of the wild *S. decipiens,* we may mention *S. hirta,* very free and coarse and large and hairy, with very large flowers on long stout shoots ; *S. incurvifolia,* with the leaves of the rosettes incurving so as to turn them almost into balls ; and *S. Sternbergi,* a handsome solid massed plant, sending up innumerable straight stems of notable cream-white flowers. It may be seen in myriads among the limestone rocks of County Clare, looking out across the Atlantic from among carpets of Dryas, threaded with azure knops of *Gentiana verna.*

S. Delavayi is a new species from China, of the great-leaved pink- headed Bergenia group.

S. depressa stands close to *S. androsacea,* but has rather large wedge-shaped leaves, densely glandular on both sides, *and cut into three blunt lobes at the tip.* These leaves tightly hug the ground, and the little rosette sends up a stiff glandular stem of 2 or 3 inches bearing a few chalk-white flowers. It is, like the other, a high-alpine of the sodden snow-borders, not easy to grow, and of no great attractiveness.

S. Desoulavyi, originally sent out as *S. carinata,* is a mix-up that stands chiefly for a small Kabschia, with quite distinct, quite loose masses of minute dark-green rosettes, and loosely set with erect- pointing needle-narrow stiff little spiked leaves. The stems are mere dwarfs, set with foliage, green, an inch or two high, each carrying one narrow-petalled yellow cup that does not open widely, and has wavy edges to the petals. The real *S. Desoulavyi* is not in cultivation. Caucasian botanists are now responsible for some eight or ten named yellow Kabschias differing only in the most microscopic and uncertain points.

S. diapensioeides is one of the loveliest and least certain of the Kabschias. I have seen whole gardensful miff off upon no discoverable cause, just as I have seen derisively healthy mats of it in positions most improbable. In nature it is a rare plant, not to be seen with any frequency until you come into the limestone ranges of the Southern Alps. Here (occasionally) in situations not open to excessive sun or rain, it nestles into the sheer walls, and there makes cushions very hard and tight and dense, of columns closely packed with microscopic fat hard grey leaves, rammed into minute rosettes at the ends, and triangular at their tips, making a wide mass often half a yard across, perfectly flat and stony, lying over the face of the cliff like a scab of silver lichen. To the touch those unyielding elastic masses give a living, pulsing, yet cold-blooded feeling, as if one were caressing the wrinkled and warted skin of some aged and venerable toad. You have the muffled consciousness of a thousand dull blunted wee prominences that give exactly the sensation of a firm and corrugated hide. Abundantly over the mat come up the little stems of 2 inches or less, carrying two or three flowers of purest white, very large and very lovely—but not particularly like a Diapensia's, any more than are the leaves. Usually it is a species purely saxatile ; but there are places on the Mont Cenis where it grows in open sandy and dusty limestone soil under the step-like ridges of the coarse grass in specially steep places, after the fashion of *S. Burseriana minor* on the neck of the Hoch Obir, the coping of rough tough grass serving (no less than the rock which it usually affects) to keep the plant free of the excessive moisture that it dreads. Here, then, it grows into enormous masses, constellated with blossoms of especial freedom and splendour, which, when those overhanging sheets are awave with whiteness, make one realise yet again that one ought always to see one's Saxifrages in bloom. For even here, in a species so beautiful, there are forms of special beauty still—with larger, ampler, whiter, and more brilliant flowers than even the brilliant type. But of the history of that lovely form which is pure *S. diapensioeides*, but that the flowers are of citron-yellow, nobody can tell. It has long been in cultivation under the names of *S. aretioeides primulina*, but clearly belongs in all respects to *S. diapensioeides*, and lacks that characteristic widening of the veins towards the notched edges of the petals that never fails to mark all the varieties of *S. aretioeides*. With regard to the cultivation of *S. diapensioeides*, it seems that in most places the prime essential is the most perfect drainage and dryness in a situation distinctly more shaded than sunny ; and the soil had better be a mixture of, perhaps, half mortar-rubble and half well-compounded light sandy loam, with enrichment of peat and leaf-mould. But it must always be remembered that if the plant appears to avoid and resent too-torrid sunshine, it also resents even more irredeemably and violently anything like dampness, dankness, or stagnant humidity either of soil or atmosphere.

S. diversifolia.—Buyers do not lose much by the inveterate error which sends out, under this name, the best of all forms of *S. Hirculus.* For the true *S. diversifolia* is at once difficult and rather dowdy with its excessive leafage. It is a many-headed mass-forming species of the high Himalayan and Chinese marshes, most variable in size and development, with many named obscure varieties, such as *S. Moorcroftiana, S. parnassifolia,* &c. The leathery egg-shaped leaves stand up in many tufts on long stalks, and are paler on the under-side, and either smooth or (more often) fringed and hairy and glandular. The stems are some 8 or 10 inches high, often much branching and always much embraced by leaves, whose number and size diminish the effect of the golden stars (which have four minute wartinesses at the base of each petal). Among innumerable developments, however, one stands out as being really desirable. This is *S. d. foliata* from Yunnan, whose especial beauty lies in the foliage, deep-purple and veined with green, thus admirably enhancing the blossoms.

S. elatior, Stein=*S. Churchilli,* Huter, *q.v.*

S. ✕ " *elegans* " (now *S.* ✕ *Irvingii*) is the name given to a seedling of *S. Burseriana* that originated at Kew, and, from cushions exactly similar to the species, produced solitary, rather less wide-awake flowers, in a dim and very pale lilac, flushed from the centre, of curiously washy and indeterminate effect, but obviously of the highest interest, as making a break so wide from the type that it is impossible not to recognise in it the influence of *S. lilacina.* It grows as readily as its parent, and has already given a secondary cross. (See under *S.* ✕ *kewensis.*)

S. ✕ *Elizabethae* is one of the most precious of early spring jewels, and of the easiest growth in any open soil and position, where it forms enormous wide mats of thorny foliage, like that of one parent, *S. Burseriana,* in general aspect (though the mass is far wider and freer)— but in colour of a deep and sombre green inherited from the other, *S. sancta,* which has also contributed to the flowers, which are in loose heads on glandular pink little stems of 2 inches or so, smaller than in *S. Burseriana,* and of a far clearer bright soft yellow than in *S. sancta,* as well as being much rounder and wider and more beautiful. They sit almost stemless in their head, and the flower-shoot has long white hairs tipped with microscopic pink glands—two characters that separate it from the larger-leaved, paler, blunter *S.* x *apiculata*, with its pedicelled primrose blossoms in a looser cluster. The only requirement of *S.* x *Elizabethae* in the garden is sometimes to be pulled to pieces and replanted, when it begins to sicken and go brown in the middle, as sometimes happens if the carpet is getting old, and about a yard across. Elizabeth, in this case, is the late Dowager of Roumania, Carmen Sylva.

S. x *Engleri*, Huter, is not the same thing as *S. Engler* (Dalla Torre). It is the hybrid of *S. incrustata* and *S. Hostii*, with the leaves of the grey and beaded rosette narrower than in *S. Hostii*, but more club-shaped than in *S. incrustata ;* they are also quite shortly and *bluntly* scalloped. The spike and flowers are intermediate; it is not specially beautiful, though useful and vigorous.

S. Engleri (Dalla Torre) is merely a robust form of *S. stellaris.*

S. Engleri (of gardens) is one of the secondary Aeizoon crosses, forming very large masses of rosettes made up of very long and narrow dark-green beaded leaves, of handsome effect, with rare and gaunt spikes of 18 inches or so, branching stiffly and scantily near the top, and rather grudgingly furnished with fat creamy flowers rather feeble by comparison with the huge cushions of the plant, and the stout unfurnished stature of the stems.

S. erioblasta is a wee Mossy living in the highest limestones of Granada, with rosettes of minutely tiny leaves, either entire or microscopically trilobed. The stems are an inch or two in height, carrying from one to three erect flowers of white or pink. (See *S. spathulata*.)

S. erosa, Pursch., sometimes offered as *S. micranthidifolia*, is a large, coarse, and ugly species of the Boraphila group, with big tufts of oblong nibble-edged leathery leaves, and branching leafy spikes of 2 feet high, carrying showers of small white bloom. It most suggests an enlarged *S. leucanthemifolia*, and is only to be admitted to the damp bog-garden, and there without welcome.

S. erythrantha calls out all our longings. It must be the jewel of its race, as well as the only red-flowered Kabschia. For it is said to be a rare form of *S. scardica*, met with on Scardus, Kyllene, the Thessalian Olympus, &c., among the type, from which it differs, apparently, neither in mass of tight and thorny little bead-edged broad-leaved rosettes, nor in abundance of goodly 4-inch stems, nor in size of the ample flowers in their characteristic loose heads almost suggestive of some very handsome big-blossomed white crucifer; but here the blossoms are not white. They are of brilliant rose-purple— in the interests of the race's future, no less in that of the garden, well worth the journey to Scardus or Kyllene in blossom-time to see them shining from afar, blood-red among the milk-white masses of their kin, thence to be collected and brought piously home, to contribute the wine of their fiery blood to a race of rosy hybrids as yet unthought of. *S. erythrantha* is quoted here under its name because, although Halaczy recognises it only as a variety of *S. scardica*, yet this red variation is so unparalleled among the white-flowered Kabschias, that there seems at least a possibility that it may be itself a hybrid of *S. scardica* × *S. thessalica*, Schott., which grows with it so freely, at least on Scardus, that imported tufts of the one are as likely as not to contain the other.

S. Escholtzii stands near *S. tricuspidata*, and is a species of Northern Asia. Than which there is no more at present to say.

S. × *Eudoxiana* has leaves and spiny tufts like that of its one parent *S. Ferdinandi Coburgi*, starry in the rosette and bluish grey, but rather longer, with two pairs of quite conspicuous lime-pits at their edge, as well as the one at the tip. From the cushion spring stems of 2 or 3 inches, carrying heads of thin and starry flowers that have sacrificed the shrill violence of *S. F. Coburgi's* yellow without gaining any advantage from the paler tones of *S. sancta*, which has, however, contributed a look of extra-spideriness to the flowers, with their displayed stamina and styles. It is an easy grower and a small neat plant—the reverse cross to *S. Haagii*, which is *S. sancta* × *S. Ferdinandi Coburgi*.

S. exarata, Vill., extends from the Pyrenees to the Balkans—a common high-alpine Mossy, widely diverse, and in the kinship of *S. moschata* and *S. mixta*. It is a small massed species, with very prominently nerved leaf-stalks, and the nerves continuing along the three blunt and parallel lobes of the leafage. This would serve to distinguish it from *S. moschata*, while from *S. mixta* it stands distinct in *not* having a dense coating of glands. At the same time it is in many ways variable, and a most uncommon plant in cultivation, many other species masquerading under its name; in all the high Alps it is abundant, making tidy clumps in the moraine-shingles, from which proceed many sturdy little stems of 3 inches or so, bearing several stars of creamy yellow that, in good forms and on well-furnished clumps, often make quite a fine effect. The name of *S. nervosa* is at least as common in gardens; but the true thing is at least as rare as the true *S. exarata*, of which it is merely an aromatic and sticky dwarf form, with narrower leaves, much more deeply cut, very nearly to their base, into three or five lobes that tend to stand apart; while the flower-stems bear a profusion of small creamy blossoms on stems of an inch or two. This plant appears to be the real *S. pentadactylis*,

Lap., which its author, in describing and figuring, suggested might only be a variety of *S. nervosa*. All these forms, being children of the high gaunt places, will want cool culture in the underground-watered moraine-bed.

S. × *Faldonside* annihilates *S. Boydii*. It is another hybrid of the same parentage, making cushions of the most beautiful blue-grey spine-leaved rosettes, from which spring a profusion of reddened stems of an inch or so, bearing great overlapping-petalled splendid flowers of pure citron-yellow, well worthy of playing pale suns to even such unrivalled white moons as those of *S. Burseriana magna* and *S. B. Gloria*, than which, in similar open conditions or reasonable devotion and regard, *S. Faldonside* is no whit less free alike in growth (though smaller) and flower.

S. × *Farreri*, Druce, has only the merit of interest to commend it. For the plant is an unshowy little thing, with creamy stars on stems of an inch or two, above rosettes of very minute three-cleft leaves. Its claim to notice lies only in the fact that it is an intersectional hybrid, found in one example by me some years ago on the Western face of Ingleborough, and even as a two-leaved seedling showing such intermediacy of character that its hybrid origin could not be doubted. The parents, as it seems, are *S. hypnoeides* and the annual *S. tridactylites*, there also abounding (together with *S. oppositifolia* and *S. aeizoeides*). The hybrid, however, is perennial, and certainly distinct.

S. Federici-Augusti, Biasol., is said by Halaczy to be the blue-grey spiny-leaved Engleria that we also know as *S. thessalica*, Schott., with a hybrid *S. Bertoloni*. (It also goes out as *S. porophylla*.) But the garden-plant grown as *S. Federici-Augusti* is another Engleria, near *S. media*, but larger and rounder in the more reflexing silver-edged grey leaves of the rosette, with a very loose glandular spire of small pink bells nodding in very large calyces of bright claret-colour and furry with glands, the colour pervading the upper parts of the corymb. Both forms grow easily in choice and calcareous conditions, and each in its quite different character is full of subtle beauty, though the broad-leaved claimant is certainly by far the finer, ampler, redder, fluffier, and more brilliant alike in growth and wide loose blossom-shower, instead of the pinched close spike of the other, beset with smaller and darker calyces and bracts. See under *S. Bertoloni*.

S. Ferdinandi Coburgi is a charming neat yellow-flowered and silver-spined little Kabschia, forming neat clumps in any open light soil, limy and well-drained, from which in March rise leafy glandular-haired stems of 4 or 5 inches, breaking out into a loose spray of some eight or ten stalked stars of a virulently brilliant yellow.

It is a notably free flowerer, and seems to rejoice in the fullest sunshine.

S. × *Fergusonii* is a red-flowered Mossy of the same blood and use as *S.* × *Guildford Seedling*—that is, emanating from the false " *S. Rhei* " —a plant of real value and ease and brilliance.

S. filicaulis is a small Himalayan high-alpine with minutely toothed foliage, narrowly oblong. The stems of 2 or 3 inches are all glandular-hairy, and much branched, each spray carrying a single flower, white or yellow.

S. fimbriata stands almost undistinguishably near *S. brachypoda*, but that the stems carry bulbils, and also two or three golden flowers instead of only one.

S. flagellaris belongs to the Trachyphyllum group, and is sadly rare in cultivation, to which it does not seem always to take kindly. It has wholly the habit of *S. Brunoniana*, but the leaves of the main rosettes are much broader, oblong-obovate, more or less glandular-hairy, more or less stiffly fringed, and often with a final spinule or bristle at their tip. They throw innumerable plant-buds on long red arching threads, and the leafy flower-shoot of 2 or 3 inches is densely hairy with glands, and carries either one bright golden blossom or several in a truss. It seems that this should have a more artificially alpine situation than is exacted by *S. Brunoniana*, and go into the gritty underground-watered moraine.

S. florulenta can never be mistaken for anything else, whether in rosette or in flower. It is a tragic and splendid old species, lingering on, alone in the race, in the gaunt cold precipices of granite here and there at great elevations in a limited district of the Maritime Alps, from the Enchastraye in the West to the Rocca del Abisso over the Col de Tenda in the East. There in the stark red-grey walls it hangs, making a broad rosette of almost uncanny splendour, with glassy-smooth leaves, quite narrow, and of perfect brilliant sombre green without the least touch of beading or silver, stiff and hard and sharply ciliated at their edges, running out into a point so acute that a healthy tuft is as prickly and ticklish to handle as holly or a bough of gorse. It has some affinities to a large rosette of *S. longifolia*, if this can be imagined spiny-pointed and of solemn emerald. But whereas *S. longifolia* always has its foliage splayed outwards and backwards against the rock, so as to receive the gifts of heaven un-impeded, *S. florulenta* always remains incurved like an angry dark-green sea-anemone, and never begins to unfurl its foliage until the moment comes for it to flower and die. This often takes many years ; the plant can live in unfavouring crannies to an enormous age, forming a deepening and ever-deepening column of dead foliage from bygone seasons, carrying the current rosette at the end, until at last the tuft has strength to flower, or else dies fruitless on its ledge, and there hangs black and stark until the winds of winter dislodge the corpse, and it drifts down on to the snow-fields far below, there to roll desolately to and fro, like some draggled tuft of a black poodle's tail. In happier circumstances, however, it is not slow to flower, but hurries rapidly to its end ; among many thousands of spikes I have never seen one sent up from an aged and unsuccessful plant. It is always in rich chinks that the royal rosette grows wider and wider, and spinier and spinier from year to year, forming a solid imbricated thorny disk of darkness in the austere precipice, of effect more tremendous than in any other of its race. And then, if happy, the saucer of rich green spines flattens out about the fourth or fifth year, and up rises the stout, leafy, and densely-glandular flower-spike, herald of the end. Late in the summer it unfolds—a grand stiff fox-brush after the style of *S. longifolia*, of rose-purple bells emerging from large and glandular sticky calyces. The spike then sets seed, scatters it broadcast, and dies. In the garden two points are to be remembered. The first is the rosette's absolute and unvarying insistence on a horizontal position. No cat hates moisture so much ; it will never be seen happy except wedged tight into the crannies of an impenetrable sheer granite preci-pice, or perhaps huddled under stones in some silt-bed into which it has seeded down, but where it will not long survive unless it can grow on its side, sheltered by rocks, with the incurving leaves shielding its heart from moisture. If this is remembered the plant is not by any means difficult to grow, in any very richly-soiled rain-shielded crevice, whether calcareous or no. But it requires the most careful handling. Like many other offensive spiky people, *S. florulenta* is extraordinarily sensitive on its own account. Its leaves are as hard and spiny as a Juniper's, glittering, impenetrable, pitiless ; yet if you bruise a leaf, break a leaf, crush a leaf, they show a delicacy like the Camellia's—blacken and flag and die, with the whole crown following in their train. So much is this the case that you can always tell the health of your specimen from its foliage; if the disk is glossy and stiff and firm and brilliantly-green, then all is well ; the moment ill-health sets in you will see the gloss die into pallor, the stiffness fail, and all the rosette go limp and towzled and dull. If, however, your treasure suc-cessfully survives, your reward, even so, is not yet. Though in nature it either hangs fire till the centuries go grey, or else (if it can have its way) hurries quickly to its end, in the garden there is no doubt that it earns its name handsomely by the heart-rending slowness with which it advances towards flowering-force. And, even when, as a doddering veteran, you see the blossom of the baby you successfully inserted fifty years before, there may well arise in your mind a doubt as to whether hope, as always, was not richer joy than any actual fulfilment. The type, of course, varies, but there is no question that the eight or ten tufts that bloomed in England in 1913 were a grievous disappointment. In the first place the spike is very stiff and stocky, in the second the calyces are very large and fluffy and baggy, in the third the petals are very short and narrow, hardly showing beyond the sepals, and, in effect, mere dim little flimsy tabs of pallid pink, weak in texture as in colour and breadth and show. So that the stout hanging spire of such bells was not received with enthusiasm or lost with regret. There still remains, however, the hope of better forms. The history of *S. florulenta* is most curious, and may be found set forth at fuller length in my book *Among the Hills*. Ardoino's account is a cento of errors that have begotten further errors (as in H. Macmillan's book on the Riviera), and the facts of the tale are these. The plant was discovered by Molinari in 1820, named and figured by Moretti in 1824. After this all trace and tradition of it was lost, and for many years the notion of a great rose-spired Euaeizoon, clinging in the stark and sunless granites round the Argentera, was taken to be such a mere myth that the name was transferred to *S. lingulata lantoscana*, an error that now lingers only in the last Kew Hand List, where the oldest and loneliest species of its race still figures as the false synonym of a variety in a wide and common type. In 1840, however, Brémond and Barla went collecting one day up the valley of the Madonna della Finestra. At lunch they foregathered at the Hospice of Our Lady of the Window with an unknown English tourist (who has always remained nameless), and afterwards the three went wandering separately among the huge cliffs and gaunt granitic needles that enclose the little shrine in a goblet of silence. At the end of the day they gathered there again to compare notes of their finds; the two experienced collectors produced mountain-flowers in goodly store, but nothing of especial note. And then the unwitting stranger opened his box, filled with a hundred things of which he knew no name. And among them lay a certain mythical stiff spike beset with hanging bells of pink ! *S. florulenta* was never lost again, but all subsequent botanists have taken their pride in having a good acquaintance with it. The ways are hard and stern and far ; yet, high up in some districts of the Maritimes there is no lack of the royal stately Saxifrage hanging from the sheer grim cliffs ; in sombre splendour of the rosette alone, the most exciting spectacle of those or any other Alps, no matter what may be the subsequent bathos of the flowers. And it must be remembered that these are not fairly to be judged by collected plants, miserable and sulky from removal, with all their hard and glossy leaves now gone limp and dull and dishevelled as an unkempt wig, sending up the flower-spike in a last pathetic fury of despair. But that same spike, a fox-brush of 18 inches, stiff and regal from the regal glossy disk of the dark rosette, would tell a very different tale of flower and colour in their normally developed force and amplitude.

S. Forbesii is an American woodland species of the Boraphila group, more worth admitting than many, perhaps, to cool corners of the garden, as its flowers are said to be pure-white, instead of dingy greenish-white, borne on stems of 2 or 4 feet high.

S. Forrestii is a new Chinese species of the Bergenia group.

S. Forsteri of gardens may mean anything that the gardener chooses. One false form is a hybrid, probably, of *S. aeizoon* and *S. cuneifolia*, that is to say, the same thing as *S. × Zimmeteri*, or closely akin, a most choice and delicate small cross with neat rosettes, and very dainty little sprays of white stars on stems of 3 inches. A quite coarse secondary Aeizoon also sometimes goes out under the name.

S. × Forsteri, true, is a hybrid of *S. caesia* and *S. mutata*, requiring care in limy soil (or moraine) and a choice open place. It is a little fine clump of delicate charm, with the flowers of *S. caesia* deepened into creamy and buttery tones by the influence of *S. mutata*, which, however, is not the dominant parent, so that the hybrid has a daintiness closely resembling that of *S. patens*, suggesting a loose and butter-coloured *S. caesia*.

S. Fortunei takes us far to China, a species of prized beauty for a well-sheltered corner, where autumn is not like to hurt the noble foot-high star-showers of pure-white uneven-rayed blossoms that appear on their fleshy branching stems in October and November, carried well above the stalked great glossy-fleshy foliage of brilliant green, cut at the edges into about seven sharp lobes. It belongs to the Diptera group, and has the characteristic short rhizomes sending up the leaves and the flower-stems. It thrives quite easily and hardily in rich soil, but must not be looked on as an indestructibly safe plant in cold or raw situations.

S. Frederici-Augusti of labels is *S. Federici-Augusti*, *q.v.*

S. fusca.—A large Boraphila-Saxifrage with kidney-shaped, deep toothed leaves on long footstalks, and a foot-high flower-stem, stiff and stout and ending in a branched dense mass of small brown blossoms.

S. × Gaudinii is a hybrid of *S. aeizoon* and *S. cotyledon*, a stalwart-growing plant intermediate between the parents, the leaves having the larger and leathery make of *S. Cotyledon's*, with the typical toothed margin of *S. aeizoon's*. The stems are many from the massed larger rosettes, red and hairy and branching from near the base, with the branches emerging from the axil of a conspicuous leaf, and ending in a truss of spotted flowers. A readily thriving commonplace in any open conditions.

S. geranioeides.—A quick and ample woody grower, one of the most delightful among the Mossies, strongly sweet-scented, and with snow-white flowers narrow-petalled and never expanded widely, closely set in rather tight clusters at the top of 6- or 8-inch stems. The foliage is most variable alike in texture, lobing and surface. The leaves, in any case, always have *long leaf-stalks that sheathe the base of the shoot*, and they are three-cleft, with *all the segments* (and *especially the laterals*) *gashed again* into more segments, that may be broad or narrow, blunt or pointed, many variations being found on the same tuft. They are usually leathery in texture, but sometimes thinner, and may be hairy with glands, or else hairless and sticky. It is, however, easy to recognise by the port of the half-opened flowers and general appearance, but, above all, by the *long and very narrow segments of the calyx*. Many pretenders to the name, however, go forth in catalogues. There is also a variety, *S. g. ladanifera*, which is even more strongly aromatic than the type, with the surfaces of the leaves varnished with a coat of scented exudation. *S. ladanifera*, Lapeyr, is now claimed in Spain as a chimæra of hybrids round *S. geranioeides*, so that almost anything Geranioid may turn up under this name.

S. Geum is the London Pride with rounded scalloped leaves standing on long foot-stalks, instead of diminishing gradually to the base as in the ordinary *S. umbrosa*. All of this Robertsonia group are common in damp cool alpine and sub-alpine places, extending to England and the West of Ireland. *S. Geum* has many varieties—*S. G. crenulata*, with leaves not sharply toothed, but scalloped ; *S. G. dentata*, with the toothing specially sharp and the leaf specially round (*S. G. gracilis* is no more than this) : *S. G. hirsuta*, a very hairy form ; *S. G. ovalifolia*, with more oval foliage ; *S. G. polita*, quite smooth and shining ; *S. G. elegans* has leaves more wedge-shaped and scalloped round their upper edge, and there is also a heaped miniature, *S. G. cochlearifolia*. Of hybrids confessed there are *S. G. repanda* (*S. Geum* × *S. rotundifolia*), with large lobed, wavy-edged big round leaves, and *S. G. glacialis* (*S. Geum* × *S. umbrosa*), with hairy intermediate foliage, free in growth, but so poor and pallid in shoot and flower that it seems hard to understand why a name so promising should have been attached to a plant so valueless. For though to live by a glacier (and even this is not a habit of the Robertsonias) is certainly not necessarily a certificate of merit, yet old and frequent associations lead a gardener to connect the name with choiceness and delicacy, if not with positive loveliness.

S. glabella makes tight cushions in damp and shady rocks at the snow-level and up to the summit of the Thessalian Olympus (and in the Alps of Naples). It is a pretty packed Mossy with firm little dense rosettes of outcurled leaves bluntly obovate and slightly cloven below, while the upper ones are fleshy and undivided. The flowers are white, on minutely glandular pedicels, and have five nerves to the obovate petals. It will require the treatment of *S. androsacea*, to which it stands in very close relationship.

S. globulifera is a Mossy, forming mats of foliage, on which, in resting-time, lies a profusion of gem-buds clothed in oblong dusky leaves, shortly fringed, but without any investment of hairs. It may always be known among the other gem-bearers by its lower leaves, which have *definite, often long, leaf-stalks,* and are themselves *tri-cleft with the lobes again cut into blunt segments.* The flowers are white and minute, half a dozen or so on the abundant small stems of 4 or 5 inches. It is sometimes sent out as *S. granatensis,* and is of quite easy culture. There is also a variety *S. g. gibraltarica,* larger and stouter, with firmer, narrower leaf-lobes, ending in a bristle. It is no less easy and hardy than the type, and in gardens is the plant that usually does duty for *S. conifera.* Finally, Oran sends us a larger-petalled form with leaves less cloven, under the name of *S. g. oranensis.*

S. × Godseffiana or *S. " l. c. Godseff "* or *S. × " sancta speciosa "* is a beautiful hybrid between *S. sancta* and *S. Burseriana speciosa,* ranking very high among the yellow Burserianas, for it is perfectly free in growth, attractive with its grey green spiny shoots, and perfectly free with goodly clear lemon-coloured flowers in loose heads on short crimsoned stems in early spring.

S. granatensis. See under *S. globulifera.*

S. granulata.—The Fair Maids of France is commoner in gardens in its double form than in its lovelier wild one, with the big gracious single flowers of snowy white inclining in a loose rare shower on stems of 6 or 10 inches, above tufts of stalked kidney-shaped leaves, dark and thick, with naked bulbils taking shelter at their base. It is a delicate sight in the alpine meadows of Teesdale, and of the easiest culture anywhere. There are two varieties, both unknown in cultivation. The one is *S. g. glaucescens,* slenderer, with smaller leaves and less evident hairs and with no bracts to the branches. The other is *S. g. graeca,* densely glandular, with the flowers gathered in a close spire. The thing sometimes sent out under this name is a variety of *S. rotundifolia.*

S. Grisebachii stands as one of the finest of the Englerias, with very handsome and broad rosettes of silver grey, ample, pointed and recurving, edged with silver, and set with red glandular hairs over their hidden surfaces. The close and graceful spike may be 9 inches high or so, white with crystalline long woolly hairs, and dense with many narrow red leaves, green at their tips ; and then hanging out a long spire of small whitish bells in large and brilliant calyces of crimson-scarlet springing from the axils of short red bracts in the same colour, so that the whole effect is that of a long inclining-topped spike of crimson, like some fine and monstrous Ajuga dipped in blood and wine, glistering and translucent in brilliancy against the sun. It is of easy and ready growth in any well-drained open limy soil in full sun, but sufficiently watered in spring. It is now, however, tending to become rare in cultivation, and no opportunity should be lost of multiplying it from its rosettes or saving its abundant seed. In the Balkans it is one of the representatives of the western-European Engleria type, *S. media,* and has leaves and leaf-columns as in that species, but very much larger, while in its close long spike it approaches nearer to the other, the spine-leaved type, headed by *S. thessalica.*

S. × *Gusmusii* (*S. luteo-rosea,* Sündermann, 1912) is a pretty pink-red hybrid between *S. thessalica* and *S. luteo-viridis.*

S. × *Guthrieana,* which is like a stunted *S.* × *Andrewsii,* is said to be a further cross of *S.* × *Andrewsii* on *S. aeizoon.* It is smaller and neater, but in fat conditions will grow into a form inseparable from *S.* × *Andrewsii,* than which, however, it is slower and less certain in cultivation. Even slower and more uncertain yet is its variegated development, with the fleshy rosettes striped with white and yellow and pink in a manner most brilliant and admirable and artificial, not damaged by the loose starry sprays of pearl-pink delicate London Prides. It is most sensitive and morbid, however, and not easy to make happy for long in the open ; whereas for pot-culture in the cool house it is quite admirable, and gives a finer as well as a more appropriate show than it ever could in the rock-garden.

S. × *Haagii* makes loose rosettes of very dark green erect little spiny foliage that clearly shows the influence of *S. sancta,* which is more dominant in this cross than the other parent, *S. Ferdinandi Coburgi.* The plant is thus the reverse cross to *S.* × *Eudoxiana,* and in both cases the small flowers on their short stems are so starry in outline, and so comparatively poor in the thin tone of their yellows, that one regrets again the use, as parents, of two species so combining the same faults of starriness and shrill colour, as *S. sancta* and *S. Ferdinandi-Coburgi*, each of which is well capable of collaborating in a far better thing, but requires to be improved, not to have its native vices confirmed and doubled. *S.* × *Haagii* grows readily enough in any choice place, and looks well in the moraine.

S. Haenseleri is a rare and handsome Nephrophyllum from the Spanish Alps, making rosettes, neat and tidy, of short-stalked, wedge-shaped leaves cloven into three or five lobes, and with bulbils nestling at the base of each. The whole clump is densely glandular and sticky, and the flowers are large and white, borne in a stately little branching candelabrum of a few inches.

S. × *Haussmannii* is a hybrid of *S. mutata* × *S. aeizoeides*. The forms of the cross fluctuate between the two parents according to their respective responsibility, and the other extreme is known as *S. Regelii*. *S. mutata*, belonging to the Euaeizoons, has close affinity with *S. aeizoeides* among the Trachyphyllums ; they both are often found together, and the result of their union is that it is by no means uncommon to collect a seedling rosette of *S. mutata* in the Southern limestones, and for it ultimately to send up a much slighter spike of much larger, though hardly less starry-pointed orange-copper flowers, which have indeed the effect of blossoms from a starved *S. aeizoeides* pinned into a youthful stem of *S. mutata*. This is *S.* × *Haussmanni*, which seems monocarpic, as *S. mutata ; S.* × *Regelii* (looser and smaller, and altogether approaching to *S. aeizoeides*, though with a reminiscence of *S. mutata's* spikes) has much more of the habit of a permanent *S. aeizoeides*, forming into loose tumbled masses of small rosettes. Their culture is easy in cool damp places of limy soil.

S. hederacea is a small annual Cymbalaria, with bright green rather fleshy foliage like that of the Toad-flax. It may be known among all its kin by the abundant stars which are *white* instead of golden. Damp places, from Sicily to Asia Minor.

S. hedraeantha is yet another name for *S. porophylla*.

S. Hervierii is a little annual Nephrophyllum from Spain, with red glandular stems and nodding white cups. It has neither bulbils nor beauty.

S. heucherifolia differs only, if validly, from *S. rotundifolia* in having its stems inclining to be smooth below, and not purple-spotted.

S. hieraciifolia lives in damp woody places of almost all Europe and America, our only alpine representative of a section prevalent in the woods of the New World. It is easy to grow in cool shady corners ; and very ugly, with ample stalked leathery foliage in rosettes,

SAXIFRAGA.

and then tall bare woolly stems of a foot high and more, ending in a leafy spike of huddled greenish-purple dinginesses.

S. Hirculus heads its group, and in its best form sometimes (called *S. H. major*) is an admirable and profuse and easy doer for moist and cool places in the rock-garden in sun (if water is abundant) or else in shade, where it may have room to form into wide tufts of bright green, oblong-narrow, undivided leafage, from which proceed many stems of 6 inches and more through mid and late summer, carrying a number of erect large flowers of bright gold, freckled with orange. The stems are set with narrowed leaves, and the species can always be told by the imperial of long dark hairs that it wears at the base of each flower-pedicel, where it leaves the stem. *S. Hirculus* is almost universal all over Northern Europe and alpine Asia, extending into England, where it is now extremely rare in some of the Teesdale bogs. In cultivation the type is distinctly as difficult, impermanent, and miffy, as the much more brilliant major-form is easy, immortal, and robust. This should be the one always sought for; it is the thing often sent out by nurseries under the name of *S. diversifolia*.

S. hirsuta is a form of *S. ligulata*.

S. hirta. See under *S. decipiens*.

S. hispidula.—As difficult as all the other wiry-stemmed Asiatic Trachyphyllums, with stiff elliptic leaves along most delicate dark stems that each end in one yellow flower whose smallness amply consoles us for the rarity and capriciousness of the species.

S. Hostii suffers in gardens from the splendour of the countless primary, secondary, and tertiary hybrids in which it has taken a hand with *S. aeizoon* and *S. Cotyledon*. It ultimately sinks into obscurity and is no more to be known. On the Alps, however, it is very recognisable, and a plant of growing attractiveness, forming wide flattened masses of large flattish silver rosettes. The grey-green leathern leaves are broadly strap-shaped, *blunt*, and silver-beaded along a characteristic margin *of rounded toothing*. The stems are about a foot high, green and rather glandular, sometimes streaked with red; they branch towards their top, shortly and sparingly, carrying large and full-faced flowers of creamy white, sometimes more or less marked with red frecklings. It may be seen on the high limestones of the Southern and Eastern ranges, as for instance in enormous abundance of enormous cushions among *Primula glaucescens* in the cool rocky places and stony banks among the brushwood by the Capanna Monza on the Grigna, no less than on almost all the cliffs at mid-elevations of the mountain, not seeming to ascend into any position of rivalry with *S. Vandellii*. Its size, its flattened mass, the *bluntness* of its

PLATE 38.

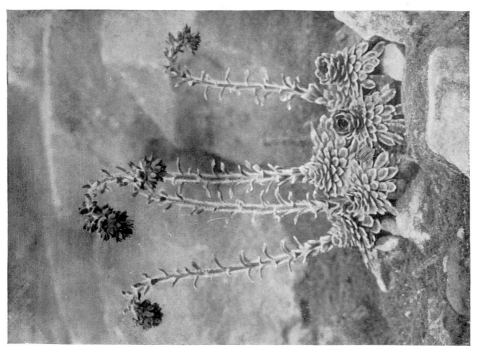

SAXIFRAGA GRISEBACHII.
(Photo. R. A. Malby.)

SAXIFRAGA × BORISII.
(Photo. R. A. Malby.)

PLATE 39

SAXIFRAGA × FALDONSIDE.
(Photo. R. A. Malby.)

SAXIFRAGA × HAAGII.
(Photo. R. A. Malby.)

outspread grey-and-silver leaves, and their *rounded beading*, clearly distinguish *S. Hostii* among its kin. In the garden it is as vigorous everywhere as it is at home.

S. Huettiana has the foliage of *S. hederacea* and the yellow stars of *S. Cymbalaria;* it may be a hybrid between the two, and comes from damp cool rocks of Trebizond and Lazic Pontus, where, however, the supposed parents are not found together.

S. hypnoeides is *nominis umbra*, a vast race, everywhere growing and everywhere varying and developing into forms so marked that they become separate races, running a long gamut through *S. spon-hemica* and *S. decipiens*, towards *S. caespitosa*. The only distinction that anchors the name to any special plant is that the typical *S. hypnoeides*, the type of all the Mossies, gathers its foliage in the axils along the stems and at their tips into oval bulbous-looking gem-balls. Other characters are the *very fine* three- to five-cleft leaves on long stalks, with the narrow *more or less fringed strips standing apart and ending in a bristle*. But at this point the species passes into cloud, and one cushion will yield almost as many variant developments as it has shoots. It is a universally-diffused Saxifrage, and its large cream-white stars *drooping in the bud* dance delicately in June over the huge mossy masses on delicate fine stems of 9 inches or so. There are, however, a few marked forms, usually often sent out by catalogues as species; among them these :

S. hyp. cantabrica has specially pointed sepals and smaller flowers than the type.

S. hyp. densa.—This is really a charming and delightful dwarf, small and close and tight in the very fine-leaved lawn, which is, and remains, of the most brilliant emerald-green throughout the year; and profuse in June, of creamy flowers on stems of 4 or 5 inches. This form is prevalent on the high limestones of Ingleborough, but always keeps its concision of character in the garden.

S. hyp. Kingii is also quite dwarf in a sheet, with downward-curving runners bearing little three-cleft leaves, and axillary gem-buds. In autumn the whole mat goes of a marked reddish tone, and is surpassed, as a neat carpet, by nothing short of *S. moschata* in its closer developments. The flower-stems are none too numerous, and about 4 inches high, carrying four or five white blossoms, pink-tipped in the bud. Nurseries often send this out as *S. exarata minor*, and *S. " planipetala."*

S. hyp. Whitlavei keeps much the same characters as *S. hyp. Kingii*, but is not so dwarf nor so close in the carpet, and does not redden in winter. On the other hand, it is much freer with its flower-stems, and they carry many more flowers—sometimes as many as a dozen to the one stalk—and these are of a clearer white. From the Mourne Mountains. And yet other forms among many that may be named, but of lesser importance, are *S. hyp. elegans, S. hyp. elongella, S. hyp. leptophylla, S. hyp. lanceolata, S. hyp. "planifolia," S. hyp. pubescens, S. hyp. recurva, S. hyp. ternata, S. hyp. arranensis,* and *S. hyp. atrovirens.*

S. imbricata.—This is a lovely little Himalayan Kabschia, in habit and in needs exactly following the high Aretian Androsaces. It makes tiny tight domes, with compressed columns of minute packed erect leaves, flattened in a facet at the end with a single lime-pit. All over the cushion, nestling into the ends of the shoots, sit stemless white blossoms among the leaves. In cultivation it is grievously rare, but much less difficult to grow than the *Androsace helvetica* it mimics, in that it is endangered by neither fluff nor down, so that perfectly-drained and sheltered crevices or moraines should readily serve its needs.

S. incrustata is the correct prior form of the name *S. " crustata,"* so commonly in use in gardens, and so often made to be, like Cerberus, three gentlemen with one name, by the additional title of *S. " cristata." S. incrustata* tends to replace *S. aeizoon* in the limestones of the Eastern Alps, where it has all the abundance of the other on the Western granites ; it is chiefly on granitic and volcanic outcrops that *S. aeizoon* appears in the Eastern ranges, but *S. incrustata* will not be found except on the calcareous. Here and there, indeed, they nearly meet, but it is odd how, in the Dolomites at least, *S. aeizoon* (if it ventures on the limestone at all), usually does so at higher levels than *S. incrustata*, holding, for instance, the Fedaja Pass against *S. incrustata* lower down in the valley of the Penia. *S. incrustata* varies in size, but is always most beautiful in its splayed-out narrow foliage of darkest blue-green gloss with a brilliant beading of silver at their edge. In no form could it ever be mistaken for any variety of *S. lingulata* (catalogues often emit it as *S. l. australis*), not only because the narrow leaves have no widening towards the tip, but also because the spike is not graceful and one-sided, but stocky and branched exactly as in *S. aeizoon*, and studded with flowers that are not loose and snowy as in the Lingulatas, but of a fat shape and a dingy creamy-white even uglier than anything in *S. aeizoon*, unless it be the very worst forms. In the garden it is as easy as the other, but valuable for the different effect of the tightly-recurving narrow dark foliage (with its remarkable pearled hem of silver) packed into dense and flattened rosettes. It freely inter-breeds, but all its seedlings, though they have more or less of the lovely clump, also have rather more than less of the stodgy and un-attractive blossom.

SAXIFRAGA.

S. incudinensis. See under *S. pedemontana.*

S. integrifolia is another ugly Boraphila from America, not horticulturally to be distinguished from *S. erosa* and *S. pennsylvanica*, but included in the same condemnation, or else in the same wild garden if you be sufficiently charitable and catholic.

S. intricata stands quite close to *S. exarata, q.v.* It can, however, be easily known apart, not only by its weaklier and rather sticky stems, but by the *dark-green colouring of the little rosettes*, and the *pure milk-white tone* of the flowers. It is endemic to high and non-calcareous rocks at medium elevations in the Central Pyrenees.

S. iratiana (a form of *S. mixta, q.v.*) is a small Spanish Mossy forming very dense but not woody-stocked carpets of bright green downy sticky foliage, accumulating in columns of dead at the base of each shoot. The tiny leaves are closely overlapping, and cut into three or five swelling lobes, more or less pointed ; there are one or two on the 2- to 3-inch stems, and the small white flowers are specially numerous, gathered round in a leafy head. It is indifferent to the rock it grows on, and is peculiar to the Pyrenees—a neat attractive little species of easy habit.

S. irrigua appears very commonly in catalogues, and very rarely in fact, *S. aquatica* being usually treated as the same thing on account of the name (even if it be the true *S. aquatica* that is sent out—an infrequent occurrence). *S. irrigua* is an annual, and a Nephrophyllum, making rosettes of handsome buttercup-like leafage, softly hairy all over, and on long stalks. Among these ascend the flower-stems, freely branching, and carrying large white blossoms, particularly effective in their snowiness against the dusk of the foliage. By an odd instinct of appropriateness its general effect recalls *S. aquatica* in the Mossy Section, with which it is so often confused.

S. Jacquemontiana comes from high Sikkim, and has golden flowers sitting almost stemless over cushions of tiny leaves glabrous below, but with a certain amount of glandular pubescence on the upper ones.

S. × Jaeggeana is an attractive hybrid, clearly owning the influence of *S. marginata*, with tumbled masses of rather larger-leaved looser rosettes of rounded leathery foliage, beautifully edged with silver ; and fine white flowers of notable amplitude and brilliance, gathered in loose heads on stems of 2 or 3 inches. An easy grower, but suggests an inheritance from *S. scardica* in its habit of dying off brown in patches.

S. Jamesii is a purple Boykinia of some 9 inches from America, for a cool shady place.

S. juniperifolia often goes out as *S. juniperina.* The error may be condoned only because the plant usually so sent out is almost always the far finer *S. sancta.* The true *S. juniperifolia* may always be known by the fact that its bruised leaves *emit a strong smell of Juniper.* The species forms flat masses of especially spiny dark-green tufts that are apt to die away brown in patches ; and the flowers appear in huddled heads on green stems in early spring, but after those of *S. sancta.* They are quite inferior, the narrow yellow petals hardly emerging from the inflated, shaggy *dark-green calyx ;* the bloom seems almost to be petal-less, and to consist only of the stamens, which are very long and stick far out in a golden spray. It clings to vertical cliffs throughout the alpine regions of the Caucasus, passing into a minute and tight-packed high-alpine variety, *S. j. brachyphylla,* from great elevations in the Eastern side of the range.

S. juniperina, Adams. See above, *S. juniperifolia,* Adams.

S. × Kellereri (Sündermann, 1912), is another new and still rare hybrid of the Engleria group.

S. × kestoniensis is a small and lovely early-blooming cross-bred Kabschia, suggesting both *S. Burseriana* and *S. marginata.* It grows readily in an open choice place, making neat tuffets of small rosettes, with rounded little grey silver-edged leaves. The flower-stems are about 3 inches high, tall for the plant ; and the flowers, carried in a loose head, are nobly ample and of the most brilliant white, appearing almost before any other of the race except *S. Burseriana magna,* yet never appearing to feel the ravages of rime or rawness.

S. × kewensis is a secondary hybrid between the " pink " *S. Burseriana* called " *Irvingii* " there raised, and *S. Federici-Augusti,* Bias. Of this it has the foliage and the six lime-pits along each leaf ; but the cushioned habit is that of *S. Burseriana,* whose influence lingers also in the larger flowers of dim lilac pallor, deepening to the centre. It should be as good a grower as its two parents in similar conditions.

S. × Kochii is a high-alpine hybrid between *S. biflora* and *S. oppositi-folia.* It has a loose and almost rampant habit, with flowers notably large and brilliant on the tumbled heaps. It answers well, if imper-manently, to cool-moraine treatment.

S. Kolenatiana, Regel, is a very different proposition from the comparatively coarse *S. cartilaginea,* Willd. It has broad pointed leaves to the rosette, and they are often red when young ; the stems are stout and red and glandular, set with more or less lanceolate red leaflets, and ending in a branched spire of which each spray carries a pair of flowers dark-red in the calyx and pale-pink in the petal, with a deeper tip.

S. Kotschyi differs from *S. juniperifolia* in having blunt and grooved leaves, limy at the point, longer and narrower than in *S. aretioeides.*

SAXIFRAGA.

The leafy small glandular-hairy stems are not stalwart, and carry a loose head of flowers on rather long foot-stalks. The blossoms are as dowdy as in *S. juniperifolia*, often deficient in a petal or two, with the same wildly-protruding stamens and in the same tone of dull obliterated yellow. It belongs to the sheer cliffs of the Cilician Taurus, and there might well be left in peace.

S. Kotschyi of gardens (*S. pseudo-Kotschyi*) is quite a different thing, but hardly more worth growing. It is a small neat Kabschia, making mounded mats of hard-pressed rounded little foliage, hard and leathery, of light grey-green with a silvered edge. The spikes are 2 or 3 inches high, carrying a loose head of pale-yellow flowers, which, though thin and starry in outline, are far better than in the true species, which stands close to *S. juniperifolia*, as does the false to an inferior yellow-flowered form of *S. marginata*.

S. × Kyrillii.—This beautiful hybrid represents the reverse cross to that which produced *S. × Borisii ;* it is the child of *S. marginata* by *S. Ferdinandi Coburgi*. The cushions are ample and erect-spined and very blue-grey, with the leaves rather broader than in the other ; the stems are many and rather tall for the tuft, attaining to 4 or 5 inches, diverging into wide and distinct-stemmed branches, bearing large and ample blossoms of a lovely clear citron-yellow—*S. marginata* having cleansed, with its purity, the shrill viciousness of the other parent's colour, and filled in, out of its own abundance, the thin outlines of the other parent's petals ; so that the result is perhaps the handsomest of the taller-growing yellow-flowered Kabschias, of which it is also one of the freest and easiest in growth.

S. labradorica. See under *S. aeizoon*.

S. laeta is *S. aeizoon intacta, q.v.*

S. laevis of gardens is an indistinct and uninteresting form of *S. decipiens*.

S. laevis, Bieb., is a rare Caucasian Kabschia like nothing else in the race, forming tufts of loose branches suggestive almost of a young and dark-green glossy *S. oppositifolia* at a first rough glance, with stiff concave little obovate leaves of deep shining emerald, narrowly edged with cartilage, and with a bristle at their ends ; the flowers sit huddled, three or four together, at the end of quite short shoots. They are yellow, but their principal effect is produced by absurdly long and spidery stamens, standing out this way and that till the whole head has the effect of a loose fluff of gold. It is not a difficult species to grow in the choice moraine or bed, but not one, apart from its variety and singularity, of any outstanding charm.

S. lantoscana. See *S. lingulata*.

SAXIFRAGA.

S. × *Lapeyrousei*, Don.   See under *S. aretioeides*.

S. latepetiolata grows with *S. Cossoniana* on the summits of the Sierra de Chiva, where, however, it is very rare, and differs in bearing no gem-buds, but forms a huddle of shoots, beset with ashy-grey foliage.

S. latiflora stands near *S. Hirculus*, and is a much finer plant than *S. diversifolia*.   The stalked lower leaves are oblong and fringed with hair, smaller than those that stud the glandular-downy stems of some 6 or 8 inches, carrying some one to three large flowers of brilliant gold. It is a marsh-species of high-alpine Sikkim.

S. latina.   See under *S. oppositifolia*.

S. leucanthemifolia represents in America the stout and ugly *S. Clusii* of Europe, and, like all these big Boraphila Saxifrages, is not worthy of much attention.

S. ligulata is a beautiful Bergenia, with the *great leaves fringed at the edge, smooth* flower-stems, and bright white or pink-tinged flowers *erect when expanded*.   These characters continue to show in the cross-breeds that it produces with others of the section.   Unfortunately the plant always blooms too early to escape the hand of the frost, and its offspring share the same fatal precocity.   In nurseries it has usually been transposed with *S. Stracheyi*, which has *hairy* flower-pedicels and leaf-surfaces *always smooth*, and is, perhaps, the hardiest and best of all the species for the garden.   *S. ligulata* has a variety, *S. l. ciliata*, which shares its vices ; and so does even its hybrid with *S. crassifolia*, *S.* × *speciosa*, which is too often nipped untimely by the chills of spring.   *S. ligulata*, accordingly, and its hybrids, should be used especially for greenhouse work, where their huge green foliage shows off undamaged, and their contrasted beauty of red stems and red buds with the noble close sprays of big pearl-white flowers achieve their effect unspoiled.

S. lilacina brings us from the Himalaya one of the loveliest of all our choice Kabschias.   It is as close and scabbed in growth as a lichen, suggesting perhaps the habit of a microscopic *S. marginata*, or, again, a fattened, flattened *S. caesia*.   From this tuffet, lonely on elongating stems of 2 inches or so, spring (in the early year) a number of large wide cups of clear lavender-lilac, with a deeper tone at their eye, and of the most strange and sumptuous loveliness.   It is of no difficulty in cultivation, in the conditions that suit the choicest jewels in its group ; and seems to do a good deal of its growing in late autumn and winter.

S. lingulata is a type, not a species.   That type is, perhaps, the most generally beautiful of the Euaeizoon group, pre-eminent in purity and grace.   The race is Southern and calcicole, being found on the lime-

SAXIFRAGA.

stones from Spain to Sicily. The distinguishing notes are the rich mats of large and out-curled leaves, very long and narrow, thick and fat and hard and leathery, widening more or less definitely to a swelling just before their tip, of deep iron-grey colour, and with a beautiful edge of silver beading or filming. The flower-spikes usually hang down, and have developed the habit, accordingly, of sending up all their branches upwards, so that the full pendent plume tends to take a one-sided effect ; and the colouring of the innumerable large flowers is of a much purer white than in the forms of *S. aeizoon*. Indeed, if their haunts and habits are thoroughly studied, it will probably be found that all assumptions of relationship between the Aeizoons and *S. incrustata* on one side, and the Lingulatas, with *S. cochlearis*, on the other, are in reality ill-founded ; and that the truer grouping will be to set the Lingulatas and *S. cochlearis* in one clan, the Aeizoons and *S. incrustata* in another. The garden-value of the Lingulatas is supreme in all their forms, all of which are often sent out as species, and all of which contribute most valuable legacies to their garden hybrids, alike in extra beauty of silvered leafage and in purified brilliancy of white blossom. All are of the easiest culture, can be as profusely propagated by cuttings, and raised from seed, as *S. aeizoon* itself. The special forms are :

S. l. australis, which is a stout and variable type of Naples and the South, with leaves of special firmness, and rather broader than in the other types. The flower-spikes are tall and well-furnished with sprays of purest white, either red-spotted or virgin, borne with greater stiffness and elasticity than in the Lingulatas of the Maritime Alps. There is an especially handsome and free-growing plant of yet larger proportions and statelier port, sent out some years since as a species from Sicily, which is clearly a form of *S. l. australis*, notable in the fat and iron amplitude of its long and very stiff well-filled-looking leaves, as in the stature and elegance of the upstanding stem that carries the snow-white flowers. This, like other developments of the type, seems especially happy on the cooler and shadier sides of the rock-work, where it multiplies its rosettes apace.

S. l. Bellardii is the central type of the group, and a treasure of singular and rare magnificence, confined to sunny and shady exposures in the Tenda district of the Maritime Alps, where it forms huge spidery cushions a yard across, and hangs in princely pennons of white from the cliffs of gneiss or limestone here and there on the very highway-side between Vievola and Tenda (always almost preferring places that only get half-a-day's visit, or less, from the sun). Its essential characteristics for the gardener are the great length of very narrow leaf, widening

289

but very slightly below the tip, of dark clear iron grey deeply grooved, muscular and wiry rather than fleshy in texture, with a brilliant margin of silver beading in the way of a toothing. These form into no rosette, but break into complicated tangled cushions, from which they rise up and stand out in every direction like those of a gigantic electrified *S. paradoxa* gone mad ; the flower-stems, yellowish or reddened, are *never glandular at all* in the type. This, however, varies, though hardly in general configuration, the characteristics of the cushion and the spikes remaining astonishingly constant, considering that seedlings are quite undistinguishable from those of the next form. The plant, however, should be seen and collected in flower ; for there are many individuals of creamier and narrower petals than the ample snowy splendours of the best—even if the creamy note be the result of ferti- lisation, when the whole spire and the flowers tend to become rather flimsy and floppety and decadent as they die. As in *S. Cotyledon*, the flowered shoot passes away, but the cushion only grows wider year by year, with more and more towsled masses of fresh dark foliage, until in the end it grows so big that one tuft is one man's burden—a bulk like a bolster. On the Col de Pesio it occurs with *S. aeizoon*, and very ugly hybrids have there resulted, magnified but not purified Aeizoons, with longer and narrower foliage displayed in a neat regular and ornamental rosette. The type *S. lingulata Bellardii* had remained so long and so strangely neglected in the garden (where it is one of the heartiest and freest growers of the race), that it has not yet had time to yield us offspring ; but, both with *S. Cotyledon* and *S. longifolia* it ought in time to yield some lovely things, contributing the added irregular beauty of its leafage, and the solid snowy purity of the flower. So far its only worthy wild hybrid has been but glimpsed ; this is the *S. Bellardii* × *S. cochlearis* cross of which one clump was seen in the slope above Briga, and which will be found treated under *S. cochlearis*.

S. l. catalaunica is a Spanish plant by now usually allowed specific rank, but, as it belongs to this kindred in beauty, it may continue to shelter here, though broader in the leaf than the rest, and approaching more in style to a great and graceful *S. aeizoon*, with pure-white flowers sometimes more or less spotted with red.

S. l. lantoscana is a firm and definite divergence of the type which passed for years as a separate species. It does occur, but *very rarely*, with *S. l. Bellardii* in the Roja Valley, but abounds exclusively farther West in the limestone gorges of the Var and the Vésubie, always local, but most abundant wherever it occurs, and showing a much more marked preference for cool and shady exposures than you will find in *S. l. Bellardii*, though it is interesting to note that the whole Lingulata

SAXIFRAGA.

group, being Southern, is much more tolerant of shady conditions than the sun-loving Aeizoons. In the valleys of the Vésubie no other form but *S. l. lantoscana* is to be seen, and on the long series of limestone wooded cliffs across the river from S. Martin it is significant to watch how, even early in the morning, shadow gains the folds and gullies from which most abundantly wave the glacial plumes of the Saxifrage. The gardener can tell it at once, when well-developed, from any well-developed form of the larger type, *S. l. Bellardii*, from the Roja Valley ; it forms true rosettes, much flatter and smaller, of much fatter and fuller less grooved leaves, curling more at the edge, swelling to a much more marked fattening at the tip, and of a wholly distinct and peculiar ochreous grey-green, filmed with silver and delicately outlined rather than beaded. The flower-stems are shorter, and rarely and only slightly glandular, but have the same graceful and abundant furnishing of large and snow-white blossoms most delicately borne in the long full cylindric spire (about half the size of *S. l. Bellardii's* best, as is the whole plant), so tantalising to see when the finest plumes of all hang derisively down from stark and impregnable precipices. The type, as in the last, remains fixed, at least in the Vésubie district ; but, as *S. l. Bellardii* takes a dwarf and stunted high alpine form (as a rule this race has no mountaineering ambitions) on the Cima Ciavraireo, between Fontanalba and the Miniera de Tenda, where it approaches a minute form of *S. l. lantoscana*—so *S. l. lantoscana* also, in an outlying district on the Sainte Baume near Marseilles (*S. Sanctae-Balmae*, Shutt.) takes a small development, thin and frail and glandular-hairy. On the limestones of Venanson the plant, like *S. l. Bellardii* on the Col de Pesio, comes into contact with *S. aeizoon*, in a very poor and squalid little calcareous type ; the resulting hybrid has quite regular and beautiful rosettes of narrow foliage, but the stems have the stiff stodginess, and the flowers the small size, the obese texture and the creamy impurity of the worst Aeizoons, to replace the graceful bending feathers of snow that are the glory of all the Lingulatas. In the garden *S. l. lantoscana* is an established favourite, which for many years obliterated *S. l. Bellardii* ; various forms have been distinguished by catalogues as *S. l. l. superba*, &c. ; there is one special development, however, extremely ready in growth, with more upstanding fuller leaves on larger and much more regular rosettes, that suggests the influence of some other species, and is called either *S. l. l. Albertii* or *S. l. l. albida*. It has, whatever its history, retained the beautiful port of the type, and is hardly less free with the enlarged plumes of purity that wave from its greater masses in early summer. And every garden that grows Saxifrages will ere long show the influence of *S. l. lantoscana* in its seedlings; most eminent is the one called *Dr. Ramsay*, a hybrid with most beautiful neat rosettes of narrower silver leaves, and stiffer upstanding stems, bearing stiffer and much less graceful spikes of larger, fatter, rounder, and less exquisite flowers of the same pure white, but with a constant central ring of much heavier red freckling than in any red-freckled form of the species. This is a quite happy grower and fertile; its seedlings show every sort of variation in the foliage, and produce, *inter alia*, most glorious giant Cochlearids.

S. longifolia.—Crown-royal they call this in Spain, where it abounds on the limestones all through the Pyrenees from the vine-level upwards. It is one of the grandest in the race—for, if it lacks the virginal glory of *S. Cotyledon* and the inimitable grace of *S. lingulata*, yet the huge silver star-fish rosette splayed tight and hard against the cliffs is superb enough picture in itself, even without those dominating regal fox-brush spires of white standing stiffly straight out from the face of the rock in a splendour almost oppressive to the beholder. It grows as freely in the garden, in any fair and open conditions, as the rest of the Euaeizoon group, and shows special gratitude for special fatness in its soil. Having flowered, alas, it seeds and dies, making no offsets; and, unless it be the only Saxifrage in the garden, hardly one of the hundreds of resulting seedlings will prove true *S. longifolia*, though they will all turn out most beautiful and valuable in their several ways, and especially in not possessing their parent's deplorable propensity to die. The form sent out as *S. l. hybrida* is an excellent type of the perennial increasing-rosetted plants that result from the natural inter-breeding of *S. longifolia* with other species; it is smaller in the accumulated rosettes, with similar but diminished spikes. And gardeners now have at command a whole series, *S. longifolia × S. Cotyledon, S. longifolia × S. cochlearis*, and so forth, forms raised by nature or art, all precious and immortal, and all so indefinite that only the most special of each should be named, and those only by strictly fancy-titles, not after the style of the so-called *S. longifolia* "*major*," which is merely a name applied, at its owner's whim, to any well-grown rosette of the type.

S. × luteo-purpurea. The only Saxifrage with a right to bear this vexed name, will be found under *S. aretioeides*.

S. × luteo-rosea. See *S. × Gusmusii*.

S. luteo-viridis of some gardens is *S. × apiculata, q.v.*

S. luteo-viridis of other gardens is an Aeizoon.

S. luteo-viridis, Schmitt, is a most distinct Engleria with small columnar rosettes of rounded lime-lined leaves; and leafy stems carrying a loose spreading head of tiny yellow flowers in large and glandular pale-green calyces. See *S. corymbosa* for its picture; but here the leaves are rounder and fuller.

S. Lychnitis is a large-flowered glandular-stemmed Hirculus from the highest Alps of Sikkim, forming tightly dense tuffets, constellated with brilliant golden stars. It stands close to *S. cordigera*.

S. macedonica does not apparently differ from *S. pseudo-sancta* (*q.v.*) except that the flowers are fewer, with broader yellow petals and often five veins instead of three.

S. Macnabiana.—This name has no owner. It is applied to a large number of intermediate Euaeizoons, all of ample stature and pyramidal inflorescence above rosettes of broadish strap-shaped leaves. The flowers should have oval, clear-white petals more or less spotted with bright red. In one form the spotting is dense and heavy, more so than in *S. aeizoon balcana*, with bigger blossoms and sturdier spike; in another, the best of all and the rarest, and the only true *S.* × *Macnabiana*, the rosette is smaller, and the constitution less certain, and the red-spotting coalesces into a crimson eye. And there are many other forms bearing the name—one a splendid and graceful secondary of *S. Cotyledon*, with ample spires of clear snow-white, gracefully-borne flowers, delicately spotted; and another a stout and useful secondary Aeizoon, stalwart and robust, with fat stars of creamy tinge, freckled with pink. In fact, when in doubt, the gardener says "*S. Macnabiana*" to every sturdy Euaeizoon hybrid, even to the third and fourth generation; but the title originally belongs to the red-rimmed beauty, which was a chance seedling, of unknown history, but probably a child of *S. Cotyledon* by *S. Hostii*, having the habit of the former and the inflorescence of the latter, but amplified. In reality this is an improved form of the thing so ridiculously known as *S. nepalensis*—when this last preposterous name is not represented by pure *S. Cotyledon*.

S. maderensis is a Mossy, once common, and now vanished. It is hairless and aromatic, with characteristic long-stalked, kidney-shaped leaves, *merely lobed and notched all round;* with large spraying panicles of white flowers on widely diverging branches. Its doubtful hardiness (seeing that it comes from Madeira) may account for its eclipse.

S. madida comes too rarely from Japan. It is a larger, stouter, fuller, more profusely-flowering version of *S. cortusaefolia*, with more bluntly-lobed leaves, and hairy all over.

S. Malyi of some gardens is *S.* × *apiculata*, *q.v.*

S. Malyi of other gardens is *S. aeizoon major*, *q.v.*

S. manshuriensis is a rather beautiful pink-flowered novelty closely allied to *S. Geum* and *S. umbrosa*—in fact a glorified London Pride of rosier bloom.

SAXIFRAGA.

S. marginata is the grandest of the truss-flowered Kabschias. It forms tumbled little mats and carpets of leathery green rounded foliage, shortly strap-shaped, with a very conspicuous edge of limy whiteness, arranged in dense rosettes. The stems, of 2 inches or more, are many and stout, reddish to a certain extent with glands, and beset with leafy bracts of the same colour. The flowers are borne in loose heads, and are goodly and ample-petalled, pure brilliant white, recurving at the height of their bloom. It grows with the utmost readiness in open limy places, having the vigour of the carpet-Kabschias, together with the beauty, and more than the beauty, of the choicest. The type varies in size and development, and varietal names have been vainly affixed. In especial, there is no difference between *S. marginata* and *S.* " *Rocheliana*," which is merely a later and therefore invalid synonym for the earlier name. But *S. coriophylla* is a marked form, being a high-alpine development of *S. marginata*, with smaller flowers on stems of an inch, which usually carries only two. The leaves also are much smaller and rounder, packed in tighter, more densely-overlapping rosettes, so that their silver margin becomes more conspicuous. It stands out as quite distinct beside typical *S. marginata*, but there is no abiding character to distinguish them. However, the thing advertised under this name in catalogues, or as *S. Rocheliana coriophylla*, is never anything more than some slightly divergent form of *S. marginata*. The true *S. m. coriophylla* may, however, sometimes be acquired by accident from nurseries, that offer it, or used to, under the name of *S. scardica*. (*S.* " *Rocheliana* " *lutea* is now being sent out ; this is a plant standing near *S. pseudo-Kotschyi*, with ragged pale-yellow stars on a fuller spike, in some ways suggestive of *S. marginata*.)

S. Maweana is now a rare treasure. It is a large lax Mossy from Morocco, which has the singular property of seeming to die away in withered strings, and then breaks out triumphantly anew in big tri-lobed, re-lobed leafage of bright soft green, producing characteristic gem-buds. The stems are leafy, and purpled at the base, sending up stout branching showers of some half a dozen or more large white flowers as big as in *S. granulata*, whose size, not less than the plant's lax habit, distinguish it from the allied *S. cuneata*, and the gemless *S. geranioeides* which is like it in shape of leaf. It must have a specially warm and sheltered position if it is to be kept happy for long. Its beauty calls for care, and its habit defies it.

S. media is the Western type of the Eastern European Englerias, that confused and confusing group. It is a limestone species of the Pyrenees, growing with *S. aretioeides* and freely hybridising in the rocks at medium elevations. It forms columnar tufts of small oval grey leathery leaves, recurving and overlapping, with a broad rim of limy cartilage. The stems are 3 or 4 inches high, red, and densely clad in glandular red-tipped hairs, that are also thick on all parts of the few-flowered, *freely-branching* flower-spray. The blossoms are small and pink, hardly emerging from the great crimson-velvet furry bells of the calyx, which in itself is as attractive as any flower. So much so that we may regret the expressive epithet *S. calyciflora*, Lap., under which it is sometimes sold; unfortunately Gouan's name of *S. media* (which seems singularly unmeaning) antedates the other by ten years, and so must stand. In the group its nearest relations seem the plant known as *S. Stribnryi*, and the other *S. Federici-Augusti*, of gardens; it offers no difficulty, but does not like torrid sun, thriving in light limy soil, or moraine, well-drained and in the less baking aspects of the rock-work.

S. Mertensiana strikes out a new line among the American Boraphilas in being really desirable, no less than of easy culture in reasonably cool and moist conditions. The basal leaves stand up on long stems, and are dark-green and nearly round, with their edges cut into wedge-shaped lobes; and in the middle comes up the widely-branching inflorescence, about 18 inches high, with each spray carrying a white, red-anthered star, and red bulbils below in clusters, till the whole effect is that of a loose generous shower of pink and white blossoms. It is rare, and ought to be quite common.

S. micrantha is a Himalayan Boraphila, shy in growth, and dowdy in bloom, and altogether unworthy of further notice.

S. micranthidifolia=*S. erosa*, Pursh., *q.v.*

S. Milesii is a variety of *S. ligulata*, *q.v.*

S. minima. See under *S. aeizoon*, of which it is a variety.

S. mixta is a small aromatic high-alpine Mossy, in the kinship, of the value, and for the treatment, of *S. exarata*. The tidy rosettes are packed with leaves, all incurving while they are young and spreading flat out when older, to show *three parallel blunt lobes* of varying length, with a *broad channel along each*, running down into the broad leaf-stalk. This channel at once distinguishes the species from all forms of *S. moschata* and *S. muscoeides*, even if it were not to be known at once by the *dense coat of white glandular hair* in which the whole plant is clothed. The flowers are of creamy colour, gathered in heads at the top of short stems of an inch or two. It is sometimes offered as *S. pubescens* (DC.); and *S. iratiana* (Schott) is a denser high-alpine variety, with the leaves sticky and more freely lobed, with stars of clearer white often veined with purple. This in its turn is often sent out as *S. groenlandica* (Lap.).

SAXIFRAGA.

S. montafoniensis is a form of *S. Cotyledon* from Montafon in the Eastern Alps. It has no special distinction ; the spikes are stiff and often red, while the small starry galaxies have more or less of red-spotting.

S. montenegrina is an Engleria, in the kinship of *S. Griesbachi* and *S. Stribnryi*.

S. moschata, Wulf., is the common dwarf little carpeting Mossy with stems of an inch or two, carrying flowers that vary from creamy-white to rose and red, all over the pleasant mats of smooth and hairless bright-green leaves, tri-cleft into long, blunt, and more or less *parallel lobes without channelling*. It is so variable a species, and with so vast a range over all the Alps, that it has been more justly named *S. varians* (Sieb.). Typically it is rather a dull little plant on the hills, the blossoms being of indecisive greenish-red or dulled-yellow tones. In the garden, however, it develops better varieties, and is of use as a carpet-plant, being so dwarf and neat and spreading in habit. But it must be remembered that most of the well-coloured red-flowered small Mossies sent out as *S. moschata* (or, more usually, *S. " mus-coeides "*) in reality belong to the range of *S. hypnoeides*—*S. sponhemica*. Some varieties of the true species are :

S. mosch. atropurpurea.—The warning in the last line is specially to be noted here, for many are the lovely sheeting Hypnoeides-dwarfs with red flowers that are sent forth as this, which is a type of Switzerland and the Carpathians, compact or loose in mat, and with blossoms of deep dark reddish tone. The characters of the species, as given above, will be the surest guide to diagnosis.

S. mosch. compacta is a densely fine carpet, with the leaves closely packed and overlapping on the short shoots.

S. mosch. glandulosa, in the possession of glandular coating approaches closely to *S. mixta*, from which it will always be told at a glance by its *unchannelled leaves*.

S. mosch. laxa is a loose variation from moister places, being more drawn out, with longer shoots, and the leaves often five-cleft. The flower-stems are longer, too, carrying more and larger flowers, of dull white. This is the true *S. Rhei*, Schott, the garden-plant that bears the name being merely a selected link in the long chain of *S. decipiens*—*S. sponhemica*.

S. mosch. pygmaea makes especially compact little tussocks, with the foliage more fleshy than in the type, and either undivided or only three-cleft. It is also especially generous with its flower-stems.

S. " muscoeides," of gardens, is always *S. moschata*, Wulf., when it is not a form of *S. hypnoeides*.

SAXIFRAGA.

S. muscoeides, All., is a distinct little high-alpine Mossy, forming tight domes of narrow succulent bright-green leaves, *quite entire and uncloven*, which die *grey at the tip and brown at the base* when they wither on the packed columns. The undivided fleshy-green linear leaves reveal its identity at once beyond all possibility of doubt. The stems are slender, 2 inches high or so, thrown up in rich profusion, and carrying two or three stars of soft white. It may be seen in every alpine chain from the Pyrenees to the Balkans; and may easily be grown in the underground-watered moraine-bed. *S. planifolia* is a synonym, the name having been applied to what is only a small stunted form of the species; and so is *S. tenera*. There is also a variety with yellow petals, distinguished as *S. m. citrina*.

S. mutata stands alone in the race, a species like no other, which has borrowed the rosettes of *S. Cotyledon*, and on Cotyledon's spike has scantily arranged a shower of blossoms stolen from *S. aeizoeides*. It is a child of the limestone in the Southern Alps, often seen in silty and shady moist places; but then, again, no less happy in the open sunny fine calcareous screes, as on the Southern slopes of the Cima Tombea, by the Bocca Lorina. The rosettes are most distinct; for though they have the size and the general shape of the leaf as you see it in *S. Cotyledon*, here the foliage is shorter, more condensed, stiffer, in a more regular and overlapping design, and of a quite characteristic dark and dull grey-green tone, with a suggestion of gloss (that gives it at once the look of a shade-loving plant), and round the edge a fine lacerated fringe of membrane. And shade-loving it certainly is in the garden—thriving heartily in moist, cool, and umbrageous corners of the rock-work, where it nobly fills a crevice with its sombre expanded starfishes of foliage. Very rarely in the garden, though, does it form more than one crown; which is inconvenient, as after flowering the plant seeds and dies as surely as *S. longifolia* and *S. florulenta* (though tufted specimens are also found of both these, but most exceptionally). In nature, however, it often makes masses of seven or eight rosettes, from which the foot-high spires of squinny long-rayed orange stars are sent up, perhaps, from two or three, leaving hope that though each flowering rosette will surely die, the cushion may perhaps continue. It is not surprising that this strange species has proved a parent both ways with *S. aeizoeides*, whose flowers it has borrowed (see under *S. × Haussmannii*). If it would do as much with *S. Cotyledon*, to whom it is equally in debt for its foliage, we should be on our way to a fine pyramid-Saxifrage with golden or lemony flowers.

S. neglecta may continue to justify its name. It stands near *S. stellaris*.

SAXIFRAGA.

S. Nelsoniana is a dense tuffet from Arctic America, with the flowers of *S. nivalis*.

S. " nepalensis."—The history of this preposterous name is probably something as follows. A handsome hybrid Euaeizoon appeared, being clearly the result of *S. Cotyledon* with, probably, *S. Hostii*, but, as was then thought, *S. lingulata*. Now *S. ligulata* is a Himalayan Bergenia, and what more easy than for catalogues to confuse *S. lingulata* with *S. ligulata ?* Accordingly, the supposed result of *S. lingulata* was transferred to the responsibility of *S. ligulata*, and, to supply it with local colour, was given a local habitation and a name, from a part of the world where no Euaeizoon Saxifrage exists (the whole group being confined to Europe and the far North, with an extension of *S. aeizoon* by the Arctic Islands into America). In cultivation the hybrid is a tall grower, stalwart and free, with varying characters suggesting *S. altissima* and *S. Hostii*, no less than *S. Cotyledon*. The white flowers are less heavily freckled with red than in the best forms of *S. Macnabiana*, which is merely an improved version of this.

S. nervosa, Vill., is a dwarf form of *S. exarata*, *q.v.* In gardens the name is often used for little Mossies of the Hypnoeides group.

S. nivalis is a rare native, and our only Boraphila. High up in the Lake country, Snowdon, and Scotland, it makes dark tight rosettes of very thick and leathery sombre obovate leaves, wavy and scalloped at their edge; in the middle comes up a naked little stem of 3 inches or so, bearing a huddled head of small white stars. It grows easily, but, apart from its interest as a native alpine, has no conspicuous beauty or charm.

S. nootkana stands near *S. stellaris* in the Boraphila group. It is sometimes called *S. stellaris Brunoniana*, and also *S. leucanthemifolia Brunoniana*. All three species, together with the Himalayan *S. strigosa*, may be held to be comparatively recent developments of a common original, probably arising in Northern Asia. The essential oddity of *S. nootkana* is that while the main branches on the sprays end in a perfect flower, the lateral ones always bear only red bulbils that drop off and propagate the plant. *S. strigosa* has the same habit, and it occasionally appears even in *S. stellaris*.

S. notata=*S. aeizoon notata, q.v.*

S. nutans comes in the neighbourhood of *S. diversifolia*. It is a tufted species of the Hirculus group, with stems of 10 inches or so ending in nodding spires of pale-yellow blossoms, whose calyces are densely glandular and dotted with black. (High alps of Sikkim.)

S. × *Obristii* is a delightful hybrid between *S. marginata* and *S. Burseriana*. It forms goodly blue-grey tuffets in any good limy place

298

PLATE 40.

SAXIFRAGA LONGIFOLIA.
(Photo. E. Heinrich.)

SAXIFRAGA OPPOSITIFOLIA.
(Photo. R. A. Malby.)

PLATE 41

SAXIFRAGA RETUSA.
(Photo. R. A. Malby.)

SAXIFRAGA STRACHEYI.
(Photo. R.B.G., Edinburgh.)

such as is set apart for the best Kabschias, and on the packed shoots spreads out narrow leaves which have the blue look and the point of *S. Burseriana*, though they are not so long and rather wider, as well as shorter than in *S. marginata*. The flower-stems are many, stout as in *S. marginata*, and red as in many forms of *S. Burseriana*, carrying numerous red-calyxed blossoms after the habit of *S. marginata*, but here they are still larger and wider, equalling all but the very finest forms of *S. Burseriana* itself.

S. odontophylla is no friend to cultivation. It is a beautiful and stately Himalayan representative of *S. granulata*, with larger leaves on longer stalks, more leathery, and with many blunt shallow scallops of picturesque effect. The noble shower of blossoms comes up in autumn, with flowers refulgently white (with red anthers), rather bell-shaped but much wider than in *S. granulata*, borne on long pedicels in graceful sprays. The plant is rare and impermanent in cultivation; it should certainly have great care and a choice sheltered place in rich cool soil, perfectly drained. It is probably not particularly hardy.

S. olympica is a Miscopetalum from Scardus, about a foot high or less, differing from *S. rotundifolia* chiefly in having the stem nearly leafless, and the inflorescence set with red glands. The white flowers, in their loose panicles, are painted with innumerable purple spots, and the leaves, which are not solid in texture nor margined, are cut into much more frequent and acute teeth. (See, however, the note under *S. rotundifolia*.)

S. oppositifolia, in all its forms, likes light open soil, with abundance of subterranean water in spring. But it is on the whole a species of generally easy culture, though in rich soils it has a tendency to grow fat and go to sleep. It is very abundant over all the mountain chains throughout Northern Europe and Asia to America, abounding more especially on the primary formations, yet as magnificent in the limestone cliffs on the Western faces of Ingleborough and Penyghent as in the high spongy beds of the Cottians, where it makes a solid sheet of purple-rose in the melting of the snow (probably, as with many geologically amphibious species, its calcareous developments are the finest). It is a species infinitely variable, though good varieties are but rarely found in the Alps of the Central and Western chains, where the dominant form is always *S. opp. Murithiana*, which tends to be looser in the habit and starrier in the more magenta, thinner star. So that, glorious as are the empurpled miles of it on the high ridges of the Alps in early summer, streaming down the dripping rocks of the Nunda in cataracts of colour, or making wide carpets in the water-logged hollows on the Col de la Croix, it is hardly ever that an individual blossom detains the passer-by with especial brilliancy of colour or rotundity of form. Far better varieties can be seen in a day on the Yorkshire fells than in weeks if not years of the central Alps. The following is a list of some more recognised developments, often offered in catalogues as species; but it must be borne in mind that some of the most lovely forms of the type are nameless, sent home by wise-eyed collectors long since, who went for themselves, and were not content with hiring some German botanist to go and rake up a few thousand indiscriminate Oppositifolias out of flower. Some of these older importations, now grown into vast masses in many a garden, are superb beyond expression, sheeted with upstanding cups of very large and comely-formed blossoms, often of a soft cheery pink that conquers the aniline-magenta tone which is so general a drawback to the species in the individual—though not in the mass, as you see it glowing far above you in cushions among the rippling and glittering water-courses from the melting snow.

S. opp. alba.—This is an albino from the worst European type; a thing mean in the star and dingy in the colour, suggesting, when in flower, an inferior Arenaria. If an albino could be found among the good forms, it would indeed be a treasure. This straggly weed, however, is no such thing.

S. opp. blepharophylla has curious large oval concave leaves, without a keel at the back, and fringed almost to the top with long incurving hairs.

S. opp. latina is a pre-eminent variety, to be known by the extra-silvery look of its extra-huddled foliage. The flowers are especially large and brilliant, even among the best.

S. opp. Murithiana is often sent out as *S. pyrenaica*. This is the dominant form in the Central and Western ranges of the Alps, and the least effective. However, the Pyrenees are supposed to be fertile in better varieties of it, and certainly the plants sent out under the name of *S. pyrenaica* by nurserymen are incomparably finer in all their forms than the prevalent type of *S. opp. Murithiana.* They are nobly free and large in growth, nobly free and large in upstanding cups, ample and well-rounded, of bright and beautiful rose-pink flowers, darker or lighter. There is also a variety called *S. opp. coccinea*, frailer in growth, with blazing blossoms which, however much they blaze, can never deserve a name that ought to be reserved for the most furious blood-scarlets; another, *S. opp. splendens;* another, called Clark's variety; another, called the Wetterhorn variety, of tight and cushioned habit; Ingleborough, besides typical large and pale-flowered *S.*

pyrenaica of nurseries, has also yielded a thin and straggly-growing form with remarkable blooms of very intense purple rose-crimson, deserving the name of *S. splendidissima*.

S. opp. Nathorstii differs in nothing from the type, except that the leaves are alternate on the shoots, so that the plant ceases to be rightfully *oppositifolia* at all.

S. opp. Rudolphiana. See *S. rudolphiana*.

S. opp. speciosa is a most splendid form. The habit is rather lax and the leafage large, the leaves themselves being blunt and keelless. The flowers are of quite exceptional size, hearty in rich rose, and very often with six handsomely-rounded petals instead of five, thus attaining quite a novel effect of opulence.

S. oregonensis is of no value.

S. pallida has almost, if not quite, passed out of cultivation. It is a Himalayan Boraphila, with a small loose rosette of scalloped leathern leaves, and one rather large flower, as a rule, solitary on the solitary scape, emerging from a dark-brown or purple calyx, and itself white, often with a basal stain of purple. It seems hard to keep, but by no means the least attractive of its dull group.

S. palpebrata is a high Himalayan Hirculus, forming neat dense tufts, with almost round small green leaves and stems of 3 or 4 inches carrying golden blooms.

S. paniculata, Cav., stands almost indistinguishably close to *S. pentadactylis*, *q.v.*

S. × *paradoxa* is a hybrid, clearly of Incrustata blood, possibly tinctured with that of *S. lingulata*. It makes cushions of especially handsome rosettes, the leaves being long and very narrow indeed, leathery and of a profound sombre iron-green, edged with a conspicuous beading of silver. It thrives anywhere, and is worth growing for the foliage alone, and only for the foliage. For the flowers are quite ugly, after the worst forms of *S. aeizoon* and *S. incrustata*—small and fat and cream-coloured, stodgily carried in close short-branched spikes on 6-inch hairy stems of dark-brown.

S. × *patens* represents a very far-sought alliance—that between two species so remote in the race as *S. caesia* and *S. aeizoeides*. It is a rare prize in nature, but may sometimes be seen where the parents abound, as for instance in the huge basin of scree and shingle below the Hubel of the Rosenlaui Glacier. It forms tidy loose tufts of small rosetted shoots, looking like those of an enlarged, relaxed, brighter-green *S. caesia*, with the oblong-narrow blunt little recurving leaves eyelashed at their base with hairs, as in *S. aeizoeides*, but dowered with an extra pair of lime-pits by *S. caesia*. The flower-stems are slender, branching into a spray of stars like those of *S. caesia,* but rather larger, and of a soft buttery-yellow or beaten-egg colour. It is a most dainty lovely little thing, quite as easy to grow in the choice bed or moraine as *S. caesia,* which, colour and relaxation and greenness and enlarged habit apart, it much more nearly resembles.

S. × *Paulinae,* to my thinking, stands high at the head of all the yellow-flowered Burseriana group, wiping out even *S.* × *Faldonside.* It is the result of correcting, instead of confirming, the faults of *S. Ferdinandi Coburgi,* with the influence of *S. Burseriana.* It has the cushions and white-powdered look at the base of the spiny spreading rosette-leaves so characteristic of *S. Ferdinandi Coburgi.* From the cushions, however, spring many stems of 2 or 3 inches, very leafy, and carrying several royally large and rounded flowers of the noblest clear-yellow, beautifully contrasting with the bluish cushion below and the tinges of glandular redness here and there among the overlapping leaves on the stem. It is a most hearty thriving delight in the conditions that suit the finer Kabschias.

S. × *pectinata* is the natural hybrid of *S. aeizoon* and *S. incrustata.* In flower it has the faults of both parents, for the blossoms on their 6-inch spikes are dowdy and stodgy and creamy; but the foliage is really handsome, elongating the dark leathern glossy leaves of *S. incrustata,* as flat but narrower, with a conspicuous (but not so conspicuous) beading; and with saw-edged scallopings along the rim that become acute teeth at the end of the leaf, after the fashion of the Aeizoons. It is as easy as the rest.

S. pedatifida stands as one of the best among the large cushion-massing Mossies. It is amazingly free, alike in growth and in flower, the blossoms being full goblets of pure-white, gathered in erect and rather close trusses of eight or ten. The leaves are on long stalks, *fringed with soft hairs;* the blade, you will see, is cut into three lobes, and the two laterals of these again are very deeply cut into two more, so that the leaf has a five-clawed look, all their tips being *sharp and narrow,* and each *starting well apart from the other,* and all pointed and undivided, giving the characteristic look from which the species has its name. No part of this plant is at all aromatic.

S. pedemontana is a widely variable Mossy of the highest rank, but far too rare in gardens, where, however, it grows and continues and flowers with the utmost ease in any light rich soil in sun or shade. In nature it is a species of the Southern granites, extremely rare in the Binnthal and the Monte Rosa district; but becoming much more frequent as you come South, till, on the high and low granites of the Maritime Alps, it is no less massive in the woodland stone-slides about the Baths of Valdieri than on the gaunt heights ascending to the Ciriegia and the Finestra passes. The type-plant makes no spreading mat, but from the crown of a woody root expands into a number of ample rosettes, made up of large and specially succulent fleshy-green leaves, short-stalked, more or less aromatic and sticky. These leaves are tri-cleft, but the lobes are all cloven again and then again, so that the effect is of a many-segmented and fatly rounded fan-shape. The flower-stems are leafy and branching, with quantities of large and rather cupped snow-white blossoms in branching sprays on delicate foot-stalks. Care should be taken with the plant in cultivation; all Mossies that do not form massed roots, but emit more and more rosettes from a woody single tap, are apt to be sensitive about excessive moisture in winter, especially when plump in texture and glandular in surface. Therefore they all, and particularly *S. pedemontana*, should be established in such a well-drained crevice (sun or shade, peat or lime, seem matters of indifference) as may let their stout trunk go wandering deep and far, while the clumped mats of their accumulating rosettes flop out in widening piles upon the rock behind which it roots. The species ranges from the Maritimes to the Balkans, and takes many forms, some of which have been recognised, and others of which are often advertised, as true species. Such are :

S. p. Baldaccii, which is *S. p. genuina*—that is to say, the nearest typical representation on earth of the abstract Platonic idea called *S. pedemontana*. This is the prevalent form in the Maritime Alps.

S. p. cervicornis is another close cushion, but here the lower leaves are less fat and ample ; they are *profoundly cut* into *much narrower jags* that stand *widely apart*, and give the plant a wholly different effect. This form is especially aromatic, less sticky than the type, and more hairy, especially at the edges of the leaves. It lives high up in Corsica and resolutely avoids the limestone.

S. p. cerv. pulvinaris is a compressed high-alpine variety of the last, and lives upon its own decay, forming very dense domes and masses on the Corsican summits, rooting into the dead and rotten packed cushion of its underlying leafage, the rosettes of the current year being small and tight in the foliage, fat and minute and lobed in tiny notches—one stout one in the middle and two stout little cloven ones on either side.

S. p. cymosa has often been hailed as a species, and occupies a far away stretch of territory, from the Banat to the Balkans. Its habit is quite distinct from that of the type, being much smaller and tighter, and the leafage all densely *clothed in long hairs*, with short stems carrying a much closer cluster of smaller and most delicate-pedicelled white flowers with the calyx-lobes rounder and larger than in the rest.

S. p. incudinensis also belongs to the Corsican summits. This makes tight and flat massed tuffets, like those of *S. p. minor*, but the leaves are smaller, with lobes shorter and fatter, the whole being much more glandular-downy, almost running to a little soft beard at the tip of each lobe. The stems, too, are beset with fine and soft curling hairiness. And no doubt there are other and many inter-grading forms, of which *S. p. aromatica*, as grown at Edinburgh, is notable for the dwarf stems and the freedom of the ample white flowers, to say nothing of the dense sticky sweetness in which the whole mat is embalmed, diffusing a warm fragrance in the sunshine that calls up all one's memories of the scented South.

S. p. minor is a common form, of less stature and more compact growth than *S. p. Baldaccii*, the type.

S. peltata stands alone in its section, and there will be found de-scribed. It is a most superb species, alike in growth and flower, and grows by the yard, with huge wrinkly rhizomes like the trunk of a baby elephant, creeping tightly over stone and soil by the side of water—and, indeed, almost anywhere. The great wide heads of large pink stars come up on their bristled pink stems of 2 or 3 feet in early spring, and then their place becomes a jungle of vast shield-shaped leaves in summer, like limp notch-edged unholy Lotus-leaves of bright rough green, a foot across, on stems of a yard and more, so tall and wild that a Monmouth might hide beneath their waving tangles if occasion called.

S. pennsylvanica is an American Boraphila, large and coarse and undeserving, with tall stout-branched stems of miserably narrow-petalled lemon-coloured little stars. It is sometimes grown as *S. caroliniana*, or as *S. marilandica;* to say nothing of the fact that several of its many variations have received varietal names, as *S. p. conglomerata, corymbifera, semipubescens*, an embarrassment of choice indeed, in the case of a dowdy wild-garden weed that is not worth choosing at all.

S. pentadactylis is yet another of the Mossies which is often offered and never seen true. It is a small lawn-forming mass, and may always be known at a glance, for it *is perfectly hairless and bright green*, but covered all over with *a sticky and aromatic exudation*. The little leaves are thick, set on grooved stalks, and deeply cut into three lobes of which the two laterals are again deeply divided, so that the five-fingered, outspread foliage, blunt-tipped and beardless, is exactly characteristic of the one species that bears the name by right. The flower-stems are short and very numerous indeed, most profusely branched, carrying sometimes as many as fifty stars of white, creamy-based, broad-petalled, clawless, and three-nerved. In nature this is a non-calcareous plant from the steep screes and cliffs of the Eastern Pyrenees ; in the garden it is unknown, every sort and kind of large Mossy being issued under the name of this rare delicacy (of which some six varietal forms are now propounded by Spanish botanists), so readily to be known by the five little narrow blunt fingers of its green foliage, perfectly hairless, yet aromatic-sticky.

S. perdurans is quoted under *S. ajugaefolia*. It is a pleasant, easy, and valuable Mossy of deep emerald foliage.

S. perpusilla is a microscopically tiny thing, forming a tuft of minute concave green leaves, smooth except for a fringe of white hairs. The flowers are yellow, arising on stems of a quarter of an inch. (Donkiah in Sikkim.)

S. petraea, Pon = *S. aquatica aprica*, *q.v.*

S. petraea, L., is an annual Tridactylite with large much-divided hairy foliage more like that of a field-buttercup. The stem is leafy and lonely, standing or flopping, and carrying a shower of white blossoms. It is a rare occurrence on the damp limestones of the Eastern Alps, but an even rarer one in gardens—and deservedly so.

S. x Petraschii stands at the head of all the white-flowered Kabschia hybrids, as do *S. Paulinae* and *S. Faldonside* at the head of the yellow ones. The tuft is only slightly glaucous, and the rosettes are made up of spreading narrow leaves keeled on the under-side, and acute at the tip. The flower-stems are about 2 or 3 inches high, yellowish, leafy, and very numerous, each carrying three or four very large and brilliant white flowers. The parents are *S. marginata* and *S. tombeanensis*—the former having contributed the number of blooms and shoots, with the smooth green tip of the leaves on the stems, which are otherwise glandular ; *S. tombeanensis* assists the fat look of the spreading foliage, and adds size even to *S. marginata's* blossoms. The hybrid is a most excellent and hearty grower, forming beautiful cosy cushions, adorned with a profusion of noble pure-white candours unusually abundant and brilliant even among Kabschias.

S. planifolia = *S. muscoeides*, *q.v.*

S. porophylla, Bert., of the Apennines and Abruzzi, is the red-flowered Engleria which passes into the Balkans as *S. Federici Augusti*, Bias. It is, in both forms, an extension of *S. media*, with rosettes and columns of overlapping broad and pointed glaucous-grey thick leaves, with three pairs of lime-pits on each side of their upper surface along the rim. But if the name *Federici Augusti* is, as Halaczy

SAXIFRAGA.

declares, a prior synonym for *S. thessalica* and *S. porophylla* too,
then it will have to embrace also the spine-leaved grey species
with the bells smaller and of darker purple, in closer spikes than the
loose branched spires and ample claret-coloured fluffy bells associated
with the broad-leaved forms. Hitherto the name of *S. porophylla*
has been associated with the spine-leaved plant called also *S. thessalica*
and *S. Bertoloni*, rather than with the broad-leaved, big-belled species,
which is *S. media*, and the true *S. porophylla*, and probably also the
true *S. Federici Augusti*. For fuller notes on the tangle, see under
S. Bertoloni.

S. × Portae offers yet another form of the hybrid between *S. incrustata* and *S. aeizoon*, with close-set, attractive rosettes of narrow
leaves widening towards the tip, where they also have a saw-edge of
sharp toothing. The stems are short, hairy and glandular, often tinged
with red, and bearing the same stodgy little ugly creamy flowers in
which the group is so fertile.

S. primuloeides. See under *S. umbrosa*.

S. Probynii, a false name for the minor form of *S. cochlearis*, q.v.

S. Prostii=*S. pedatifida*, q.v.

S. pseudo-Kotschyi is the due name of the plant described earlier
under *S. "Kotschyi"* of gardens, q.v.

S. pseudo-sancta, Janka, comes quite close to *S. juniperifolia*, from
which it is impossible to distinguish it (except by its greater and more
universal healthiness), so long as there are only the dense mats of
fine dark spiny shoots to judge by. The flowers, however, are wholly
different, though carried on exactly the same stems; for they are
both larger and brighter, with oval three-nerved petals of rich yellow,
emerging clearly from a very baggy green calyx, fluffy with glands,
and with sepals much inflated and of light yellowish-green. So that
these little greenery-gallery clusters make far more of an effect on
their many little 2-inch stems in early spring, than do the dowdinesses
of *S. juniperifolia*. This species often serves in gardens for *S. sancta*.

S. pulvinaris is a form of *S. pedemontana*, q.v.

S. punctata is a North-Asiatic Boraphila, with tufts of long-
stalked kidney-shaped leaves, broadly toothed. The stem branches
only at the top into few-flowered sprays, the blossoms being white
stars with a large purple ovary in the centre.

S. × pungens is a hybrid between *S. marginata* and *S. juniperifolia*;
the result gives small cushioned tufts of packed and tiny dark-green
rosettes of the Marginata type, but minutely tiny and so closely overlapping that hardly more than their tips are visible. They are not
blunt, however, but with a minute firm point. The stems are 2 inches

306

high **or** so, carrying several yellow flowers intermediate between the parents, but not capable of competing in purity, size, substance, and charm with *S. Paulinae* or *S. Kyrillii*. It grows readily enough, however—but no more so than do they all.

S. purpurascens.—This may be known among the Bergenia Saxifrages by the leaves, smooth and glossy, and *without any hairy fringe*, with blossoms purple and *always nodding*, on *foot-stalks always hairy*. These qualities it also contributes in greater or less measure to all its offspring. It is a really handsome species, and the parent of garden hybrids yet handsomer. In nature a wet-ground plant, it prefers, like so many others of similar tastes, a very sandy soil in cultivation, but is not particularly profuse or free or ample as a rule. The leaves have a lovely gloss, and an edge of red which afterwards overflows the whole surface till it looks like a shining slice of raw liver. The stems are stout and always dark-red, the flowers densely crowded, on hairy pedicels, and of brilliant deep rose-purple—the latest of all in the race to appear.

S. pyramidalis is a sham name for some specially ample-spired types of *S. Cotyledon*. It has no separate characters.

S. ramulosa, from the Central and Western Himalaya, has all the habit and look of *S. imbricata*, with stems, however, of 5 or 6 inches, carrying white flowers singly or in pairs, on glandular-hairy foot-stalks. The overlapping leaves are smooth and stiff and blunt, and pitted with lime. (Kabschia.)

S. ranunculifolia.—This, as sent out, always proves to be *Romanzoffia sitchensis*, which is not even a Saxifrage at all. The real plant makes a tuft of long-stalked kidney-shaped leaves which are cloven into three wedge-shaped segments, and then these again gashed and lobed ; at the base of each stem is a cluster of stalked naked bulbils, while the species may always at once be recognised by the dilated sheath with which the stalks of the stem-leaves embrace the main trunk. This, in size and habit, recalls *S. granulata*, but that the white blooms are rather smaller. It needs the culture of *S. granulata* in a rather cooler and damper spot ; but is very rare indeed in gardens, owing to the persistent imposture of the Romanzoffia.

S. recta. See under *S. aeizoon*.

S. recurvifolia=*S. caesia* (a name from the Pyrenees).

S. × Regelii is the reverse cross to that which has given *S. × Haussmannii*. Here the influence of *S. aeizoeides* so far prevails over that of *S. mutata* that its loose tufts of narrow dark-green leaves have quite the look of *S. aeizoeides*, but that they wear a few faint lime-pits inherited from *S. mutata*, as well as modified spires of orange-coloured stars after the same tradition. It thrives as readily as all this group in the same conditions, but is not the equal of *S. Haussmannii* in amplitude and size, though freer, smaller, and more spreading in growth.

S. × repanda is a hybrid of *S. Geum, q.v.*

S. retusa is the most precious jewel of the Porphyrions. It is a neat and creeping miniature, to be seen only on the highest granitic moors of the Graians, Cottians, and Maritimes (also through the Alps of Salzburg to the Carpathians on the one hand, and Westward to the Pyrenees on the other), lying over the sere brown turf like dropped necklaces of living ruby. It suggests a very fine and frail *S. oppositifolia* in habit, creeping flat in densely matted shoots in the sparse moorland herbage, packed close with pairs of tiny oval leaves, dark-green, glossy and leathery, from which abundantly stand up little brave stems of 2 or 3 inches, carrying some half a dozen flowers in a head, rather starry in the petal, so that the effect is of a short and fluffy rosy spike. For the petals are pink, and the spraying stamens of a yet brighter shade, so that the whole head has a delicate and feathery brilliancy of colour and effect. And forms of yet more special radiance may be discovered among the abundant type in the highest places of the Southern granites in July; that called *S. retusa maritima* is merely trying to explain that it came from the Maritime Alps, not at all that it wants to live in the sea. In cultivation this species, though so high an alpine, though so limited in distribution, and non-calcareous in taste, proves by far the easiest of the group—an even more certain thriver and flowerer than *S. oppositifolia* in many places, having no fads about soil, but liking best a rather cool mixture of spongy porous peat and loam and chips, in a corner of the garden not too sunburnt, and adequately supplied with water. Here it will continue to grow on quite happily from year to year without further notice, and send up its dainty 2-inch cluster-heads of spidery red and rose towards middle and later summer.

S. × Reyeri is a natural hybrid of *S. sedoeides* and *S. tenella*. It is a greenish-flowered little high-alpine of no value.

S. × rhaetica is a hybrid of the Aeizoon group, to be found in the Bernina district—a plant of fine growth and ample port, not unlike that of *S. Hostii*, and of similar heartiness, though perhaps of less worth. And indeed, since every rock-garden is now a compendium of all earthly Alps, so far as Saxifraga is concerned, these natural hybrids or intermediate species hovering on the edge of *S. Cotyledon, S. aeizoon, S. altissima,* and *S. incrustata* have lost a great deal of their value, except for the intrinsic interest that each may possess. But when *S. longifolia* and *S. lingulata* take a hand, the garden becomes a better nursery for finer things than ever the scattered range of the larger Saxifrages in the Alps can produce.

S. Rhei, Schott. See under *S. moschata.*

S. "Rhei" of nurseries comes into the long line between *S. decipiens* and *S. sponhemica*—a most valuable Mossy, well-beloved in every garden, where its soft and paling large pink flowers have yielded by now many other forms of an eclipsing brilliancy of colour, yet unable to surpass their parent in gentle charm. For some names, see under *S. decipiens*, that justly-named yet pardonable Proteus.

S. rigescens is a small Trachyphyllum of especial charm, with neat green tufts of foliage, and brown flower-stems of 4 inches or so, carrying sprays of a few especially large and well-rounded blossoms of pure and brilliant snow-white, having more the appearance of an Aeizoon spike. It is of hearty habit, and flowers in May.

S. Rigoi is a specially free-growing bud-bearing species that may best be described as an enlarged and improved version of *S. globulifera*, with much finer flowers, two or three to a stem, and as large as those of *S. aquatica.*

S. rivularis may very rarely be seen by stream-sides far in the Scotch highlands. It is a valueless and difficult weedlet, like a weakly, diminished, and quite inferior tiny-flowered form of *S. cernua.*

S. rocheliana=*S. marginata*, *q.v.*

S. rotundifolia is now considered the whole of the Miscopetalum group. It is that abundant Saxifrage of the damp alpine woods and stream-sides, with ample rather fleshy-green kidney-shaped lobed leaves on long stalks, and ample leafy branching pyramids of 2 feet high or less, with sprayed clouds of pink-freckled white stars, with *white anthers* and *sepals that never reflex* (these two last qualities serving at a glance, among many others, to distinguish it from all the London Prides). It is universal throughout the Alps, and has taken many forms, some of which have often been treated as species. Two of these are *S. chrysosplenifolia* and *S. heucherifolia*, *q.v. S. r. repanda* is by some held a synonym of *S. r. chrysosplenifolia*, and by others separated on account of the white hairs that clothe the leaves. *S. r. glandulosa* (*S. Heuffellii*, Schott; *S. angulosa*, Schott; *S. lasiophylla*, Schott) is specially tall and specially branching and specially glandular with hairs. *S. r. fonticola*, on the other hand, is small and neat and very pretty, quite hairless and with densely-spotted flowers in few-flowered sprays, the laterals always overtopping the central one. And there are two plants sometimes sent out as *S. "graeca,"* and *S. rhodopea*, both of which appear to be forms of *S. rotundifolia*—in all its varieties an easy and delightful summer-bloomer, for cool places,

SAXIFRAGA.

bogs, lake sides, and shady moist exposures. *S. olympica* stands only doubtfully apart.

S. Rouyana is an Aragonese alpine of the Nephrophyllum group, coming near *S. granulata*, with foliage deeply lobed.

S. Rudolphiana remains aloof as a perfectly distinct species from *S. oppositifolia*, which yet it in so many ways suggests. It is a most minute form, never ramping, but forming tight and perfectly flat masses, often a yard across, of wee wee packed and serried little shoots (much greener than in *S. oppositifolia*, too) that have the aspect of hundreds of microscopic rosettes squeezed in a carpet, and peppered all over with royal cups of brilliant magenta rose-purple flowers sitting stemless on the mass and staring boldly up to day. It is a rare species, but very abundant in its home, where it often carpets all the bare and open basins of fine moist shingle in the highest granitic Alps of the Hohe Tauern; as, for instance, in myriads on the ranges round the Great Glockner, not as a rule ascending to the rocky topmost ridges, but loving the finest shingles and silt-slopes in the snow-filled hollows of the hills. In cultivation it is certainly dainty, but can be made to thrive happily if planted in a choice corner of the underground-watered bed, in company with the rarest plants of similar tastes, in a spongy mixture such as that prescribed for the smaller and more difficult high-alpine Gentians (if the water cannot be achieved special care must be taken that the plant has a cool position, as it hates being sunburnt if there is not a protective emanation of moisture from below). Indeed, on the heights of the Pasterze one wad of *S. Rudolphiana* will often contain as well both *S. androsacea* and *Gentiana imbricata*. In spring all these treasures are truly grateful for a top-dressing of fine sand and leaf-mould, to repair the ravages of winter and yield a little added stimulant for summer.

S. saginoeides makes a most charming little cushion of small bright-green foliage as fine as a Sagina's—as its name so truthfully informs us. All the stems are rammed together in the mass, over which are studded the rosettes of tiny and grass-fine emerald leaves; and the tuffet is beset with golden stars, borne singly, each on a very short leafy and glandular stem. It is an extremely rare prize in cultivation; a high-alpine of the Himalaya, belonging to the Hirculus group, and requiring the same treatment as recommended above for *S. Rudolphiana*.

S. × Salomoni is a hybrid of old standing and high favour, between *S. Burseriana* and *S. marginata*. The massed rather looser tufts have the blue tone and spiny look and erect leafage of *S. Burseriana's*, but the leaves themselves are broader, almost equalling those of

S. marginata. The reddish flower-stems are abundant, some 3 inches high, carrying four or five large and vase-shaped open flowers, like those of *S. marginata*, made even yet larger and more brilliant in their pure whiteness by the influence of *S. Burseriana.* It is a splendidly free grower, and of the easiest cultivation, spreading rapidly into wide masses.

S. sancta stands as one of the most valuable of the furnishing Kabschias, and brings joy to the heart all the year round with its wide carpeting masses of serried green and hearty leaves, short and strap-shaped and spine-pointed, with pitted broad edges of silver beading ; no less than in the early year when these are obscured by innumerable solid stems of 2 or 3 inches (which afterwards elongate and go red), carrying loose trusses of *smooth and hairless-calyxed* flowers, each on a distinct pedicel, with bright-yellow oval three-nerved petals as long or longer than the broad, blunt, and yellow-green segments of the calyx that afterwards go red like all the stem. In gardens this most useful and pleasant plant thrives with the utmost ease and permanence in any decent soil and open place. It belongs to Eastern Europe and Asia Minor, and may be seen in the damp marble rocks at the summit of Athos. Sometimes an inferior species is sent out as *S. sancta ;* this is *S. pseudo-sancta, q.v.,* which belongs to the highest shady rocks, wet from the melting snows, in the mountain region of the Balkans. This has less brilliant blossoms, with spidery stamens and not so much else, protruding from baggy and *very gland-ular calyces,* and arranged in a short little huddled spike instead of in a loose distinct-pedicelled head. The leaves also are narrower and more keeled, and the whole mass approaches much more in dowdiness and darkness and uncertainty of tenure to *S. juniperifolia.*

S. sarmentosa is another greenhouse Diptera Saxifrage, also called Mother of Thousands, with showers of uneven-petalled pink and white flowers, hairy round leaves, fleshy and variegated and stalked, and innumerable long red runners at the end of which fresh tufts develop, so that the plant spreads without pity wherever established.

S. scardica is represented by every sort of impostor in the garden, where the true species is as rare as it would be valuable. The usual impostor that goes out in its stead is a small form of *S. marginata,* but it is sometimes also impersonated by *S. × Salomoni.* The real *S. scardica* is a most beautiful and distinct Kabschia, standing nearest in the race to *S. Vandellii,* but about twice the size in all its parts, with masses of rosettes built of small tight sharply-pointed and splayed-out leaves, of special spininess though rather broad, bluey-grey, and rough with little teeth at the base, and a thick marginal pitting of lime-pits all round the edge. From this arises a number of pale stems, very tall for this group, about 5 or 6 inches high, carrying a quite characteristic bunch of splendid white vase-shaped flowers in a loose-stemmed cluster that somehow gives the effect of not belonging to a Saxifrage at all, but to some lax-headed Crucifer with blossoms of great size borne in a scattered flattish head, instead of in the spike, tight or showery, or in the branching sprays, more usually characteristic of Saxifraga. The foliage, too, is unusually pretty, even among the Kabschias, being made up of those broad-pointed grey-and-silver leaves, arranged in masses of hard and rather flattened tight rosettes. It belongs to the stony places on limestone high up on the Thessalian Olympus, and also on Scardus, where it grows in such close communion with the blue spine-leaved Engleria called *S. thessalica*, with spikes of red bells from red bracts on red spikes, that imported clumps of the one are as likely as not to contain fragments of the other, suspicion thus being raised as to the hybrid origin of the red *S. scardica*, called *S. erythrantha*, q.v. In cultivation this beautiful Kabschia, rather later in flower than the rest, is perfectly easy, free, and successful in light calcareous loam in an open and well-drained place, perhaps disliking extremities of sun-heat, unless the water-supply below be especially well regulated; for the plant's one fault in cultivation is its tendency to die off brown in patches if excessively sunburned or otherwise displeased.

S. Schmidtii is a form of *S. ligulata*.

S. × *Schottii* (Sündermann) is a hybrid, akin to *S. Gusmusii*, between *S. luteo-viridis* and *S. Federici-Augusti*. It is the handsomer of the two, and one of the finest rosy Englerias.

S. Schraderi, Sternb., is a notably free-growing and free-flowering Mossy closely allied to *S. hypnoeides*, and, through the five-fingered form of this, making a link with *S. decipiens*. It is *not aromatic*—a most important point, distinguishing it from some developments of *S. trifurcata*, which otherwise it might be taken to resemble; and another point to mark is that the *stems of the leaves* have a *fringe of hairs*. These notes at once remove it from all the invariably aromatic forms of *S. geranioeides*, which are also universally hairless and universally sticky. The long-stalked leaves of *S. Schraderi* are smooth and bright dark-green, on elongated shoots; they are first of all divided into threes, and then all the lobes may, or may not be, again twy-cleft or tri-cleft into narrow diverging strips—the *re-gashing of the middle lobe* distinguishing it at once from every form of *S. pedatifida*. The flowers are snow-white and large, borne on long free-branched reddish sprays, with long petals and very narrow-pointed calyx-segments. The commonest name for this in gardens, where it grows with the rampancy of *S. hypnoeides*, is *S.* " *ceratophylla* " (*q.v.*), which it isn't.

S. sedoeides is a difficult and quite worthless small high-alpine, forming lawns of tiny packed green leaves, acutely narrow, undivided, and fringed with fine hair at the edge, scattered in long divergent shoots above a mass of dead leafage in coarse clusters. The little stems are very frail, about an inch high, carrying from one to five minute and feeble spindly stars of greenish-yellow. No other species resembles this weakly thin high-alpine of the limestone ranges, like a delicate Polytrichum, slack and frail and minute, but not in the least like any Sedum ever seen. It is a plant that no treatment satisfies, and no gardener desires. There is also a variety with purple flowers, called *S. s. Hohenwartii ;* and the typical species was long cultivated as *S. aretioeides*, a brilliancy with which it has no more relationship than Jane Eyre with Jane Austen.

S. Seguieri is yet another little high-alpine dowd of no deserts, but this time resembling a miniature form of *S. androsacea*, with tiny leaves, more or less fringed, narrowly spoon-shaped and always *undivided*, arranged in dense cushions from which spring flower-stems of less than 2 inches bearing some one to three feeble yellowish stars, with the petals hardly as long as the sepals. It likes the uppermost peat-beds in stony places by the melting snow, but is a thing to recognise by this description and pass gladly by.

S. Sendtneri. See *S. aeizoon cartilaginea.*

S. serpyllifolia, on the other hand, may be much longed for, and, when acquired, cultivated with reverence in the choicest underground-watered bed among the choicest gems. For (unlike *S. diapensioeides*) it is, in habit, domed tuffet, leaf, and white large flowers alone on little bare stems of an inch or so, an exact repetition of *Diapensia lapponica*, hailing from the same situations in the Siberian Altai and Northern America.

S. serratifolia. See under *S. umbrosa.*

S. sibirica is a Nephrophyllum that gives us pause. It has the habit of *Adoxa moschatellina* or *Romanzoffia sitchensis ;* a frail small species with weakly and often flopping stems rising from tufts of brilliantly green ivy-shaped leaves on long white stalks, with large white blossoms, slightly drooping, on fine stems in fine sprays. *S. sibirica* has a delicate daintiness of charm, and in reasonable conditions of good well-drained soil, in cool and duly-watered position in shaded aspect, is as easy to grow as it is hard to come by.

S. Sibthorpii, Boiss. and Sprun., is one of the best among the annual Cymbalaria Saxifrages. It makes a neat and perfectly hairless tuft of small and rather fleshy kidney-shaped leaves, bright-green and glossy, with five rounded lobes, and brown stripes. It is very generous indeed with its fine little stars of rich gold, *spotted with a paler shade*, all through the summer, and may be known by these from all allied species, no less than by *the reflexing calyx*. It is abundant in cultivation under the false name of *S. Cymbalaria*, Linn.—a wholly different thing (*q.v.*)—and sows itself freely in cool moist corners. The confusion of name is accounted for by the fact that this is *S. Cymbalaria* (Sibth. and Sm.), a much finer and larger-flowered golden Southerner than *S. Cymbalaria*, L.

S. soldanellaefolia of gardens is a neat and tiny clumped affair standing close to *S. cuneifolia*.

S. spathulata, from Northern Africa, is a gem-bearing Mossy, quite easily to be known by its narrowly spoon-shaped leaves, fringed at the edge and *perfectly untoothed, uncloven and undivided*, except in the rarest cases. The buds are nearly round, enveloped in obovate dusky leaves webbed with hairs from their edges; and the flowers are small and white on short stems in sprays. Like many others of its habit, such as *S. conifera* and *S. Reuteriana*, it is rather difficult to grow, and as often missed as seldom mourned. The thing that usually goes out under the name is a form of *S. decipiens*. *S. erioblasta*, *q.v.*, from the Spanish Alps, is a stoutened variety of this, with the gem-buds invested in longer hairs.

S. × speciosa is a garden hybrid between *S. Cotyledon* and *S. aeizoon*. It makes concise clumps, that do not spread much, of very handsome rosettes, dark-green in the leaf, and beautifully beaded; the flowers are borne on stocky spikes of 6 inches or less, rather stiffly, and are large and solid, of brilliant pure-white. It is a treasure, but Latin varietal names ought not to be applied to hybrids unless a whole race is to bear it and the description be stereotyped—a task impossible of achievement. There is also under this name a hybrid in the Bergenia group.

S. × splendida is said to be a hybrid of *S. longifolia* and *S. Cotyledon* —one among so many. It has stout spikes of 6 inches or so, in the ugly and impure creamy tone of the worst Aeizoons, but larger; and the silver-beaded rosettes of narrow outspread leaves, green and lustrous, are quite specially attractive.

S. sponhemica is the name for a group of lavish-growing Mossies that on one side fade into the fine-leaved *S. hypnoeides*, and on the other into ampler-lobed *S. decipiens*. It forms the usual wide soft masses, and may be either compact or loose. In the typical state (so far as there is one) it is like a more slender *S. decipiens*, of more delicate habit, with the leaf-stem generally flat, and the leaves three-cleft or five-cleft, but sometimes undivided on the long runners, and with the lobes narrow, tapering *and pointed, never blunt*, and ending in a bristle. The flowers are many, of greenish white or cream, on tall fine stems, and are usually nodding in the bud. To the garden-varieties of this, its hybrids and its kaleidoscopic forms, there is no end.

S. Spruneri stands close to *S. marginata*, and as the species is officially unknown in gardens, it may be wondered whether this is not the pretender that often does duty for *S. scardica*. It forms enormous and very dense hard level mats in the upper region of Parnassus and Olympus, with columnar leafy shoots packed together, of oval leaves only a quarter of the size of *S. marginata's*, minute, densely overlapping, leathern, hard, and blunt, with a little point at the rounded tip, flat and faintly keeled, with a band of grey cartilage round them, and a dim fringe at their edge, and a rare lime-pit here and there along the margin. The many stems are about an inch high, set with glandular leaves, and carrying several brilliant white vases, a little smaller than in *S. marginata* itself, of which, as it has all the habit and beauty, it ought also to have the requirements and robustness.

S. squarrosa has something in its cushion that recalls those of *S. diapensioeides*, but on a very very much minuter scale, and much more green than grey. This, in fact, is the smallest of our Kabschias, making flat hard masses as dense and low as a lichen's, and having all the look of a hoary green lichen in the lower limestones and cool rocky or mossy places of the Dolomites. It is always far smaller and tighter than *S. caesia*, which in the Dolomites usually lives higher up ; and it may always be known not only by the greener tone, but by the compressed minuteness of the crowded shoots, on which the microscopic leaves are so serried that, although they overlap and recurve, only the tip of each, with its lime-pit, is exposed, so that the mass is hard and elastic with a thousand little unyielding blunt points to the touch. The stems are glandular all over, most threadlike and dainty, rising up in multitudes from the carpet in summer. They are 3 or 4 inches high, and delicately branch to carry several large white flowers, candidly wide-open and round in the petal. It certainly surpasses *S. caesia* in charm and brilliancy, and in the garden is at least as easy and hearty, if not easier and heartier, in any light limy soil, well-drained yet cool, whether in sun or shade ; so long as it can reasonably be watered, the plant is quite happy and tightly spreads from year to year. In the Alps it will not be seen West of the Dolomites, but there abounds at alpine, rather than high-alpine elevations, often especially abundant on mossy rocks in the woodland region, as on the dank tremendous walls of the Serraj de Sottoguda. From the Dolomites it ranges East-ward into the Carpathians and the Karawanken, where it seems to ascend higher upon the mountains; there, on the crest of the Hoch Obir, I found a most unusual variation with flowers of clear pale-yellow, without suggestion of hybrid blood about the growth's other details, and with neither *S. mutata* nor *S. aeizoeides* there present to con-tribute any golden influence.

S. Stabiana is a small neat carpeting form of *S. aeizoon*—the same as *S. Sturmiana*.

S. Stelleriana. See under *S. bronchialis.*

S. stellaris is a native bog-plant and generally distributed all over the Northern world, with various closely allied species or sub-species—*S. leucanthemifolia, S. Clusii, S. Engleri,* D.T., &c. It varies widely accordingly, and sometimes its branching sprays produce only bulbils. And there is a beautiful quite dwarf form of the high summits in rather dry places, with only a single large pearl-white blossom to the short scape, and this with a dusting of gold against which the rose-red anthers make a brilliant delicate effect. Such also are the flowers of the type, only carried in light branching sprays on stems of 4 or 5 inches, above a rosette of obovate wedge-shaped leaves, toothed towards their end, and of a leathery dark-green consistency. So it may be seen in every bog of the alpine and sub-alpine region (of Europe and England and the far North); and so it should also be seen in every garden that can arrange for the conditions of soaking boggy moisture in spongy soil on which it always and everywhere insists, declining in the garden to put up for long with even the most well-meant of substitutes.

S. stenopetala=S. aphylla, q.v.

S. Stracheyi is the second of the Bergenias, with a fringed eyelash to the great green leaves, as in *S. ligulata.* But here the pedicels of the blossoms *are hairy and not bald,* while the many larger blossoms, up-standing in their ranks on the wide and spreading head, are pure-white, cream-coloured, or tinged with pink. This, with *S. crassifolia,* is by far the best and easiest of the Bergenia-species for culture out of doors; being, with its variety *S. S. Milesii,* the last of the line to come into flower. In nurseries the two names, *S. ligulata* and *S. Stracheyi,* have got transposed, each upon the wrong plant; so that the useful, easy, and hardy true *S. Stracheyi* has acquired the bad name that rightly belongs to the uncertain *S. ligulata,* which has little if any use for outdoor culture, not only on account of its constitution, but because of its incurable precocity of flower. Whereas *S. Stracheyi* comes two months later, and may always be known also by the *hairy pedicels* of the blossoms; just as all hybrid Bergenias with fringes of hair to the leaves must have the blood of either *S. Stracheyi* or *S. ligulata*.

S. Stribnryi is a very handsome and large-rosetted Engleria, for the same culture and of the same beauties as the rest. Indeed, it has more than many: for its chief, if not its only, distinction from the variety *Federici Augusti*, Biasol., of *S. media* lies in the fact that the big fluffy purple calyx-bells are not carried in even the loosest spire, but on widely-divergent sprays from the 5-, 6-, or 8-inch stems, in lax and ample showers. There are interesting hybrids now between this and the stricter-spired species of the group.

S. ✕ *stricta* may also be found in lists as *S. crustata hybrida*. It is another cross in the race of *S. incrustata*, with the same lucent and packed rosettes, but built of stiffer and much handsomer, shorter leaves, more sharply beaded, and sending out laterals so freely as soon to form a brilliant carpet. The stems are many, about 5 or 6 inches high, brownish and glandular, generously branched, the branches each carrying but few flowers and often only one, so that the family fault of overcrowding is avoided. The flowers, too, are good, large and ample-petalled, and of a clear cream-white that easily escapes the dowdy tone into which *S. aeizoon* so often falls. It is the most admirable sample of its group, and was formerly grown at Oxford under the name of *S. caesia*.

S. strigosa comes from the Himalaya if it were wanted. Which it is never likely to be, for it is a hairy Boraphila in the kinship of *S. stellaris*, with a tendency to produce gem-buds in the axils of the leaves on the flower-stem. It is dowdy in appearance, difficult in temper, and tender in constitution.

S. ✕ *Stuartii* stands close to *S. media*, but has bells of clear yellow; there is also a pink-flowered form.

S. Sturmiana is a useful mat-forming dwarfish development of *S. aeizoon*.

S. subverticillata comes quite close to *S. laevis, q.v.*, but the bright-green leaves are both longer and narrower, seeming to be arranged in whorls along the shoots, and not roughened at their edges. The yellow spider-anthered flowers are much the same, but carried on longer foot-stalks, so as to form a much looser truss. It lives high up in the damp limestone cliffs and caves of Daghestan.

S. ✕ *Suendermannii* is a name given to the other extremity of the hybrid produced by *S. Burseriana* ✕ *S. marginata*. The type *S.* ✕ *Obristii, q.v.*, resembles *S. marginata* in habit and aspect; while this one approaches much more nearly to *S. Burseriana*, though smaller and laxer in the tuffet, as well as broader in the leaf. It is a free grower too, and particularly free with its short stems carrying usually only one large flower, like those of *S. Burseriana*.

S. taygetea is a small and dainty little clumped species in the kindred of *S. rotundifolia*, with roundish stalked scalloped leaves of pale colour and thick texture, topped by 8-inch showers of loose pink and white stars. It thrives in a cool place like the others.

S. tellimoeides almost escapes out of the family of Saxifraga into that of Boykinia. It has a fat creeping rhizome, and five-lobed leaves, often as much as 9 inches across, and veined with brown, on long stalks, after the style of a modified *S. peltata*, with one or two more leaves set here and there up the stout 18-inch stem, that is brown in colour, and ends in a truss of eight or ten large whitish flowers with long velvet petals. It thrives easily in rich soil in a rather cool out-of-the-way place, and blooms in July and August.

S. tenella belongs to the Trachyphyllums, and makes conspicuous mats of delicate bright-green moss in the Julian and Styrian Alps, carpeting the ground with slender shoots, clad in needle-narrow little leaves of clear translucent emerald, minutely fringed as a rule, and each ending in a bristle. The many 4-inch stems, fine and dainty, come up in summer as in the rest of the group, and loosely branch to carry some half a dozen or more little stars of bright clear white. It is a ready grower in good cool soil, and makes a most brilliant and lovely mass.

S. thessalica, Schott, is either something or nothing. It ought to represent the close-spiked and spine-leaf-rosetted Engleria, with baggy little bells of claret-crimson, in a much more dense head than most, which is imported in the mats of *S. scardica*, and sometimes is sent out as *S. Bertoloni*. On the other hand, it is also declared to be a synonym of *S. Federici Augusti*, Biasoleto, which, as represented and grown, is little more than a development of the broad-leaved, large-belled, and loose-spired *S. media* of the Spanish Alps. See notes under the other names in this tangle. This ought to stand distinct as the only Engleria with rosettes of narrow spinous leaves, and small flowers in a denser spike than in any of the rest except *broad-leaved S. Grisebachii*. But the whole group is difficult and tangled in gardens.

S. thysanodes is a variety of *S. ligulata, q.v.*

S. tombeanensis is perhaps the most fascinating of all the several-flowered Kabschias. It stands midway between *S. diapensioeides* and *S. Vandellii*, making harder tighter mats than any other species, of minuter leaves, fat and serried and bluntly pointed, standing up in a dense array like those of *S. diapensioeides*, but of microscopic size and much greener colouring, with delicate glandular hairs to be seen with a lens all round their margins. The stems are finely glandular too, about 3 inches high, or less, carrying several flowers of dazzling whiteness, and even larger than those of *S. diapensioeides,* above a cushion so much smaller that they seem enormous. It is a species of the most venerable rarity, only to be gaped at from below, here and there on some of the starkest precipices of South Tyrol. It takes its name from the Cima Tombea, where it shared those blazing cliffs with *Daphne petraea,* until exterminated by a German vandal. The extermination, however, is not complete. Here and there it may still be seen on the Tombea, occasionally in a low and open place ; and on one outstanding bluff the reverent may take joy in the sight of three splendid tufts of the Saxifrage freely growing and seeding on a cliff where no German or any other Hun will care to tread. And there are a few other stations for *S. tombeanensis,* but not many : here and there along the line of Baldo, and elsewhere in that immediate region round the head of Garda. But nowhere else is it to be found in the world, and even there is a plant that has a sad propensity to die off brown in patches of the tuft, though it does all in its power to secure health by seeking, as it seems, only the hottest and sunniest aspects of the limestone cliffs, exactly after the habit of *S. Vandellii,* but not at all in the taste of *S. diapensioeides.* In the garden it grows happily in sunny places in light and limy loam, but its tiny crusted grey-green shoots are so minute and glandular in their tumbled hard masses that they seem mysteriously to invite the invasion of moss, which, if it comes, has to be picked out laboriously with pins, as otherwise it overlays and extinguishes the Saxifrage. If dissatisfied the dome will die off in parts, as it does at home ; nor is it in cultivation always as profuse of blossom as *S. diapensioeides.* It is so concisely small, and so extremely deliberate in spreading, that it should have the very choicest of spots, immediately before the worshipping eyes of all beholders who know what they see.

S. tosaensis blooms in later summer, with white flowers on stems of 8 inches or so. It should have a sheltered and warm place in moist soil, for it comes from the province of Tosa in South Japan, and may not prove soundly hardy. It belongs to the large-leaved section of *S. tellimoeides,* approaching to Boykinia.

S. tricuspidata lives far away in the Arctic North. It is a most distinct Trachyphyllum, to be confused with no other species. It makes a spreading massing clump like the others, but the stiff and dark-green foliage is wedge-shaped and *cut at the top into three toothed lobes,* each with a bristlish point—bristles sometimes appearing also in a fringe down the edge of the leaves. The flower-stems carry a few creamy stars dotted with yellow, throughout the summer and early autumn. The three-cusped leaves at once jump to the eye, and prove the species; which grows as readily as the rest, and has yielded various hybrids sometimes called *S.* × *arguta* and *S.* × *trifida*.

S. tridactylites.—Our own common spring-blooming annual, the Rue-leaved Saxifrage, has no place in the garden except to give a diminished picture of what we shall see if we are tempted by the names of *S. controversa, S. Blavii,* or *S. adscendens* in catalogues.

S. tridens is a quite dwarf and small alpine Mossy, from the Apennines, growing sweet-temperedly in cool and peaty soil, where it forms cushions of tiny and close-huddled ground-hugging rosettes, with bright-green, three-toothed minute leaves very scantily endowed with hairs, and sending up *very short* stems of milk-white stars. Its big brother in the race is little *S. androsacea*, to which it stands in much the same relation as does *S. depressa* from the Balkans, from which it emerges distinct in its yet more pygmy dimensions, especially short stems, and scanty endowment of hair; but of which it may almost be taken as the Western development, both being sub-species, or even mere varieties, of the widespread *S. androsacea*.

S. "tridentata" is the most fatuous of catalogue mistakes for *S. tridentina*, which is the grandest of all types of *S. Burseriana, q.v.*

S. × *trifida* is a hybrid between *S. tricuspidata* and *S. tenella*, with the foliage tri-cleft after the fashion of *S. tricuspidata*, but broader and not so deeply and sharply cloven as in *S.* × *arguta*. It will take the culture that suits the parents; hybrids and parents too are pretty dainty things (for cool soils and well-drained moist beds), rather than dazzlers of any dizzying distinction.

S. trifurcata is the true *S. ceratophylla* of Dryander, and has also borne the names of *S. Schraderi* and *S. paniculata*. It is a specially handsome, free-growing, woody-stemmed Mossy, quite easy and luxuriant and spreading and popular. It *is perfectly hairless all over*, but in the typical form the long-stemmed rich-green leaves, thick and leathery, and cut and curled like a stag's horn, are coated with a *balmy viscid sweat*, and the whole plant is strongly aromatic. The flowers are nobly large and white, borne in generous widely-branching sprays, usually of reddish colour, that tend to flop, so that the blossom-boughs, to hold their flowers upright, have all to twist round and come up in what looks like a one-sided spray. It can be mistaken for no other species, for its loose and branching panicles of bloom at once distinguish it from the closer clusters and the longer, less open goblets of *S. geranioeides*, to which, in some of its forms, it sometimes approaches.

S. triternata, of Glasnevin, is an entrancing but curiously miffy

SAXIFRAGA.

small Aeizoon, with rare delicate spires about 5 inches high, of softly-blushing pale-pink flowers.

S. turfosa is a new Chinese Hirculus from Yunnan, with typical yellow stars, and rather the habit of *S. diversifolia*, except that if made happy in a cool and peaty spot it will freely send out runners and so increase on the face of the earth.

S. × tyrolensis stands so exactly midway between its two parents, *S. caesia* and *S. squarrosa*, that it is by no means easy to distinguish it from a laxer specimen of the one or a tighter of the other. It may be seen among them in the cool limestone silt above the Tre Croce di Rimbianco on the way to the Forcella Lungieres. In the garden it hardly grows as well as its parents, and has a slow and grudging habit surprising in a primary cross. So that, as its beauty does no more than compete on even terms with that of its two vigorous and thriving little originals, it is not a treasure to be passionately pursued.

S. umbellulata belongs to the high alps of Tungu. It forms rosettes, and then sends up leafy stems that vary between 2 inches and 8, with four or five golden flowers in a head, or umbel, on elongate and densely glandular foot-stalks of 2 or 3 inches.

S. umbrosa.—The London Pride, or Pratting Parnell, or Prince's Feather, has its place only in the wildest, most worthless and outlying corners and rough margins of the rock-garden. It gives also the following varieties, all of varying value for shady places, and often advertised as species:

S. umb. Aegilops is like a crested monstrous London Pride, with erect narrow leaves, twisted and scalloped and cut. It must be grown in full sun if it is to keep its rather morbid character; if planted in the shade it soon goes back to *S. umb. serratifolia*, from which it seems to have sported. In moist places the short flower-stems are almost shaggy.

S. umb. cuneata has rather narrower foliage than the type, tapering markedly into the leaf-stalk.

S. umb. Melvillei advances towards *S. Geum*, for the leaves are nearly round, and their stalks nearly bare. The flowers have no special distinction.

S. umb. Ogilvieana is the finest of the larger London Prides. It is an Irish form, characterised by the deep, handsome scalloping of the foliage, which takes specially rich tones in winter; and gathers into very full and neat rosettes, the long oblong leaves contracting suddenly to their base. This variety is notably free, too, in flower, and the stems are ruby-red, while glistering brightly in the sunshine the ovaries of the starry pinky blossoms, freckled with darker dots to half way up the petal.

S. umb. primuloeides is a much dwarfer, carpeting version of the last, and is incomparably the most delightful of all. This makes a neat and charming little massed colony of copious growth, with mounded rosettes of dark, down-lying, wavy-edged fat foliage, and countless 8-inch loose showers of brilliant soft-pink stars on pinkish stems in early summer—a beauty of the greatest willingness and charm, yet never becoming too rampageous for its place, as is the way with the others of the group, unfitted for anything but a wild and worthless place.

S. umb. serratifolia, or *S. umb. acanthifolia*, is merely an ordinary London Pride, with especially coarse saw-edges to the leaves, which, in shady places, tend to develop long leaf-stalks.

S. umb. variegata makes bright colours of pink and white and green, especially in winter, but tends in all soils, even the poorest and sunniest (but quite certainly and promptly in richness and shade) to revert to type—a trait displeasing to all who love such freaks.

S. valdensis is an extremely rare prize. There is hardly a catalogue that does not offer it, or a nursery that possesses it. For the thing which so many gardeners under this name cultivate and label and display, is nothing but *S. cochlearis minor* in its smallest huddled forms. There is, however, some excuse for the error, at least as far as the tuft is concerned. For the two species do make something of the same effect in the foliage at a first glance, though a second very soon shows that the leaf-tip of the impostor is widened but *flat*, while in the true *S. valdensis* it is more or less *puffed up and fat* as well. To say nothing of the fact that in all forms of *S. cochlearis* the flowers are borne on almost glandless and smooth fine stems in loose spires of 4 or 5 inches, whereas in *S. valdensis*, which is not an Aeizoon but a Kabschia, they are clustered up a densely-glandular stout stem, and collected in a fewer-flowered closer truss. The true species is also extremely rare in nature, no less than in the garden, only to be seen in one or two hot and sunny cliffs of schists and disintegrating granites high in the Cottian Alps, thus differing from all other Kabschias, not only in its alpine proclivities, but also in its love of non-calcareous formations. No one who has seen it can ever mistake it again. In the case of the small forms of *S. cochlearis* the tiny blue-grey leaves stand erect and apart, in a looser rosette, in a looser clumped mass of rosettes. If you put your hand over it you will feel a number of little points, yielding elastically to the touch ; they never curl outwards in a tight mass, as do those of *S. valdensis*. This, in its native rocks, forms the tightest, hardest and smoothest domes of the race, the leaves being narrower and rather longer than in *S. cochlearis*, of a darker grey-green, with a more definite beading of lime-pits round their edge ; they fatten at the tip a little, and widen less, and never (unless drawn up in the shade) stand up or apart in the rosette, but lie unrolled out upon each other so close and firm that your hand feels only a rounded smooth ball under the palm. The flower-spikes are much more numerous than in any variety of *S. cochlearis ;* they come on glowing little ruby croziers from the humped globe (often as large and domed as the segment of a football), with all the profuseness of an Aeizoon ; they are 4 or 5 inches high, stout and richly furry with red glands, carrying some six or twelve large and pure-white flowers in a rather tight truss. The affinities of *S. valdensis* are said by some to be with *S. caesia*, a relationship which is by no means obvious in nature, where the dense masses and balls of out-rolled blue-grey rosettes do indeed suggest afar off a very much tightened and enlarged and compressed *S. caesia ;* but the abundant, stout and ruby-furred glandular stems with their handsome burden of white blossom look rather towards *S. aeizoon* in their vigour and abundance, while the design of truss and bloom takes us back to Kabschia again. In cultivation the plant is quite easy, and rather uncertain. It will soon, however, once suited, grow away contentedly in any well-drained crevice, in sun or shade, in lime or peat—its curious restriction to the rotten schists and sandstones of the Cottians being evidently no part of its essential character, which seems to breathe from every pitted pore a love of lime as keen as that of any other species in the group. Nor does its equally apparent desire for full sun appear to be any rigid characteristic either ; I have known many a clump die off in the full light, and others thrive happily in limestone crevices and damp aspects of a cold and sunless cliff. Its principal requirements are good drainage and careful planting.

S. valentina differs from *S. trifurcata* in being slenderer altogether, with narrower stalks to the leaves, smaller flowers, and sepals and lobes of the *foliage blunt instead of sharp*. From *S. paniculata* it can be distinguished not only by its smaller flower-sprays and slenderer growth, but also by more deeply-cut leaves with blunt strips *that do not stand away from each other*. It is a beautiful large Mossy of most lavish blooming habit and big white blossom. The whole plant is *perfectly hairless and sticky ;* the woody stems are densely clad in old dead leaves, and spread into wide cushions of lustrous, loose, and living green. The leaves stand on long stalks, and are profoundly cut into three lobes, blunt and very narrow, with the lateral lobes again gashed, and none of the segments starting widely apart from the rest.

S. Vandellii can only be seen wedged tightly into the highest, starkest, hottest and driest limestone cliffs of the Lombard Alps, from the Adamello in the East to Livigno in the West. It forms enormous rounded masses, as firm as rock, and densely, painfully thorny—not to be touched or sat on unadvisedly—of specially close-rammed rosettes built of iron-hard narrow-triangular emerald foliage, spike-pointed and fringed at the base, and edged with cartilage, but only faintly pitted with lime, and altogether much greener in effect than those of any other Kabschia. It has no real affinity to *S. Burseriana*, but stands quite close in the race to *S. scardica*, of which it has exactly the massed habit and the firm prickly cushions; but here they are greener and harder, the leaves narrower, darker, sterner, more upstanding, serried and thorny. The flowers, however, have precisely the same effect; they come up on innumerable glandular stems of 4 or 5 inches, branching at the top into the same curious loose wide heads, like a Crucifer's, of magnificent white vase-shaped blossoms, standing each on a definite foot-stalk in a simultaneous cluster. As in all the rest there are finer and inferior forms; but the type is always a wonder and an awe, when you see the round dark masses of lucent sombre green clinging high and hard, above your head, in the impregnable cliffs of the Grigna, and waving at you in scorn their drooping tassels of white bloom—that bow the pale stalks beneath their weight, and afterwards, with stem and all, assume a series of yellow tones fading into amber. It is no easy thing to collect either, owing to its incurable propensity for precipices; but supports removal well, and soon becomes re-established. In cultivation it wants careful planting in a sunny, warm, and perfectly well-drained situation, between cliffs of limestone (if possible), or perhaps in a limestone moraine. It is not always very quick about starting, and seems to have a strong dislike for superfluous moisture, or dankness, sunlessness, or darkness of any sort.

S. varians=*S. moschata*, q.v.

S. veronicaefolia. See under *S. atlantica.*

S. virginiensis is a by no means interesting American Boraphila, with branching stems of about a foot high, carrying showers of white little stars (double ones, in an improved garden-form), above rosettes of toothed oval leaves on short stems, dark and leathery. It is usually ignored, though a place might more readily be made for it in a cool out-of-the-way corner than for its better known and more popular variety, *S. pennsylvanica.*

S. viscidula is a glandular tiny Hirculus from high-alpine Sikkim, standing near *S. Lychnitis*, but smaller in the golden stars, which are also carried one to three on a stem instead of always lonely.

S. × *vochinensis* is a garden name for a hybrid in the group of *S. aeizoon* and *S. incrustata.* It has the usual beauty of dark-green and beaded rosettes, and the usual fault of stodgy outline and rather creamy tone to the flowers, which are freely borne on their spikes of 6 or 9 inches.

S. × *Wallacei.*—This is undoubtedly the grandest of our Mossies, whether in growth or habit, in flower or out of flower. And it is a garden hybrid, having nothing whatever to do with *S. Camposii,* of which catalogues still obstinately persist in making it a synonym, continuing to perpetuate the original error of the *Botanical Magazine,* which figured the plant (T. 6640) under the name of *S. Camposii,* Boiss. and Reut.—a species at that time not in cultivation, and even now not common. The parentage of *S.* × *Wallacei* remains unknown ; dates make it unlikely that *S. Maweana* had any share in it, and one of the most probable parents is *S. trifurcata.* With *S. Camposii* it has no relationship at all. The hybrid was raised at Edinburgh, from seed purporting to be that of *S. Maweana ;* but the attribution is unconvincing, if on no other ground than that *S.* × *Wallacei* is said to have been growing at Kew in 1867, whereas *S. Maweana* was not introduced till 1869. In any case *S. Wallacei* is the pride and joy of every garden in every season and situation, with its wide billowing masses of rich and comfortable-looking ample green leaves, cloven five times or more to the base of the blade ; the stems and shoots all have a tendency to redden, and the flowers are pure white, of enormous size and amplitude, produced in generous branching sprays that hide the whole green wave in early summer with a crest of refulgent snow.

S. Willkommiana, Boiss.=*S. pentadactylis, q.v.* (*S. valentina* was once reckoned a variety of this, as originally described).

S. Wulfeniana is very rare indeed in cultivation, being always substituted by *S. retusa,* of which, in point of fact, it can only be retained as a stunted and compressed high-alpine form from the Eastern ranges [*S. Wulfeniana,* Schott=*S. retusa,* Gouan], standing to the type in much the same relation as *S. Rudolphiana* to *S. oppositifolia,* and, as it has the same habits as *S. Rudolphiana,* possessing also the same difficulties of temper in cultivation, though capable of being made happy if the same exactions are satisfied. When at last it blossoms, it will be seen to differ from the average type of *S. retusa,* not only in having a much smaller denser tuft, but also in sending up no spikes, the little rosy stars sitting solitary, almost flat to the cushion, even as do the vinous-purple cups of *S. Rudolphiana.*

S. yunnanensis is a new and unproven Bergenia Saxifrage from Yunnan.

S. Zeleborii is an obscure species or hybrid in the Aeizoon group,

SCABIOSA.

from the Eastern Alps, of no outstanding merit, producing white flowers in spires of 6 inches or so.

S. Zimmeteri is a really lovely and far-fetched little hybrid from the Pusterthal, with *S. aeizoon* for one parent, and *S. cuneifolia* for the other. The result is one of the daintiest of small jewels, often quoted in catalogues, but not there to be trusted. It grows readily in any reasonable conditions of soil and light, making neat rosettes of spatulate leathery leaves of pale green, with an edging of grey cartilage derived from *S. aeizoon*. The blossom-shower is delicate and dainty as in *S. cuneifolia*, and of about the same stature—some 5 or 6 inches. But it is much better furnished, and the flowers are stars of white with orange anthers, uniting the elfin grace of *S. cuneifolia* with the handsomer foliage due to the influence of *S. aeizoon*, lying down in neat and overlapping-leaved rosettes after the Aeizoon style, but much broadened at the end, and of that characteristic leathern pallor of green.

Scabiosa.—This race, as a rule, is large and weedy for the rockgarden. Nor are the annual species to be admitted, while the larger herbaceous ones are offered in catalogues. Of smaller kinds, *S. graminifolia* is really most beautiful and a pure joy on a ledge of the rock in dry, well-drained soil, warm and limy, in a hot and sunny place. It is a species of the Southern Alps, woody-rooted and forming wide flaccid mats of long narrow leaves, like swathes of soft grass, pale-green and shimmering with a close coat of silver; over this, on bare stems of 6 or 9 inches, play rich wide flower-heads of lilac-lavender all the summer through, making a lovely effect above the silver mass. In the same line of beauty are also *S. silenifolia* (violet), *S. lucida* (more ordinary, with feather-cut leafage and pinkish flowers), and *S. vestita*. *S. magnifica* (or *Knautia*) grows about a foot or 18 inches high, and has spreading heads of pink; *S. integrifolia* is but half a foot, with tight and rayless velvety heads of yellow; and *S. Webbiana*, from Ida, is dwarf also, with wrinkled roundish root-leaves in cushions, and heads of white blossom on stems of 6 or 9 inches through later summer. Very beautiful and very rare though is *S. sphaciotica*, from the wood-limits of Cretan Ida and the mountain-tops, in sandy places. It is perfectly dwarf—a rosette of practically undivided silver leaves, narrow and oblong, almost the same length as the many rather weakly short stems which each carry a head of pink flowers. (This is also *Pterocephalus tomentosus*, as Pterocephalus is sometimes called Scabiosa.) And, finally, there is *S. pyrenaica*, of larger and looser habit, with feathered silver foliage and larger blue-lavender flower-heads than our own wide and flat-headed *S. Columbaria*, which is so beautiful as a native rock-plant, in crevices of the limestone cliffs. All these bloom through later

326

summer, and all are to be raised from seed, and all will like (and some demand) a sunny and well-drained place.

Schivereckia podolica stands quite close to *Draba*, but the flowers are of pure and brilliant white, borne in bunches on leafy stems of 5 or 6 inches, above rosettes of silver foliage, in the spring. Seed, and a sunny place. An improvement of this is *Sch. Bornmuelleri*, which is no less soft and silky, but even tinier in habit—only about 2 inches high, and much more profuse in flower. *Sch. iberidea* is *Ptilotrichum cappadocicum, q.v.*

Schizocōdōn soldanelloeides.—This is Iwa-kagami, the Mirror of the Mountain ; sometimes it comes in from Japan clinging round the root of some collected Azalea, torn from the mossy woodland places where it lives among the rocks ; or may be seen in the flower-fairs of Tokio, in forms that make the gardener's heart go dry with longing, so bushy and stalwart are they in their tufts of rounded leathern foliage, deeply, darkly, beautifully glossy green ; and so noble in the port of their 9-inch stems, beset with hanging wide bells, fluffily fringy, of sweet shell-pink, flushed and lined inside with blurs of ruby crimson. It is the most glorious of woodlanders ever seen, but in England, grow it never so widely—and in the Wisley wood there is a mass a yard across—neither stems nor leaves have learned to repeat that free and stately carriage, but incline to remain a little stunted and huddled and screwed. The difficulty of its culture is that of Pyrola's also, and so many other woody-fibred woodland species—the difficulty of getting good rootage and established plants to start with. But, if this can be achieved, Schizocodon will thrive quite readily in light rich soil consisting almost wholly of leaf-mould, mixed with stones, in situations as shady, for choice, as you can find. It blooms in early summer, and may be raised from seed by dint of the greatest care. There is one other species ; *Sch. ilicifolius* is probably distinct, with much more violent holly-like toothing to the leaves, which in *Sch. soldanelloeides* are much rounder in outline and smaller and more regular in the toothing. *Ilicifolius* is also frailer and paler ; and there is also an alpine form of the type, with only a dim serration to the leaves.

Scillas are dealt with faithfully and descriptively in catalogues.

Scoliopus Bigelowii is a Rocky Mountain plant, standing near the Dog's Tooth Violet, with the same marbled foliage, and a flower of green and pink, standing solitary on a stem of 5 or 6 inches. It blooms with Erythronium, and may have the same treatment.

Scopolia.—These are strange things, attaining 12 or 15 inches, and producing, very early in the season, abundant big bells, like a Belladonna's, of lurid metallic browns and purples, most curious and witch-like in effect. They may be planted in rough and rather shady corners of no high importance. Among the species, all to be raised from seed, are *Sc. carniolica, Sc. japonica, Sc. tangutica,* and *Sc. lurida.*

Scorzonēra.—In this race of the Salsifies two species only are of special merit (if two they are indeed). These are *S. rosea* and *S. purpurea.* The former is a rare but locally abundant beauty of the Southern limestones, in open meadows, making tufts of grassy narrow green foliage, from which stand up, all the summer through, delicate stems of 6 inches or so, each carrying one erect Dandelion of soft clear pink. *S. purpurea,* of the Eastern ranges, heightens its stature to 8 inches, and its colour is of a more burning carmine rose. And, if a contrast be wanted with these, there is *S. austriaca,* similar in stature to the last, but with blossoms of brilliant gold. These are all easy of culture in any open warm place in light soil deep enough for their abysmally long tap-roots ; but they are apt to slip gradually away, and their best effects would be got by planting them in broad masses, associated with *Campanula rotundifolia* in one of its forms. Seed.

Scrophularia.—None of these are really worthy of cultivation, so far as the race is likely to be generally known. *S. Hoppei* in the Alps, however, has a certain quaintness, attaining 18 inches or 2 feet, with feathered green foliage, and multitudinous minute helmets of hot blackish brown, with golden anthers. Any stony poor place would be suitable for sowing the seed of this straight out, and making no more fuss with it.

Scutellaria.—These Labiates are all of ready culture in open warm corners in light soil ; and their whorled sprays of largish helmeted long flowers in shades of blue and pink and white have a value of their own through the late summer and autumn, even if their wearers, like so many of the family, are rather wanting in elegance of deportment. *C. alpina* is a really handsome plant, for example, of floppish rather square stems, and large whorled heads of violet hoods and white lips ; it may be seen in special abundance and very fine form on the wayside rocks at the summit of the Mont Cenis Pass, &c. ; there is a roseate variety sometimes called *S. lupulina* or *S. lup. bicolor* ; as well as an albino. The effect of the plant is that of some generously glorified and relaxed and enlarged floundering Brunella. *S. baicalensis* is the same thing as *S. macrantha,* near the last but more erect, with rounder leaves and stems of 18 inches, and flowers of clear blue. *S. orientalis* is minutely dwarf, about 2 inches high, with flowers of yellow and gold ; *S. rupestris* attains 8 inches, and has violet helmets, while *S. japonica* has the same height, but flowers of dark purple. *S. minor* is no taller than these last, with pink blossoms, but *S. peregrina* rises to 15 inches or so, with casques of imperial violet. *S. albina* is its match in height, with flowers of yellow and yellowish tones. The ridiculous name *S. indica japonica* stands for several things, chiefly a form with erect stems, crowded with spires of huddled and rather narrow little blooms ; the true *S. japonica* is a much more delicate, weakly-stemmed attractive species, with softly hairy leaves of greyish tone, and larger scattered flowers of rich colour, that charmingly adorn a rocky ledge in late summer and autumn with the long open-lipped trumpets of purple-blue.

Sedum.—This vast race, as a whole, is curiously uninteresting : as is felt even by catalogues, that do their best, yet can't say much, and take refuge in an inextricable welter of synonyms and pseudonyms. Nearly all Sedums are of easy culture in open poor places— often far *too* easy in cultivation, and yet more deplorably easy of propagation. The race is much too large and dim for us here minutely to discriminate. There are, however, several main types, alike of habit and growth, with species that may be taken as typical. In the first place there is the fleshy-stocked section, with erect leafy stems and flowers usually rather dingy ; this may be exemplified in *S. Rhodiola*, and easily grows in any light and deep soil. Then there are the smaller sheeting rock-plants of low massing habit, such as *S. acre* and *S. album ;* the trailing green mat- or carpet-forming section, with starry radiating heads of flower, that may be seen exemplified by *S. spurium* in every cottage garden ; another group of the same habit, but with rounded and glaucous foliage ; and finally the type that forms loose masses of shoots, beset with numbers of narrow leaves, fleshy and round in section, with stems of 8 inches or so, and uncurling heads of branched blossom that open out like the tail of a scorpion. The type of this is *S. rupestre* from our cottage walls. In these later days a large number of species has been sent in from Mexico, with more, it is said, to follow. The hardiness of these in most English gardens is open to the very gravest doubt, and it will be understood that here I do no more than quote the vendor's description, such as it is, with a note that the word Mexico spells danger, and that the names are unverified.

S. acre is our common little golden Stone-crop, useful for rough places, and everywhere abundant.

S. acutifolium makes mats like *S. gracile*, of shoots very densely set with cylindric leaves. The stems are 3 or 4 inches high, and both greyish leaves and white flowers (blunt-petalled and in a large head) are considerably bigger. It may be pictured, roughly, as a smaller-growing *S. album*, with larger leaves (*S. Calverti*, Boiss.).

S. adenotrichum grows from 3 to 9 inches high or long, with the glandular-downy leaves rosetted at the base of the stems, which often diverge into drawn-out branches, and are loosely set with acute-petalled white stars banded with pink. (Sikkim.)

S. aeizoon is close to *S. kamschaticum*, the yellow-flowered *S. spurium*, but is not so creeping, smaller in all its parts, and with more numerous golden blossoms packed into a tighter, flatter head of sprays, nestling among the uppermost stem-leaves that overtop them all round.

S. alamosanum is bright pink, about 2 inches high, and blooms in late summer. (Mexico.)

S. Alberti blooms in early summer, with white flowers, and stems of 4 or 5 inches.

S. album is a typical weed of the race—really valuable, and yet perfectly pestiferous in its powers of propagation ; so that, within a year of receiving two squashed sprigs in a letter, you will be casting it out of your garden by cartloads, and yet never seeming to see any signs of clearance. Every fragment grows with fearful rapidity, forming matted masses of stems beset with innumerable minute sausage-like grey-green leaves ; the flower-stems rise up in profusion in June to a height of 6 inches or so, and uncoil the typical radiating heads of the group, beset with white stars. It serves as the picture of many, and is as hard to be got rid of as love or lime.

S. algidum is a flat-leaved plant of the Rhodiola group, with erect stems of some 6 inches, beset with flat narrow green leaves, and ending, in July, with a head of pinkish blossom.

S. allantoeides attains 6 inches, is yellowish, and comes from Mexico. One should judge its leaves to be like a sausage.

S. alpestre is like a most inferior *S. acre*, with fewer, smaller flowers, packed among larger, more numerous and fatter foliage. It may be seen all over the Alps.

S. alsinaefolium is a 2-inch annual with white flowers.

S. altissimum grows to 10 inches, with leafy stems and heads of yellow flowers in later summer. It makes almost a bush on the hot walls of Southern Europe.

S. amplexicaule.—The stem-boughs of this end in a cylindrical gem-bud, and the leaves widen at the base, to clasp the stem in a sort of white sheath of membrane. Otherwise it is much like the last.

S. Anacampseros lies about on the Alps with long round trunks, quite naked, but, towards the tips of the shoots, packed with leathery, grey-green, obovate leaves, thick and fleshy, the stems rising some 6 inches or more to show these quasi-rosettes, topped with flattish domes in summer of dim purply-pink stars.

S. Andersonii attains 4 inches, and has white flowers.

S. anglicum is a very pretty and choice little native—quite low and

PLATE 42

SAXIFRAGA STRIBNRYI.
(Photo. R. A. Malby.)

SEDUM ANGLICUM.
(Photo. R. A. Malby.)

PLATE 43

SEDUM SEMPERVIVUM.
(Photo. R.B.G., Edinburgh.)

SEDUM SEXANGULARE.
(Photo. R.B.G., Kew.)

matted, with fat leaves like elongated bluish globules on the 3-inch stems, that bear a branched head of rather large and most attractive pearl-white stars.

S. annuum is not only annual, but a minute yellow-flowered worthlessness at that.

S. anopetalum stands in the group of *S. altissimum* and *S. alpestre*, and is a plant of scant merit, with thin stars of pale yellow.

S. asiaticum belongs to the Rhodiolas, and has no special value, forming masses, however, with many stiff stems of 8 inches or more, sturdily arising from the stock, densely set with outstanding dark green narrow leaves, and ending in late summer with muffled heads of rather indeterminating-coloured whitish-yellow or pinkish flowers.

S. Athoum stands 4 inches high, and has blossoms of flushed white.

S. atratum is the very ugly little metallic dark-tufted annual Stone-crop of the high Alps, with minute flowers of dingy pallid tone.

S. atropurpureum is a tall-growing Rhodiola of 18 inches, with heads of pinkish flowers in late summer.

S. atrosanguineum can hardly be called more than a rather slender variety of the common Orpine, with erect stems beset with large scattered leaves, oblong and fleshy and coarsely toothed, ending in a spreading head of pink or purple bloom in late summer. But here the whole plant is of dense metallic purple or brownish-black.

S. azureum = *S. caeruleum*, *q.v.*

S. Beyrichianum comes from America, and is 8 inches high, with white blossoms in July.

S. bithynicum keeps the same hours and colour, but is only half the size.

S. boloniense is a dwarf 2-inch Stonecrop of Southern Europe, with yellow flowers through the summer.

S. brevifolium has various forms, but in all is one of the race's brightest jewels. It is very minutely dwarf, with bright green or pur-plish little leaves, like drops of colour, packed tightly to the twisting, mat-forming shoots ; the stems are about an inch high, or a trifle more, bearing sprays of large oval-petalled blossoms, each distinct on its tiny footstalk so as not to look crowded. In Corsica they are brilliant pink, in the stony places of all the Spanish mountains they tend to be pearl-white or flushed, with purple anthers, and a band of deeper colour to each petal.

S. bupleuroeides is an ugly Indian plant, in the way of *S. elongatum*.

S. caeruleum is a brilliantly green little annual, with multitudes, all through the summer, of small many-rayed stars of clear pale-blue, unassuming but attractive.

S. callichroum is a dainty small plant like *S. anglicum*, but rather frailer, and with rosy flowers, keeled with purple. It forms pleasant colonies beside the springs, and in damp places, high up in the Alps of Persia.

S. carpathicum flowers in August, white, on 10-inch stems.

S. Cepaea (*S. spathulatum*, W.K.), makes long narrow spires of pinkish-white blossoms in July, on weak stems of some 6 inches, set with stalked leaves either opposite or in whorls. It has no notable merit, and abounds in stony places of the mountain region all over Europe to the Levant.

S. Clusianum blooms in June. It is a plant of 2 inches, from the Abruzzi, with white stars.

S. collinum = *S. rupestre*.

S. compactum, from Mexico, makes a mass a third of an inch high, with golden flowers.

S. confertiflorum has neither beauty, permanence, nor value.

S. coriaceum grows about 10 inches high, with lax sprays of pinky-purple. It is a Himalayan plant in the group of *S. Rhodiola*.

S. corsicum is a form of *S. dasyphyllum*—usually the distinct variety *S. d. glanduliferum*.

S. crassipes is an uglyish Himalayan Rhodiola about a quarter of a foot tall, with heads of pinkish green from June through late summer.

S. crenatum stands quite close to *S. spurium*, but is wholly hairless and has blunt pink petals longer in proportion to their calyx.

S. crenulatum is an Indian Rhodiola, with specially dense cymes of pink or purple flowers, at the top of erect stems beset with white-margined large-toothed leaves, scalloped along the edge.

S. creticum is a monocarpic species in the lovely line of *S. pilosum*, making House-leekish rosettes, 2 or 3 inches across, almost from the base branching into a great dome of nearly globular pink flowers that never open out their glandular petals. (From the lower stony places of Crete.)

S. Crista-galli is only a cockscomb-leaved form of *S. rupestre*, very monstrous and frightful.

S. cruciatum has stems of 8 inches, and whitish flowers in July.

S. cupressoeides stands 6 inches high, has pinky-white flowers, and comes from Mexico.

S. cyaneum takes its name, not from the flowers (which are pinkish instead of the rich sky-blue that one had hoped), but from the no less lovely glaucous-blue tones of the little many-stemmed 3-inch tuffet, tinted with a soft lilac bloom at the top of the blue stems that spring from oblong-obovate basal leaves almost arranged in rosettes of blueness, thick and fleshy, with narrower-oblong and quite narrow leaves warming to a powdered lilac-rose as they ascend the tiny stems towards the sprays of roseate stars, delicately blending into the pink and blue tones of the whole weak-stemmed clump. (Eastern Siberia, &c.)

S. dasyphyllum is a most rare native (common in South Europe— far more so, indeed, than *S. anglicum*) resembling *S. brevifolium*, but slighter; and the fat globules that stud the two 3-inch frail stems, are of a bluish tone. The whole plant stands near *S. anglicum*, but the pink or cold-white flowers are smaller and more numerous on the looser spray, which is glandular-sticky towards the top, while the leaves are rarer and very much fatter, like swollen grey quinine capsules.

S. debile calls itself a poor thing, not without justice. It is sadly feeble, 3 or 4 inches high, with close forked sprays of yellow.

S. divergens is a contemporary, but half a foot high, with yellow blooms.

S. diversifolium blooms in July. It is only 2 inches high, with blossoms of rosy-white.

S. Douglasii rises from quarter of a foot to 12 inches in height, with flat leaves set up the stems and keeled beneath; and with open spires of yellow stars.

S. elongatum differs in little from *S. Rhodiola*, but that the leaves lack that plant's one attraction in their blue-grey tone.

S. eriocarpum has flowers of dullish white all through the later summer, on stems of 4 inches or more.

S. erythranthum is a rubbish like *S. atratum.*

S. erythrostictum is nearly 2 feet high, and only greenish at that.

S. euphorbioeides closely resembles *S. algidum* , but is taller—about a foot high, with leafy stems, and the yellowish flowers arranged in a short spire, not in a head.

S. Ewersii is singularly charming, with quite short and more than half trailing stems of nearly a foot, set at intervals with large oval-rounded smooth-edged leaves in pairs, of a lovely tone of pale powdered blue, and in good contrast with the domes of ruby-crimson blossoms in which the shoots conclude in late summer. Its range is from Siberia to Kashmir: and it thrives like a weed.

S. Fabaria is merely a weaker form of the common Orpine, *S. Telephium*, with smooth carpels, and the upper leaves wedge-shaped to the base, instead of oblong.

S. farinosum comes from Madeira, and therefore is not to be too blindly confided in. The plant is very lovely, and bloomed with powder, about 4 inches high, with stars of white blossom.

S. fastigiatum is a larger-flowered *S. quadrifidum*—a plant of many stems of 2 or 5 inches, with close-set cylindric little leaves on the shoots and none on the branches, which carry from one to five red flowers, often with only four rays. (Arctic Russia.)

S. Forsterianum is a most doubtful name, representing some small local or climatic variation of *S. rupestre*.

S. gelidum suggests a quite dwarf neat *S. Rhodiola*, differing from *S. quadrifidum* in having flat oblong little leaves, often toothed, and much smaller than in *S. Rhodiola*, but with the same rose-scented sweet fat rootstock, emitting slight flopping stems of 2 inches or so, that end in heads of yellow flowers, purpled at the petal-tips.

S. gemmiferum produces blossoms of brilliant fine pink, on shoots of 4 inches, in July and August.

S. glandulosum is a neat and dwarf Sardinian, with pink-white stars on sprays of 2 inches high or so, in June.

S. glaucum, sometimes called *S. hispanicum*, because it is never found in Spain, is more or less of an annual, with one-sided sprays of specially creamy flower with black anthers and six petals, pointed and starry. The whole plant is 2 or 3 inches high.

S. gracile stands not far away from *S. album*, making the same dense masses of shoots, packed with the same cylindric green leaves, which here are much larger though the stems are much shorter—not more than 3 or 4 inches high, and densely leafy, smooth and green and matted, sending out lax starry heads of three to five rays that bear white flowers with red anthers. It is found in dampish stony places high in the Alps of Asia Minor.

S. Greggii declares its height to be a foot, and its flowers yellow, and its home to be Mexico.

S. Griffithii makes a weak and hairless clump, springing from a rosetted basal tuffet with perfectly narrow leaves *on* the stems of 6 or 9 inches, unlike those of *S. adenotrichum*, though it has the same sharp-pointed whity-pink petals, but the flowers are borne in a rather dense spire, involved in leafy bracts.

S. Grisebachii has no attractions.

S. gypsicola has no more.

S. haematodes offers finer things in its name than its pallid bloodless tints perform. It grows a foot high, and is a stiff leafy thing with flowers in heads of dim and indeterminate pinkishness.

S. heterodontum is a small Indian Rhodiola, with stems of 2 inches or so from the fat stock, beset with ample margined leaves with deep sharp toothing at their edge, and ending in very dense heads of pink or white blossom in July.

SEDUM.

S. Hildebrandii comes from Southern Europe, and is about 8 inches tall with sprays of bright yellow blossom.

S. himalaiense stands close to *S. atropurpureum*, a coarse and weedy plant, differing chiefly in the greater laxity of its deep-purple-flowered cymes, ample and leafy, and about a foot high or more.

S. hirsutum wears glandular down over the whole growth, and is otherwise like a diminished *S. album* with pink flowers.

S. hispanicum=*S. glaucum, q.v.*

S. hispidum=*S. hirsutum.*

S. humifusum comes from Mexico, and lies on the floor, and is no more than 2 inches high, with yellowish blossoms in July.

S. humile is a quite minute Rhodiola from the highest alps of Sikkim, sending up many stems of an inch or two set with narrow-oblong foliage, and ending, usually, in a solitary large flower.

S. hybridum comes a twin to *S. aeizoon*, but its *pistils are green* after flowering and not empurpled, while the shoots never branch before they reach the concave-rayed head of yellow. It runs about and creeps freely, blooming in July.

S. ibericum=*S. stoloniferum, q.v.*

S. integrifolium=*S. Rhodiola.*

S. involucratum belongs to the same style as *S. spurium*, making wide running mats of branches that end in dense heads of specially starry-pointed white flowers, with the last scalloped leaves standing like a frill round the blossom-clusters.

S. japonicum senanense is a little reddish-leaved *S. acre* with splayed heads of white stars, which is found on the rocks of Japan.

S. kamschaticum is the well-known orange-coloured *S. spurium* that makes so good a companion for it in the garden, blooming (as does all the group) in later summer. There is a variegated variety of this.

S. Kirilowii is said to have red flowers in July and a height of 8 inches.

S. Kotschyi makes no appeal for admittance.

S. laconicum is a most inferior version of *S. acre*, verging towards the worthlessness of *S. annuum* and not unlike it.

S. Lampusae lives in crevices in Cyprus. It is a monocarpic rosette in the way of *S. pilosum*, but with pink flowers in a very narrow branching *spike* of a foot or 18 inches high.

S. latifolium is a variety of *S. maximum, q.v.*

S. Liebmannianum is 2 inches high, with yellow blooms in August. (Mexico.)

S. linearifolium is an Indian Rhodiola, with erect stems of 4 or 5 inches, densely set with overlapping narrow-oblong leaves, some

SEDUM.

half an inch long, and ending in a head of six or eight large white flowers.

S. Listoniae has a graceful habit, and belongs to the group of *S. spurium*, with matting stems of some 4 to 8 inches, set with perfectly entire and toothless little obovate fringed leaves of which the lowest on the shoots are about an inch long. The flowers are pink and as large as those of *S. spurium*, with narrow pointed rays. It lives in Caria, Angora, and Bithynia.

S. littoreum is a dimly pink little annual of no merit.

S. longipes comes from Mexico. It has yellow flowers, grows to 8 inches, and blooms in August.

S. lydium affects mossy damp places and stream-beds at sub-alpine elevations in the mountains of Lydia and Caria. It is only 3 or 4 inches high, forming dwarf and creeping mats of shoots very thickly set with fat little cylindric leaves, and altogether after the style of *S. album* and *S. gracile*, with fatter foliage than this last, and the flowers borne on branching sprays so compressed and tight-packed that it seems a solid head of pink stars with black anthers, as large as in *S. album*. Be careful of *S. lydium* in lists.

S. magellense has short tufted weakly stems of 4 inches or less, more or less unbranched, and set rarely with fat and fleshy obovate spoon-shaped leaves which are mostly huddled at the base; and concluding in an erect few-flowered spire of whitish-pink flowers, with narrow pointed petals, gathered by ones or twos on erect footstalks. It pervades the Eastern European region, taking its name, however, from Monte Majella in Central Italy.

S. Maximowiczii blooms in late summer and has stems of 18 inches, with heads of golden yellow.

S. maximum is a giant of 18 inches to 2 feet, with stiff stalks and broad egg-shaped fat leaves, and terminal heads of whitish flowers with reddish tips in August and September. Not particularly good.

S. mellitulum is a Mexican of 3 inches or so, with yellowish blossoms.

S. micranthum is pink, and only 2 inches high, but has little worth.

S. microstachyum is a miniature of *S. Lampusae*, only about 2 or 3 inches high. It lives in the crevices on the North side of Troödos in Cyprus.

S. Middendorffianum has linear narrow leaves, and clusters of golden blossoms, lying about on weakly shoots of 6 inches or so in July.

S. mite stands indistinguishably close to *S. sexangulare*.

S. montanum=*S. anopetalum, q.v.*

SEDUM.

S. multiceps produces many heads of white flowers on 3-inch stems in August and September.

S. nanum is without worth.

S. neapolitanum has stems of 2 inches all the summer through, with flower-stars of clear bright pink.

S. neglectum is one of the yellow-headed kind, about 4 inches high, like *S. acre*, and blooming all the summer.

S. nevadense is a diminished version of *S. villosum, q.v.*

S. Nevii makes a spreading tuft of 3 inches or half a foot, with alternate leaves, and three divergent rays to the flower-heads, and these are set densely with pointed-petalled white stars in summer.

S. nicaeense is a pale-yellow Sexangulare of no special charm.

S. obtusatum makes notably brilliant little clumps and masses of leaves which are packed bulging ovals or rhombs of brilliant succulent emerald in early summer, on stems of bronzy crimson, a tone which in ever-increasing fire gradually gains the whole plant, lasting through the winter, and in summer contrasts well with the golden blossoms in their rayed heads on stems of 3 inches or so in July. An American, like *S. Nevii.*

S. obtusifolium makes a hardened stock from which issue short green stems of 2 or 3 inches, smooth and green and fat, closely packed to the tips with amply obovate blunt small red-veined leaves a trifle scalloped at their edge, and diminishing in size to the tip of the shoots, where the flowers are loosely borne on two or three divergent sprays, being pointed-rayed stars of white. (Caucasus, &c.)

S. ochroleucum is little more than *S. anopetalum, q.v.*

S. olympicum only differs from *S. magellense* in having narrower leaves ; it is an Eastern development of the species.

S. oppositifolium is almost exactly *S. spurium,* but the pinkish-white petals are broader and less pointed, and the leaves, in their pairs, are blunter at the end. (From the stony high places of Caucasus and Persia.)

S. oregonum has erect stems of half a foot or less, beset with narrow foliage of brilliant green, and ending with heads of yellowish-pink.

S. ovatum is whitish in the bloom, and about 6 inches in the stem.

S. oxypetalum stands 8 inches high, has yellow flowers in July, and comes from Mexico.

S. pachyphyllum is a compatriot of the same stature, but produces its pink bloom a month later.

S. palaestinum has neither use nor merit.

S. pallidum stands close to *S. glaucum,* but has smaller flowers, with five rays to the flower instead of six, and these more abruptly pointed at their tip. The colour is a dim uncertain pink.

S. Palmeri is 8 inches high and yellow in the flowers, which it produces in July and August. It comes from Mexico.

S. pedicellatum is a Spanish plant of no value.

S. pilosum, on the contrary, is perhaps the loveliest of the race. It forms clumps of fat and densely downy rosettes exactly like those of a soft and middle-sized Sempervivum, from which arise at the end of May stout little trunks of 2 inches or less, very thickly set with spreading foliage, and unfolding into a round shallow dome of the most deliciously clean and crystalline soft pink, bells of waxy texture and much more suggestive of a Kalanchoë from Fairyland than of anything else we know in this comparatively unrefined family, so generally (with handsome exceptions) to be described as "honest and active but most unattractive." *S. pilosum* comes from the rocks of Armenia and Caucasus, &c. In cultivation such a jewel should be planted in colonies in the foreground near eye-level, on a sunny ledge in light and well-drained soil, with plenty of stones ; it is of quite easy temper, but the flowering-trunk always dies after flowering, even though it may be hoped that, as in *Saxifraga Cotyledon*, the lateral rosettes with which it surrounds itself may survive. In any case it seeds and germinates copiously, so that seed should always be kept coming on.

S. Pittoni is a garden form of great minuteness, being only a bare inch high, with white galaxies in July.

S. populifolium is an exceptional Orpine, with many weakly purple stems of a foot, set with long leathern leaves like a Poplar's, ending in hawthorn-scented roundish heads of pinky-white flowers from May to September. It is very useful, but by no means devoid of brilliance, elegance, and charm. (Siberia.)

S. potosinum comes from Mexico, and is 4 inches high, with yellowish flowers.

S. primuloeides is a most curious and rather pretty species, recently introduced from China, but named, as it seems to me, with a quite singular disregard for propriety of comparison. It makes low huddled wide bushes of 2 or 3 inches high and many more across, of shoots close-packed with fat oval-pointed leaves, flattish and grooved, of dark metallic tone that excellently throws up the white flowers that appear to sit singly in the ends of the shoots, and are closed pointed bells almost suggesting single blooms of some Bell Heather, though the description of it by the advertiser as being like a "glorified White Heather" is almost more misleading than its specific name, as suggesting long airy spikes of white small blossoms, instead of the solitary bells snuggling here and there in the low wide mass of sombre foliage. It grows readily and is quite hardy, but not always, I think, particularly generous of its blossom. And see Appendix for others.

S. pruinatum is a valuable Sexangulare-Sedum from Spain, with fine blue-grey foliage, and spreading heads of golden bloom in summer on stems of 8 inches or so ; for a hot dry rock.

S. pruinosum is still finer, being a glorified *S. rupestre* from Italy, with glaucous-blue cylindric leaves standing closely up the 8-inch stems, which end in gracefully uncurling scorpion-tails of bright gold stars.

S. pulchellum has a singular beauty, following these last in style, but with foliage of bright succulent green, and unrolling scorpion heads of lovely rose-pink flowers that continue far on into the late autumn and even to the winter. It comes from rocky places in Virginia and Georgia, and was long found a disappointing surprise in the indestructible wiry section of the race to which it seems to belong. For it throve but feebly and impermanently in the nice hot dry suntraps considered essential to its kin. But the truth of the matter is that this species—so Rupestrish in look, had it not that warning lush greenness—is really addicted to damp and rather cool hollows ; accordingly, in underground-watered beds, or at the edge of tap or pool, it will prosper most heartily, and flower freely, and continue in comfort from year to year, now that it is no longer to be starved and baked to death on the arid and blazing rocks that make the life of so many other species in this group.

S. purpurascens is another gloomy and unattractive Orpine, with stems of 15 inches or so, set with toothed oval leathern leaves of bronzy tone, and ending in heads of dowdy pink-purple flowers in late summer.

S. purpureum is yet another, being a variety of *S. Telephium* itself, from Siberia, with the whole plant of deep purplish colouring.

S. quadrifidum is a many-stemmed stiff Rhodiola of 4 or 5 inches, thick with almost cylindric leaves on the shoots, and then with leafless branches carrying from one to five red flower-stars, that often have only four rays, to justify the name. (Arctic Russia, &c.)

S. reflexum stands extremely close to *S. glaucum* and *S. rupestre*, but is rather larger in all its parts than the last, with bigger flowers looser on their sprays. In England the pseudo-wild species (a rare " escape ") may be known by the down-turned leaves on the flowering shoots. *S. glaucum* occurs in the South, and has more erect and spreading foliage and flowers in a paler shade of golden yellow.

S. repens=*S. alpestre, q.v.*

SEDUM.

S. reteroideum = *S. amplexicaule, q.v.*

S. rhodanthum has a name which announces beauties that the plant does nothing to fulfil. It is a stout Rhodiola, from streamsides all up and down the Rockies, sending out a great number of stiff stems of a foot or 18 inches, densely leafy with crowded foliage flat and narrow and lucent dark-green. The flowers are small, of indeterminate whity-pink, in axillary clusters at the tops of the stems in July and August. Quite a pleasant " furnishing " Sedum, but should never have been called " Rose-flower."

S. Rhodiola.—The Rose-root is typical of its group. You may see it in the high limestones of Ingleborough, as in most other considerable mountains of the globe, forming immense woody swelling root-stocks that have a distinct scent, if you tear them, of damask roses gone bad ; from these spring unbranched stout stems of 6 inches or so, set with ample and rather incurving oval flat leaves, deeply toothed on the upper half, and very thick and fleshy, of blue-grey tone. The blossoms are yellowish and insignificant, in close rounded heads at the tops of the stalks in summer, more or less enclosed in the uppermost leaves.

S. rhodocarpum has 8-inch stems, yellow flowers, and a home in Mexico.

S. roseum is a beautiful little rooting matting species from Caucasus and Daghestan. It spreads with short fine rooting stems, and the other shoots are as fine as threads, 1 or 2 inches tall, set with opposite pairs of quite minute flat blunt-oval leaves, continuing almost to the huddled lax irregular sprays of flower-stars, which are white inside, and with a pink flush outside, deepening to a rosy rib down the back of each petal.

S. rosulatum makes no fat stock, but the obovate spoon-shaped leaves are rosetted below, and set here and there on the stems of 3 or 4 inches, that bear weak and straggly scorpion-tail heads of pedicelled white stars. Common in Afghanistan and Kashmir.

S. rubens is a valueless little annual Crassula, with red foliage and small greenish flowers.

S. rupestre is the largest and brightest of English Sedums, unfurling scorpion-tailed heads of brilliant golden flowers, on 10-inch stems beset with cylindric glaucous leaves. It may be seen on many an old wall up and down England. It is not to be distinguished from *S. reflexum* except by its slightly diminished size in all its parts, and its flowers sitting *tight to the sprays*, instead of having each a tiny foot-stalk. *S. Forsterianum* is the same thing—a variety built up on variable and local conditions.

S. sanguineum has but little worth.

SEDUM.

S. sarmentosum comes from China and Siberia. It is a creeping thing, about 4 inches high, with yellow flowers in summer.

S. Selskianum is half a yard tall and has yellowish heads of blossom in July.

S. Semenowii will always be found, most likely, to be *Umbilicus Semenowii, q.v.*

S. Sempervivum is also sometimes called *Umbilicus* or *Cotyledon Sempervivum,* or *Sedum sempervivoeides.* There is no wonder that this strange and brilliant plant has puzzled its god-parents. It stands nearest to *S. Lampusae* and *S. pilosum,* making a big and hard rosette of very fat fleshy fringed leaves, dark iron-green in colouring, deepening to bronze, and with a touch of light at the top, precisely resembling that of a Sempervivum of the Calcareum group, but for the much greater fatness of the foliage and the more flattened outline. This rosette sends up in summer a stout leafy stem of dark bronzy tone and some half a foot high, more or less, breaking at the top into a wide spray of bell-shaped flowers in the most dazzling shade of pure blood-scarlet, vivid and velvety, standing out with double ferocity against the metallic darkness of the leafage. This must be grown in the same conditions as suit *S. pilosum,* in places of especial light and heat. It dies even more certainly after flowering, and seed should be matured, collected, and sown with care. Its brilliancy stands alone in the race, as does that of *S. pilosum* in a more delicate and gentle line. But they are neither of them Sedums to the eye. *S. Sempervivum* lives in the Alps of the Levant, where it attracts so much attention that those who have the mania of popular names may call it *Hasereti tchitchek,* if they please, without further application to Wardour Street.

S. senanense. See under *S. japonicum.*

S. sexangulare is not common in England, though scattered; and nowhere truly wild. It is merely a much glorified and more brilliant *S. acre,* with slender leaves, proportionately longer, and lacking in the extreme acridity of *S. acre's* flavour; it may, however, be only a splendid variety.

S. Sieboldii is an evergreen, with weaklyish stems ascending 6 or 10 inches. They are set with margined roundish or heart-shaped foliage, standing horizontally out, and end in heads of bright pink flowers spotted with green, in summer. It is a typical Rhodiola from Japan, useful rather than lovely.

S. spathulifolium has especial charm. It is a neat little clumped mass, with broad fat leafage of huddled spoon-shape or rhomboidal design, and powdered with a lovely bluish bloom that well enhances the radiating sprays of bright golden stars that come up on pinkish

341

stems of 2 or 3 inches from June to September, all over the crowded tuffets of the plants. (Colorado.)

S. spectabile carries the name of Rhodiola to the head of the race. It is a truly superb species, with its noble stout stems of 18 inches or so, set with very ample flat-toothed foliage, leathery and firm, of the loveliest powdered blue-grey, and ending in that huge massed yet delicate head of chalk-pink flowers in September, October, and November, so dearly beloved by all the lingering insects that the disgraceful intoxication of the bees upon its blossoms affords yet another warning to the young, such as may so freely be drawn from this deplorably immoral insect, once mistakenly accepted as the type of modest and industrious excellence (whereas no German officer, combined with no murderous suffragette, could quite unite the apian iniquities of cruelty and intemperance). There are other garden forms and improvements of *S. spectabile* (which is sometimes offered under the name of *S. Fabaria*—a vastly inferior thing, *q.v.*), such as the more vivid-coloured plant called *S. s. atropurpureum*, and another, " Brilliant." They all thrive excellently and for ever in deep rich soil in open sunny places, and make portly stiff bushes of blue and rose-capped splendour in the last and saddest days of the garden, when life has not yet wholly given up the struggle, nor death yet wholly triumphed.

S. spurium.—This is the type of so many useful species, and one of the most useful and common itself, to be everywhere seen in poor soils and places, even under trees, making long flopping mats of its rooting sprays, set with pairs of glossy toothed leaves, and ending in rounded starry heads in high summer, and for a month and more to come, of large pinky star-flowers of typical blurred rose (as if they had been left under water rather long), or else of a yet more blurred and diaphanous pinkish-white. There is also a brighter form called *S. s. splendens.*

S. Stahlii grows about 4 inches high, has yellow flowers, and comes from Mexico.

S. stellatum has no merit. The purplish flowers are particularly narrow and thin in the ray, borne on two or three scorpion-tail recurving branches, on stems of 7 inches or so, set with obovate wedge-shaped scalloped foliage. A common annual of Southern Europe.

S. stenopetalum makes a tuft of 3 or 4 inches, densely set with leaves, and especially so on the sterile shoots. The flowers are pinkish-white, carried in dense compact sprays. Quite common in the American alps.

SEDUM.

S. Stephani is a dwarfer *S. Rhodiola* with longer flowers and narrower less-toothed leaves.

S. Steudelii is of no special value.

S. stoloniferum (*S. ibericum*) stands near *S. spurium*, but lives on damp rocks in Pontus, Caucasus, and Persia, where it freely flounders with its long rooting stems, with blunt rhomb-wedge-shaped leaves, with wavy scalloping at their edge, ending in lax, leafy, and divergent-sprayed heads of similar pink flowers, narrow and pointed in the star, but a little smaller than in *S. spurium*.

S. subulatum comes near *S. acutifolium*, but has slenderer, smooth, cylindric leafage of glaucous-blue tone. The stems are 3 or 4 inches high, and the sprays of the flower-heads are so condensed that there seems to be a rather close head of white blossoms, of oblong blunt petals, running to a little point, and connected with one another at the very base. (Stony places of Transcaucasia, &c.)

S. telephioeides comes from Siberia, and, when it has so frankly acknowledged that it is exactly like *S. Telephium*, no catalogue need be at the pains to say much more.

S. Telephium is the Common Orpine, standing as a useful type for many a useful and charmless species in the race. The stiff stems are a foot high or more, several from a hardened stock, and set with scattered oblong or obovate leaves, large, and leathery-fleshy, and dark green, fiercely waved and toothed at the edge. At the top the stem branches into a spraying head, not a tight dome, of more or less purplish flowers. It blooms in later summer, and might without difficulty be more effective than it is, the habit being a trifle rank, and the bloom neither bright nor beautiful. There are many varieties, some with foliage empurpled to enhance the gloom of the blossom, and *S. Fabaria*, Koch, is simply a slenderer state of the species; which is abundant on English rocks and walls and hedgerows, and often as an escape from cultivation, being a plant that it is impossible to kill; so that, cultivated for many centuries, every scrap cast out into the world has rooted for itself and made fresh colonies.

S. tenellum differs for the worse from *S. lydium*. It has the same habit, dwarf and neat, but with shorter, broader leaves, and the flowers rather smaller, white inside at first until the outward flush gains the interior also. The petals are hardly longer than the elongated calyx-segments, and the stars are borne not in scorpion-tail branches, but gathered into what seems a much denser head. It is a pervasive commonplace of the Persian Alps and Caucasus.

S. ternatum belongs to the rocky woods from Connecticut to Georgia, &c. Its stems are from 3 to 7 inches, studded with flat wedge-shaped leaves, whorled in threes at the base, but growing rarer and more oblong as they mount the stalk to where the flower-head divides into three rays, beset with white stars in early and mid-summer.

S. testaceum is another American, said to be 4 or 5 inches high, with pink flowers in July.

S. tibeticum is an Orpine from the Himalaya, with smooth stems of some 6 or 10 inches, bearing lax spires and sprays of pinky-purple flowers usually five-rayed, unlike those of *S. quadrifidum.*

S. Treleasii comes from Mexico, blooms in August, and has yellow blossoms on stems of 10 inches or a foot.

S. tricarpum is a scatter-rayed golden-starred species from the woods of Japan, rather suggesting a brilliant Chrysosplenium, and with only three ovaries to each flower.

S. trifidum stands among the very few Sedums that are exacting and difficult to please. In cultivation it is both rare and cherished, but quite common at mid-elevations of Kashmir and Sikkim, where it grows on all the rocks and old trees of the mountain woodland. It is a smooth plant of a foot high at the most, but usually much less, with oblong leaves 2 or 3 inches long, irregularly waved and lobed, or else regularly feathered into one or two pairs of narrow blunt lobes, green, and rather shining. The flower-sprays are leafy and branched, carrying pink stars in July, well spaced in the spray, each on a distinct foot-stalk.

S. tristriatum stands near to *S. dasyphyllum* in looks and needs and habits. It is a thing of 3 inches from the upper stony places of Crete, with three darker stripes on the pale petals.

S. trullipetalum is about 5 inches high or less, with narrow outstanding foliage packed and overlapping on the stems that end in dense spires of whity-yellow flowers with a very long claw to the root of the petal. The rosetted basal leaves are more ample, and there is no stock.

S. turkestanicum blooms in late summer, and should have pink flowers on stems of 4 inches or so.

S. Verloti comes from Southern Europe, attains 4 inches, and has yellow flowers, but not much merit.

S. villosum is only an annual, but a most charming jewel, here and there to be seen on the damp moorland rocks of the Yorkshire highlands. It makes tiny clumps of basal rosettes, built of tight, fat little cylindric leaves, green and fleshy and glandular-downy, so that they are soft and velvety in effect. The stems are leafy too, 4 or 5 inches high, more and more glandular as they rise to where they

SEMPERVIVUM.

break into sprays carrying only a few rather large waxy flowers of
soft clear pink in early summer, with a stripe of deeper rose to each
petal.   It should be established in cool, damp, and rocky places, there
to be let seed itself about at will.

S. virens is only a Southern form of *S. album.*

S. Wallichianum from the Himalaya blooms from June to August,
grows half a yard high, and has yellow flowers.   It is not likely to be
found a species of value.

Selaginella.—Of these quaint little creeping Club-mosses several
may be grown for their bright-green shining carpets in cool places,
where they persist through the winter and turn russet.   Pieces
should be taken off the mass in autumn to be sure of their safety.
Species that may be grown are *S. Douglasii, helvetica, Braunii, selagi-
noeides (S. spinosa)*—all of them pretty and pleasureful coverers of light
sandy vegetable soil in a cool place.

Selliera. See **Goodenia.**

Sempervivum.—The Houseleeks form a vast family, most
minutely differentiated, often confused, and often interbreeding.
They are all of the easiest culture and the loveliest effect, at least so
far as their carpets and masses of rosettes go,—green, blue, violet,
ruby ; or of all shades commingled ; or cobwebbed till they are like
Ping-pong balls in cotton wool.   Their flowers are not always of equal
merit—whirling large catherine-wheels gathered in wide heads on stout
stems in summer, but sometimes rather dull and indeterminate in tone.
However, there are few things in the rock-garden so valuable even for
their flowers, as are the Houseleeks for their massed rosettes alone.
Any sunny place and any light and rather rich soil, perfectly drained,
and thoroughly sunburned, will bake them as happy as the centuries
are long.   A terrible notion was started some years ago, and gained
an astonishing prevalence which even now still lingers ; it used to
cause these wretched plants to be inserted on rocks in kneaded pats
of manure and clay.   No more prejudicial or preposterous treatment
could be imagined ; the manure goes sour, and the plants, unable to
penetrate the hard unwholesome mass with their roots, do not, indeed,
always immediately die (for it takes more than difficulty to kill a
Sempervivum), but they sit sullen in a hump, and make little or no
increase ; until at last, when you awake to the wisdom of moving
them, you are able to see the sickness and infertility of their sluggish
rootage in that odious medium.   Not, indeed, that they are hostile
to food, or that a little stimulant does not mightily help them to start
on inclement ledges and bare rock-faces, but above all they dislike
hard impermeable stuff such as this caked mixture produces.   Let a

345

SEMPERVIVUM.

blend be prepared, then, containing a quarter of old and well-rotted manure, *thoroughly broken up*, and mixed with three times its bulk of mingled mould and rich light loam, so that the compost will be firm without being armour-plated in its adamantine impenetrability when it settles, and the roots of the Houseleeks will be able to rove through it happily and unimpeded. Once started they will never need any further care again, except in the dividing of old masses that may have gone lank with a tendency to die from the centre. They are all lovers of the fullest sunshine, high on the hottest banks and turf of the Alps, or in old walls—not, as a rule, a rock-haunting race, and much preferring, for the most part, the springy slopes and steep well-drained acclivities of tough elastic peat in which you will find *Trifolium alpinum*. The list of available Houseleeks is enormous, but there is much confusion in gardens and catalogues, nor are by any means all the species, so nicely segregated and created by the botanical eye, of any special distinctness in the horticultural, among the others from which they have thus minutely and delicately been divided by the botanist. And even such catalogues as give long lists of Sempervivum usually omit to provide much information as to the size and special qualifications of each plant : a consideration of great importance when it comes to being saddled with the huge rosette of a Tectorum when one has wanted for a given ledge the neat small globule of an Arachnoideum, yet been unable to tell what make or shape of plant you were buying, from the jejune snippets of description which is all that the space in catalogues can afford. Therefore, since alphabetical lists may elsewhere be found, notably (and to the Sabaean and dispiriting bewilderment of the amateur) in M. Correvon's *Plantes des Montagnes* (where Houseleeks are found aligned, like Banquo's descendants, in page after page of unilluminated polysyllables), it may prove more convenient here to adopt, instead, the botanical system, which means that kindred species are gathered together, so that one can compendiously state the qualities of a group, instead of its members being scattered far and wide down the column, according to the exigencies of the alphabet, so that each has to be separately treated, and pursued by raging eyes to its lair among cousins with whom it has nothing in common but the link that binds Monmouth and Macedon (and a glance at the Index will save all inconveniences of reference).

PLATE 44.

SEMPERVIVUM CILIATUM.
(Photo. R. A. Malby.)

SCUTELLARIA INDICA (var. JAPONICA).
(Photo. R. A. Malby.)

PLATE 45

SEMPERVIVUM ARACHNOIDEUM.
(Photo. R. A. Malby.)

SEMPERVIVUM DOELLIANUM.
(Photo. R. A. Malby.)

PLATE 46

SEMPERVIVUM FIMBRIATUM.
(Photo. R. A. Malby.)

SEMPERVIVUM FUNCKII.
(Photo. R. A. Malby.)

SEMPERVIVUM.

CLASS I.—RHODANTHAE.

Flowers red, all their parts in twelves.

GROUP I. *Ciliata.*—Leaves of the barren rosettes *fringed at the edges only. The rosettes all large and ample,* several inches across, with noble *leaves of green or violet or glaucous-blue,* with a *red tip.*

S. tectorum is the common Houseleek, and in foliage as fine as need be. It has darker varieties called *S. t. atropurpureum, atrorubens,* and *atroviolaceum,* all sometimes offered as species. It has also, on the Bernina, begotten a hybrid with *S. Wulfeni* which is perhaps the most wholly beautiful in foliage of all the large and smooth-rosetted dark Houseleeks. This is *S. × Comollii,* with very royal rosettes, blending blue and violet in a most wonderful combination of bloomy metallic colouring, darkening outward to the sharp leaf-tips in a deep glaucous-purple that goes of a yet more sombre tone in the winter. Other garden varieties or wild forms of *S. tectorum* are sometimes sent out as *S. affine, S. beugesiacum* (perhaps a species, but close akin), *S. Bungeanum, S. grandiflorum, S. ornatum, S. pallescens* (pale green in the leaf and bright pink in the flowers), *S. laetevirens, S. marmoreum* from Athos, *S. juratense* (quite near to *S. tectorum,* but a month earlier in the production of smaller flowers), *S. brevirameum* with notably large rosettes, *S. rupestre,* and *S. speciosum.* All these are very handsome; all these have the habits and the noble rosettes of the species, and this section of the group. As have also the following, that have no claim to be more than garden forms of the Houseleek : *S. bicolor, S. cupraeum, S. densum, S. glaucum, S. pulchrum, S. majus, S. tenellum,* and *S. violaceum*—variations whose names explain them. Rather smaller than this should be the rare *S. × Fontanae,* being a hybrid between *S. arachnoideum* and *S. tectorum ;* and *S. × adenotrichum* is another hybrid, with dim *S. montanum* for its other parent.

S. Boutignyanum (*S. alpinum*), with its variety *S. adoxum,* the inglorious, comes from the Pyrenees, and has large flowers of pale rose in wide heads of 6 inches or so. *S. pyrenaicum* is a Pyrenean version, with paler flowers still.

S. arvernense is taller in the stem, but has the usual large and red-tipped rosette. It belongs to Central France and the Western Alps.

S. calcareum.—This is one of the most important large plants in the race, and is often offered under the comic name of *S. californicum.* Now no Sempervivum exists in America at all ; the race is practically confined to Europe. *S. calcareum* is singularly beautiful with its large rosettes, which are specially ample and fat, specially neatly packed, of a lovely glaucous-blue, with an abrupt dark purple tip to each leaf. Other Houseleeks, species or varieties, coming near this, but lacking the empurpled tips, are *S. Lamottei*, with even taller stems of 15 inches (*S. racemosum* is merely a longer-leaved, more pointed, and expanded *S. calcareum*) ; *S. glaucum*, a beautiful thing from the Simplon, with rosettes of 2 or 3 inches across ; *S. Schottii*, from the Tyrol ; *S. atlanticum*, a lonely outlier from its race on *Atlas* (perhaps the name *S. "californicum"* arose from a muddle between this plant, presumed to have something to do with the *Atlantic*, so that against this was set the fact that California looks out over the Pacific, and must therefore have a Sempervivum of its own to match the other side of the Continent). *S. triste*, often seen and sold, is a garden form or hybrid, standing close to *S. calcareum*, though rather more like *S. tectorum* in the more splayed rosette, which is here of a very deep and doleful metallic purple-brown that has earned the plant its name.

Now we come to members of the same group, but of much smaller habit and rosette. These are : *S. Greenii*, from the Eastern Alps, with reddened tips to the neat leaves of the rosette (a diminished *S. calcareum*, as is also *S. parvulum*); *S. Verloti*, a plant of Dauphiné, by some authorities ranked as a hybrid between *S. tectorum* and *S. montanum ;* and *S. Funckii*, from the Tyrol—these last two lacking any red tips to the leaves, and *S. Funckii* remarkable for the brilliant emerald green of its rosette even in winter. Its flowers are enormously large and wildly fringy stars of pale poor pink with a darker stripe in each petal.

GROUP II. *Pubescentia.*—Leaves of barren rosettes *downy on the surface* as well as being fringed as before, but *without spreading tip* of hairs to the leaf. Parts of the red or pink flowers as before. *Rosettes smaller.*

S. montanum.—This is a common alpine species, with mats of middle-sized glandular rosettes of a dull green, profusely emitting young, and, like many another, often squeezed lopsided in their mat ; and a few very big whirligig flowers of a perfectly dull and ugly dead rose on stems of 6 inches or so. *S. Burnati* is a larger version, and *S. serpyllifolium* a tiny one, while *S.* x *Theobaldi* is a hybrid, with *S. Wulfeni* for its other parent.

S. anomalum is a garden plant, with the leaves of the rosettes gone dark.

SEMPERVIVUM.

GROUP III. *Barbatula.*—Leaves fringed and *tipped with a tuft of hairs.* The rest as before.

S. Pomellii is placed by some as a hybrid between *S. arvernense* and *S. arachnoideum,* with rosettes of middling size.

S. fimbriatum, with loose rosettes of rather soft pointed leaves. Besides the points that separate the two groups, this may easily be known from *S. montanum,* with which it often grows, by its looser rosettes, and the much broader and less spidery petals of its brighter pink flowers.

GROUP IV. *Arachnoidea.*—Dwarf *small rosettes* with the leaves all interwebbed with more or less of *cottony fleece from tip to tip.*

S. arachnoideum is certainly the most important of the smaller rock-garden species. It is a really lovely little jewel, no less in its masses of neat woolly-white balls than when among them rise up stems of 3 or 4 inches in summer, expanding sprays of large and comfortable twelve-rayed stars in the most glowing shade of ruby rose, shining on the hot banks of the Alps like little catherine-wheels of living red light, above the crowded whiteness of the globules below. No heat can ever be too great for this plant—the hotter, the happier. In the mountains it is certainly a species that prefers the non-calcareous formations; it is very abundant, but also very local, and may be seen in carpets in many a warmer exposure at rather low elevations in the Southern ranges, on walls and banks, for choice, but never in the higher alpine turf in company with the large-rosetted species. In the Southern Alps, as the warmth grows greater, so does the density and whiteness of its cobwebbing, until, in the Maritimes, it turns as snowy as wool, and may be seen on the black and crimson porphyry ledges of the Roja valley in hot places, lying like dropped shreddings of a fleece, unrecognisable as a plant in its congeries of little snowy globes, until the spraying heads of scarlet-rosy whirligigs rise up above in brilliant and flaming contrast. This is the lovely form called *S. a. transalpinum.* Another variety, often quoted in catalogues, is *S. Laggeri,* which, in gardens, seems to be merely a rather larger variety of *S. arachnoideum.* In the limestone regions of the Jura this species is replaced by the quite similar but much less cobwebby *S. Fauconneti,* which establishes a connecting link between these small Houseleeks and *S. montanum.* Another close cousin is *S. barbatulum* from the Eastern Alps; *S. a. bryoeides* is a mere form with specially minute and serried rosettes; and another very tiny miniature variety is *S. a. Cottettii;* while another most specially woolly development from the Eastern ranges is called *S. Pilosella ;* and yet another, from the Southern granites, has flowers of particularly flaming red that have earned it the name of *S. sanguineum.* The species too has hybridised all over the mountains, and all the following crosses must be understood as having something of bright colour, white webbing and neat-massed small habit, derived from *S. arachnoideum*—*S. Pomellii,* see above ; *S. piliferum (montanum × arachnoideum), S. × Thomayeri (S. hirtum × S. arachnoideum), S. × lautareticum (S. rupestre × S. arachnoideum), S. × Morellianum (S. calcareum × S. arachnoideum*—inheriting a double allowance of beauty) ; *S. Heerianum, S. rubellum (S. Boutignyanum × S. arachnoideum*—the same cross) ; *S. roseum (S. arachnoideum × S. Wulfeni) ; S. × Fontanae,* see above. (*S. pseudo-arachnoideum* is a kindred development of the Western Alps.)

S. Doellianum stands so close to *S. arachnoideum* as sometimes to have been held a mere variety. Its differences, however, are for the worse, the flowers being of a duller pink, the rosettes looser, and more splayed out, and distinctly less cobwebbed—in fact with only quite a few threads from tip to tip, and a small beard on the point of each leaf. (Tyrol.)

S. oligotrichum, Baker, is another species in the same group.

GROUP V. *Chrysantha.—Flowers yellow or yellowish.*

S. Wulfeni.—Very handsome large sea-green rosettes, very heavily fringed at the edge, but otherwise wholly smooth—not unlike those of the Houseleek, except in the peculiarities of colour, &c. The stout stem of 10 inches unfolds a glandular-stemmed sprayed head of large pale-yellow purple-eyed flowers like whirling angry Sea-anemones. This species is scattered about in the high turf of the granitic Alps, often forming wide masses. There is a sad-flowered hybrid between this and *S. montanum,* called *S. × Widderi ;* and another version of the same unpromising cross is *S. × Huteri.*

S. Gaudini has specially handsome rather large rosettes of narrow leaves, handsomely incurved at first, and then opening wide, but not violently pointed, all fluffy with glandular hairs and of brilliant green sometimes reddened at the tips ; the stout stems are 10 inches high, unfurling great steady stars of clear pale-yellow. It is a remarkably handsome species of the Italian Alps in the high slopes, and demands open-ground treatment with us in hot places.

S. Braunii differs from this last in being much smaller, with the pointed-leaved, littler rosettes always kept open, quite neat and well-packed in effect. The stems, too, are pleasantly slender, and not crowded with leaves, about 4 inches high, carrying not a sprayed head so much as a scant cluster of bright and large comfortably-rayed flowers of richer yellow, almost suggesting some small and stiff golden-flowered Adonis in their stolid lines. (Alps of Styria.)

S. ruthenicum has small stars and broader leaves in the same style; and *S. Laharpei* is a garden form.

S. Pittoni has tongue-shaped leaves clothed in long glandular hairs and shortly pointed, to build its medium-sized rosette, every leaf having a purple patch at the tip. The flowers are pale yellow, and the plant is extremely rare on the serpentine rocks of Kraubat in Styria.

S. grandiflorum, Haworth (for *S. grandiflorum* of gardens is apt to be a mere variety of *S. tectorum, q.v.*), is one of the finest of all the yellow Houseleeks, as figured in the *Bot. Mag.*, T. 507). But the history of the treasure and its home are both obscured in the past, and as for its present whereabouts we may make the same inquiry as about the Thane of Fife's late lady.

CLASS II.—DIPOGON.

Parts of the flowers in sixes.

S. Heuffellii (*S. patens*) has smallish yellow flowers, but they are not wildly and beautifully fringy as in the foregoing. Its habit is of medium size.

S. Reginae Amaliae has all the habit and handsomeness of a big bronze-purple rosetted *S. tectorum*, but can always be known by only having the parts of the *flower in sixes instead of in twelves*, no less than by the smallish pale-yellow blossoms in their spraying heads on stems of 10 inches. Queen Amelia is so far gone in glory that I cannot now tell what she was queen of, or when, or where; but her Houseleek is more enduring, and lives on in the East of Europe, outliving queens and dynasties alike.

S. arenarium (*S. Kochii*) has its young offsets *always rolled up in round balls*. It is a small neat thing, but the green rosettes are quite imposing with their many points, when at last they splay out, and the stout little flower-stem of 2 inches uncurls its scorpion-tail branches thick-set with cream-pale large flowers that do not open out but keep a ragged urn-shape in their packed recurving sprays. It is a plant of South Tyrol, Styria, and Carinthia.

S. soboliferum follows the same example of keeping its young involved in balls, a fashion followed by all prudent mothers ; and is, in general effect, a smaller version of the next, with erect yellow-pale bells.

S. hirtum, however, has no feeling for balls, and its young rosettes are not wrapped up in them, but go forth into the world in full expansion. The rosettes are neat, unfolding so amply that at last they give almost the effect of a tropical Nymphaea with hairy green petals, so long and pointed and independent are the fleshy emerald leaves. The flowers are of a clearer yellow than in the last, not exhausted and made anaemic by the strain of balls upon their mother-stem, which is about three times the size and height of *S. arenarium* and *S. soboliferum*—as indeed is the whole plant, which forms broad flat masses in the rocks and walls of the Eastern Alps.

Senecillis carpathica (Senecio glaucus) is almost a Senecio, and extremely handsome with its long stiffly-upstanding oval-rounded leaves of clear glaucous-blue, about 18 inches high. The flowers are large and yellow, in a rather close shower at the top of a yard-high stem ; they make a contrast with the leaves, but are not themselves of any startling beauty. *Senecillis* thrives readily in deep rich loam in a shady aspect, may be multiplied by seed or division, and blooms in the later summer.

Senecio is perhaps the largest single family in the world, and perhaps the most uniformly hideous and weedy, with some of the most noble exceptions. It is as much temperate as tropical, as happy on the Equator as on the Alps. Before, however, we deal with the alpine group there remains a section of herbaceous plants that cannot here be omitted, as they are such noble adornments of the bog and waterside. They are all of tropical enormousness of habit, some with huge showering heads of bloom, others with fluffy spires, others with tall spikes of big flowers or tall close tails of little ones. They are all quite easy and vigorous, verging on the voluminousness of weeds ; they all like cool deep and rich soil ; they nearly all bloom golden in late summer, and they are all to be freely multiplied whether by division or seed. I name only the best, as at present known, most of them being comparatively new arrivals from China. *S. aconiti-folius* (*Syneilesis*) has flowers of dim pink in loose spires on branching stems, above very deeply finger-cut foliage of ample outline. Much nobler is *S. clivorum*, one of the finest in the group, with huge leaves like those of a super-Coltsfoot on long stems, whose masses are sur-mounted by great branching showers of very large flowers of the richest gold ; this has a dwarfer variety, *S. c. subcrenatus*, that however is more huddled in the spray and rather less ample in the bloom. In the same line is the magnificent *S. japonicus* (*Ligularia japonica* or *Erythrochaete palmatifida*), but rather more light in the habit, with splendid leaves of refreshing shining green deeply cut into five or seven fingers, and overtopped by sprays of noble blossoms of intense golden-orange. Other Ligularias, like huge Coltsfoots, with aspiring yard-high spikes of yellow, are *S. macrophyllus* (suggesting a giant Senecillis), *S. sibiricus*, and *S. stenocephalus*. *S. Doria* is the same thing as *S. macrophyllus*, and *S. suaveolens* is sometimes called *Cacalia*. It is a smooth plant of a yard or two, with narrow leaves and dense spikes of dirty-white flowers faintly fragrant. *S. Faberi*, from China, is rather a weed too, with piles of coarse pointed leafage, and small mean heads of small mean flowers in small mean sprays, at the top of stems more than a yard high. *S. Przewalskyi* has most beautiful glossy foliage, deeply and sharply fingered, and gashed again in long divergent pointed lobes. The flowers are quite minute, soaring aloft in a narrow little mangy spike of 2 or 3 feet, drooping at the tip. *S. Veitchianus*, however, is one of the most superb, well furnished with flowers of light yellow towering above masses of enormous Coltsfoot foliage; while even this is beaten out of the field by *S. Wilsonianus*, which unites the spiked huge habit of the last with the very much larger and more brilliant flowers of *S. clivorum*, so that you get masses and jungled acres of giant Coltsfoot from which in abundance tower stout and strapping Campanili of 5 feet or so, well spaced in their rich store of radiant wide suns of orange. Wholly different in character from this is *S. tanguticus*, which is a most terrible and inexorable weed, never to be got rid of when once introduced, but most effective in a wild cool place, with loose and fluffy spires of tiny golden blossom in clouds, suggesting a yellow Artemisia or Macleaya, on stems of 3 or 4 feet, set with delicate and finely-feathered foliage, dark above and light beneath. And there are still many more species, but Senecios should always, if unknown, be seen in bloom before being bought. And see Appendix.

Of medium-sized Groundsels the most important are *S. pulcher* and *S. Doronicum*. The former comes from Colorado, and closes the year with immense flowers of flaming carmine-purple on thick stiff stems of a foot or two, above very leathery fleshy foliage of dark-green, narrow-oblong, and very stiffly and fatly waved and toothed and gashed and scalloped along the ledge. It is a superb species, though stolid and obese in habit; and is quite hardy, though the lateness of its blossoms is a fault, as they so often get wrecked. It should, accordingly, have as hot a place as possible, in a soil that shall be both rich and cool, yet light and perfectly well-drained and deep. *S. Doronicum* is a favoured but most variable species of the higher Alps, of which the most often cultivated form is a rather lush and spreading plant, with oval green leaves rather soft and hairy in texture, and abundant large flowers of no better a yellow than the clear gold of Arnica. This form I have never seen on the Alps, where its habit is usually to make a clump of two or three crowns at the most—more refined and much less leafy in appearance. However, in the high granites of the Maritimes it tends this way, alike in greenness of looser leaf and yellowness of blossom ; on the Mont Cenis the flower is still golden and great, but the leafage is perceptibly harder, more fleshy and leathery, and of a greyer waxy green, leading on to the Oberland form, which is the finest of all, and truly well-bred, with a single crown (two or three at the most), of ribbed and cobwebbed stiff stems, carrying two or three very large flowers of a very rich deep orange, above a tuft of long-stalked basal leaves, white beneath and of hard leathern consistency, in a beautiful tempered tone of dark iron-grey with a hint of fleshy gloss. In all forms it is easy to grow in any light soil and any open place, and is the best of the larger alpine Groundsels (together with its kindred *S. Gerardi*, *S. Lagascanus*, *S. renifolius*, *S. persicus*, and splendid leathern-rosetted glossy *S. eriopus*). *S. campestris*, *S. alpestris*, *S. alpinus*, *S. spathulaefolius* are not plants of any arresting worth or beauty, although this last, and *S. campestris*, of which it is a variety, have at least the romantic interest of straying onto Micklefell, where may be seen the basal tufts of entire woolly leaves, with uprising stems of a foot or more, carrying heads of large clear-yellow flowers, broad in the ray. And in the same style is *S. aurantiacus* (*Cineraria*), with the same entire leaves, greyish or grass-green, but heads of brilliant orange blossom (as has also, in the same style, *S. erubescens*).

Of the more alpine *Senecios* or *Cinerarias* a marked group is formed by the white-leaved species that belong typically to the hot South, where they have developed the snowiness that is so fine and clear in *S. candidus* and in *S. Cineraria*, so commonly in use once as a bedding plant on account of its whiteness. The Senecios of this group all have the lobed and feathered or fern-like foliage of grey or white ; they all require dryness and lightness of soil and perfect drainage, and all the sun they can get (they answer to the call of the moraine) ; and they are all comparatively insignificant in the flower, though their hoary and often aromatic foliage is quite enough to secure them admittance. *S. leucophyllus*, from non-calcareous rocks of the Spanish Alps, has white leaves of rounded oval outline, beautifully frilled into rounded lobes ; the flowers are yellow, gathered in heads on stems of some 4 to 8 inches (it is found by some cultivators to have a special tendency to rot off at the neck) ; *S. Boissieri*, from the Alps of Granada, is a tight silky-silver tuffet with rayless blossoms on stems of 2 or 3 inches ; *S. incanus* is the common silver-grey Groundsel-cushion of all the high Alps, very pretty in the deep-toothed oval little leaf, and perfectly boring in the flower ; *S. carniolicus* is like it, but of a greener grey, much larger and longer in all its parts, with shallower lobes to the drawn-out leaves ; *S. uniflorus* is a higher alpine, from the summit-ridges, packed and small, with foliage especially white and not so specially lobed, and one large orange-golden bloom sitting close to the tuft on a short stem—the best effort of the group in the way of blossom. While *S. trifurcatus*, probably the prettiest of all, exactly suggesting a pale-yellow *Chrysanthemum alpinum*, so far baffles our hopes by lingering coyly in the marshes of Tierra del Fuego.

But the hills have far richer things to give us in the fine-leaved alpine Groundsels. These form almost woody root-stocks, flopping or creeping over the high-alpine and sub-alpine turf in stony places, with bright dark-green foliage, lucent and hairless, very finely cut and curled and feathered. In *S. adonidifolius*, the least worthy of the group, the stems are about 8 inches high, and the flowers are of brilliant yellow, but the whole effect of the plant is not so brilliant as in *S. abrotanifolius* from the Engadine and Eastern ranges, which flounders about with its shoots that may be a foot long, ferny with dark glossy emerald leaves, and with loose upcast heads of a few nobly large and well-built blossoms in the most glorious shade of orange flame-colour, making the finest possible comparison in the garden, when established in light rich peaty soil, well-drained and nourished and helped with stones, in company of *Campanula alpina* or *C. rotundifolia*—or (as is the fashion that is so beautiful in the high turf of the Engadine) scattering its furious scarlet suns under the hanging pale bells of *Campanula barbata*. But much more valuable and choice even than this last, and quite the most precious of its race for the rock-garden, is *S. tyrolensis*, replacing the last (and perhaps only a variety) on the limestones of the Southern and Eastern Alps, most general in the Dolomites. It is much neater and more compact in habit, with smaller more finely, tightly-curled fern-fronds of glossy emerald, and the same fiery splendours of flower in rather ampler heads upon less straggling sprays. This is a real treasure for any choice place and companionship, its colour loudly clamouring for pale Campanulas to cool it. The flowering moment is in June and July ;

and both these last can either be multiplied by seed, or by pieces taken off the rambling shoots, which are much tighter and more condensed in *S. tyrolensis*.

Serratula.—These are tall-growing summer-blooming plants close to Centaurea. None is worth troubling about except *S. coronata* and *S. atriplicifolia*. The first likes dampish shady places, and has stems of 2 or 3 feet, set with feathered foliage, and carrying loose clusters of purple great Hard-head flowers. The second is an astonishing and remarkably handsome thing, preferring warmer and dry places. The lower leaves are heart-shaped, arrow-barbed, and the stately stems bear big lonely horizontal or nodding Thistles, in late summer, of so austere and sombre a purple as to seem almost black and hollow-eyed against the greyness and silvery effect of the plant.

Sheffieldia repens. See **Samolus.**

Shortia uniflora and *S. galacifolia* belong, the one to Japan, and the other to America. It is sadly difficult, as with most woodland plants, to obtain sound and moving roots of these; but when they are acquired, the race will thrive in light rich vegetable soil, whether in sun or shade—sun being recommended to ripen the redness of *galacifolia's* foliage, while shade seems much more invariably indicated for *S. uniflora*. The former sits quiet in a wide tuft, with rounded glossy leathern leaves on stiff stems, among which stand up the lovely pearl-pale five-lobed bells in spring and early summer, lonely on their stalks of 4 or 5 inches. There is also a rose-pink form, and both the species and the variety are now becoming rare in their native woods, where they grow in the light vegetable soil among the Galax which they so greatly on a smaller scale resemble in habit of clump and leaf, though firmer and stiffer and thicker and more leathern.

S. uniflora lives far away in the dense woodlands of the Japanese Alps, and is a much more unquiet straggling wandering fairy, and therefore more difficult to collect with adequate rootage. It is smaller in habit than *S. galacifolia*, too, with thinner leaves, much more than ever like a little Galax, standing out on their fine stems along the rambling branches, from which arise a profusion of flowers larger and lovelier than those of *S. galacifolia*, in a warmer tone of pearly flesh, like awakening Galatea. It is undoubtedly a difficult thing to establish; sound plants that have got over the distemper of home-sickness should be at any cost procured, then put out in light vegetable soil, with a few chips and very loose perfect drainage a foot or 18 inches below (it might even be well to give them a spring-mattress of besoms and branches 18 inches down, as if they were frame-violets), under the fringe of some such light-growing evergreen as *Pinus montana*. And, beautiful as was the original *S. uniflora*, that called *S. u. grandiflora* bears flowers of almost twice the size and quite twice the freedom ; it seems uncertain whether this is not the truer type of the species. The race stands quite close to its cousin, *Schizocodon*, and will inter-breed—though most careful division (if you dare) of established clumps (if you can achieve them) will always be the readiest way to increase your stock of a treasure so rare and subtle.

Sibbaldia procumbens and *S. maxima* (or *cuneata*) are worth-less little greenery-yallery carpeters, between Potentilla and Alche-milla, but more reminiscent in effect of a thready and starveling Alchemilla. They may be grown, if wanted, on non-calcareous rock-work near water in cool shady and well-drained places. But for precautions so choice most gardeners will prefer plants more choice to match.

Sibthorpia europaea is a valueless half-hardy Scrophulariad from Western Europe.

Sida napaea and *S. dioica* are two big malvaceous weeds from America, with white flowers. They are for the seed and treat-ment of the next, but much less valuable.

Sidalcea.—These tall Mallowy wands belong more rightly to the herbaceous border ; they will be found in all catalogues—*S. candida, S. oregana* (under the false name of *S. malvaeflora*), and *S. Listeri*—all bushy handsome things of a yard or more in height, with lavish show of silky pink or white Mallows throughout the late summer.

Sideritis.—These are woolly-velvety Labiates of the South, requiring great heat and dryness, which they do not requite with any corresponding brilliancy of blossom. Smallish in habit, and therefore most suitable for the hot rock-garden, are *S. condensata*, with stems of 4 inches, and yellow flowers in September ; and *S. euboea*, flowering at the same time, on stems two inches taller. Others, rather bigger, for higher places on sunburnt banks, are *S. spinosa* and *S. libanotica*.

Sieversia is hardly, if at all, to be distinguished from Geum, either in looks or needs. The names, in catalogues, are often changed. *S. anemonoeides* is a pretty creeping species from Kamchatka, with solitary fine flowers ; *S. glacialis* is hairy and one-flowered also, with golden blossoms that cheer Siberia. And *S. Rossii* usually appears in lists as Geum. It has handsome feathered shining foliage, and brilliant yellow blossoms on long stalks. There is also a quite dwarf variety of this in Tchuchtchuland, called *S. R. humilis*.

Silēnē.—In spite of having lately lost two of its brightest jewels, this huge and artificial family still retains some valuable rock plants, of delicate rather than dazzling charm, among hundreds of worthless and weedy species of which an enormous number are annuals into the bargain. The race is predominantly Southern, and is often being split and re-divided ; the following list includes *Heliosperma*, and, besides omitting all worthless annuals and all the ranker tall-growing herbaceous species, will try to warn the buyer against less worthy perennials in a vast race of low general average attractiveness, yet too often having its many species advertised in lists without comment.

S. acaulis is perhaps the best known and the most generally praised of all alpine plants. I can never feel that the praise is deserved, nor that the species really merits quite such sedulous attention in the garden, where so many things of far higher merit could be cultivated with a tithe of the labour bestowed to suit this cushion of rather crude little chalk-pink stars, which in the garden will rarely, if ever, be induced to be more than an attractive neat flat mass of glossy almost spiny-leaved close-packed rosettes, with a greater or less (usually less) lavish allowance of comparatively pallid blossoms in summer. At the same time, this is a merely personal feeling, and to many people *S. acaulis* is gracious as the Grail ; nor are the huddled masses of colour that it makes on the Alps (from end to end, from England to America, from the Arctic circle to the Southern Alps), on lime or granites, anything but a joy to behold as you see them lying in sheets of sheer pink in the upmost shingles and rocky ridges, or making a shot-silken effect of rose, in little grassy folds of the final alp, interthreaded with fine grass, and blotted here and there with *Gentiana verna* in spring, or *G. bavarica* a month later. Yet its colour is never clean, however brilliant ; and, in many of those high places, if you go a little higher yet, you come upon the no less solid but perfectly pure pink mats of *Androsace alpina,* so clean and gentle and well-bred in their unsullied radiance that one sickens evermore of the Silene, despite one's best intentions and honest feelings of admiration—always compelled as they are, by the memory of the Androsace, to feel a blatancy and an underbred shrillness about the colour and even the habit of the Silene. However, in the garden they are both memories, and likely to remain so. The Silene will at least *grow* with the utmost readiness almost anywhere in the sun, in light soil, and makes very fine cushions of lucent emerald moss ; in the moraine it does quite well, and looks its most characteristic, and often flowers more freely than elsewhere. In the garden there are various forms of it—one with white blossoms— such of them as they are (a poorish thin variety not at all uncommon in the hills) ; and another with yellow morbid foliage, called golden, because it is not green. The variety *S. a. exscapa* is usually seen at higher elevations than the type, and is a specially miserable little thing, making enormous masses, into which all over are rammed minute squinny pink stars much smaller and less glowing than in the species. As for the *elongata* form, this is now acknowledged by Dalla Torre as a species.

S. alpestris stands high among the best and most valuable of the family. It likes a cool and not too sunny place in rich light soil, and there it rambles loosely far and wide, with tufts of long-oblong narrow leaves of bright and shining green ; from the shoots here and there, all the summer through, rises a profusion of delicate branching stems about 6 or 8 inches high, firm, and yet most dainty in effect, sticky with glands as they ascend, and carrying wide showers of far-spaced lovely white stars with fringy petals, very rich and pure in effect. It is a common plant of damp places at rather low elevations in the limestones of the Carpathians and the Tyrol, while on the granites there develops an absolutely paludose form, of extreme loveliness, growing in the stream-beds and sphagnum mats under the Great Glockner, and producing sheaves of blossom in the most exquisite shades of clear pure rose. And there is also a double-flowered version of the white type. All forms and types of *S. alpestris* seed abundantly (like all the race) and can also be multiplied at any time by division.

S. alpina is a name that can be ignored.

S. aprīca is declared to come from China, to attain 8 inches, and to have flesh-pink flowers in June.

S. argaea is a minute Eastern species, barely 2 inches high, with white stars in June.

S. Armeria is an annual of the South, with heads of chalky-rose bugles, on stems of a foot or so, enhanced by pairs of ample and rather stem-embracing narrow-oval leaves of glaucous-blue. In the moraine it seeds itself from year to year, and grows very much smaller and more delicate, so that it has real charm and value, flowering when there is apt to be a feeling of emptiness there, throughout late summer and on into the autumn.

S. Asterias, with a variety, *S. a. grandiflora*, is also an annual, but larger, taller, bushier, in the same style of display.

S. auriculata is an alpine tuffet, with pointed leaves and white flowers lonely on short stems, emerging from a baggy calyx.

S. Borderi is a small lawn-forming species, mossy and dense, peculiar to the rocks of the French and Spanish Pyrenees in the alpine zone. It makes close masses, with hairy little spatulate leaves, and quite short stems, more and more sticky towards the top, where it unfolds two or three bright pink flowers with deeply cloven lobes in a large calyx.

SILENE.

S. Boryi makes a matted tuffet of very narrow small grey leaves, with many stems of some 3 inches or half a foot, each carrying one or two pale-pink flowers with bifid petals. (From the high rocks and alps and open bare places of the Sierra Nevada.)

S. bryoeides has no right to separate rank from *S. acaulis,* unless that the petals of the pink stars that crowd its flat and glossy mat are not notched, and its seed-capsules are a little shorter. It is a plant of the Jura.

S. caespitosa stands near *S. Saxifraga,* and, like all that group, has not any special brilliance or beauty, though the wide matted masses of shoots have their furnishing value, and the countless frail stems of 8 inches or so carry flowers of pale dim pinky-white.

S. californica is always a rare species, even in its own country; and, in ours, like many of its transatlantic kin, requires deep light soil, rich and well-drained, in a sheltered sunny place. In habit it is loose and lax, with branches of 10 inches or so, flopping from the central root-stock, set at intervals with pairs of rather sticky oval-pointed leaves, and branching into sprays that each carry a single flower, huge and ragged, and of the most astonishing velvety scarlet, in a dark calyx. It blooms all through late summer, and should be most tenderly watched, and have its abundant seed collected and sown each season in case of accidents.

S. Campanula differs in nothing from *S. Saxifraga* for garden effect. It is a plant from damp shady places of the Maritime Alps, making great masses of fine soft narrow-pointed leaves; and the countless stems spraying out their flowers of dim white, dirtied beneath with brown, are *not sticky towards the top,* as in *S. Saxifraga.*

S. capillipes is another in the same persuasion from the Levant.

S. caucasica stands closely akin to *S. vallesia,* to which refer accordingly for its portrait. It has no startling merit.

S. chromodonta is a delicate little thing of damp rocks and cool mossy places in the same charming style and kinship as *S. pusilla.*

S. ciliata approaches *S. Borderi,* but is larger and less attractive, making lawns of bigger but no less hairy leaves, and carrying cloven-petalled flowers of white or pink in stout hairy calyces on stems of 9 inches or so, with one, two, or three blossoms, all turning the same way.

S. cordifolia forms a glandular-sticky tuft, with broad leaves in pairs on stems of some 4 to 8 inches, each carrying one pretty pinky blossom of delicate flat starry shape, only slightly cloven in the lobe. (Maritime Alps.)

S. Correvoniana is the double form of *S. elongata,* Bellardi, *q.v.*

SILENE.

S. dianthoeides is a species from the grassy alps of Caucasus, **where** it forms dense perennial mats of foliage, and sends up its flowers in dense heads, like those of some clustered Pink, on stems of 6 inches or so.

S. Elizabethae has gone away into *Melandryum, q.v.*

S. elongata, **B**ell, is a close cousin of *S. acaulis*, but differs so magnificently from that poor cousin as to have earned specific rank. It is almost confined to the districts of the Western Graians, extending into Dauphiné, and eastward as far as the Simplon, growing at times almost to the exclusion of the type, from which it stands aloof in making larger, looser, handsomer mats, covered with *much larger and brighter flowers* of much richer outline, and emerging from the tuffets on quite definite little stems of 2 inches or more, instead of sitting almost close in a carpet. It is a plant of singular opulence and beauty of effect, and in cultivation is neither better nor worse to grow than the type, though incomparably more desirable. There is a double-flowered form called *S. e. Correvoniana*, and the wild type may be seen abounding in the rocks by the roadside on the top of the Mont Cenis Pass, and there recognised by eyes that would otherwise be bewildered to see *S. acaulis* so very much finer, ampler, and more splendid than usual—almost like mats of glowing little single Carnations depending from the shaly cliff.

S. eriophorum (Heliosperma) is the correct name of *S. Veselskyi* (which is also called *S. Heuffleri* and *S. glutinosum*). It is quite a good thing all the same, like a combination of *S. alpestris* and *S. quadrifida*, making an upstanding fine bush of 6 or 9 inches, all in a tangle of very thin sticky-stemmed sticky-leaved branching sprays, with innumerable stars of white blossom all the summer through, in the way of *S. quadrifida*, but more numerous, and in a much more intricate fine mass. It grows easily in any cool open soil.

S. exscapa. See under *S. acaulis.*

S. glutinosum=S. eriophorum, q.v.

S. Graefferi=S. ciliata, q.v.

S. Griffithii is not of great merit.

S. Hayekiana is exactly after the habit and scant beauties of *S. Saxifraga, q.v.*

S. Heuffleri=S. eriophorum.

S. Hookeri is a specially beautiful species, on the contrary, even taking rank above *Melandryum Elizabethae.* It comes from California, and appreciates light open soil or moraine, in a sunny, warm, and well-drained position. Here it forms a tuft or clumped tuft from a central taproot, after the fashion of Archduchess Elizabeth's Melan-

SILENE.

dryum, but that the leaves are very finely long and narrow, grey with down, lying laxly out on the ground in wide star-fish rosettes of unequalled delicacy; round these rosettes, all through the summer, spring countless stems of 2 inches or so, each carrying one enormous gaping flower of the softest and truest pink, with white rays from the throat in a secondary star, and the petals so deeply cut into long narrow pointed lobes, that the blossoms seem to have ten beautiful long fringy petals standing out in a regular catherine-wheel like some enormous Sempervivum flower of steadied flame and purified rose-pink. The only enemy of this plant is excessive damp in winter; for sunny and well-drained places, or suitable moraine, it is one of the most important prizes ever brought over, and, though now it roars upon us as a novelty, was first introduced in 1873.

S. humilis should be as valuable as the last when it comes to hand. It lives in the high schistose screes on Tufandagh in the Eastern Caucasus, and may be pictured as a smaller, tidier version of *S. Schafta*.

S. Keiskei is a Japanese species, approaching to the flopping habit of the Americans. It has weakly narrow leaves and ample handsome stars of well-coloured flowers, with the petals cloven in rounded lobes not quite to half their length.

S. Kitaibeli is like *S. Saxifraga*, but taller and more graceful in habit.

S. laciniata comes from California, and gives an idea of the glory possessed by *S. californica*, to which it is declared inferior. It has a deep central stock, that must be planted in light rich soil in a warm place, very deep and perfectly drained; this emits a certain number of narrow leaves, and a few quite weakly flopping stems of 8 or 10 inches, carrying on their branches all through the summer enormous flat and double-pointed rayed stars of flaming vermilion. Like all this group it has a feeble constitution in England, to match its feebleness of stem (which prevents it from ever producing any unanimous effect of flower), and the best way of making sure of it is to save the seed with diligence each season.

S. Lerchenfeldiana is a smooth and blue-grey little plant of decumbent habit, and the highest attractions, which may be seen trailing about in the cliffs of the Balkans, and throwing forth a perennial profusion of charming clear pink stars on graceful and delicate stems throughout the summer.

S. libanotica has white flowers on 6-inch stems in summer.

S. maritima is our own Sea-Campion, from the coasts and high-alpine inland cliffs. It is quite easy to grow, and, in fact, inclined to sow itself too freely in the garden; for, though its leafy blue-grey stems

PLATE 47.

SHORTIA GALACIFOLIA.
(Photo. R. A. Malby.)

SILENE HOOKERI.
(Photo. W. Irving, Kew.)

PLATE 48.

SOLDANELLA ALPINA.
(Photo. W. Irving, Kew.)

TANAKAEA RADICANS.
(Photo. R. A. Malby.)

of 6 inches or so, prostrate on the ground, are pretty enough with their large crimpled white blossoms, yet they lack refinement and effect. Nurseries advertise a *rosea* form, which has flowers of a dim and washy magenta-pallor. And there is also a double form which has the untidy fatness of the border Pink, *Mrs. Sinkins*.

S. monachorum is a tiny variety of *S. quadrifida*, from cool rocks of the Balkans, where it sends up its little white galaxies all through the summer on stems of 2 inches.

S. Moorcroftiana is an Indian species, emitting stems of some 12 or 18 inches, from a woody stock. It has no value.

S. multicaulis has long tapering narrow foliage, and forms itself into grey tufts, from which arise many stems of 8 inches or a foot, carrying either one solitary pink flower, or else two or three in a short spray at the top. (It is general in the Rockies.)

S. nevadensis lives in high crevices, and is like a dwarf *S. italica*.

S. norica is a local development of *S. acaulis*, without much distinct value.

S. odontopetala forms dense rosetted tufts in the sheer rock-walls of Lebanon and the Levant, from which, springing below the rosettes, come stems of 6 or 8 inches, more or less (for the type is most variable), bearing white stars in July.

S. olympica belongs to the kindred of *S. dianthoeides*, growing in a mat, with clustered white flowers on a rather taller stem.

S. oreades comes close under the shadow of *S. Saxifraga, q.v.*

S. Orphanidis emerges from it handsomely. For, though a wide loose tuft and cushioned mass of small fine foliage like *S. Saxifraga*, the countless flowers on their delicate stems of 10 inches or so are larger and whiter and more attractive. (It lives in the summits of Athos.)

S. parnassica is a yet taller-stemmed plant in the way of *S. Saxifraga*, with stalks of 8 inches or so.

S. pennsylvanica has the basal leaves nearly hairless, spatulate, and tapering to a hairy foot-stalk. The stems are half a foot high or thereabouts, carrying clustered pink flowers from April to June.

S. petraea = S. alpestris, q.v.

S. pharnaceifolia is cluster-headed above a close cushion, with white flowers on stems of 4 inches, in July.

S. pudibunda. See under *S. quadrifida.*

S. pumilio has gone away into *Saponaria, q.v.*

S. pungens makes dense tuffets in the sheer cliffs of Armenia, and has white flowers on stalks of half a foot.

S. pusilla is a most dainty, lovely species for a cool corner on the shady side of a limestone rock. It is like a miniature of *S. quadrifida*, with glossy tufted masses of very small glossy green leaves, narrow and fine as moss ; and the flower-stems are as fine to match, about 2 or 3 inches in length, coming up in such profusion all the summer through, that the plant is hidden in a cloud of small virginal white stars with regular jags to the petals.

S. quadrifida (*S. quadridentata*) is an abundant plant in shady places, cool damp rocks, and path-sides in the limestone Alps, and in the garden enjoys moist and shady rockwork no less, where it makes a delicate effect, being thready-frail and loose in habit, twice the size of the last, but no less dainty, with quite narrow little glossy green leaves, and branching airy stems that vary from 2 inches high to half a foot, and shower forth, all the summer through, multitudes of star-flowers of very pure bright white, with four regular little teeth at the edge of the petals, giving the blossoms a charming cog-wheel effect. There is a variety of this, with broader leaves and rose-coloured flowers, which is found on primary rocks, and is rare. Owing to its modest habit, this blushing maiden is called *S. q. pudibunda* (*Heliosperma*).

S. Reichenbachiana blooms in May, with 4-inch stems, and white flowers.

S. Roehmeri stands near *S. olympica*. It is a mat-forming plant of Macedonia, with stems of half a foot, bearing clusters of white blossoms in that dirty isabelline tone affected by so many of the race.

S. rupestris is only biennial, but may easily be raised yearly from its abundant seed. For it is a really pretty species, often to be seen in rough places and dry open slopes in the granitic Alps, where it forms little leafy bluish-green tufts, with rather broad oval-pointed foliage, and stiffish stems that vary between 3 and 10 inches, waving and branching in quite a different effect from the lacy and cloudlike daintiness of the Quadrifida group, or the taller and well-balanced elegance of *S. alpestris*, yet quite effective in their sturdy neat way, with sprays of milk-white flowers ample in the petals, which are only very slightly lobed (if at all), instead of being cut into teeth, so that they look mild and cosy and solid. It flowers persistently through the summer, and the milky whiteness often passes into tender pink. In the garden it should have a sunny place in well-drained peaty soil or moraine, with abundance of chips, but no lime.

S. Saxifraga is the type of many, and common in all the ranges of the Southern Alps. It makes a great loose cushion, on very thin woody flopping stocks that develop into masses of innumerable pointed narrow leaves of brilliant grassy green, from which rise ascending sticky stems in perpetual profusion through the summer, wiry and fine, and most graceful in their slender port and multitudes, each carrying an erect, notch-petalled flower, of middling size and of a dim greenish-white, with a dirty reverse of brownish tone. It is quite easy to raise and grow, and has a certain daintiness rather than any brilliancy of show or charm.

S. Schafta is perhaps one of the rock-garden's greatest assets in late summer and autumn, when the profuse leafy tufts and wide masses of 4 or 5 inches are covered for months on end with the profusion of its large rosy-magenta flowers in dark calyces. So lavishly does it grow, indeed, and so riotously bloom, that it loses the refined air of endurance which ought to be associated with an alpine perennial, and takes on the look of some bedding annual, ebullient in blossom because ephemeral. And there is something a little crude and un-alpine too about the lushness of its leafage. It is, however, a plant of the easiest culture anywhere, and free of seed ; so that, with its free and tardy flowering habit, it becomes a species of high value.

S. Sendtneri has whitish blossoms, on stems of 10 inches or a foot, in July.

S. Smithii is a tufted mass in the way of *S. Saxifraga.* This is *Saponaria caespitosa* of the Flora Graeca.

S. spathulata hangs unattainable in the cliffs of the Ossetian Caucasus, in little densely sticky tufts, from which come stems of 2 inches or so, each bearing three large flowers of bright rose-purple, with the petals deeply cloven.

S. stellata=*S. ciliata, q.v.*

S. subulata, like *S. stentoria* and *S. rhyncocephala,* is a dwarf of no value, with tiny flowers.

S. tatarica=*Lychnis viscaria alba nana.*

S. tejedensis comes nearest to *S. Boryi,* but is hoar-frosted with sticky greyness all over.

S. vallesia is another interesting type, which may be found running in the warm granitic crevices of the Cottian and Maritime Alps, &c.— a local species, though of wide distribution. It is quite dwarf, with rather large paired leaves, oval-pointed and very sticky, of light but dull green colour, and soft lax texture—not so much gathering into masses as a rule, but emerging in little low shoots of an inch or two along the cracks of the rock. The whole growth has a robust and rather lush look, and the flowers are borne on leafy stems 3 or 4 inches long, and often much less, two or three to the spray, or sometimes only one. The fatness of the long calyx gives high hope of the blossoms, but such optimism goes unrewarded, for these, when they do unfurl (which they do not properly do except at evening), though rather large, are not big enough for the leafy plant, and are of dim greenish-white inside, with a reverse of dull brownish-red, repeating those of *S. Saxifraga* in doubled size, and with the petals much more deeply cloven.

S. Veselskyi=*S. eriophorum.*

S. virginica, the Fire-pink, is most splendid, but by no means easy to cope with perennially, and, like the others of the group, by no means usually long for this world. It should have a very deep-soiled and perfectly-drained place on a sheltered open slope, with a warm aspect. The soil should be a rich light mixture of peat, loam, leaf-mould, and sand, made spongy and loose, and diluted with chips ; into this the plant will happily send its vast root, and the crowns will break into tufts of long rather thin narrow spoon-shaped oval leaves. From these will spring or flop the frail slender stems, in summer, branching into sprays that carry here and there at rare intervals and in steady succession enormous flat flowers of violent crimson-scarlet, rich and velvety, with the oblong petals deeply cloven.

S. Zawadskyi (*Melandryum Zawadskyi*) makes the richest promise, with its beautiful basal rosettes of dark green lucent leaves, looking like the clump of some Arthritic Primula, and no less easily to be cultivated in any light soil, in sun or shade. But the upstanding stems, of 4 or 5 inches, unfurl in late summer, one above the other, three or four quite uninteresting greeny-white flowers sometimes a little tinged with pink, in a style that blends *S. maritima* and *S. vallesia* in one unsatisfactory combination.

Sisyrinchium.—These small Irids have beauty in their neat clumps of Iridaceous or rush-like leaves, no less than in the persistent profusion of their satiny bells or stars of blossom. The race belongs mainly to the New World, and, though many of the species are small and charming, some of them are large and ugly, in the way of *S. striatum*, which makes almost the growth of a stiff Bearded Iris, with crowded spikes a foot high or more, of straw-yellow flowers of the feeblest effect. *S. angustifolium* (sometimes called *S. bermudianum*) is the best-known Blue-eyed Grass—a name that is really apt to its lavish grassy tufts and clumps, with the little sword-blade leaves seeming to erupt at their tips into an unending profusion of delicate blue stars. It is the type of a large American group, all in the same way of charm, of which the best are *S. anceps* (*S. gramineum*), *S. montanum*, *S. arenicola*, *S. Farwellii*, and *S. atlanticum*. Yet this invader is abundant in the wild and woolly West—not of America only, but of Ireland, running riot among the grass in damp cool places of Kerry and Galway. Here it has long been known ; but of late years has

From **JACK DRAKE**

INSHRIACH ALPINE PLANT NURSERY
AVIEMORE, INVERNESS-SHIRE, SCOTLAND

Tel.: KINCRAIG 211 207   Station: AVIEMORE

28 April 1958.

M MISS ETHRIDGE
18 LAUDER RD
EDIN 9

1 SISYRINCHIUM (yellow) diffol.og

P & P   3/6
           2/-

           5/6

Paid

AVIEMORE INVERNESS-SHIRE, SCOTLAND

successfully invaded England also. In cooler, moister parts of the rock-garden or waterside it promptly establishes itself, and seeds with such profusion that it is soon far away in the water-meadows, puzzling the cows. It is much to be wished that the same could be said of *S. grandiflorum* and *S. filifolium*, for these rare treasures have a beauty that baffles words. They are both rush-leaved plants; *S. grandiflorum* is North-American, and likes cool peaty soil, where it is soon at home, forming clumps, widening from a creeping root, of delicate upstanding foliage of rich green, from the tallest of which, some 6 or 9 inches high, the first lengthening of the days in February elicits a succession of most noble hanging bells in a deep and flashing imperial violet, shimmering and sheeny in the silken exquisiteness of the texture, and continuing their succession far on into the spring and early summer. It is so breath-taking a beauty in its byzantine magnificence of colour and fineness of Coan texture, that one can hardly turn away to look at the white variety, which is lovely and delicate and lustrous in its way as a sunlit pearl in dreamland. But she has not yet, in her lucent satin, won to the yet serener grace of the Fair Maid of the Falklands, who more suggests the pale and gentle ghost of Desdemona or Deianeira—a frail exquisite growth of those gaunt moors and rolling stretches, smaller and finer than the last (but for the same treatment in cool peaty soil, with abundance of chips and drainage), darker in its tone of green, and with a stature of 6 inches or so. It hangs out wide diaphanous bells of a white so delicate that they seem fairy cups of blown glass, freaked and lined with dark threads fused in the hyaline texture of the crystal as it sprang from the pipe of that dark rush-like stem, and swelled into a goblet, and now swims delicately in the air, as if it were a bubble about to float loose from its moorings, and set sail home to fairyland. There are various other hardy, and many more half-hardy, Sisyrinchiums (such as rush-like *S. odoratissimum*, with trusses of pale and deliciously sweet long tubes of white blossom, at the top of the green and milky stems): but after *S. grandiflorum* and *S. filifolium* they fall into a huddled dim crowd behind, among the obscurer ruck. And it may wisely be remembered that an unknown Sisyrinchium may often prove to be a *Marica* lurking in ambush for the unwary.

Smelowskya calycina (or **americana**) is a close and charming high-alpine Crucifer, from the Rockies, making dense cushions of leaves an inch or two in length, and finely, sharply feathered; close among which sit short close spikes of pink or white blossoms, each about half an inch across, and with the petals clawed at the base. This shall go into the choice moraine.

Smilacina.—These, on the contrary, are for the bog, or for rich cool soil in shady woodland places. They stand near Solomon's Seal, with the same creeping rhizomes, but with fluffy spires of white stars at the ends of the shoots. *S. racemosa* is the tallest, nearly a yard high very often, and especially handsome with its ample glossy-dark leaves alternating up the stems, and then the ample cone-shaped creamy plume in May and June, followed by berries like vitrified drops of bright blood in autumn. *S. stellata* is much dwarfer, with whitish flowers much more scattered and starry in their loosened and scantly furnished head, produced much later in the summer, about August, and followed by berries of green and black. *S. trifolia* is not more than 4 inches high, with white stars in May ; and the relationships of the race may be gathered from the fact that *Clintonia borealis* sometimes bears the generic name of *Smilacina* instead.

Sobolewskya clavata is an Eastern Crucifer of a foot high, with long spikes of pure-white flowers in midsummer, and heart-shaped leaves below, on long stems, and a general dishonouring likeness to *Sisymbrium Alliaria*, though far more refined. *S. lithophila* is wiser in taking Hutchinsia for its model, and achieving the same effects in the same easy conditions, with white flowers in spikes on stems of 5 or 6 inches.

Solanum Dulcamâra is a native climber, with clusters of violet and gold flowers. It yields a dwarfer and unaspiring form in China, called *S. d. "nanshan"* ; and *S. Sinclairii* is a quite tiny miniature of the next, which I here mention, because *S. tuberosum* was warmly recommended to some enthusiastic rock-gardening friends of mine, as being a really beautiful thing of about 15 inches or 2 feet, rather leafy, but with fine foliage and profuse heads of very large rosy-blue or white flowers, with a rich golden pointil, carried unremittingly all through the summer, and of the finest effect. Accordingly they purchased seed and raised it with great care, and planted it out with more, in the choicest of places, expecting their reward of beauty. And they got it, too, precisely according to the fair and unadorned promise ; only they had omitted to enquire the more vulgar name of the plant—which is "Potato."

Soldanella.—In moist cool soils in open yet cool exposures and atmospheres, the Soldanellas are both hearty and immortal. And why anyone should have wanted to change so lovely a name into "Moonwort" is not clear ; but even Parkinson seems to have shared (reluctantly) the general and enduring craze for forging foolish English names for species that are *not* English (and therefore make such pallid pretences seem even more pretentious than before), a craze that has had its ironical result precisely and solely upon such races as had beautiful and not ugly generics of their own to start with. No eminent person has yet coined a Wardour Street Ruskinianism for Smelowskya, Boenninghausenia, Tchihatchewia, where such might have been useful and admitted ; while the beautiful grace, aptitude, and euphony of " Saxifrage," " Anemone," " Campanula," and " Soldanella " cry shame upon the ancient effort or far-fet preciosity of " Moonwort," " Bell-flower," " Windflower," and that most fatuous of all affectations, " Rockfoil." Fortunately these quirks have long since faded out of favour, and even catalogues only do them rare lip-service sometimes at the heading of a race, but in the body of the page follow the fashion of all sensible people, among whom such nonsense is never heard : everyone who is able to grow a Soldanella or a Saxifrage being able also to call it by its own easy, simple, and beautiful name. The Soldanellas, then, are all of the easiest growth in the conditions described ; often prospering mightily in the open border in alpine climates, and filling the bed with their massed little round and glossy leaves like shining emerald leather. If they would do as much with their flowers all would be well. In point of fact, if they are shy of blossom, I think the fault may often lie outside their own responsibility. Every winter shows the curled bloom-spikes nestling freely down among the bases of the leaves, and rejoices the heart of the gardener with their appearance. And it may be that they also rejoice the eyes of slug or mouse, whose passion for such a tit-bit may be the reason why spring still shows the gardener nothing more than foliage, and the promise has evaporated into greenness unmitigated. Or it may be the changes and chances of our English winter. In any case the buds are far more often formed than developed, and far more often formed than despairing cultivators believe. It would be as well, therefore, to keep the Soldanellas protected against the winter rains with slabs of glass, and also to keep a careful eye open for depredators, who seem to look on the youngling buds in their earliest stages as we on whitebait. In the race there are six species, and many hybrids ; the species shall first be dealt with, and then their crosses.

S. alpina (*S. Clusii*, Schm. ; *S. occidentalis*, Vierh.) is, of course, the best known, thanks rather to its name than to its habits, for it is hardly the member of the race best worth knowing. And yet it is a plant of overwhelming beauty as you see it veiling all the margins of the melting snow with wide films of violet, spreading day by day, till the whole dank brown earth, dark and sodden, becomes a sweep of shot silk in shades of blending umber and amethyst. It is essentially an alpine, *not a sub-alpine species*, occurring only upon the high and open hills, and there in quantities so enormous as to colour the world. It is much smaller and more compressed in habit than *S. montana*, and forms into dense mats and lawns and masses of smaller rounded leaves, *perfectly untoothed* at the edge. The stems are only some 3 inches or so, carrying smaller, fewer *deep* flowers, freaked inside with crimson, and of narrower, straight-sided outline, fringy like all the family indeed, but not opening wide into the ragged splendid saucer of *S. montana*, and carried towards the tops of the stems, instead of here and there, in the much looser and more lavish spray of that much more noble and sumptuous plant—a species that has so undeservedly been obscured by its inferior cousin that in most popular handbooks, such as Stuart Thompson's *Alpine Plants of Europe*, and Correvon's *Atlas de la Flore Alpine*, there is no mention of it at all, despite its unquestionable regality in the race. In cultivation *S. alpina* will do with more water, though no less easy than the others ; and will be especially happy in the underground-watered grit-beds, that remind it of the deliquescent snowfields where it dances in its maddest happiness. It would be happier still with us, indeed, if we could give it the snow-carpet that it loves with so warm a heart in winter as to generate (according to romance) heat enough of its own to melt the coverlet and come poking through into the world before the whiteness has gone.

S. hungarica has *S. carpathica*, Vierh., and *S. pyrolaefolia*, Schott, Nyman, &c., for its discarded subsequent synonyms. The second one is to be regretted, for it neatly sums up its habit, which otherwise is smaller in stature than *S. montana*, with fewer lessened flowers of a bluer-lavender, on a stem of some 4 or 5 inches. Its leaves are usually perfectly smooth-edged, instead of with the remote scalloping that is practically invariable in the other. *S. hungarica* is wholly oriental in its distribution, coming no further West than the Hochschneeberg and the Raxalpe below Vienna, and ranging thence through all the Carpathians to the Balkans, in the same situations as *S. montana*, at the same sub-alpine elevations. In gardens it is rare: in catalogues obscure.

S. minima (*S. austriaca*, *S. cyclophylla*, Vierh.) has the same narrowed bell and shallow fringe as in *S. pusilla*, but is a smaller treasure yet, hardly ever achieving more than one flower to a stem of only an inch or two. It may always be known, stature and flower apart, by the fact that its very fat dark little round leaves *are almost like flat salt-spoons* on their stems, *perfectly round in outline;* whereas in *S. pusilla* they swell into an open and very shallow, but quite definite rounded lobe on either side, so as to be of a kidney-

370

shaped design. The flowers, too, seem always to be as pale as the other's only sometimes are ; they are the daintiest wee bells imaginable, fine and frail in shape, waxy and sturdy and crystalline in their texture, dancing across the damp hollows and stream-basins of the Eastern limestones, and down into the Abruzzi, preferring the finest turf (rather than stony places), which the plant fills with shining masses of minute foliage, over which hover, in the family profusion, pale or snow-white bugles, lined with streaks of violet inside. This, again, revels in the underground-watered bed ; and of this, as of all the race, it has well been said that no Soldanella can have too much moisture in summer, or be kept too rigidly dry in winter (*cf. S. pusilla*).

S. montana is certainly the grandest species of all, and in cultivation certainly the one most rarely seen. It does not affect great elevations, preferring moist and rather opener places among the brushwood and coppice of the Alps from end to end (especially, as some say, on the limestone), widely varying, but always to be easily recognised by its especial amplitude, and *singleness of tuft or clump*. It is large and loose in growth, with perfectly round leathery dark leaves, usually with a certain *amount of vague scalloping at their edge;* from the clump arise stems of 6 or 9 inches, carrying some half a dozen immense lavender-lilac blossoms of particular shallowness, widely open and wildly fringy, with recurving open edges, borne here and there at spacious intervals up the stalk. It is a most stately species, and far too rarely seen in cultivation, where, however, it is yet easier and more lavish than the rest. In catalogues it sometimes appears disguised as *S. Clusii* (Curtis), *S. major* (Vierh.), *S. alpina* (F. W. Schmidt), and *S. villosa* (Darracq).

S. pindicola lives on the actual summit of Pindus, on serpentine rock, in company with *Pinguicula hirtiflora;* and differs from the last in its yet taller and stouter habit, but essentially in its own peculiarity of having the *under surface of the leaves* of a *pale hoary grey with pitted minute dots.*

S. pusilla (*S. Clusii*, Gaud.) typifies a new group of only two species, easily known, *S. pusilla* and *S. minima*. All the rest have wide-open bells, ampler or narrower, but always *wide*, and always *deeply fringed* to at least half the depth of the bell. But *S. pusilla* and *S. minima have long tubular little bells*, with only quite a *neat and shallow toothing* at the edge, much more in the way of frilling than of fringe. *S. pusilla* is a fine small neat plant, forming wide masses, and occurring almost as abundantly as *S. minima*, but usually in damper and stonier places at the same alpine elevations, although they often overlap. The stems rise some 2 to 4 inches above the tiny fat kidney-shaped leaves, smooth-edged, outspread, and of glossy dark green ; and hang out one or two lavender-lilac flowers of the typical elongated tubular bell-shape. Apart from its smaller size and difference of configuration, the bloom is usually of paler colour than in the rest ; and in the Dolomites (where it comes upon the limestone that it does not universally prefer), it fades to a pallor almost snowy, and the little bells chime ghostly in their uncounted millions in the steep and stony screes above Misurina in the summer, springing from their glossy mats in the close coign of dankness between each block, till all the slope becomes a-flicker with its multitudes.

The different species often overlap, and a long chain of hybrids has arisen, as easy and as beautiful as their parents, but as rarely seen in gardens as in catalogues, which have only lately begun to recognise their existence, and are yet in pardonable difficulties about their names. Here, then, they are, up to date :

S. × *Wiemanniana* (*S.* × *vierhapperi*, Janch) has *S. alpina* and *S. montana* for its parents. It stands intermediate, with no streakings in the throat of the widely-expanded and irregularly wildly fringy flowers. Sometimes their foot-stalks have the longer impermanent glandular hairs of *S. montana*, and sometimes the small more sessile glands of *S. alpina*.

S. × *lungoviensis* stands between *S. pusilla* and *S. montana*. It is a smaller *S. montana*, with an added touch of depth to the more tubular and yet crazily-fringed bells, and on their foot-stalks glandular hairs that do not fall off as in *S. montana*.

S. × *Richteri* (*S.* × *transylvanica*, Borb.) is the hybrid of *S. pusilla* and *S. hungarica*. The flowers are two to the little stems, and compromise, like the rest, between the shallower ragged bowls of the one parent and the longer, smaller, frilled bells of the other.

S. × *hybrida* (*S.* × *media*, Brügg.) is perhaps the most beautiful of any, borrowing from the small scale and exquisite soft colouring of pale *S. pusilla*, and also from the deep fringes, taller habit, and internal streakings of *S. alpina*. It may be seen abounding in the high woods of the Brenner district, filling the moss-cushions with its shining round little dark leaves, and hanging out everywhere a dancing chorus of the loveliest ample and swelling waxen bells of clearest pale lilac, longer than in *S. alpina*, wider than in *S. pusilla* (so that a delicate cone-shape results), frilled most exquisitely from the mouth, and streaked inside with five blurred lines of crimson-violet velvet that achieve the final note of its especial and endearing charm. The influence of *S. alpina* is seen in the increased stature, size, and the two, or even three, flowers to a stem of 2 or 3 inches ; that of *S. pusilla* in the longer shape of the pale bells, never fringed to more than half their depth, and rarely as deeply as that.

SOLDANELLA.

S. × *Handel-mazettii* (*S.* × *Aschersoniana*, Vierh.) is the hybrid of *S. minima* and *S. montana*; it may be seen on the Austrian limestones, and imagined as being much in the same way as *S.* × *Richteri*, the influence of *S. pusilla* being here replaced by that of *S. minima*.

S. × *Ganderi* (*S.* × *Wettsteinii*, Vierh.) is the only one of the hybrids that has yet strayed into catalogues. The parents, here, are *S. alpina* and *S. minima*, so that their child may be imagined as having very much the same elfin loveliness as *S.* × *hybrida*. The bell, however, though of the same size and dainty streaking, has the yet paler colouring contributed by *S. minima*, and the plant is always to be at once known by the rather long-stemmed leaves, that, on their larger scale, keep exactly the perfect roundness and salt-spoon effect that is so characteristic of *S. minima*. This is not an uncommon hybrid in the Dolomitic limestones of South Tyrol, being found among its parents in great abundance (as are most of the crosses). It is, in effect, like a doubled and tri-flowered *S. minima*, taller and stouter, with the ampler bell more deeply fringed to half its length.

S. × *neglecta* (*S.* × *Jancheni*, *S.* × *mixta*, Vierh.) has *S. minima* and *S. pusilla* for its parents, so that, between beauties so similar, nothing specially distinct could have been expected to emerge in the way of fresh beauty. The flowers, however, solitary on their stems of 3 or 4 inches, are both larger and longer in the bell than either parent's, and the whole plant seems to have developed a special robustness and amplitude in its small way, retaining the salt-spoon leaves of *S. minima*, by which chiefly, among the millions of its progenitors, it may be known. It may be seen on the high limestones of the Karawanken, the Hochschwab, &c.; records of all these hybrids can no doubt be still widely extended, but that of *S.* × *neglecta* from the Pasterze is doubtful, as *S. minima* is not thought to occur in the Hohe Tauern. Of all the species there are, of course, albinoes, especially valuable in the case of *S. montana*, and only less so in that of *S. alpina*; not so much to be desired among the paler tinier blooms of *S. minima* and *S. pusilla*, though very beautiful indeed when you see a mat of those tiny huddled leaves hovered over by little fairy bells so waxen-white that they look as if they were carved from the snow to which they owe their beauty. Division is the ready means of propagating all Soldanells, which can be taken to pieces with the greatest ease, but only slowly, and with uncertainty, be raised from their abundant seed. All clouding and confusing synonyms have here been given, in due order, to the several species whose personalities obscure each other and multiply in catalogues; and it is proper also to note that *S. crenata* and *S. sinuata* are synonyms for—of all impossible things in the world—*Schizocodon soldanelloeides* ! whose soldanellishness, indeed, is only of the most superficial, vague, and general order, not standing for a moment any inspection nearer than a dozen yards.

Solenanthus stylosus comes very close to *Cynoglossum*, with the same needs and habit. It is a hairy Esau of some 12 to 18 inches high, from Central Asia, with dark-purple flowers crowded on the uncurling sprays, which lengthen out afterwards in fruit. It blooms in summer, and is an admissible but not indispensable thing for an open and rather unvalued slope of the garden.

Solidāgo indeed gives us a change, from the most elfin of alpines to the coarsest of woodland weeds. None the less, the Golden Rods have their value, in some eyes, for lighting up the darkening glades of the garden in autumn with their lavish sheaves of rather crude yellow flowers. There is an enormous botanical diversity of species, offering Rods of every shape and size, but such of these as are obtainable will always be found described ; for no catalogue could hope to sell a Solidago without giving clear and detailed promise of the plant's distinct charm among the huge ruck of its relations. *S. Shortii* is among the best of the tall kinds, growing 5 feet high, with lateral sprays of especially lavish flowers that give ample pyramids of yellow stars, with weeping lateral boughs ; and *S. aspera* is like a very delicately bowing Spiraea of spraying gold ; but all the species of this large persuasion are meant for the large wild garden or border only, to fill the rough dank places of the wood, in company with the wilder Michaelmas Daisies. For the rock-garden, however, there is a minutely dwarf form of *S. Virga aurea*, which is really pretty, being the typical common Golden Rod, but reduced to a stature of 3 or 4 inches, whose huddled conglomerations of golden stars in autumn have an almost cheering effect, though hardly alpine. And there are other dwarfs, in *S. nana, S. pygmaea,* and *S. arctica ;* but these are comparative giants of 8 inches or so, not lacking on their smaller scale the weedy coarse look of the race ; but *S. brachystachys* is neat, and only half a foot high, while *S. Cutleri* is a very high-alpine from the Rockies, repeating the neat packed pleasantness of the condensed *Virga aurea.* It is sometimes called *S. alpestris,* a name which is also given to that form of *S. Virga aurea* that is found in Central Europe—not in any way differing for the better from the tall and leafy type, even if it differs at all : so that *S. alpestris* is a name to beware of in lists.

Sonchus.—Usually the Sowthistles are names before which the gardener shrinks in affright, and orders dynamite ; but *S. grandiflorus* is a fine stalwart species of the Chatham Islands, growing sturdily 5 feet tall, with portly sprays of purple flowers ; while, in the wild bog, room might well be made for the stately and extremely rare native, *S. palustris*, of much the same stature and succulence, with ample heads of yellow in late summer, and rich handsome foliage like the double-barbed blade of a narrow spear-head. It makes a fine associate for its no less sumptuous and no less rare cousin, the Bog Rag-wort, *Senecio paluster* (*S. paludosus* is not so tall, and only an annual or biennial), in wild and marshy places among flags and reeds and bulrushes. Spain, meanwhile, sends us a wholly different thing in *S. spinosus*, with a variety often sent out as *Acanthosonchus cervicornis*. Under these sonorous syllables cowers a tight and tiny mass of thorns about 3 or 4 inches high at the most, very branching and woody-stemmed, with a few narrow toothy green leaves springing from the base, and spines and scales making up the rest of the pile, which is beset with little yellow flowers like those of *Lactuca muralis*. As its habit suggests, this is a plant of the hottest, driest, and stoniest places on the coasts of Granada, Africa, and Egypt,—typical desert-species,—and in England should not be trusted to endure for too long in one stay, even though not nearly so miffy, exacting, or tender as its aspect and capricious carping look of unfriendliness would lend one to expect. It blooms quietly and persistently, too, all the summer, and can be quite readily increased by division and cuttings from the base ; so that, altogether, there might easily be unworthier candidates for admission to sunny stony slopes or moraines in the rock-garden.

Soyeria hyoseridifolia=Crepis tergloviensis.

Sparaxis pendula (and var. **pulcherrima**)=**Dierama pendulum,** *q.v.*

Sparganium.—These are water plants of ramping habit and broad soft foliage like a lush ample grass, and strange round fluffy heads of green flower clustered on stems of various heights in summer. They make no show, but are useful for filling shallow waters and edges of marsh ; *S. affine* and *S. minimum* have floating stems, and are smaller than the rest, which are usually a foot or two in height, rapidly spreading into invasive flaccid tangles.

Spathyema foetidum=Symplocarpus foetidus.

Speirantha convallarioeides is a small Chinese woodlander, with creeping rhizomes, and stems of 6 inches, and leaves like those of a little Lily of the Valley ; and then erect bunches of twenty or thirty scentless little white flowers. It should have the shady rich treatment of the Valley-lily that it so resembles in look and habit.

Sphaeralcea Munroana, sometimes also called **Malvastrum Munroanum,** is a useful but rank Malvad, floundering or upstanding, with stems of a yard or so, abounding in grey-haired ivy-shaped leaves, and ending in abundance of bright scarlet mallows from May to November. It is a thing to propagate by seeds or division, and to plant only in the hottest and most sheltered faces, high up on the ledges of the largest and sunniest rockwork, where it can send its roots deep and deep into very light and perfectly-drained soil, while its branches continue to flap and flop their weakly length over the cliffs, and clothe the ledges in their slack and scarlet-fingered embrace.

Spigelia marilandica has been much served ; on account, one supposes, of its difficulty. For, when at last successfully achieved, in the bog treatment accorded to *Gentiana asclepiadea*, its effect is not brilliant in England (whatever may be its beauties in Maryland), when up comes the stem of a foot high or so, set in pairs of green oval-pointed leaves, quite like those of the Willow-gentian, and ending in bunches of erect trumpet-shaped flowers, red outside, and yellow within, late in the summer. In England, when it flowers, it is usually of a dingy Gentian that it has the effect—of some strange parti-coloured Gentian, in hues unheard-of, but not brightly or successfully adopted. It may, however, be capable of better things, but is certainly a mimp in English culture, perhaps pining for the warmer climate of Maryland, and American sunshine, to bring out the fire of its colour; even as it is wanted to elicit the full blazing bloodiness and flame of the Castillejas.

Spiraea.—This vast family is filled with shrubs, but also contains innumerable herbaceous plants for damp and cool rich soils, invaluable for bog, wild-garden, or border. (See also under *Astilbe*.) Among these the first is *S. Aruncus*, a royal pile of splendid foliage, and then wide towering plumes of cream 4 feet high and more, above the sprayed pyramid of the sumptuous wrinkled leafage outspreading in flat ample tiers. It is very common in all the sub-alpine woods and meadows throughout the mountains of Central Europe, in some places forming round bushes so huge and high that they serve as boundaries and hedgerows to the little patches and fields carved out for culture high on the laps of the great hills. It hates being moved or divided, but is otherwise a thing as noble for the wild garden as it is easy and everlasting. There is also a form of it called *S. A. Kneiffii*, not nearly so vigorous and tall and stout, with skeletonised foliage of the most elegant and filmy effect. The species is sometimes called *Aruncus silvester*, and there are others of the far East rather resembling it ; *S. astilboeides* (*Ast. japonica*) comes from Japan and is only about 2 feet high, in the same style, with rather looser plumes of whiter flowers ; and this again has a variety *S. a. floribunda* of especial amplitude, with leaves of glancing green. The common Meadow

SPIRAEA.

Sweet is the type of the next group, and it would not be easy to find a lovelier plant for the waterside. It has purple-leaved varieties, and one with rosy flowers. *S. kamschatica* is the friend that we all learned to know and love long since as *S. gigantea*; it is simply a Meadow Sweet of 6 feet high and more, with magnified and splendid five-lobed (not feathered) leaves, of clear green, and those overwhelming stems topped by a wide foaming crest of creamy-white in summer. It freely seeds itself, and is too gorgeous and tropical and rapid for any use but that of making jungles in the bog-garden, where grown men could play hide and seek. There is a variety with empurpled foliage, and another with flowers in lighter and darker tones of creamy-pink. Another superb Meadow Sweet, but exactly like our own in stature and feathered leafage and looser spraying crests of blossom, is *S. lobata* from America, with flowers in the richest shade of raspberry-fool pink, which deepens to a note in which the allowance of fruit is much larger and that of the cream much scantier, so that the raspberries richly prevail in *S. l. venusta*, often offered as a species, but a form of *S. lobata*, especially opulent and ample, not only in colour, but in growth and flower. And even *S. lobata venusta* has a garden form, sent out by catalogues that wish to be correct, as *S. lobata venusta magnifica*, from which compilation of epithets the portrait of the plant may be imagined. *S. palmata* is different, though in the same bog-garden style. This has the wide five-lobed green leafage of *S. kamschatica*, rather than the dark feathered leaves of the Meadow Sweet, and the sprayed flower-heads have the same wide and foaming effect, though their stems be only some $2\frac{1}{2}$ feet high. The flowers are of almost pure raspberry-and-red-currant-tart-juice colour, with hardly more than a drop or two of cream to lighten it, most sumptuous and appetising to see in summer, when the rich jungles of the colony are awave beneath one's eye in their ample flattened wide billows, so different from the more upstanding, scattered, stiffer, sprays of the Meadow Sweet and *S. lobata*. In gardens, too, there is a mysterious treasure often advertised as *S. digitata*. This is no more than *S. palmata*; but what nurseries ought to mean by it, and usually do, is a most lovely variety of the type, with so compressed a habit that the whole thing, flower-head and all, is hardly 6 inches high, though undiminished in size of blossom, richness of colour, or dainty magnificence of crest. The foliage, too, is more deeply lobed, and the flowers continue far on into late autumn, so that it is the most precious of jewels for a moist cool corner on the choicest rockwork, never ramping nor becoming invasive, but sitting close in a neat clumped pyramid of leaf and flower. There are also other varieties of *S. palmata*, of the same or greater stature than the yard-high type, with blossoms in differing degrees of sweetness and light. These are distinguished in catalogues as *S. p. elegans* and the magnified *S. p. maxima*. And quite close to this stands *S. purpurea*, whose name must arouse no false anticipations, for it belongs to the brown-purple veinings with which the leaves are blurred and diversified, while the fine foam-heads of flower are pink as in all these last, and with the leaves up the stems of the same ample verge and pointed lobes. And finally, in this group there is our own *S. Filipendula*, with a taller and handsomer form with double flowers, and also a pink one ; this likes much drier and sunnier places than the rest, and on many a sunny down of England may be seen making a rosette of finely feathered and ferny dark green leaves, springing from the ground in their rosette, and rather like those of an unsilvered *Potentilla anserina*, until it has sent up its slim and nearly naked stem, breaking into a wide foam of cream-white bloom in early summer. See Appendix.

Of shrubs in this race there is no end, and, with China now emptying over us its shoe as if we were Edom, their number is daily increasing as their desirability and distinctness lessen with their multiplication. Here there is no place for such ; all catalogues that sell them sufficiently commend and describe them. But *S. crispifolia* (often appearing in the same list as *S. bullata*, as if the two names meant two plants instead of only one) is a valuable bushling for an effective corner of the rockwork, very stiff and upstanding in habit, with many little stark boughs, beset with stark dark rough leaves, strangely blistered and twirled and quirled, and ending in many small dim heads of flowers of fluffy pink in later summer, the whole thing not being more than some 10 inches or a foot at the most. Much more in the way of the rock-garden, however, is *S. caespitosa*, which breaks away from the traditions of all the rest, and makes dense wide mats of silvered undivided little narrow leaves (like those of an *Antennaria dioica* that has lost much of its silver), in any sunny well-drained place in perfectly light stony soil or moraine ; and from this, from early summer onwards, sends up spikelings of fluffy white bloom on stems of not more than a few inches. This is an American, as is also another pleasant thing, often called *Eriogÿna pectinata*, but in reality *S. pectinata*, however little it may look it. This is Mrs. Sprat to Caespitosa's Jack ; for it likes cool moist soil in a rather shady situation, where it forms tufts of very fine and ferny shining green foliage, rather suggesting *Saxifraga hypnoeides*, and emitting runners, with tufts of leaves, that strike root and widen the colony ; the spikes of woolly-white flowers come up on stems of a few inches in summer, and the plant is a treasure for the cool damp rockery, although it is so much a traitor in deserting the traditions of Spiraea in order to plagiarise the prettiness of a lax-growing Mossy Saxifrage. Much the most lovely, however, of all the Spiraeas we at present possess in the rock-garden is *S. decumbens*, sometimes also sent out as *S. Hacquettii*. This is a true shrub, and a perfect miniature of *S. arguta*, but not more than 3 or 4 inches high, running finely about among the sunny stony places of the limestone screes of the Dolomites, with little arching shoots set delicately with small and well-proportioned toothed grey leaves, and bearing loose galaxies of milk-pure stars throughout the summer on bending sprigs and elegantly-spaced sprays of 4 or 5 inches, half flopping and half standing, but always of incomparable charm and sweetness of aspect. This most lovely little species runs freely about with underground roots, and, in ledge or slope of the well-built rock-work in a sunny place and light limy soil or moraine, soon forms colonies of a foot across and more, never crowded, but always inimitably graceful in the wiry archings of its fine frail wiry stems, beset with such small blue-grey leaves, and so lavish in the sprayed loveliness of the snow-pale flowers.

Stachys.—This family of Hedge Nettles, like so many of the Labiates, is much too generally coarse and dowdy for the rock-garden, usually with woolly fat foliage, and whorled spikes of dull dead-nettle-flowers on gawky fat stems in summer and autumn. There are, however, two plants of preposterous merit emerging unexpectedly in this coarse dim race (catalogues can chant the charms of the rest).

S. corsica is completely dwarf and neat and green, forming a wide and very quickly-spreading dense carpet of shining emerald little leaves, close upon which through all the summer sits such a profusion of large and blushing flowers that the whole mass becomes and remains a sheeted field of soft and creamy flesh-pink, clear and pure and fine in texture as well as in colour. It can obviously be multiplied at any moment to any extent ; it is faithfully hardy, but likes a dry sunny place in specially well-drained light loam, where it can have room to spread into a carpet so close and thick and wide that fairies might give a dance there among the untellable multitudes of those flowers, tinged to warmth like the first promise of the sun on far-off snowy ranges. Taller than this is *S. lavandulaefolia* from the Caucasus, and in need of the same sunny situation and light soil on the rockwork, where it forms creeping woody masses of shoots and subterranean runners, sending up prostrate stems that make a dense tuft of grey velvety foliage, from which spring whorled spikes of purplish-red flowers in summer.

STAEHELINIA.

Staehelinia.—This is a race of sub-shrubby woody Composites for hot dry corners of hot dry rockwork, where they form bushlings of whitened foliage, set in later summer with narrow flowers. *S. dubia* belongs to Southern Europe and is about 15 inches high, with blossoms of purple-rose ; *S. uniflosculosa* is the prettier, from the burning hills of Greece, with a stature of some 8 inches, and flowers of clearer pink. Seed and cuttings.

Stanleya pinnatifida is an American Crucifer of about 2 feet high, for a warm dry place in poor soil ; it has feather-cut fine foliage and freely branching spires of golden-yellow flowers from May to July. It may be raised from seed, but has no particular value.

Statĭcē.—The Sea-Lavenders are eminently a race of the South, developing into vast bushes in the Canaries, from the modest little size of our own *S. ovalifolia* (*S. auriculaefolia*, Vahl.). As a family, considering their provenance and their taste for hearing what the wild waves may be saying, by the sterile sands and salty marshes of the Southern seas, the Statices are a family of astonishing willingness and ease in cultivation, taking to good fat loam anywhere in the open garden, with a zeal as warm as if they had not chosen in nature to plough the sands. Catalogues freely offer the herbaceous-border species, of which quite the best is *S. latifolia*, with very handsome evergreen foliage, and clouds of lavender a yard high and a yard across through the later months of the summer. Rather smaller, but beautiful, and, like all these, so especially valuable as helping to fill the voids of autumn, are *S. eximia*, *S. altaica*, and *S. Gmelini*—this last with splendid glaucous-blue leaves and swathes of dark-purple stars. *S. incana* (*S. tatarica*) has loose foot-high showers of bright ruby-red (or variable) blossoms above rosettes of decorative leaves (it has a neat compacted *nana* form) ; and *S. speciosa* with our own native *S. Limonium* blooms earlier, in May and June, and is worthy of a place. There remain, however, a vast number of smaller species, of the most gracious and well-bred effect on the rockwork, not the least charming being *S. minuta*, with an indefinite number of variations ; but the type is the tight little Sea-Lavender that sits in the crevices of the Mediterranean coast, and has specially delicate rare-flowered flights of lavender blossoms in winter, on sprays of 3 or 4 inches above the clumps of small rosettes made of hoary-grey spoon-shaped leaves, minute and elegant. Like so many of these Mediterranean plants, it is perfectly hardy in the garden, but takes some years to learn how silly it is to try and flower in the middle of an English winter. *S. spathulata* is one of the beauties of the race, growing to 6 or 8 inches, with fine blue-grey persistent foliage, and notably brilliant blossoms of purple and white.   Equally magnificent in a new style is *S. undulata*, which makes perfectly smooth hairless downless tufts of wavy-toothed foliage, from which rise foot-high stems breaking into big heads of flowers especially large, pure white, and frilled in great chaffy stars of an even more brilliant snowiness to complete their effect.   This lovely thing is found along the coast from Attica to Puerta de Despeña-perros in Spain.   Of smaller species there are many of similar charm among themselves, all well-deserving of more attention than they get ; for few things could be prettier than our own *S. lychnidifolia* (*S. auriculaefolia,* Vahl. and Benth.), and the still neater and tinier *S. reticulata,* which almost approaches the daintiness of *S. minuta.* But among these species there is wild confusion, so closely are they allied, and the name Auriculaefolia, for instance, is so generally applic-able that it has been generally applied—as, to *S. ovalifolia* and *S. Gerardiana* (*S. ovalifolia* having also been called *S. globulariaefolia*). The picture, then, to be made of all these, is of a basal tuft of neat and grey-green leathery oval leaves, from which rise spraying loose showers of everlasting flowers in chaffy cups, which though of no brilliant effect in their muffled lilac-lavender, are yet of a delicate grace especially their own, and specially valuable in *S. Costae* from Catalonia, whose dainty stems have an arched and bending habit.   *S. corymbosa* is a variety of *S. lychnidifolia,* while there are many more in the same kinship, all quietly well-bred little plants of airy effect on the rockwork, where they bloom in summer and late summer, and should be exposed to full sunshine in a well-drained light soil, and there propagated by divisions pulled from the many-headed crowns, or else by seed.   The glory of the whole race, however, is *S. caesia* from the salty wastes of South-eastern Spain, forming mats and dense masses of small spoon-shaped leathern leaves, densely hoar-frosted with lime till they seem rimed with blue and white ; from these ascend a number of stems sometimes a yard high, breaking into the noblest and amplest pyramids of purple that the family affords.   And, no less regal than this, and even more germane in its growth for the rock-garden, is *S. insignis,* which has the same amplitude and beauty, but is of much dwarfer habit, and with the leaves of dark olive-green, hardly limy at all.   (It is a rare species of Southern Spain.)

Stellaria.—The Stitchworts make no pretence to liveliness, but for shady cool places on the rockwork there are several species that either flop and flounder along, or form tufts of fine foliage studded with an interminable succession of white stars in summer.   Of these *S. bulbosa* and *S. radicans* are of bigger, looser habit, while *S. ruscifolia* and *S. cerastioeides* are clumps of some merit.

Stenanthium.—These are large Liliaceous plants in some ways suggestive of Veratrum, but certainly more graceful, sending up in summer their narrow and sword-like leaves, and then running up in a noble bending tasselled spire or plume with drooping branches, all heavy with countless flowers that open greenish, and then pass, in the course of their long life, to pure-white and pale-rose, making an effect of amplitude and rich tenderness unparalleled in pictures. All this, however, is rather an account of what they ought to do than of what they actually do. *S. robustum* causes convulsions in catalogues; they foam with enthusiasm like the flowers they depict. But, plant it never so well in damp rich soil in a warm and sheltered corner, the *Stenanthium* rarely does any such thing as dazzle, but produces mangy draggled feathers at the best, of tassels that rarely emerge from their dim and greenish tone. The race is American, and probably the special sunshine of that continent is necessary to ripen the temperament of its members. Other species of less value are *S. angustifolium*, which does not get beyond being whitish, and *S. occidentale*, which is of dwarfer habit, not more than a foot high, with spikes of blackish-purple.

Stenosolenium saxatile stands between Arnebia and Eritrichium. It is a Siberian species, very hispid and hairy and branchy, with oblong narrow foliage and elongated sprays of blossom in summer along the ends of the branches. The flowers are long in the tube, and of rich violet-purple.

Sternbergia.—These are well known—the lovely golden Autumn Crocus of the South, with masses of glossy rich strap-shaped leaves, and abundance of flowers in September, rich and solid in their texture as in their pure golden colour, seeming as if Colchicum had been corrected by Tulip, and the result were these gleaming goblets sitting close to the ground through the saddest hours of weeping autumn. Sternbergias should be planted in good deep rich soil in a warm sheltered place and there left alone for ever. The amplest is *S. macrantha;* and other species are *S. colchiciflora* and the old *S. lutea. S. Fischeriana* has the unrivalled originality of blooming in early spring instead of late autumn.

Stobaea (or **Berkheya**).—These are large stalwart thistlish thorny biennials, of handsome coarse effect for rough sunny banks, growing a yard high and more, and blossoming in late summer. *S. membranifolia* has heads of straw-yellow, and *S. purpurea* proves its name only a flattery, and not a lie.

Stokesia cyanea is a beautiful American Composite, growing a foot or 18 inches tall, in deep and light soil, very well drained, and in a hot aspect. Its flowers are like a compromise between a China

Aster and an Artichoke, of clear delicate blue (or white in the Albino). Unfortunately it produces them far too late in the season for their development ever to be successful ; so that the plant was useless for English gardens until the Continent invented a form called *S. c. praecox*, in which the fault was corrected, and the flowers produced betimes in autumn.   Seed, division, or root-cuttings.

Streptolīrion volubīle is a new climbing Asiatic Commeliniad of no special value, rambling for a yard or more, with little white flowers among the long-stemmed and more or less heart-shaped leaves.

Streptŏpus.—This family is almost pure Solomon's Seal, for the same treatment and of the same sumptuous charm, but having wide branches instead of the one arching stem.   *S. amplexifolius* is often to be seen in the alpine woods, and has small white Solomon-Seal-bells in early summer, often growing nearly 3 feet high, and brilliant with red berries in the autumn.   There are several other species, especially in the mountain forests of America ; among which *S. roseus* stands out, by virtue of having bells of purplish-pink.   It has a lesser habit than the last, being only about 18 inches tall ; *S. longipes* returns towards the exaltation of *S. amplexifolius;* and the Japanese form of *S. ajanensis* has yellow stars.   Division and seed.

Stylophŏrum diphyllum (once called **Meconopsis petiolata,** DC.) is a pretty Golden Poppy-wort, to be raised freely from seed and planted in rich light soil in a rather shady place, or on the edge of woodland, where it will make bushes of handsome smooth green leaves, finger-lobed to the base in veiny divisions each like an oak-leaf.   The stems are a foot or 18 inches high, carrying throughout the summer daintily-stemmed large golden Celandines springing only just clear of the stalwart leafage, either solitary or several, from the summit of the stalk.   This is the Yellow Celandine Poppy of America, sometimes offered under the false name of *S. ohioense.*   There are two other species from the Alps of China : of these *S. sutchuenense* is very handsome, of much the same stature and configuration as the last, with the same comely plump flowers of gold ; but the whole clump is clad in a fur of long russet hair.   The only remaining species, *S. lasiocarpum,* belongs to Central China, where its bleeding root is valued as a drug, and the plant is called Human-Blood-Wort.   It has the same height as the rest, varying between 6 inches and 2 feet.   But the flowers are rather smaller, gathered in bundles of four or five, above the leafage, which is of thin texture, feathered to the base on either side, and with the end lobe largest.   These all bloom in summer, and there is no other *Stylophorum,* for *S. japonicum* of catalogues is *Hylomēcon japonicum,* though precisely similar in prettiness and needs.

SUKEROKIA.

Sukerokia.   See **Heloniopsis.**

Sullivantia Ohionis is a dim little whitish Saxifrage-cousin from America, to be grown at need in a cool, shady, and quite moist place.

Swertia.—This is a curious race in the alliance of Gentiana, but wholly unlike. All its members are inhabitants of marshy meadows over the alps of Europe, Asia, and North America, having their oval-pointed leaves arranged in pairs, and sending up unbranched stems of 6 inches or a foot, breaking, in summer, into a loose pyramid of erect and wide-open large stars of blossom with ample pointed rays. The best-known type is *S. perennis,* the only species of our European Alps, where it may rarely be seen here and there in boggy places and peat-mosses of the open alpine pastures. It is also the only one to be at all commonly cultivated in English bogs, being a lush-looking grower of about a foot high, with flowers of a curious wet-slate-colour, freckled with darkness. There are countless other species, few, if any, in cultivation : from America might come among others *S. palustris,* *S. congesta,* and *S. scopulina*—this last with four-pointed stars of dark blue. And from the Levant, *S. longifolia,* *S. Balansae,* *S. Aucheri* (yellow), and *S. lactea* with whitish-lilac flowers, four-rayed, on stems of 6 inches. And, from the Himalaya, so many species, and so remote, that they are hardly worth recording, seeing that the charm of the family lies in its quaintness rather than in any brilliancy of tone, so that there is little fear but that new species of merit will be at least adequately described in catalogues that may some day offer them. All may be raised from seed, with the delicacy and care attaching to the seed-raising of almost all Gentians ; and when established, divided at pleasure. See Appendix.

Symphyandra.—This race suffers like Adenophora from coming so very close beneath the tyrannous shadow of Campanula, which obliterates all rivals, or, rather, forbids all approach. Yet Symphyandra might well be thought of as Campanula, for in beauty the members of this group (separated only from the other by minute botanical differences) are easily the peers of the best Campanulas. They are all plants of the Caucasus and Levant, all quite easy to raise from seed, all quite easy to grow in light open conditions of the rockwork, all of the most well-bred and delicate loveliness, and all blooming in late summer, when their beauty gains an added value that it hardly needs.

S. armena may be pictured by a little diminishing the noble purple bells of *Campanula Raddeana ;* it has the same graceful spraying stems of 6 inches or a foot, here arching or flopping, and branching into laterals that each carry three or four violet flowers nodding upon their thread-fine foot-stalks. The lower leaves stand up from the stock on long stems; they are heart-shaped egg-shaped, coarsely and irregularly toothed. Leaves and blooms alike are smaller than in the rest of the race, and the plant hangs happily at home in the sheer cliffs of Georgia.

S. cretica lives in the rocks of Sphakia, &c., with stems of 18 inches or so, smooth, hairless, and pale green, with pale-green heart-shaped leaves on their stalks, rather deeply and crudely toothed. In the flower-spire the large nodding bells are solitary, each on a very short foot-stalk, only one to a spray in the short loose pyramid of eight or nine blossoms.

S. Hoffmannii is a taller thing than these last, attaining 18 inches, and carrying white bells. It is the only member of the race, as we know it, that prefers a rather cool and half-shaded place on the rockwork.

S. lazica is another 18-inch species, quite weakly and elegant in the stem, hugging the cliffs and grottoes of Lazic Pontus, and there making tufts of the usual heart-shaped egg-shaped leaves, downy-green, and sharply toothed on their long stems. The blossom-sprays are graceful and pendulous and long-drawn-out, carrying towards the end a very loose and delicate fountain of some half a dozen or more trumpet-bells of enormous size, 3 inches long, and of a ghostly glassy white, swinging daintily each on a long fine foot-stalk of its own.

S. ossetica approaches the unparalleled magic of the next, from which it chiefly differs in being perfectly hairless and downless, even brighter in the green of its leaves (which are often longer, and usually more pointed), and with stems of a foot or so, less lavishly branching and hanging out chimes of loveliest blue.

S. pendula.—It is many years since I have considered this strangely neglected plant (which no one else seems able even to see) as easily the most beautiful thing of its kind that the garden holds in August. It is a copious grower and quite immortal, making huge root-stocks from which spring such a multitude of fine branches that they pile up into a mounded mass, 2 feet across, of bright-green foliage, oval-pointed and crimpled and toothed. From this, in late summer, imperceptibly emerges a corresponding multitude of fine and finely-branching flower-stems, lying down upon an heap like the waters of the Red Sea, or straying forth in cascades upon the ground. And on these, for three months without intermission, are borne unending processions of large long bells in the most wonderful glassy shade of pale and translucent yellow-white, faintly and most exquisitely green like some sainted Primrose in glory. So diaphanous and subtle is the tone and texture of those flowers, that I know nothing like them in the garden for the hyaline miracle of their make, seeming blown bells of rarest Murano, tinkling along the ground in their incomparable multitudes, and shining with a pale glow-worm glamour of their own among the brighter and more earthly green of the amassed foliage. This most noble treasure will grow for ever in any deep rich soil and any open place, but its best altar of worship will be a deep ledge of light soil on the rockwork, a foot or two above eye-level, that the profuse and elfin beauty of its great bells may never fail to elicit the full measure of the adoration for which they so sedulously ring out from July to October. It should be planted, too, with its blue twin *S. ossetica*, that the contrast of delicate tones might yet further, if possible, enhance the unearthly beauty of those Serene Transparencies of crystal.

S. Wanneri hugs the rocks of Roumania, the Banat, Transylvania. It is about 6 inches or a foot long, and its boughs always cling tight to the stone, after the fashion of the saxatile Campanulas, such as *C. Elatines*. The leaves are roughish with hairs, oblong-narrow, sharply toothed, and almost gashed, the basal ones diminishing to the long leaf-stalks. But there are a few leaves on the stems also, and the sprays branch into lateral shoots, all carrying flowers, so that they become a thyrse or ample spire of nodding long bells of imperial violet and imperial magnificence.

Symphўtum.—No Comfrey is in place on the rock-garden, for which their coarse, hairy, leafy, Borragineous habit wholly unfits them. But in the wilderness they are superb, and all the following should be grown, since they need no culture, and reward neglect so handsomely with their bunches of uncurling multi-coloured bugle-bells in spring and early summer; *S. asperrimum*, yard high, with flowers of violet-blue; *S. bulbosum*, yellow, and only 8 inches tall, quite fitted for a choicer place, as is also *S. canescens*, which makes a little bush of 18 inches or so, with very many branching and clear-borne bunches of beautiful clear-yellow flowers suggesting the Golden Drop to which it stands so near in blood; *S. caucasicum* is another Anak of 3 feet, with blossoms of pink and blue, but *S. cordatum* is quite small, not exceeding 6 inches, and begging, accordingly, to give the rock-garden its chimes of creamy-white; *S. peregrinum* is a handsome red-flowered stalwart of 3 feet, and *S. tauricum* is half the height, with its white blossoms continuing on into September and October; while *S. tuberosum*, again, is smaller yet, not much exceeding 10 inches, and bearing yellow bugles in June. Half-shade in the rough light wilderness among the undergrowth for all of these but the smallest; and all can be originally raised from seed, and subsequently multiplied by division.

Symplocarpus foetidus.—The Skunk Cabbage of North America is a goodly ornament to any large bog, where it grows readily and for ever, forming into close and immemorial clumps. In early spring, almost stemless, appear the huge stinking Arum-flowers of dim and livid purplish-green. After these are gone develops the splendid leafage of oval smooth leaves 2 feet high on their stalks, and nearly a foot across. But be careful how you approach it unguardedly; the plant has taken a wrinkle from the animal world; and any part of it, if scraped or bruised or otherwise annoyed, emits (as its popular name forewarns) the characteristic savour of what, in German, is so aptly known as the Stink-beast.

Syneilesis aconitifolia=**Senecio aconitifolius,** *q.v.*

Synthyris.—This is a group of small American alpine Scrophulariads, making tufts of neat foliage, and sending up flowers in little fluffy spikes, sometimes suggesting a condensed and much more refined Wulfenia with a stem of only 3 or 4 inches. All the species that are worth growing thrive readily in cool rich soil, not liking a situation too torrid in climates where the sun is hot in summer; but here succeeding with equal heartiness, whether in sun or shade, and gladdening spring with the show of their curious furry spikes. The best perhaps of all, and the best known, is *S. reniformis*, which makes the most engaging tuffets of round leaves, very dark leathery-green and scalloped neatly round the edge; among these in April springs up a profusion of lovely fluffy spikes of clear violet-blue flowers. In *S. pinnatifida* the leaves are feathered, and the stems are taller, rising to some 8 inches, with dainty plumes of blue. This lives in the high rocky cool places of Idaho and Wyoming; sharing its home with *S. alpina*, of the same rich blueness, but with elliptic little scalloped leaves. *S. plantaginea* has the same height as *S. pinnatifida*, but blooms a month later, in May, with flowers of a pinker tone of blue; and *S. Bullii*, which is ugly and dull yellow, serves as a warning to the young that they should not buy undescribed new Synthirids without caution.

T

Tanacetum.—The Tansies are intensely aromatic-leaved Composites with rayless heads of yellow flowers like fluffy golden buttons in summer. They are easily divided and raised from seed, and thrive even excessively in any sunny place in open soil. Most, however, are too large in habit for the rock-garden, and not good enough for any other. Among the smaller kinds, however, that are useful on hot banks of poor dry ground is *T. adenanthum*, a novelty from China, with spreading neat masses of fern-fine silky-white leaves, emitting a profusion of golden knops. And other small-growing species of more or less merit are *T. nivale*, which is specially white in the leaf, and only 6 inches high ; *T. argenteum*, and *T. Kotschyi*. They are, all of them, neither more nor less interesting than the Santolinas to which they are so closely allied. But see Appendix.

Tanakaea radicans is a most pleasant little Japanese plant for light rich woodland soil in a comfortable cool corner, where, if it is happy, it will soon throw out runners freely from its main tuft of fringed-looking elliptic-pointed toothed leaves, leathery and richly green, from which ascend in summer stems of 6 inches, ending in loose fluffy spires of white blooms like those of a miniature Spiraea.

Taraxăcum.—Dandelions are not desired, as a rule, in a rock-garden. Without difficulty *T. Pacheri* and *T. alpinum* from the Alps may be cultivated for the sake of the hills they come from ; and with still less difficulty may they be omitted. The common *T. dens-leonis*, too, as it grows as a weed in the streets and waste places of Tokio, has the interesting peculiarity of being white in the flower instead of golden, while high up beside the glaciers of Kasbek, between 8000 and 11,000 feet, lives the only really brilliant Dandelion. This is *T. porphyreum*, with the usual habit, and flowers of medium size profusely produced on stems of 4 inches. But they are of intense violet-purple.

Tchihatchewia isatidea.—The beauty born of this murmuring sound has passed into the countenance of a rare monocarpic Crucifer from sunny rocks of the Levant, which there forms ample fat rosettes, and sends up stout and crowded pyramids a foot high or so, with large flowers of delicate waxy pink that have exactly the sweetness of *Daphne Cneorum*. In cultivation it has never done any good, but in many experiments has always proved a mimp, and by now has probably wholly passed away. In nature it must surely be extremely beautiful and encouraging to see, but in the garden it evidently has that sense of exile and consequent sullenness that is often found among the alpine Thlaspids of which it is the giant cousin. It ought to be raised from seed, and tried yet again in a sunny slope of the moraine.

Tecophilaea Cyanocrocus?—No, no. Let salesmen say what they will, this glorious Gentian-blue Crocus from Chili is quite impossible of general cultivation in England.

Telekia, the more correct name of *Buphthalmum, q.v.*

TEUCRIUM.

Telephium Imperati, with its smaller and smaller-flowered form called *T. I. orientale*, has branches that splay flat along the ground, set with pairs of thick and oval sea-blue leaves, with heads of greenery yallery blooms in summer. It may adorn a hot dry slope, but has neither brilliancy nor any look of refinement. Seed.

Tellïma grandiflora is a large-growing Saxifrage from North America, only admissible to a cool out-of-the-way corner of the wild garden in rich soil, where it will make wide tangles of Heuchera-like foliage, sending up, well above it, bare stems of a foot or two in thick abundance, set all up in a narrow slim spire with well-spaced blossom-cups of dim greenish-white or rusted green in May and June. They have a certain grace of effect, indeed, and their profusion is pleasant, but while the mass of foliage is handsome, this and its kindred species are not things to be passionately pursued, except for the filling up of a dank and worthless place in wood or wild.

Tetragonolobus siliquosus = Lotus siliquosus, *q.v.*

Teucrium.—The Germanders are not specially interesting or beautiful Labiates. The taller ones, indeed, are not worth troubling, but for making carpets in some cool place one may well use *T. montanum*, which is so common in the Alps, with its low-massed shoots of 3 or 4 inches, ending in a crowded head of pale creamy-lemon-coloured blossoms, rather large for the plant, and making a fine effect by their mass. In the same way is *T. pyrenaicum*, which, however, has the hairy scalloped leaves along the shoots more rounded and ample, so that the effect of the flowers, lilac in the hood and creamy in the lip, is diminished by the enveloping effect of the fat foliage, soft and velvety-green. Pretty, too, for crevices of the rockwork should be *T. Paederota*, which is a miniature of the Veronica which bears that name, and whose fluffs of blue blossom are so effective in the cliffs of the Dolomites, hanging from their glossy sprays of dark leathern leafage. Another dwarf yellow-flowered Germander is *T. aureum*, of 4 inches or so in height. *T. hyrcanum* belongs to the larger growers, and makes a bushy mass of 8 inches or so, with many long upstanding spikes, very furry and dense, like a happy kitten's tail, and packed with little purplish-red flowers in summer. The smaller members of the race may be imagined from a certain general resemblance to the Bugles ; they are all intensely bitter, and in general use as digestives ; as for pretty pink *T. marum*, gardeners will be well advised not to admit the Catnip, for the stomachic qualities of this are known to others than humans, and every cat in the county will come to parties on it every night, with such stimulating effect that not only does *T. marum* vanish beneath their attentions, but also every other plant in the place gets uprooted in the insensate gambollings produced by their intoxication, or else oppressed by the slumbers of the later stage, when the Bacchants usually choose *Eritrichium* or *Gentiana bavarica* for their beds.

Thaleia dealbata is a most handsome water-plant of the Southern States, not always hardy or prompt of bloom in the cold waters of inclement climates, but desirable for a sheltered and sunny corner in shallow still pools; with great oval upstanding leaves of a smooth and bloomy glaucous tone, contrasting with the brief feathered sheaf of blue flowers that unfold as late as possible on a stem of 2 or 3 feet.

Thalictrum.—This race, though not strictly alpine, contains a number of plants notably beautiful and useful for the rock-garden, whether it be with the effect of their very delicate Maidenhair Fern foliage, or with their sprayed fluffy stars of blossoms that are often brilliant and nearly always delicately charming. The race is quite easy of culture in almost all its members, in any good rich loam in an open place ; blooms in spring and early summer, and may readily be raised from seed or multiplied by division in spring.

Th. adiantifolium is an exceptionally fine-foliaged variety of the variable *Th. minus, q.v.*

Th. alpinum is the tiniest of the race, a little plant so modest and meek that it is not easy to catch sight of it in the highlands or the alps, whether of England, Scotland, or Europe, where its few small leaves stay close to the ground, and a bare stem rises some 4 or 6 inches high, nodding beneath a loosely arranged burden of perhaps half a dozen rather large and tasselly flowers of dim greeny tone. It should have a choice place in the underground-watered bed, in stony gritty peat, and has interest but no conspicuousness.

Th. anemonoeides=*Anemonella thalictroeides, q.v.*

Th. angustifolium belongs to the ugly group of the family, with stiffish displays of yellowish blossom in July, on stems of a yard high.

Th. aquilegifolium, on the contrary, is by far (at present) the most generally important of the race. It is most abundant in the moister meadows of the Alps, where sometimes its varying fluffs of lilac, rose-amethyst, and cream appear to fill the fields with multi-coloured foam, as on the slopes to the North of the Mont Cenis Lake, where, at so high an elevation, the plant has grown into a more condensed habit, the light and lovely maidenhair foliage of emerald green (large and rich as in a stiffened *Adiantum farleyense*) lurking below, while the stems rise in their millions some 15 inches or less, each bearing a dense billow of indistinguishable volume, from pure white to a velvety rose-purple. In the valleys far below it becomes much ampler, and so may be seen in any English border in cool moist soil in the sun, waxing prodigiously in a noble sprayed pyramid of clear green, above which goes soaring many a leafy stately stem of 3 or 4 feet, branching into fluff after fluff of white or creamy foam far on into the summer. It seeds with such profusion and grows so heartily that it ought to be planted in wide drifts by every pool and moist place, in the company of its old neighbours, *Trollius, Paradisea Liliastrum, Gentiana asclepiadea,* and *Campanula rhomboidalis.*

Th. Chelidonii is a type of some very beautiful species that want a little extra care. They seem to require a light and specially stony soil in a sunny place, loose and well-drained, not poor, but neither hard nor heavy, with water flowing freely beneath in the early year. In such conditions will *Th. Chelidonii* be happy, with tufts of fern-fine foliage about 6 or 9 inches high, emitting a stiff loose spire of single flowers unusually large for the race, being about an inch across, in lovely contrast of the four ample sepals of delicate rose-lilac against the soft citron fluff of the stamens. (It belongs to the high Alps of Kulu and Sikkim.)

Th. Cornuti=*Th. dasycarpum, q.v.*

Th. dasycarpum (*Th. Cornuti*) lives in moist open places in the woods of North America, where it grows a yard high, with flowers of yellow.

Th. Delavayi has the habit of a very tall aspiring *Th. minus,* with lovely fine foliage, wiry and bluish and bronzed, in spraying narrow pyramids of 18 inches or so, tipped by short airy showers of cream-and-lilac blossom in the way of *S. Chelidonii,* but hardly half the size. It blooms far on into the summer, and should have the care of *Th. Chelidonii,* in a position especially sheltered and sunny.

Th. dioicum is a North American for a cool place, attaining only some 6 inches, with blossoms of whitish tone in May.

Th. dipterocarpum is the most magnificent of all in the Chelidonian group, and to prosper as it wants, should have the stony soil and subterranean moisture in warm places which this section prefers, and on which this particular member insists. The plant is more than twice the height of *Th. Delavayi,* and has absurdly little leafage for so graceful and aspiring a stem of 4 or 5 feet, which branches towards the top into several long spires and loose sprays of lovely ample flowers in shades of rose-lilac, whose blunt clear softness of tone contrasts perfectly with the beaten-cream-and-egg colouring of the stamens. (China.)

Th. Fendleri is an American of some 2 feet high, with yellowish sprays in July.

Th. flavum, Th. foetidum, and *Th. glaucum* belong to the ugly side of the family, being, indeed, stately and stalwart with handsome fine foliage of glaucous blue-green. But the crowded and multitudinous blooms are packed in tight stiff spikes and heads of yellow, rather coarse and rank in effect—though obviously useful for the wild garden, where they will grow 5 feet high and more, blossoming in the summer. (*Th. flavum* is a native.)

Th. majus and *Th. minus* are simply larger and smaller forms of the Wild Maidenhair of our Northern limestones. The specific name is *Th. minus*, but the type varies distractingly, and yet another of its forms is the especially fine-leaved *Th. m. adiantifolium*. All developments of the species will grow almost anywhere, and though their dishevelled and wild showers of little brownish tassels in summer have only their wind-blown grace to commend them, the foliage is always a pleasure to see, and never more so than when it sprays from the Cliff at Ingleborough in a finer and more wiry grace than it retains in the fatness of the garden.

Th. orientale is a specially lovely plant from the Caucasus, hardly more than 4 or 5 inches high, with flowers of rich clear pink in May.

Th. petaloideum (*Th. baikalense*) has great distinctness as well as great distinction of habit; the leaves are exactly like those of a stunted Columbine in effect, of darkish green; and the rather stiff stems rise firmly up in summer to a height of a foot or 18 inches, bearing wide clusters of large upstanding solid flowers of ample ivory-white sepals, most solid and striking in effect. It thrives with kindly heartiness in any open soil, and blooms usually from the middle of summer onwards. And among the many other species that might be named are *S. purpurascens*, from North America, which has blossoms of reddish-purple tone on stems of 2 feet, far on into the autumn; *Th. saxatile*, suggestive of a little 4-inch *Th. minus*, from the European Alps; greenish *Th. sibiricum*, with a stature of 2 feet; and foot-high, ivory-pure *Th. tuberosum*, from South Europe, producing its lovely flowers in May.

Thermopsis.—The Sham-Lupines are border plants by right, and until they are well-established in rich light loam, well-drained and in the sun, for several years, they will not show their best face to the world. They are large and erect bushy plants of 2 or 3 feet high, with long Lupine-spires of yellow from the middle of summer onwards; and should be raised from seed, as they dislike being worried at the root, and transplanted and divided. *Th. caroliniana* can attain a height of 6 feet; *Th. fabacea* only that of a yard; *Th. montana* is of the same height, as also is *Th. divaricarpa* and *Th. rhombifolia*; while *Th. lanceolata* is the baby of the family, with only some 12 inches to its credit.

THLASPI.

All the species have a handsomeness, but they also have a large lushness and crudity that detracts from their value.

Thlaspi.—This little race of Crucifers can easily be told from all others of the family, except Lepidium and Iberis, by their *membrane-winged seedpods;* and from Iberis and Lepidium by having *more than one seed in each cell. Th. montanum, Th. alpestre,* and *Th. alpinum, Th. brevistylum,* and *Th. praecox* are all prettyish little tufted bright-green plants of the Alps, with heads of white flowers in spring on leafy stems of 3 or 4 inches ; they are not, however, by any means perennial, and are not of any moment in the garden (though pleasant in stray remote corners of the moraine)—by no means adapted to come into competition with the beauties of the race, among which are found some of the best-beloved jewels that the highest shingles have to show.

Th. affine makes a close dwarf tuffet high on Scardus, set with white flowers with anthers of creamy-pink.

Th. Andersoni has flowers of white or pink in wet places of high Alps in Garhwal and Kumaon.

Th. bellidifolium stands near *Th. rotundifolium,* but emits no caudicles or wandering shoots from the neck, sitting tight on Scardus in closely-matted cushions of fat and bluntly-paddle-shaped little fleshy dark leaves, crowned with flattish heads of lovely sweet-scented rose-purple blossom. When acquired it must be cultivated in the moraine, like all the group here treated, and allowed ample water flowing beneath its feet in spring, to make it think that the snows are melting once more in its former home. I say, when acquired, for a most frightful weed has lately come forth under this name—a rosette of ample glaucous leaves, sending up a stem of several inches, with microscopic flowers of dingy white.

Th. cepeaefolium is the choicest of tiny treasures in this treasurable group. It is never found except on the high granites of the far Eastern Alps, very rare, and almost confined to the Raibl Thal in Carinthia. It is a frailer, more upstanding spindly miniature of *Th. rotundifolium,* but never running nor forming such rosetted clumps ; the tiny leaves being narrower and much sparser and smaller, concentrating their energies in much more lavishly decorating the many little fleshy 2-inch stems, which are taller, and more tidily furnished-looking than the larger and laxer though shorter ones of *Th. rotundifolium.* And these leafy stems spring straight from the neck of the tuft, bearing tight *rounded heads* of delicately-sweet little flowers of lilac-mauve. For greatest care in the choicest foreground of the moraine, in full sun.

Th. Haussknechtii and *Th. papillosum* are white-flowered high-alpines of the Levant, of the same style and habits as *Th. alpinum.*

Th. Kotschyanum has only a life of two years in the high screes of Elburz, where it attains 2 inches from its tuffet, and lightens the stony places with ample heads of fine white bloom.

Th. limosellaefolium is the rarest and yet the easiest to grow of all the shingle-Thlaspids. It is confined to the high places of the Maritime Alps, on the granite of the upmost folds and passes of the mountains in the group of Argentera and Enchastraye. It has much the same general habit as *Th. rotundifolium*, though it does not wander, but forms a looser and upstanding clump of leaves which are narrow, long, spoon-shaped, brightly green and of ordinary commonplace texture, as they are of ordinary commonplace colour (instead of affecting the packed fatness, the round outlines, the fleshy firmness, the dark and livid iron-grey gloss of *Th. rotundifolium*). It looks, in fact, much more like a tuft of Lamb's Salad, strayed up unadvisedly into those grim and silent desolations. The flowers are very beautiful; a profusion of stems, 2 or 3 inches high and sometimes more, spring from the clump and bear flattened domes of most delicious sweetness in lighter and warmer rose-lilac tones than those of *Th. rotundifolium*. Both plants, indeed, have a rare winsomeness; their cosy and comfortable habit, their packed heads of dainty and fragrant bloom so huddled and friendly in those high and friendless places, the delicate brightness of their colour in the wildernesses of grey or russet stone to which they so confidingly nestle, all combine to earn them a most special place alike in one's heart and in one's moraine. In cultivation I believe *Th. limosellaefolium* to be easier and freer than *Th. rotundifolium*, which it so successfully replaces in the crude high granites of the Maritimes; it strikes with delightful readiness from summer cuttings, which next year are much more hearty and heartily-blooming tuffets of rosy fragrance than the parent tuft; so that this might prove the best way of cultivating all the high-alpines of this race—by treating them as annuals or biennials, and keeping a constant supply of cuttings coming on. There is a white form, too, of *Th. limosellaefolium*, which I found in the upmost shingle of the Boréon; it is amazingly ready and vigorous alike in growth and flower; but, though a really pretty and pure thing, there are so many pure and pretty white things among the Alpine Crucifers, that one cannot think the Thlaspi has acted for the best in relinquishing its own especial and essential charm of soft sweet rosy-mauve.

Th. microphyllum is only an inch high, with very tiny rosettes, tight and dense, of minute smooth-edged leaves with heads of white flowers adorned with purple anthers. It lives beside the snows on Parnassus.

THLASPI.

Th. nevadense is a smooth and bright green tuffet, many-rosetted, in the shingles and highest crevices of the Sierra Nevada, with all the small obovate leaves entire, or just a little scalloped. The many stems are 2 or 3 inches high, carrying large heads of large white blossoms.

Th. ochroleucum copies *Th. montanum* and bears its yellow flower-heads on the musical slopes of Helicon.

Th. pumilum is sometimes called *Hutchinsia pumila*. It is a Caucasian plant, exactly like *Th. rotundifolium*, but with white flowers.

Th. rotundifolium—the *Iberidella* of bygone years—is the special treasure and glory of the highest shingles throughout the Alps, but always more especially on the limestone or sandstones, where, from its great tap-root, it forms, by means of shoots beneath the shingles, wide mats of tuffetted rosettes of fat, dark, broad little oval leaves, thick and fleshy and waxy-smooth, and of a livid iron sombreness of colour, over which are borne in summer, in a profusion that hides the mass, great *flattened heads* of large and most deliciously-fragrant flowers of tender rosy-lavender. It is a most widespread and most abundant high-alpine of the dreary shingles and wet stony places by the birthplace of the streams in the uppermost hollows of the hills. But it is also quite local and rather variable. For instance, in the Mont Cenis it is both sparse and comparatively poor, straggling in form, and dotted here and there, instead of colouring the stone-slopes as it does when you get East into the Dolomites, where, in the most austere places, such as that amphitheatre of huge emptiness up behind the Grasleiten Hut, under the overwhelming walls of the Antermoja and the Kesselkogel and the Great Valbuon, all the slopes are set with those fragrant rosy tuffets, concise and ample and free, cushions of lilac sweetness breaking the pale white desolations with little ringing cries of colour in that vast home of silence. And thus it is, too, through-out all the screes of the Dolomites, even in the very highway-sides on the crest of the Falzarego Pass, abundant and rich and lovely as in no other range that I can call to mind, though on the Grigna it is also abundant and beautiful, even if much looser and more straggling in form ; while on Baldo it haunts the roughest shingles only, and is only occasionally there to be seen at its best. In the garden it wants all the reverence accorded to the rest, and deserves it far more than all except *Th. limosellaefolium, cepeaefolium*, and *bellidifolium* (of what persistent plagiarism are these three most beautiful members of the race accused by their names !) It should have sunny calcareous moraine of ample depth, with water flowing far beneath ; then there is little doubt of its prosperity and generosity with its lovely flowers ;

THYMUS.

it should also be kept going with relays of cuttings, as with *S. limo-sellaefolium.*

Th. stylosum is sometimes offered as *Noccaea.* It is a dainty, neat little green impermanent tuffet with heads of rather spidery-looking lilac-rosy blossoms in earliest spring, and seems to like a rather cooler and less sunny aspect of the moraine than those affected by the rest, which, so long as they are adequately supplied below with water (which sends up its emanations through the soil and so makes a protective envelope of coolness round the plants on the surface), always enjoy all the light and air that may be going, and will not, on the Alps, be found in the danker and colder exposures of the high shingles.

Th. Szowitsianum is a biennial like *Th. Kotschyanum*, from damp places in the Levantine Alps, but it grows a foot high, and has quite loose spires of white blossom.

Th. violascens attains only to 4 inches, and has flowers of whitish lilac in the mountains of Asia Minor.

Thymus.—The first of all Thymes is, of course, the common one, than which, for a carpet in hot sunny slopes and levels and walks, there could never be anything more sweet and desirable. And, as with this, so with the rest ; let them have light well-drained soil and the fullest sunshine, and they will all continue to thrive imperturbably. For they are all children of the smiling South, and bring with them into exile the hot fragrance of the Mediterranean hills ; they may all be multiplied from cuttings like kitchen herbs, and used for the stuffing of all hot gravelly poor places, even as one of the family serves as a stuffing for ducks. For, whether they be bushlings or whether they make carpets, they are always charming, no less in their leafage than when enriched with their innumerable little lipped flowers of rose or white or carmine. In the race they stand close to Satureia, Micromeria (that was), and Calamintha ; from the four names a general picture of the group may be painted in the mind. Of the carpeting Thymes, which we will take first, the first of all is *S. Serpyllum.* But of the Common Thyme there are many varieties that have received names ; botanical variations (each as valuable as the type, whatever its particular eccentricity may be) are *Th. S. latifolius, nummularius, Marschallianus, Ochrus, Schaubardii, Kotschyi, squarrosus.* Many of these are offered as species. Of garden varieties we have the brilliantly coloured *Th. S. coccineus,* the yet deeper-toned *Th. S. splendens,* and the beautiful small-habited and larger-flowered purity of *Th. S. albus ;* to say nothing of that densely woolly grey form, *Th. S. lanuginosus,* which is more lovely in the leafage than in the rather rare pinky flowers, and which is sometimes sent out as a variety of *Th. Chamaedrys.*

Then, of low-growing creepers in the kindred of *Th. Serpyllum* are *Th. odoratissimus, comptus, cappadocicus, villosus, latinus* (quite flat), *nitidus, marginatus, pannonicus,* and *azoricus* (some of these coming suspiciously close under the shadow of *Th. Serpyllum*). *Th. striatus* (*Th. Zygis*) is a trifle stiffer and leafier and larger, with larger flowers, leading on to the next group of more upstanding small neat bush-thymes, of which *Th. Chamaedrys* and *Th. citriodorus* are the best known types, this last having a silver and a golden variety often used for edgings, and borrowing for its enhancement the scent of Aloysia. Another plant of special sweetness where all are sweet is *Th. Piperella*, with fat and stiff little twigs; and yet another, *Th. Herba-barona*, whose especial fragrance is of seed-cake, most delightful to those who rightly appreciate that dear confection. *Th. teucrioeides* from Parnassus is a weakly bushling suggestive of *Calamintha alpina*, specially branchy, and rising up all over at the ends to show off its tiny pink flowers. *Th. hirsutus* is pink too, and makes the most lovely tight small tufts after the habit of *Galium olympicum;* while yet another tidy close clump is built by *Th. micans*, starry and wiry in effect; and less so is *Th. Funckii* from Murcia, which makes a stiff concise grey mound. *Th. Billardieri* goes back towards *Th. Serpyllum*, and flops and creeps and roots freely as it goes forward like the serpent on its belly, covering the ground in a carpet of very narrow tiny leaves, fringed with white hair, that enhance the twinkle of the rosy blooms. And *Th. Cephalotes* is the most brilliant of all the bushlings—a most dense and branching downy mass of 4 or 6 inches, with the leafy grey cushion all odorous of camphor, while the flower-bracts are dense too, and brilliant purple, enclosing blossoms of contrasting brilliant pink.

Tiarella cordifolia.—The Foam-flower is the delight of shady banks on the cool rock-work or wood garden, where it makes tufts of its handsome delicately-green five-lobed leaves, and sends out runners far and wide with more; while from the mass in June there rises a profusion of diaphanous pinky bare stems of 6 or 8 inches, ending in a little fluffy spire of white blossom like a Spiraea's, warmed by the Cochin-China-hen's-egg colour of the anthers. It is perfectly easy to grow in such conditions, and rooted runners can be taken off at any time. There is, however, a giant form, *T. unifoliata*, also an American, that grows three times the size, but sits quite close in a widening clump, as it were a Heuchera, with upstanding spires of yet creamier-warm foam all through the full summer, on stems of 18 inches or more. This does not require coolness and shade, but appreciates the richest soil it can get, in open bed or border. *T. purpurea* is a dark-leaved form of *T. cordifolia* with pinkish flowers, and *T. polyphylla* is a smaller frailer species from Bhotan and Nepal, of noted daintiness, indeed, but not, like *T. cordifolia*, combining extreme elegance with indestructible vigour and ubiquity.

Tofieldia.—This is a family of minute bog-Asphodels, with small fluffy spires of greeny-yellow flowers on stems of 4 or 5 inches. *T. palustris* (*T. borealis*) may be seen in the alpine marshes of Teesdale, and the larger taller *T. calyculata* in all the wet meadows of the Alps; and there are smaller species, such as *T. alpina* (a variety of *T. calyculata*), *T. glacialis*, and *T. rubescens*. They are all quite without showiness, but have a certain charm of their own for those who remember the alpine marshes, and in their own would like to repeat the effect. A very wet and very loose gritty spongy soil is that in which the Tofieldias will be happy.

Tollmiaea Menziesii is a small and rather dowdy Saxi-fragaceous Woodlander from California, striking a compromise between Heuchera and Mitella, with 10-inch loose sprays of dingy greenish flowers, high above the typical and handsome Tiarelloid foliage of the whole group. The root-leaves form knobules at the end of their stems, which strike root when they drop dying to earth, and so propagate the plant excessively, considering its unattractiveness.

Townsendia.—This is a beautiful family of dwarf and usually high-alpine Asters from the Rockies, that require specially gritty, rather rich soil, but quite light and stony and especially well-drained, with abundance of water below, while growing. (Seed, and division of clumps.)

T. exscapa (*T. sericea*) is a packed mass of silky-grey little narrow oval leaves, on which sit conspicuous fine wide Asters of white or pink or purple, on stems of about an inch in June. Even closer and tighter is the habit of its variety *T. e. Wilcoxiana*, where the leaves are darker and hardly silky, while the flowers are of lavender-blue—their only possible detraction being that, so to speak, their eye is a trifle large and fat for the eyelash of their florets. Neither species nor variety is a plant of the mountains, but belongs, instead, to the plains.

T. formosa (*T. pinetorum*) has thin foliage, and otherwise makes exactly the picture of a rather dwarfish *Aster alpinus*. It lives in the mountains of New Mexico.

T. grandiflora grows from 2 to 8 inches high, forming tufts of quite narrow long paddle-shaped leaves, and sending up in June abundant noble violet Asters nearly 2 inches across. (Wyoming and New Mexico.)

Tozzia alpina is a singularly rare and ugly little Scrophulariad with minute and squinny yellow flowers, that may be seen, and hastily passed by, in the damper places of the turf in the Maritime Alps, &c. It is like an inferior Eyebright ; no less impossible to cultivate, and far more dowdy.

Trachystēmon orientale = Psilostemon orientale, *q.v.*

Trautvetteria palmata is a rather dim Japanese Ranunculad of the woodland, growing 2 feet or a yard high, with handsome ample foliage, hand-shaped, with toothed ample fingers. The stems of blossom come up in summer and break in radiating bunches of fluffy whitish flowers, the whole plant rather suggesting a Thalictrum with the foliage of a Cimicifuga. Any good rich soil in a cool place will suit it, and the clump can easily be divided in spring.

Trichopetalum gracile = Bottionaea thysantoeides, *q.v.*

Tricyrtis.—These strange plants have all the same resemblance, differing chiefly in their stature, so that one picture may suffice to express their almost inexpressible quaintness. From a short stock they send up more or less arching stems of a foot or two, embraced by dark hairy leaves, corrugated and oval-pointed, which from their axils almost all the way up emit large and evil flowers, very late in summer as a rule, or autumn, built on the scheme of a lily, but wried by perversity into an almost Aubrey-Beardsley freakishness of outline and heavy waxen texture and livid sombre colour of putrid pinks, freckled and spotted with dark purple till their name of Toad-lily is felt to be apt. They like the treatment of Trillium, and with the Trilliums should be planted and there left undisturbed for ever, in a rather warm corner, however, that their flowers may develop betimes, for often they are nipped in the bud by autumn. *T. hirta* (*T. japonica*) is the best known ; but a better plant is *T. macropoda*, if only that it blooms earlier, in June and July, in rather closer sprays. Much smaller and quite dainty and charming in its sinister way is *T. Hototogisu*. Pronounce this " hototongeese," and think of it accordingly as meaning the nightingale of Japanese woodlands, a frail 6-inch stem or so, set rarely with heart-shaped leaves, and bearing several flowers only, in a loose spray, notable and noble for the delicate build of the plant.

Trientalis europaea is a very dainty little Woodlander, which may with care be grown in light rich vegetable soil in a cool and shady corner of the garden, and may with a good deal more difficulty be happed on in the alpine glens of England and Scotland, where its delicate stem, set with a Herb-Paris-like whorl of some half a dozen soft oval-pointed leaves of bright green, make a charming effect, even if it were not for the exquisite pearl-pale Chickweed blooms that continue to hover over it through the summer on the finest of thready foot-stalks. America, as with its railway accidents, so with its plants, is never content until it has outdone the Old World in largeness of scale ; accordingly there is an American development of this, called *T. canadensis*, corresponding to the American forms of Linnaea and Maianthemum, in being rather stouter and larger and more robust than their effete and overbred relations of the outworn Old World.

Trifolium.—The huge family of Clovers does so much for fodder that it feels dispensed from service in the garden ; so that, out of its innumerable species, only three or four can even be admitted to the rock-work, and even these are still more easily omitted without loss to anybody. On Parnassus lives a little clover, *T. Parnassi*, that makes close carpets of fine green, and has flower-heads of bright pink as large as a pea. Twice the size of this in all its parts is *T. caespitosum*, and light open slopes might well be found where they might both be more welcome than any of the large Clovers anywhere in the garden, though sometimes, as for a curiosity, space is found for *T. ochroleucum* and *T. montanum* and our own very rare *T. stellatum* with a stature of a foot or so and dowdy heads of soft and starry fluff. Yet another dwarf is *T. polyphyllum* from the Caucasus, with carpet habits and heads of clear rose in June ; and for hot and value-less places we might use the dark-leaved form *atropurpureum* of our common white Clover, or even, more suitably, golden-headed little *T. badium* of the Alps, while *T. rubens* is a bush of a foot or two with dense whirligig-heads of purple-red in June and July. But, take it all in all, the race is of singular unimportance in the garden, and even the one true alpine, which is also the best of the family, is not of capital value there. For *T. alpinum* is not often seen in gardens, though of easy culture in light and stony peaty soil on hot and well-drained banks. Yet it is handsome enough, with its packed masses of large folded trefoils of long, thin and narrow-pointed light-green foliage, close upon which, on bare stems of 2 or 3 inches, sent up in profusion, are carried amply-furnished and gracefully-furnished heads of enormous flowers, by far the largest in the race. Yet their dim pink-ness has precisely that lack of brilliancy which is so common a fault among the Peaflowers. It is just between the notes, as Papilionaceae so commonly fall out of tune—neither softly pale, nor clearly bright, but just a murk of mild and muddy mauve. Even the pallid forms and the creamy albino have the same fatal fault of indeterminateness and inefficiency of tone. *T. alpinum* is an abundant species of the open Alps, which, indeed, its dense turf goes far to compose. For over all the undulating folds of the granitic and non-calcareous ranges it lies like a cloak, and the miles of the moorland are springy with its masses beneath the tread, while over the edges of all the hill floats keen the warm and heady vinous scent which is the essential smell of the mountains, and owes its whole force and sweetness to the exhalations of the Mountain-clover in every part. It is curious, indeed, how obstinately utilitarian this family is, and how unfriendly to the merely æsthetic values of life. Even the alpine member of the race declines to be essentially ornamental, and achieves the miracle of being decently dowdy among the brilliant galaxies of the wild hills, where brilliancy is almost a *sine qua non*. Yet still even this Clover, despising ornament, insists on being useful : that pungent sweetness is the bouquet of many a cherished liqueur ; and the Alpine Clover is no less important in their composition than the Alpine Worm-woods ; while that intoxicating vinous warm sweetness wafted across the upper lawns on the Alps is enough of itself to earn our affection for the plant, when, in some dull day or some low valley or dark London street, the nose suddenly calls up a memory of that nipping haunting smell, and instantly the high bare hills appear in sight, decked in all the sere and austere majesty of the mountain-spring, chill and brown and elastic beneath feet that now in an instant are treading the resilient odorous mattresses of the Trifolium once more, with the wind of the snow coming cold and sweet into one's face, instead of the blasts of skimming motors as one tramps the unyielding flags of Eaton Square.

Trigonōtis radicans is a pretty little Borragineous plant, for cool shady places in moist and spongy stony soil of perfect drainage, where it will form rooting fine mats with wandering stems, and these be generous with slight sprays of blossom like lilac-pink Forget-me-nots. It is a rare novelty from Manchuria. And Japan offers us yet another woodlander in *T. Guglielmi*, with running stocks and small heart-shaped glossy-green leaves, and tall loose showers of white blossom like little rounded stars.

Trillium.—For all the Wood-lilies a cool, deep, and very rich woodland soil is wanted, and they detest torrid sunshine as much as they detest drought ; there is no actual need, however, to treat them as bog-plants, their desire being only towards the damp and spongy conditions of rotting vegetable matter in opener places of the deep American woods ; though *T. grandiflorum* is quite equal to a little extra moisture at the root, and, like all the rest, loves loose old leaf-mould with keenest devotion. Yet they are not impatient or greedy plants, as anyone will realise who has seen the mileage of the Hokkaido, filled with a brake of 2-foot-high bamboo, but with a dense springing undergrowth in the early year of snowy Trillium trefoil-flowers, arising in multitudes from soil so packed with the greedy runners of bamboo that those who know that insatiate race will realise how little moisture or richness is there left in the ground for the poor Wood-lilies, which yet contrive from season to season to make those sere brakes look as if drifted snow were still occupying the ground beneath.

T. acuminatum has large flowers of inferior greenish white on its 8-inch and very amply-trefoiled stem in April.

T. cernuum has leaves of especial breadth, and the stalks only attain 6 inches or so, while the rose-white flowers have wavy edges to the three petals.

T. declinatum has the whole habit of *T. erectum*, and the stalked flower. But the blossom is white, and horizontally borne, instead of shamelessly erect as in the uglier species.

T. discolor=*T. sessile Wrayi.*

T. erectum is not only ugly, but stinks. It grows 10 inches high, and above the dark full foliage the flowers of dirty brown stand brazenly up on a foot-stalk in April. There are also forms with white flowers, passing on towards *T. declinatum*.

T. erythrocarpum=*T. undulatum, q.v.*

T. grandiflorum is the best known and best beloved of the lot, a plant unsurpassable anywhere for heartiness of habit, charm of manner, and refulgent purity of bloom. In any cool rich soil it will grow and spread from the solid fat knops of its root, sending up fleshy stems of 10 inches in abundance, set with the unvarying trefoil of ample lustrous emerald-green smooth leaves, and topped by the single blossom of especial size, especial fullness of the three petals, and especial glory of pure ribbed whiteness, that often fades to a serene pink, and in one form is even of a serene pink from birth to death. It unfurls in the first days of June, or the last of May, and at the sight of it in old masses the heart of the beholder opens and shuts like Mrs. Caudle's when she saw a rose. It wants no more than the treatment of the Wood Anemones, and should be planted everywhere by the thousand, and made a wild weed; its only fault being that its excessive beauty and goodness attract as much love (though of the cupboard variety only) from slugs and mice as from gardeners.

T. nivale, with *T. ovatum* (if, indeed, this last be truly distinct), are minute tiny gems for choicer treatment in a more prominent shelf of the cool rock-work; they only grow some 4 inches high or less, and bear large flowers in May of dazzling whiteness, carved from the snows by which they spring, and from whose melting tears they reincarnate its vanished purity in their blossoms.

T. petiolatum is twice the height, with white flowers that do not, however, enter into any competition with those of *T. grandiflorum*, though they have their value, as coming a month earlier.

T. pictum=T. undulatum.

T. pusillum is the Benjamin of the lot, so minute as not to exceed a couple of inches ; a treasure for the daintiest of places, which it will rejoice with snow-born thimbles in the Spring.

T. recurvatum and *T. sessile* stand quite close together. They have both large and very handsome foliage marbled with brown and green, appearing in the dawn of the year, before the others are waking. Close and stemless on these, stand up large flowers with the upstanding petals rather narrow, and never opening widely out. In the types these flowers are of varying tones of blackish brown, by no means attractive, but the form *T. sess. californicum* (sometimes sent out as *T. giganteum*) is very handsome, for the stature is taller, and the outline bolder, and the brave big half-opening pointed-petalled blooms are of clear creamy white (at least in the garden-form known as Snow Queen), making a fine effect as they rise up from their noble marbled glossy leaves in March when all the other Wood-lilies are still abed. There is yet another variety, of less merit, called *T. sess. Wrayi*, with greenish blooms. The type is usually sent out instead of this form, which is also sometimes called *T. discolor.*

T. stylosum is a plant of 10 inches, with most lovely soft-rosy flowers in April or May.

T. undulatum, however, is, after *T. grandiflorum*, the royalty of the race at present, and unquestionable sovereign of the smaller species. It is the plant usually offered under the names of *T. pictum* or *T. erythrocarpum*, and well repays the choicest of culture in the choicest bed of gritty cool rich peat in shade. Here, if kept in mind of the cold damp places it affects in American woods, it will send up, in spring, dainty stems of 4 inches or more, unfolding a refulgent large wavy flower of purest white, swinging gracefully above the leaves, and stained inside with stripes and blurs of rich crimson at the base of the virginal petals.

Triteleia uniflora is to be found in all bulb-lists ; but there is nothing lovelier in spring than wide masses, in a sunny place, of its countless narrow leaves of lush and flopping texture and bright soft green, from which rise the innumerable bare stems of 4 or 6 inches or more, each carrying a single ample erect flower, curiously suggesting tobacco blossom, of a delicate milky-white, that after the fashion of milk often goes delicately and palely blue, but smells more sweet than any milk that ever came from any cow on earth. It is a plant of Argentina, but absolutely hardy and easy to establish on warm open banks where the bulbs can ripen and multiply with their usual generous rapidity.

Tritoma.—This is the wrong name of Kniphofia. But *K. Nelsoni* is a real gem for the rock-garden, and particularly noble on a projecting high ledge in the sun, in deep and very well-drained loam, rich and light, where it will make abundant masses of long and narrow dark grass; and then in September and on into November, send up an unceasing profusion of little flame-spires of a foot or 18 inches high, dainty miniatures of its great cousins, of the same flaring glow and scarlet fire, so startling on the cold grey rocks in October when all the garden is going dank in death. This precious plant is rarely found in catalogues, and yet more rarely found true. It is a jewel indeed, and, though perfectly hardy if properly placed, is thankful for high and dry places in the fullest sunshine. *K. rufa* is in the same dainty way, but tenderer in colour and flame, and rather taller, with shorter looser spires, attaining 2 feet or so. It has, however, a more catholic constitution than the last, and blooms earlier. Another lovely little thing is *K. pauciflora* of a foot or two, most dainty in habit, with its torches loosely dropping sparks of pure golden flame in late summer. These have all been hybridised with each other and with *K. Nelsoni*; *K. × corallina* is one result of combining the charms of some with the earlier bloom of others; and catalogues have already produced more, named after the nobility, nurserymen and others; and will continue, without doubt, to utter more. The value of them all is supreme; for, with their grass-fine foliage like that of a miniature dark-green Pampas of unheard-of elegance, and their dainty upstanding flames of clearer or more violent hot fire, they offer exactly the aspiring line that suits the upper ledges of the larger rock-garden, and gives especial bulk and majesty to the long lines of its composition, seeming to lift it to Andine heights; to say nothing of the intrinsic beauties of the gracious fine torches themselves, or their cunning choice of exactly the most best-timed moment for their appearance in late summer and far on into autumn, when fire-heat is so much wanted among the chilling cliffs of the dying garden. They are all of perfect ease to grow, once well-planted and left alone for ever in deep warm soil in their places; yet the miracle remains that the average rock-garden seems to be quite unaware of these miniature, delicate-habited, hardy Torch-lilies, while their stout crude cousins are cherished excessively in the herbaceous borders beyond.

Trollius.—The Globe-flowers are too well known for description. And catalogues nowadays are full of larger and larger, brighter and brighter hybrids, so that this list shall concern itself only with some of the species—premising only that the one need of the whole race is deep rich soil, moist and cool and adequately supplied with water. The generic likeness of the race is strong, and small differences, as a rule, separate many of the species, in the course of the race's extension from the mountain-woods of Europe, across the stretches of Asia to America.

T. europaeus shall be the type for comparison, as being our own and the best known—a plant of the alpine meadows all the ranges over, often occurring in such abundance in damp places that you may see whole acres shining with the bland and moony citron of its unbroken mass of bloom, with the hot gold of Caltha flaring in a mass no less unbroken below, so that the marsh is a dazzling tumble of shot shades in lemon and orange. It is little less common, though not in masses so dense, in the Alps of Craven and Teesdale, where its orbed moons of pale yellow float like globes of ghostly light across the riotous carpets of the pastures in June, thick with *Geranium sylvaticum* and waving Forget-me-not and Potentilla and Mountain Pansy. Such associations, then, are what would best suit its unearthly luminosity in the garden—to be planted in drifts, and wild stretches, with *Paradisea* and *Campanula rhomboidalis*, and *Thalictrum aquilegifolium* and *Gentiana asclepiadea*, and many another well-beloved glory of the mountain-meadows, such as even *Lilium Martagon* and *Aquilegia alpina*.

T. acaulis is a tiny treasure from the high Himalaya, with widely open buttercup-flowers of gold, rather than globes (after the fashion of *T. laxus* and *T. patulus*), standing lone and erect on unbranched stems of some 5 or 6 inches or less. It should have choice treatment in the gritty and underground-watered moraine-bed.

T. altaicus again has the yellow blossoms gaping open instead of globular as in the Globe-flowers. Note that it has the Globe-flower's height of some 12 or 15 inches, and much the same foliage. But the styles at the flower's heart are dark purple; the outstanding sepals, of brilliant yellow, are some five to fifteen in number, and the mean, tiny, barely visible petals inside are more or less shorter than the central fluff of stamens, which accordingly quite obliterates their inconspicuousness.

T. americanus is often advertised as *T. laxus*, and has a pale variety sent out as *T. laxus albiflorus*. This is a weaklier Globe-flower of the typical form, rather frail in growth, about 2 feet high, and with balls of pale-yellow blossom that often verge through diluted shades of lemon-water-ice towards a tone that only the grossest flattery could call white.

T. asiaticus is like a slightly taller *T. europaeus*, but the leaves are more finely gashed, and of a deeper bronze-green tone, while the flowers are of brilliant gold, loosely opening, instead of folding into a ball, with the tiny petals standing above the stamens in a different style and proportion from that of *T. altaicus*. There is a yet larger form of this that goes out in gardens under the name of *T. giganteus*, and also as *T. Fortunei* or *T. Loddigesii*.

T. aurantiacus. See under *T. hybridus*.

T. chinensis is another development from further Asia, growing 2 feet high, with flowers of dark yellow.

T. dahuricus is taller still, and more light and vivid in colour.

T. dschungaricus has all the habit of *T. europaeus*, but the golden globes are tinged with mahogany brown on the outside.

T. europaeus.—See above, at the head of the family. There are endless varieties of this plant, and many of those recognised as species are little more than local developments. Conspicuous is one called *T. e. napellifolius*, which is taller and larger than the type, very free in blossom, with globes of glowing orange yellow. A paler one is flattered with the title of *T. e. albiflorus*, and gardens also distinguish a form which they call *T. e. grandiflorus*. In nature the species, so unendingly abundant, seems to vary extraordinarily little in habit or colour. In many millions of many seasons I have only once seen a variation, into pale soft butter-colour, at the edge of citron meadowsful of the type, below the Little Mont Cenis.

T. hybridus is the all-embracing name of the innumerable crosses between the last and the looser-flowered and more richly orange Asiatics. There has resulted a long chain of superb intermediate plants, of 2 or 3 feet high, most generous of large and usually rather lax flowers, in oranges and gold of varying intensity. All these are praised adequately in catalogues under the names there given them, of Excelsior, Orange Globe, Fire Globe, &c. &c., and the strain also holds the enlarged and half-orbicular Globe-flower of deeper colouring which is often called *T. caucasicus*; as well, no doubt, as many another that sometimes figures as a species.

T. japonicus, like *T. pumilus*, has the flower like a great golden buttercup, widely open, with five ample golden sepals extinguishing the almost invisible wee petals inside.

T. laxus=*T. americanus*.

T. Ledebourii is a plant of 18 inches, with yellow blossoms which are not globes, but have five broad sepals widely open, and, inside, the little insignificant petals standing up above the stamens.

T. lilacinus (also called *Hegemone lilacina*) is the jewel of all—a treasure from high damp places on the mountain tops of the Altai. It is a most lovely small thing, about 4 inches high, with the lobed and feathered leaves of the family, but with noble many-sepalled flowers of lovely lilac-blue, about 2 inches across, shooting into blossom with the first dawn of spring, and then never scattering, as in the others of the race, but still clothing the seed-vessel about with the fifteen or twenty faded tabs. This great rarity is a capricious little creature too, and must have a corner in partial shade, where it may be established in very loose spongy and gritty soil of peat and leaf-mould and coarse sand and many stones, with water flowing abundantly beneath during the time of development, to keep it in mind of the dank marsh hollows of the highest Altai, where it leaps up from the first influence of the melting snows. No pains would be too much to make it happy.

T. patulus has wide orbs of pale yellow, on stems of about a foot.

T. polysepalus is 18 inches high, with fully furnished flowers of clear yellow.

T. pumilus is an easy-going dwarf plant of 6 inches or so, for the rock-garden, that has lost all right, like so many others, to the name of Globe-flower, for the sepals of rich yellow stand quite flatly out more straight than in any buttercup. The flowers appear in sprays above the pile of fat leaves, cut into three plump and overlapping lobes, with plump irregular shallow lobings or scallopings. *T. p. yunnanensis* is a fine thing, larger and more complicated than the species; but somehow the simpler shorter stems and smaller scale of type-*T. pumilus* better suit the contrast of bright flat flowers above the tuft of dark and comfortable little leaves; so that the species, neater and in better proportion of flower to foliage, almost lonely on their shorter stems above the glossy leaves, has a better and more well-bred look than the taller and more lavish sprays of *T. p. yunnanensis*, above an ampler leafage, that with the added length of stem, violate the balance between the size of the 9-inch or foot-high tuft and its comparatively smaller flat flowers of bright gold.

All these can be raised from seed, but the work is slow and precarious, for Globe-flowers rarely germinate until the year after their sowing, and even then take two or three seasons to reach their fair development. On the other hand, they detest, like all clumping Ranunculads, to be disturbed and divided and harassed at the root. And, in any case, if seed is to be sown, it should be sown as soon as possible after gathering, the Ranunculads having germs that feed rapidly upon themselves and consume away; so that prompt sowing with all of them is most advisable, that you may get the unexhausted vigour of the vital force thrown immediately into the development of the young plant.

TROPAEOLUM.

Tropaeŏlum.—The three hardy perennial tubers of this race ought to be planted very deeply indeed, not less than 8 or 9 inches down, in specially light warm soil, in a specially warm place high up on the rock-work, that thus their roots may be secure, and their flopping fat arms of foliage come trailing down for the just display, all through the summer, of their innumerable flowers. *T. patagonicum* has hooded blooms of violet-purple and yellow ; *T. pentaphyllum* of a dead dull purple ; and *T. polyphyllum* is of a rare beauty with long fleshy trails, clothed in lovely folded fat foliage of glaucous-blue, with a profusion of little Nasturtiums of the richest golden yellow in admirable con-trast. As for the Flame-flower, *T. speciosum* is no rock-garden plant, but may easily be established on the cool side of the border, in rich soil, there to wreathe the hedge or the old yew-tree with swathes of scarlet fire through the later summer, growing longer every year, and every year extending the field of its invasions.

Troxĭmon alpestre is an American Composite of no par-ticular interest, that insatiate enthusiasts may grow in damp but sunny places in light soil between stones, where it will drive deep its long root-stock, and form tufts of smooth and feathered foliage, from which in summer arise the hairless stems of 2 or 3 inches, carrying yellow flowers. *T. grandiflorum* is less interesting still, with stems of a foot high and larger flowers.

Tulipa.—No race has diverged into directions more marked than this. Fat, in bed and border, sit hundreds of garden-hybrid Tulips that have sometimes sold the glory of their race for comfort, and in other cases, such as the May-flowerers, have acquired the garden-comfort by virtue of a yet added grace of port and glory of colour. But the remaining species will risk no betrayal of their better selves, and the rock-garden (and all its mice) is eager for many and many a lovely and hearty Tulip, that only has to be planted on some sunny slope and there for ever left alone to continue and increase and be happy ; though not all the Levantines are equal to the labour, in our unripening climate, of doing much more than replacing their annual bulb by that which is to yield beauty again next season. There is place in the rock-garden for the tall species, such as *T. Gesneriana*, but these will be found in catalogues, which also deal faithfully in due time with blazing novelties in the same line, such as *T. Hoogiana*. But in between the two extremes there are a number of smaller treasures whose names are often seen, and whose presence in the garden is much to be desired, though their precise symptoms are sometimes beyond the power of the unguided enthusiast to discern. Therefore this list proposes to deal compendiously, in their botanical precedence, with the smaller and more dainty species especially suited to the rock-garden; and pass by on the other side of the more ascertainable catalogue-species and the most obscure group of Neo-Tulips that has apparently erupted quite newly from the soil of Italy and swum unbeknown into the ken of bewildered botanists.

T. australis is often sent out under the name of *T. Celsiana*. It is a lovely thing of some 6 or 10 inches, quite like our own *T. sylvestris*, but not so tall, and with all the segments of the goblet, sepals and petals alike, of the same size, and shaded heavily on the outside with brown. In cultivation it is very widespread and popular, blooming early in the season and spreading readily. In nature, too, it is very widespread, in the higher alpine meadows of the South, and varies greatly; in particular there is a dwarf form that climbs high in the Maritimes and earns its varietal name of *T. a. alpestris*. It is wonderful to stand under the pale darkness of a cloud on the rolling bare moors above the Boréon in July, when the brown sere turf is illuminated in the gloom with many million little sparks of lemony light from the cups of the Tulip standing bold and erect in their galaxies on delicate stems of 2 or 3 inches.

FIRST GROUP: NAKED FILAMENTS AND CONE-SHAPED FLOWERS.

T. Oculus solis is the stalwart Sun's Eye scarlet Tulip of the South, standing sturdily 10 inches or a foot in height, and early in blossom.

T. praecox is that other surprising great 12- or 15-inch Tulip of Southern vineyards, the outsides of whose flowers are blurred and dead and dull in the flat-sided triangular-looking bud, like the underside of a butterfly's wing, in no way preparing one for the satiny fury of pure scarlet that presently unfolds, staring out into the world with a menacing wide pupil of blackness. It may stand for a type of the even more inspiring glories, alike within and without, of the similarly sturdy novelties, *TT. Tubergeniana, Fosteriana, Miqueliana*, and *Willmottiae*, so savagely blazing at the end of Spring that eye can scarcely bear the furnaces of their vast expanded flowers under the sun.

T. montana (*T. armeniaca* and *T. Boissieri*, Regel.) is a plant of much lessened size, as a rule about 6 inches high, though able to attain a foot. It is otherwise a smaller repetition of the last, but its leaves are usually twirled sickle-wise in a sidelong curve, and have waved edges, while the smaller bell-shaped flower of scarlet glares straight upwards at the sun. It has a lovely little dwarf alpine form of 3 or 4 inches called *T. m. Julia*.

T. chrysantha offers us a golden-yellow *T. montana* from Afghanistan, with the added advantage that its bulbs are savoursome and nourishing as a chestnut.

T. sogdiana has similar flowers, but of half the size, and the leaves have no wave at the edge.

T. Clusiana is the special treasure of the Riviera, where it is now becoming sadly rare, but was not so long ago to be seen still abundant in an old Olive-orchard forgotten in the heart of Cannes. It is a ready grower, but hates being in a pot, as it has a curious habit of pushing the new bulb far down below the old one. In cultivation it is ready and easy : a plant of inimitable grace, with its fine slender growth and fine narrow pointed foliage, ending in the very long pointed bud, all a flush of broad musty-pink bands down the pale reverse of the segments, that ultimately in May and June (with us) open into a wide star of six long points, softly and coldly pearl-white, with an eye of bluish darkness at the heart.

T. Eichleri is also *T. Julia* (Haag. and Schm.). It lives in Transcaucasia and has all the qualities and habits of *T. praecox*, but the foot-stalks of the flowers are finely downy instead of being perfectly smooth.

T. suaveolens, Roth., has nothing to do with *T. sylvestris*, of which it is made a synonym in catalogues, although it even stands in a different section of the race. It is figured in the *Bot. Mag.*, T. 839, and is a dwarf Tulip of South Russia, with downy leaves as long or longer than the flower-stem, and rather flattened. The blossom is big, with very wide-awake spreading bells of gold or scarlet ; or sometimes scarlet with a margin of gold.

T. boeotica lives by Parnes, and in the seaward fields of Boeotia. It is about a foot high and bending in the stem, and downy, with nobly large wide flowers of intense purple, with the three inner segments running to a sharp tip like a tail. And each has a yellow-bordered oblong blotch of blackness at its base. It has a dwarfer variety with even larger blooms, called *T. b. eriantha*, from the mid-alpine regions of Malevo in Laconia.

T. undulatifolia (*Bot. Mag.*, T. 6308) has a stem of 6 or 9 inches, and is quite like *T. montana*, but that the stem is finely downy, and the segments of the flower specially long-pointed, suddenly drawing to a tail-tip at the end. The star-cups are pure scarlet and held sturdily erect. From the fat fields at the foot of Tartalos in Ionia by Smyrna.

T. Greigi, with its ample grey leaves marked with broken blurred

PLATE 49.

THLASPI LIMOSELLAEFOLIUM.
(Photo. R. A. Malby.)

TROLLIUS PUMILUS.
(Photo. W. Purdom.)

PLATE 50

TULIPA PERSICA.
(Photo. R. A. Malby.)

lines of brownish black, beneath the immense and amazing goblets of vermilion that are its blossoms, is well known among the greater and most gorgeous Tulips of the rock-garden. It likes a specially hot and well-drained place, but is never a species easy to keep suited for very long, as the strength of our summers is not enough to hearten it fully for next year's bulb, but its succession gradually dwindles away. Also the plant has miffinesses of its own.

SECOND GROUP, ALL WITH FLUFFY FILAMENTS AND BELL-SHAPED FLOWERS.

T. saxatilis is a Cretan, of wholly distinct aspect, with ample soft leaves of peculiar smoothness and brilliant green gloss. The stems are about a foot long or more, and usually carry a couple of deep and beautiful bell-shaped flowers of soft clear rose with suffused and melting yellow base (*Bot. Mag.*, T. 6374). Its only trouble in England (where it grows heartily and spreads, yet can but seldom be induced to flower) is that it seems to want a situation of intense sunshine in a soil so light and stony that it will have no chance of going to sleep in luxury, but will be forced to wake up to its softly lovely chimes in May. As for *T. Beccariniana*, which is a repetition of this, but with flowers of pearly whiteness flushed with rose, this will not trouble the gardener as much as he would like ; it is only known from one specimen, found near Lucca many years ago and never seen again.

T. sylvestris is our own wild Tulip, quite common, so far as its notable grey pointed leaves are concerned, in many an orchard of the midlands and the West, extending even into Yorkshire, but always so parsimonious with its blossom that even in a good year an acre of foliage will show but one or two golden bells in April and May. The stem is about 10 inches or a foot high, and the plant may be known from all its like by the *nodding blooms*, golden without and within, with the three outer segments curling backward at the tip. In the garden it grows and spreads and flowers admirably, and even seeds itself about ; especially in the slightly improved form that is often sent out as *T. florentina*.

T. orphanidea lives in the damp fields of Dekeleia, Arcadia, and Attica. It stands near the last, but the leaves are quite narrow and *bright green* instead of glaucous-blue, as long as the flower-stem or longer ; while the flowers are purplish outside, golden within, and narrower altogether in the petal (*Bot. Mag.*, T. 6310).

T. Hageri is among the Royalties of the rock-garden Tulips,—

together with the little wavy-leaved dwarf star-Tulip of blood-scarlet, called *T. linifolia,* and the 6-inch taller butter-belled or pale citron *T. batalini;* to say nothing of that harbinger of spring, *T. Kaufmanniana,* which sits almost close on the bare earth in wide Water-lilies of flushed rose and pearl and salmon and cream in the early morning of the year, as if they were evoked memory springing through the soil, of some summer sunset of long ago on far-off unforgotten snows. *T. Hageri* quickly increases into a close and many-stemmed clump with masses of long and very narrow bright-green rather wavy-edged leaves lying straight outstretched upon the ground; while from the clump rises a number of fat 6-inch stems, each carrying a single bold and erect little starry bell, which in the type is of a rather blunted fire-copper-colour outside, though scarlet and black-blotched within; but, if you import your bulbs from Parnes, where it grows with *T. orphanidea,* they may often give you strange breaks of the most ravishing sunset-rose or irradiated apricot, of a rich and melting purity unparalleled for tender richness in the race. Catalogues offer a form called *T. Hageri nitens,* which is a more flaming variety of the species indeed, but is no relation to these last.

T. pulchella is a little beauty of only 3 or 4 inches, and specially free with its flowers, which are wide bells of a uniform rosy-purple *within and without,* blotched with black at the base. The leaves are narrow-oval, sickle-twisted and outspread upon the earth, and the plant may be found high up in clayey places in the Alps of the Cilician Taurus.

T. Lownei continues the beautiful dwarf tradition of the group into which we are now come. It is only 3 inches high or so, and very free, no less than the last, with its gaping bells, beside the snows of Lebanon and Hermon. It has, in fact, all the look and habit of the last, but the flowers are of soft *whitish tone inside,* and the reverse of the three outer segments is darker in tone of purple than the purple reverse of the three inner ones, which, with the white inner surface of the bell, gives great richness and variety to the little flowers, springing three or four from one bulb in April.

T. bithynica is the species called in gardens *T. acuminata* and *T. cornuta.* It stands near *T. pulchella* in general habit, but departs from it wholly for the worse, being a plant of some 10 inches or a foot, with very long pointed tails to all the flower-segments, which are dull red outside and scarlet within, carried brave and erect in April and May. This is found beside the snows of Transcaucasia, Cadmus of Caria, &c., and is the *T. turcica* of some authorities, but not the true *T. turcica,* Roth., which is a form of *T. sylvestris*—unless indeed it be, according to Grisebach, a garden development of this same *T. bithynica.*

T. violacea is the same as the last in all respects, but that the blossoms are violet and the filaments of the anthers considerably shorter.

T. Biebersteiniana is quite close in all its charms and ways to *T. australis* in the earlier section, but may be known at once by the *bell-shaped* golden flowers, nodding before they open, no less than by their fluffy filaments.

T. humilis lives in the sandy places of Eastern Persia, and is indeed humble with a stature of 3 or 4 inches. The flowers are pale-purple inside, and reddish-green outside. *T. crispatula* is a variety of this.

T. cretica may be seen on all the high summits of Crete. It is a most dainty little treasure, with very narrow small sickle-shaped leaves, huddled and spread out at the base of the stems of 2 or 3 inches, each carrying a single erect bell of pale pink, pearly white within.

T. biflora attains 6 inches or a foot. The leaves are flat and narrow, standing up and spreading outward instead of lying down meekly along the earth, and the stems are so far better than even the promise of their name that they can carry as many as four or five flowers, which are erect bells of greenish-blue tone, white on the inside, with a yellow blotch at the base of the segments. It lives on the limy alpine heights above Schiraz in Persia, and ranges thence far away through Iberia and Russia to the Siberian Altai.

T. oxypetala is a rare species of Taurus, with leaves twice as broad as in *T. Clusiana*, and more or less wavy. This Tulip has affinities with *T. baeotica* in the earlier group, but here, besides the fluffy filaments, the whole plant is quite without down. The large erect blossom is pink, with the three outer segments recurving, while the three inner ones stand firmly up in a three-pointed cup; and the whole amply bell-shaped goblet is carried erect.

And there remain, of course, innumerable other species of interest or beauty; this list being merely meant as a help among some of the more valuable kinds for the rock-garden as already known, but always to be supplemented by further discoveries, and by ampler treatment of the larger sorts in catalogues and other aids to knowledge.

Tunica olympica is but an unvalued annual.

Tunica prolifer is **Dianthus prolifer,** an annual of egregious worthlessness.

Tunica Saxifraga is one of the most precious of perennials, making a dense and woody permanent root-stock, from which there springs and floats every year an airy cloud a foot high, and more across, of thread-fine branches in a haze of green, bearing delicate tiny pink Pinks in an unimaginable profusion from June till the end of the year. It is a universal plant of all the dry sunny banks of the Southern Alps down to the level of the Mediterranean ; where its little stars may everywhere be seen in dry places by the roadside, never fearing sun. It varies, however, and many of the wild forms are thin and squinny and poor ; in the garden it develops the loveliest amplitude, and grows infinitely larger and finer in every way than it does in the starvation-diet of dust and sunshine that it endures in the hills. No fatness, however, seems to impair its permanence, and, though it always looks and does its best in the fullest sunlight, it by no means insists on this as a condition of its comfort. It can be raised by the thousand from seed, and special forms may be secured by division and cuttings. Of these a pinch of seed will develop you several beauties, of larger flower, of brighter soft pink, or more vivid veining, or sometimes of pure white. And there is also a double form, which has the advantage of not being safely hardy or permanent.

Tunica xylorrhiza=**Gypsophila ortegioeides**, *q.v.*

Tussilago.—Great as is the value and the size of the large Coltsfoots, their place will never be in the rock-garden, and they are indeed by far too vast and invasive for anything but the wildest of woods and wildernesses and bogs.

U

Umbilicus.—This race stands so squeezed between *Sedum* and *Sempervivum* that at various points the species overflow. On the whole it is to *Sempervivum* that the Navel-worts more closely stand allied, most usually forming rosettes after the same fashion, but rounder, and often thorny in their succulence. The flowers, however, are generally borne in tapering spires, though also sometimes in looser sprays. Their requirements may be held general ; they are all lovers of dry hot rocks in nature : and in the garden, the driest hottest rocks are what they imperatively need, the lightest and most perfectly drained of soil, in the hottest sunlight that the garden affords. They may be raised from their fine seed, and, though the flowering rosette will die, the plant may usually be continued from its offsets. The flowers are borne in summer and on into the later months : sometimes they make a charming show to match the charm of the rosettes, but often they are shorter than the calyx, or of dim tones that give no effect.

U. aeizoon is a most delightful little thing, with massed tiny rosettes like those of a Sempervivum, quite small and huddled, made up of tongue-shaped tiny fleshy leaves, fringy with hairs. The stems are some 2 inches high or so, carrying a radiant spray, not a close spike, of a few brilliant-golden deeply-cleft flowers, after the starry style of Sempervivum, and borne after the spreading fashion of such Houseleeks as *S. hirtum*, but on stems minutely downy. It blossoms all through the later summer, and has its home in the high rocky places of all the Cappadocian Alps and Cilician Taurus.

U. chrysanthus is a quite hardy easy pleasant species to deal with, and is often sent out under the name of *Sempervivum chrysanthum*. It is almost a repetition of the last, but twice or three times the size, making masses, in any open warm soil, of handsome downy-haired rosettes of bright green, much fatter than in those of *Sempervivum Gaudini*, and looser in the leaf, but not greatly dissimilar in general effect. The pubescent glandular stems are 6 inches high, coming up by the side of the rosette, and open into a sprayed Sempervivum head of ample starry flowers of soft yellow, rayed with red, less golden in colour than the last. Other species in this neighbourhood, whose dullness of flower or insecurity of habit unfits them for cultivation, are *S. Haussknechtii* and *S. platyphyllum*, from regions too southerly and hot for hope; and *S. oppositifolium*, which would not be, in any case, to be desired.

U. Cotyledon = *U. pendulinus*.

U. elymaiticus has specially dense rosettes, almost smooth and hairless, of tongue-shaped spoon-shaped fat leaves with a long diminution to their base; the flower-stems bear a freely branching shower of yellow blossoms that are not as good as they might be, for they are only half the length of the calyx. For the same reasons, beware of *U. globulariae-olius*, *U. serratus*, *U. persicus*, *U. ciliolatus*, and *U. horizontalis*.

U. leucanthus, from the drier places of the Ural, denies its right to the name by bearing abundant flowers of pale flesh-pink, three times the length of their calyx, on many one-flowered sprays in a noble pyramidal shower above the handsome hostile rosettes, with each packed leaf ending in a sharp incurving spine.

U. libanoticus makes clumps of handsome glaucous foliage, dimly toothed at the edge. The tall spike is rather one-sidedly furnished with hanging bells of bright pink-purple, leaving their calyx far behind.

U. Lievenii is a good perennial, with all its leaves almost cylindrical. They soon fall from the 10-inch flower-stems, which carry dense heads of rather one-sided sprays set with most handsome large flowers, like fine waxen tubes of pink, no less than four times the length of their forgotten calyx. (Turkestan, Persia, Ural, Altai.)

U. pendulinus is our own Navel-wort, so common with its round glossy leaves in the walls of the South and West, though not specially entrancing with its loose spires of pendent greenery-yallery little bells. It has, however, the romance of being a lone exile from the rest of its family, happily cast into the shade in more senses than one.

U. Pestalozzae makes beautiful rosettes of glaucous-blue leaves, dimly toothed here and there at the edge. The flowers are pale pink, twice as long as their calyx, and so making a dainty show as they hang out in rather one-sided sprays, on their stems of only 4 or 5 inches, in the cliffs of Berytagh, Cadmus of Caria, &c.

U. Semenowii throws up a foot-high spike of pink and white flowers, in a dense leafy spire like a cat's tail not yet angry to the very tip. They do not emerge far from the foliage, but are pink-and-white, while the rosettes of thorn-tipped and fatly fleshy foliage are handsome, and especially prolific of younglings at their base.

U. Sempervivum is by no means the same thing as *Sedum Sempervivum* (though it does pass as *Cotyledon Sempervivum*). This has rosettes of blunt fat spoon-shaped leaves, attenuated to their bases, and fringed with a toothed margin of membrane rather as in *Saxifraga mutata*. The blossoms are borne in a sprayed shower in one-sided rows along the sprays: in colour they are purplish, and minutely warty on the outside, like all the plant.

U. spathulatus spreads freely on the high Alps of Sikkim, sending out many rosettes on stolons from the central clump of broad paddle-shaped leaves, and is generous, too, with its stems of flower, about which gardeners still know too little.

U. spinosus is picturesque and well known, forming round close rosettes of notably tight and fleshy spine-tipped metallic dark-grey foliage, in a spinous ball, round the base of which emerges an encouraging number of babes, gathered in a neat circle round their mother. The stems are some 4 inches high, opening their yellowish flowers in July. Like all the others it loves summer sun, and yields to nobody in detestation of winter wet.

Urospermum Dalechampii may be liked by people who affect Hawkweeds. It makes, in any sunny open soil and site, large loose masses a yard across of silvery hairy foliage, rather feathered at the base, ample and abundant; and up above, on bare stems of a foot or 15 inches, arises, all the summer through, an unceasing procession of erect Hawkweeds or Dandelions of brilliant yellow. It can be divided more readily, as a rule, than grown from seed, and is a plant of furnishing value rather than choice charm.

Uvularia.—This little family of Woodland Bells has now been split up by American botanists—who may be considered to have the right, as their country has a monopoly of the race—into *Uvularia* and *Oakesia*. However, for the gardens of the humble Old World, it may be enough merely to mention the fact, lest catalogues some day catch out the unwarned, by hysterical proclamations of *Oakesia* as a novelty, even as one, the most effusive of all, has lately proclaimed the ugly, half-hardy, long-known, and long-disliked *Campanula colorata*, in the wildest tones of rapture as a beautiful and new and hardy perennial! *Uvularia*, at least, does not deserve such condemnation; these are all really dainty things for rich woodland soil in shady places, where they suggest little frail Solomon's Seals, with very much larger bells of creamy-yellow, which hang out in spring and early summer from the ends and upper axils of the graceful sprays, of 10 inches or a foot, set here and there with more or less glaucous oval-pointed leaves. The most generally brilliant is *U. grandiflora*, which in even an open cool border will form masses a yard through and a foot high, abounding in the beauty of its pendent creamy-yellow bells in May. Similar is *U. perfoliata*, with the leaves more in number, and more closely clasping the stem. And others in the race are *U. puberula* and *U. sessilifolia*. There is a variegated-leaved plant, looking like a tiny Dracaena, which is sometimes sent out as *Disporum sessile*, which may have reference to *Uvularia sessiliflora*. The collected clumps have that interesting trait that I have already noted about those of Cypripedium; for they evidently grow and root only in the superficial vegetable richness of each season, their thready whitish rootage running out flat on all sides from the little tubers. And see Appendix.

V

Valeriana.—The large Valerians have hardly any attraction at all, even for the wild garden; but the race, at the other extreme from the gawky dimness of these, affords us several high-alpines of minute and meek charm, not specially showy, but of a pleasant and unassuming prettiness. They are all plants that spread and establish quite readily in light soil, and especially in moraine, where their mild presence and the evergreen foliage of some makes its best effect. They are easy to divide at any time, and bloom through summer into the later months.

V. arizonica, on the contrary, is an early riser; producing heads of not very brilliant pinkish flowers on the mats of partly feathered leafage in March.

VALERIANA.

V. elongata is a leafy little Valerian of no attraction beyond its fragrance, whose greenish flower-spires of 4 or 5 inches may be seen above the loose and shining clumps of dark green foliage here and there in the high limestone crevices and screes of the Southern and Eastern ranges.

V. celtica is the famous Nard. All over the occasional alps where the Speik abounds, its collection is an occupation and almost a ritual, and the intensely sweet little plant (in all its parts), serves for embalming, incensing, and disinfecting. It spreads in the high turf, especially on non-calcareous ranges, and, where found, is most profuse. The small oval leaves, diminishing lengthily to their base, are bright green, springing in tufts from a woody thick stock that wanders far ; the grooved brittle stems rise up 4 or 5 inches in early summer, bearing a loose spire of small and perfectly dull stars of dirty brownish-yellow.

V. globulariaefolia lives in the Pyrenees, and attains 3 or 4 inches, bearing rather large heads of pink blossom above the basal clumps of small leaves, which are oval and undivided, while those on the stems are feathered like those of a scabious. Here also the stem is grooved, and the plant intensely sweet.

V. longiflora is another Spanish mountaineer of the same habits and size, but blooming, not in May and June only, but far on into the later summer.

V. oligantha stands 6 inches or more, and has the common weedy look that so blunts the attractions of so many Valerians, whose descriptions would be found alluring, while their realisation would sadly disappoint, such is the lack of personality and distinction in the family.

V. saliunca is better than the last. It makes dense masses of oval small undivided leaves of dark green in the high places and stony ridges of the granitic ranges here and there, and sends up in summer flattened heads of pink flowers, intensely sweet, on many stems of 2 or 3 inches.

V. supina, however, is not only the one species of the race for which the rock-garden positively asks, but would always, in every race, be accounted a treasure. It is not a common species, but may be found in rather cool and damp slopes of broken soil and scree and mud, in the high places of the Eastern ranges (as in the great couloirs along the side of the Schlern, descending into the gloom of the Bärenloch), making wide packed masses of small dark oval leaves, fringed with fine hair, and virtually toothless at the edges ; these are almost hidden from view by the profusion, in summer, of almost stemless heads, loose and well-arranged, of comparatively large and solid and distinct flowers

418

of a waxy pearly pinkness and the most entrancing fragrance, embalming the air as one passes. This beautiful and blessed little mass thrives happily in the moraine, and quickly spreads; it should, however, in hot dry climates, be well supplied with water, and set in a rather cooler aspect; also, for the advantage of one's own eye and nose, it is as well to have it close in reach of both on a high ledge. It is the only Valerian that counts in the rock-garden (*V. olenea*, from Daghestan, however, has similar stature, and so may have similar charm); after this all the others that are sometimes advertised— *V. tripteris*, *V. saxatilis*, *V. alpestris*, *V. saxicola*, *V. montana*, *V. tuberosa* need only be thought of as names to be avoided, unless, indeed, one wants to encumber one's garden with weeds no better than the common *V. dioica* of England.

Vancouveria hexandra is a most beautiful Epimedium, with the ample leafletted leafage of the race, soft bright-green in colour, and much more graceful, wide, airy, and light in habit than any of the others. The flowers, which are small and creamy, come up on stems of 10 inches or a foot in summer, in the most delicate and dainty loose showers, so that each little star seems to float pendulous on the air by itself. It is a perfectly easy grower, under the conditions that suit Epimedium, and soon its creeping root-stock fills a cool shady ledge with its vivid spraying foliage. There is now also a form, or subspecies, which differs in having the leafage rather more condensed and leathery, especially beautifully goffered round the leaflets, and turning to shining red and russet on the upper surface, while the under side is of a contrasting glaucous-blue. To add to these attractions, this form is evergreen, instead of dying down in winter like the typical *Vancouveria*. It is, perhaps, a new species.

Vella spinosa is a strange angry small Crucifer, which, on the limy cliffs of Granada, especially above the sea, makes tiny spiny bushes of 6 inches high or so, intricately branching, and having hardly a leaf to its name, but perhaps a very few very narrow fleshy little ones here and there. The plant, like so many others of the hot places, makes up for this lack of amenities by its exuberance in defence; being a hedgehog of thorns, and with a sharp spine terminating every twig, along which, in summer, sit yellow flowers veined with violet: it is the *Piorno di Crucetillas*. There is also another species, rather less fierce, of a foot high or more, and set with round small leaves of deepest green to enhance the brilliant yellow of the blossom: this is *V. pseudo-cytisus*. Both species should be kept for the hottest and driest places in the most well-drained and warm-soiled slope, and should have hostages taken in autumn, by means of cuttings.

VERATRUM.

Veratrum.—These vast-foliaged portents are the curse of the cows in all the high meadows of the Alps, where you may see their towering masses of corrugated stiff oval leaves, like those of some giant *Gentiana lutea* (and often deluding the unwary with the resemblance), until with summer, here and there upon the clumps, develop the stalwart branching spikes of 3 or 4 feet high, of which every bough is densely packed with stars of blossom which, in every form and every species, are in varying degrees of unmitigated dinginess, greenish, yellowish, or of a grubby brownish-black, that do not atone for the venomousness of all the plant, nor lead us to be tempted (even by its generous and statuesque port), to pine for Veratrum in the garden; where, however, the race will thrive, of course, indestructibly in any deep soil, and in any not *too* torrid aspect. Nearly all Veratrums offered are forms of *V. viride*; the true *V. Loebeli* lives in America, and is neither known nor wanted over here.

Verbascum.—The Mulleins, again, are rather weeds of the brick-field than treasures of the rock-garden. Some of the statelier species are noble objects for the border, however, and may be found abundantly proclaimed in the catalogues of their growers and raisers. Almost the only common species at all adapted for the smaller rock garden is *V. phoeniceum*, with a modest habit of 18 inches or 2 feet, and loose spikes through later summer of large flowers in varying shades of violet, rose-lavender, or pale white. *V. pumilum* is but a biennial, and lives far away in the dry places of Anatolia. None the less it is pretty; being some 10 inches or half a foot high, with hoary foliage and flowers of bright yellow, spotted with purple. *V. Pestalozzae* is a yet more genuine candidate for the rock-garden, being a plant of the Lycian Alps, 4 inches or half a foot high, and soundly perennial, wrapped in tawny wool, with notably wrinkly leaves and woolly yellow blossoms. Seed of every Verbascum is profuse and easy to raise, and none requires more cultivation than open soil and sunshine for its prosperity.

Verbena.—No Verbena worth the growing is really safe and hardy and capable of permanent establishment in the average English rock-garden. Various species, however, are advertised from time to time, and may be grown in the hottest slopes as half-hardy annuals, and propagated yearly by cuttings, kept indoors, if such a course be considered allowable; for, though these often have a bloody and a fiery gorgeousness of colouring, they do not surpass the ordinary bedding Verbenas of commerce (which they exactly, on a slighter scale, resemble); and, if we are to adorn the rock-garden with the one, then why not with the other? And, once we open the door to bedding

420

annuals, there seems no valid plea against furnishing all the rocks with Perilla, Alternanthera, and Pelargoniums, as if it were carpet-bedding at the Crystal Palace.

Verbesina Purpusii is a Mexican alpine, only to be trusted in very light and chipful soil, in very warm and sheltered corners. It is hardly worth all this trouble ; it makes loose tufts of oval basal leaves, and then sends up in summer long naked stems of a foot or so in rich abundance, gawkily standing out this way and that, and each carrying a single flower, like an inferior *Arnica montana*, with a rather conical eye, and not quite counterbalancing the ebullient mass of leafage at the base, so different from Arnica's neat flat rosettes.

Vernonia.—These are gigantic perennial Eupatoriums or False Hemps from America, with stems of 6 feet or more, bearing tasselled sprays at the top, of intense and vivid violet. They will grow in any wild cool place, and wax mighty and thick into tall waving jungles, but their flowers are usually behind the times in England, except in specially warm and sheltered places, and get cut off in November before their prime. There are many species : those best known are *V. noveboracensis*, and the even more wealthy-blooming *V. arkansana*.

Veronica.—This vast and on the whole undistinguished race has nevertheless provided us with a large number of most brilliant treasures for the rock-garden, alike among those that stand up and among those that lie down ; and it may roughly be said that in clean open soil and open sunny exposure there is not a single *Veronica* that is not easy to grow, and often, indeed, rampageous and inde-structible. Having done this, however, and amply furnished our edgings and rockwork from the Old and the New World, *Veronica* has overflowed into Australasia, and there developed (besides rock-jewels) a new, most perplexing family of wholly different aspect—repellent leathern bushes with hard dead-looking foliage often of a metallic cast-iron look, or else with no apparent leaves at all, but scaly stiff branches and tentacles like gigantic club-mosses on some panto-mime scene of the Lower Regions. These are in a state of perilous confusion at present ; but, as many are valued by some for " furnish-ing " in the rock-garden, where they are most of them tolerably hardy, this list proposes first to deal with the normal and respectable species, herbaceous in look if not in deed, that abound in the Old World and the New ; and then, more cursorily, to run through the list of the more desirable New Zealand shrubs and treasures, clinging, however, to the hand of Cheeseman without question, as the gardener's best clue in the labyrinth of these almost indecent bushes—plants that are no plants, but lifeless imitations of living things, forged by Hephaestus out of dark metals in the underworld, and as vital (but far less attractive) as the little bay-trees and orange-trees of painted tin that one buys at Marshall and Snelgrove's to adorn the dinner-tables of one's friends. (And see Appendix for Chinese *V. pyrolaefolia*, &c.)

V. ageria (*Paederota ageria*) is a local rock-plant of the Eastern Alps, with long clusters of straw-yellow flowers, not very pretty, hanging from the crevices, at the ends of stems of some 4 or 6 inches, in summer. The leaves are in pairs, dark green and smooth, narrow-oval, toothed, and pointed.

V. aleppica is weakly in its stem of half a foot or 12 inches, which tends to flop in a diffuse mass. The regularly-toothed leaves are larger than in *V. orientalis*, which otherwise the plant resembles; and the flowers are pink. Following the example of *V. orientalis*, it has good value.

V. Allionii has been indiscreetly praised. It is a mat-forming species, covering wide spaces on the high turf of the Mont Cenis and the Southern Alps, with creeping shoots after the fashion of our own *V. officinalis*, set densely with regularly-toothed pairs of thick leathery green opaque leaves lying flat in the ground. The shoots root as they go, and finally, in early summer, from the axils near their tips, send up dense and fluffy-looking spikes of dark sapphire flowers, huddled in a blur of blue about 2 inches high on a naked stem. It is a rare thing, though locally abundant, and quite easy to cultivate in any open stony slope. But it is not exciting enough for the language that has sometimes been deployed upon it, and its principal charm, in reality, is that the little leaves can be brewed into a most excellent and salubrious tea.

V. alpina deserves prosecution for its false pretences. Under this name we expect something better than this peculiarly dingy small weed with its large hairy pairs of oval leaves on the weak creeping stems of 2 or 3 inches, that end in a parsimonious little parcel of diminutive flowers in a pale lymphatic shade of slaty-blue. (It is universal in the European Alps, and a special rarity in the Scotch ones.)

V. americana is a species near *V. Beccabunga* and of no value at all.

V. apennina is a lovely jewel and a notable improvement on the rather dim *V. serpyllifolia*. It lives in the damper rocks and beside the mountain springs in Castile and the Apennines; a species with prostrate and abundantly-rooting shoots, with almost sessile pairs of egg-shaped little leaves, and a generally robuster habit than the other, with looser spires of larger flowers in a much more brilliant tone of blue, making, ultimately, a wide carpet after the fashion of *V. repens,* but beset with a firmament of much brighter coerulean stars. A cool, moist place will clearly comfort it, when caught.

V. aphylla leads one to expect nudity and brilliance, but rewards one with especially leafy small tuffeted rosettes of oval hairy leaves in dull pale green, with hairy *naked stems* of 2 or 3 inches, carrying a small cluster of promptly-evanescent flowers, in varying shades of lilac-blue or violet. It is a general species of all the Alps, in dampish high places, from the Pyrenees to the Levant, but nowhere has it any brightness or beauty.

V. armena makes a many-stemmed tuffet of weakly stalks from the hardened stock. They are set with pairs of curled-edged little leaves, feathered in specially fine slits, and the flowers are bright blue, borne in short loose spires.

V. assoana is no more than a form of *V. austriaca.*

V. Aucheri huddles itself into very small dense tight tufts and cushions of minute white-velvet leaves, egg-shaped and deeply toothed. The stems are cotton-fine, set with foliage, and packed into an intricate tangle ; they are about 3 inches long, and large lonely blossoms of blue or white emerge, each by itself, from the axils at their end. This dainty beauty lives in the high screes of Demavend.

V. austriaca comes near *V. latifolia,* from which it differs in having the leaves feathered on either side to the base. It is a downy feeblet, usually flopping, about 8 or 10 inches long or high, with these pairs of rather large oval feathered leaves, and then from their uppermost axils pairs of loose spikes of large bright blue flowers only just not large enough always to redeem the plant from the charge of leafiness.

V. Bachofeni is a North American of no merit.

V. Beccabunga stands for the common Brooklime, which there is no need to introduce into the garden from every English stream-bed.

V. bellidioeides has all the faults of *V. alpina* in a rather more obvious form, as the plant is larger in all parts. The leafy hairy rosettes of largish daisy-like leaves, so often seen in the Alps, are of a dead grey tone, and the little blooms, packed sparingly in a head at the top of a hairy and rather leafy stem of 4 or 5 inches, are of a dim and pallid dull blue. *V. lilacina,* Townsend (*V. Townsendii,* Gremli.) is no more than a form of this, especially glandular, with stem-leaves larger, anthers nearly white (instead of yellow), and blossoms of a dowdy slate-colour.

V. Biebersteiniana is an 8-inch species from South Europe, blooming in June, with spikes of blue flowers.

V. bombycina makes a neat tuffet of lovely woolly whiteness, so close is the clothing of its tiny narrow-oval leaves, from whose shelter emerge red stars, either lonely, or in sprays of several. This is a charming moraine treasure; at home it shrinks into the highest crevices of Makmel of Lebanon.

V. Bona-rota (*Paederota Bona-rota*) acts as the "double" of *Phyteuma comosum,* whose dark and glossy deep-toothed leaves are vaguely imitated in general design, and absolutely in their gloss and dark yew-green colouring by those of the *Veronica*, which at once, however, is seen on nearer approach to be a quite different thing in all its habit, and wholly downy. It runs along freely in every crevice of the Southern limestones, hanging out from the chinks a fringe of pendent shoots about 4 or 5 inches long, each ending in a longish fluffy-looking cluster of longish flowers of rich clear blue. It may be grown in the garden in open stony ground, but is even better in the moraine, or with a crevice at its disposal to fill. It blooms in high summer, and, like the Phyteuma, is no friend to excessive torrid sunshine.

V. caespitosa has the lovely habit of *V. bombycina*. It makes a dense pin-cushion of greyish and rather woolly shoots, set with tiny very narrow blunt leaves rolled over at the edge. The stems, among the leafy shoots, are thread-fine, and all entangled, and so short that the flowers hardly emerge from the mass, but sit, bright big stars of pink, in their woolly calyces, close over the surface of the little cushion. This beauty lives on the summits of the Levant, and on Lebanon achieves a variety called *V. c. leiophylla,* which is wholly woolless but for the inflorescence. These should both have the devotion that waits on *V. bombycina,* which they both reward by blooming in May and June, according to the fashion of the family.

V. cana is an Indian alpine of 6 inches or a foot high, with slender unbranched stems only most sparingly furnished with leaves, here and there in rare couples. The loose flower-sprays are about 3 inches long, from the tips of the shoots as well as from the uppermost axils, and the bright blue blossoms are each about half an inch across.

V. canescens makes a great change from the last. This is so minute and so dim that you never notice that your piece of broken ground or your sandy bed has been overrun by tiny pervasive shoots, set with pairs of microscopic glandular oval leaves of a blunt invisible green, running flat across the surface here and there; until in July you come round one day and find that whole space peppered with single speedwell stars of delicate clear china blue, that have all the look of having been scattered there from some overhanging spray of *V. Chamaedrys.* But this is *V. canescens,* suddenly sprung to light again, as is its pleasant way, when you are quite sure you lost it in the winter, and know too well that its own place knows it no more. For this lovely little New Zealander—which now never lets you again forget its presence till autumn has long been dark on the garden—turns out not only an easy and a hardy plant, but has the happiest way of seeding itself about in the most unexpected places here and there, where you would never yourself have dreamed of putting it, nor of hoping to see it thrive in a carpet. It lives at home in the dried margins of lakes and pools in both the Islands, and up to 3000 feet in the mountains ; its perfect adaptability to our country is such a pleasant miracle that pieces of the mat should always be secured and potted up in autumn, lest trust in the miracle should betray you, as trust in miracles invariably does, if carried too far.

V. carnea is a form of *V. spicata* with pink flowers.

V. caucasica (*V. ossetica*) has stems of 5 or 6 inches or more, rather crisped and glandular. The leaves are oval, but feathered to the base in gashed lobes. The flowers are pearly-white with a striping of lilac, borne in a very loose and widespread showery spray throughout the later summer. Several doubtful names of catalogues may belong to this species.

V. Chamaedrys.—You would not need to search catalogues far before you came on many an uglier thing than the common Speedwell.

V. chathamica belongs to the group of New Zealand shrubs, but comes here because its habit of ramping forward flat upon its belly is so picturesque ; till the ground, or the cliff-wall, becomes a dense sheet of its rock-hugging shoots, set closely with oval-pointed foliage of a beautiful light glaucous-green, and emitting little spikes of blue flowers in the latest days of summer. It is quite hardy in any reasonably sheltered place, and will strike with the utmost readiness from cuttings.

V. cinerea makes lax trailing cushions and masses and rooting carpets of short shoots, all of ashy-grey velvet, with the narrow-oblong toothed leaves rolled together along their edges, and the ascending branchlets about 3 or 4 inches long, sending out from their upper axils rather loose spires of pink blossom throughout the later months of the summer. The flowers, to judge by the statements of some lists, appear sometimes to vary to blue. It stands near *V. caucasica* and *V. orientalis*, but differs, among other points, in the fact that the shoots root as they go.

V. circaeoeides is a name for a species in this group, with a pleasant habit of weakly 8-inch stems, set with veiny toothed rhomboidal leaves, often of russet and bronzy tone, and specially loose sprays in the later summer of pearly-white flowers veined with pink, that give a faint suggestion of an enlarged Enchanter's Night-shade, to justify the plant's improbable name. It is as easy as all the rest in any open soil and site.

V. commutata makes widely-ramifying mats after the way of *V. Allionii*—a crisply-downy creeping thing, with the lower leaves in their pairs hardly cut at all at the edge, while the upper ones are feathered into fat and quite toothless regular lobes all along, with the largest at the end. There are always two spikes sent up from the axils towards the end of each shoot, on a longish bare stem of an inch or two, ending in a close mass of erect-borne blossoms of bright azure, with stamens of deep violet, huddled on their very short foot-stalks into a mass. (It is a native of Southern Aragon, on the Sierra de Javalambre, taking a special form that bears that name.)

V. crassifolia is one of those tall 2 to 3-foot herbaceous Veronicas with spikes of blue in late summer, for which the border may be thankful, but with which the choice rock-garden has few close dealings.

V. cuneifolia (*V. dichrus*, Schott, is the Villosa variety of this) makes a downy tuffet, and the foliage is smaller than that of *Teucrium Chamaedrys* or the Germander. It roots as it goes, and the ascending stems of 2 or 3 inches are thread-fine, emitting longish and usually lonely (not paired) spires of blue flowers, with a white margin, in June and July.

V. deltigera has dainty stems that vary between 6 inches and thrice that height. They are weakly uprising, leafy, hardly branching, and set with oblong egg-shaped pairs of leaves, more or less deeply toothed. The broad-lobed blooms are about three-quarters of an inch across, and their spires, of 3 to 6 inches long, are notably numerous, springing from the ends of the shoots as well as from the upper axils. (Western Himalaya.)

V. dentata is a little blue-flowered form from the Jura, about 2 inches high, but not of any special worth.

V. dichrus is a downy variety, *V. c. villosa*, of *V. cuneifolia*, *q.v.*

V. elegans is no more than a garden form of *S. longifolia*, with terminal spikes of pink, and a stature of 10 inches or a foot. These plants like a dampish place, and bloom through the later summer months, thus atoning for the rather commonplace look of their crowded upstanding spikes of brightly-coloured flowers.

V. erinoeides=*V. thessalica*, *q.v.*

V. euphrasiifolia comes quite close to the downy variety of lovely little *V. telephiifolia*, from which it differs only in not having seed-pods rather heart-shaped, but perfectly oval. It is a delightful prize still held in store for us by the Alps of Persia.

V. fragilis comes as a near neighbour to *V. cuneifolia*, but the

PLATE 51

VERONICA SATUREIOEIDES.
(Photo. R.B.G., Edinburgh.)

VIOLA BOSNIACA.
(Photo. R. A Malby.)

stems are especially dainty and fine and frail, while the spires of white
bloom are short and scantly furnished, springing from the tips of the
shoots no less than from the axils. (South-eastern Alps of Persia.)

V. fruticulosa cannot be reckoned more than a variety of the
beautiful *V. saxatilis*, but it is quite distinct for the garden, a neat
half-woody little branching mass of much bolder and more erect
habit, some 6 or 8 inches high in a bush, with oval foliage, thick and
fleshy, crowded with hairs, towards the edge especially, and always
untoothed at the rims. As the stems ascend, the small oval leaves
grow smaller, and all the upper part of the plant is sticky with glandular
hairs. The stems go off into a much more marked, longer spire than
in *V. saxatilis*, and the flowers, instead of being of royal blue, are softly
pinkish with darker veining. It is a choice thing for the garden, and
may be seen in all the Southern alpine chains, but very rarely in
Switzerland (as in the Alps of Scotland), except on the limestones
of Engelberg, and about Dôle in the Jura. Its whole look, more
bushy with long pink spikes, makes it wholly different from the floppy
V. saxatilis with its loose clusters of rich sapphire.

V. galatica is 6 or 9 inches high, weakly ascending from an almost
woody base. Its relationship is with *V. Chamaedrys*.

V. gentianoeides bears a rather ridiculous name, but is none the
less a useful and pleasant species among the coarser Veronicas that
are fitted for the garden. It makes large tufted masses of loose smooth
leafage, long and oval, of bright glossy green (there is a variegated
form). From these, in summer, arise many spikes of 10 inches or a
foot, tidily yet not tightly set with large flowers of palest blue with
a hem of deeper colour. It is a stately and beautiful creature, and well
deserves its place.

V. Hendersonii = *V. longifolia subsessilis*.

V. incana.—Even more may be said of this than of *V. gentianoeides*.
It is a Siberian and Caucasian species making wide clumps of most
handsome toothed oblong leaves of silver-grey, from which, in summer
and late summer, rise spikes of 6 or 8 inches, densely furnished with a
fluffy-looking mass of rich violet-blue blossom, in beautiful contrast
with the dense-plated silver of the foliage. Like the last, and like all
Veronicas except the highest alpines, this species spreads and thrives
profusely in any open place, seeds well, may be divided afresh almost
every day of the week, and is as admirable for a border or even an
edging as for the rockwork itself.

V. incisa is a great 2-foot stalwart from Siberia, with flowers of pink
or blue in June.

V. japonica is a form of the closely allied *V. sibirica*.

V. Kotschyana makes a tufted bush to the goodly height of 2 or 3 inches, with many weakly-rising stems, and packed and more or less overlapping little eyelashed leaves, very narrow, fleshy, upright, and rolled over along their edge. The blossom-spikes are about an inch and a half long, well-furnished with pink stars of flower in June. It comes from the alpine and high-alpine crevices of Taurus.

V. kurdica comes quite close to *V. orientalis*. It forms a neat mass of 2 or 3 inches, and its especially large blossoms of brilliant blue stand off from the main spire on longer and more widespread foot-stalks. (Mountains of Armenia and North Persia.)

V. laciniata is a stalwart of little moment for the rock-garden, living in Siberia, and attaining 18 inches, with spikes of blue throughout the later summer.

V. lanuginosa huddles in tight woolly tuffets on the high Himalayan passes. It has minute round leaves, woolly all over, and packed into a woolly cushion of 2 or 3 inches high, in which sit the small blue blossoms with their uppermost lobe comparatively large and round.

V. latifolia is a common sight across Central Europe—a tall leafy rank weed with erect axillary sprays of blue in early summer.

V. laxa has no merit.

V. longifolia ranges across Europe to America. It is one of the spike-flowered section, and a handsome plant of 18 inches or so, nobly showy for the border, with its abundant cat's-tail spires of lilac-purple; with innumerable garden varieties in shades of white, rose, and violet. It especially likes a rather damp place, and blooms in June and July.

V. macrostēmon lives in the Arctic regions, where it repeats the packed neat charm of *V. nummularia*, but the huddled tiny rounded upper leaves on the tiny wandering shoots are saw-edged or scalloped, the upstanding spike of an inch or two is downy, and bears its blue flowers in a rounded head that afterwards lengthens out.

V. melissaefolia is like a Germander Speedwell of 2 or 3 feet high.

V. minuta makes a most lovely carpet, after the dense fashion of *V. repens*, but that the flowers are bright blue. The species stands near *V. telephiifolia*, but the leaves are not fleshy nor brittle, while, on the other hand, they are much more slender. It will only be found, like Prometheus, on the highest summits of Caucasus.

V. montana grows about 4 inches high, and has blooms of a dim powder-blue.

V. monticola comes from the Caucasus, and is a really valuable plant in the terminal-spiked group of *V. incana*. This stands about 8 inches high, with long spikes of brilliant azure in June.

V. multifida comes as a twin to *V. orientalis*, with leaves cut into deep featherings, and the flowers of pink or pale-blue from stems of 5 or 6 inches, diffuse and spreading.

V. nummularia grows into neat wandering fine lawns in the Pyrenees. The naked stems go rambling, and are woody at the base, sending up small shoots of an inch or so, packed with overlapping tiny round-oval leaves, smooth-edged, thick, and rather fleshy, with an eyelash of hair at their rim. The blossoms are large and lovely, packed in heads of soft blue at the tips of the upstanding shoots, with four lobes to the corolla, and a heart-shaped pod succeeding each.

V. nivalis is another of the valueless little dirty sad-blue Squinnies, after the fashion that this race seems to take, at least in Europe, when it strays to alpine elevations.

V. officinalis is common enough in the open woods for the garden to be spared its presence. It is a pale peer to *V. Allionii.*

V. orchidea makes a terminal spike of blue flowers on stems of nearly a foot high. It is not more than a variety of *V. spicata.*

V. orientalis, which has served as the picture for so many nearly-allied species, makes a loose and flopping mass of weakly stems of some 6 or 8 inches from the central stock. They are set with pairs of oblong wedge-shaped toothed greyish leaves, and send out from the upper axils, in summer, one pair or two pairs of short sprays of blossoms, pink or blue. It is a common Speedwell from the drier rocks in the Alps of Asia Minor; and, in the garden, the type of a useful and interesting group, of which it is itself one of the most brilliant members. In gardens it fears no foe in the way of the hottest sunshine, and is often sent out under the name of *V. alpina*—a vastly inferior article, as we have seen.

V. Paederota makes huddled downy masses of 2 inches or so, with packed fleshy small foliage in the precipices of Persia, from which depend the heads of tubular bloom in summer.

V. paniculata is 18 inches high, with rather slack growth and sprays of blue blossom in June.

V. pectinata makes prostrate velvet-hoary mats of rooting shoots beset with obovate leaves, regularly deep-toothed, and arranged in pairs lower down, but solitary and very rarely opposite each other on the flower-sprays, as these arise profusely in May and June, some 5 or 6 inches, carrying large flowers of pale blue. It lives in all the shady places of the hills from Byzantium away through Asia Minor.

V. peduncularis belongs to the Caucasus, where it grows 4 inches high or so, with pearly-white stars lined with rose in May.

V. petraea has some affinities with *V. alpina*, but is a very great improvement on that dismal little weed. This forms into wide sheets and masses, with tiny wedge-shaped oblong or elliptic foliage, minutely downy, and either entire at the edge, or, more usually, with a few small teeth. The bloom-shoots are some 4 or 5 inches long, and over the whole mass, not in pairs, but lonely from an upper axil of each branch, they spring in summer, bearing a loose shower of large and ample flowers of real heavenly blue, of a rare effect when the wide sheet of green is played over by this dancing galaxy of clear colour.

V. pinnata is another of the tall and less interesting leafy Speed-wells from Siberia, attaining 18 inches, with blue blossoms in July.

V. polifolia is a hoary-grey tuffet from Lebanon, built of 3- or 4-inch shoots, dense with oblong-narrow tiny leaves, regularly toothed and rolled over at the edge. The flowers are pink, in close short spires.

V. Ponae has small worth. It is a hairy leafy woodlander from damp places of the Pyrenees, growing about 6 or 8 inches high, with a specially loose shower of poor pale-lilac flowers at the top of the stems, clad, in the usual woodland way, with pairs of large soft leaves, oval-pointed, toothed, and rank in effect.

V. prostrata is not the same as that variety of *V. Teucrium* which also passes in gardens under this name, as well as under the no less false one of *V. rupestris*. It is near *V. Teucrium*, however, and accord-ingly a plant of high value, making diffuse and microscopically downy masses, and differing from the other in its leaves, which *are very narrow and acute*, joining the dwarfer stems each by a distinct *wee foot-stalk*. The abundant spires of intensely blue (or white) blossoms are shorter, too, and all the lobes of the *flowers are blunted instead of being pointed and starry*. It has the same garden use and garden charm of profuse blossom in the summer, and is more suited for a forward place on account of its slightly less rampageous habits.

V. pyrolaefolia. See Appendix.

V. repens has quite special charm, however, above most others; this lovely little Corsican, in any warm level place in good light soil, in sun or shade, immediately makes perfectly unbroken soft sheets of vivid green many yards across (so that it should always be planted for the broadest effects), and these, all the summer through, are veiled by a dense abundance of very pale-blue, almost whitish flowers, sitting flat in the foliage till hardly anything can be discerned but the moonlit unanimity of that carpet. It seeds abundantly, and every pulled-off fragment grows. No cover more delicious for bulbs of medium strength could be imagined, but the effect, in itself, of a dozen square yards of the *Veronica*, either in its unadorned beauty of emerald green, or veiled in its luminous grey shroud of blossom, is a thing to make the gardener praise and give thanks. There is a variety,

VERONICA.

V. r. macrocarpa, with pink flowers in the Sierra Nevada ; and the type gives a diminished picture of its yet lovelier azure cousin *V. apennina*.

V. rosea is nothing but a form of *V. austriaca*, with pink stars, and yet ampler leaves feathered deep in broader segments.

V. rupestris of gardens is the variety *V. T. dubia* of *V. Teucrium*, although its splendour is such that there may seem to some more *dubia* than *Teucrium* about such an assignment.

V. satureioeides is a flopping little mountain species after the habit of *V. saxatilis*, from the mountain tops of Dalmatia. It may be known botanically from *V. saxatilis* by the foot-stalks of the blossoms shorter than their bracts, as by the *five segments* of the calyx ; but for the gardener it is a wholly different plant, lying down in large masses, with the shoots beset by bigger, leatherier, darker, rounder, more obviously scalloped leafage, often almost concave ; no less than by the generous and rather crowded heads of large flowers from the tips of the shoots. These flowers, however, are of a dull and sullen leaden blue that greatly depresses the value of what is otherwise a neat and easy and useful alpine Speedwell for drooping over the edge of a rock or bank. It blooms, however, much longer than the other, to make up as far as it can for its lack of equal brilliance.

V. saxatilis, when all is said and done, still stands aloft at the head of our alpine Speedwells. It is a thing as delicate as it is superb, a quite weakly, woody-rooted species, flopping its boughs about for 3 or 4 inches this way and that, and then uprising in shoots clad with pairs of oval, leathery-fleshy leaves of intense and shining dark-green. But, intense as their colour may be, it is as nothing to the intense azure of the large and sadly short-lived stars in which the shoots conclude, opening a few at a time in the loose spray. They are like rare illuminated jewels of blue, sparkling in scattered handfuls on all the rocks and open bare slopes of all the high Alps of Europe even into Scotland ; and, for a final touch of coquetry, they have brilliant yellow anthers, and a white-pale eye, rimmed with a ring of vivid crimson. It seeds and grows with perfect zeal, yet never invades ; so that it is well to admit it to the choice places that its choice and rare loveliness deserves.

V. scutellata, *V. serpyllifolia*, and *V. officinalis* are all natives and unfitted for the garden ; only the last would serve the same uses as *V. Allionii*, rambling neatly over the ground with pairs of pale-green scalloped leaves, and sending up spires of pale blue flowers in summer, on stems of 2 inches or so. (See *V. officinalis*.)

V. senanensis is a pretty wandering species from the upland fields of Japan. It has oval-pointed, toothed leaves on long petioles at the base, and on shorter up the erect stems of 5 or 6 inches that end in a loose spray of large pale blossoms veined with a richer lilac.

V. sessiliflora is a Siberian of 2 feet high, with flowers of dark deep bluish tone in August.

V. spicata is a rare native, and in its native state pretty, when it wanders with fine shoots over the lawns of Cartmel, and sends up dense little fluffy spikes of dark-blue after the fashion of *V. Allionii*. However, it varies most copiously, and is usually so much taller as to be a treasure beloved by borders, where the rock-garden need not be concerned to grudge it. There are many varieties in shades of white and pink and purple : through all the summer they are all in flower : but the only one with which we have much business is the aforesaid neat small form *V. sp. alpina*, not more than 4 inches high in stem and spike.

V. spuria is a terminal-sprayed tall species of no value.

V. Stelleri in the meadows of Japan makes no successful attempt to rival *V. Chamaedrys*.

V. stenobotrys is a *V. melissaefolia* with narrower foliage.

V. surculosa comes nearer to *V. cuneifolia*, but has the *flower-sprays much shorter and denser, the head remaining oval even in fruit.* These come up on quite short stems from the shorter shoots of the tuft, and are much more usually produced in pairs, carrying blossoms of bright azure, erect on their tiny foot-stalks in the spike. The downy leaves are rather long, wedge-shaped obovate, with two or three scallopings on each edge. *V. surculosa* lives in stony places high up in the Cilician Taurus, and in the garden is as free and easy and pleasant as the rest of the group.

V. taurica is a small compressed form of *V. orientalis*.

V. telephiifolia has most especial daintiness. It lives on Ararat, but not at all less happily in our gardens, where it makes flat sheets of tiny rosettes, built of minute rounded almost fleshy foliage in the most lovely shade of glaucous-blue. From this, in summer, arise very short stems of 2 or 3 inches, bearing an oval spray of clear blue blossoms. This should have a place among the choicest things in select bank or moraine, and may be most readily multiplied by separation of the shoots. There is also a variety *V. t. pilosula*, from Transcaucasia, which is apt to have the leafage a trifle larger.

V. Teucrium is *V. prostrata* of Smith's *Prodromus* (not of Linnaeus), and has given birth to that most superb of garden Speedwells, the thing sent out as *V. "rupestris,"* and better to be known as *V. T. dubia*, whose cataracts of growth, and crowded spires of intense azure, are the joy of every garden, big or little—a form of indestructible vitality, rooting and thriving as it goes, with such profusion that there is no trusting it in daintier company. The leaves are stemless on the stalk, narrow-oblong, bluntly scalloped or sometimes here and there with teeth ; the stems are crispulous with a minute wool (the whole growth is faintly downy), and the flower-sprays are sent up in one pair or two pairs from the upper axils of every shoot, and the noble brilliant-blue corollas on their erect foot-stalks in the spike *always have the three lower lobes sharply pointed* (in *V. prostrata, q.v.,* they are always *blunt*). *V. austriaca* differs from this in hardly anything but the greater narrowness of the leaf. Both species are European, and this one abounds from Spain through all Europe to Asia Minor and Russia. It varies widely, and nurserymen have lately sent out a compacta-form, which, if it does indeed belong to *V. Teucrium* (they attribute it impartially to *V. "prostrata"* and *V. "rupestris"*), should be a tidy and delightful prize for select places in the foreground.

V. thessalica (*V. erinoeides*) makes as good a copy as it can of *V. Kotschyana*, and only differs from that lovely neat jewel, in having its small rhomboidal leafage *toothed at the edge*, and in wearing its flower-spikes from *the tips of the shoots, singly*, instead of in pairs, one on either side from their uppermost axils. It is a high-alpine of Greece, living near the snows on the Thessalian Olympus, Kyllene, Parnassus, &c.

V. thymifolia sometimes shares the same heights. It is a velvety close tuffet, rooting as it goes, standing in close relationship to *V. kurdica*, but differing in the carriage of its blue blossoms, which are borne in *most dense head-like spikes*, packed together on stems of 2 or 3 inches. The little leaves are very narrowly oblong, swelling to the tip, and, because it lives on the summits of Crete, the plant has sometimes been called *V. cretica* (Pall.), as well as *V. teucrioeides*, and *V. tymphrestea* (Boiss.).

V. urticifolia has no use or value. It is a form of *V. latifolia ;* both may quite commonly be seen in the damp places of the alpine woodland—tall, lax stems of 15 inches or more, set with pairs of large, hairy, oval-pointed, toothed leaves, which emit from their upper axils, in one or two couples, loose spraying showers of pale-pink flowers that, though pretty in themselves, make no effect against the weedy flaccid stature and the too lush and slack leafiness.

V. virginica is another tall woodlander, about a yard in height, with the foliage arranged in whorls, and long, slender, terminal spikes of blossoms that are sometimes violet-blue or pink, but in one form white. It is not a thing of choiceness or merit for the rock-garden ;

though perhaps admissible to the cooler places of the wilderness, blooming, as it does, in the later summer.

Veronicas (New Zealand).—These are usually more or less hardy, but by no means all are to be universally trusted. They succeed, however, for their time, in any good, light, rich soil, and make good growth of evergreen foliage, though often too shy of their flowers, which are due to appear in autumn and late summer. They can all be multiplied endlessly by cuttings. The following list will deal with them in their botanical succession, so as to avoid the necessity of repeated description, and also give a clear chain of differences and comparisons, which ought, by setting each plant among its likes, to give a picture so recognisable as to compensate amply for the complications of reference that so arise, in the disordered jumble of the alphabet. Nor will more than a selection here be made, for fuller trial, from among such species as ascend into the mountains, so as to give higher ground for hope of hardiness.

V. Lewisii is a downy, pale green shrub, with short, broad sprays of notably large stars.

V. venustula grows only 6 or 9 inches high, with four segments to the calyx, and sprays of white blossom emerging from the ends of the shoots.

V. diosmaefolia has the same colour and arrangement of flowers, but the calyx has only three segments. It is a neat shrub with narrowish foliage of bright green, making an upstanding mass which is usually some 2 or 3 feet high, but may reach 15 feet.

V. Colensoi of the *Bot. Mag.* and of gardens is false, but what the true species might be nobody knew. It is *V. Hillii*, Col.

V. rigidula is a stiffish little bush from 6 inches high to 2 feet.

V. elliptica has very large elliptic leaves of pale green, on short foot-stalks. The white flowers are veined with purple and sweetly scented. It seems to be *V. odora* (Hook.).

V. buxifolia has the same shape of leaves, and they are similarly packed and overlapping up the stiff branches, but here the foliage is glossy, and the big white blooms are scentless.

V. Mathewsii makes a bush of 2 feet high or 4 feet, with goodly spikes of white or purple flowers. It is sometimes called *V. Traversii* in gardens, but is stouter and more leathery in the leaf, with larger spikes as well as larger flowers.

V. Balfouriana came by a favour of the gods from some unknown place, out of seed that was raised at Edinburgh. It is a lessened *V. Traversii* with smaller leaves, edged with red, longer sprays, and very much finer flowers of pale violet.

VERONICAS.

V. Darwiniana stands close to the next, but the leaves are glaucous-grey and without a keel underneath.

V. Traversii is one of the hardiest of all, indestructible as any native, forming vast bushes of perfectly neat unvaried pudding-bowl design, admirable for the formal garden as odious anywhere else; its stiff, straight shoots are set with bright, dark-green foliage; and their upper axils eject in summer a noble profusion of white blossoms, carried in rather looser and more graceful little spires than the fat and fluffy cat's-tail spikes that have so dowdy an effect in so many Veronicas.

V. subalpina follows quite close. It is a much-branched, erect shrub of some 3 to 6 feet.

V. vernicosa has an inclination to flop, on the contrary, with its branches of 2 or 3 feet long. It is *V. Grayi* of gardens, and others close in this relationship are *V. obovata* and *V. monticola.*

V. Cockayniana has flatter spreading leaves, glaucous-grey beneath; the branchlets are downy, the plant a bush of 2 or 3 feet, and the flowers white, with well-rounded lobes.

V. anomala makes slender branches 4 or 5 feet long, empurpled at the tips, with redundant spreading foliage, as in *V. patens*, larger than the spikes of pink or white blossom.

V. decumbens flops and spreads into a diffuse mass a foot or two across. The branches are of polished ebony-purple, and the leaves are flat and green with a red edge; while the spires of bloom are graceful, each small white star having a foot-stalk.

V. Gibbsii leads us close to the next, from which it differs in having its foliage more pointed, and fringed with long, white, woolly hairs. Otherwise its habit is the same, and it makes a stiff bushling of a foot or 18 inches, with spikes of white sessile flowers.

V. carnosula is the one of this section most usually offered. It is a formal and lifeless-looking stiff bush, varying between 6 inches and 3 feet, and the type of many, with its unyielding boughs beset with fat, fleshy, rounded-oval leaves, like flaps of dull hard metal, over-lapping and smooth and leathern; the upper axils so freely emit spikes of white sessile little flowers, that the ends of the shoots make the effect of being one crowded pyramid of blossom.

V. amplexicaulis differs only in having ampler leafage, which is more or less heart-lobed and stem-embracing at the base. The spikes, too, are larger and often broader in effect.

V. pinguifolia hardly differs at all from *V. carnosula*, except that the leaves are sometimes edged with red, and the capsules are always plain oval-oblong instead of heart-shaped.

V. Buchanani is almost the same thing.

VERONICAS.

V. pimeleoeides makes a very branching and more or less flopping bush of slender sprays, usually downy, from 3 to 18 inches in length. The leaves are small and loosely arranged and of glaucous-blue, and the sessile flowers in their spikes are violet in tone.

V. Gilliesi is a prostrate plant (with varieties *V. G. minor*, and *V. G. glauco-coerulea*), with tiny flowers and the leaves densely tiled upon the shoots.

V. tetrasticha forms depressed patches, often a foot across. The blossoms are small and white, in sprays of two or four from near the ends of the branchlets, on which the leaves are so close-packed and plated, in four rows, clutching the stems in a close ring, that the effect is of a four-sided scaly stem, each side being even slightly concave, according to the hollowed shape of the leaves. This is the first species we come to, of the scale-boughed and apparently leafless group that tries to imitate Cypresses and Salicornias and Club-mosses.

V. quadrifaria is the same thing, but slenderer and more wiry, with still smaller flowers and the sides of the square stems perfectly flat.

V. tumida makes the same sort of patch, but the leaves are fat and swollen in their close rows, so as to seem bulging through a mesh.

V. tetragona has bolder ways, and stands more or less erect, a shrub of 6 inches at one end of the scale or 3 feet at the other. The blossoms sit atop of the shoots in little huddled heads, and the thick shiny leaves, fluffy-woolly at edge and base, are tiled tightly down as before, so as to produce rigidly four-square stems, with the suggestion of a Dacrydium.

V. lycopodioeides is the same thing, but the stems are not so much merely squared as sharply four-angled. The leaves, too, are broader, narrowing more suddenly to a bluntish point.

V. Hectori is a small, robust plant in the same line, not usually more than a foot or so in development, with the very thick, leathery foliage packed along the stems until they are perfectly smooth and *cylindrical instead of squared*—this point being its great distinction from all these last.

V. salicornioeides is more slender in the bough and *always perfectly erect*, with yellow-brown branches, and the usual terminal huddles of small white stars. The species that bears this name in gardens is *V. propinqua.*

V. Armstrongii is more spreading and branched than either of these last, from which it otherwise only differs in having the leaves *just standing free from the stem at their tips*, though otherwise welded into the usual tight round sheath.

VERONICAS.

V. propinqua (*V. salicornioeides* of gardens) can always be known from the real Simon Pure to whose name it pretends. For, while it has the same dimensions of a foot or two (and a tortuous habit, sometimes decumbent), and the same tight, scaly boughs, yet, as in the last, the fat, leathery, fringe-edged *triangles of the leaf-tips stand free along the stalks*, which are thus not the perfectly smooth, scaly, club-moss branches of the other. We are now emerging more and more with each species from that close-scaled habit, even as before from the spreading, rounded, metallic leafage of the Carnosula group.

V. cupressoeides continues the process. This stands very near indeed to the last, but is a much closer, neat, tight, round shrub of 2 or 3 feet or more, built of quite slender, cylindrical, green branchlets, minutely downy, and set only here and there with pairs of little pointed leaves, suggesting the scales of a Cypress. The small flowers are pale blue.

V. Haastii makes a flopping, woody, twisted mass of densely-leafy, four-sided branches a foot in length, or less or more, the leaves being thick, pointed, and fleshy, standing out in their four rows, and not sheathing the stem. The blossoms are small and white, in dense heads or squashed spikes at the tips of the shoots.

V. epacridea stands next door the last and fades into it, but the leaves recurve their tips on the same four-sided branches, and usually have a thickened margin of red.

V. Petriei lies meekly down, rising up at the end of its stems of 3 to 6 inches. The little leaves are not close, but lax and spreading, with their stalks sheathing the tiny trunk. Each branchlet ends in a spike-like head of blossom, beset with a great number of blunt and very narrow leafy bracts.

V. dasyphylla lies flat down, and is a stiffly leathern, woody mass of four-square stems some 2 to 6 inches long, and ascending an inch or two at their tips, to carry one large terminal lonely flower. The downy, concave leaves, closely packed in four rows, in spreading over-lapping ranks, are welded pair to pair, and so sheathe the stem.

V. macrantha stands erect, a foot or two in height, and sparingly branched. The leaves (by now we have got to quite normal foliage again) are oval and bluntly-scalloped, very thick, and smooth, and fleshy, and glossy, with a thick edge. From the axils of the ends of the shoots spring sprays of some half a dozen fine big blossoms of pure white.

V. Benthami is in the same line, but the stems are quite naked below, and densely crowded towards their tips with flat leathern leaves, edged with white down. The flowers are bright-blue, in sprays from the points of the branches.

V. erecta comes close to *V. Hulkeana.*

V. × Fairfieldii is a hybrid of garden origin, which may be a result of *V. Hulkeana* and *V. Lavaudiana.*

V. Hulkeana stirs to warmth even the most frozen heart towards the New Zealand Veronicas. Not only is it supremely beautiful, but it is so supremely graceful as well. It makes delicate bushes of three feet or more, slender to the point of frailness and spindliness ; the branches are set with fatly-fleshy scalloped oval leaves of a clear and softly dark-green gloss ; then from these spring out and up on protracted bare stems, carrying them handsomely clear of the leafage, long broken spires of crowded big flowers in a lovely shade of lavender-blue, giving the effect, on their tall, elegant stems, of bunches of double Lilac in August and September. This beautiful plant is much rarer in the New Zealand wilds (where, unlike these others, mountaineers, it declines to ascend above 500 feet) than in the New Zealand gardens ; in ours, most lamentably does it fail to be trustworthily hardy, but should have a warm, sheltered place against wall or rock, with cuttings securely rooted off in August, and kept safe.

V. Lavaudiana is a species of only some 3 to 9 inches, lying down for the most part, till its tips rise up to show the wide 2-inch dome of blossom, made up of many crowded, small-flowered spikes. The stems are not free with branches, and are rather densely set with obovate, scallop-toothed leaves, sternly leathery, of a dark-green, usually margined with red.

V. Raoulii (we are now getting into the true realm of rock-garden New Zealanders) is another weakling of the same kidney, with widely freely-branching stems of 6 inches or a foot. The leaves are of yellowish green, outspread and rather long on their leaf-stalk, otherwise as in the last ; as are the flower-domes.

V. pulvinaris utterly breaks away from all previous traditions by making a perfectly dense, massy, mossy tuft in soft round cushions of 2 or 3 inches across, with oblong, very narrow little leaves that are neither fleshy nor leathery, but quite normal, with long white hairs on both surfaces above their middle and at their toothless edge. Over this greying tuft of gentleness the large white salver-shaped flowers, with five or six lobes to the corolla, sit by themselves solitary at the tips of the shoots from which they scarcely emerge.

V. Thompsoni is the same, but a little bigger and broader in the leaf, not so hairy, and with a longer tube to the flower. Its effect is that of *Myosotis pulvinaris*. These should all be jewels of moraine.

V. ciliolata advances another step from the last, with stouter branches, and leathern foliage fringed from the middle with long, stiff, white hairs. The blossoms still have five lobes to the corolla.

V. loganioeides, though a name common enough in lists, is one of most obscure meaning. It *should* be a dwarf shrubling of 6 inches or a foot, with weakly-flopping and arising stems almost fluffy with loose, soft, grey hairs, with leathery small oval keeled leaves of dull green, packed closely into opposite pairs up the shoots, and either smooth at the edge or with a little tooth or two on either side. The rather small flowers are borne in ample domes from the tips of the shoots, made up of many clusters from the upper axils.

V. linifolia is really a beautiful and valuable plant, quite outside the run of its predecessors. In gardens it often stands as *V. filifolia*, and is a herbaceous perennial of perfect ease and hardiness, sending up each year a fuzz of countless fine stems in a cloud of greenery some 6 or 9 inches high, befogged with innumerable fine leaves on long petioles, that blend in the grassy cloud-effect of the whole; and this vivid nebula, all the summer through, condenses a constant galaxy of daintily-borne stars, of delicious blue or white or pale pink, hovering in flickering flights of sparks from the green mist of the mass. Any comfortable place in any comfortable soil will suit this admirable charmer, which can be multiplied by division or seed.

V. Catarractae is no less a treasure, and no less indestructibly hardy. It is a charming species, weakly flopping and arising, with its sparingly-branched stems set sparingly with little, thickish, ovate-narrow pairs of leaves, *coarsely and sharply toothed.* From a final axil of each shoot comes up in summer one long, incurving spray of 6 or 9 inches, loosely set with an airy sprayed flight of large flowers in shades of white or pale pink. It is a most variable thing, and there can be little doubt that the beautiful and perfectly hardy *V. "Bidwillii"* of many gardens belongs in reality, either as child or variety, to *V. Catarractae*, which is always safe and vigorous in wide, loose masses in any reasonable place on the rockwork. (Other variations are called *V. C. diffusa* and *V. C. lancifolia.*)

V. Lyallii is a smaller and more prostrate version of the last, with small smooth leaves, *so broad as to be almost round*, with two or three blunt toothings at either edge. It roots as it pleasantly advances, and sends up delicate, erect sprays of 5 or 6 inches in late summer, daintily balancing a loose spray of large white blossoms veined with pink. This species, again, is widely variable, and one development is called *V. L. suberecta ; V. Lyallii* of the *Bot. Mag.* 6456 is a larger and more erect grower altogether, with bigger flowers, and bigger *egg-shaped* and pointed foliage. It is possibly an intermediate between *V. Lyallii* and *V. Catarractae*.

V. Bidwillii.—The true plant exactly copies the *small round foliage* of the last, but on a still smaller scale, making a closely matted, tight creeping mass, with the leaves *quite distant on the shoots, and very minute*, almost sessile, oblong-egg-shaped, and either smooth at the edges or with two or three coarse notches. The flower-flights, too, are much longer and more erect, emerging from the axils, but some way below the ends of the shoots, and aspiring straight up, some 6 or 9 inches, with flowers pretty much the same as in *V. Lyallii*, from which, however, it can be always known by its close, prostrate habit, longer blossom-sprays, and smaller foliage. It is a haunter of the river shingles, and in England is hardly ever seen true ; the genuine species not bearing the reputation of perfect hardiness.

V. Hookeriana is stouter and stiffer in all ways, with stout glandular-downy sprays of fewer and larger blossoms, white (or veined with pink in the variety *V. H. nivea*), and gathered by half dozens or so in a wide shower at the top of the stems. The leaves are rather thickly placed on the flopping arising mass of branches ; they are particularly stiff and rather large, leathery in texture, oblong, and with coarse scalloping at their edge.

V. Olseni stands quite close, but is altogether slenderer, with less down and more stars to the spray. It is probably intermediate between *V. Hookeriana* and *V. Catarractae.*

V. spathulata comes nearest to *V. Hookeriana*, from which it differs in being more depressed and branching in the mass, while the spoon-shaped leaves have little foot-stalks, instead of sitting almost stemless to the stem. The sprays are shorter, too, double the length of the foliage, carrying the same flowers of white or pearly pink. The whole growth is smaller and more prostrate, making quite dense, flat carpets and mats.

Thus *explicit valde feliciter Liber Veronicarum Novae Zelandiae;* for, at the one end of the scale there remain behind us only large shrubs, with which we can have no concern ; while in front at the other, are only a few worthless or obscure plants, such as *V. Cheesemannii*, a minute and small-flowered alpine tuffet, round and grey in the 2-inch cushion, whose effect, when a-bloom, is that of some small Euphrasia ; *V. plebeia*, which creeps but has valueless little dulnesses ; for *V. Anagallis* we need not go so far afield ; and the unsurpassable *V. canescens* has been promoted into the ranks of the Old-World Veronicas—a rather invidious preference, when the beauties of *V. pulvinaris*, *V. linifolia*, and *V. Catarractae* are called to mind.

Vesicaria.—This is a scanty and shiftingly-furnished race of small, woody-stocked, rosette-leaved Crucifers, standing cousins-german to Alyssum, and rejoicing in like conditions of sun and open light soil, which they reward with similar loose showers of golden blossoms in spring (from which afterwards, abundant seed can be procured to increase the stock). *V. cretica* is *Alyssum creticum; V. Kingii* is *Lesquerella Kingii;* and *V. alyssoeides* is *Physoptychis gnaphalioeides.* Even *V. reticulata* should more rightly be called *Coluteocarpus reticulatus.* It is a dwarf, smooth tuffet with stiff leaves to the crown, diminishing very lengthily to the base with a few sharp teeth along either edge, and giving the large rosettes of fringed foliage, perched on their woodyish trunks, a look of special distinctness. The flower-sprays are well furnished, about 6 or 8 inches high, and their brilliant golden burden is succeeded by large, round, bladder-pod seed-vessels. This is of the easiest culture in any sunny bank or wall. Of true *Vesicaria,* however, its departure leaves us with only *V. montana, V. graeca,* and *V. digitata. V. graeca* is a copy of the last, and yet more closely still resembles an Alyssum of the Saxatile type, though slighter and sturdier in growth, carrying the same golden sprays about a fortnight later than those of *C. reticulatus. V. digitata* is a smooth and glaucous-grey rosetted plant of an inch high, from the schistose Alps of Eastern Caucasus, with a strong likeness to *Iberis carnosa;* and *V. montana* is a prostrate creeping species from the Alps of Colorado, with rosettes of roundish stalked leaves, set with starry hairs, and spires of golden blossom of decent size and show.

Vicia.—No Vetch is a high or true alpine, because the short season of the mountains does not admit the development of long-stemmed vegetation, least of all of such rambling rampers as are most of the Vetches; among which, for brilliancy of blue flaming bunches, it is not easy to parallel our lovely hedgerow weed, *V. Cracca.* The best of the race, however, is *V. unijuga* (*Orobus lathyroeides* or *Ervum gracile*), from Siberia, which does not ramp or climb, but forms a perfectly erect wiry clump of some 12 or 15 inches in any good open soil and situation, bearing most lovely flowers in June, of the most brilliant blue. *V. pyrenaica* creeps finely with little blunt-leafleted leaves of bright green, and single largish violet-purple blossoms in their axils; *V. argentea* may be seen in the upper granitic schists of Catalonia and Aragon, where it makes tufts of velvety silver, sending up stems of a foot or more, that do not climb, and whose leaves, accordingly, have no grappler at their end. The flowers are large, gathered in one-sided heads, with the sail whitish and veined with violet, while the darker keels are tipped with purple. *V. Orobus* is quite near this, and perhaps its original type, green and not silvery. *V. aurantiaca* is now *Orobus*; *V. venulosa* grows 18 inches or 2 feet in the rocky places of Elburz, and has pink flowers tipped with violet; *V. ecirrhosa* makes a pale-coloured plant with many stems of 5 or 6 inches, carrying each four or five large flowers of a lively violet blue, above the short and ungrappling foliage; *V. alpestris*, like the last, is an alpine from the high stony places of the Levant (where the longer season admits of a Vetch's development); it is a lovely species of the same many-stemmed habit, flopping or drooping, and creeping as it goes; the profuse stems are 4 to 6 inches long, bearing one-sided sprays of eight or nine large and splendid violet Pea-blooms; *V. multicaulis* has almost the same beauty. But the finest of all is *V. canescens*, which colours all the slopes of Lebanon above the Cedars, from afar off, with a tapestry of fallen sky. It is an erect grower of 8 or 10 inches, with many stems clad closely in silver wool. It is in all ways more robust than its kinsman *V. argentea*, with larger foliage and blossoms of brilliant and dazzling blue. Very similar is *V. Greyana*, from the dry alpine slopes of the Cilician Taurus; but this has pointed rather than rounded leaflets. It is also firmer in the stem than their frail cousin *V. variegata*, from the Alps of Pontus, which on many weakly stalks of 6 inches or a foot, has large flowers variegated with blue and white. All these Vetches will arise profusely from seed, and thus are best propagated. All will grow well in any warm, open, stony loam, and all will bloom brilliantly in the height of summer.

Villarsia nymphaeoeides is a really pretty but terrible water-weed, that in a year or two fills your pond with floating leaves like those of a tiny water-lily, among which sit solitary, all the summer through, fluffy, five-pointed, starry cups of golden yellow. Other species sometimes offered are not safely hardy. For *V. Crista-galli* see *Menyanthes*.

Vinca.—The periwinkles are useful furnishers of backgrounds, rather than prominent adornments of the garden. There are many varieties of the Greater and the Lesser Periwinkle, *V. major* and *V. minor*. There are also neater growers in *V. acutiflora* of South Europe (clear lilac), *V. difformis* of Portugal (clean blue), and the yet neater 8-inch *V. libanotica*. But the supremely beautiful Periwinkle of the family, worthy of the choicest garden, is the too-seldom-seen *V. herbacea*, which is a true herbaceous plant, dying away in winter, and in spring sending out over the slope of rock very long and very slender branches, rooting at the ends, and set here and there with slender, pointed leaves in pairs, and bearing in spring and again all through the summer most lovely clear delicate stars of blue that sometimes on cool or grassy banks make the whole expanse a shimmering galaxy. This really charming thing will thrive rampageously in any open place or wild, but is best, in raw climates, on an open sunny bank in light, good soil, which it will then hide under the fine weeping curtain of its rambling rooting sprays.

Vincetoxicum alpinum (Cynanchum vincetoxicum).— This is that rather ugly weed so often seen on hot, dry, stony screes and cuttings in the Alps, growing about a foot high or more, with the fine stems beset by ample oval-pointed leaves of leathern texture and dark dead green (rather like a Dog's Mercury copied in morocco leather) ; at the top these break in summer into axillary clusters of dimmish little creamy long-throated stars. There are many species and varieties, with blossoms in varying degrees of dinginess, down to reddish black and blackish red. They might be grown in specially barren hot places of the garden, where there is only stone ; yet it would not be difficult to think of many plants more worthy of admittance even as "furnishing," except perhaps in the case of *V.* (or *Asclepias*) *speciosum* from the Levant, with large flowers of crisped purple velvet in the axils of the ample crisp-velvet foliage.

Viola brings this alphabet to the last great dragon in its path. No race is more fertile of more exquisite beauty, but no race is also more fertile in dull and dowdy species. And, unfortunately in these later years, the enormous multitudes of American violets have taken (no less than American heiresses) to overflowing into our continent undescribed, so that we have no idea, when we buy, whether the new name will give us another *V. Rydbergi*, or merely some dingy little woodland worthlessness of no account. On the other hand, European botanists have taken to subdividing some of our own species, until we rush eagerly to purchase *V. Eugeniae*, only to discover, when the bill has at last been paid, that we have secured merely a form of *V. calcarata*, with which our garden is already paved. On all counts, therefore, of complexity and confusion, no less than of multiplicity and varied loveliness, the race must be dealt with in due order (with a general ruck of undistinguished undesirables to be found by the consulter herded under *V. viarum* and *V. magellanica*, in case a given name on which he wants enlightenment is not to be found occurring in its alphabetical place). The cultivation of Viola either offers no difficulty at all, in the case of nine species out of ten, that merely require open cool loam to grow in, and there are happy for ever ; or else, in the tenth, offers so much that hints may be occasionally suggested for these that will not be necessary for the others—especially as among the problems are some of the most peerless beauties of the

VIOLA.

family to be found. The main blooming-time is in spring and early summer, but various species, American and subalpine, continue on into the later months. All Violas can be raised from seed, but the method is slow and often chancy, and by far the better propagation is by division or by cuttings, which, especially in the case of the more lavish-growing species, root as easily as if they were Pelargoniums in a bottle. And remember, all violets are extra variable.

V. adunca is an American woodlander, with leafy stems and rooting runners, and ample egg-shaped foliage, and big violet violets varying to white, with a darker form, *V. a. longipes.*

V. aetnensis stands as a form of the cruelly diverse *V. calcarata.*

V. aetolica comes very close to the lovely *alpestris* form of *V. tricolor,* but differs from it wholly for the better in having a soundly perennial root. The sepals, too, are never narrowly lance-shaped, but always short, broad triangles. *V. aetolica* makes a pleasant, low, loose mass with abundant lavender-lilac paling pansies on upstanding stems all through the summer. There is also a variety *V. a. heterosepala,* with rather larger petals of golden yellow, and narrowing more towards their base. These all grow fast and easily, as may be imagined, as any bedding Viola.

V. affinis lives in the moist fields and woods of North America. It makes a tuft of narrowly heart-shaped leaves drawing out to a long, thin point, which come up with the flowers, and are almost hairless like the whole clump, scallopy-toothed, and sometimes even irregularly, wavily cut at the edge. Its violets are purple with a white eye. Sometimes it stands as *V. venustula.*

V. alpestris is a big-flowered lavender Heartsease of annual habit, and a variety of *V. tricolor.* For its picture, see *V. aetolica.*

V. alpina is one of the rarest and most important of all the mountain species, a most lovely thing, almost exactly intermediate between a violet and a pansy. It is a plant hardly ever to be seen in a catalogue, yet one of quite singular amphibious beauty in the family, and in cultivation perfectly easy to grow and keep in any good, light, rich soil, mixed with peat and limestone chips, with such various enrichments of sand, leaf-mould, loam, and old manure as the zeal of the cultivator may prompt, in a ledge or slope on which the sun falls freely in the later and modified half of his daily round, but which is also well secured against excessive aridness by pipes or care. Here it forms a delightful neat close tuffet of rounded, heart-shaped little leaves on long stalks (all springing from the one central crown), dark, smooth and glossy green, with broad rounded scalloping along their edge, and a few microscopic hairs in each scallop; from the

444

neck, among these, on stems of 2 or 3 inches in May, arises a profusion of very large violets, or rather small pansies, well above the neat and tidy clump of foliage, and, in themselves, of a rich and glorious purple, with blotches of violet darkness radiating into the petals from the rim of the white eye ; the two lengthily oval upper petals stand apart from each other, too, so that the flower gets the look of an alert and prick-eared little purple rabbit. It is indeed a most precious jewel, and in the garden of a vigour equal to its beauty, though it never throws any runners, and can only be multiplied from seed, or most careful division of the main crown ; in cultivation, like *V. calcarata*, it does not seem always and everywhere to be as lavish as it should of its imperial well-built blossoms, with their rounded and comfortable petals of exaggerated violet-design. They both, it seems, want to be ripened for flower by a perfectly dry resting-time in winter, followed by a soaking wet period of development when the snows are weeping themselves profusely away through the mountains of the world. The casual wanderer is not likely to come upon *V. alpina ;* it is a species of the far Eastern Alps, where, in the turf and sometimes even in the rocks of the limestone ranges, it replaces *V. calcarata.* It is lavishly abundant within its range ; occupying all the grass of the Styrian and lower Austrian limestones, in company with *Campanula alpina, Dianthus alpinus, Primula Clusiana, P. minima, P. auricula,* and *Androsace lactea ;* it then has a patch of profusion in the Western Carpathians (on the Tatra and Mount Choc, &c.), and after that has no further habitation on earth, except the caterpillar-curve of its profuse distribution along the high limestones of Transylvania. It has a charm distinct from all violets, and from all pansies, yet partaking of both, and doubling them all.

V. altaica is one of the great-great-grandmothers of our garden Pansies. It stands near *V. calcarata,* making looser, freer masses, with abundant noble pansies, continuing through the summer, of lilac, yellow, mauve, or purple, with a shorter spur than in *V. calcarata,* and shorter, broader leaves. It is a plant from the alps of Asia Minor and the Altai, as easy and hearty as its descendants suggest.

V. arborescens is a most curious small woody-trunked tree-violet of 6 or 8 inches high. Here and there wander the grey trunks across the ground, arising at their ends to produce tufts of narrow little long-oval leaves, with a profusion of lavender-blue violets. It is a rare species and very delicately lovely, only found in the dunes and sandy places and open seaward woods of the South of France, &c. ; in cultivation it is not known at all, the pretender that bears a misleadingly similar name, *V. arborea,* in catalogues, being nothing more than a horrid trunked form of the sweet Violet which you trail up a stick and then call the Tree Violet, flamboyantly proclaiming its lanky lack of charm.

V. arenaria has one station only in England, on the Widdybank Fell, but over the sunny slopes of fine alpine grass, as, for instance, on the Mont Cenis, is quite common and charming, well worthy of the garden, though it is only a tiny tufted violet, with small, rounded, pale leaves, and a reckless profusion of dear little comely rounded flowers of lavender-lilac on stems of about an inch or so.

V. atlantica = *V. Brittoniana, q.v.*

V. atriplicifolia has small yellow violets in the woods of North America, but does not seem a species of special value.

V. Beckwithii offers us rich rare beauty, with its magnified violets, of which the two upper petals are of deep purple, while the rest are of pale soft whitish lilac, veined with darkness and bearded with gold. They stand high on their stems of 5 or 6 inches above the bold, broad, heart-shaped violet-foliage, and their lower petals are nibbled at the edge. It lives in the Sierras of California, and when caught should be cosseted accordingly.

V. bellidifolia comes from sub-alpine regions of the Rockies; it is a minute stem-forming plant of 2 or 3 inches high, with a generous abundance of little violets, lighter in the three lower purple-veined petals than in the upper ones.

V. Bertoloni = *V. cenisia, q.v.*

V. Bielsiana is a Transylvanian form indistinguishable from *V. tricolor.*

V. biflora runs across the Northern hemisphere, lighting up all the cool and shadowy places of the Alps with the dancing golden sunlight of its little flowers like fallen sparks of day into the green dimness of forest or path-side. It should have the same cool hollows in moist and gritty soil in the garden; where it will impermanently make itself at home and take to running about and illuminating the un-promising places with its flickering pale glints throughout the summer. It can easily be divided, or raised from seed; in the alpine woods it often makes whole wide carpets of shivering fire, as for instance in the deep and solemn ancient woods of the upper Boréon, where the silent forest is almost noisy with the crackling of its innumerable golden flashes, uttered daintily by pairs above the sheeted masses of pale kidney-shaped leaves, in such a bewilderment of brilliance that all the dappled distance of the woodland is a dance of golden daylight under the dark.

V. blanda of some authorities is *V. pallens.* *V. blanda* of others is

VIOLA.

also *V. amoena* (Leconte), a stemless species from beside the mountain streams of North America, sending out running, rooting shoots, and abounding in sweet-scented white violets.

V. bosniaca gives us one of the most important contributions that this generous race has brought us in recent years ; and, indeed, with *V. gracilis* and *V. bosniaca*, we have no need to complain of Viola. This has almost the lush and ready massed habit of a bedding Viola, but up the flopping stems, all the summer through, is produced an endless succession of brilliant little elongated Pansies of flaming vinous rose-mauve, a colour indescribably brilliant and in itself delightful, but which requires the greatest care and forethought in its associations. No such forethought or care are required by the plant, which thrives handsomely and perennially in any light good soil and open place, readily multiplied by cuttings as well as by seed.

V. Brittoniana lives in the moist sandy places along the Atlantic coasts of North America, and is also *V. atlantica* (Britton), and *V. septemloba* of other authorities. The earlier leaves of its clumps are reddish underneath and roughly toothed, the later ones are kidney-shaped in outline, but then cut into some five to nine ample lobes. The flowers are noble big violets of brilliant purple, with a brilliantly white eye. One authority states that they continue through the later months of summer.

V. Bubanii is a variety of *V. lutea* from the Pyrenees, with long pansies of intense purple, and the whole growth more or less silky-haired.

V. caespitosa is a doubtful mountain-tuffet of the East, like a condensed high-alpine *V. tricolor*.

V. calaminaria is a unique form of *V. lutea*, abundant by the lead mines of La Gueule in Belgium.

V. calcarata.—This is *the* alpine Pansy, veiling all the hills for miles and miles in hazy films of gold and lavender, and making a riot of colour in the fine turf of June such as no pen nor brush can paint, of a hundred million pansies in every shade, from pure white through yellows of softness, subtlety, and violent gold, to tender lavender and on into the richest imperial violet, interrupted everywhere by the crashing azures of *Gentiana verna*, with the dropped dark indigo trumpets of *G. latifolia* coming into the chorus like deep solemn notes of music in the clangour of lilting colours, lightened with the tinkle of Potentillas, and softened by the dim-grey universal hum of Globularia, till the whole is an orchestra of glory fit only for the accompaniment of passing gods. Not always, however, for the passing man ; for one who writes with facile fluency about flowers, stood there upon a

447

golden day in June, with his feet planted right and left on a Gentian and a Pansy, and, looking out across that illimitable ocean of loveliness with a peevish eye, said, "I don't call *this* much of a display!" So back he went to study carpet-bedding in Balham. *V. calcarata* is abundant and universal in the high turf of all the Alps, until on the Eastern limestone its place is taken by the wholly different *V. alpina.* The Spurred Pansy runs and ramps through the herbage far and wide, with its frail and thready shoots, sending up here and there its tufts of little, oval, scalloped, smooth leaves, and the great flowers on their stems of 2 or 3 inches. So current is the habit of its growth, indeed, that it becomes most difficult to collect, never staying long enough in one place for us to be able to get well-rooted morsels off some choice variety; and making it even hard work to get good pieces of the plant at all, unless you look out for some open shaly bank or crumbling slope of earth near the path-side, where the absence of rivals may have coaxed the Pansy into a concise and clumpy mood. In the course of its vast range, indeed, this evasive tendency of the Viola occasions much woe to its admirers, for few beauties vary more widely into forms and colours more delectable. There are comfortable, fat-faced forms, and thin, lean, angular ones; some have the lower lip dropped and triangular and long as an embittered Puritan's; others are flattened till they are as jolly as the jovialities reflected in a broadening mirror; some are large and stately and ample, while others are little and thin and delicate and starry. In colour, too, they vary no less distractingly, for, apart from the general wide range of tones (in which at any moment you may come upon something special, either in clarity or intensity), you may also happen on strange beautiful thunder-and-lightning blends of citron and bronze and violet, or sometimes, though very rarely indeed, on one with pansies of a pure but muffled sad flesh-pink. None of these, when got, are inferior to the type in ease of cultivation; *V. calcarata* is a marvel of vigour in any rich, open soil in which it can have a sufficiency of water. In some gardens it seems shy of flower—a fact that may account for the preposterous rarity in cultivation of this, one of the most brilliant of all alpines and one of the heartiest in growth; but in others it forms sheeted masses of its green as lavishly besprent with its royal glowing pansies as if it were the commonest of bedding Violas. These admirable plants it imitates, too, not only in the freedom of its growth, but also in the freedom with which it will strike from cuttings; so that in a year or two, you could have whole edgings of some chosen and cherished variety. But these varieties, besides the pain their habit gives to the collector, are hardly

VIOLA.

less of a trial to the cultivator. For botanists are perpetually sub-dividing them and giving them names, which the nurseryman seizes on at once, and sends their wearers out unannotated, as species, so that the zealots of Viola are for ever buying *V. calcarata* under unrecognisable and expensive epithets. One of the most important and oldest of these is *V. Zoysii*, which is no more than a thin-flowered yellow form of the type, with a deep notch in the lower petal. Other named but vague developments, all belonging to *V. calcarata* in major or minor habit, and all of them, accordingly, plants of the greatest beauty, are *V. elongata*, *V. Eugeniae* (these two being the same large development of the species), *V. corsica*, *V. aetnensis*, and *V. nebrodensis*.

V. calycina has the leafy tufts of the common Pansy, but is probably perennial, with flowers in the way of *V. rothomagensis*, but yellow. It is a diminished version of *V. olympica* from the meadows of Pisidia, differing in the size no less than in the broad, blunt lobes of the calyx.

V. canadensis is a variable plant from the woods of North America, making long and leafy branches of a foot or 16 inches, with heart-shaped, saw-edged leaves, and abundant large violets of very pale colour, almost white, with a yellow heart and a veined fine flush of purple from their base. It is a widespread species, and among the many forms it takes are the small and deep-coloured *V. c. scopulorum*, and the most magnificent, perhaps, of all its group, the brilliant *V. c. Rydbergi*, an inestimable easy treasure for good open soil in the garden.

V. canina needs no introduction to the garden. It has innumerable varieties, all of which, with the type, are quite as well worthy of the garden as many a rarity that there lifts a brazen and expensive face of ugliness. Among these are *V. c. stricta*, an upright growing form ; *V. c. Ruppii* or *Hornemannii*, a form from damp meadows, with especially broad-petalled flowers of clear blue-violet ; *V. c. lancifolia* (*V. lusitanica*), with very starry violets of light blue, not at all lilac or mauve ; *V. c. Jordani*, narrow in the leaf and dainty in the long lip ; *V. c. stagnina*, an English bog-plant, rather coarse and straggling, with white or deathly pale blossoms ; *V. c. Schultzii*, a special rarity from Alsace, which outrages its family by having blossoms of pale yellow, melting into white ; *V. c. pumila*, another rarity of damp places, and a pretty little plant of striped pale-lilac flower, and *V. c. elatior*, a fine and large development, with big violets of soft lavender.

V. cenisia is *the* High Alpine Pansy, whose lovely purple faces, with their golden eyes and delicate black-pencilled moustache, you may often see twinkling at you across the desolate expanses of the last and highest shingles of all, in the upmost folds of the mountains where the

449

streams are born of the snow. Far and far through the scree the Viola sends its thread-like wandering roots, often growing among blocks so big, and roaming so insatiably, that it becomes almost impossible to gather up the remote ramifications of its rootage. It may always be known by its habitat, where no other Violet dwells, no less than by the dainty purple pansies here and there, and the small, silky, iron-dark leafage of little, oval, scarcely scalloped leaves, nestling among the stones and taking very much their own powdered sombre greyness. It is a local but locally abundant high-alpine, the type of that most difficult and lovely group. It is not, however, I think, by preference a limestone species, as sometimes stated; on the Mont Cenis, at least, its name-place, it is most glorious in the last screes of the primary rocks that descend from the Nunda and Mont Lamet and all that vast amphitheatre of precipice which falls in sweeps to the Clear Lake; and in the Oberland is hardly less lovely in the highest sandstones of the Schwarzhorn, there also among the typical non-calcareous high-alpines, such as *Ranunculus glacialis*, *Geum reptans*, *Androsace alpina*. In cultivation *V. cenisia* is sadly pernicketty and precious, fitted only for the underground-watered moraine, but there prospering among its old friends, if experiment be made with sound and well-rooted pieces. It is unalterably faithful to the high elevations, rarely if ever descending in the river-shingles like the rest, though here and there in the stony sweeps and rubbish-dumps below the Hospice of the Mont Cenis a strayed reveller of a tuft may very occasionally be found lying in a compact flare of purple, concise and clumped in habit as it cannot be far up among the barren rocks of the mountain. In many ranges of East and West *V. cenisia* is replaced by other species or developments of the same mountaineering habit. Both *V. comollia* and *V. valderia* are reckoned as mere varieties of *V. cenisia;* yet their habits and beauties are so much their own that the gardener will always treat them as being separate species, and as special species they will here be found in their places, although no claim to specific rank is thereby made for them. In the Pyrenees, however, exist one or two other forms, called *V. Lapeyrousei* and *V. vestita* (they are probably one), which are more densely tufted and less inclined to wander, more silky grey, too, in the clumped rosettes, almost to the point of being velvety; while the stems and the whole growth are stouter and stronger than the frail, delicate loveliness of *Mammola rupina* in her typical form upon her original and typical mountain.

V. chelmea is a pallid little palustris Violet from Greece.

V. Clementiana (*V. grandiflora*, Griseb.) stands quite near to

VIOLA.

V. altaica, but has yellow pansies of half the size with longer spurs. It differs, on the other hand, from *V. calcarata* in having the spur no longer than the petals, while the leaves are also narrower. It is an alpine development on Scardus and Olympus ; each main branch of Viola has its main habit at each elevation, shading into many developments in different countries and ranges, all appearing to emerge from some far-off and vanished original ; thus, in the lowlands, *V. tricolor* shifts and eddies like Proteus ; at alpine elevations *V. calcarata* is the type of many ; and in the last and highest places of all, *Mammola rupina* is the type of more, in East and West alike, but only in the Old World.

V. comollia is one of these, and the most distinct and brilliant. It is unfortunately a very rare plant indeed, confined to one or two screes in the Orobian Alps, where it runs about among the stones after the fashion of *V. cenisia,* but that its leaves are elliptic or rounded, and perfectly untoothed, while the nobly large flowers are sweetly fragrant, and of a flaming vinous rose, more rich than even in *V. bosniaca,* with the same opaque reverse of nankeen yellow to the petals. It will take the same treatment as *V. cenisia* in cultivation, but its rarity and preciousness are such that any nurseryman who steals into possession of a piece divides it up as minutely as if it were unicorn's horn, so that never does the buyer get hold of a fragment with any strength in it left to live. And it is not always easy, in any case, to make even full-rooted plants of the high-alpine stone-pansies feel at home : if they are rootless there is no chance at all.

V. conspersa (*V. labradorica* of lists) makes a leafy-stemmed, long-armed plant in cool places, emitting in summer a quantity of pale violets on stems from the axils of the straying sprays, above rounded, scalloped leaves. It is also known as *V. Muehlenbergii* (Torr.).

V. cornuta replaces *V. calcarata* in the Pyrenees, but otherwise is only known about Grammont in Savoy, until we get to English borders, where this star-flowered alpine Pansy is one of the best-known in the whole race, forming rich masses of blossom on their long stems all the summer in a blaze. There are many varieties, some with white flowers, and one, " George Wermig," with dark violet ones ; then there is the whole race of Tufted Pansies, which are the children of *V. cornuta* by *V. tricolor ;* there is a neat thing called *V. florariensis,* too, which blooms all the year round, with large lilac pansies, and is a hybrid between *V. cornuta* and *V. rothomagensis ;* and finally, in these later days, there is a yearly growing procession of intermediates between *V. cornuta* and *V. gracilis.* Indeed, if these pansies and violets are grown in any garden, it is never safe to weed even the paths, lest mules as good as any of these, or better, may there be turning up unbeknownst, the range of hybridisation and fertility being so incalculable in the family that attempts at affiliation soon become vain. Nobody can tell the origin of one of the quaintest things of all, called Bowles's Black. This is a little bushy plant of Tricolor blood, with abundant small pansies of dense black-violet velvet throughout the season, thriving anywhere, and sowing itself freely, and incidentally hybridising again with any lutea-gracilis- cornuta- or calcarata-cousin that may happen to be handy. All the children of all the parents have their place, but they form too cloudy and vast a race for constant naming, and are often so blurred from the distinct beauties of their blood, that the utmost they can ask of the gardener is not to root them up, unless they have sprung in a place too precious and prominent.

V. corsica is a form of *V. calcarata*.

V. crassifolia lives in the highest stone-slopes of the Lycian Alps. It is a tiny tufted plant between the shingles, with microscopic little fat oval leaves, perfectly smooth and toothless and glossy. The purple pansies are about half the size of *V. cenisia's*, and have a shorter spur and narrower wing-petals than its even closer but larger-pansied cousin, *V. nevadensis*.

V. cretica comes in the way of *V. palustris*, with rounded leaves, and rather small pale violets.

V. cucullata makes ample handsome tufts of almost hairless pointed great heart-shaped leaves, among which on tall stems spring a large number of large handsome violets of clear rich blue deepening to the throat and sometimes white, very round and solid in the petal, and so most hearty and full of face. It is a thriving New England species, popular and widespread in cultivation.

V. Cunninghamii need have no hold on our longings. It is a New Zealand species without special attraction.

V. Curtisii is a false name for the biennial *V. sabulosa* from the Channel dunes, a Tricolorous small pansy with the upper petals purple, and the lower ones wedge-shaped and yellowing to their base.

V. declinata = *V. Dubyana*, q.v.

V. delphinantha seems very difficult to grow, and not much fun when grown, as it does not flower readily, nor give notable pleasure when it does. It has all the look of a rather miserable Delphinium as it arises on Athos and Olympus, with specially narrow leaves and erect stems.

V. delphinifolia is a name for an American woodland violet with divided leaves suggesting a Larkspur's.

VIOLA.

V. dichroa should be a dear little thing, forming very neat round tufts in the alps of Turkish Armenia, from which it sends up quantities of tiny, round-faced, yellow- and pale-blue pansies, in the way of *V. calcarata* but about a quarter of the size.

V. dissecta is a Siberian Violet, coming in between *V. pinnata* and *V. pedata*, with rather the size and form of the latter; a thing, therefore, of choice, for a select place in the cool and stony moraine.

V. Dubyana (*V. heterophylla*) stands near *V. valderia* in the group of *V. cenisia*. It is a most distinct and beautiful species, rarely to be seen here and there in the open stony patches of soil, rubbly track-sides, or fine sunny limestone screes high up in the Alps of Lombardy. It has lovely staring starry purple pansies, longer and thinner and more violet-like than those of *V. cenisia*, and much more resembling those of *V. valderia*, to which the plant is closer, too, in its longer stems and radiating habit from a single fine white tap-root, never running out into wide or ramifying clumps. It is an easy-going moraine treasure, of far better constitution, however; fine and frail in the silky-greyish leafage, with outstanding blossoms all the summer through. It should always be kept going from seed, and never trusted to abide too long in one stay.

V. elatior is a form of *V. canina, q.v.*

V. elegans comes close under *V. lutea*. It is a blue-and-yellow mountain Pansy from Switzerland.

V. elongata is also *V. Eugeniae*, a larger form of *V. calcarata*.

V. epipsila is no more than an improved *V. palustris*.

V. erectifolia (*V. gomphopetala*, Gray) makes a neat tuft from a single tap-root, with erect-standing, elliptic-narrow leaves of 3 or 4 inches long, on stems of about the same length. The flowers are large golden violets, veined with darkness, and this beauty shines in the high Alps of Colorado.

V. Eugeniae. See under *V. elongata.*

V. Falconeri is a Himalayan version of the Dog-violet, with leaves dotted with black glands, and bigger, finer flowers than *V. canina's*.

V. filifolia lives in New Zealand, and may easily be allowed to stop there.

V. flavo-virens = *V. linguaefolia, q.v.*

V. florariensis. See the note on *V. cornuta.*

V. fragrans, on the contrary, should be eagerly pursued into the high screes of Crete, where it makes velvet-grey clumps of very narrow-oblong blunt little toothless leaves, and sends up very large sweet-scented pansies of pale violet and yellow.

V. glabella should be a big yellow violet of 8 inches from Colorado.

VIOLA.

V. gomphopetala = *V. erectifolia, q.v.*

V. gracilis lives only in Macedonia and the mountains of Asia Minor, the plants of South Italy and Greece being impostors. No garden introduction of the last century has been more lovely and delightful than this violet, in the habit and of the vigour of *V. cornuta*, much neater in the dense upstanding armies of its blossom, and with its rather nobler and profuse great violet-pansies of the most shimmering imperial purple velvet, with a tweak to the petals that gives each flower an inimitable butterfly grace. It grows with the utmost readiness in any light soil, rich and open, and can be propagated from cuttings like any bedding Pansy. Seed sometimes yields a creamy-citron-coloured form, but much more often proves the influence of other species in the garden on the impressionable nature of the Gracious Pansy. And, though these mules are always going forth under pompous names, such as Purple Robe, &c., and though they are all definitely larger and stouter purple pansies of much beauty, they have utterly lost, for that look of fat rounded solidity, the freakish, elfin loveliness of *V. gracilis*, no less than its intensity of dark and velvety violence.

V. gracillima is a large-flowered, purple form of *V. lutea*, with the lower leaves huddled together, and the pansies standing out on long stems of 7 inches or so.

V. grandiflora = *V. Clementiana, q.v.*

V. hastata is a small and delicate leafy-stemmed American woodland violet.

V. hederacea is the delicacy which for so many years has been called *Erpetion reniforme*. The New Holland Violet does not deserve the reputation for miffiness and tenderness that overclouded it—most probably and reasonably because it was Australian, and good things are less rare out of Galilee than hardy ones out of Australia. In any light rich soil, rather moist if not shady, this violet makes wide, running, clumped carpets of neat and vivid kidney-shaped bright-green leaves, from which, all the summer through, on naked stems of 2 or 3 inches, springs an incessant show of rather starry little purple violets, fading definitely to white at the tips of their petals, with a most distinct effect of personality and grace. In due time the plant seeds itself all over the bed, and both young and old alike seem astonishingly resistent to our climate, though for safety's sake it is no bad thing to dig off a clump or two from the fringe of the colony, and pot them up securely through the winter.

V. heterophylla = *V. Dubyana.*

V. hirsutula lives in dry, rich American woods, a small plant with dainty, heart-shaped, silver leaves, purpled underneath, and hugging the ground ; while, above, its violets rise on taller stems in spring.

V. hirta.—The English scentless violet is not nearly enough used in the garden. In all its many forms *V. hirta* is quite distinct, and quite beautiful, with its peculiar leaves, elongate and narrowly heart-shaped and hairy, and its abundance of violets well above them in crowds in spring. There is an albino of the type, and the species varies on the one hand into the development called *V. sciaphila,* which more affects the woodland, and is very nearly hairless, with large, ample foliage and flowers, and *V. Thomasiana* of high downs and open ground, which is minutely small and neat in every part, with almost triangular little hairy leaves, and sweetish violets of lilac or rose or mauve-purple. Between the two and into the type there are many gradations ; one of the values of the species, for a sunny and unthought-of place, is that it never runs and ramps, but sits secure in its tidy clump.

V. Hornemannii = *V. canina stricta, q.v.*

V. incognita.—The unknown violet is an American woodlander that deserves no closer intimacy, any more than do *V. fimbriatula, V. sagittata, V. emarginata,* and *V. renifolia.*

V. ircutiana has tufts of leaves like those of a common Daisy, and violets of red or pale purple colouring.

V. Jooi is a lilac-pinkish-flowered little violet from the limestones of Transylvania, standing close to *V. prionantha.*

V. Jordani. See under *V. canina.*

V. labradorica, Schrank (for which in so many lists *V. conspersa* does duty), is a dwarfer species, and almost hairless, with the blades of the leaves hairyish on their upper face, and the leaves themselves *always blunt instead of tapering to a point.* As a rule its violets are of deep purple, and it haunts cool places through North America. (Allow, in these notes, for the inveterate variableness of all violets.)

V. lactea is a pallid form of *Viola canina.*

V. lanceolata is a form of *V. adunca.*

V. lancifolia (*V. lusitanica*). See under *V. canina.*

V. Lapeyrousei. See under *V. cenisia.*

V. latiuscula springs in open places of the rich, dry woods of North America. The earlier leaves of the tufts are rounded-heart-shaped, but the later ones are much bigger, about 4 inches across, very broad, and then running to a quick, sharp point. Its violets are large, and noble in their imperial colour.

V. libanotica is like a smaller version of *V. hirta.*

VIOLA.

V. linguaefolia makes a plant of about a foot high, with tongue-shaped foliage, and bright yellow violets.

V. lusitanica = *V. canina lancifolia.*

V. lutea is the delicate and lovely little mountain pansy that in the English alps by no means inadequately replaces *V. calcarata*, and turns the meadows of Teesdale into a foaming sea of pansies, smaller indeed, but no less rich and undulating and diverse in their colour-shades, from the pallor of first dawn to the richness of Nero's cloak. In the garden *V. lutea* is indestructible and perpetually in bloom, but tends to hybridise almost too freely with the Tricolors and Cornutas, producing endless fatter and more golden versions, called Golden Drop, &c., which have changed the long, thin daintiness of *V. lutea's* pre-Raphaelite face, for such rounded obesity as soon shades on into nothing more elegant than the fatness of the bedding Violas, in which *V. lutea* has indeed had so large a share. Only wild types of this, accordingly, should be grown, and these grown on again from cuttings.

V. Lyallii has white flowers, and seems to be the best of the rather feeble violets offered us by New Zealand.

V. macedonica stands quite close to *V. tricolor;* but yet closer to *V. vivariensis*, in that it is soundly perennial. It straggles among the ferns on the hills of Macedonia, a blue-purple pansy of 12 inches, differing from the others, too, in that its petals stand widely apart the one from the other, so that the pansy-face has a wild and startled expression.

V. magellanica comes from very far away in the Antarctic Islands, where it plays at being a *V. odorata* with yellow flowers. Others of this remote race are *V. ovalifolia, V. sericea, V. argentea, V. Commersonii.*

V. magellensis makes yet another of that wonderful and beautiful group that calls *Mammola rupina* mother. For this is a most tiny huddled miniature of *V. cenisia* from high sandy places on Majella in the Central Apennines.

V. minuta has similar relationship, but fills a missing link between *V. cenisia* and *V. alpina.* It is a neat and lovely velvet-grey tuft of almost round, tiny, scalloped leaves on short stems; its purple pansies are smaller than in *V. cenisia*, and the scalloping on the leaves much more pronounced. To *V. alpina* it approaches, among other points, in its condensed clumped habit, which it practises in the high Alps of Kasbek and Iberian Caucasus.

V. mirabilis cannot live up to its name. In the alpine woods it makes trunky rank tufts of clawed and finely divided foliage, among which spring comparatively insignificant sweet-scented pale violets.

V. missouriensis lives in the river bottoms of its native State, and forms clumps of broadly heart-shaped, pointed leaves, coarsely toothed, from amid which spring pale violets with a white eye surrounded by a flush of deeper purple.

V. montafoniensis has no especial merit or distinctness.

V. montana is a form of *V. canina*.

V. multicaulis (Britt.)= *V. Walteri, q.v.*

V. multifida is more or less of a twin in needs and looks and habits to *V. pinnata*.

V. Munbyana is a useful 6-inch purple pansy perpetually in bloom, from the Alps of Greece.

V. nebrodensis.—A form of *V. calcarata, q.v.*

V. nephrophylla (*V. vagula*) haunts the cold, dank bogs of the North American woodland, and is almost smooth and hairless, with clumps of kidney-shaped, rounded leaves, of which the latest developed are broadly heart-shaped and dimly scalloped here and there. Its violets are fine and large, and rich in deep colour.

V. nevadensis replaces *V. cenisia* in the highest screes of the Sierra Nevada. It is an even less rosette-forming plant, and much less hoary with hair, with the leaves egg-shaped, rather than oval-heart-shaped or broadly oval. Its lovely pansies are of a reddish violet-blue with a radiating eye of gold. It wears a look of *V. crassifolia*, but has larger flowers, and a longer spur, and wider lateral petals, so that the blossoms are fuller in outline.

V. Novae Angliae is cousin to *V. septentrionalis*, but has the foliage narrowly triangular and pointed, instead of being blunt at the tips. Among these, in the river shingles of New England, arise the many variable violets.

V. nummulariaefolia is one of the race's choicest jewels. It lives only in the highest turf and open rocky places of the Corsican mountains and the Maritime Alps, where often it forms wide, close mats creeping along from its one tap-root, in a mass of shoots along under a big stone in the bare slope, and emerging in dense tuffeted lines of minute rounded leaves, very dark and fleshy and glossy, in cushions that neatly outline the boulder's base. From these shoots in summer come a bewildering abundance of short stems carrying the loveliest round pansy-violets of a quite peculiar shade of clear and brilliant periwinkle blue, freaked and with a diversity of deep violet-black lines that give a wonderful effect of wisdom to those clear little plump blue faces, so profusely squatting close upon their tuft. In cultivation *V. nummulariaefolia* requires first of all rather careful re-establishment in the sand-bed, for it is so precious that the nurseryman who will send out well-rooted specimens is almost as rare as the Violet itself; but then, in the underground-watered moraine, or specially stony and well-drained peaty slope, it will grow ahead with a neat heartiness the more embarrassing that it seems as if the plant considered this was grace sufficient, without the added courtesy of putting forth a flower. No doubt, like so many of its equals on the high hills, it wants an absolute resting season of drought in winter to ripen it for an adequate display of bloom in summer. And never, I think, will it show quite the condensed, dark, glossy mass of tight tiny leaves covered with quite that condensed crowd of serene and cheery countenances, which make such a bewildering patch of beauty on the high moors and in the rocky-silty slopes of the Col de Pra in early June, when there is yet no sign of life over the sere dead moorland, but the dawning steam of sweetness from *Trifolium alpinum* arising in the nipping clear snow-air, and the pale coerulean jewel-work and gentle mosaics of the Viola lying here and there in slabs of pure colour amid the brown barrenness of a world yet hardly stirring from its sleep.

V. Nuttallii is one of the finest yellow-flowered violets. In the prairies of the Northern States it throws abroad its leafy branches set with oblong narrow foliage, almost toothless, and tapering downwards to the leaf-stalk, along which a flap of leaf continues on either side. The flowers are of bright yellow, often richly purple on the reverse.

V. ocellata is a particularly brightly-painted form or cousin of *V. canadensis*, making a noble clump of erect stems above the leaves in California, 6 inches or a foot high, bearing large violets nearly white, with the two upper petals bright purple on the reverse, while the rest are lilac-white or creamy, veined with violet, and with a pencilling of violet beard. It is as beautiful as *V. Rydbergi*.

V. odontocalycina bears a close resemblance to *V. cenisia*, but its spur is shorter, and it forms close tufts of huddled and overlapping little fleshy foliage of grey velvet, blunt and toothless at the edge, emitting big pansies of clear blue-purple with a thick, blunt spur, that light up the high stony places in the Alps of Armenia.

V. odontophora has no merit to pine for.

V. odorata is the Sweet Violet, of which no more need be said. There are countless varieties, but in particular, for the rock-garden (the rest are too stout and rampant, as a rule, or too florist-fed in fatness) there is the pretty, small-flowered, yellow variety, which is, indeed, most lushly and largely leafy for its blossoms, yet produces them in such profusion as to make it worthy of admittance to some not specially valued, shadyish corner in rich soil. It may be offered as *V. sulfurea* or as *V. Vilmoriniana*.

PLATE 52

VIOLA DUBYANA.
(Photo. R. A. Malby.)

PLATE 53

VIOLA CALCARATA.
(Photo. R. A. Malby.)

VIOLA HEDERACEA [ERPETION RENIFORME].
(Photo. R. A. Malby.)

VIOLA.

V. olympica has a neat small habit in the way of *V. rothomagensis*, differing from *V. tricolor* in being perennial, as well as in being a tidy cushion of green, from which spring the purple and varied flowers of the Heartsease, with the spur twice as long as in *V. rothomagensis*. Its home is in the pine region of the Bithynian Olympus.

V. oreocallis.—The Hill Beauty of North America is a pretty little tufted violet, though hardly deserving such an invidious name.

V. orphanidis makes leafy lush masses of softly, loosely silky leafage sending up on weakly branches a succession of blossoms like those of *V. cornuta*, but smaller and less brilliant, even as the habit is laxer and more leafy.

V. orthocĕras has much the habit of the last and of *V. cornuta*, but its blooms are twice the size, while its habit is more prostrate than that of *V. cornuta*, flopping along for a foot or more, and sending up large short-spurred pansies of yellow and purple, with wide and spreading side-petals as in *V. orphanidis* and *V. olympica*, all being species of Caucasus or Russian Armenia or Macedonia.

V. pallens is a pale North American woodland violet that is often called *V. blanda* by modern authors.

V. palmata springs in spring from the rich, dry places of the American forest. Often the earlier leaves are ordinary and undivided, but the mature ones are handsomely cut into some five or nine lobes, and the big violets are often more than an inch across.

V. palustris is common in flat bogs and marshy levels of England, with ample, almost round, long-stemmed leaves, and tiny pale flowers almost as round in outline as the leaves. It serves as the type of a vast group; e.g. *V. nephrophylla* (*q.v.*) is an improved cousin of this, that sends out no runners, and so does not grow so rank.

V. papilionacea also loves the moister places. But this is an American, forming a stout clump of very broad, heart-shaped leaves, amid which rise up violets of deep purple with a white eye.

V. Patrinii ranges across Northern Asia to Japan. It is a dainty little tufted violet, with quite narrow and saw-edged, oval leaves, forming smooth and hairless clumps that never send out runners. The dainty violets are usually of clear lavender blue, but the plant is wildly variable. It ranges far down on the dusty plains of China.

V. pedata has always been a problem for the cultivator. Even in its own States of America, if brought into the garden from the fields or bank-sides where it abounds (as in the sandy levels of Long Island), the clump soon mimps away in exile. In England it has occasioned as much discussion and correspondence almost, as its beauty is worth.

VIOLA.

On the whole it seems likely that a sandy and perfectly-drained wood-land mixture, light and free, but specially rich and clammy and well watered from below in spring, will best appease the plant's home-sickness, if only it be enshrined in some place not too open to the furies of the sun. (New pieces will pay for being potted for a season in thumb-pots, and nursed up in a frame beneath a light covering of manure through the winter, in a shady aspect, and with the sashes kept on when the weather threatens frost.) Yet different treatments succeed or fail with it in different places, and sometimes it thrives in moraine, and sometimes in pure sand. In any case it is well deserving of all the trouble it gives, so delicately beautiful are the tufts of quite dwarf and dark bird-clawed foliage; and so splendid the noble orange-pointilled ample violets with back-turning upper petals, hovering on their 2- or 3-inch stalks like golden-bodied butterflies of a lucent blue lavender, which is hardly improved in the form *V. p. bicolor*, where the two backward-lying upper petals are of richest violet velvet, making a royal contrast with the bland melting lilac of the lower, and the springing point of fire from the flower's heart. There is also a lovely and purely virginal albino form. There seems, with us, little propagation except by division, and those clumped fleshy stocks are by far too precious to be harried, supposing they have lasted on for two or three seasons, and formed into a comely clump of three or four crowns.

V. pedatifida is a most variable plant, but has the same handsomely divided, bird-clawed foliage, this time further adorned by prominent fan-shaped veins. It forms clumps from a vertical stock, and the flowers are solid and goodly purple violets on stems of 8 inches. It belongs to the prairies of the Northern States, and includes two marked developments, at least, in *V. p. Bernardi* and *V. p. indivisa*.

V. pedunculata comes from California, where it forms ruffling fields all gold one minute and all bright brown the next, as its blossoms ripple under the wind. It is a most lovely species for a sheltered, warm place in light, rich soil, where, from its stocks, it sends up normal Sweet-violet leaves, firmly upstanding and rather squashed down in outline till they are like a flattened heart with a few forward-pointing fine jags towards the tip. High above these, on stems of 6 or 8 inches, goes sailing an incessant fleet of very large and very round violets of pure gold, with the two uppermost petals veneered on the reverse with mahogany, so that the field of flowers under the sun laughs innumerably in alternate twinkles of flame and flickers of brown between the breezes.

V. pinnata is a rare treasure of the Alps, a frail thing and rather difficult to grow, the only one of our alpine violets with divided foliage after the fashion of *V. pedata*. Here and there on the stony slopes of the high ranges, in the screes and often under the fringe of a mountain pine, may be seen springing among the stones that most delicate clump of smooth and very finely gashed and bird-clawed foliage. It is yet more rarely seen, too, than it need be, for *V. pinnata* is a shy, elusive nymph, hurrying up to life immediately the snows are gone or going, hastily throwing up, on stems of 2 or 3 inches, her little intensely sweet violets of rosy lilac, pale lavender, or white ; and then, by June, having borne and ripened even her inconspicuous tiny utility-flowers, she is gone to rest again, invisible in the heart of the stone-slope. In the garden nothing will usually serve her for long but sandy and rich moraine-mixture in a rather shady aspect, and copiously watered from below when the violet is beginning to expect the mountain to be cool and moist about her feet ; there is little question of multiplying this rare and dainty elf, no sooner come than passed again ; who is as capricious and full of airs and fads as the incomparably more brilliant and beautiful *V. pedata*, towards which, indeed, she seems to have aspirations, as we may now see. For,—

V. p. chaerophylloeides in the mountain woods of Japan makes a far jump from the meek inconspicuous grace of its type, towards the regal splendour of *V. pedata*. For it is much larger and firmer in habit, much nearer to *V. pedata* than to *V. pinnata*, and its few flowers are much larger, of a hot, translucent, amethystine lilac. When the sun goes down on the mountains, and sends his last slanting beams in ruddy scarlet among the saecular columns of the Cryptomerias above the Tombs of the Regents, the whole air is filled with beams of red fire and powdered gold, kindling the young scant foliage of the undergrowth to a dappled flicker of green flame ; the bending buds of the lilies glow like ghostly jade, the arched sprays of Kerria carry ranks of dazzling suns, and here and there on the rich brown earth the little Crowfoot Violet gleams and burns as if enchanted into the very likeness of a living amethyst with a heart of fire. Unfortunately the plant seems to have all the miffiness of the type, besides being dishearteningly difficult to import alive.

V. poetica waits for her master's inspiration on the high-alpine slopes of Parnassus. This is a most lovely and dainty small mountain Pansy of noble purple on stems of an inch or two, close in the relationship of *V. crassifolia*, and so coming into the family of *Mammola rupina*. It makes clumps of quite minute, almost bald and fleshy little rounded leaves on rather long foot-stalks, and the rich, blue-purple pansies have a thick spur, and are taller on their stems than those of tiny *V. crassifolia*, although they are not quite so large.

VIOLA.

V. polychroma is only a Tyrolean form of *V. tricolor*.

V. primulaefolia makes tufts of foliage in the American woodlands and far across Asia, but its pale violets, veined with darker tones, are not nearly so large and worthy as those of *V. Patrinii*, its cousin german.

V. prionantha has its outstanding little long-heart-shaped leaves very vigorously toothed, and forms dainty clumps from which stand out pleasant small violets usually of fine purple. It is a plant of Northern China and Japan.

V. pseudo-gracilis is the version of *V. gracilis* that comes to us from Southern Italy. It is a bright and beautiful free-growing blue-purple Violet-pansy enough, in the kinship of *V. cornuta*, but not to compare with the blazing violet darkness and the freakish fairy faces of *V. gracilis*.

V. pubescens is a downy small species of the American woods, almost exactly repeating *V. biflora* in habits and requirements, but that its little golden violets are veined with purple and often solitary on their stem instead of being twins.

V. pumila. See under *V. canina*.

V. pyrolaefolia has its far home in Patagonia. It makes beautiful neat tufted masses of egg-shaped and roughly-hairy toothed leaves, and hurries precipitately into bloom with its big golden violets on slender stems of 4 inches or so, well above the foliage, and pencilled on the lower lip with delicate veins of dark red. It should have a choice and well-guarded and half-shady place in cool and well-drained vegetable soil with plenty of grit.

V. Raffinesqui is an annual Pansy in the way of *V. tricolor*.

V. Reichenbachiana.—This is the limestone development of the type-species, *V. silvestris*, the common Dog Violet of the woods; it often has the lower petal purpler than the rest.

V. Riviniana, on the other hand, is the non-calcareous development of the same Wood Violet.

V. rostrata fills the cool shady places of the woodland about Quebec. The leaves are all rounded-heart-shaped, the upper ones rather more pointed, and all of them quite smooth and a little inclined to be saw-edged. The numerous long-spurred violets spring clear of the 6-inch branches on their tall stems, and are lilac-blue with a deeper blotch at the base.

V. rothomagensis.—The Rouen Violet makes neat small tufts of concise habit, from which the whole length of summer calls a succession of tidy little lilac pansies, the mass of the plant being some 8 inches high.

VIOLA.

V. rotundifolia is a stoutly running thing, quite prostrate in growth, with rounded-heart-shaped leaves, minutely downy at flower-time, and with wide vague scallopings at their edge. The flowers are bright yellow violets, and their three lower petals are veined with brown. It lives in the cold woods of North America.

V. Ruppii. See *V. canina stricta.*

V. Rydbergi is an especially brilliant form of *V. canadensis, q.v.*

V. sabulosa = *V. Curtisii, q.v.*

V. sagittata is a stalwart North American Violet of 10 inches, with lavender-lilac flowers and arrow-head foliage.

V. sarmentosa is the same as *V. sempervirens,* an evergreen Californian Violet with yellow flowers.

V. scabriuscula comes quite close to *V. pubescens* and *V. biflora,* though it is usually larger and leafier and rather coarser than the Two-flowered Violet. It shades into *V. pubescens,* but the leaves are earlier, some one or three from the base, and then three or four stems, shorter, leafier, and less downy than in *V. pubescens.* Like the rest of the group, it haunts the cold, damp places of the mountains. It is a much better garden-plant than *V. biflora.*

V. Schultzii is the very rare pale-yellow Alsatian form of *V. canina, q.v.*

V. sciaphila. See *V. hirta.*

V. scopulorum is a condensed, diminished, and deeply coloured variety of brilliant *V. canadensis.*

V. Selkirkii makes clumps of handsomely scalloped leafage much too large, as a rule, for the huddled little lilac violets; it is a small and rather delicate thing, running underground.

V. septentrionalis has variable flowers. It lives in the moist open woods of America, beneath the pines, for instance, and may be known from *V. Novae Angliae,* among other things, by the invariably *blunt end* to the heart-shaped foliage. It is remarkably pretty.

V. silvestris is the woodland cousin of our Dog Violet, abundant in every copse.

V. sororia has the same ample clumped habit as *V. papilionacea,* and occupies the moist places of Northern America even to the very dooryards. It is a variable species; the leaves are often largely triangular from their heart-lobed ample base, but sometimes rounded and running abruptly to a point. The stems of the many purple violets are about the same height as the leaves.

V. spathulata is a Caucasian tuffet of no especial merit.

V. speciosa copies in all things *V. macedonica,* but has larger flowers.

VIOLA.

V. splendida comes out of Southern Italy, and is a beautiful lax and spreading ramper, after the way of a rather looser and more prostrate *V. cornuta* which has reminiscences of *V. gracilis*. The handsome Cornuta-flowers are generously borne from the decumbent branches on long foot-stalks through the summer, and *V. splendida* is a pleasant addition to the garden, though hardly satisfying the hopes aroused by its name. There is also a really pretty cream-white form more justly called *V. eburnea*, thus indicating an affinity with *V. gracilis*, whose purples go to cream, while the bluer lilac of *V. cornuta* goes to a cold paper-white. Cuttings should always be taken of *V. splendida* in autumn, as, though it thrives and spreads quite readily in any light, warm soil in summer, it is not always tolerant of raw, wet winters.

V. stagnina is a rank and whitened form of *V. canina, q.v.*

V. Stoneana lives in the moist woods of America, and is notably handsome among the handsome lobed-leaved violets of the New World. It makes clumps of foliage, cut into some three to nine segments, and the big purple blossoms have an eye of denser darkness.

V. striata has become well-diffused in cultivation, while so many of its betters still linger in the wild woods of America. This is a rank and straggling thing, of the leafy-stemmed group, abundant in foliage, amid which, all the summer through, it emits quantities of rather inconsiderable cream-white violets lined with purple. It is useful to fill a cool place, but has not so much intrinsic merit as many a form of *V. canina* and *V. silvestris*.

V. suavis (*V. tolosana* and *V. Beraudii*) is an especially fragrant white-eyed development of *V. odorata*.

V. subvestita need not trouble our pulses from its far-off home in the Rockies.

V. sudetica is a large violet or white form of *V. lutea*, with the petals often toothed. It can be half a foot or 18 inches high or long, and may be seen principally in the Vosges.

V. sulfurea. See under *V. odorata*.

V. Thibaudieri is a Japanese of no value.

V. Thomasiana. See under *V. hirta*.

V. triloba shades in and out of *V. sororia*. Sometimes the leaves are undivided, sometimes they have three or even five deep lobes. They are of sombre purple at first, but as the deep violet violets, paler on the reverse, begin to hover over the clump, the foliage assumes a tone of yellowish green.

V. uliginosa is but a dim little marsh violet of the far North.

V. uniflora, in the wilds of Siberia, bears small golden flowers in the kinship of its more handsomely endowed twin-bearing cousin, on branches of 4 inches in the early year.

V. valderia.—The sinking fires of the race leap up once more towards the end, with the last of our great alpine Pansies. *V. valderia* is no more than a variety of *V. cenisia*, yet it is hard to sink its identity, no less for the unusual beauty of its name, than on account of the treasure's own character. It is a very rare form, peculiar to the schists and granites of the Maritime Alps, North and South of the Argentera, revelling at far lower levels than would ever be tolerated by the austerer-tempered *V. cenisia*, and never ascending into the high and barren places of the hills, where alone you may hope for *Mammola rupina*. It lives, however, in the same rocky screes and river-shingles among the coarse blocks ; not running about, but forming a single straggly tuffet from a single tap-root. Otherwise, though the foliage, thoroughly villous, is of a greener colouring, the habit of the plant, except in that most important point, does not diverge greatly from that of *V. cenisia*, but the sham leaves at the base of the real ones are undivided and like wee leaves themselves in *V. cenisia*, whereas in *V. valderia* they are cut and gashed into some half a dozen unequal lobes, of fringy effect along the stems. It thus has so much in common with *V. Dubyana*, which it also resembles in its singleness of root. The flowers, however, are precisely the purple and soft lavender-violet pansy-faces, comfortable yet not plethoric, of *V. cenisia*. Their two side wings, and the lip, have a pencilled moustache and minute imperial of black velvet, that give special intelligence to their expression, as the little brilliant countenances smile up from the raw and rosy granite débris with their delicate twinkling eyes of gold. In cultivation *V. valderia* has long given more trouble than *V. cenisia* and *V. nummulariaefolia*, owing principally to its softness of habit, that makes it abhor travel to an inordinate degree. It so dislikes a journey that it usually arrives as jam. However, this unpleasant surprise (for the low proclivities of the plant had made one hope it more invincible and hearty than any other of this high-alpine race), once faced successfully, *V. valderia* will grow as well as the best in specially sunny open moraine, and continue to delight the whole summer with its gentle purple pansies. It takes its lovely name, like the synonymous Potentilla, from the Baths of Valdieri, deep under the northern shadow of impending Argentera. Unlike the Baths, however, the violet sits in the sun ; and in the sun always, low or high, it will always be found luxuriating in the limited district where it developed long ago before the days of the great glaciers, and clung to life through that trying time, by digging its feet deep into the grits of the granite. On the seaward side of the range it is especially profuse, always to be seen prospering in open stony places of the hot slopes, anywhere a little above the level of Saint Martin Vésubie, and ascending as high as Our Lady of the Window, where its tuffets are peculiarly neat and well-furnished. It never attempts the limestone, as it seems ; but on the upmost ridges above Saint Martin it becomes so abounding that all the lighter grassy places are full of it, and the arid hillside is made a shivering dance of its little pansies, till, on the Col de Pra, going down into the solemn head of the Gordolasca Valley, it is abundant in the open lawn itself, as if it were *V. lutea* or *V. calcarata*. Yet its happiest homes are those in open, stony ground, where it can have the whole place at the disposal of its tuffet. *V. valderia* is so generous in bloom as to be no Methuselah in cultivation : albinoes also occur, yet are but sickly souls, with more than the type's distaste for foreign travel.

V. variegata is a 6-inch pallid violet of Siberia, standing near *V. dissecta*, but with its foliage undissected.

V. vallicola (*V. physalodes*, Gray) cultivates valleys in the Central Rockies, where it loves the moister, cooler corners. It has a spreading stock, from which it sends out a few stems of half a foot or less, with larger golden yellow violets than in *V. Nuttallii*, veined with purple, each about half an inch across.

V. vestita. See under *V. cenisia.*

V. viarum is a North American of no outstanding charm for the garden ; and in the same rather dim ruck come *V. renifolia*, *V. lanceolata*, *V. macroceras*, *V. imberbis*, *V. ovata*, *V. kamschatica* (a twin to *V. Selkirkii*, if not the same), *V. incisa*, and *V. Gmelini*, which has good-sized violets, indeed, that make one hope there may yet be jewels in this heap, though the sifting out of many such has already amply stored this list with violets as well as pansies. Of these, again, *V. tricolor*, the Annual Heartsease, gives us many forms and names, such as *V. bannatica*, *V. arvensis*, *V. segetum*, *V. Kitaibeli*, *V. hymettia*, *V. demetria* : together with other and more worthless annuals yet, in *V. modesta*, *V. ebracteolata*, *V. occulta*, *V. parva*, *V. pentadactylis*, &c.

V. Vilmoriniana. See *V. odorata.*

V. vivariensis, however, is a frail perennial Pansy, starry-faced and of clear blue, with the lower petals rayed with gold, standing out from the plant on long, fine stems, in the counties of Drôme and Ardèche.

V. Walteri (*V. multicaulis*, Britton) has the same brilliant purple violets as *V. labradorica* (Schrank), first of all springing from the central tuft, and then from the prostrate leafy stem. It lives in the rocky places of American mountain woods, and its leaves are rounded-heart-shaped and scalloped, often veined with darker green.

V. Wiedemannii is a larger and more graceful version of *V. palustris*, from the Alps of Anatolia.

V. Willkommii comes near **V.** *mirabilis*, and has little worth.

V. Zoysii is merely a form of *V. calcarata, q.v.*

Vittadenia australis, from Australasia, trails quite happily about in any light and well-drained soil in a rather sunny, sheltered place, adorning all the later summer with clouds of blushing daisies, springing lonely on long stems in unceasing profusion from the low and finely-branching mass. Far more dainty and delightful still is the even freer and richer-blooming little pink and white daisy, *V. triloba* (*Erigeron mucronatus*). This is one of the best of edging plants, and its riot of blossoms continues in unceasing elegance from June until they are finally sent home by the frost. Seed, division.

W

Wahlbergella.—A worthless group. See **Melandryum.**

Wahlenbergia.—The treatment of this divided and unnatural family has always been confused and arbitrary; and, for the sake of convenience, we have here left all the cluster-headed group under the name of *Edraianthus*. There still remain, however, two quite clearly separated sections; first of all, and close to *Edraianthus*, the single-flowered prostrate or cushion-forming plants of the Adriatic coasts, the happy home of *Edraianthus;* and then the large group of accepted Wahlenbergias, many of them valueless and miserable annuals (we take no account here, for instance, of *W. nutabunda*, or *W. homallanthina*), while the rest attain their best development in Australia and New Zealand, where the family fate of confusion seems to have overtaken them. For the sake of avoiding unnecessary bewilderment, let us take these first, then, and throw in at the end that strange and lovely little outlier of the race in the marshes of England and Wales, which would feel so much more at home if left quiet under its old name of *Campanula hederacea.*

W. albomarginata, Hook. fil., has some dozen leaves, all in a rosette at the base, and nearly an inch long, broadish spoon-shaped and green, quite smooth but for a trifling hairiness on their edges and foot-stalk, and earning their white-margined name by having a definite rim of redness often extending to the reverse. The stems are some 2 to

8 inches high, one to five from a rosette, and each bearing one delicate flower, vase-shaped, of white or blue, about an inch or more across. This is the garden-plant that passes under the name of *W. saxicola;* it has a minute alpine form, not more than an inch high, with drooping bells, called *W. a. pygmaea.* It is a variable, but always lovely thing, with its very fine threadlike stems, either tall with large white diaphanous vases, or small with little blue ones; and thrives in light open loam in the sun, but not parched, where it flowers all through the summer, and should have tufts taken off and potted up for safety in autumn, in case an English winter should be too much for this wonderfully accommodating New-Zealander.

W. cartilaginea is a small perennial from New Zealand, not more than 3 or 4 inches tall, with short, sturdy stems, each bearing one big sweet-scented white blossom, cloven into five lobes to the base, and no longer than the enclosing segments of the calyx. The leaves are all gathered at the base of these in rosettes; they are broadly, bluntly spoon-shaped, quite toothless, about an inch long, and especially thick and leathery, with a yet further thickened white rim of cartilage at the edge that makes *W. albomarginata* more than ever a thief in its deceitful name. This, like all others of this Australasian race, should have choice, light, gritty soil, with plenty of stone, plenty of water, and plenty of care.

W. congesta is densely tufted, instead of loose in the arrangements of its rambling rosettes. The leaves, too, are rounder in their outline, and the flowers are smaller than in the larger types of the last, about half an inch wide, pale-blue cups on frail stems of an inch or two. Its essential personality rests in the proud fact that its seedpod *is always round,* instead of obconical as in the last.

W. gracilis. See *W. vincaeflora.*

W. multicaulis, Benth., has sometimes been called *Campanula capillaris.* It is a perennial, with a great number of erect stems a foot or two in height, usually each carrying one smooth small bloom, but sometimes branching so as to carry more. Though their multitude and the cloudy effect of the slender-stemmed bush has its value, they are but little, and the plant is hardly worth pining for, even were it hardy like the rest, which can hardly be hoped, as it comes from Australia. *W. m. dispar* is a no more useful variety of the species.

W. saxicola, DC. (the names are endlessly confused in gardens; no less of this species than of the next; and solid earth gives way beneath the feet of the venturesome, when Cheeseman's Manual is found no longer a sure guide). This is a perennial, with about a dozen obovate, spoon-shaped tiny leaves, perfectly smooth and green on both sides, and more or less faintly toothed at the edge, narrow and more or less pointed, arranged quite stemless in a loose rosette at the base. The perfectly smooth and naked flower-stems are delicate and slender, rising some 3 or 4 inches, or much less, from the tufts, bearing each one dainty little bell-shaped flower of *bright light blue*. It should have the treatment of the *W. albomarginata* which so often shares or usurps its name in gardens. It is a species of Tasmania.

W. vincaeflora, Decaisne.—This came into cultivation through successive years in a cloud of false names and notes of exclamation. It is, though perennial, a thing of curiously lush and annual look; from a thin base sending up such a profusion of rather lanky stems, about a foot or 18 inches high, that in summer the whole becomes a tossing bush of large cup-shaped flowers of peculiarly clear light blue, which would be even more acceptable than they are brilliant if only they did not have so flimsy an air, as if the garden were being fraudulently furnished with annuals. Catalogues still at times call it *V. gracilis*, and offer various named forms in which the gawkiness of habit is sometimes wholesomely corrected, as in the rather more compact and very much more expensive, but not otherwise in the least degree different *W. v. minor*. The genuine variety, *W. v. littoralis*, differs only in having all the leaves uniformly narrower, and always in opposite pairs instead of sometimes alternate. And all these will thrive for the time in light, open soil, and flower in a profuse blaze of light-blue beauty through the later summer; their description insists on their perennial nature; but in the garden their loose ephemeral habit, and mangy base make it extremely hard to believe in. Nor do they appear often to seed. So here ends the list of *Australasian perennials* in this race.

W. hederacea calls us high into the moors and marshes of England and Wales, where it trails its delicate length, and unfolds tiny, ivy-like leaves of bright green, and then, throughout the summer, on thread-fine stems, hangs forth such a profusion of dainty clear-blue bells that all the marsh goes softly blue. In the garden *W. hederacea* must not be planted by itself, or else it proves rather hard to establish. A moist place should be chosen, by stream-side or pool, where sedges and grasses are already at home. Then among these (they should not, obviously, be of the coarsest) the *Wahlenbergia* should be inserted, so that it may twine and clamber and faint in coils among the herbage as it does on its own hills, and feel itself in a marish jungle of the mountains, where it may wander in and out secure, and throw up those delicious gentle bells in a continuous humble display of colour.

We come now to the *Wahlenbergias* of the *Dalmatian district*—

close cousins to *Edraianthus*, but that each flower-stem, whether long or short, *carries only one blossom*, instead of a plethoric huddle that ruins their effect.

W. Oweriniana stands overshadowed by the next, from which it differs obviously in being a much smaller cushion in all its parts, with smaller lilac blooms sitting tight into a smaller tuffet of tinier leaves, which have the further specific distinction of being *perfectly smooth and hairless on their upper surface*. It ranges much further east, being found in the mountains of Daghestan; a most rare and little-known species, which should surely be a most choice jewel for a choice place in sunny limestone rockwork in specially light and stony limy loam or moraine.

W. pumilio.—This is the jewel of the family. Multiply the last by two or three, imagine tuffets of pure silver 8 inches across, built of spiny, glistering, pointed little leaves, with their upper surface coated in silvery close-piled silk, and their mass in early summer hidden from view beneath a dense settlement of great lilac-lavender cups, sitting close over the cushion and gazing sturdily up to the day. Such is *W. pumilio* on the highest limestone summits of Dalmatia; and such, without the slightest difficulty, is *W. pumilio* perfectly prepared to be in any well-drained, choice, warm place in the garden, in any limy light loam full of stones; but most especially in the moraine, where its silvered cushions wax round and fat and full immediately, until summer makes them hide themselves in a veil of purple bells, as it were a silver table set with myrrhine goblets for a party of deplorably bibulous fairies (for such lucent amethyst vessels could never hold so dull a drink as dew). In such conditions the plant is one of the easiest of Alpines, as it is certainly one of the most lovely. In firm rock, indeed, it will not even ask for sun, but on the northerly Cliff at Ingleborough is now six years old in a wide mass of flopping stems from a microscopic crevice in which a rooted cutting was inserted long since. For by cuttings is the best means of multiplying this beloved treasure, that hardly ever seems freely to set seed with us.

W. dinarica (*W. pumiliorum* of catalogues) may be best pictured by imagining the last, grown in close shade and drawn up. It is looser in the cushion, the leaves are longer, less silver, and often almost bristly with hairs; while the purple vases do not sit tight to the mass, but stand off it on slender and rather weakly stems quite evident very often to the eye. It is no less, however, a lover of open mountain-tops than the last, and no less easy in the garden, though a species of inferior value, not only on account of the less brilliant habit, but because the average size of its largest flowers is hardly larger than that of *pumilio's* smallest.

W. serpyllifolia has a much wider range than these last, up and down the hills of Servia and Bosnia. It is by far the most splendid of all, especially in the form that originated at Ingleborough, and has to be called *W. s. major*, because it possesses great satiny-purple bells of twice the size of any other form, even though the wild type be so ready and hearty in cultivation that it always develops finer blossoms than in nature. It may always be known by the loose flopping habit of its smooth, rich, red-purple stems of 5 or 6 inches, springing out on all sides in early summer from the central rosette of oval little green lucent leaves, fringed with hairs at the edge, but otherwise quite smooth and glossy except in the rare hairy variety, *W. s. pilosula.* At the end of the stems in early June, hanging in a mass over the edge of a warm limestone rock, develops a corrugated bud of reddish varnished black, which opens into an upstaring bell of the most fulminating imperial violet, in a texture like the finest shimmering silken lining to the Emperor's robe. The blaze and glory is Byzantine in its sumptuousness; unfortunately, however, it is not Byzantine in the longevity of its majesty; but in a fortnight all is over, and the plant does no more except make shoots that can be freely made into cuttings. It is of astonishing ease and good temper in the garden; but seems eager for more cosy conditions than the arid chips of the moraine. It grows its heartiest indeed (in tangles of shoots often a foot across) in a sunny aspect, in very rich and light limy loam, which should be well watered all through the summer and spring, and should, of course, be as perfectly drained as every other part of the garden. Its best place is on a slope or ledge at eye-level, where the regal bells can immediately affront your vision with the full dominance of their display; a particularly good association is with *Saxifraga cochlearis* or *S. l. lantoscana;* let these occupy the back of the ledge, and then their snowy plumes will be waving in the precise moment when, in front, the violet cups of the *Wahlenbergia* are overflowing the bed, in rich droppings of purple down the face of its rim of rock.

W. Murbeckii leads on from the last towards the Cluster-heads; and is probably a hybrid between *Edraianthus Kitaibeli* and *W. serpyllifolia.* It has much smaller and more pointed leaves than this last, and the violet bells on their single stems have five or six widening pale bracts just below, while between the lobes of the calyx there is the little toothed appendage which is usually lacking in *W. serpyllifolia,* always lacking in *W. Oweriniana,* always present in *W. pumilio, W. dinarica,* and *Ed. Kitaibeli* (in complete or modified form). The picture and possibilities of this rarity, however, need not greatly concern the cultivator, as, up to the present, only one specimen of it has ever been seen—more than twenty years ago, on the alpine heights of Velez Planina.

Waldheimia tridactyloeides is a delightful Composite from the high moraines of the Altai, wriggling far and wide among the stones, and emerging in little clumps of small, fleshy, three-toothed leaves, huddled in a rosette, on each of which sits a big rose-pink Aster or Townsendia, ampler and more splendid of effect than the last, as the rays are twice as long as the disk is wide. It lives in the upmost shingles of Alatau by the birthplaces of the streams, and should have a place in the choicest part of the underground-watered moraine-bed.

Waldsteinia.—These are delightful little plants, too, but of a quite different kindred. For they stand between *Geum* and *Potentilla,* and make, in any soil, the most admirable and freely-running carpets of handsome green foliage, from which are thrown up loose few-flowered sprays of large golden strawberry-flowers in early summer, and on spasmodically through the season. *W. geoeides* has simple kidney-shaped leaves without divisions or lobings, and does not send its runners roaming over the face of the earth ; *W. sibirica* has three-lobed leaves irregularly cut and toothed, among which, as the frail stems wander, come up sprays of two or three round-petalled yellow blooms, often divergent twins from a stalk hardly higher than the foliage ; *W. lobata*, *W. fragarioeides*, and *W. trifolia* (*W. ternata*) are all most useful and charming ground-coverers in much the same style ; *W. fragarioeides* and *W. trifolia* are more especially attractive, very freely roaming, and easily to be divided at any moment, with their running clumps of three-lobed leaves, with the segments irregularly toothed ; and then, in early summer, their specially graceful and abundant inclining sprays of golden stars, reaching their perigee in a long and lax succession of brilliance.

Weldenia candida must be looked to with care ; for it is a high-alpine of the Mexican Mountains, only to be trusted out in deep, light, and perfectly-drained soil in a warm and sheltered position. And if glass or boughs are put over the spot in winter when the plant has died down, it is not to be imagined that the *Weldenia* will resent that attention, but the more securely in spring will it again send up, from its long radish of a root, its unfolding rosettes of smooth and pointed, narrow, succulent leaves, like those of some wee unfolding glossy pine-apple, among which sits for some weeks on end a succession of three-petalled, rounded little flowers of extraordinary diaphanous white, like the ghost of a snowy Tradescantia long since drowned, very quickly come, and yet more quickly gone again, but succeeding themselves in such profusion that there is never a moment bare of their translucent trefoils of living and shimmering light. *Weldenia* is still rare and horribly expensive; yet the beauty is worth more than the pounds demanded in payment. But, alas, there is as yet no question of multiplication; this can only be achieved by division, and one would as soon divide one's grandfather's corpse as an established clump of such a treasure.

Willemetia stipitata is a Hawkweedish plant of 15 inches and little worth.

Wulfenia.—These are Scrophulariads of a factitious preciousness, because one of them happens to be a famous rarity of the Gailthal, where, however, it has earned the expressive name of Cow's Walk by its abundance. *W. carinthiaca* is a handsome thing enough, but rather coarse and rank, quite easy to raise from its abundant seed, and quite easy to grow in any rich, deep, and rather moist kitchen garden soil or border, where it makes solid clumps and extending colonies of upstanding, thick, smooth leaves, of bright glossy green, lengthily oval, and elegantly scalloped and crimped at the edges; among which in summer come up crosier-like stems of 10 inches or more, unfolding a dense nodding spire of blue flowers (or pink or white) in the way of *Veronica Bona-Rota*. *W. Amherstiae*, from the Himalaya, has much less value and brilliance. The rosettes suggest a limp *Horminum pyrenaicum*, and the flower-spikes a starred and spindly version of that rather dismal weed, with purpled long blossoms drooping at intervals from dark calyces, up the stem of some 5 or 6 inches; *W. orientalis* lives in the rocks of Northern Syria, and comes nearest to *W. carinthiaca*, but the foliage is yet thicker and more leathery and more intensely smooth and glossy; and *W. Wallichii* is said to be a Himalayan species of much smaller stature than the rest, bearing lilac-blue flowers in June and July, like the rest, on stems of only 4 inches or so. These all should have the soil and fatness appropriate to *W. carinthiaca*, though in rather choicer places on the well-drained rockwork, where the Cow's Walk is too large and rank to be admitted, no matter how rare and handsome and corpulent.

Wyethias are big yard-high Composites from America, that copy Helianthus. *W. angustifolia* and *W. mollis* might be admitted to dampish cool corners of the wilderness.

Wyomingia. See under **Aster.**

X

Xatartia scabra is a hideous and extremely rare Umbellifer, from the schists of the Central Pyrenees.

Xerophyllum asphodeloeides makes tough wiry dense tufts of grass in the sand-barrens of America, from which arise stems of a foot or two, bearing a spire of large and solid white Asphodel flowers in a most curious and penetrating pure tone of rich waxed-ivory solidity, peculiarly dazzling when you see them aspiring to the sunshine in open places of the woodland. Large and sound imported clumps of this should be procured, instead of the nurseryman's fragmentary single crown; and then they should be planted, either in sun or shade, in very rich and light soil, very lavishly mixed with sand. Here, if let alone, the plant will thrive and increase for ever, growing every year more lavish with its towers of lucent ivory in June.

Z

Zahlbrücknera paradoxa is a quite ugly and rather miffy and tender little green-flowered Saxifrage, flopping and creeping in damp, cool places on the rockwork, where it has, however, the decency only to be biennial at best.

Zauschneria californica, with a yet finer variety, *Z. c. splendens*, has close relationship with the Oenotheras. In light, sandy soil in a sunny place it makes wide grey many-stemmed masses of tall and slender stems of 18 inches, more or less, carrying all through the later summer a long profusion of brilliant hanging vermilion trumpets not unlike a Fuchsia's in effect, on the countless wand-like sprays. But cuttings should be secured in autumn.

Zephyranthes.—Much ink has fiercely flowed in the past over the question as to whether even *Z. candida* was hardy. There can be no doubt that the La Plata Crocus, in light and sandy soil, in a hot border against a vinery, and in a warm, dry climate, may be both hardy and free, and intensely beautiful, with its dark, glossy, grass-like foliage, and its profusion in late summer and autumn of glistering wide white crocus-stars with a rich heart of gold. But there can be no doubt, also, that this display is not to be counted on, and that the plant is not one of any general use for the outdoor English garden. As this, then, is the only one that even makes the faintest

PLATE 54

WAHLENBERGIA PUMILIO.
(Photo. R. A. Malby.)

PLATE 55

WAHLENBERGIA SERPYLLIFOLIA.

(Photo. R. A. Malby.)

claim to being hardy, there is little use in dilating on the similar and yet more startling splendours of rose-pink *Z. gracilifolia, Z. rosea, Z. Julia*, or pearly *Z. versicolor*, or the snow-pure royal Atamasco Lily, *Z. Atamasco.* Intending buyers, in saving their pence, will also be saving their tears.

Zizia aurea and **Zozemia absinthifolia** are both Umbellifers, in varying degrees of dim ugliness or quaint prettiness according as your fancy prompts. Their charm lies only in their fine green foliage, for which they may be, perhaps, admitted to the gardens of the curious.

Zwachia aurea comes very close to Lithospermum and Moltkia, but the segments of the golden-yellow corollas stand erect, instead of opening out into a star. It will like sunny sites, probably in light soil; and is a Borragineous species of no special interest, from the Balkans.

Zygadēnus.—These are smaller and less brilliant, but still quite elegant cousins of Xerophyllum, also from North America, but perfectly easy of culture here in light, rich soil, rather cool and inclined to moisture, but thoroughly drained. Here they willingly throw up their frail leafage, and then, in summer, their stems of a foot or less, carrying a loose pyramidal spire of rather large waxen stars of greenish or creamy white. The most greeny ones are *Z. glaucus* and *Z. chloranthus* (the plant sometimes grown in our gardens as *Z. elegans*); white and waxen are *Z. Nuttallii, Z. glaberrimus*, and *Z. Fremontii;* in *Z. angustifolius* the snow is said to flush; and yet another species is *Z. leimanthoeides.*

APPENDIX.

MECONOPSIS.

NEWER SPECIES AND FURTHER NOTES.

Meconopsis aculeata now divides into two definite forms, of which the commoner, *M. a. normalis*, has flowers on short pedicels, and the lobings of the foliage blunt or rounded ; the other form, *M. a. acutiloba*, is very much rarer, with *long* flower-pedicels and the leaf-segments triangular. *M. Guglielmi Waldemari* is merely a variety corresponding to *M. horridula's* relation to *M. racemosa*—that is, with no central spike, but the blooms all springing separately from the base, each on its own stem ; it has not yet occurred in cultivation. Much more interesting is *M. a. nana*, a most distinct and charming thing, which forms dense cushions of foliage from a mass of fibrous roots instead of the typical carrot ; the whole plant is on a much smaller scale than in the type, not more than 5 inches high. Like the type, though, it seems biennial.

M. argemonantha makes a rare colour-break in the race. It stands close to *M. primulina*, but the leaves are rather suggestive of a dandelion's, and the flowers are pure white, with yellow anthers. But *M. argemonantha* is still but scantily known, and not within grasp of the gardener at all.

M. Baileyi is another collector's species, so far unknown to the cultivator, and indeed but incomplete in the specimens. Nothing yet appears as to leaves or roots, but the blue flowers are four-petalled and on solitary stems, with golden anthers, several or many from each crown of the tuffet. *M. Baileyi* comes in the group of *M. bella*, and will therefore most probably prove perennial.

M. concinna from Yunnan is also in the kindred of *M. bella*, but has quite narrow foliage much less divided, and a capsule opening in deeper cleavages. It is a very charming little plant, of stony limestone pastures and cliff-ledges, with flowers of deep purple-blue, each on a stem of 3 to 6 inches from the tuft, which, alas, has all the look of being biennial. This we may hope for, as Forrest has collected it.

M. decora already rejoices one lucky cultivator. It is a most interesting, strange Poppy, having at once a look of the Aculeata Group and of the Robusta. In other words, it is a tallish-growing species, with a spire of golden-anthered blossoms of pure white, borne on graceful delicate footstalks. The style, however, is long, instead of short as in the Robustas, while it has soft hairs instead

APPENDIX.

of the prickles of the Aculeatas. *M. decora* came from the Eastern Himalaya, and was at first supposed a mere albino of *M. aculeata :* but proves in reality a perfectly distinct and most desirable species, though probably of biennial tendencies.

M. eximia belongs to the Mekong-Salween Divide, and is a monocarpic little Poppy, very close in habit to my own *M. lepida* of the Primulina Group, but obviously differing in its fat capsule, and in the vesture of bristlish hairs in which the whole growth is vested, stem and leaves and pods and all. It is a lovely ornament of the open alpine pasture-lands, with nodding flowers of rich blue-purples, with greyish-yellow anthers.

M. Forrestii, again, is similar in style—some 6 to 15 inches in height, with pale-blue flowers. In bloom the flower-stems stand widely out from the main stalk, but in fruit the whole growth develops even to the height of 2 feet, and the capsules on their stems stand straight up along the spike, pressed close to the central trunk. The anthers are orange yellow, in the specimens, though described as being blue, and this lovely Poppy also we shall owe to Forrest, though whether we retain it or no depends upon ourselves. For, like the others of the Primulina Group, it is biennial.

S. Guglielmi-Waldemari is merely a state, unknown in cultivation, of *M. aculeata, q.v.*

M. impedita holds a medium position between the groups of *M. bella* and *M. primulina*. In appearance it comes much nearer to the former, a biennial tuft of solid, deeply lobed and feathered little leaves in dense clusters, emitting a number of remarkably graceful stems, some 6 to 15 inches high, each bearing a beautiful pendulous flower of deep blue, with yellow anthers and almost invariably 4 petals. *M. impedita* haunts open stony ridges of barren limestone, and approaches *M. Henrici* not only in its length of style, but in its biennial temper. *M. Morsheadii* is best taken for the present as a mere variety of *M. impedita*, but rather thinner in the texture of the leaves, and with larger blooms of paler colouring.

M. latifolia has at last emerged from under the shadow of *M. sinuata*, of which it was once considered a mere variety, and may as such be often seen grown in gardens. In reality it is a distinct and most beautiful species, in appearance suggesting an *M. Wallichii* of rather smaller dimensions, with pendulous flowers of lovely pale azure, and golden anthers to enhance them. Not less notable is the foliage, not so softly hairy as in the Robusta Group, yet not quite so harshly as most of the Aculeatas ; and cut, not lobed, into deep and handsome featherings. The dark purple-black stigma at once marks out this splendid Poppy from *M. aculeata*, while the shape of leaves and capsule separate it definitely from *M. sinuata, which is not yet in cultivation at all. M. latifolia* throws out such odd growths at the base, and in the lower leaf-axils up the stem, that there seems a fair hope that it may prove perennial, or learn to become so.

M. lepida, one of the choicest treasures of my travels, will be found in the Appendix devoted to their trophies.

APPENDIX.

M. Morsheadii. See under *M. impedīta.*

M. Prattii admits a further note, in reference to my journey of 1915, and the distribution of *M. racemosa, q.v.* It is *M. Prattii* and *M. Prattii* alone of the Prickly Group (unless F 735 does indeed prove, as I hope, a new species) that occupies the Da-Tung Alps and the regions above Chebson Abbey, somewhat vaguely given as the source of the original specimen on which *M. racemosa* was based. And in the Da-Tung, *M. Prattii* is not so saxatile as in the Min S'an, but abounds in the open alpine turf at great elevations, with flowers of richest azure but a rather flimsy habit. In the rocks it also grows, however; and in one place 3 beautiful rose-coloured forms appeared, and in another an albino, of dingy and unattractive tone. Few things could be more beautiful than the high passes in August, when all ablaze with clouds of violet Delphinium, from which in serried myriads rise the azure spires of *M. Prattii.* Single radical flower-stems occur sometimes in this species round the base of the main stem, and in the Min S'an Alps it takes a form with very long pedicles, which may conceivably be another species.

M. Psilonomma, another of my own jewels, will be found in the same Appendix with *M. lepida.* It has lamentably failed in cultivation.

M. quintuplinervia evidently has its centre of distribution in the Da-Tung Alps, where it is of an abundance and a beauty quite stupefying, all over the high lawns. Variations are very rare, but I have seen six-petalled forms, and three times found the most beautiful albinoes: one slope yielded tones of vinous mauve, and there is a development of extreme loveliness, in which the flower is a soft clear turquoise, with only the faintest iridescent suggestion of lavender remaining.

The Petrograd specimens include, with the true *M. quintuplinervia,* many sheets of a quite different Poppy from the Szechuan March — a beautiful biennial of the Primulina Group, recalling *M. Psilonomma,* but hairier and with several (and even many) flowers on the scape.

M. racemosa may always be known from *M. Prattii* by its golden, instead of creamy, anthers. It seems that one specific name ought to include *M. horridula* and *M. racemosa* as fluctuating forms of a single species. The original specimen on which Maximowicz based *M. racemosa* is said to be labelled as coming from Chebson (Chobsen) Abbey on the Western foothills of the Da-Tung Alps. But, in examining the specimens of *M. racemosa* in the Petrograd Herbarium, I was not able to find any indication of this locality, all those given referring to the ranges south and west of Sining, and away to the Koko-nor. This exactly bears out my own experience: in the Da-Tung Alps I never saw a sign of *M. racemosa,* the prevailing Poppy of the high grass and shingles being exclusively *M. Prattii,* while Chebson Abbey could in no case be the haunt of any Prickly Poppy at all, sheltering as it does in the green foothills, some 4 to 6 miles distant from the great Alps behind. On the other hand, the Poppy brought back by Purdom from the ranges of Kweite and the Koko-nor, was unmistakably and universally the genuine *M. racemosa,* darker-blue in colouring, and golden anthered, in forms as often as not reverting wholly or

APPENDIX.

partially to the trunkless, many-flowered development which is typical *M. horridula.*

M. rudis has yielded what appears to be a variety: *M. r. intermedia*, with the flowers all springing from the base as in *M. horridula.* This plant, however, exists only in fragmentary specimens, and is still so obscure that it need not concern us at present. Meanwhile I also suspect that what some gardeners are now calling *M. "Wardii"* is merely *M. rudis* on some occasions, and *M. speciosa* on others. *M. rudis* has dark prickles, an orange stigma and yellow anthers, while *M. Prattii* has pale prickles, the stigma greenish, and the anthers creamy white. This alone should serve always to differentiate these two species at a glance.

M. speciosa is yet another Prickly Poppy in this group, whose blossoms are a disappointment in our gardens. Its feathered foliage distinguishes it immediately from *M. Prattii*, *M. rudis*, and *M. racemosa*, while there are but few and small bracts beneath the flower shoots up the main trunk, instead of the numerous and conspicuous ones that mark the spires of *M. aculeata*, *M. sinuata*, and *M. latifolia.* Otherwise, it has the same habit as this assemblage of blue Poppies. (The garden-plant of this name is ugly, and may be false.)

M. venusta holds out better hopes than most of being perennial. It is a cousin of *M. bella*, and so close in general appearance to *M. concinna* as to suggest at first being a mere variety. But here the leaves are feathered into rarer rounded lobings (*very* rarely entire); from the tuffet of these arise stems of 6 to 14 inches, each bearing a big four-petalled blossom of deep wine-purple with orange anthers. It loves the same situations as *M. concinna*, and is distinguished by the depth to which the valves of its capsule open when ripe. As yet another of Forrest's treasures, it should ere long be in all our hands.

M. "Wardii" has been much too prematurely proclaimed and issued. It seems at present most probable that there is *no* real *M. "Wardii,"* and that everything sent out under this name belongs to *M. rudis*, *M. Prattii*, *M. speciosa*, or even *M. racemosa.*

PRIMULA.

ADDENDA, AND FURTHER INFORMATION.

So many are the new Primulas now pouring in on us from China and the Indian Frontier, that panting type toils after them in vain, and these volumes should have a supplement every month if they are to continue up to date. However, here is the latest news, to July 1917, of fresh species in this race, hardly now to be recognised, many of them, under the freakish Greekish names in which they are pranked out, in the deficiency of any more Latin ones. Indeed, so many of the new Primulas have Greek names, and all the new Meconopsids have Latin ones (except my own *M. Psilonomma* : I am not responsible for *M. "lepida,"* whom I myself had planned to call *M. Eucharis*), which seems, to my taste, a reversal of propriety. But under any name, no doubt, these new Primulas will smell as sweet. As soon as we have got them, that is; while many are now fluttering into our reach, yet many more still exist only as dry and often fragmentary specimens in a Herbarium, shadowy foundations of new species that may ultimately be found impossible to maintain.

P. acclamata. See my Chinese Appendix.

Primula aemula is a very splendid species from open mountain pastures of Yunnan; and possibly, therefore, sharing in the "softness" of constitution which is the one bane of the beautiful treasures that hail from such southerly regions, when translated to the cooler, lachrymose conditions of England. *P. aemula* stands nearest to *P. reflexa* and *P. orbicularis,* and is a stout and stately splendour, with several remote tiers of brilliant satin-sheening golden stars up its tall stems, after the general style of *P. japonica* and *P. helodoxa* (though in reality this species belongs to the cousinship of *P. Maximowiczii,* but lacking the reflexed petals of *P. szechuanica* and *P. reflexa* in that group). The basal rosette is large and ample, with fleshy narrow-oblong foliage of a foot in length or so, minutely toothed at the edge, and absolutely without powdering or down of any kind.

P. alsophila. See my Chinese Appendix.

P. alta represents *P. denticulata* on the hills of Yunnan, and unfolds its downy foliage, together with its heads of lavender-purple blossom, in February, attaining a foot or more in height.

P. annulata is a delicate little thing only existing hitherto in dried specimens. It has a look of *P. yunnansis,* and yet more of *P. bella*; but from the first is distinguished by a ring round the mouth of the flower, and from *P. bella* by the lack of whiskers in its throat.

P. Calderiana is yet another of the Primulas long sunk in the welter of *P. obtusifolia.* It is perhaps at best only a microform of *P. Gammieana,* with fewer smaller flowers, with dark-purple calyx, and the corolla not velvety outside. It is common on peaty hill-tops in Sikkim, and its purple blossoms are very variable in colour.

P. celsiaeformis exactly describes itself. It is a near relation of *P. blattariformis* in the rather coarse group of *P. malvacea,* and is just like a purple-flowered Mullein with long-stalked foliage. But the variety *Duclouxii* of *P. blattariformis* has now been promoted to specific rank as *P. Tenana, q.v.*

P. cephalantha stands very close in prettiness, difficulty and impermanence to *P. pinnatifida,* but quite distinct in the Muscarioid Group by its special hairiness, which prevents it taking on the bright green look of *P. pinnatifida.* Its flower-head, too, is more of a spike, and yellow meal develops, as in *P. aerinantha,* on the 10–inch scape and the seed-head as it ripens.

P. chionantha takes us back into the clan of *P. nivalis,* and is one of the grandest in that grand group, a superb tall plant, hairless and yellow-powdered, with tier over tier of large pure-white stars, ravishingly fragrant. It can attain almost a foot and a half on the open alpine meadows of Western Yunnan, is very eagerly to be desired, and thrives handsomely in rich soil.

APPENDIX.

P. citrina. See my Chinese Appendix.

P. compsantha stands close to *P. minor*, but is still obscure in position. It lives on the open stony pastures of Yunnan, and is a small dainty thing, with stems of 4 to 5 inches rising from a rosette clothed at the base in relics of dead leaves. The head carries four or five rather trumpet-throated flowers, said to be pink, and with a greenish yellow eye, whiskered with hairs.

P. conspersa. See my Chinese Appendix.

P. coryphaea calls out our utmost longings to the open granite summits of the Burmese mountains, where it forms wide carpets in coarse sandy soil between drifts of dwarf Rhododendron—a tiny lovely species in the group of *P. bella,* with white-fluffed throat and blossoms of rich blue-violet. But how hardy will it prove ?

P. Farreriana, my noblest new species of 1915, is one of the most magnificent of the nivalis clan, and haunts only the dark sunless chines of granitic or limestone precipices at great elevations in the Da-Tung Alps. It is, indeed, astonishingly saxatile for its appearance : it makes stocks as thick and fat and succulent as any leek's, so wedged into the dark corners and danker crannies of the precipice that one wonders how it can find room or nourishment. The foliage is ample and splendid, of deepest glossy green, and white with meal beneath ; the stout stems just emerge above, carrying some half a dozen very large and deliciously fragrant blooms, of palest lavender blue, which fades in time to a French grey from the central 10-lobed star of white, in clear contrast to the profound claret-purple of the tube, which, when the flower is seen full-face, gives the effect of an almost black eye.

P. fasciculata recalls little *P. tibetica,* but has its orange-eyed flowers of bright rose, rather larger, and always solitary, quite stemless in minute tufts, constellating the high bogs in Western Yunnan.

P. florida is a neat, tidy plant, with a tight head of large blossoms almost disproportionate to the small rosette from which it is borne aloft on a stem of 4 to 5 inches. They vary through tones of lavender, and are fragrant. *P. florida* has some look of *P. stenocalyx,* and is a lovely species from high and stony limestone pastures of Western Yunnan.

P. fragilis forms moss-like patches in half shade on calcareous cliffs in Upper Burma. It is a wee delicate thing, clothed in golden meal, and upturning from its minute mats its solitary flowers of pale purple.

P. Gageana plays but a small part in our present hopes. *P. Gageana* lives very high up indeed in the Alps of Sikkim, in the bogs. It is a smaller but hardly less beautiful version of *P. Kingii,* but with oblong blunt leaves and different lobing of the corolla ; which, however, has much of the dark claretty tone and the fleshy downiness that is so remarkable in *P. Kingii.* The stem is about 8 inches in height, with a head of 1 to 8 pendent blooms : but, alas, *P. Gageana* exists only so far in one set of dried specimens.

P. glandulifera is yet another in the group of tiny tufted Primulas round *P. minutissima,* and yet another still only known by a dried specimen or two. It is so close in fact to *P. Stirtoniana* and *P. minutissima* as hardly to be

481

distinct in the gardener's eye (especially as he possesses none of them), though very much so in the botanist's.

P. Harrissii stands in the very shadow of *P. rosea*, but is smaller, and with leaves and flowers unfolding together.

P. helvenacea flaunts its tall and stately stems of thin-textured violet flowers in the cliffs of the Mekong–Salween Divide, and is allied to gorgeous *P. calliantha*, though distinguished at once by its long-stalked small-bladed leaves.

P. indo-bella explains itself. It replaces *P. bella* in Bhutan, where it forms dense cushions of inter-ramifying stolens and wee frail rosettes, close over which are constellated the fat and fleshy stars of blue blossom.

P. leimonophila loves the pastures in Hunan, at Yo-jô, but has not yet come into ours. It is a remarkably lovely plant, in the general clan of *PP. Gageana, Kingii, argutidens*, and *amethystina*. It swings out a one-sided head of drooping bells in a rich tone of Prussian blue.

P. lhasaensis may be no more than a larger form of *P. Jaffrayana, q.v.*

P. meiantha is actually annual or monocarpic. It is a small-flowered Burmese plant in the Malacoeides Group, but its annual habit and squinny minute blossoms sink it below further consideration.

P. melichlora is known only from a set of specimens, and is a cushiony, woody-rooted yellow-mealed cousin to *P. spathulifolia*.

P. minor is a charming tufted alpine, which may best be described as a miniature of unparalleled *P. pulchella*, but with leaves mealy on the upper surface, and rounded undivided lobes to the round-faced lovely lavender flowers, borne few in a head. It loves open and rather dry exposures on the mountain slopes of Adundz' and under the rocks.

P. nemoralis has violet flowers and soft leaves in the forests of Yunnan, and stands near *P. sinuata* in the chain of *P. sonchifolia*.

P. oresbia, apart from its dense vesture of white meal on the underside of the leaves and on the inflorescence, might almost be *P. incisa*. And to the aggregate of *P. incisa* it more certainly belongs than as yet to any earthly garden. It seems to be very pretty, but specimens and descriptions of *P. incisa* itself are not satisfactory or unanimous. The group links on the Soldanelloids with the Bellae.

P. petrophyes, though with structural differences, may by us be taken (if only we could get it) as virtually a diminutive and alpine state of *P. leimonophila, q.v.*

P. philoresia is a little matted loveliness from near Adundz' (A-tuntzu), and is so exactly like a smaller version of *P. dryadifolia* that it might be taken for a mere variety, were it not that its wee leaves are hairy above, while each flower, long-tubed from its calyx, stares straight up from its nest in the mat of foliage, instead of arising several on a stem.

P. prionotes only exists in specimens for us, and is so far the only Indian Sikkimensis-cousin with purple flowers.

P. pseudo-malacoeides explains at once its uses and affinities. It is slenderer and smaller in flower than the type.

APPENDIX.

P. radicata is a dwarf high-alpine from Chitral, in the group of *P. rosea*, with brilliant blossoms, each sitting solitary in rosettes of very thick leathery foliage.

P. Reginella is my only new Primula, except *P. Farreriana*, of 1915. In point of fact *P. Reginella* has several times been collected before, but now only for the first time (by my specimens) made capable of separate recognition. It is an exquisitely lovely minute gem of the very highest grassy arêtes only in the Da-Tung chain, very local indeed, but occasionally sprinkling the sere pale turf at 14,000 feet with the sparks of its tiny flowers of richest rose with a golden eye, springing close by twos and threes, from the microscopic tufts of glossy emerald leaves that lurk in the lawns and under the little ridges of the fell-slope. *P. Reginella* stands almost undistinguishably close to *P. tibetica*, but is always quite powderless and lucent, whereas *P. tibetica* (Watt notwithstanding) is invariably mealy (they say), particularly in the young foliage. *P. Reginella*, in point of fact, distinct and exquisite little queen of loveliness though it is, has suffered much from confusions. Particularly interesting is its confusion with *P. pumilio*, for which at first I took it, expecting to find it pumilio, and nothing else. *P. pumilio* rests on one sheet of specimens in the Petrograd Herbarium, and on that page are arranged 4 dense rectangular patches of specimens. Of these the first alone represents the real *P. pumilio*, a squatty tuffet, with a stalk, however short, and a head of flowers ; the second and third samples consist almost wholly of *P. Reginella*, and the last entirely so. In the same Herbarium *P. Reginella* may also be found lurking under *P. diantha* and *P. sibirica*. In sum, it suggests a wee dwarf form of my brilliantly rosy sibirica cousin F 507, and will be a treasure of delight in cool finest turf, or in specially choice safeguarded corners of the underground-watered bed.

P. rhodantha is a rare plant, in the immediate group of *P. rosea*, but distinguished by stalked leaves, a stem hardly longer than they, and the slender footstalks of the flowers themselves. It is a distinct species, formerly reckoned a mere variety of *P. rosea*.

P. riparia I found on beck banks about Chago, on the Tibetan Alps, in 1914. It is a worthless little squinny-flowered thing in the aggregate of *P. neurocalyx*, and in appearance suggesting a starveling of *P. obconica*.

P. rosiflora lurks in the shadow of *P. elegans* and *P. rosea*, but here there is hardly any stem at all, and the flowers have each a long footstalk and a lobed central ring.

P. rupicola is still obscure, but seems near *P. Souliei*, and bears up its heads of golden-eyed rosy flowers on 3-inch stems on the boulders and open stony pastures of Yunnan.

P. sciaphila connects *P. bella* and *P. indobella*. It is very rare, only one sample having been so far seen, a massive patch in dank shade of mossy granite cliffs in Upper Burma. It is larger than the similar *P. coryphaea*, with darkish purple flowers over the carpet, which suggests that specially neat mat form of *P. bella* which is differentiated as *P. nano-bella*.

APPENDIX.

P. seclusa is a coarse-leaved cousin of *P. mollis*, with profusion of bright pink flowers, fading irregularly outwards in the lobes. It loves deep and damp shady gullies in the rain-zone of the Burmese forests, and may therefore maintain a just and fixed displeasure against the conditions of life in the open in England.

P. sinomollis differs chiefly from its eponym in having slenderer stems and a much smaller calyx. It stands even nearer to *P. cinerascens*, but has bigger crinklier leaves, and tall stems particularly lavishly endowed with tiers of blossoms. It will want the same conditions as the rest, and be no more hardy.

P. stolonifera, pervading the boggy stream sides in the Lichiang Alps, may be figured as a fine many-stalked *P. denticulata*, with globes of fragrant golden-eyed flowers of lavender. But it differs immensely in throwing out long stout stolons on every side, and thus ramifying into a notable jungle of clumps.

P. tanupoda exists in only one specimen, and seems to stand between *P. sibirica* and *P. tibetica*. It is mealy, according to the invariable character of *P. tibetica*, indeed, but its flower is larger and does not reflex in fading. However, we may defer meditations on *P. tanupoda's* character until the plant itself has materialised.

P. Tenana differs from *P. blattariformis*, of which it once was only held a variety, in short soft foliage, deeply roundly lobed, in a wool-less stem, shorter pedicels, and smaller flowers.

P. viola-grandis. See my Chinese Appendix. It is by far the smallest of its group, a mere big violet indeed, as compared to the great wide-throated Gloxinias of *P. Elwesiana* and *P. Delavayi*.

P. Waddellii may be but a microform of *P. Stirtoniana*, and anyhow, is based on specimens so scanty that at present we need bother about it no further. It should have one solitary flower squatting tight in the powderless rosettes of its carpet.

P. Waltonii cries aloud to be collected from its home on the high gaunt hills of Holy Lhasa. Only two sheets of dried specimens are so far known ; but this promises to be a beautiful Sikkimensis cousin of tall stature, powdered with yellow meal, and swinging out a splendid shock of lilac-violet blossoms in a lavish head. In fact, though one of the rare non-yellow species in the group, it is *exactly* like *P. sikkimensis* in effect, differing only in the colour and shape of the blossom, and in the form of the calyx.

P. Wardii is what used to be called *P. sibirica chinensis*, a collector's commonplace all through the Alps of Western China. It is also what is usually grown as *P. sibirica*, but a very much finer thing than that feeble little plant, being in fact more of a glorified, magnified *P. involucrata* with soft lavender-rose flowers, but otherwise of identical needs and habits, and the same clean, entrancing fragrance. It has proved a most precious introduction, and of the freest, heartiest temper in cool moist soil. The real *P. sibirica* still awaits unravelling. In the Da-Tung Chain I found a plant which is clearly the one formerly regarded as a passage between *P. tibetica* and *P. sibirica*. But if even *P. tibetica* be still very variable and obscure and aggregated, it is certain that it is separated by a real gulf from *P. sibirica*. My Da-Tung Primula (F 507), however, though with the saccate bracts of *P. sibirica*, has something the look of a drawn-up spindlified *P. tibetica*, being a thin frail plant, with 2 or 3 flowers on a 4- to 5-inch stem, richly rosy as in *P. rosea*, and with a golden ring. It has clearly nothing to do with *P. Wardii*.

P. Woodwardii is the prior and proper name of *P. blattea*, *q.v.*

REPORT OF YEAR'S WORK (1914) IN KANS AND TIBET.*

IN spite of all the perils and tragedies with which the Kansu-Tibet border seethed in the earlier part of 1914, neither the " White Wolf " nor local insurrections succeeded in at all frustrating our botanical expedition. On 13th April we left Tsin Chow, a bygone imperial city of South Kansu, and struck almost due south for Kiai Chow. The way ran through loëss country, largely cultivated, and over high open downs. The two most important finds were *Farreria* Sp. (*novum genus*), Balf. fil., twice occurring on the barren fells; and—yet more important if possible—the first (as I believe) record of *Viburnum fragrans* as a wild plant, scantily appearing in the hilly copses south of Shi-ho. At Kiai Chow we entered upon the arid country of the Hei Shui Jang, or Black Water River, a justly named voluminous tide of filth, which, in all its course between Siku and Bi-gû, where it joins the White Water (the Bei Shui Jang) runs through a series of loëss and sandstone ravines, hedged in on both sides by vast arid downs of loëss. The climate here is African in heat and drought : I have made a point of sending samples of all good seeds from this region to Mr. Benbow, secure that at least at Mortola they will do well, whatever be their fate in the damps of England. Kiai Chow, during our short stay, yielded only the lovely little *Iris Henryi* and *Paeonia Moutan*.

Leaving Kiai Chow (pronounced in every province differently, but usually Jié-Jo †) on 25th April, we continued southward down the grilling ravines of the Black Water towards Wên Hsien, crossing the Fung S'an Ling Pass the day before our arrival, and there making acquaintance with two treasures in *Pleione* F 4 and *Primula* F 300. This pass separates the Black Water from the White Water, which flows beneath the acacia'd walls of sunny Wên Hsien in unsullied purity, to join the Black Water a little farther east, at Bi-gû. On 3rd May we rode out of Wên Hsien, striking due westwards up towards Tibet. Ere long the White Water deserted us, and our way continued up the East Road River to Di-er-Kan, the first Tibetan village. Hence, on 6th May, we turned sharp to the right, and up over the huge forested and grassy flank of Chago-Ling, the pass over the great limestone range that had now for two days past been peering

* Written in Lanchow, December 1914. See also, for a fuller history, " On the Eaves of the World " (Arnold, 1917).

† I usually diverge from the official Romanised spelling of Chinese names, which in all cases seems nicely calculated to give them as they are *not* pronounced.

at us above the vast loëss hills on our right. Here, of course, the climate is cool and alpine, and enormous virgin forests clothe the mountains—a strange sight, after many weeks of bare and arid loëss. This range is one of the enormous ripples in which the Kwun Lûn dies away eastwards into China. It runs roughly parallel to the Min S'an farther north, and between them intervenes a ridge of some 10,000 feet, cutting off the Black Water from the Satanee River. From the heights of the pass at last the big snows came into sight, the Satanee range, on whose final vertebrae we stood, towering away to the left in magnificent peaks and wildernesses of white, while in front, over the intervening mountains, rose the overwhelming mass of Thundercrown, sheer above Siku,—last outbreak of the Min S'an splendours which, to match those of the Satanee, unfolded themselves westward in ever-increasing magnitude far away into the wild heart of Tibet.

All this gorgeous country, being alpine, is despised by the practical-minded Chinese, who abandon it wholly to the savagery of unkempt Border tribes. We had trouble accordingly at Chago, left it hurriedly on 8th May, and by 13th May were ensconced comfortably in a small temple at Satanee, in a friendly village under Chinese sway. From this, however, when we had just begun to get our teeth into the riches of the snowy range, now just opposite, we were driven by a general Jehad organised from Chago by the monks, under the conviction that our investigations were annoying the mountain spirits. The White Wolf was now raging in Kansu, and our position was critical. However, we decided on the least of the many threatened evils, and made straight over the intervening range to Siku, on chance of finding the rumour false that declared the Wolf in full possession and the town sacked.

On 22nd May we entered the storm-tossed little city of Siku, sitting so snug beside the Black Water, embosomed in groves of willow and persimmon, with gaunt and sunburnt hills of loëss all around; and behind, overhead, the colossal impending mass of Thundercrown and the huge ridge in which, after Thundercrown, the Min S'an dies away eastwards as the Satanee range dies away eastwards from Chagola. Reference to a map will show that we were now once more quite near Kiai Chow, having rejoined the Black Water a little farther north-west, and thus described a long and irregular narrow rectangle down through the last descending tip of Kansu. Berezowski, it will be remembered, had visited both the Siku and Satanee districts in 1886, spending the winter zoologising at Satanee; while at Siku they vividly remember him to this day, as having stolen a moon of theirs that lived in a stone and was never seen after his departure. Even the Herbarium yield, however, of the Potanin expeditions, is still for the most part a *rudis indigestaque moles;* these districts have proved very fertile of interesting and beautiful plants, many of which are probably new to herbaria, and yet more of them to cultivation.

Siku, Shi-ho and Wên Hsien were the only three towns of South Kansu left untouched and unvisited by the White Wolf. All the early summer Siku sat secure in utter isolation, cut off from all intercourse with the ravaged outside world, and sufficiently occupied on its own account with repelling

APPENDIX.

invasions from wild Tibetans, who seized the chance of the general anarchy to come up against it from the mountains a few miles west, which, though (like all this border) called " China " and " Szechuan " on maps, are, in reality, pure Tibetan, owing allegiance only to uncontrolled Tibetan princelings or to the august remoteness of Lhasa. In the intervals of repelling these alarms, then, we were able to spend a happy six weeks exploring the fastnesses of Thunder-crown and the great ridge. Thundercrown runs up to some 15,000 feet, and the ridge is little more than a thousand feet lower. Though the conditions are alpine here, and every cloudless day for weeks in succession breeds a thunderstorm in the afternoon (hence the name Lei-Go-S'an—Thundercrown), yet the high Alps feel the influence of the loëss barrens far below, and the Ridge is dry for its altitude—much drier than corresponding elevations in the Satanee range to the south, or the main Min S'an to the north-west, towering as they do over cool woodlands and scantily-cultivated alpine valleys. On the Siku ridge woodland and luxuriance are only found in the huge ravines that disembowel the flanks of the mountain, and finally debouch all together in the wide shingle flat of dead rivers that sweeps down to Siku, where the lost waters of the range all come bubbling up again in springs like diamonds, amid the dappled shade of willow and poplar.

On 6th July we left Siku, rode east some 20 miles down the Black Water, and then struck straight away north, up through the gorges of the South River (the Nan Ho), which here joins the Hei Shui Jang, cutting itself a way down through the last fading battlements of the Min S'an range.

On 10th July we reached Minchow, on the northern side of the Min S'an barrier, in a country now quite changed—of rolling green dish-covery grass downs, with a curious feeling of being in a saucer on the roof of the world. Whereas Siku, home of fig and palm and pomegranate and persimmon, sits sunning itself at 4500 feet, Minchow stands 2000 higher in a cold, damper, and less kindly climate, where palm and pomegranate are strangers. So now we moved westwards, along the Tao River, up to the dilapidated little Tibetan city of Jô-ni, where for some time we fixed, exploring the foothills of the main Min S'an mass, which lies across the river, some 60 miles south, approachable only by long, open, wooded valleys, river-channels from the endless undulating downs of lush hay above on either hand. Here the moist chill summer is much the same as our own, but the winter, of course, is of a far more adamantine hardness. Loëss still lingers on either side of the Tao, but is no longer in evidence in the landscape, which is here, more especially in its upper reaches, of a quite special character, owing to grass only growing on the south side of the folded downs, and forest only on the northern, with a perfectly definite line of cleavage, diversifying the emerald sea of waves, from one aspect, with stripes and rims of darkness ; while from another, a dark world of forest alone appears.

On 21st August I returned alone to Siku for the seed harvest, while Purdom worked in the Tibetan valleys and highlands. He rejoined me at last on 16th September, and after our headman had successfully returned from Wên Hsien with Primula and Pleione, we all adventured back again over the hills to Gahoba and Satanee, pleasantly and placidly exploring the Satanee Alps till at last the alpine winter came crashing finally down on 18th October, and the snowfall drove us back again to sunny, torrid Siku—the change being equivalent to that of Torbole or Garda from the Stelvio. From Siku we made our final ascent of Thundercrown in quest of *Delphinium tanguticum,* and then Purdom hurried north again for odd jobs in the Tibetan Alps, while I remained to finish a few final collections at Siku. On 30th October I also bade a last sad farewell to this delicious little corner of sunshine, and rode northward to join Purdom at a small village nearly opposite Jô-ni, whence on 13th November, the country and the green hills being now all gone brown and sere and dead in winter, we all moved up northward over Lotus Mountain towards Lanchow, there to spend the dead months, after a well-rounded season, in which, after all its storms and stresses, there have been only two downright failures to regret—*Iris Henryi* and *Farreria* Sp.—neither of which was it possible to attempt.

As for such cultural hints as I give, these, of course, are purely conjectural, and based on my local observations. The foregoing itinerary is meant to suggest the various climates of the districts I have this year explored, and the stations given for various plants will serve to identify each with its own conditions. Generally speaking, these northerly ranges should give no such legacy of tenderness as is bequeathed by the warm wet atmospheres of Yunnan and Szechuan that have bred us so many disappointments. The Satanee range has a climate close akin to our own north country conditions, with a very hard winter. Yet harder is the winter and damper the conditions in the vast grasslands of the Min S'an Alps. Between the two lies the hot loëss region of Siku, and it is from there alone that we may expect its plants to want favouring circumstances of drought, heat, sunshine, and a hard stony soil. The Thundercrown ridge, however, with its daily shower, stands far above the circumstances of the hot loëss at its feet; and its children will take the culture of the general high-alpine flora of the Min S'an, to which indeed they belong, though cut off from their kindred upon a remote and insulated mass of limestone. And this last word reminds me of a last caution. For whatever the information may be worth, both the Min S'an and the Satanee range are essentially calcareous, so that, except where a special caution is entered, it may be taken that all the following plants are calcicole in nature.

Adenophora.—These beautiful Campanulads take the place of their august cousins in the alpine grass-lands of Tibet, having all, more or less, the habit of *Campanula rhomboidalis,* though with longer and stiffer displays of bells. One common species has showers of poor little almost globular flowers, with far-protruding style; a second is an improvement, leading on to the next, F 235 (? *A. Potaninii*), a really lovely thing which should be of the easiest culture in any healthy open place. It has crisped, deeply dentate, incanescent foliage, and noble branching panicles of big blue bells, far better furnished and more elegant than in *C. rhomboidalis*. This abounds in the grass-lands of the T'ao River district, colouring the hillsides in August. F 354 is very similar, but appears shorter and stiffer in the spike. It hails from a different district, from the alpine herbage in the valley opposite to Satanee, and I have not seen it in flower. Finally, F 492 will not yet be distributed, as I think it may prove identical with F 235, being from the same region, a pinch of winter seed collected from the dried capsules on the crest of Monk Mountain.

Allium.—In no race are the Alps of Kansu and Tibet more prolific. Of the commoner and cruder sorts I have taken little note, and, even among such as I have considered beautiful, the seed may sometimes yield confusion. F 165 is a narrow-leaved species, with spraying heads of pink stars on stems of about 5 inches in high summer. It abounds in South Kansu, and in the sub-alpine turf above Siku, though it is possible that two species are concealed under one number here. Even more possible is it that even more species may be concealed under F 222, the most important of the lot.

Allium cyaneum.—I greatly suspect that this name embraces several of the lovely bluebell-blue Garlics that so abound all over the Alps of South Kansu and Tibet, dotted freely in the hot alpine herbage (with close heads and colour), or forming mats on the ledges of cool limestone cliffs (with spraying heads of celestial stars), but always and everywhere, even on the highest ridges to which they ascend, objects of greatest charm and elegance and delight in August. It should not be easy to fail at home with *A. cyaneum*, already introduced by Potanin through Petrograd, but never yet fully realised in English gardens. F 258 occurs rather higher than typical *A. cyaneum*, in the alpine turf of the Min S'an. It is not a match for its blue rival, being a Garlic of 5 or 6 inches, with a tight round head of yellow blossoms in July and August. F 304 is not yet capable of distribution; a bulb or two were sent home, but this pretty thing blooms so late in October that I was not able to get more than two or three doubtfully ripe seeds. It is a delightful little species, making a pair to the cliff-haunting form of *A. kansuense;* for it grows only on cool shady ledges of the limestone, where it forms mats and sends up numbers of 3- or 4-inch stems, each carrying a loose, radiant head of a few soft pink stars. This is found about Siku; and about Siku too the last, and perhaps the best, of this year's Garlics. F 305 is a high-alpine, only seen at some 12,000 to 12,500 feet, growing in the upper slopes of the great limestone screes on Thundercrown, in very hard caky loam, overlaid with small chips. It *may* prove only a development of *A. cyaneum*, but I am definitely inclined to believe it a distinct species. It grows in tight little colonies, has long reddish, deep-set bulbs, and rather nodding heads of the loveliest Puschkinia-blue blossoms on stems of 4 inches in mid-August, of colour much paler and softer than in any form of *A. cyaneum* (unless it was a frost which had bitten them into that beauteous pallor). And the last of our blue Garlics is F 321—a most dainty little grassy thing of 4 inches, the whole tuft breaking into a shower of rather dark-blue heads. This was collected by Purdom from shallow shelves of soil in the limestone rocks of Lotus Mountain; blooming in August–September no seed could be got, but its discoverer, ascending the mountain in the snows of February, hacked out three or four tufts from 3 feet of ice. (*A. Purdomii*, Sp. *nova*.)

Antennaria Sp.—A universal moorland wayside weed all over Kansu, with umbels of white everlastings on 8-inch stems, only really silvery and attractive when the seed-fluffs are gone, leaving the naked receptacle a glistering flat star. It is rather a dull rubbish.

Androsace longifolia (F 94).—I gave this plant too high rank among my possibilities. In appearance the most delicate and glorious of high-alpines, it is so far from being alpine at all that it is only found at low elevations in the loëss district, affecting particularly steep and torrid banks of iron-hard loam, or loamy shingle, where it forms wide carpets of splayed-out dark-green rosettes, snowed under in early May with a profusion of stemless big white flowers that give it the effect of an albino *A. alpina* glorified beyond recognition. It is always found by itself, on cliffs and scarps and banks uninhabitable to most other plants, and it never ascends much above 6000 feet, luxuriating on the burning slopes about the Black Water round Siku at 4500 feet. *A. longifolia*, in fact, turns out so lowland a species as never to be either happy or hardy in England by tepid conditions. It is of extraordinary beauty, and though technically a Chamaejasme, because it sometimes has 2 flowers or more to its microscopic stems, usually gives much more the idea of being a specially-superb Aretia, specially lavish in its carpets of flat snow.

A. mucronifolia (F 319) returns to the tradition of the family, and is a very high alpine, never found except in the last fine turf on the crests and ridges at 13,000 to 14,000 feet, along the Min S'an. Here it makes fine clumpy masses of wee rosette-balls, from almost every one of which in August springs a ½-inch scape unfolding a domed round head of some 3 or 4 milk-white flowers with a golden eye, piling each mound of rosettes with snow, and showing the wild sheep of Tibet exactly how hawthorn smells in England. Now that *A. longifolia* has preferred so successful a claim to queen it in gardens over all the Aretias, a place is left vacant for *A. mucronifolia* to take sovereignty over all the villosa-Chamaejasme Group. For indeed it is a supreme loveliness, wholly different in effect from the last. It bloomed, unfortunately, too late for seed to be got, and a pinch of last year's germs collected on Thunder-crown in June were too untrustworthy and few to be distributed ; our hopes at present rest on dormant masses sent home in the winter. (Photograph.)

A. Engleri proves a pretty little Andraspid, exactly like an annual version of *A. carnea*. It constellates with its tiny pink heads the sandy waysides along the enormous levels of the Honan Plain in earliest April.

A. Delavayi has been exhibited at Edinburgh, and so may some day be to be hoped for. It is a lovely Aretia, forming dense masses of tight pilules, beset with stars of soft pink. Its habit and general form (but for the solitary flowers of the Aretia Group) recall *A. mucronifolia;* but yet more closely does it recall our own *A. alpina*, which it replaces in similar situations beside the everlasting snows in the high Alps of Yunnan.

A. tibetica (F 246).—This only doubtfully occurred to me in the Siku

APPENDIX.

district, but becomes abundant as soon as you get north, and up the valley of the Tao River—a lowland species, like *A. longifolia,* never ascending, but delighting to grow on the precipitous lip of loam-banks along the waysides. It is always happy, but does not affect shady aspects; while in the sunny ones that it prefers, it likes best to flop in a cushion from the overhanging loam-cliff, while above it sprout forth a few fine sprays of Aster or Artemisia that keep off the full fury of the sun. I was too late to see it in flower, but it appears to vary between white and pink by all accounts (possibly containing two forms or species). From its lowland habit of pointed-leaved rosettelets, and their generous profusion of well-furnished 3-inch scapes, as doubtful a future in gardens might be foretold for *A. tibetica* as for *A. longifolia,* from exactly the same hot and un-English conditions (and so far suggesting a flattened-out mass of *A. tibetica* as almost to justify its ancient name of *A. sempervivoeides tibetica exscapa*). Figured English specimens seem to me to give no idea of the real beauty and elegance of *A. tibetica*—at least it was long before I could believe that they represented the same species, as I have this year seen it abounding, neat and graceful in habit.

A. tapete (F 128).—Has not yet been collected, as it so exactly mimics *A. helvetica* that no one would be thankful for yet another wool-dowered miff of the Aretia Group. *A. tapete,* however, grows into far larger masses than *A. helvetica,* and is so closely clad in silver grey as almost to have the argent hoar of *A. hirtella.* It is universal in the high limestones above 12,000 feet, hugging the sheer precipices and flawed rock-walls exactly after the style of *A. helvetica.*

Anemone Sp. (F 91).—This is a most magnificent Anemone, clearly in very close alliance to *A. narcissiflora,* and indeed a mere development. It is, however, a far grander plant, forming many yard-wide masses on the *open ledges* of the bare limestone cliffs at 9000 to 11,000 feet, always out of reach, and often impregnable. Here, amid colonies of soft leaves, it emits 8-inch stems, carrying sometimes only 1 flower (in this case as large as in *A. silvestris*), but usually 3 or 4. These are of a clear snow white, shining from afar like arrested flakes of snow, all up and down the enormous precipices of Thundercrown. It is, as I say, no joke to get at, and it seems to have an eccentric way of dropping its carpels green. Nor have its seedlings any tendency to grow or thrive. F 91 I have only noted on Thundercrown; it is purely (and very oddly, for its size and lush, soft habit) a high-alpine of the exposed cliffs, ascending in wizen form to the topmost crests, but never coming lower than some 8500 feet. Its full glory is from the end of May to the end of June.

Anemone vitifolia Var. (F 436).—It is a fashion nowadays to give specific names (such as *hupehensis, moupinensis,* etc.) to all these local developments of universal anemones. For the typical form of Kansu-Tibet I will as yet make no such claim. It is a tall-growing and very luxuriant plant, with a profuse display of rather fat-faced flowers of pale pink, abounding in all hard, hot, and stony places at low elevations throughout South Kansu and up the Tibetan border. It loves river-shingles and sun-baked stony fields, but never affects the woodland.

APPENDIX.

Aquilegia Sp. (F 280).—Quite different from *A. ecalcarata*, as we grow it from Japanese seed ; this should be no other species. It abounds in the sub-alpine river-shingles and coppice of the Kansu-Tibet mountain regions—a dim little quaint dinge, with showers of small chocolate Columbines in June.

Arisaema.—Of these great Aroids, two abound in the rich or stony woodland places of the Siku-Satanee Alps. Of these I believe F 283 to be *A. triphyllum*, and F 420 to be *A. ringens*. The former has 3 big folioles, and makes an impressive sight in deep and sheltered woodland places ; while F 420 has a more elaborate leaf-frill, and the spathe of scarlet fruit is dazzling in the October woodland. Neither, of course, is really choice or specially attractive, but impressive in the right place.

Aruncus Sp. (F 386).—This is a superb thing, precisely replacing *Spiraea Aruncus* in the Alpine copse-fringes, dingles, and hedgerows in the Satanee Alps. It is, however, of much slenderer growth, developing only 2 or 3 stems from the crown, and the blossom panicles, opulent and arching, leave all efforts of *S. Aruncus* far behind, attaining often to a generous yard in length, and even more.

Aster (F 131).—A small, single-flowered high-alpine Aster, which runs happily about in the topmost screes of Thundercrown, with stems of 2 or 3 inches, and gold-eyed purple daisies. The first lot sent under this number covers the far more beautiful and important F 226—a treasure of the same habits and tastes, but with much larger blossoms, occurring on the highest shingle-crests of the main Min S'an. (Painting.)

Aster Sp. (F 156).—This Aster occurs on level and very stony lawns of scant turf just above Siku, in the debouchure of the gorges (and ascending to about 8000 feet in crevices of hot rock-slopes). It forms carpets of smooth-looking, almost glaucous foliage in rosettes, from which spring 6-inch stems in June, carrying a scattered flight of some 4 or 5 large flowers of a very tender pale lavender, so faint as to be almost of a soft grey in effect, as the flowers sheet the distance. But *A. oreophilus* is not winter-hardy in damp English soil.

Aster Sp. (F 173).—This exactly copies *A. diplostephioeides*, but differs in having its 7 or 8-inch stems beset more liberally with quite narrow-pointed leaflets inclining to expand at the base. The large marguerites of rich lavender unfold in July-August, and the upper grass-ridges of Tibet, imperialised in a rippling ocean of these glorious, golden-twinkling Asters, while among them flare the furious flapping scarlet flags of *Meconopsis punicea*, offer a sight that not even the Col de Lautaret can easily efface. F 173 is general on the high grassy lands of the Tibetan border, between 8500 and 11,000 feet, stuntifying into a very concise, neat, large-Astered form on the uppermost turfy summits, where it has a far-off look of *A. alpinus* on far-off hills. (*A. limitaneus*, Sp. *nova*.)

Aster Sp. (F 174) is more local than the last. I have seen it rare in the Tibetan valley of Mirgo, here and there among the grass, and very abundant in the alpine hay of the Bao-u-go Valley, at some 10,500 feet, never seeming to ascend to the wind-ruffled heights of the great ridges above, where F 173 is no less happy. It is a superb beauty, recalling *A. Falconeri* in the profusion of its especially long and narrow rays of deeper violet-blue than in the broad-rayed lavender face of F 173. The leaves are rather long and narrow, too— soft and rather pointed; leaflets sit alternately up the stout 12 to 15-inch stem, and the whole plant is green and hairy. The single flower is enormous, with an eye of intense vermilion orange, clouded round by a Saturn's ring of chaffy fluff. Its fringy, ragged grace is after a very different carelessly regal style of magnificence from the rather smug and fat-faced complacency of lovely F 173. (*A. Farreri*, Sp. *nova*.)

Aster Sp. (F 131), a sufficiently dear and dainty little alpine Aster, occupies the upper screes of Thundercrown; but further north-west, in the heart of the range, its place is taken by F 226, a jewel pre-eminent among the best, with much larger golden-eyed purple marguerites piercing everywhere on their 3-inch stems, from the gaunt shingle-slopes of the upmost Min S'an. This little plant is hairier (especially at the base), with a grey pubescence, and the basal leaves in F 131 are usually more spatulate and clearly-stalked. None the less, and allowing for the floral super-eminence of F 226, I fancy that they might both prove forms or developments of one species; standing to each other as does Primula No. 22, from the main range, to Primula No. 10, an outlying type from the isolated and outlying mass of Thundercrown, which has also bred Aster F 131.

Aster Sp. (246).—We now move into the group of *A. acris*. All the warm bare loëss banks, hedge-cliffs, and city embankments from Jô-ni away down the South River Valley (not extending to Siku) are coloured in early July with this Aster, which forms a tight, neat-domed bush of many stiff and sturdy stems about 1 foot or 18 inches high, and twice as much across; solid all over with domed heads of little lilac-lavender stars, making a rare effect of rich colour and concise, almost artificial, tidiness. (*A. Thunbergii;* rather tender.)

Aster Sp. (F 200).—This abounds on the hottest, barest loëss hills and stony torrid slopes about Siku. It is woody at the base, intricate and very fine and wiry in leaf and habit, forming low filmy, heathlike masses, beset with little lavender Asters of great charm in August and September. Whether the number includes two species or not I cannot be certain, as the plant's true character is hard to decipher, owing to its always being so pitilessly cropped by goats on those Saharan hills. It is not, as thus seen, brilliant, but may prove much more so in goatless gardens; and anyhow, even at its most hard-bitten, has the fine and feathery charm of *Felicia abyssinica*. Seed has been collected from the best forms only. (*A. hispidus;* rather tender.)

Aster Sp. (F 455).—Seems like a much glorified version of the last, from similar hot situations farther down the Black Water. It is probably nearer, however, to *A. turbinellus*, forming low, wiry, half-decumbent masses, with profusion of large and brilliant flowers in October, on very long, stiff pedicels. Seed from the finest forms only.

Aster Sp. (F 456).—This replaces F 246 in the Siku district, blooming six weeks later, at the beginning of September. It is notably Galatelloid, with

APPENDIX.

fewer stems than in F 246, forming no bush and set with broader foliage of glaucescent tone. The flower-heads are lax, the flowers comely and of a thick and chalky lavender. Its height is from 6 to 8 inches, and its beauty conspicuous and serene. Treatment, &c., as for F 246. (*A. sikuensis*, Sp. *nova;* not hardy.)

Aster Sp. (F 458).—A rather weedy wayside Aster about Gahoba, whose very brilliant flowers, however, may look much better when the mass grows under good culture, to a thick clump of soft, greyish stems of 10 to 14 inches. I find some of these "back-end" Chinese Asters intensely puzzling; each district seems to have its own form of what is, probably, one pervasive species. There is a straggling Michaelmas Daisy with the habit of a poor *A. Thomsoni*, from cool, damp groves and rill-sides about Siku, which may have affinities with F 458; as, indeed, may also F 455, though this is less likely, as the affinities of F 455 are rather with F 290.

Chinese Asters of 1914.

Alpine Group	F 131, F 226	Acris Group	F 246, F 456
Diplostephioid Group	F 173, F 174	Turbinelloid Group	F 290, F 455

Astilbe Sp. (F 385) is possibly only *A. Davidi.* It was abundant in a small stretch in the cool stony bottom of the great Siku gorge. The only flower-spike, however, that I saw opening (and a mutilated one at that) seemed to be of a pale soft pink. F 384 abounded in the alpine open turf above the Da-hai-go in the Satanee range, and is perhaps the same, though its habit seemed a trifle larger, and its spike (all I saw of it) longer and heavier.

Boea hygrometrica Sp. (F 261) is very general throughout the hotter lower loëss region of South Kansu, haunting the cooler vertical faces of black primary rock (or hollows round the feet of boulders) all up the course of the Black Water, always in a strictly horizontal position, and there making a precise copy of *Jankaea Heldreichii* in the flat and shaggy silver-haired rosette, until in July up spring a number of naked 4-inch scapes, each expanding into a loose flight of pendant little narrow Streptocarpus-flowers, of Streptocarpus lavender, most beautifully contrasting with the shining silver rosette below. It is a thing of the greatest charm and daintiness, and ought to prove a treasure for our gardens in typical Ramondia-places and attitudes, in the cooler walls of the rock-garden, not exposed to excessive rain, and apparently preferring non-calcareous rock. There is a wee relation of this, not collected, with rare scapes of an inch from rosettes of an inch wide, which I have only once seen, forming enormous flat masses and curtains on certain cliffs just beyond Wên Hsien above the White Water, where it grows all curled and wizzled with the drought. (Flower unknown.) (*Boea* does not prove at all winter-hard in England.)

Callianthemum Sp. (F 73).—This, as collected in May from damp cool ledges in the Satanee Alps, had low outspreading foliage, very glaucous and beautiful, with outlying stems of 2 to 3 inches, and very large flowers of a most melting China-blue, suggesting a discarnate *Anemone blanda*. The seed sent out under this number was collected from a plant of precisely similar habit, abounding in the earthier parts of the big limestone screes on Thundercrown; I have none but a philosophic doubt that they should prove identical. Seed is very hard to get; the carpels fall while yet green, and you have to quest around each clump to detect the green nutlings lurking here and there in the chinks of the shingle; and then the catching them becomes an agitating business, for if not caught at the first pounce, they dive deeper and deeper among the pebbles every moment, and are soon completely buried from view. So hard are these wee nuts, and so evident their purpose in dropping prematurely, in order that the husk may wilt and rot below ground, and give the nucleus full time to sprout, that in the artificial conditions of the garden it would be well, I think, cautiously to split open the nut, and extract the kernel to be sown. (*C. Farreri*, Sp. *nova*.)

Cimicifuga Sp. (F 445).—This very superb thing lives luxuriant in the alp-meadows about Jô-ni, and far up into the Tibetan highlands, extending southeast to the Thundercrown gorges, where it is rare and poorer in the drier circumstances. The basal volume of foliage is ample, sumptuous, glossy, and splendid; from this arise in August the stately stems of 6 to 7 feet, deploying a great foaming spout of cream-white blossom in a broken panicle, suggesting *Spiraea Aruncus* on a quadrupled scale of glory. This will clearly repay the very richest conditions of culture, in a moist but sunny spot. (Can it be *C. racemosa ?*)

Convolvulus Sp. (F 99).—Such a very lovely little mound of silver-grey thorns this is, starred in June with inset blossoms of the softest hot, clear pink, perfectly clean and pure. It is a dense hedgehog, usually of about 4 inches high and 8 to 10 inches across; but, where safe from goats, occasionally doubling its dimensions, and developing quite a woody trunk. No Levantine could be lovelier; it lives on the hottest, driest slopes of the hot, dry loëss hills about the Black Water, and is not hardy. (*C. tragacanthoeides*.)

Corydalis Sp. (F 113).—This is one of the much-boomed Chinese Corydalids of late years—a lush rank mass of blue adiantoid foliage, with tall spikes of pallid yellow flowers and a noxious stink. I cannot admire it; it especially affects the slag-dump-like avalanches of filth that here and there descend in cataracts of unpleasant, slimy chaos from the hills about Siku.

Corydalis Sp. (F 37) is general all up the Boreler, in beck-shingles and alpine turf and scrub-edges. It is a weakly, gracious thing of annual look, about 6 inches high, with scant fine leafage, and flower-spires of the most dazzling pure azure, occasionally varying to straw-colour. Unfortunately, seed of Corydalis is often hard to catch on the hop, and I have not yet succeeded in getting any of this beauty. (*C. curviflora*.)

Corydalis Sp. (F 254) lives only in the topmost screes of the great mountains, huddling close with fat and lovely leafage of glaucous-blue, emerging from which unfold large heads of very large flowers of pure white, but lipped and helmed with sky-blue, and with a black eye. It smells most deliciously, too, of Lily-of-the-Valley, and its tuffets of sky and snow make a wonderful effect as they dot those gaunt arêtes of the Min S'an in August, amid the hovering velvet butterflies of *Delphinium tanguticum*. Seed was unluckily not procurable ; our hope depends on dormant tubers sent home in the winter, and ere long to be distributed, if all goes well. (It didn't; this is *C. melanochlora*.)

Corydalis Sp. (F 418) is a version of F 113, living on the loëss cliffs round Minchow, and differing for the better in having larger flowers of a clear, decisive yellow. There is not yet enough seed to distribute, as almost all the pods were discharged by the time I got back to Minchow. (I take no count here of various other species seen—gawky, dull weeds, lush and ephemeral, of no value except for the Herbarium.)

Cotoneaster Sp. (F 148).—This is perhaps the most important of all. I have only seen it at one point, in the limestone bottom of the great Siku gorge, where, growing and resting and re-rooting as it goes, in almost pure limestone silt, it ramps perfectly tight and flat along the floor, moulding each boulder in its embrace, and developing a carpet many yards across of refulgently glossy and apparently evergreen rounded foliage, among which glows in September and October a richly-scattered profusion of brilliant scarlet fruits like holly-berries peppered over a lucent ground-willow, with here and there the amber leaves of autumn enhancing the sombre gloss of the carpet's green and the flashing wealth of its bejewelment of berries. These were red and ripe on 28th August ; they were yet larger, redder, and more brilliant still at the latest back-end of October. It is *C. Dammeri radicans*. In any case it is certainly new to my experience, and should prove a prize of most special preciousness, whether for its own beauty, sheeting a slope, or as covert for delicate Daffodil and Crocus.

? **Cremanthodium** Sp. (F 10) has pretty little kidney-shaped leaves, and single golden senecio-stars on stems of 4 to 5 inches in March to April. It abounds in all cool and mossy places of the sub-alpine woodland throughout South Kansu. The seed, however, eluded our notice.

? **Cremanthodium** Sp. (F 212) lives in cool moist ledges under limestone cliffs (such as cry aloud for Soldanella) at high elevations in the Min S'an. Its glossy foliage is beautifully crenelate, and it carried several bell-shaped yellow flowers to a 6-inch stem (thereby making its name yet more doubtful) in August.

? **Cremanthodium** Sp. (F 239) is, I believe, merely the last, repeated under a new number, unless it be a different and divergent form with more flowers. This cannot yet be distributed.

Cypripedium Sp. (F 58 and F 85).—This is the great Red Slipper of the sub-alpine slopes and copses all up the Border, peculiarly magnificent near Satanee, on loose soil of a coppice, burnt out some two seasons ago. These Slippers in the relationship of *C. ventricosum-speciosum* are still very obscure and tangled : whether this be *C. Franchetti* or *C. fasciolatum*, or neither or both, I cannot yet pretend to discern. It is a plant of stout and leafy stem, from the upper foliage of which escapes the voluminous baggy blossom, densely

APPENDIX.

lined in rose-crimson on a dead-white ground, and with a pouch of deeper flush. Striking as is this bloom, there is a Cypripedium, form or species, occurring rarely in the Siku gorges (where the common leafy stalwart does not appear) which yet surpasses it—a thing of smaller, slighter growth with few leaves, and those near the base of the 8-inch stem, leaving free play to a long and rather woolly peduncle supporting an *enormous* bulge-bagged blossom of very much deeper colour, especially in the uniform maroon crimson of the inflated round lip (? *C. fasciolatum*). This is represented only by specimens and a painting; of the others I sent home pods to an orchidist to raise. (The last is *C. tibeticum.*)

Cypripedium luteum (F 138) is a most glorious plant, precisely copying *C. Reginae* (*C. spectabile*) in all points of stature, amplitude, and habit, but that the comely round flowers are of a clear yellow, with a waxen sulphur lip. The segments are sometimes mottled with a few fleshy stains, the lip is freckled within, and the staminode in some forms, but not all, is, or goes, of a rich chocolate which gives Proud Margaret her especial look of well-fed intelligence. The Red Slippers haunt the scrub and copse edges up to about 8000 feet, and there begins *C. luteum*, occasionally joining them, but beginning thus at the top of their distribution, and ascending for nearly 1000 feet higher. We saw it in bud amid the overblown Red Slippers opposite Satanee in the end of May, and peasants, seeing us pick the red ones (which are powerful magic) told us also of the yellow; in the Siku gorges the plant occurs handsomely, and Purdom has a record of it from a wood beyond Minchow. It grows behind Siku, in sudden outbursts: here a great patch, or an abundant colony, and then no more. Usually it likes a half-shady slope, in and out among scant scrub on the edge of a glade; but I have seen it magnificent in shallow moss and mould on the top of a boulder in dense fir-tree shade; while one of the finest and yellowest drifts of all was growing in hard fibrous loam among coarse turf in fullest sun; while in the loose, burnt humus opposite Satanee it was trying to rival *C. californicum* in stature. From all this it should result that Proud Margaret should easily, in any fair conditions, impart an ample share of pride to her possessor, so long as he remembers that, for all her resemblance in style to *C. Reginae*, she is *not* a bog-plant like the Queen-Slipper, but a haunter of light woodland fringes in the cool well-watered Alps of China. Dormant crowns of this have been copiously sent, and I hope the Sleeping Beauty will ere long satisfactorily awake. (But she never did.)

Cypripedium Sp. (F 139) has not been sent. It is a wee, running thing, with pairs of leaves, and stems about 2 inches high, and green-segmented half-open tiny flowers, with a lip of brilliant waxy gold, whelked and warted and buckled like Bardolph's nose. It careers about occasionally in mossy grass in opener places of the mountain woodland, in such close association with *C. luteum* as often to run in and out among its stems. It has not only the exotic look of a wee Catasetum, but a Catasetum's heavy and cloying exotic scent of aromatics. I only noted it once, in the Siku gorges. (*C. Bardolphianum*, Sp. *nova*.)

APPENDIX.

Cypripedium margaritaceum is a very rare species, occurring on almost pure limestone in pine-woods of the Mekong district. It is stemless as *C. acaule*, with a pair of ridgy purple-blotched leaves, from which arises a 4 to 5-inch penduncle, carrying a waxen morbid bloom of yellowishness beclouded with maroon, and covered in shining purple hairs. The lip is long and of a less copiously maculate yellow.

Daphne Sp. (F 11) (? *D. tangutica*).—This is abundant all over South-West Kansu, from Shi-ho away to Siku, in the lowest alpine zone, amid very light scrub, and usually preferring a slightly-shaded cool aspect in soil that may be yellow loam, or mould, or turfy peat, or limestone detritus. It ascends to some 7500 to 8000 feet on the moorland ridges above Ga-hoba, and above Siku is as finely developed among the calcareous *débris* at the debouchure of gorges as is *D. alpina* among that about the Lago di Loppio. It forms a neat, rounded, low bush, about 15 to 24 inches high, and rather more across, with the foliage, and after the style of, a small *D. indica*; and the masses of lilac-pale blossom appear in April, filling the air with fragrance, especially (as it seemed to me) in the later afternoon, and followed at the end of June by a brilliant clustered show of glowing vermilion fruits.

Delphinium Sp. (F 253).—Referring to "The English Rock-Garden," I find that *D. tanguticum* stands closely related to *D. caucasicum*, and, from the similarity of their styles and sites, I therefore have to conclude that F 253 is *D. tanguticum* and no other. It is a noble beauty, confined to the limestone and shalestone screes along the upmost gaunt arêtes in the Min S'an extending down to Thundercrown. Through the shingle it threads and spreads, and over all the grim slope hovers in August a flight, as it seems, of enormous violet-purple butterflies, flitting close over the stones, with wide-fluttering silken wings, and a black eye, and a body furred with white and gold. These single-flowered 2-inch scree Delphiniums are none of them known as yet in cultivation; they make an absolutely new tradition of beauty in their race, and should be at home perennially in the moraine. Of the larger species so abundant up and down the Border, I will not here speak; none, I think, offer any really valuable contribution to the garden. F 243, however, of which one rather doubtful pod was secured on Thundercrown, is another high-alpine species of the screes, with some 2 or 3 flowers on a low-squatting stem among the foliage, and, though large, of a rather indeterminate lilac-purple, with a rather dulling downiness of pubescence on their parts. (F 253, in the garden, tends to grow gawky and pallid.)

Dianthus.—This race is very ill-represented in the Tibetan Alps. *D. squarrosus*, or a species closely akin to it (F 389), abounds in the upper grasslands, while on Lotus Mountain, low down, occurs a small red-flowered Clusterhead (F 352).

Dicranostigma Sp. (F 1) is a Great Celandine, abounding on precipitous field-banks and walls of the loëss right away from Honan to the Tibetan border. It makes a very handsome basal rosette of richly glaucous-lobed foliage, like a blue Ceterach, from which arises a profusion of stems in April, showering forth golden-yellow Poppies over a long period, in sprays of some 8 to 12 inches high.

Disporon pullum (F 60) is a singularly beautiful woodland treasure, first seen on the Feng S'an Ling, and thence abounding sporadically throughout the lower alpine forests of the Satanee-Gahoba district. It has all the branching habit of a Streptopus, and grows about 10 to 12 inches high, hanging out clusters of the most exquisite waxy Lapageria-blossoms, with golden anthers. These ring out their chimes in mid-May, and the growth afterwards develops and expands a little, replacing the flowers with bloomy black-blue berries in October. Obviously the treatment of Streptopus and Polygonatum ought handsomely to satisfy a beauty so nearly related, and delighting in the same rich, cool, woodland conditions. Its effect is, indeed, more that of Uvularia ; most unluckily, though the seed of this lovely plant was all good, none of it, so far as I know, germinated.

Farreria Sp. (F 19a), (*novum genus*, Balf. fil.), or *Wikstroemia Farreri* (Balf. fil.), is a singularly lovely little ground Daphne, with clusters of bright citron-yellow flowers, twice met with on the high, bare loëss downs of South Kansu, April 18 and April 20. Unfortunately seed could not be got, and roots were un-negotiable. There is another species, F 71, brilliantly golden, but of quite inferior merit, which abounds in rocks and dry coarse alpine turf on the Satanee ranges, between 7500 and 9000 feet ; this also appears so shy in seed that none could be found, though occasionally, as on burnt-out ribs of rock, its evidence was plain, in small compact young plants.

Gentiana Sp. (F 25) is abundant all over South Kansu and the Tibetan Border, ascending to 8000 feet, and luxuriating in any open, sunny position wet or dry, but especially profuse in river-shingles and fallow fields. In its second year the seedling forms a glossy crown, like that of some stout *G. verna*, and in the third this becomes from March to November an endless display of bright azure stars on long tubes. The ovary matures at the tip of an exaggeratedly protruded style, as the flower withers ; its two lips quickly gape, and the seed is gone. This fashion seems common among the better Gentians of the Border.

Gentiana Sp. (F 217).—This number covers a most beautiful Gentian, very abundant in the higher alpine turf of the Min S'an, where it literally turns the turf to a sea of blue with the profusion of its pale clear water-blue trumpets, most delicately lined with darkness on their outside, and poising each singly at the end of the whorled-foliaged stems that spring in such masses from the crown. The species either varies or includes two species. Seed sent as F 217 was for the most part collected on Thundercrown ; the Min S'an type is to all intents and purposes the same, but differs conspicuously in having a very much larger ovary. This last has also been sent as F 332. Seed is borne as in the last, and the heyday of the bloom is in August. (*G. hexaphylla :* a success.)

Gentiana Sp. (F 220).—This is quite like *G. frigida*, but taller and in every way better developed, growing about 8 inches high, with 6 or 8 large long straw-coloured trumpets in August. It is general all along the line of

APPENDIX.

the Min S'an, from 11,000 to 14,000 feet, growing for choice in the cool alpine turf, usually on steeper barer banks than those affected by the luxuriant mossy-looking masses of F 217. Seed very doubtful, and not distributed.

Gentiana Sp. (F 267).—Unfortunately blooms too late in September for seed to have been got. It grows only on rock towards the highest summits, between 12,000 and 15,000 feet, and there forms wads of foliage like *Melandryum Elizabethae*, close on which lie stemless the *enormous* trumpets of lavender blue.

Gentiana Sp. (F 303) stands close to *G. Kurroo*. It is, however, rather smaller, and more leafy, with flowers much more numerous along the flopping 6- to 8-inch stems in September, rather smaller, and of an intense rich sapphire velvet. It grows all along by the waysides, in the banks and little level lawns beside the road in the Jô-ni district, not ascending above 8000 feet, and hugging always the flatter places of the loëss region, in such hard dry loam and in such open sunny places as those preferred by *G. cruciata*. (*P. Purdomii*, Sp. *nova*.)

Gentiana Sp. (F 332) represents the large-ovaried species from the Min S'an, of which the Thundercrown development has been sent out as F 217. (This proves *G. Farreri*, the glory of 1915.)

Gentiana Sp. (F 442) comes from the Min S'an grass-lands, and was harvested by a Chinese collector. No more can be said; it is perhaps one of the hideous cluster-headed Gentians of the Macrophylla-mongolica Group that so abound in the Chinese Alps, and are yearly collected in huge bales for "medicine."

Gentiana Sp. (F 443) is a pretty annual, from the high alpine turf all along the Min S'an. From its frail crown it sends out a few frail prostrate sprays, supporting at intervals, perfectly erect, very long-tubed five-pointed stars of clear straw yellow, of charming effect among the grass in August.

Geranium Sp. (F 201).—There are many field Geraniums up and down the grass-lands of Tibet, but none of them likely to be of any garden value—rather weedy herbaceous things for the most part, akin to *G. sylvaticum*. F 201, however, is of quite a different kidney—being a high-alpine species, found only in the topmost screes of shale or limestone at 13,000 to 15,000 feet, where it abounds in such masses as to cover the whole vast expanse of desolation with the fluttering flights of its innumerable big flowers of palest pink in August, crowded on footstalks of 2 or 3 inches, all over the concise clump of each plant, making mounds of soft pallor all up and down the desolation. In effect it approaches nearest to *G. argenteum*, but is much neater, much more lavishly be-blossomed, and in colour of an even paler and more evanescent pink. It is the only important Min S'an alpine which does not seem to extend down to Thundercrown; and its season is so awkward that it was only after great difficulty and exertion that two seeds were hacked up out of the ice-locked adamant of the mountain in autumn. Runners, however, have also been sent, and it is to be greatly hoped may survive the journey. (Photograph.)

Hedysarum Sp. (F 103) occurs in big stretches down the river-shingles of the Black Water, between Kiai Chow and Wên Hsien, but its main distribution seems higher up, about Siku, where it luxuriates on the hot, hard, bare, and shingly hills of loëss about the town, and even wanders north about a day's journey up the Nan Ho. It is a most beautiful plant, forming low masses of glaucescent foliage from a woody trunk, from which rise foot-high racemes, very graceful and delicate, beset with large blossoms of rose-purple-crimson in a long and elegant flight. Its bloom is in May, and the prickly rough burrs that hold the seed await the frosts of November before they dry up and fall. (*H. multijugum.*)

Incarvillea Sp. (F 34).—With greatest uncertainty did I here include this plant, which stands away from Incarvillea in having very minute seeds, wadded up in white fluff in long and very narrow pods (*Amphicomearguta*). It is a most handsome thing, herbaceous from a huge woody stock, with straight 2-foot stems set with voluminous glossy foliage, and ending in big flights of lovely rose-pink little Allamandas, clear and brilliant, in May. This I have only once seen, and only in the hottest of walls and stony banks in the hot and parching region about Wên Hsien, on the banks and embankments of the White Water.

Incarvillea Sp. (F 89) lives in the hot limestone ledges of the Thunder-crown foothills at 7000 to 8000 feet. It is magnificent in flower, and probably is *I. compacta.* Unfortunately, all seed had fallen by the time our collecting began.

Incarvillea Sp. (F 97) has weakly branches of a foot or so, set with finely feathered ferny foliage, and bearing from May to November a steady flight of lovely citron-yellow Allamandas. Its home is round Siku, on the very walls themselves, and on the hottest and driest and barest exposures on the hot, bare, dry loëss hills about the town. (*I. Przewalskyi fumariaefolia*, or new species.)

Incarvillea Sp. (F 268).—This may be the same as F 89, but has quite a different taste in habitats, not haunting ledges of rock, but open broad patches of soil by the track-side ascending over the foothills of Monk Mountain. It is reported a superb rose-red *I. compacta* cousin, and the seed-scapes are 8 to 12 inches in height. I can say no more ; *ipse non vidi :* coll. W. Purdom.

Indigofera Sp. (F 266) is but doubtfully Indigofera at all. It is a perfectly prostrate trailing plant, sending out from its crown 3 or 4 branching naked-looking sprays of 12 to 30 inches long, hugging the ground, and densely set in late August with very brilliant crimson-purple blossoms that suggest a much improved and flatly repent *Cytisus purpureus.* This lovely thing occurs in the Nan Ho Valley, and abounds all over the hot loëss hills about Siku, on steep banks, and at the edges of stony fields, paths, etc.

Indigofera Sp. (F 312) is one of the loveliest. It haunts only the hottest, barest, driest, stoniest slopes of the torrid downs about the Black Water, where it forms neat and very dense, intricate, woody bushlets of 6 to 8 inches high and twice as much through, spinous and stiff, lacy with elegant tiny leafage, and hanging out pairs of little pea-flowers of brilliant rose-pink in June, along the many brief pungent sprays. Goats, despite its spininesses, keep it sedulously cut into shape ; it especially loves to have plenty of stone and shingle in its loam, and luxuriates beneath the Akropolis of Siku, where the rude forefathers of the hamlet lie for centuries exposed, each in his collapsing coffin of wood, poised among the Indigoferas upon the pebbly slope of the hill.

Iris Sp. (F 19) (*I. Henryi*) is a charming little grassy frailty that runs about in the coarse hot turf, midway on the blazing hills about Kiai Chow, and in April decks their gullies with a galaxy of milky-white (or sometimes palest blue) Moraea-flowers, giving the whole effect of Triteleias, but with a peacock-eye to the fall. Unfortunately, even if seed is set, it was not possible this year to procure any.

Iris Sp. (F 29) is a type of the ensate Iris which forms by mats all over the loëss downs and path-sides of China, with thin flowers of blue on 4-inch scapes in April. Several of the later numbers may refer to this species, or to others closely allied in the same group.

Iris Sp. (F 124) (*I. goniocarpa*), if it does not include two distinct species, begins first in the rock-ledges of the Feng-S'an Ling above Wên Hsien, is seen below the town on hot bare banks outside the wall, and again on rock-ledges and in and out among scant scrub above Chago—a grassy lovely Iris, suggesting a smaller *I. unguicularis*, with the brindlings and feline mottlings of *I. tectorum* over its broad and crested lavender falls. But it then, if the same, erupts in enormous abundance over the mid-alpine turf of Thundercrown, from 10,500 to 12,000 feet, enamelling all the sward with its delicate flowers. Abundant as it is, however, this plant marks a comparative failure. The summer was torrid, the pods were gone before we guessed, and instead of millions of seed we only acquired a dozen or so, not yet distributed. F 270, however, marks an obscure Iris, which may or may not be this, collected by Chinese retainers in the main Min S'an, where this species, if it exists, was long over before we got there.

Iris Sp. (F 90) (*I. goniocarpa*) occurs at lower elevations than the last on the same Thundercrown turf, filling the much coarser longer grass on the hot dry slopes at 7000 to 8000 feet, often, in opener places, developing quite a fan of grassy foliage, with dozens of fine 6-inch stems, each balancing a single lovely flower with lavender standard-blade and a fall of waxen pure white, heavily margined and mottled with richest violet velvet. Even worse luck have we so far had with this; arduous and prolonged research yielded only three capsules, and in these only two seeds still preserved a promise of vitality (May–June).

Iris Sp. (F 177) is a cousin of *I. prismatica* from the highest grass-ridges of Tibet, with rather thin flowers of plum-colour and dark blue in August, from its fine dark grassy nets of foliage.

Iris Sp. (F 276) lives on the hottest bare banks of loëss about Siku, and again crops out in the Nan Ho Valley. It is a strange Moraeoid species, with fans of broad tectorum-like leafage, and tall, very graceful branching stems of 12 to 24 inches, displaying erect flowers, rather small and fugacious, of velvety texture and greyish tone, the falls being mottled with hazel-brown on a pale background. It blooms in July–August and is soon ripe in seed.

Iris Sp. (F 413) is a small species from level loëss pans on the Akropolis of Siku. It belongs to the type of F 29, but seems much littler and slighter in every

APPENDIX.

part, with flowers (unknown) springing almost stemless from the crown, 2 or 3 often on 1 welded scape.

Iris Sp. (F 414) is a relation of F 29, abounding on the bare loëss in the open valley-bottoms of the Tibetan ranges opposite Jô-ni, at some 9,500 to 10,000 feet. Its lingering flowers in August were blended of blue and white, and offer good hope that the plant may prove as valuable as it is certainly floriferous. (*I. Farreri*, Sp. *nova*.)

Iris Sp. (F 415) was collected by our Chinese headman as being the same as F 19, which is no more nor less than *I. tectorum* (abounding in huge masses all over the cool grassy downs between Shi-ho and Foo-er-gai), but the fat and purfled pods he brought seem to me in many ways so distinct from those of *I. tectorum* that I can but send it out with this caution, though I am unable to suggest what else it might be, especially as it was not collected in the tectorum district.

Isopyrum grandiflorum (F 96) is so universally abundant in all the cool high-alpine limestone cliffs as to have been, in the end, but too slackly collected this year—especially as its seeds are so minute and its capacious capsules so capricious. Such seed as is distributed will want most careful raising. The species is very beautiful, with cushions of tiny columbine foliage, and big golden-hearted flowers that are not blue, as often said, but of a dense waxen texture, and milk or skim-milk colouring, only rarely deepening to any blue tone. *Isopyrum* Sp. (F 293) cannot yet be sent out. It occurs in the Monk Mountain district (flower unknown) and differs from *I. grandiflorum* in greener rather larger foliage, and in a distinctly bigger rounder seed. *Ipse non vidi :* coll. W. Purdom. (*I. Farreri* beats all, and was introduced in 1915.)

"Kennedya" Sp. (F 184).—This absurd name I apply for convenience, as nothing else so paints the effect of this plant, with several wiry 10- to 12-inch stems in August springing from the crown, and ejecting on fine peduncles, rich racemes of brilliant blue violet peaflowers from all the upper axils, more brilliant yet for their rich red-purple calyces. It is abundant throughout the alpine grass-lands of Tibet, extending south into the Satanee range. (*Vicia unijuga*.)

Leontopodium alpinum, the common type of the European Alps, is an abundant wayside weed over all the loëss lands of South Kansu, but there are at least two sub-species or forms of much greater merit from more alpine stations.

Lloydia Sp. (F 87) (*Ll. alpina*) has not yet been sent. It is lovely in all the cold crevices of the higher limestone cliffs, swinging out glassy bubble-bells of pearly white with dark lines, larger and fuller, and much more beautifully borne, than in *Ll. serotina*. (Sent in 1915.)

Lychnis Sp. (F 265) abounds in hedgerows and waysides down the Nan Ho Valley and even across the Black Water, and up to some 7000 feet in the foothills of Thundercrown. It is like a gigantic Ragged Robin of 2 or 3 feet, making a lovely haze of rose amid the pale-blue swathes of Adenophora, with *Lilium tigrinum* flashing out in blots of orange fire. (*Silene Fortunei*.)

APPENDIX.

Meconopsis.—I do not know the authority or diagnosis of *M. Wardii*, but the two following Poppies are both clearly new since Fedde's monograph in the *Pflanzenreich*, and I cherish hope accordingly that one certainly, and both probably, may prove to be distinct new species. Both are biennial, both belong to the Primulina Group, both stand at the Delavayi-end of that group, and both appear to be of very limited range.

Meconopsis Sp. (F 123) (*M. lepida*, Sp. *nova*) inhabits the upper alpine banks and ledges on Thundercrown, markedly preferring the cooler westerly aspects. It is not found in the open turf, but often occurs at its fringes round the base and up the gullies of little limestone outcrops in the huge grassy flanks of the mountain at 12,500 feet, not steadily abounding, but appearing in sporadic outbursts. It is a most lovely little biennial of some 4 to 8 inches, with all the narrow, rather glaucous foliage at the base, and the naked stem carrying from 1 to 6 large flowers, made up of some 6 to 11 rhomboidal petals of lavender purple silk, arranged in a whirling catherine-wheel round the creamy crowded boss of stamens. These flaunt their frail and filmy loveliness in June; unfortunately by the end of August the seed was so unanimously fallen that barely enough could be collected for distribution in even the smallest quantities. However, it should germinate well, and must then be copiously raised again; nothing more daintily beautiful exists in the race, as you see its great whirling heads poised delicately amid the fine grasses, the golden Gageas and Fritillaries, the innumerable purple Irids that enamel the grassy rocky ribs of Thundercrown. (The Dainty Poppy.)

Meconopsis integrifolia (F 92) is very magnificent and portly in the highest turf of Thundercrown, standing stiffly up in early June with its huge lemon-pale globes in sumptuous but rather graceless and gawky candelabra of colour. Here, as I say, it loves the long high-alpine hay at some 12,000 to 13,000 feet, and is found in no other situation but over all the open flanks of the grassy slopes, where its bloom is at its height before the herbage is well up, while still the Alps are sere and brown. No meadow, however, is too coarse for it; and, at its lower limit, at some 7500 to 8000 feet, it luxuriates amid the coarsest tangle of tall Asters and Berberids, the Asters, in September, enclosing the huge upstanding pods of the Poppy in a lush jungle of leafage and blossom. (The Lampshade Poppy.)

Meconopsis quintuplinervia (F 118) has already been figured in the *Chronicle* from an *in situ* photograph on Thundercrown. It is indeed a gracious and lovely thing, with its single bell-shaped flowers of softest lavender-blue swinging high upon their bare stems above the group of pale-haired, greyish foliage crowded in the turf below. The supremely important point about *M. quintuplinervia*, however, is that it is undoubtedly perennial, and thus forms a grand addition to the garden, where there is as yet no perennial Meconopsis except *M. grandis* and *M. cambrica*. This beautiful treasure inhabits the finer (as a rule) alpine turf of Kansu-Tibet border, between 9000 and 13,000 feet. We first met it, still dormant, amid the snows on Chago-ling; on Thundercrown and all up the Min S'an it abounds, as also, in amazing profusion, in the northerly ranges of the Da-Tung. In the Minchow district it trenches on cultivated land, and there, at the edges of culture-patches on the rounded green hills, it becomes quite unrecognisably splendid in the steep enriched embankments down the slope, waxing into masses of foliage a foot across and almost as deep, with 40 or 50 great swaying vases of lavender all hovering at once, on 1 or 2 feet stems, above the tangle of leaves below—thus making it evident that *M. quintuplinervia*, while it should answer happily to fair alpine cultivation, should also be handsomely responsive to specially generous treatment. It blooms from June to August; on Thundercrown there was a notable little rocky grot which in June was filled with a rose-scented jungle of rose-pink Peonies, above and amid which floated the innumerable expanded blue butterflies of the Poppy. The number of petals, though usually 4, can often be 6; and it may be noted that the original diagnosis seems to have been made from specimens smaller than the usual type of *M. quintuplinervia*, and far inferior to the best. (The Harebell Poppy.)

Meconopsis Prattii (F 136).—Seed was distributed as *M. rudis*, but this glorious blue Poppy is *M. Prattii*. In Fedde's key to the race, *M. rudis* has stem-leaves up to the middle of the spire, while *M. racemosa* has neither bracts nor stem-leaves at all. Unfortunately, in the diagnosis of *M. racemosa*, a full description is given of the stem-leaves already declared to be non-existent! My quite different Kansu plant, sent out as *M. rudis*, is undoubtedly *M. Prattii*, and *M. Prattii* alone. The specimens and seedlings will, however, repay investigation, as these two Poppies are not as yet of any final and absolute distinctness. F 136, at least, takes two clearly-marked forms; so far as I can judge, from Thundercrown up into the foothills of the Min S'an, it is a dense and stocky plant forming a close 8- to 10-inch mace of gorgeous dawn-blue blossoms, woven of silk and opals. In the highest craggy Alps above Ardjeri it takes a new character; the stems are taller, darker, barer, the pedicels are very much longer, so that the inflorescence is a loose and irregular broken flight of flowers, instead of a solid huddled mass. (This may, of course, be merely a later stage of blossom, yet had to me the look of a clear varietal, if not specific, difference.) All the seed sent belongs to the stocky Thundercrown form; in every variety this Poppy (or Poppies), it must be noted, stands apart from all its grass-loving kin, in being always and only found in the gaunt screes and stone-slopes and precipices of the highest limestone or shaly ridges from 12,000 to 14,000 feet. In other words, it is born and made for the moraine, and there should be sown again and again, that its biennial splendour may annually repeat the glory of light with which its dense spires of amassed azures illuminate the vast and lifeless stone-slopes on the highest crests of Tibet. Every part of the growth is virulently prickly, and the fierce hardened thorns of the fruiting stage make its sturdy pyramids of capsules an agony to collect, unless with a mailed fist and a pair of tongs. (Painting and photograph.) (The Celestial Poppy.)

Meconopsis punicea (F 175) far surpasses all English description and all English effort, as you begin to see it, bloodily flaunting in and out of the scantier

APPENDIX.

coppice in the Tibetan valley-bottoms opposite Jô-ni, first appearing at some 10,000 feet and thence ascending to the high grass-ridges, haunting the glade-edges and light bushery of the glen, until in the open hayfields it rages furiously over all the hill, between 11,000 and 13,000 feet, dappling the distances with blood like any Poppy in an English field; and, in the little grassy hollows along the crests, hovering in flapping flags of vermilion above the rippling sea of golden-eyed purple Asters. For in England those dim flags of scarlet flop; on the Tibetan Alps they blaze and flap—huge expanded stiff goblets or wave-winged butterflies of incandescent blood, that compel from me a palinode to my previous rather cold description of *M. punicea*, as alone I had hitherto known it, showing no trace of its own true sinuous and serpentine magnificence. This glory of the upland open hayfields, and scant cool coppice of the lower region in the cool Tibetan Alps, should be sown broadcast at home in moist rich soil amid pleasant neighbours, with loose scrub of *Pinus montana* all about to keep off excessive heat and drought; it is invariably biennial, from a slight weak tap, and does not extend out of Tibet into the warmer drier Alps of Thundercrown, nor southwards (so far as I could find) into those of Satanee. (Painting and photograph.) (The Blood Poppy.)

Morina Sp. (F 215).—A doubtful name; in any case it is a pretty Morinoid Labiate, with glossy spinous-edged foliage, and stems of a foot or so, with close heads of cream-coloured blossom in August. It haunts the higher grasslands of the Tibetan Alps at some 11,000 feet; and, though not special, has a meek attraction.

Myosotis Sp. (F 245) is very general all over the drier regions of South Kansu and Tibet, the seed having been collected on the walls of Jô-ni. It is a small annual-biennial species, forming little low tangles of quite prostrate sprays, beset from March to September with a profusion of light blue stars of a peculiar soft loveliness like that of Omphalodes. Carpeting a sandy patch round the foot of a big boulder it looks really beautiful in its quiet way, and ought, though not of high importance or startlingness, to give a great deal of modest pleasure in suitable poor and gravelly levels, for preference in fullest sun. It is miffy and short-lived.

Onosma Sp. (F 3) has not been collected. It fills all the torrid banks, in the torrid region of the Black Water and the Nan Ho, with low clumped masses of narrow grey foliage; from which, in April, unfurl croziers of long pale blue bugles, very pretty, but not large enough, and with the unfortunate notion of attempting a copy, at all points, of the supreme and inimitable *Lithospermum graminifolium*.

Ophiopogon Sp. (F 302) (*O. kansuensis*) occurs at one point in the Nan Ho Valley, on cool ledges of rock, or at the track-side, or about the roots of light scant scrub- -forming evergreen mats of very dark, wiry grass-fine foliage, from which spring 6-inch spikes in July, unfolding a spire of lovely crystalline and waxen stars, seeming as if carved out of lavender or rose-flushed ivory, and followed by balls of blue-black fruit in November. I considered it a most lovely, dainty thing. In cultivation it is very slow and reluctant.

APPENDIX.

Oreochăris Henryana (F 262) grows in similar sites, but not only likes cool ones as markedly, but is much more partial to damp atmosphere, and even to a certain damp in its soil; growing magnificent on dank mossy limestone rocks in the depths of the Mö Ping cañon, and often abounding—as in the debouchure of the Siku gorge, and at intervals in the lower reaches of the Nan Ho Valley—on very steep banks of a stony, rather clammy silt (which grows a certain film of earth-moss characteristic of such cloggy cool surfaces) from which it spreads happily in and out of the lower fringes of scant scrub and herbage, always preferring an aspect steep to the point of being sheer. Here the rosettes are dully green and only hairy, resembling exactly that specially sinuate form of *Ramondia pyrenaica* which is called *R. p. quercifolia.* The scapes are slightly shorter and stouter than in Boea, with fewer and much larger flowers—little thimble-shaped inverted Gloxinias in a charming blend of shrimp-pink and coppery flesh-tones, borne in a flying panicle in August. It ought to prove easier than F 261, and at least as delightful, in similar situations; both continue their mimicry of Ramondia in having quite microscopic seed, which should be carefully sown accordingly on a silty surface and most tenderly watched. (This also, worse luck, is delicate; will neither thrive nor survive out of doors.)

Paeonia Sp. (F 67) (? *P. Beresowskyi*) abounds between 8000 and 9000 feet on the Alps of Thundercrown and Satanee—not a woodland plant, but loving grassy stony dells and glades on the open alp, in a way that carries one back to the pink Peonies on Baldo. F 67 is in my eyes a species of singular charm and delightfulness; it has voluminous lucent foliage, and stems of 12 to 20 inches, carrying several flowers in all sorts of clear and clean tones of rosy pink, light or dark, with a golden eye of stamens, and so intoxicating a fragrance of roses that all the hill becomes a rose-garden as you go by its generous jungles of large and lovely blossom in May and June.

Pleione Sp. (F 4) is an Indian Crocus of extraordinary beauty. It was only seen at one point of the Feng-S'an Ling, deep down in a profound slaty river-gorge, heavily shaded and perfectly sheltered, so that I dare not yet assert its hardiness. Here it grows in big masses, up and up on the shelving ledges of the dark cliff, in the accumulated leaf-mould fallen from the trees above. On 28th April it was but just opening; yet already, such is its prodigality of blossom, the twilight of the cliff was aglow with countless bright blots of colour from its clumped blossoms of crimson-purple, with their great lips crested and ridged with pure vermilion. Several bulb-mats of this were sent home; but none arrived alive.

Pleione Sp. (F 158) is no less rare, but not so brilliant a thing. I have only once seen it, growing on the cooler face of an inaccessible church-big boulder high up in the mouth of the Siku gorge, where, on the ledges of vegetable mould, it grew in little clusters of 2 or 3 bulbils, rooting along in the surface-carpet of a small dry Selaginella that here covers all the shelves of the cliffs. It has corrugated leaves of bright green, and the flower, so far as I could judge from one glimpse of a lingering bloom in early June, is pretty and spidery and pink, suggesting a gigantic Bletia, carried solitary on a stem of 4 inches, not more than one, it seems (and not always that), being produced from each small tuft of foliage. A seed-pod has been sent, and also a few pseudo bulbs, collected by a coolie striding barefoot along the face of the boulder, as a fly walks lightly along the ceiling. This, also, died of the home-journey.

Polemonium Sp. (F 141) is general up the Border, in all characteristic Polemonium places, in river-banks, and shingles of the lower alpine region, and in and out of the light alpine glades and woodland. It is probably only the tanguticum variety of ubiquitous *P. coeruleum*, but is very much more graceful than the type, with loose and scattered showers of blossom on stems of 12 to 24 inches, from early summer onwards. Only a small pinch of seed was after all collected, from high in the Siku gorge; so that F 141 will probably not be distributed till the resulting plants of this have next season yielded their abundant crop.

Polygonatum Sp. (F 274) (? *P. roseum*) is a dear little fine-leaved whorled Solomon's Seal of 4 inches or so, that freely spreads into carpets of its larch-like shoots, in the opener alpine places and scant turf round the base and ledges of rock-ribs on Thundercrown, etc., beset with starry flowers of mauve-pink in June, which are followed in autumn by berries of brilliant glowing blood-colour.

Potentilla Sp. (F 188) is that fruticosa-Veitchii type, of which there are now so many in cultivation. The pure white *P. Veitchii* is abundant all over the foothills of the Siku Alps, etc., and only towards the highest limit, in the turf at 12,000 feet, does it seem to pass into a yellow form. At least, and until closer investigation decides differently, I am inclined to assume that all this large range of white-golden fruticosa-Potentillas belong in reality to one species. As you advance into the Tibetan Alps opposite Jô-ni the type gets better and the bushes larger. The valley bottoms are filled with masses of deep and brilliant gold, while a little higher up the white form comes into fuller possession, and the grassy folds of the box-pleated upper Alps seem as if mounded with masses of snow in August in their couloirs, with banked dark forest on one side and the emerald open lawn on the other, in which the Potentillas are so profusely peppered in bushes of 2 or 3 feet, concealed from sight by their blossom. The deep golden type passes into the pure white by innumerable gradations of cream, amber, citron, and butter-yellow—intermediate colour-forms (or hybrids); seed sent out embraces all these, having been collected not only from the snowy and golden extremities of the type, but from a little bank in the Mirgo Valley, where every link between them was in rich abundance and the loveliest blend of every shade of saffron, sulphur, and cream —it being specially noted that the paler forms were perceptibly paler and greyer in the seed-husk than the rich brown of the yellower forms. All these should make masses of lovely, small, tight bushes, and deserve to be planted in big sweeps amid grass on the fringes of woodland and shrubbery, where in

APPENDIX.

August they ought to mimic snow and gorse as they do on the cool green mountains of Tibet.

Potentilla Sp. (F 214) is a real gem of a very different kidney. It belongs only to the highest alpine earth-pans and cliffs on the crests of the Min S'an and Thundercrown at 14,000 to 15,000 feet, where, on the bald, bare loam it forms tight, massive hassocks, often a yard across, of bright, lucent-green foliage, so finely divided and curled as to make the effect of some hairless glossy small Saxifrage of the Ceratophylla Group, amassed into a tight, hard dome. So the plant grows, from a thick, woody trunk; and in mid-July the whole hump is covered with a galaxy of almost stemless single little golden stars, in shape and size and colour like those of a diminished *P. verna*, with a blotch of orange at the base of each citron-yellow petal. This compact beauty, in fact, makes a golden third in a trinity with pink *P. nitida* and snowy *P. Clusiana*, though even tighter and harder in its masses than *P. nitida*. (*P. biflora:* a failure.)

Primula.—In this great race 1914 has been delightfully fertile, the Nivalis-Maximowiczi Group being especially well represented. Several most interesting extensions of races or groups have been recorded, and I cannot help suspecting that Nos. 1, 5, 6, 10, 13, 15, 22, 23 may prove to be good new species. So far as I can discern, the season has yielded 25 species, new or old, though perhaps one or two of these may fade into others, and certainly there are more than one concealed under No. 19. (Written in 1914.)

Primula Sp. No. 1 (F 38) should certainly belong to the Davidi Group, but that it utterly lacks the brown investiture of scales, and in all its habit and habits precisely repeats *P. acaulis*, with clumps of crisp, crinkly, sharp-toothed leaves, with pale veins, a lettuce-like succulency, and a microscopic veneer of green-velvet glands. From this rises a scape of 2 to 4 inches, bearing a loose olyanthus head of large and lovely rose-mauve flowers in March, with a ten-rayed eye of green and white from the pale throat. Not only does this plant repeat the tufts of the Primrose, but it also occupies the typical Primrose-sites in all the forests from Chago-ling to the gorges of Thundercrown, between 7000 and 8000 feet, growing in the opener places of the woodland, by path-sides, on lightly-coppiced banks, or in the wide, flat stretches of *Anemone nemorosa*, dappling the ground beneath deciduous trees. It loves the clammy rich loam of the Primrose too, but especially luxuriates in rotten timber, forming magnificent crowded colonies in the moss along aged and decayed windfalls in the forest. The calyx, with its lobes, pedicels, and scape, lengthen and stouten and amplify remarkably in seed. For this, owing to our enforced flight, we had to depend on specimens hurriedly dug up in the woods of Satanee, carried off in boxes, and grown on to ripen in the hot backyard of the Yamên at Siku. On this accordingly I build no great hope; but plants have been since sent, which I trust may be enough to introduce so really first-class a Primula into cultivation, where it has all the look of thriving robustly and permanently. So far, it is the only general woodland Primula, exactly taking the place of *P. acaulis* in its limited region. (*P. hylophila*, Sp. *nova:* a failure.)

APPENDIX.

Primula Sp. No. 2 (F 39) is very hard to place ; it is best pictured by imagining a scape of soft-mauve *P. hirsuta* applied close upon a rosette of *P. farinosa* or *P. frondosa*. It is a charming species, and abounds on cool, mossy rocks and cliffs in the woodland zone of the Chago-ling-Satanee Alps, penetrating across to Thundercrown, where it is commonly seen in the boulder-crevices from 8000 feet to the actual gaunt summits of the ridge, where it is still in bloom at the end of June—long after the May-flowering specimens of Satanee have passed into seed. It is purely a saxatile plant, of cracks and crannies, and dies away in autumn to a beautiful fat knop of creamy-white, the same soft powder on the reverse of the foliage finely enhancing the blossom in spring. It is only at its best, goodly in form and rosette and freedom and flower, in the Alps opposite Satanee ; about Chago-ling, and throughout its strange distribution over the open flanks of Thundercrown, it seems to miss the cool and mossy dampness of the woodland cliffs, and is universally thin and starved in growth, with only 2 or 3 blooms to a scape, instead of the possible 8 that it can attain to in the sub-alpine river glens of Satanee. (*P. scopulorum*, Sp. *nova :* rather tender ; perhaps contains two species.)

Primula Sp. No. 3 (F 33) is clearly a microform of *P. obconica*—an interesting record of so remote and northerly an extension of the group. It is a small, dainty clump, with gracious little scant umbels of mauve-crimson blossom ; three tufts were first seen on a steep, grassy rill-bank above Chago on 6th May, and then a whole bank, cool and overhung with slight coppice, was seen studded with delicate specimens on the descent from Chago to the Satanee River on 8th May. It proved impossible to get either seeds or plants of this —a failure with which I am glad to compound for success with so many more brilliant and important species. (*P. riparia*, Sp. *nova*. See above.)

Primula Sp. No. 4 (F 40) is interesting, as being the plant previously recorded from Kansu, *P. Loczii*, from Szechenyi's tour in the Kweite Alps, right away north of this region. In my experience it is confined to the district round Ga-hoba, where, on the high moorland ridges confronting the huge Satanee Alps, it abounds on all the myriad little willowed hummocks and dimples of the fell, not only in the mossy banks, but out upon the fine open turf itself in sheets. Above Ga-hoba it is sporadic on the higher ridge behind, and its last occurrence was in one big patch just below the crest of the Mö-Ping Pass, on the further side. It is a charming, pretty thing, like a glossy dwarf and perfectly powderless *P. farinosa*, with the curious quality of throwing out a number of rooting stolons from the central crown, and so forming rapidly, where satisfied, into a thick wide carpet. It blooms in early May, and is a lovely reminder of *P. farinosa*, in *farinosa's* pet situations, on the cool, grassy fringes of the woodlands and fell coppices about Ga-hoba. Seed was late and very scant ; my chief hope lies in dormant crowns despatched in December. (None too hardy.)

Primula Sp. No. 5 (F 61) belongs to the Polyneura Group, but is, I think, of special interest as bridging the gulf between this section and that of *P. septemloba*. Unless I am wrong, *P. septemloba* lives in the cool upper woodland

510

of the Satanee Alps, while across the intervening range abounds *P. lichiangensis* on the warmer, drier slopes and boulder edges of Thundercrown. That intervening range, with the foothills opposite Satanee, is the home of Primula No. 5, a most lovely species, far superior in grace and charm (as I think) to *P. Veitchii* and *P. lichiangensis*, of which it has precisely the soft foliage and lush woodland habit (it is singularly small and frail in the crown); but its beautiful big flowers of vinous rose are not flat stars but shallow saucers, and instead of being borne in stiffly-upstaring umbels, are carried loosely and gracefully in an almost pendulous and one-sided spray, in general effect recalling that notable wide-faced form of *P. viscosa* which yields *P.* × *Crucis* to *P. marginata* on the Col de la Croix. (Occasionally, but very rarely, a second tier of blossom unfolds above the first.) Above Satanee P. No. 5 occurs happily, though rather stunted, in the hot crevices of sunny primary rocks from which coppice has evidently been cleared; but its real home is in deep, cool places and mossy river-banks of the woodland, and it is particularly fine and lovely in the dense darkness of a little Bamboo-brake in the forest zone of the Satanee Alps, growing in very rich clammy loam, consisting almost wholly of decayed vegetation. Here it blooms in early May; October seed proved too scanty to distribute, but I hope that dormant crowns may also help to increase the stock. (*P. Silvia*, Sp. *nova*.)

Primula Sp. No. 6 (F 74) (*P. viola-grandis*) is especially beautiful, important, and interesting. It is a very far northerly and most unexpected extension of the weird Omphalogramma group, with solitary flowers like gigantic monstrous violets or Pinguiculas before the full expansion of the leaves. Hitherto the most northern species of the group has been *P. Franchetii*, which is rare in the Alps of the Mekong-Salween, very far to the south, in uppermost Yunnan; the nearest relation to *P. viola-grandis*, *P. Delavayi*, lives yet further to the south, on the flanks of Tsang-s'an, and differs, *inter alia*, in having its stems beset with brown membranaceous bracts. Thus the whole depth of Szechuan intervenes between the older Omphalogrammas of Yunnan and their new cousin of Kansu. *P. viola-grandis* has already been splendidly figured in the *Chronicle*, so I need not expatiate on its prognathous great blue-purple blossom, with ears laid stiffly back, and lip stuck stiffly out (but the bud opens a regular star of intense violet, lightening to a more lucent tone as it opens out, and the segments set to work reflexing and protruding). It only remains to describe the enormous subsequent expansion of the foliage, which develops heart-shaped blades like those of a fat *Viola hirta* or *V. odorata*, but densely thick like flannel, of very dark opaque dusty green with paler veins, lying flopped about on the black soil, too heavy for the elongated fleshy footstalks of glandular pinkness. *P. viola-grandis* may, perhaps, prove easier than its cousins; but it has a very rigid choice of habitats. It is never found except up cool, westerly-facing, shady exposures of big limestone cliffs in the Alps of Satanee and Thundercrown, hugging the underside of ledge-sods in clammy moist soil of loam or vegetable mould, and descending freely into the upper reaches of the Siku gorges, where they go lost at last in sombre inaccessible cañons of gloom and dankness

APPENDIX.

Usually it is found in clumps here and there, its piercingly refulgent violet flames hovering like blue sparks of electricity in May from the gloomy walls; but in one station I know, higher up on the open Alps of the Ridge, it so abounds in little western couloirs and on a little turfy saddle beneath the cliff, so runs riot in loam or red earth or peat-mould, and so gaily flickers in and out of the minute 3-inch Rhododendron scrub, that those few and limited stations are all a shimmering dance of Violets in early summer, and there at least the plant gives better hope of a robust and hearty habit. As might be imagined from its preposterous flower and length of tube, it is a poor, scant seeder, hardly 5 per cent. of the blooms (which are not by any means sent up from every crown either) resulting in the tall 6- to 8-inch seed-stem and its round capsule atop. I was late upon its final scene too, so that the distribution of seed will have been sadly niggardly. However, I felt profoundly grateful and fortunate to get what I did, the 4 or 5 last capsules lingering on the mountain side, with the seed lying loose in its saucer, at the mercy of any moment's flow of wind, or dash of hail. In autumn the whole thing dies back to a white scaly bud like a wee bulb of Lilium; some of these have also been sent, and I hope may arrive alive. (Painting and photograph.) It never germinated.

Primula Sp. No. 7 (F 86) is almost certainly a cousin of *P. lichiangensis*, and as such I have not troubled to collect it for general distribution, it being by now so generally grown. I do not very greatly love or admire it. Its interest lies in this far northerly extension of its original distribution in the Alps of Yunnan. It abounds at mid-elevations on Thundercrown, not at all avoiding hot dry flanks and exposures, but growing for choice in scant sunny scrub, deep woodland, and along the be-shrubbed brows of cliff or boulder, from which its stiff and starry umbels of bright and golden-eyed magenta pink flaunt or flap with fine effect in May. In the main Min S'an its place is taken by F 197.

Primula Sp. No. 8 (F 116) is a most gorgeous species of the Nivalis Group. Purdom originally collected it on the foothills of Monk Mountain, and it was shown by Veitch at the 1913 Conference under the false name of *P. "purpurea,"* Royle—*P. purpurea*, Royle, being an invalid synonym for *P. nivalis macrophylla*. Now F 116 differs absolutely and utterly from every form of *P. nivalis* in being completely smooth and glossy, and devoid of powder in all parts of its growth. It forms a deep woody stock, sheathed in brown membrane, and ending in a few fat white roots; this supports a cabbage-like tuft of dark green foliage, and an 8- to 12-inch stout stem, carrying a great head of deep violet stars in June, on pedicels so distinct and slender that the cluster is a rayed wheel of blossom, not a piled dome. It grows in the open coarse turf of the Alps, dotted here and there, between 9000 and 13,000 feet, blazing from afar amid the lavender and gold and citron of the other reigning flowers that constellate the grass. Its long stock, and the rough herbage and steep slopes that it affects, indicated that it might prove to possess a typical nivalis-sensitiveness to the least deficiency in drainage or moisture. All turf-Primulas, in fact, should, I think, be treated as such in cultivation, their coarse

APPENDIX.

enveloping mat of grass and rootage equalising their moisture in summer, and draining it uniformly away ; while in winter it dies down upon their dormant crowns like a dry thatch, over which springy mattress lies the warm coverlid of the winter's snow. I should, indeed, make an Alpenwiese on a raking but well-watered slope, for nearly all the Nivalis Group, and especially for the forms of *P. nivalis* itself. P. No. 8 (*P. Woodwardii*) is a joy to collect, with stalwart oval pods of hearty brown, standing starkly up from the moorland on length-ened scapes of a foot and more ; two lots have been sent, as 116a and 116b, on the chance that the Monk Mountain form may perhaps prove in some way different from that of Thundercrown. *P. Woodwardii*, however, despite fore-bodings, grows very easily and vigorously and permanently with us, even developing a white eye, which greatly enhances the beauty of the violet flowers. It is one of the best Primulas from China.

Primula Sp. No. 9 (F 121) is a unique occurrence, which yielded no seed, and of which I have one sod here in Lanchow which may possibly get no further. We found it only *in* the little mountain track ascending Thundercrown, between 9000 and 9500 feet, where, in clammy, limy loam it grew in wads and clusters like seedling boxesful of groundsel (and by no means, in their earlier stages, unlike). The majority seemed packed seedlings ; only here and there arose the delicate 5-inch scapes in June, bearing flowers intermediate in appear-ance between *P. longiflora* and *P. farinosa*, but much nearer the former, round-faced, purple-tubed prettinesses of soft pink, above the minute leathern-grey foliage huddled on the ground. Abounding as it does in its limited area, it must seed and germinate copiously ; but not perhaps every season, since in 1914 not the trace of a capsule was anywhere discoverable. It is a dainty, pleasant thing, with its remarkable long-tubed flowers swinging horizontal, usually in pairs ; I suspect it of being very close indeed to F 168, from higher up the mountain—and perhaps a mere microform. But F 168 is a larger, finer plant in every way, with bigger, rounder flowers of milky pink ; it does not grow in mats but in isolated crowns, and the shorter corolla-tubes are yellow and not purple. (This is a minor form of *P. gemmifera.*)

Primula Sp. No. 10 (F 122) is a most important and beautiful species of the Nivalis Group, which, however, instead of a long, perilous neck with a few roots at the end, breaks straight, in hearty crowns, from such a mat of stout red fibres, ramified into such a mesh of white rootlets, that you can weed it up in big sods like groundsel from the slopes of bare fine silt where it lives, between 12,000 and 14,000 feet on Thundercrown, occasionally flaunting from the cliffs in big aged masses, but usually dotted about all by itself, over the otherwise bare earth-pans, beck-shingles, and loamy patches of scree beneath the crests, which it illuminates with its stout-pedicelled, domed (and often 2-tiered) heads of big lavender-blue stars in June, on stout powder-white scapes of 3 to 10 inches, rapidly lengthening in flower and fruit. Its pods are very long, straight, narrow-drainpipe-shaped, flat-ended, and pallid in colour, going transparent at the top, as in *P. Maximowiczii ;* the lovely flowers have a strong scent of an old apple-cupboard haunted by mice. It should prove an easy doer in loamy well-watered moraine, and never shares its home with other vegetation nor descends to less gaunt and barren places. It has so close a relationship to P. No. 22 from similar heights and situations in the main Min S'an, that I dare not yet quite propose it as a separate species, or more than a local development on its isolated mountain mass. In P 22, however, the foliage is taller, more advanced with the flower, more upstanding, revolute, dark, leathery, opaque, and stiff, with more powder in its young stage, and a clear white line of powder round the under margin of the mature leaf, such as is very rare indeed on the much more explanate, glossy, succulent, bright-green foliage of P. No. 10. (Painting and photograph.) (*P. optata*, Sp. *nova;* as yet slow and reluctant.)

Primula Sp. No. 11 (F 133) was suspected to be *P. flava*. This gracious and glorious canary-yellow-headed beauty, lush and sub-tropical-looking in thin and powdered foliage, has been figured in the *Chronicle* beyond need of more description. It looks as if it had a sturdy constitution, yet in nature is most rigidly restricted to the dry and powdery limy silt on the floors of overhung (and, for preference, sunless) grottoes and crevices of the limestone cliffs at 9000 to 10,000 feet, from Thundercrown away up all the Border ranges, ascending to 14,000 or 15,000 feet in open crevices and crannies, where, however, it still markedly prefers the cold and overhung aspects, and is anyhow always wizen and compact by comparison with its luxuriant development in more comfortable cavities lower down. Here, and here only, untouched by sun or rain, it grows superb and lax as in the photograph, seeding copiously over the fine silty surfaces, cool and powdery, of the dusty grotto-beds. It is *P. citrina*, of which I believe *P. flava* to be only a xeromorph. It lives, but does not thrive.

Primula Sp. No. 12 (F 187) is *P. conspersa*. It was collected first by Purdom in 1911, and has been commented on in the *Chronicle*. It is not found at all until you reach the Minchow district, and ranges westwards, thence into the foothills of the Min S'an, not mounting or descending from some 8500 feet, where it occupies precisely the situations beloved by *P. farinosa*, on the damper grassy hillsides and in the small, marish folds of the fells, and in level damp places beside the mountain streams; precisely copying *P. farinosa* too in its whole effect, except that the scapes are usually 9 to 12 inches high, and carry 2 or 3 superimposed tiers of blossom. (So that, in sum, it is exactly like a much taller, several-tiered *P. farinosa*.) In the Tibetan Alps it blooms from early July; it is not absolutely a biennial, for specially stout crowns can be found preparing next year's leaf-bud at the base of the seedling stems; but by far the larger majority of seeding plants die in the act, and it is as a biennial that *P. conspersa* had better be grown in England, wherever *P. farinosa* is happy, with a yearly sowing of seed broadcast over fine moist turfy tracts. (Painting and photograph.)

Primula Sp. No. 13 (F 168) is a particularly beautiful species, very closely allied to *P. sibirica*, but differing absolutely, I think, in having its daisylike foliage always dentate, and its scapes and pedicels always powdered—to say nothing of its much more moderate stature of some 5 or 6 inches only. The August-borne blossoms are very large and comfortable faced, and fat and round, of a melting, milky pink with a yellow throat and delicate fragrance. This charmer begins in the moister upmost silt-slopes of Thundercrown (where it has a strange little offshoot or poor cousin, in P. No. 9, 2000 feet lower down the mountain), but its main abundance is in the Min S'an, very high up, at 12,000 to 13,000 feet, where it loves the open earth-fans of the steep fell-sides, densely dotting the fine loam and shingle with its solitary crowns, so frail and scant of root; but thence even spreads by myriads into the finer Alpine turf all round, and sends its seedlings far down into the valleys beneath, where their results occur in little colonies or bright specklings of colour, along the grassy or shingly levels of the beck-bottoms in the gorges and cool glens and shady places, very different from the naked exposure of the high-alpine heights where it is at home in the barer moister slopes and channels of clammy and stony calcareous loam. (Painting and photograph.) (This is *P. gemmifera*.)

Primula Sp. No. 14 (F 191) is *P. Maximowiczii*. This, the big reddish hyacinth-flowered, many-tiered stalwart, has an enormous range over all the grassy Alps of Northern, Central, and Western China. Let it be noted that this must surely be both hardy and soundly perennial (unless where it may flower itself to death), but that it is a typical turf-Primula of nivalis habit, and therefore would be best if grown in grass on a cool, well-watered, and perfectly-drained slope, kept rigidly dry in winter. Stagnation and clogging damp will be its detestation, especially in the over-rich soil which it would clearly appreciate in summer. I have not yet seen it in flower, but it abounds in the hay of the cooler slopes on the Tibetan Alps, not descending to the flat and sedgy glen bottoms like *P. Purdomii*.

Primula Sp. No. 15 (F 178) is a most charming little species of the woodland group, but quite (I think) distinct. It runs freely about with light, frail runners, in the profound cold moss-banks in the highest Tibetan forest, towards the summit of the ridges, at some 12,000 feet, covering the deep beds of leaf-mould with a carpet of sharp-lobed, bright-green foliage, above which spring dainty little scapes of 4 or 5 inches in July, each usually flourishing, on long, fine pedicels, a pair or more of charming rose-mauve flowers, wide and flat and starry, with a pale eye and darker tube. It has a most especial daintiness and charm; and its divaricate calyx-lobes make its assignation uncertain. A later lot of seed distributed as F 464 is almost certainly F 178 beyond shadow of doubt; but as it was collected by a Chinese collector I have thought best to avoid the possibility of a confusion. (Painting and photograph.) This has a certain look of *P. kisoana*, but is clearly distinct, if only in the much longer and finer pedicels and better blossoms. (*P. alsophila*, Sp. *nova*; it is symbiotic with a fungus, and has failed.)

Primula Sp. No. 16 (F 193) is doubtful, and distributed only under a caution. It is a most precious find of Purdom's—a glaucous-grey, erect-leaved, clumping Primula of the Nivalis Group, with the habit of the rest, but blossoms of *soft* *yellow.* Only seven specimens of this were originally seen in 1911, on one high grassy crest of Tibet, in company with *P. Maximowiczii* and *P. Purdomii.* On Purdom's return to the station in 1914 the flower was over, and the two solitary plants discoverable in seed could not therefore be *positively* guaranteed to be this new yellow Nivalis, though the probabilities in their favour are so large as almost to amount to certainty. (Seed of the next number yielded chiefly this.)

Primula Sp. No. 17 (F 192) is the unsurpassable and worthily named *P. Purdomii.* This Queen of the Nivalis Group belongs to the high grasslands of the Tibetan Alps opposite Jô-ni. Though I have not been dazzled yet by the spectacle of its bloom, I have been interested to watch its habit (they say it flowers best in alternate years), and to note that, while it is a typical turf-species of the Nivalis cousinhood, like *PP. Maximowiczii*, P. No. 16, P. No. 8, yet it has idiosyncrasies not shared by the others. It is perceptibly more local, and, though it may often freely be found in the folds and slopes of the vast upper hayfields, it has a clear liking for more level (that is to say, more moisture-retaining) tracts, such as small flat stretches along the descending ridges, and especially for the sedgy cool flats in the upper stretches of the valleys, beside the cold and brawling ice-green becks of the Min S'an. No hay or rushy turf can be too coarse and dense for it, it seems; its need is evidently the even distribution of damp by the grass roots in summer, and then, in winter, a thatch of yet more special depth and dryness under the dry snow than that required by all the others. It is a noble and robust grower, very different from the small (yet how beautiful!) specimens shown at the Conference. I have seen the seed-scapes at least 2 feet high, with some 30 stalwart erect pods. It was first collected by Purdom in 1911, and exhibited at the Conference of 1913.

Primula Sp. No. 18 (F 194) is *P. tangutica*, one of the few really frightful Primulas—so ugly that only under protest have I sent any seed at all, though it abounds with P. No. 13 in the highest earth-fans of the Tibetan Alps, in habit like a small untidy *P. Maximowiczii*, with Maximowiczii's larger redder flowers reduced to wispy starved little ragged stars of dull chocolate and brownish black.

Primula Sp. No. 19 (F 195) requires very careful watching, as this number contains certainly two distinct species, and possibly four. The number stands primarily for *P. stenocalyx*, which I think is undilutedly genuine in the earliest lot of seed sent under the name (and already germinated)—a most beautiful species of the Auriculate Group, with lush flat rosettes of glabrous foliage, in the vertical cliffs and shingle-walls of the lower Tibetan region about Jô-ni, and short scapes of an inch or two, generously furnished with large and deliciously fragrant flowers of rosy-lavender. It was first collected by Purdom in 1911, but has never yet been shown. Unfortunately, we were too late in the Min S'an for its flowering season, and as our reports had a certain ambiguity as to the difference between " form " and " species," it was only too tardily that I discovered that at least one supposed " form," from the Lotus Mountain, was in reality a distinct species of similar stature, but with densely white-powdered foliage (*P. dealbata*, 1915, Sp. *nova*); which leaves me suspecting that the same may ultimately have to be said of another so-called "form" from Monk Mountain. Accordingly, I have labelled all sendings of *P.* "*stenocalyx*" with the name of their district; and advise that all these be kept apart and carefully watched, as possibilities are so many. It even, I believe, will be found to include a few stray seeds of P. No. 20, from collected crowns sent down with the true cognata's, to ripen their pods in Jô-ni. In the earliest lots, however, which alone were large enough for general distribution, I am certain that *P. stenocalyx* will be found pure, and possibly unalloyed except for the Lotus Mountain plant, which undoubtedly comprises the majority, if not the whole, of the second sending. (*P. cognata* is a chimæra, it seems.)

Primula Sp. No. 20 (F 196) is blurred with the last, and very scanty in supply, even if sent at all. It need not be regretted; it is a starveling little thing, replacing No. 2 in the highest cool cliffs and grassy rock-ledges of the uppermost Min S'an. It has the puny look of *P. yunnanensis*—a feeble tiny rosette, and a scape of an inch, more or less, with 2 or more flowers. These we never saw, unless some rather attractive starry recurving blooms of lilac-mauve from the great Ardjeri gorge did indeed represent this species in a stout and drawn-up form (for here the scape had attained 3 or 4 inches, and the abundant crowns seemed stronger than up above. It was here growing in damp cool silt, very loose, about the feet of great boulders in the shade, at the mouth of the ravine).

Primula Sp. No. 21 (F 197) may perhaps contain two species, of which only seed from Rou Ba Temple has been distributed. As I know the plant, in the cool silty grottoes and shady boulders of the Ardjeri gorges, it stands in very close alliance to *P. lichiangensis*, precisely repeating its habit and foliage, and, though I think it distinct, differing distinctly for the worse, in rather anæmic pallid stars of blossom—though this may be only because the flowers were then, at the beginning of August, in their final stage of disappearance. In any case, *P. lichiangensis* gives the picture and the rule for this and also (whether it be the same or no) for the parent of the other seed sent under this number—a woodland species from forest banks about Rou Ba Temple and opposite Jô-ni. It is distinct from *P. Silvia*, and a quicker, freer grower, though inferior.

Primula Sp. No. 22 (F 248).—For the differences between this superb species and its smaller cousin, see under P. No. 10. P. No. 22 makes robust and clod-forming clumps of stiff upstanding foliage all over the gaunt consolidated silt beds and hard earthy shingles of the uppermost arêtes of the Min S'an, in the same sort of places chosen by P. No. 10 on Thundercrown, but growing much stouter and more abundant, often making quite a waving jungle of its stalwart stems over gaunt slopes where no other living thing occurs. It weeds up in sods like a groundsel, and roots in the same rampageous manner as P. No. 10, with the same long, pale, and chaffy pods, though I fancy it more rarely super-imposes a second flower-tier on the first. The flower is so far unknown; judging by P. No. 10 it should be a glorious Nivalis of lavender-purple, and, to judge by captured crowns now emerging from their biscuit-tins in Lanchow, it sends them up (after the leaves are well-developed) with profusion, and grows with imperturbable vigour and copiousness of clump. Seed was barely mature, and *may* prove unsatisfactory; but I hope that dormant plants may also arrive and in good condition. This has thriven much better than *P. optata*.

Primula Sp. No. 23 (F 273) has especial value, as being our only representative of the spiked Giraldiana Group. It is a most delightful find of Purdom's, rarely occurring on mossy slopes of a river-ghyll high on Lotus Mountain, with pine-trees well up above it on either side. I have only seen it in dry and seeding specimens; it appears to me perfectly *glabrous*, a wonderful and unique promise of prosperity in a Muscarioid Primula; its white-powdered stems, in capsule, are a foot or more in height, and it bears lovely little bells of lavender-blue, with the intoxicating fragrance of its group. (*P. aerinantha*, Sp. *nova*.)

Primula Sp. No. 24 (F 300) was, in point of fact, the first of all our Primulas to be found. It was already out of flower when we descended from the Feng S'an Ling upon Wên Hsien on 28th April, and Purdom had the happy idea to diverge up to the foot of a high-swaying little Staubbach of a water-spray that shot down over a great westerly-facing cliff to the left; and there, all up the ledges, found this Primula growing in great wads and masses of the neatest little mealed rosettes, from all of which shot sturdy scapes of an inch or two, carrying such sturdy pedicels and calyces as to give good hope that the flowers will be sturdy and large to match. The umbel seems to carry 4 to 6 blooms in a wide head; as yet I cannot assign this almost unexamined but most distinct species to any particular group, unless it be that of *P. Sertulum*. The buds on collected plants here have unfortunately gone " blind," but I hope seed will prosper, and a cool rather damp cliff-crevice ultimately reveal the species in the beauty I feel safe in foretelling from its neat massed habit and doughty little scape. (No seed germinated.)

Primula Sp. No. 25 (F 192) is almost certainly *P. septemloba*. I found it, in the very end of all things, on a cool loose-soiled bank at a cliff's foot, high up in the Alps of Satanee, with scant willows growing about. Everything of it was gone to mush, except the sere stiff scapes of 8 inches; but the very numerous crowded erect pedicels of these suggested obviously the drooping flowers of *P. septemloba*, and amid the decayed leaves could be discerned the relics of *acute* lobing, such as you get in *P. septemloba* and P. No. 15, but not in the more gently-rounded divisions of the Polyneura Group. The plant, however, had bad luck; the collecting-box was not prompt enough in recognising its specific claims, and its large root-masses got mixed up with the frail crowns of P. No. 5, while the 7 seeds which alone the exhausted capsules yielded were so carefully put away as never to be found again. It will no doubt turn up among the sendings of P. No. 5, but is in itself a much less important species, already known, and not pre-eminent, as it is closely rivalled by *Cortusa Matthiolii*, as delicate a thing and an older friend.

APPENDIX.

Primula Sp. (F 464) is almost certainly P. No. 15.

Primula Sp. (F 465) **(Chiappa)** is a doubtful woodlander, but is almost certainly P. No. 21.

Nivalis-Maximowiczii Group	*P. Purdomii* (17).
	P. Maximowiczii (14).
	P. tangutica (18).
	P. No. 8 (*P. Woodwardii*).
	P. No. 10 (*P. optata*).
	P. No. 22.
	P. No. 16.
Davidi Group	P. No. 1 (*P. hylophila*).
Omphalogramma Group	P. No. 6 (*P. viola-grandis*).
Giraldiana Group	P. No. 23 (*P. aerinantha*).
(?) Souliei Group	P. No. 11 (*P. citrina*).
Farinosa-Auriculata Group	P. No. 4 (*P. Loczii*).
	P. No. 9 (*P. gemmifera minor*).
	P. No. 12 (*P. conspersa*).
	P. No. 13 (*P. gemmifera*).
	P. No. 19 (*P. stenocalyx*).
	P. No. 19 (*P. dealbata*).
Polyneura-Septemloba Group	P. No. 5 (*P. silvia*).
	P. No. 7 (*P. lichiangensis*).
	P. No. 21.
	P. No. 15 (*P. alsophila*).
	P. No. 25 (*P. septemloba*).
Incertae Sedis	P. No. 2 (*P. scopulorum*).
	P. No. 20.
	P. No. 24.
Obconica Group	P. No. 3 (*P. riparia*).

Rodgersia aesculifolia (F 132) is perfectly magnificent in the richest, coolest, and darker aspects of the great Siku gorge, growing 4 or 5 feet high in the corners under the cliff, with enormous metallic foliage and foamy white blossom in crest over crest to the summit of the spumy pyramid—by far the most superb of Rodgersias when in such form, and completely vanquishing the utmost effort of Astilbe and Spiraea. It is general all over the lower alpine coppice of the Siku-Satanee ranges, and, above Siku, even lingers handsomely on hot dry hills of coarse grass, from which the woodland has been pitilessly cleared for many generations.

Salvia Sp. (F 169) is a magnificent herbaceous plant of 3 or 4 feet, abounding in the lower alpine turf of the Tibetan highlands away down to Satanee. It is a stalwart and stately grower, and in August bears large heads and whorls of large and very richly violet-purple, which in our gardens unfortunately deteriorates.

Salvia Sp. (F 227) is very common in low hot dry places all up the Border.

APPENDIX.

It is rather a rank and ugly thing, coarse and flopping, with voluminous flannelly foliage and weak stems of a foot or so, bearing loose spires of dim baggy-belled flowers of vinous mauve in summer.

Saussurea Sp. (F 337) I had not meant to send for anyone but Mr. Bowles, that lover of curious delights. However, as the quantity is sufficient, all may have their share, for what it is worth, of this odd thing which, perfectly tight to the ground in barer places of the upper alpine turf of Thundercrown and the Min S'an, there produces a fat head of (probably) quite dowdy flowers, followed by the plant's one attraction, a wide gleaming collarette of silver-smoke, which when ripe detaches itself all of a piece and floats away upon the air like a filmy cigarette ring. No other Saussurea attracted notice (and this, only by its seed), though there is a flannelly-leaved one (if Saussurea it be) on the highest bare stone-slopes of the Min S'an, with Primuloid rosettes of grey foliage, and fat great buzzle-heads of undistinguished (so far as one could foretell) flower.

Saxifraga.—Take it all in all, the Saxifrages of this part of the Border are not brilliant in flower, nor profuse in variety. Of the Kabschia Group one species only; of the Porphyrions doubtfully one (out of flower and indecipherable in the topmost cold limestone crags of the Min S'an); the bulk belong to less interesting sections, and have so far yielded only one first-class plant.

Saxifraga Sp. (F 73) is our one Kabschia; it is a neat and beautiful thing, forming masses like those of a rather lax *S. valdensis*, on which are applied solitary-blossomed stems of *S. marginata*, making a fine effect when the domes are covered in May with 2-inch stems each flourishing a full-faced snowy flower. It haunts cool aspects of the upper limestone cliffs from Satanee to the Min S'an, never appearing in other situations, and varying, like all its group, in brilliancy and amplitude of blossom. So scant a pinch of seed was alone procurable that it will not yet be available for distribution (and never came up).

Saxifraga Sp. (F 200) is by far the most important, this year, of its race. It is a most splendid clump-forming species of the Hirculus Group, very profuse in stems of 6 to 8 inches, beset with rather conspicuous glaucous-grey foliage, and expanding into generous corymbs in July, of noble citron-yellow flowers with a deeper golden base. It abounds in all the higher alpine turf of the Border, between 10,000 and 13,000 feet, and ranges from Thundercrown up on to the lusher cooler flower-fields of the Min S'an, where amid the pale blue surf of Gentiana F 217, its rich tufts of grey and gold make an effect of perfect beauty. (A quite inferior cousin, of the same group, often accompanies it.) No other species was really worthy of note or collection, though F 216 was a wee green moss with golden stars, that had a delicate gaiety in cool moist rock-ledges up the valley opposite Jô-ni.

Sedum.—Of these the greater majority here are, as elsewhere, dull and uninteresting plants. F. 238, however, is a prettyish little thing, from the topmost bare screes of the Min S'an and Thundercrown, being like a small and dainty *S. rhodanthum* of 3 or 4 inches, with the fine-leaved shoots each

APPENDIX.

ending in a fluffy head of white sodden-looking flowers in August (*S. Farreri*, Sp. *nova*). I cannot be certain if this will be to be distributed, as I cannot decide whether it is identical with F 322, or whether this number covers a cousin from similar sites and heights, still more like *S. rhodanthum*, with small dull reddish flowers on stems an inch or two taller, and more freely produced, than in the last.

Sedum Sp. (F 336), however, if really Sedum and not Umbilicus, is a truly beautiful thing. It seems special to very hot stony banks about Siku, and in the little town itself grows in such abundance on every roof that the groove between each ridge of tiles becomes a solid channel of its lovely blue-pink metallic glaucous foliage, fat and cylindric, but in colour like a bedding Echeveria's, from which in late August profusely arise dense fox-brush spikes of 6 to 10 inches, breaking into serried pyramids of little coldly-white or pinkly flushing stars. The flowered crown of this expires in seeding, but the mass of the plant continues unperturbed, as in *Saxifraga Cotyledon*, and it ought, in hot dry places, pebbly and parching and poor, to introduce quite a new charm into our gardens, unaccustomed to such a style of beauty in Sedum.

(?) Serratula Sp. (F 432) is a handsome but quite coarse thing, common in open moorland fields all up the Border at low elevations, growing some 3 to 5 feet high, and expanding, in August, in a spreading compound head of brilliant magenta-purple fluff like a gigantic Ageratum. In sunny rich stretches of the wild garden it should make a fine effect.

Stellera Sp. (F 93) is so named at Kew, but I find no other trace of a pink Stellera. In any case, whether really Wikstroemia or any other Daphne-cousin, this charming thing may be described as a herbaceous woody-stocked Daphne, springing abundantly in all the high hayfields of the Tibetan Alps, ascending to 11,000 feet, but no less happy in coarse dry turf on the hot and sun-baked foothills of Thundercrown. It springs in a moss of glaucous-leaved shoots to a height of 8 to 12 inches, forming a compact dome of growth and blossom, each undivided stem ending in June and July in a compact dome of fragrant pearl-white Daphnes with a centre of varnished ruby-red buds. It is evidently poisonous as the rest of the family, for in the Tibetan hayfields the cattle pass it deliberately by, as they pass by buttercups in England. Its seed is scanty and doubtful, and hard to catch; it may not be sufficient for distribution. Young plants should be most carefully guarded from root-disturbance. (It is not very ready or hearty in cultivation.)

Stellera Sp. (F 112) may just as easily be Wikstroemia or Farreria. It is a willow-leaved, brilliantly-green sub-shrub of woody base, usually sprouting herbaceously to a height of about a foot, with undivided stems ending each in a loose thyrse of bright-yellow Daphne-flowers in June. On the hot bare loëss downs, to which it is peculiar (I know of it only on the torrid hills of Siku, extending up to Lodani, and a little way up the Nan Ho), it is compelled to this habit by being pitilessly eaten back by the omnivorous goats; where let alone I have seen it develop into a branching bush of some 3 or 4 feet. The seed drops while still its envelope is green, and though lavish in germination,

APPENDIX.

must be spared root disturbance in later stages. (This, I think, has generally failed.)

Swertia Sp. (F 334) is but an annual, I fear, and may indeed be nothing more than a specially fine Asiatic development of *Pleurogyne carinthiaca*. It abounds in the open turf all over the upper Alps of the Min S'an and Thunder-crown, from 9000 to 14,000 feet, and is really most beautiful in September, forming loose 6- to 8-inch pyramids of large wide saucer-shaped flowers of a lovely soft clear electric blue, growing in exactly the same turfy open slopes that breed Pleurogyne above the Glocknerhaus. But this is so attractive as well to deserve an annual sowing, in light grass or little interstices of turf.

Veronica pyrolaefolia is a most pleasant Chinese Speedwell, running about comfortably over the ground after the fashion of *V. officinalis*, with shoots clad in rather large soft rounded leaves, and sending up in summer croziers of blossom exactly suggesting a Lily-of-the-Valley that has gone of a soft lavender blue. It is a very valuable garden plant indeed.

THE END

PRINTED IN GREAT BRITAIN BY THOMAS NELSON AND SONS LTD